MOESIA

BLACK SEA

THRACE

ippi Neapolis

Amphipolis

pollonia SAMO-
THRACE

BITHYNIA and PONTUS

Mysia

AEGEAN

Troas
Assos

Mitylene

Pergamum

Thyatira

ASIA

Sardis

Smyrna Philadelphia

Hierapolis

Ephesus Colossae

Laodicea

Miletus

SAMOS

Trogyllium

PATMOS COS

Cos

Cnidus

SEA

ns

Rhodes

RHODES

Salmone?

CRETE

ix? Fair Havens

CAUDA
CLAUDA

SEA

LIBYA

Ancyra Galatia Tavium

Pessinus

Antioch

Phrygia

Iconium

Pisidia Lystra

Derbe

LYCIA

Perga

Attalia

Patara

Myra

GALATIA

CAPPADOCIA

Lycaonia

CILICIAN
GATES

Tarsus

PAMPHYLIA

Seleucia

CILICIA and SYRIA

Antioch

CYPRUS Salamis

Paphos

Sidon

Tyre

Ptolemais

Caesarea

Joppa

Gaza

Damascus

Jerusalem

Alexandria

EGYPT

ARABIA

New Testament Story

An Introduction

David L. Barr

Wright State University

Wadsworth Publishing Company
Belmont, California
A Division of Wadsworth, Inc.

Religious Studies Editor: Sheryl Fullerton
Assistant Editor: Liz Clayton
Editorial Assistant: Cynthia Haus
Production Editor: Deborah O. McDaniel
Managing Designer: Merle Sanderson
Print Buyer: Barbara Britton
Designer: Ingbritt Christensen
Cover: Ingbritt Christensen

Printed in the United States of America   19
1 2 3 4 5 6 7 8 9 10—91 90 89 88 87
ISBN 0-534-07284-4

Library of Congress Cataloging-in-Publication Data

Barr, David L.
  New Testament story.

  Bibliography: p.
  Includes index.
    1. Bible. N.R.—Language, style.   2. Narration in
the Bible.   3. Story-telling (Christian theology)
I. Title.
BS2370.B37   1987   225.6′6   86-18969
ISBN 0-534-07284-4

Acknowledgments

🕊 🕊 🕊

Quotations from the following sources are reprinted with permission. Pages on which quotations appear are given in parentheses.

Unless otherwise noted, the Scripture quotations contained herein are from the Revised Standard Version of the Bible, copyrighted 1946, 1952, 1971 by the Division of Christian Education of the National Council of Churches of Christ in the U.S.A., and are used by permission. All rights reserved.

American Philological Association: Excerpt from *Secundus the Silent Philosopher*, by Ben Edwin Perry, 1964. (p. 231)

Augsburg Publishing House: Excerpts from pp. 134–135 of Eusebius *History of the Church From Christ to Constantine*, ©1965 G. A. Williamson. Reprinted by permission from the 1975 Augsburg Publishing House edition. (p. 329)

Baker Book House: Excerpt from *The Liberated Gospel: A Comparison of the Gospel of Mark and Greek Tragedy*, 1977. (p. 165)

E. J. Brill: Excerpt from *An Introduction to the New Testament*, by A. F. J. Klijn, 1980. (p. 327)

Cambridge University Press: Excerpt from *The Setting of the Sermon on the Mount*, by W. D. Davies, 1966. (p. 186)

Collins Publishers and Eerdmans Publishing Company: Excerpt from *Christian Reflections*, by C. S. Lewis, edited by W. Hooper, 1967. (p. 339)

Doubleday & Company: Excerpts from "First Enoch 42," "Second Enoch 3," and "Apoca-lypse of Zephaniah 9" from *The Old Testament Pseudepigrapha*, edited by James H. Charlesworth. Copyright © 1983 Vol. I by James H. Charlesworth. "Psalms of Solomon 17" from Vol. II of *The Old Testament Pseudepigrapha*, edited by James Charlesworth. Copyright © 1985 Vol. II by James H. Charlesworth. Reprinted by permission of Doubleday & Company, Inc. (pp. 246, 271)

Fortress Press: Excerpts from *What Is Redaction Criticism?* by Norman Perrin, 1969; and *The Problem of History in Mark* by James M. Robinson, 1982. (p. 145)

Harvard University Press: Excerpts from various books in the Loeb Classical Library. (pp. 35, 36, 46, 62, 63, 71, 78, 79, 89, 106, 121, 146, 167, 168, 210, 214, 230, 247, 249, 268, 275, 287, 291, 292, 300, 308, 311, 332)

Indiana University Press: Excerpts from Apuleius' *The Golden Ass*, translated by Jack Lindsay, 1960. (pp. 64, 277, 315)

John Knox Press: Excerpts from *Intrepreta-tion: A Bible Commentary for Teaching and Preaching*, Vol. on Romans, 1985. (pp. 44, 254)

KTAV: Excerpt from *The Fifty-Third Chapter of Isaiah according to Jewish Interpreters*, by Adolf Newbauer and S. R. Driver, 2 vols., 1969. (p. 192)

National Association of Baptist Professors of Religion: Excerpts from "By Land and By Sea: The We-Passages and Ancient Sea Voyages," in *Perspectives on Luke-Acts* by Vernon K. Robbins, edited by Charles H. Talbert. Special Studies Series #5 (1978): 215–242. (p. 231)

W. W. Norton & Company, Inc.: Excerpt from the translation of the Pseudoclementine Homilies in *The Writings of Saint Paul*, The Norton Critical Edition, edited by Wayne A. Meeks. (p. 130)

Penquin Books Ltd.: Excerpts from *The Dead Sea Scrolls in English*, by G. Vermes, pp. 82–83, 92–93, copyright © G. Vermes, 1962, 1965, 1968, 1975. Reprinted by permission of Penguin Books Ltd. (p. 102)

Scholars Press: Excerpt from *A Sourcebook of Texts for the Comparative Study of the Gospels*, by D. Cartlidge and D. Dungan. (p. 158)

United Bible Societies: Excerpt from *A Textual Commentary on the Greek New Testament*, by Bruce M. Metzger, 1975. (p. 165)

Wadsworth Publishing Company: Excerpt from *Judaism: Development and Life*, by Leo Trepp, © 1982 by Wadsworth, Inc. (p. 161)

Westminster Press: Excerpts from *New Testament Apocrypha: Volume One*, by Edgar Hennecke, edited by Wilhelm Schneemelcher; English translation edited by R. McL. Wilson. Copyright © 1959 J. C. B. Mohr (Paul Siebeck), Tubingen; English translation © 1963 Lutter Press. Excerpts from *New Testament Apocraphya: Volume Two*, edited by Wilhelm Schneemelcher and Edgar Hennecke; English translation edited by R. McL. Wilson. Published in the U.S.A. by The Westminster Press, 1966. Copyright © 1964 J. C. B. Mohr (Paul Siebeck), Tubingen. English translation © 1965 Lutterworth Press. Used by permission of the Westminster Press, Philadelphia, PA. (pp. 126, 127, 128, 130, 271, 321)

*It is my hope
that this work might honor
Fred and Marie Barr,
whose love brought me to be,
and
Howard and Ruth Dunlap,
whose love freed me to become.*

Contents

જી   જી   જી

Introduction

Chapter 1

Chapter 2

Chapter 3

Chapter 4

Chapter 5

Chapter 6

Chapter 13

Preface

৯ৡ ৯ৡ ৯ৡ

Just because we lack imagination is no reason to think that the ancients did.

Amos Wilder (1976:53)

Those who talk of reading the Bible "as literature" sometimes mean, I think, reading it without attending to the main thing it is about; like reading Burke with no interest in politics, or reading the Aeneid *with no interest in Rome. That seems to me to be nonsense. But there is a saner sense in which the Bible, since it is after all literature, cannot properly be read except as literature; and the different parts of it as the different sorts of literature they are.*

C. S. Lewis (1958:2–3)

The degree to which we moderns are shaped by books is difficult to overemphasize. Our rooms are littered with them—at least my study is as I finish writing this. It is hard to remember that books are a relatively recent invention, barely five centuries old. Before Gutenberg printed the Bible from movable type in 1456, most of our forebears worked with handwritten manuscripts, a far different medium. Even with printing, books did not become widely available until the invention of a machine that manufactured paper, early in the nineteenth century.

A whole new way of studying the Bible developed in conjunction with this new technology. The first printed Greek edition of the New Testament was published by Erasmus of Rotterdam in 1516, under the title *Novum Instrumentum,* meaning a new instrument. Other study books soon followed: dictionaries, concordances, lexicons, atlases, commentaries. These new instruments made it possible to analyze the biblical writings in ways never before possible. They have allowed us to move closer to their original contexts and meanings than has been possible since the third century. Today we know more about the Corinth of Paul's day than has been known for a thousand years—a momentous gain, indeed.

But there has also been a significant loss. With the emergence of this new print technology, the Bible became an object of silent study. When copies were scarce, people studied the Bible by reading it aloud, discussing it, telling its stories. It was a living book carried by the living voice. This is certainly how all the New Testament writings were originally presented and how they were most often experienced until modern times. This silencing of the Bible, brought about by the widespread availability of books, has made it a distant work for many people today.

Another, more subtle, change resulted from producing the whole Bible as one book.

When we encounter the various writings bound together in one volume, we easily fail to distinguish between the kinds of writings contained in the Bible. We have forgotten how to listen to a gospel, a letter, a farewell speech, a revelation. Nor does it help much that our schools have so largely abandoned the study of classical antiquity, so that ancient forms of rhetoric and religion are foreign to students today.

In a small way this book hopes to compensate for some of these losses while capitalizing on the great gains of the past two centuries of biblical studies. The pursuit of this goal has called attention to four issues: orality, rhetoric, context, and literary technique. This book explores the *oral nature* of the New Testament world and, especially, the extent to which good stories were told and retold. It surveys the stories in, and behind, the New Testament writings and analyzes those writings as a set of interacting stories, not just as discrete documents.

The dominance of oral media in that world mandates serious attention to the art of rhetoric, the stylized means of persuasion so highly developed by the ancients. Hence, this book emphasizes *rhetoric*. The introduction identifies the various kinds of rhetoric practiced in the ancient world, and the chapters that follow show how the various authors employed them.

Attention to rhetoric demands that we also be concerned about the *historical and social contexts* of these writings. Ancient rhetoric was more than the use of certain stylistic devices; it encompassed the whole setting of communication: speaker, speech, and audience. All three are implicit in the rhetorical product, and we must explore all three when we study each of the New Testament documents. So that the reader may better grasp this context, numerous quotations from other ancient writings are included to illuminate the documents studied. A separate chapter on the historical setting has not, however, been included. I have pursued the more ambitious goal of integrating such historical information into the discussion of each writing where it is most appropriate.

This book also emphasizes the *literary nature* of all the New Testament documents, be they letters, narratives, essays, or more specialized genres. Insofar as possible, these writings are compared with others of a similar kind to show what the ancients may have expected to hear from such writings. Each is also examined for its overall structure, its use of particular literary devices, and its "story."

The idea of story works in a number of ways, but one predominates: each of these writings existed within, and attempted to proclaim, the charter story of the faith of these early believers. The men and women who listened to these writings explained their world by telling stories—of how the world came to be, how it has fallen and may be redeemed, how it will eventually end. For those who wrote and heard these works, that was the story of Jesus. We endeavor to hear their stories.

Thus, Chapter 1 explores what may be known about the stories of Jesus *before* the documents were written, while Chapter 13 reflects on the meanings Christians found in these documents *after* they were collected into a canon. In the intervening chapters, each New Testament writing is studied in its approximate chronological order and in conjunction with other writings of a similar type. They are not all discussed in equal depth; space forbids. With Paul, for example, two letters (I Thessalonians and Romans) are studied in detail, while the others are treated in sufficient depth to enable the interested reader to proceed to independent study. In each case, our study provides a sense of the overall work and its historical and social context, focusing on important sections. Further resources for study are also provided, beginning with the most basic works, then listing the standard commentaries, and proceeding to advanced studies suitable for term projects or other serious research.

A reading guide and a set of study questions are also provided for each writing, so that even beginning students may read the biblical literature with a sense of direction. It is my firm conviction that one cannot tell another what a work of literature means, for meaning emerges only in the reading of the literature itself. The goal of each chapter is to enable the reader to read the New Testament document for herself or himself. To try to understand a work of literature by reading *about* it is—to take a phrase from David Ben-Gurion—like kissing one's bride through the veil.

If this book should serve to remove some of the veils that too readily blind us to the beauty and power of these writings, it will have been worth the labor of its making. That labor was not entirely mine, of course. And genres being what they are, this is the place to thank those without whose assistance this book would not be.

To the many readers who read and commented on parts of this manuscript, I owe a great debt, especially to those students in several classes who patiently read (and criticized) various chapters, thereby saving their colleagues from many unintended obscurities. Then there are my colleagues who offered many helpful suggestions (and even a few I did not find so helpful). My special thanks to Dennis Smith (Oklahoma State University) who read the entire manuscript in both its earliest and latest stages and offered many suggestions for improvement. Numerous others read parts of the manuscript in various stages of its development. I specifically want to thank: Catherine Albanese (Wright State University), Irvin Batdorf (United Theological Seminary), John Carey (Florida State University), James Carse (New York University), Charles Thomas Davis (Appalachian State University), Arthur Dewey (Xavier University), Robert Fowler (Baldwin-Wallace College), Gene Gallagher (Connecticut College), Robert Hann (Florida International University), Judith Kovacs (University of Virginia), Shirley Lund (Boston University), Elizabeth Struthers Malbon (Virginia Tech University), Grant Osborn (Trinity Evangelical Divinity School), Edmund Perry (Northwestern University), Vernon Robbins (Emory University), Robert Straukamp (California State University), and Charles Talbert (Wake Forest University).

Thanks are also due Veda Horton, secretary in the Department of Religion at Wright State University, who graciously provided many small services that enabled this project to move forward, and to Robert Dorris, my student worker, who has labored many hours to help me master the bibliography.

The staff at Wadsworth Publishing Company has been most refreshing. My thanks go to Miriam Nathanson, who first saw the potential of this book in my oral descriptions of what I wished to accomplish; to Sheryl Fullerton, who patiently shepherded the manuscript into its present form; and to Debbie McDaniel, who oversaw the production stages of the book. Each in her own way made a demanding job more bearable.

Finally, more than thanks are due to Judith, Elizabeth, and Nathaniel, who not only endured the many evenings I spent at my desk instead of in family pursuits, but also assisted in all the ways a family might in such a labor—especially by their unfailing support and love.

Common Abbreviations

ๆ๑   ๆ๑   ๆ๑

ATR   *Anglican Theological Review*
            Published by the Episcopal Divinity School, Cambridge, MA
            02138

BCE   Before the Common Era (same dates as BC)

CBQ   *Catholic Biblical Quarterly*
            Published by the Catholic Biblical Association, Washington,
            D.C. 20064

CE   Common Era (dates the same as AD)

f or ff   The following page or pages, verse or verses

GP   *Gospel Parallels*
            B. H. Throckmorton, ed. Nelson, 1967

IDB   *Interpreter's Dictionary of the Bible*
            4 vols. with supplement. G. A. Buttrick, ed., Abingdon, 1962,
            1976

JAAR   *Journal of the American Academy of Religion*
            Published by the American Academy of Religion, Chico, CA

JBL   *Journal of Biblical Literature*
            Published by the Society of Biblical Literature, Denver, CO
            80210

JR   *Journal of Religion*
            Published by the University of Chicago, Chicago, IL 60637

JRS   *Journal of Roman Studies*
            Published by the Society for the Promotion of Roman
            Studies, London WC1H 0PP

JSOT   *Journal for the Study of the Old Testament*
            Sheffield, England

Loeb   *Loeb Classical Library*
                Harvard University Press. A series of the works of most
                ancient Latin and Greek authors with the original language
                and an English translation on facing pages

NT   *Novum Testamentum*
                Published by E. J. Brill, Leiden

NTA   *New Testament Abstracts*
                Published by Weston School of Theology, Cambridge, MA
                02138

NTS   *New Testament Studies*
                Published by Cambridge University Press in conjunction
                with the *Studiorum Novi Testamenti Societas*

OCD   *Oxford Classical Dictionary*
                Published at the Clarendon Press, 1970

Par.   Parallel references in the other gospels

SFG   *Synopsis of the Four Gospels*
                Published by United Bible Societies, 1972

TAPA   *Transactions and Proceedings of the American Philological
                Association*
                Published by the APA, a professional society of scholars in
                classics

TDNT   *Theological Dictionary of the New Testament*
                10 vols. Gerhard Kittel, ed., G. Bromiley, trans., Eerdmans,
                beginning in 1964

VT   *Vetus Testamentum*
                A journal for study of the Hebrew Scriptures, published by
                E. J. Brill, Leiden

ZNW   *Zeitschrift fuer die neutestamentliche Wissenschaft*

Chronology of the
New Testament World

Dates	Events	Writers/Writings	Palestine	Roman World
BCE				
323	Death of Alexander		Beginning of Hellenistic Age	
200			Seleucid rule	
190				
180				
170				
168	Persecution of Antiochus			
		Daniel	Maccabean rebellion	
160				
		Septuagint completed (300–150)		
150				
			Pharisees and Sadducees begin to be mentioned	
140				
130				
120				
110		I Maccabees		
100		II Maccabees		
90				
		Dead Sea Scrolls written (about 150 BCE–CE 70)		
80				
70				
		Cicero (106–43)		
63			Pompey enters Jerusalem Roman control	
60				
50				
44				Assassination of Julius Caesar

Dates	Events	Writers/ Writings	Palestine	Roman World
BCE				
40				
37			Herod the Great King of Judea	
30				
27				Augustus rules–36*
20				
10				
4			Death of Herod Archelaus/Philip rule	
CE				
6		Hillel and Shammai Philo of Alexandria (30 BCE–CE 45)	Direct Roman rule of Palestine	
10				
14				Death of Augustus Tiberias rules–56*
20				
26			Pilate rules (26–36)	
30	Death of Jesus Paul at Damascus			
37				Death of Tiberias Caligula rules–25*
40				
41			Herod Agrippa made king	Death of Caligula Claudius rules–51* Jews expelled from Rome
50		Seneca (1–65) Paul (?–64) Thessalonians Galatians/ Corinthians	Felix rules (51–59)	Death of Claudius
54		Philemon/ Philippians Romans		Nero rules–17*
60			Festus rules (59–62)	
62	Death of James			
64	Fire at Rome			

* The numbers after the emperors' names indicate their age at the beginning of their reigns.

Dates	Events	Writers/ Writings	Palestine	Roman World
CE				
	Persecution–Death of Paul, Peter ?			
68		Colossians ?	Judean War	Death of Nero
70		Mark	Destruction of the Temple	Chaos–three emperors Vespasian rules–60*
		Josephus (37–95) *Jewish War*		Death of Vespasian
80				Titus rules–40*
		Ephesians ?		Death of Titus
		Matthew		Domitian rules–30*
		I Peter ?		
		Luke-Acts		
90	Council of Yavneh			
		Jewish Antiquities John		
96		Apocalypse *I Clement*		Death of Domitian Nerva
		Dio Chrysostomos (40–112)		Trajan rules–45*
100		Pastorals ?		
110		Ignatius' letters Pliny (61–112) Letter to Trajan		
117				Death of Trajan
		Gospel of Peter ?		Hadrian rules–41*
120				
		Papius *Letter of Barnabas* II Peter ? *Didache*		
130				
		Basilides Polycarp's *To the Philippians'*	Second Jewish revolt	
140		*Apocalypse of Peter* ?	Bar Kochba Jerusalem made a Gentile city: Jupiter Capitolinus	Death of Hadrian Antonius Pius rules– 51*
150		Justin Martyr (100–165)		

Dates	Events	Writers/ Writings	Palestine	Roman World
CE				
		Marcion		
		Valentinus		
		Acts of Paul		
160				Death of Pius
				Marcus Aurelius
				rules—40*
		Tatian's		
		Diatessaron		
170		Irenaeus (130–202)		
		Hegesippus		
180				Death of Aurelius
				Commodus rules—
				19*
		Dio Cassius		
190		*Acts of Peter* ?		
		Clement of Alexan-		Death of Commodus
		dria (150–215)		Septimius Severus
		Tertullian (160–240)		rules—48*
200		*Mishnah*		

Any ancient chronology is, obviously, only an approximation. The dates assigned to the various writings are uncertain. A question mark indicates extreme uncertainty. The dates of rulers and writers are more sure; most are taken from the *Oxford Classical Dictionary* or the *Interpreters' Dictionary of the Bible*.

New Testament Story

Not by History Alone

❧ ❧ ❧

A Literary Reading of the New Testament

Learning to Hear the Bible

Discovering the Original Meaning

The Learning Process

Resources for Further Study

Introduction

This book about stories will be better understood if I begin with a bit of my own story. I grew up attending a small church in rural Michigan, a church that delighted in the Bible. We had a community of people who really liked one another: adults, young people, kids, old people. We studied the Bible diligently and understood it to be "our story."

I am afraid we often confused the biblical story with our rural American assumptions about life. We naively applied the Bible directly to ourselves with a devotional and wholly uncritical reading. Our doctrinal sieve carefully sifted out any ideas that did not agree with our own notions. Yet I learned to delight in the Bible and found in it a new and fascinating world. I devoted my life to its study.

LEARNING TO HEAR THE BIBLE

The longer I studied the biblical writings, the more complex they appeared. As I learned to ask disciplined questions, I found unexpected and exciting answers. Eventually I became convinced that we who claimed to regard the Bible so highly were really not listening to it. Though we accused others of neglecting the Bible, we insisted that it always say what we had predetermined it would.

As I struggled to understand the Bible, I encountered a bewildering array of modern approaches, some with names I could barely pronounce. But these approaches were important, for they aimed to uncover what the biblical writings meant in their original settings.

The World behind the Text: History

Much effort in modern biblical studies has gone into the task of building a realistic understanding of the specific settings in which the various writers worked. Today we have reasonably precise pictures of the situation of most of the New Testament writers. Pursuing my studies, I learned to hear the voice of Matthew, and to distinguish it from that of Mark or Luke or Paul. I heard them telling their own stories, and I was alternately fascinated, frustrated, bemused, shocked, threatened, enchanted, offended—but never bored. Eventually, I became a teacher, a convenient pretext for continuing the study of this enigmatic book.

The Danger of Obscuring the Text

Yet teaching the New Testament has had some unexpected and even undesirable results. Too many students feel frustrated but never fascinated, threatened but never enchanted. They learn only enough to spoil their innocent piety. Intimidated by the enormous effort of historical interpretation, they leave the study to professionals. Instead of an exciting drama, many people today find the Bible a closed book.

Sometimes I hear my colleagues discussing this problem—usually in whispers, more freely at some late-night gathering. We have reversed the miracle of Cana: we have turned the wine into water. The historical-critical method is shipwreck, some say; we must find a new paradigm for biblical studies. We lament the sorry state of biblical literacy, feeling vaguely to blame. Ironically, however, nearly to a person my

Roman Coin from about 70 CE This seated figure represents Judea (as the inscription says), seated in a pose of mourning. It marks a very significant event for the study of early Judaism and Christianity: the destruction of Jerusalem by the Romans in the year 70. Before that destruction, Jerusalem was the center of the Christian movement, which thus maintained strong ties with Jewish people. After 70, Christians looked to other centers and became less and less Jewish. Knowing which writings came before, and which after, this event will be important. (Hirmer Verlag, Munich.)

colleagues refuse to go back. Their own experience of the critical study of the Bible has been liberating, even if not always satisfying. However cantankerous we may find the historical Paul, for example, few of us are willing to exchange him for the infallible Paul of our childhood. We find that the historical understanding of these texts is an indispensable place to begin.

The Role of Historical Studies

A historical understanding of a text is one that is appropriate and likely for the historical situation in which the text was composed. We make the basic assumption that an author was trying to communicate something meaningful to the audience for which he or she wrote. This approach attempts to discover who wrote the text, when it was written, and what issues it was intended to address in its own time. Only when we grasp the historical situation of both author and audience can we hope to understand the message communicated.

The great strength of the historical method in all areas of study has been to free us from the tyranny of our present situation by showing us the past. In literary studies, historical method creates distance, and thus objectivity, between the reader and the text. Such disciplined objectivity will allow us to hear truly what the biblical writers intended to say.

But this distance can also become a problem. Historical study can create such a chasm between us and the text that we forget that those human beings were very like us and wrestled with problems we encounter today.

The Role of Social Analysis

Many contemporary scholars are finding ways to overcome the limitations of historical analysis. One such approach investigates the social world of these texts, attempting to place each in its specific social context, concerned not merely with "who" and "when" but also with "how" and "in what kind of society."

The major advantage of social analysis methods is that they bring to life the real world of social interaction in which the early believers heard these texts. They focus our attention on the practical, political, and social questions these texts involved. Such analysis reveals that the texts do not deal with ideas alone; the ideas relate to actual lives of real people. Yet this very concern with the real world can be misleading, if it ignores the literary and imaginative character of these writings. It may also overlook the great beauty, artistry, and intellectual daring of these writings.

Both historical and social analyses are indispensable to the goals of this book and both will be used in the discussions that follow. But the primary purpose of this study is to bring these ancient texts to life as works of literature. This book is written for all who wish to hear afresh the stories of the New Testament writers.

The World within the Text: Literature

Before the historical and social study of the Bible developed, less than two centuries ago, people naively lived in the stories of the biblical text. They delighted in them. Today we need to recapture some of their delight without their naiveté. In fact, a major current movement in biblical studies is attempting this by means of a literary study of the texts.

The Danger of Distorting the Text

One problem with approaching the Bible "as literature" is that a good deal of the Bible is not literature, at least not in the aesthetic sense in which that word is commonly used. No work of the New Testament is written in poetic form. Nor is there much attempt at literary embellishment or ornamentation so common in the literature of that age. There is nothing like the attempt of Lucretius, the Roman philosopher, who wrote an extensive philosophical poem about 50 BCE. He explained:

Ɗ Ɗ Ɗ

My art serves a higher purpose. A doctor who wants to get children to drink a bitter medicine first rubs a little honey on the rim of the cup. The children, unable to imagine what lies ahead, drink the medicine, lured on by the sweet taste of the honey. So they are taken in, but not ensnared, for they are healed by the medicine. So too, philosophy often seems bitter to those who have not drunk deeply at its wells; most people avoid it. That is why I have written this work in poetry, the honey of the muses. My purpose is to lure the mind so that, once engaged with these ideas, it might be led to a true insight into the nature of the universe. (On The Nature of The Universe, *I.920, free translation*)

Because so much of the New Testament lacks such conscious literary technique, literary approaches have tended to be selective, concentrating on the narrative literature and more especially on Luke, a writer with great literary skill. This has limited the usefulness of literary analysis and distorted the subject, for the nonnarrative writings of the New Testament have greatly influenced the religion, art, literature, and history of the West. In fact, literary analysis has frequently neglected the most influential voice in the New Testament, that of Paul. Paul wrote letters, not stories, and very little of our modern literary criticism has been designed to deal with letters.

Letters as Literature: Structure and Story

Yet letters were a recognized literary genre in antiquity; much of the enduring fame of Cicero (106–43 BCE) was based on the more than nine hundred letters he published. Seneca (who was Paul's contemporary) and Pliny (in the generation after Paul) saw the value of publishing their letters. Literary theorists even developed rules for letter writing, and the composition of suitable letters was a routine exercise in the schools. Not only were students expected to be able to write an appropriate letter on a specific subject, but they were also expected to be able to write in the styles of the great masters. Topics ranged from the personal to the political to the philosophical, and included an enormous business correspondence.

In the ancient world, letters were written documents and oral performances. Here we need to consider each aspect.

As written documents, we can apply the same techniques of literary criticism to these letters that we apply to other writings. Two aspects of the letters will concern us: their structure and the stories they reveal.

In Paul's time the structure of a letter was relatively fixed, and it will pay us to give careful attention to how Paul followed that pattern and how he deviated from it. In addition, the letters contain an arrangement of words and images, allusions and quotations, logical argument, and liturgical design. Each letter must be studied for its overall shape and pattern, and for the way that pattern reflects the writer's approach to life. The letters must also be examined for the stories they present. The letters are not stories but they do reflect the stories of their writers and the story of what God had done in Jesus, as each writer understood it.

The word *story* has a certain ambiguity. It refers to a "series of events that are or may be narrated" (*Oxford English Dictionary*). Thus, while a story actually told becomes a narrative with a plot, the same story could be told in a variety of narratives with different plots. One could tell a story from the beginning and tell it "in order," or begin in the middle or even at the end, filling in the earlier incidents with flashbacks or reports. But the important point is that the story is separate from the narrative that relates the story.

This larger sense of story provides the dominant metaphor for this book. Our age is accustomed to analyzing human behavior in a variety of modes, a tendency greatly enhanced by the division of our universities into various disciplines. But the ancients had no universities and no disciplines. An educated person studied all available knowledge, from philosophy to astronomy to medicine. Today we tend to explain things in terms of disciplinary perspectives: history, literature, sociology, theology, psychology, anthropology, and so on. Of these, only the first two had been invented in antiquity, and they in a very elementary sense.

This is not because the ancients did not think and speak about the same things we do (social groups, ideas, self-understanding, for example), nor were their theories necessarily inferior to our own. There is much psychological insight in the Greek tragedies, for example, but in the form of stories told. Nearly all ancient literature and history, and a good deal of philosophy and religion, involved the telling of stories. Consider, for example, how the ancient Jews confessed their faith. They did not formulate theological doctrines or even write logical creeds. Listen:

≥ ≥ ≥

A wandering Aramean was my father; and he went down into Egypt and sojourned there, few in number; and there he became a nation, great, mighty, and populous. And the Egyptians treated us harshly. . . . Then we cried out to the LORD the God of our fathers, and the LORD heard our voice. . . . (Deut. 26:5–10)

This is not theology but a summary of a story, the kind anthropologists call a charter story because it provides the warrant for Jewish life. In a similar way, the story of Jesus, especially the story of his death and resurrection, was a charter story for his followers, for these foundation events provided meaning for their lives—their charter.

The gospels present their own accounts of this charter story, but some version of it was assumed by both the writers and the audiences of the New Testament letters. This sacred story was the ultimate source of all the ideas, arguments, and actions found in the letters. Thus we need to acquire some sense of this basic story before beginning our study of the individual letters. Chapter 1 sketches the basic shape and content of the Jesus story.

We must listen for the stories even if what we read seems to be about ethics or ideas. Too often, interpreters of the letters have gotten caught up in the argument and forgotten to hear the story. They have debated Paul's attitude toward women based on the following kind of passage:

≥ ≥ ≥

But any woman who prays or prophesies with her head unveiled dishonors her head—it is the same as if her head were shaven. . . . That is why a woman ought to have a veil on her head, because of the angels. (I Cor. 11:5, 10)

How often have interpreters debated Paul's ideas without noticing those angels standing over in the corner! In what sort of story did Paul and these early Christian women live that they had to be aware of such heavenly guests? Can the ideas ever make sense unless we discover the story behind them?

Notice that the meaning of *story* has shifted slightly: it now includes not only the charter story of Jesus but also the community story of his followers as well, what we might call history, sociology, and autobiography. It is impossible to talk about Paul's letters without telling stories: He had been forced to leave Thessalonica, was worried about his followers there, and so wrote to them. He was in jail and met a runaway slave and needed to write to his master, Philemon. He had been challenged in Galatia by opponents who discounted his authority and needed to defend himself. These are the ways every commentary must speak, though writers usually hide the extent to which they are making up stories by simply labeling it "Introduction." In this sense, the letters contain a story of Jesus, and of Paul, even though they do not contain narratives.

We may illustrate this meaning from our own experiences. Each of us has a story, in the sense that we understand our lives in a connected fashion and relate them to some larger meaning. In fact, each of us lives in several stories—the story of our nation, our school, our family, our circle of friends, our sense of the real purpose of life. These larger stories provide the framework for our personal stories. Remembering our stories enables us to appreciate how the ancients understood their lives. In the following pages I have chosen not to speak of the theology of Paul, or of his psychology or sociology, though elements that correspond to these modern concerns will be discussed. Instead, we will speak of Paul's stories concerning himself and his communities, and his larger story of Jesus, which I think are more appropriate categories for this introductory approach. As your own study advances, you may wish to ask more modern questions, but begin by listening for the stories.

Our notion of "story" is thus a broad one: it includes the stories told in narratives, the charter story implied in the letters as well as the narratives, the community stories that the letters and narratives reveal, and the personal stories of the individual writers. There are strong correlations between charter, life, and personal stories: each level of a story implies and reflects the others. We will understand the letters only if we understand their story contexts.

Obviously, this will be easiest to do when we come to the gospels, which are not only stories but also narratives. Revelation, too, is largely narrative. If story is so basic, should we perhaps begin with these narratives and work backward to the earlier nonnarrative literature? This is a possibility, but it has the major disadvantage of interpreting an earlier age by a later one. We must not assume that Paul's story of Jesus was simply equivalent to one of the later gospels. We must not use the gospels as a standard by which we judge the other writings. It is not that the narrative literature controls the earlier letters, but that both the letters and the narratives rest on basic stories of Jesus and of the communities. We must endeavor to hear these stories.

Oral Literature: Understanding Rhetoric

Hearing is the proper verb in regard to the ancients, since nearly their whole experience of literature was aural. Whether public or private, reading was done out loud. Even much later, in the fifth century, Augustine tells us he was bewildered that Ambrose was reading without pronouncing the words (*Confessions* 6.3). People simply did not read silently. If we pay attention to the wording, we will not find reference to readers in ancient texts; they speak of the "hearer" of the message (for example, Rev. 1:3 and Heb. 5:11). Publication consisted of reading the work aloud at a public gathering. No doubt this was also the way in which Paul's letters were encountered by their earliest audience. In fact, it is likely that all the literature in the New Testament was first presented orally.

This orality of the documents means that we must strive to hear them and not simply to read them. Read them out loud. Even in translation they make a different impression when encountered as a spoken word. This orality also implies that we should not be overly subtle with the meaning we find. Examining carefully and at leisure the fine points of a written text is quite different from hearing it read without having a text in front of you. Interpretations that depend on nuances of text or on minor changes in wording should be approached with caution.

Because the letters were originally presented orally, our analysis of them must include as a central component a study of how the ancients were trained to speak and listen, the study of rhetoric. Training in rhetoric was a basic part of the educational process, and since the time of Aristotle (384–322 BCE) students were taught that an oral presentation involved three distinct elements: speaker, audience, and discourse. The speaker had to demonstrate his own character (*ethos*), stir the emotions of the audience (*pathos*), and present a logically convincing case (*logos*). How these three effects were achieved depended on the situation in which one spoke. Ancient rhetoric was always situational.

The rhetoric of conflict   Ancient rhetoric was developed in three primary situations. First, there were the speeches in the courts of law. This judicial rhetoric sought to influence the audience to make a judgment about something that had happened in the *past*. In ancient law courts, the jury consisted of all interested citizens and was usually very large. (For example, a jury of over five hundred men convicted Socrates.) Verdict was by majority vote. Since citizens originally represented themselves, they needed to know how to speak well. If a plaintiff failed to gain a conviction, he was liable for the amount for which he had sued. Consequently, judicial rhetoric was the most highly organized form of ancient rhetoric; prosecution and defense represented its positive and negative forms.

The rhetoric of decision making   Another kind of rhetoric developed in the popular assembly, what we would call the legislature. Again, the speaker sought to influence a large body of people, but now the wisdom of some *future* action

was under debate in this deliberative rhetoric. Again, there were two possibilities: the exhortation (we ought to do this) and the dissuasion (we ought not).

The rhetoric of exhortation   A third kind of speech, found in a variety of contexts (political, philosophical, religious, and social), sought to demonstrate a certain truth. The funeral oration, for example, sought to demonstrate the virtue and excellence of the departed in a eulogy or encomium. But there was also a negative form, the invective, which sought to denounce some person or vice. This demonstrative rhetoric sought to persuade the hearers to hold some view toward a certain person or action in the *present*. The three kinds of rhetoric are described in Table I.1.

We will observe examples of each of these kinds of rhetoric in the New Testament writings, but a word of caution is in order here. While the ancients had a passion for clear and logical distinctions in theory, in practice these three forms of rhetoric often overlapped, and any given presentation might use more than one. Nevertheless, attention to the kinds of rhetoric employed will help us determine the structure of the writings and perceive the stories behind them.

The World of the Text: Historical Literature

What follows is not simply literary analysis. Because this study involves documents of a history and a culture far different from ours, any comprehensive attempt to understand them must be also a study of history and of society.

Though I have assumed that the original meaning of these texts is somehow the most important or most interesting understanding of them, not all literary critics would agree. Early in this century a new school of literary criticism developed in reaction to the overwhelming concern of previous critics for historical and biographical interpretations of the literary texts. The older criticism argued that one could only understand

Table I.1   Kinds of Rhetoric

Name	Context	Situation	Time Concern	Technique	Degree of Complexity	Purpose
Judicial rhetoric	Courts	Conflict	Past	Narrative Case Proof Rebuttal	High	To persuade to the speaker's viewpoint
Deliberative rhetoric	Assembly Legislature	Deliberation	Future	Proposition Proof	Moderate	To decide an issue
Demonstrative rhetoric	Public meetings (schools, funerals, holidays, etc.)	Exhortation	Present	Maxims Lists	Low	To demonstrate that something is so

Shakespeare if one related his plays to incidents in his life. The New Critics, as they called themselves, argued that works of literature are autonomous and independent: once an author sends his poem out into the world he loses all control over it. The whole meaning of the poem is found in the poem, according to these critics.

In one sense this is true. What an author intended to say does not have priority over what he or she actually said. Sometimes they say less than they intended—sometimes more. Only close analysis of the writing will reveal its meaning. Ultimately, justification for any interpretation of a text must be the actual content of the text.

In another sense, this concentration on the text alone is false, because it is impossible. It appeared possible to the New Critics only because they dealt with nearly contemporary texts written in English. Paul wrote to the Galatians: "Christo sunestauromai; zo de ouketi ego." No one can interpret this text by itself; we cannot even translate it into English without a historical consideration of what these words meant in Paul's time. Even when translated ("I was crucified with Christ; I no longer live."), they make no sense unless

we understand both the general historical practice of Roman crucifixion and the specific historical event of the crucifixion of Jesus. Yet even with that knowledge the meaning of the sentence is not obvious. Clearly, Paul was not crucified with Christ; clearly he still lived. We need to know more about Paul, his general view of the world, his religious practices, his relation to the Galatians, and the specific problem he was addressing in Galatia when he formulated these words. Such historical investigation is indispensable for an understanding of these texts. Without it we will continue to read our own ideas into the text—a far less interesting enterprise.

DISCOVERING THE ORIGINAL MEANING

Our goal, then, is to hear these documents in something like their original key: to try to understand what they may have meant to their original hearers. This implies two further considerations. First, it implies that our concern is with the ancient world. Though it may be important to discover what the New Testament means for us today, this study is about something overheard; it seeks to unravel other people's meanings. This approach allows us to achieve some distance and a critical perspective on issues and ideas.

This does not mean that what we read will be irrelevant for our time. Reading about other people's problems can prove useful for the insight it provides about our wholly different problems. The foundation on which all later interpretations must be built consists of deciphering and ultimately understanding the meaning of the work in relation to the time when it was written.

Problems to Be Overcome

Second, our goal implies that we can listen to these writings in somewhat the same way as the original hearers. But three obstacles stand in our way: We speak a different language (these writings were all in Greek); we live nearly two millennia later (the intellectual and historical changes present even greater differences than those between Greek and English); we bring different expectations to the texts.

Language

A moment's reflection will show how great the gulf is that separates our age and experience from the ancients. In English, the noun *faith* and the verb *believe* imply two quite different kinds of activities. To have faith implies a religious stance toward the world; to believe refers to holding ideas to be true. The Greeks spoke of *pistis* and *pisteuein*, using the same root word for both noun and verb. In both cases the root meaning was to trust. This language problem is great. Words like "Lord," "Savior," "law," and "love" must be interpreted according to their first-century context.

One way to minimize this problem is to read from several modern translations, especially those that attempt a nonliteral interpretation. Several modern versions attempt English translations that are the equivalent of the *ideas* expressed by the Greek (a theory of translation called dynamic equivalence). These translations produce varied results, from rather strict paraphrases (*Today's English Version*) to very loose paraphrases (the *Living Bible*), with others forming a middle ground (Phillips' translation). The problem with a translation based on the theory of dynamic equivalence is that there is no check on a translator who misjudges the original meaning, then radically alters the text by inserting his or her own views (as happens frequently in the *Living Bible*).

Other modern translators use what is called a theory of word equivalence, attempting to find English words that correspond to each of the Greek words in the original. This technique produces a fairly literal, but not always easily understood translation. The translators of the *King James Version* (1611) used this approach, as did the translators of the modern descendant of that version, the *Revised Standard Version*. Other modern translations (the *New International Version,* the *New American Bible*) are based on the same philosophy. I strongly urge that a modern literal version be your constant companion in the study you have undertaken. An even better strategy would be to read from a variety of translations, some literal, some paraphrased. When serious differences emerge, consult a good commentary that discusses the reasons for such differences.

Time

More than language stands in the way of our understanding the ancient world. Think about all the inventions, conveniences, and ideas that have so shaped our modern consciousness: computers and telephones, printing and universities, sociology and critical historiography, psychology and democracy. (A few free cities with democratic systems existed in the ancient world, but the vote was limited—usually to the wealthy, always to the men.) All these changes and much else that we now take for granted were unknown in antiquity. We must be careful not to leap too easily from our experience to that of the ancients.

Roman Dress The toga was the formal dress of the Roman and also the garment in which one would be buried. It seems to have been a large semicircular cloth (perhaps 18 feet along the straight edge and up to 7 feet deep). It was a dignified, but not very convenient, dress, and several emperors had to enforce its use on public occasions by law. The third figure from the left, showing his side, reveals his tunic—worn under the toga outdoors or by itself indoors. It was a short shirtlike garment falling perhaps to the knees. Women added an additional skirtlike tunic that reached to the feet. Senators and knights were allowed to add colored stripes to their togas. (Alinari/Art Resource, New York.)

Expectations

A third, equally important, obstacle to understanding these texts is one we might miss because it lies within ourselves: we experience these texts in a way impossible to their first hearers. We experience them as a collection, but their original audience encountered them as individual writings. Modern people view the New Testament in various ways (some regard it as Scripture; others consider it infallible; still others view it as just another book). But for its first hearers, the New Testament was not a book at all. Even so basic a concept as *New Testament* did not exist when these works were produced.

The New Testament as a canon These writings were heard one at a time, not as part of a collection. When Paul wrote his second letter to the Corinthians, he could not assume they had

the rest of his letters with which to compare it—
he was not even sure they had understood his
first letter to them (I Cor. 5:9–12). We, too, will
encounter these writings one at a time. Only later
(Chapter 13) will we consider the collection as a
whole.

Today we regard the forms of these writings
as unusual. People no longer write gospels. Even
our letters are different. If someone were to address a letter to us in the manner of Paul, we
would be quite surprised and, perhaps, a little
amused. But Paul employed the letter-writing
techniques common in his day. We will only understand what Paul's correspondents may have
understood when we can imagine what this type
of writing meant to people then.

Kinds of writing   Clearly we approach different kinds of writing differently. A letter from a
friend you dated in high school will be read with
an expectation different from the one you bring
to the reading of this book. And the way you
read both of these will differ from the way you
read a comic book. Various kinds of literature
(what critics refer to as genres) demand different
kinds of reading. We have been programmed by
our general experience of life and literature to
expect different things from various genres: science fiction is different from history, and both
differ from romance.

With what expectations did the earliest hearers of a gospel approach that text? How did their
expectations differ when they heard a letter? Did
their expectations vary if they knew the author
of the letter? These are not easy questions to answer; yet it is useful to raise them so that we may
realize some of the difficulties we face in reading
these documents as they were originally read. We
can then begin the process of developing a sympathetic imagination on which all successful
interpretation is built. The first step is to be aware
of the great river of language, history, and literary expectations that separates us from those
original hearers. Only then can we begin to build
the bridges necessary to carry us across to their
side.

Approach of This Book

The tools used to construct these bridges will
consist of a thorough historical investigation of
the context of each writing, an examination of
the social situation from and to which it spoke,
and a careful literary analysis of the text of the
documents themselves.

This presents a dilemma: how should the history, culture, and literature be presented? Two
options exist: start with the history or start with
the literature. Traditionally, textbooks begin with
a chapter on the history of the period, then go
on to explain the historical context of each writing before actually reading it. I resist such an
approach for two reasons—one practical, the other
theoretical.

On the practical side, I have not found such
a method useful in my teaching. My students were
rarely able to recall the relevant information useful for understanding a particular writing from
the rapid survey of the period I provided during
the first few days of the term. They had no reason to remember what a Stoic was because they
did not know why it would be important. Thus,
it seems more practical to discuss the historical
situation only when it is important for understanding a particular writing. Where the same information is important to several writings, I will
resort to cross references.

On the theoretical side, I object to putting the
history before the literature because it implies a
false view of education: that I know the conclusion you should come to and need only lead you
to it in a logical way. It views the scholar as a
wagon master who could lead the wagon train
safely to California because he has been there
many times before and knows the safe paths. This
is a false image of the scholarly task. Scholarship
is a quest for understanding, not a means for supporting preordained conclusions. The scholar is
more like the local scout who is willing to ride
out ahead of the wagon train, discover the lay of
the land, locate a few watering holes, and warn
of potential dangers.

In this study we will always begin with the

text of the biblical writing. Reading that text will lead us to consider the historical and social circumstances of both writer and audience, and understanding those circumstances will make us return to a further reading of the text. It is a circle, but I hope not a vicious one.

THE LEARNING PROCESS

While reading the following pages, you will often find it necessary to put this book down and turn to the biblical writings themselves. This is as it should be, for a work of literature can never adequately be summarized. The most we can do is to point to things we have found useful and say, "Consider this." This book is filled with such pointing, combined with the rich insights of other scholars and my own musings on the text. It will never be my intention to tell you what it *really* means. I pursue the more ambitious goal of providing you with the resources necessary to arrive at your own interpretation.

As you learn, do not be surprised if some of your previous ideas about the New Testament are challenged. That is an inevitable part of the learning process. But, as one of my professors admonished, don't understand too quickly. Do not immediately assume that your earlier idea is completely false just because some new insight seems to call it into question. Do not presume that the new way of reading the writings fol-

lowed here must be wrong because it is at odds with your earlier understanding. To do either would abort the learning process.

Once, when planning a trip through northern Pennsylvania, I did some reading about the Moravians and planned to visit one of their settlements near Bethlehem. I learned that the Moravians are an egalitarian community, according everyone equal status in life and in death. Thus, they do not permit grave markers of different sizes. Imagine my bewilderment on visiting a cemetery and finding many different sizes of gravestones. Fortunately, while wandering around the cemetery, I met the old caretaker who explained to me that while Moravians recognize no social distinctions, they do recognize innate status differences based on the age that a person had attained at death. Babies, children, adults, and the old all had different sized memorials. My earlier understanding was not wrong; it was only partial.

This is the process of learning: First we are ignorant; then we learn something and understand something; then we learn more and what we understood previously is challenged. We may feel ignorant again, but it is a higher-level ignorance. When we learn more, we may be able to reconcile our earlier understanding and our new knowledge or to choose between them. This process never stops as long as we keep learning. Running into an old caretaker every now and then doesn't hurt either.

RESOURCES FOR FURTHER STUDY

These resources will supplement each chapter, enabling you to advance your study as far as your interest takes you. They are each arranged from the most basic works to the more advanced. The form of citation is simple, using only the author's last name and the date of publication. Complete data may be found by consulting the comprehensive bibliography at the end of the book. Where it seems helpful, the title of the book is also included in these resource sections.

Three excellent introductions to the basic issues discussed in this chapter are now available:

Kennedy, 1984, *New Testament Interpretation through Rhetorical Criticism.*
Krentz, 1975, *The Historical-Critical Method.*
Petersen, 1978, *Literary Criticism for New Testament Critics.*

On the issues involved in social analysis, see:

Kee, 1980, *Christian Origins in Sociological Perspective*.

Malina, 1981, *New Testament World*. An anthropological approach.

   More advanced works with extensive bibliographies include:

Abrams, 1953, *The Mirror and the Lamp*.
Booth, 1961, *The Rhetoric of Fiction*.
Chatman, 1978, *Story and Discourse*.
Frei, 1974, *The Eclipse of Biblical Narrative*.
Hirsch, 1967, *Validity in Interpretation*.
Kennedy, 1972, *The Art of Rhetoric in the Roman World*.
Malina, 1986, *Christian Origins and Cultural Anthropology*.
Meeks, 1983, *The First Urban Christians*.
Peterson, 1985, *Rediscovering Paul*.

Scholes and Kellog, 1966, *The Nature of Narrative*.
Wellek and Warren, 1956, *Theory of Literature*.

   The ancient critics are analyzed by:

Grube, 1965, *The Greek and Roman Critics*.
Russell, 1981, *Criticism in Antiquity*.

   English translations of the more important works can be found in:

Gilbert, 1962, *Literary Criticism: Plato to Dryden*.
Russell and Winterbottom, 1972, *Ancient Literary Criticism*.
Smith and Parks, 1967, *The Great Critics*.

   Complete translations appear in the Loeb Classical Library Series. Rose, 1951, *A Handbook of Greek Literature*, is still useful.

The Story before the Writings

ಇಲ ಇಲ ಇಲ

Storytelling in Earliest Christianity

The Ancient World

The Stories of Jesus

The Basic Story

Resources for Further Study

1

Imagine that we could travel back through time. Before the invention of modern communications, we would notice how isolated people were, how long it took to find things out, how hard it was to confirm rumors. As cars disappear, the world becomes enormous. Few people travel; those who do spend months just traveling. As machinery disappears, the number of laborers multiplies. Most of them are directly involved in food production. Cities shrink; eight out of ten people live in the country. Before the development of sociology and psychology, people's inner lives take on new significance. Dreams are thought to be as real as the waking world, possibly more so. As we move back before the age of science, the world itself comes alive. No longer interpreted by mathematical formulas, or seen as a machine, the world becomes a new creation every day. Miracles are not considered violations of the laws of nature; they are simply a novel way for God to do what he does all the time.

The social scene has changed dramatically. The gap between rich and poor looms large; there are few in the middle class. People's lives are pretty much predetermined; they can expect to do exactly what their parents have done before them. Government is never chosen; it is simply there. There are no nations, only the local government and the faraway imperial power. Nor is there any distinction between church and state. The church sanctions the power of government and the government in turn enforces the rules of the church. Few people learn to read and write since books are the property of the privileged few, available mainly in the monasteries.

THE ANCIENT WORLD

Let us move even further back—before there was one religion, before the great population migrations ended the last vestiges of the Roman Empire—back to the times of the Caesars. Cities expand once again; some have millions of inhabitants. Though travel increases as trade and a money economy prevail, it is still a lengthy and distracting endeavor. Most people never travel more than thirty miles from where they were born, but the small minority who do, range widely over the new roads and shipping routes established for the military. The military is everywhere: the Romans have a standing army of more than three hundred thousand men. Constant wars occur along the frontiers of the Empire and repeated rebellions within it. Large numbers of legionnaires are on the roads, and many are stationed in the various provinces; numerous cities have been founded just to accommodate those who retire from the army after twenty years of service. There are two cultures. A high literary culture flourishes among the upper class in large cities. Most people have a basic education and can read and write (probably in Greek), but few own books (which had just been invented) or scrolls; many are functionally illiterate. For entertainment, a large city provides a music hall (possibly seating five thousand), a public theater (perhaps seating twenty thousand), and a sports arena (perhaps seating fifty thousand). The sports are related to warfare: wrestling, boxing, sword fighting, animal fighting, and so on. The athletes are a mixture of

Theater at Ephesus   This large, well-preserved theater could have seated 24,000 people for cultural and civic meetings. Acts portrays a town meeting in this theater that turned into a near riot while Paul was in Ephesus (19:23–41). Such theaters were found in every major city in the Roman Empire, and in many smaller ones as well. The detailed photo, on the facing page, shows the front of the theater, including the seats of honor (four rows up) and the altar. Every theater included an altar to the God Dionysus, patron of song and wine, and each performance opened with a sacrifice in his honor. (Photo by author.)

professional gladiators, criminals, and slaves (though a person could be all three at once).

Religion is everywhere. The games usually commemorate a religious festival. The theater, dedicated to the Greek God Dionysus, begins with a sacrifice. Public life, from politics to the trade guilds, to the public baths, is permeated by at least nominal devotion to the gods. Private religion involves devotion to the gods and ancestors of the household, as well as more esoteric cults. New religions from the East seem to spring up daily in the big cities. One meets Persian magi, Indian gurus, Egyptian priests, and Jewish merchants and magicians everywhere. Magic and astrology dominate the lives of most people as they strive to overcome the general feeling of helplessness that marks an authoritarian society. Every day in the marketplace one hears philosophers proclaiming their versions of truth and freedom. Cynics mock the culture and the prominent citizens of the day. Neo-Pythagoreans play music,

offer mystical numbers, and plead for nonviolence. Stoics proclaim reason and self-control. And the common people go about their daily tasks much as their ancestors have done for generations.

Stories are told. When the Emperor Claudius dies, people tell how his death had been forecast by omens: the lightning that struck his father's tomb, the comet that clearly foretold the death of the leader. Things did not just happen, they were part of a larger plot: all of life was a story.

A Storytelling Culture

Once there was a philosopher named Secundus, who was called Secundus the Silent because he never spoke. The reason for his silence was a very grave mistake he made as a young man. Having studied philosophy abroad, he adopted the Cynic philosophy and became a vagabond. He let his hair and beard grow, and when he re-

turned home he was not recognized by the servants or by his mother. His Cynic teachers had taught him that all women were corrupt; the ones considered chaste were only those who had not yet been discovered. He decided to test this idea by trying to arrange a tryst with his mother. When he succeeded, he shamed her by revealing his identity. Unable to bear the disgrace, she hung herself. Then Secundus decided that too many evils resulted from free speech and took a lifelong vow of silence.

Another story concerns a philosopher honored by Alexander the Great, who came to him and offered to grant him anything he desired. "Then stand aside," replied the philosopher, "so I can see the sun."

Stories like these were told in all sorts of settings: in schools, at parties, over dinner, at an inn, or simply while walking down the road. We easily forget how time-consuming travel was in the ancient world—and how boring. A good traveling companion who knew many stories was valued highly.

Numerous tales were told to entertain; many have survived in various collections. Often they were about faraway places, daring exploits, or grotesque events. One such tale concerned the steward of a large estate who was entrusted with all his master's property. His wife discovered that

Greek Dining This scene from a large bowl shows a Greek dinner party in a late stage. The men are drinking wine from bowls while they recline at table. There are no women present, a Greek but not a Roman custom. The lyre player on the right could be providing music, but more likely is telling a story—one of the ancient tales or a praise poem he has invented for the host. (Alinari/Art Resource, New York.)

he was having an affair with another woman. Enraged, she first destroyed all his account books and everything she could collect from the storeroom. Finally, she killed herself and her infant son. The master was so upset with his erring servant that he ordered him arrested, then had him stripped and smeared with honey and tied to an old fig tree in which a large colony of ants made their home. There he hung until those murderous creatures picked him quite clean. The dry white bones may be seen hanging there to this day, they say.

Such storytelling ran the gamut of human activities from education, where the stories of Homer's *Iliad* were the basic text, to politics, religion, travel, and entertainment. Professional storytellers would be hired to entertain after dinner parties and other special events. Thus, storytelling was an integral part of all aspects of life.

The earliest Christian stories were heard in such an environment. Before we begin the study of the writings of these early believers, we need to understand something of the stories behind them. In this chapter we will sketch in broad outline the development of early Christianity and consider some of the evidence of how the stories of Jesus were preserved and used. Then we must probe these stories to learn why they constituted good news (which is what "gospel" means). We will see that the basic shape of the Jesus story as a narrative of Jesus' words and deeds, culminating in his death and resurrection, reflects the oral proclamation of the church.

To tell these stories and to interpret Jesus to their audiences these believers made use of certain models, or ideal figures drawn from earlier Jewish tradition—models such as Messiah and Son of God. We will analyze four such models and see how they helped interpret Jesus. Finally, we will try to reconstruct the elements of the basic story of Jesus as it was probably told in the years immediately after Jesus' death. This is a tentative enterprise, since no written sources are available from this period. But that the story was *told* is certain, so we can know, or at least guess, something about that story and its tellers.

Storytelling among Christians

Jesus and his disciples had taken dinner at the house of a friend. As they reclined at the table, a woman unexpectedly anointed Jesus with a large amount of very costly oil—in the manner of anointing a king. The disciples were shocked at her extravagance. But Jesus came to her defense:

❧ ❧ ❧

She has done a beautiful thing to me. . . . Wherever this gospel is preached in the whole world, what she has done will be told in memory of her. (Matt. 26:6–13)

And so for more than nineteen hundred years her story has been told. The story itself holds the clue to its own preservation. Notice the two verbs: *preached* and *told*. A fundamental aspect of early Christian preaching was telling stories, and this story was part of the earliest Christian proclamation of the gospel.

This is not surprising. Such storytelling was an integral part of Jewish culture long before, and long after, the first century. Nearly a thousand years before Jesus, for example, a prophet in the royal court, a man named Nathan, had to confront the king on critical charges: adultery and murder. Avoiding a direct approach, Nathan told him a story about two men and a pet lamb (see 2 Sam. 11–12). The king was taken in by the story and condemned himself. This power of a story to take one in makes it an effective tool for those who would persuade others.

Stages of Development

That Jesus himself told stories of a most remarkable kind seems certain. These stories are called parables. No one before had ever told stories quite like them. From them we gather some of our most authentic information about Jesus.[1] In the parables we find an intense expectation of the coming of God's kingdom and a challenge to see that kingdom in the little things of life: the little seed, the woman making bread, the farmer hiring day laborers.

1. For a justification of this and the other historical judgments about Jesus expressed in this section, see Chapter 13. See also Jeremias, 1963:11 and TDNT 5:747.

Jesus himself seems to have been an enigmatic figure, little understood by his contemporaries. He showed great religious zeal, yet associated with some of the least religious elements in his society. He had been baptized by John, but went off on his own, apparently not making baptism a part of his own ministry. He gathered an enormous crowd of followers, taking twelve—symbolizing the number of the original tribes of Israel—into an inner circle. He does not seem to have addressed, except under pressure from others, what was considered the major issue of the day: how to respond to pagan Rome, the new ruler of Palestine, the sacred land.

He did not live long. He probably died in his thirties after a ministry of only a few years—perhaps even as short as one year. He died, ironically, at the hands of the Romans under a charge of insurrection. But that was not the end.

His followers burst forth with an extraordinary energy, telling all who would listen about this Jesus. They believed he was still alive (I Cor. 15:4–5), had overcome death (Acts 2:24), and was still with them (Matt. 18:20). They saw his words and deeds in a radically new way, believing that all the promises in their Bible had come true in him. We know little about those early days; not a single written source has come down to us from the first two decades after Jesus.

The first written sources appear around 50 CE: the letters of Paul. Though Paul has left us more records than any other early Christian, we know surprisingly little about him. He seems to have been born in Tarsus, a Greek city in what is today eastern Turkey. He was Jewish, perhaps the son of a Jewish slave who had been taken in war and carried off to Tarsus. If so, his father was an industrious person, probably a leather craftsman, who gained his freedom and, with it, Roman citizenship.

Paul received a good education, in both the Greek and the Jewish traditions. Some say that as a young man he went to Jerusalem, where his father's sister may have lived, to complete his Jewish studies. In any case, this young Paul bitterly opposed those followers of Jesus who were proclaiming Jesus to be a new way to God. But in the process of this opposition Paul himself was transformed—called, he believed, to carry the news of this Jesus to the Gentiles. He began to travel and to proclaim Jesus.

There must have been dozens of people like Paul, though we know little about them. They left little documentary evidence, because they operated primarily in an oral medium, telling stories. Even Paul—who never actually tells stories in his letters—seems to have been familiar with such stories. For example, when he had a problem at Corinth with how to celebrate the Lord's Supper (Communion), he responded to it as follows:

ᔍ ᔍ ᔍ

The Lord Jesus on the night when he was betrayed took bread, and when he had given thanks he broke it, and said, "This is my body which is for you. Do this in remembrance of me."

He added more details (I Cor. 11:23–26), but this sample is sufficient to see that he was familiar with a story about Jesus' last meal and used it to meet a problem. Further, he expected his hearers at Corinth also to know the story. This is not surprising, for it seems very likely that stories of Jesus' last supper with his disciples were told repeatedly whenever his followers gathered to celebrate that meal in communion.

There would have been hundreds of stories like this about what Jesus did, and many more stories retelling those he told; a great number were later written down in various collections. When and where they began to be written is not easy to discover. The ones we possess (the four gospels) all date from the last third of the first century, but there is reason to suspect earlier sources, many of which were quite different from the four gospels.

Yet the quest for written sources overlooks the most important fact about these earliest believers: they lived in an oral culture. Stories about Jesus existed long before there were any written gospels. Before trying to reconstruct some elements of these oral stories, we will consider the more basic question: who were these storytellers in the decades between Jesus' time and the writing of the gospels?

The Early Storytellers

Let us reconstruct the situation. Jesus lived in Palestine and probably spoke Aramaic, a language related to Hebrew. In his time, Aramaic was the native tongue in Palestine, Syria, and Babylon. Many of these people (and possibly Jesus) also spoke Greek, and many Jews could at least read Hebrew (which Jesus probably did). Most of the Jesus traditions would have developed in this setting—primarily Aramaic, with some Greek and Hebrew—and many of the sayings seem to have an Aramaic background.

Nevertheless, all four New Testament gospels were written in Greek, for by the time they were written the story of Jesus had spread to all the major cities of the Roman Empire and many, perhaps most, of his followers were Gentiles.

The years between the time of Jesus and the writing of the gospels were a time of tremendous change, when the stories about Jesus crossed profound barriers of language and culture. This translation was very complex: not only did the storytellers have to find Greek words with which to express the ideas, they also had to make the stories relevant to their Gentile hearers. This may be seen in minor and major details. People in Palestine, for example, understood the special significance of the fig tree, but when the saying was translated for other regions the teller simply said "every tree" (compare Mark 13:28 with Luke 21:21). It made sense in Palestine, where dirt-roofed houses were common, to speak of digging through the roof (Mark 2:4), but Greco-Roman houses had tiled roofs and the story was translated accordingly (Luke 5:19). At the other end of the scale, certain Jewish categories such as Messiah and Prophet would not make sense to Gentiles, so new categories, such as Lord and Savior, had to be developed. Trying to trace such transformations is a fascinating, though inconclusive, endeavor. We will consider more details when we study the gospels. But who were the people responsible for this monumental work? Who were the tellers of these stories?

On the one hand, the answer is everybody. Earlier, we saw how common storytelling was in this ancient culture. Surely people told the stories of Jesus as they walked on the road (Acts 8:39), sat at dinner (Acts 2:46), stood in the marketplace (Acts 17:17), and worked at their trades (Acts 18:3), among many other things. Though Paul's letters preserve the names of some of these people, we know little else about them.

While individuals remain obscure, we do know something about the kind of people they were. When Paul was having some difficulty maintaining order in one of his churches, he chided:

༄ ༄ ༄

Now you are the body of Christ and individually members of it. And God has appointed in the church first apostles, second prophets, third teachers, then workers of miracles, then healers, helpers, administrators, speakers in various kinds of tongues. (I Cor. 12:27–28)

Clearly, this is not a list composed by an administrator, judging by how far down the list administrators appear. It is a list drawn up by an apostle. Nevertheless, the ranking that Paul gives here was not disputed and was probably widely accepted (for a somewhat different list, see Eph. 4:11). Though we can no longer be sure of the precise function of each office, the first three, which are explicitly numbered, are reasonably clear.

Apostles were those "sent," the root meaning of the term. In this case they are sent by Jesus, his representatives. In the first instance this was the twelve disciples, but Paul clearly counted himself among those especially commissioned by the risen Christ (Rom. 1:1; I Cor. 9:1–2), and included others as well (I Cor. 15:7; Rom. 16:7). The office of apostle was probably claimed by numerous others (II Cor. 11:13, 12:11). Understood to be Christ's emissary, the apostle possessed a very powerful authority, an authority Paul exercised continually (I Cor. 4:9, 9:1–2; Philem. 8; I Thess. 2:6). When we read Paul's letters, we must understand that they were the letters of an apostle (as he asserts in every letter but Philippians).

Prophets also had a special relation to Christ; through them the risen Christ spoke to his community. Our clearest example of a New Testament prophet is the scene in Revelation 1 in which the risen Jesus appears to, and speaks with, the prophet John. Some of the early prophets are known by name (such as Agabus, Judas, and Silas—Acts 11:27, 15:32), others by some special designation (such as the four daughters of Philip—Acts 21:9), and many more only by allusion (Acts 13:1).

Because they were understood to be inspired by the same Spirit as the ancient prophets, they had the special task of studying the writings of these earlier prophets for their testimony to Christ (I Pet. 1:10). Unlike the apostles, prophets continued to be active well into the second century, as works like *The Shepherd of Hermas* and the *Didache* show. A major issue in late first-century and early second-century works is to distinguish between true and false prophets.

The office of teacher seems more prosaic than those of apostle and prophet since it depended less on inspiration and more on hard work. It involved high authority and great responsibility (James 3:1). The model for this office was twofold. Jesus was the model teacher; in fact, half the New Testament references to "teacher" concern Jesus. There were also teachers in the synagogues. Though the exact work of the teachers is hard to determine, they were probably responsible for instructing new converts and gathering groups of disciples whom they trained to carry on their work. Teachers were probably the most sedentary of the three groups. Apostles and prophets seem to have imitated the nomadic lifestyle of Jesus.

Apostles, prophets, and especially teachers would have told stories about Jesus as they went about their tasks: preaching, leading worship, catechism, debates, celebration, justifying their behavior, and so on. In these typical life situations the individual stories were told and retold until someone wove them into a connected narrative—a gospel. Though the process by which the gospels were put together remains obscure, one interesting theory has emerged from a careful study of the sermons in the book of Acts.

THE STORIES OF JESUS

Only the few stories of and about Jesus preserved in gospels remain. Written in the last third of the first century, thirty-five to sixty years after Jesus, they represent the culmination of years of telling and retelling, of forgetting and inventing, of condensing and elaborating. The gospels are a veritable patchwork of such stories, woven together in beautiful and daring ways to produce a larger story. Yet these patches, the individual units of tradition, existed long before the gospels were written. Like the story of the woman with the oil, they were told while proclaiming the gospel. The gospel writers shaped this material, developing it into a larger story.

Shape

On the day of Pentecost, the story goes, Peter was inspired by the Spirit and stood up to proclaim publicly his faith in Jesus, who had been executed some two months earlier.

æ æ æ

Jesus of Nazareth, a man attested to you by God with mighty works and wonders and signs which God did through him in your midst as you yourselves know—this Jesus, delivered up according to the definite plan and foreknowledge of God, you crucified and killed by the hands of lawless men. But God raised him up, having loosed the pangs of death, for it was not possible for him to be held by it. For David says concerning him . . . thou wilt not . . . let thy Holy One see corruption. (Acts 2:22–28)

This short synopsis of the first "Christian" sermon may or may not represent what Peter actually said that day, but it surely characterizes the preaching typical of that first generation.

Four characteristics of that proclamation are worth noting: first, it is wholly devoted to telling about the man Jesus; second, it focuses on his death and resurrection, which form the core of the proclamation; third, the death and resurrection are set within the context of what Jesus had done (especially the "mighty works"); and fourth, the whole is enhanced and confirmed by appealing to the Hebrew Scriptures, which are said to refer to Jesus. By this appeal to Scripture the "story of Jesus" was extended backward to the time of beginnings. Later we will see that by connecting the resurrection with the new age the preachers also extended the story forward to the time of the end. Ultimately, the story of Jesus encompasses all human history.

Now let us fill in the outline that Peter's sermon provides us: We must not imagine that ancient speakers would be content with a general allusion to Jesus' mighty deeds. They would tell the stories. Since a sermon might last for an hour or two, there was ample time to elaborate (see Acts 20:7). So too, the stories of Jesus' betrayal, trial, and death would be told. It seems likely that these stories formed a connected sequence well before the present gospels were written, for the sequence is remarkably alike in all four. Many scholars believe that the general shape of the Jesus story as it came to be recorded in the gospels was developed by the generation of preachers whose pattern is evident in this excerpt from Acts.[2] We must be careful not to assume that this earliest preaching was identical with the present content of the gospels. As we will see, the present gospels are products of the late first century and each transformed the story of Jesus to fit the situation it addressed. Yet some basic story of

Jesus' life, death, and resurrection is presupposed in the earliest Christian literature we possess. It seems likely that the shape of the earliest Jesus stories is reflected in the synopses of apostolic preaching found in Acts (namely: mighty deeds + suffering + death + resurrection). Can we learn more about the content of this earliest preaching?

Substance

The very complicated question of whether and to what extent the stories about Jesus in the gospels go back to the earliest believers must wait until we have carefully studied the gospels themselves. What we want to know now is how these earliest believers explained Jesus to their contemporaries.

There are many ways to explain something, but the most common process involves two factors: placing the new thing within a context that is already meaningful to the one you are teaching, and then adding new information that refines the understanding.

A story recorded in the gospels tells of Jesus walking with his disciples. Suddenly he interrupts them with the question, "Who do people say I am?"

They reply that there are many different opinions. "Some say you are John the Baptist; others say Elijah; others believe you are one of the prophets."

"But who do you say that I am?"

"You are the Messiah."

The various versions of this story differ as to how Jesus responded to this reply (Mark 8; Matt. 16; Luke 9). This brief incident reveals the problem Jesus' earliest followers faced: how ought they to understand this enigmatic figure? It was not enough simply to repeat the stories about him; some means had to be found to interpret those stories, to make sense of what Jesus did, to solve the enigma. This little story also reveals their strategy for understanding Jesus.

---

2. A thesis known as the *Kerygmatic* (pronounced care-rig-ma′-tic) *hypothesis,* from the Greek word for preaching *kerygma.* See Dodd, 1951.

Jesus' earliest followers interpreted him within the context of certain models, or paradigms current in their time. As we now use paradigms, or ideal types to make sense of certain individuals (an Einstein, a Gandhi, a Florence Nightingale), so these people applied paradigms to Jesus: Elijah and Messiah. Both were drawn from the Hebrew Scriptures, which, as we saw from Peter's sermon, was believed to apply in some direct way to Jesus.

These Scriptures, roughly what Christians today call the Old Testament, comprised the Bible of the early believers. Though a few of our writers demonstrate their knowledge of these Scriptures in Hebrew, most quote them from the common Greek translation of their day, the *Septuagint*, a Greek word for the number seventy (and it is often referred to as the LXX, the Roman number seventy). The name derived from the legend that it was translated by seventy scholars, who worked independently for seventy days to produce seventy identical translations. Actually, it was translated over the course of a century with a good many variations. But the legend makes its point: this is a worthy translation, which has the same divine authority as the original. Most people seem to have the accepted the point, if not the legend.

These highly authoritative Scriptures were now seen to be referring to Jesus. Luke tells a story that illustrates the point. Two of Jesus' followers are traveling in the days after the crucifixion. As they walk along, they are joined by a third person who gets them to tell him stories about Jesus. They conclude their stories by saying, "We had hoped that he was the one to redeem Israel. . . ." His death seems to have destroyed that hope. The stranger, whom the reader knows to be Jesus, replies:

๛ ๛ ๛

"O foolish men, and slow of heart to believe all that the prophets have spoken! Was it not necessary that the Christ should suffer these things and enter into his glory?" And beginning with Moses and all the prophets, he interpreted to them in all

the scriptures the things concerning himself. (Luke 24:25–27)

Two highly significant conclusions about earliest Christianity may be drawn from this story. First, the death of Jesus confused his followers and left them at a loss to explain him. Second, the solution for them lay not only in their experience of Jesus as having risen but also involved the new meanings they discovered in the Scriptures, which they now understood to apply directly to Jesus.

Reading and Reflection

Imagine you were a follower of Jesus and were confused and disappointed at his death. Now read Isa. 52:13–53:12. Imagine having seen the crucifixion, then read Ps. 22.

Understanding Jesus was a two-way process: what they read in the Scriptures helped interpret what Jesus said and did; and the words and deeds of Jesus reshaped the meaning formerly attached to the Scriptures. Thus Psalm 22 helped interpret the desolation of Jesus, making even his nakedness meaningful (Ps. 22:18). At the same time, their experience of Jesus gave new meaning to the psalmist's telling God's praises to "the ends of the earth" (Ps. 22:27; see Matt. 28:18–20).

We can see this same two-way process at work in one of our earliest statements about Jesus, probably a fragment from a traditional story that Paul quoted in the opening of his letter to the Romans, we read:

๛ ๛ ๛

The gospel of God [was] promised beforehand through his prophets in the holy scriptures, the gospel concerning his Son, who was descended from David according to the flesh and designated Son of God in power according to the Spirit of holiness by his resurrection from the dead, Jesus Christ our Lord. . . . (Rom. 1:1–4)

Notice the use of Scripture, the appeal to paradigms (Son of God; descendant of David), and the appeal to the Jesus tradition (the resurrection). This dynamic interaction produced the earliest understanding of Jesus.

Now let us briefly examine four of the most influential paradigms that scholars have discerned in the earliest traditions about Jesus. We have access to these traditions only in later written sources, especially Acts, Paul's letters, and the gospels, but they did not originate in these documents. They stem from the oral traditions behind the writings.

The Messiah

This is one of the earliest and most pervasive of the models used to interpret Jesus. The Greek word for messiah is *Christos,* which in time came to be treated as Jesus' second name: Jesus Christ. *Messiah,* meaning "the anointed," was originally applied to the high priest (Lev. 4:3) and then to the king (I Sam. 9:16). It soon became a synonym for the king (Ps. 2:1–2), who was understood to have an eternal covenant with God: there was always to be a son of David to sit on the throne of Israel (II Sam. 7:12–14; Ps. 89:3–4). But it did not happen that way.

When the Babylonians conquered Israel, they obliterated the monarchy. Centuries passed. Israel lived in subjection to the Gentiles, with no king (except for that usurper Herod, who was not even a full-blooded Jew, let alone a Davidite). Expectations grew that God would act, send the anointed, overthrow Gentile domination, establish his kingdom. This hope is vividly expressed in a pious work of the century before Jesus, *The Psalms of Solomon:*

❧ ❧ ❧

Lord, you chose David to be king over Israel, and swore to him about his descendants forever,

that his kingdom should not fail before you. But, because of our sins, sinners rose up against us. . . .
See, Lord, and raise up for them their king, the son of David, to rule over your servant Israel in the time known to you, O God.
Undergird him with the strength to destroy the unrighteous rulers, to purge Jerusalem from the Gentiles who trample her to destruction. . . .
There will be no unrighteousness among them in his days, for all shall be holy, and their king shall be the Lord Messiah.
(Psalm of Solomon 17:4–5, 21–22, 32; quoted from Charlesworth, 1985.)

The overthrow of evil and the establishment of divine rule is *what* the Messiah was expected to accomplish, but *how* he was expected to do this was never agreed upon. Some saw a divine warrior; at least two leaders of rebellions against Rome (Judas the Galilean in 6 CE and Simon bar Kochba in 135 CE) were each acclaimed as the awaited Messiah. Others viewed the coming Messiah as an essentially religious figure, as did those Jews who wrote the Dead Sea Scrolls. Some expected a heavenly figure; others a mortal man. We will examine this great diversity of opinion in more detail when we study Matthew's gospel.

What, then, did it mean to associate Jesus with this paradigm of the Messiah? Primarily, it connected him with the coming of God's rule or kingdom and the associated overthrow of evil. We have very little evidence that this was often understood in a political sense. For just as the understanding of Jesus was shaped by this paradigm, the meaning of the paradigm was transformed by the experience of Jesus. What had been conceived of as a political transformation was now understood as a spiritual transformation. They were free, now not from Roman power, but from the power of the Evil One (see Matt. 6:9–13). Stories of Jesus healing people or casting out demons would serve as visible demonstrations of this conquest.

Difficulties arose in associating this model with Jesus. Even though Christians redefined the meaning of Messiah, people continued to expect a new David (or son of David), an earthly king. But instead of destroying the wicked, Jesus himself had suffered and died—a fate never associated with Messiah before the development of Christianity. Further, the political implications of the Messiah's victory over evil had subversive connotations, for "Messiahs" tended to be rebels fighting against the power of Rome. In addition, this messianic idea was unique to Jews; Gentiles were not expecting a messiah. As Christianity spread among Gentiles, the Messiah concept had limited power to explain Jesus, because the concept itself had first to be explained to those outside Israel. While the paradigm of the Messiah explained much about Jesus, it left other things obscure. Other paradigms were needed, especially to explain his suffering.

The Suffering Servant

This enigmatic figure arises out of the complex prophecies of Isaiah. Four "songs" celebrate the fate of the Servant of Yahweh: he would bring justice to the nations, bring light to the nations, bring healing and forgiveness, and, most of all, he would suffer. (See Isa. 42:1–4, 49:1–7, 50:4–11, 52:13–53:12.) But the Servant's suffering would be redemptive: for "with his stripes we are healed" (Isa. 53:5).

In their original context these songs seem to have been an attempt to explain the harsh suffering of Israel's exile: it was not for sins, but for the healing of the nations. One song explicitly identifies the Servant and Israel:

And he said to me, "You are my servant,
Israel, in whom I will be glorified. (Isa. 49:3)

But in the long history of this tradition, the Servant became an ideal type—God's perfect servant. And in the experience of these early be-

lievers, Isaiah seemed to describe exactly the fate of Jesus:

He was despised and rejected by men;
a man of sorrows, and acquainted with
grief. . . .
Therefore I will divide him a portion with the
great,
and he shall divide the spoil with the strong;
because he poured out his soul to death,
and was numbered with the transgressors;
yet he bore the sin of many,
and made intercession for the transgressors.
(Isa. 53:3, 12. Read the whole song.)

This paradigm made sense of the most difficult aspect of the Jesus tradition—his suffering—and transcended the Messiah title in another way: it pointed to the Gentiles, the nations, as the object of healing and forgiveness. It is no accident that the first story in Acts to portray an outreach to Gentiles uses this paradigm: Philip uses the passage about the suffering servant to tell the Ethiopian eunuch "the good news of Jesus" (Acts 8:26–35; see also I Cor. 15:3; Phil. 2:7; Matt. 12:18–21; Mark 1:11).

On the positive side, this model showed Jesus' suffering to be part of the divine plan, purposeful and redemptive. Yet the Suffering Servant ideal focused almost exclusively on the death of Jesus and tended to limit his significance to the past. It lacked a way to deal with his life and teachings; other paradigms were needed.

The Final Prophet

Although a few individuals in Israel continued to claim prophetic inspiration, the great age of prophecy ended hundreds of years before the time of Jesus. But there were traditions that prophecy would once again flourish in the last days (see Joel 2:28–32, used explicitly by early Christians in Acts 2:14–21). More especially, there were traditions based on the saying in Deuteronomy 18:15 that God would send another prophet like

Moses, in fact a second Moses. This new prophet would renew the revelation from God and restore his people to holiness. As Moses marked the beginning of Israel's life, so the new Moses would mark a new beginning. He would inaugurate the reign of God.

A related notion was based on the tradition that another prophet, Elijah, did not die but was instead carried off by God (II Kings 2). Some thought he would return in the last days to witness and restore God's people (see Mal. 4:5–6, 3:1). We should not imagine that these traditions were firmly fixed. There was great variety. Matthew apparently knew a tradition that included the return of Jeremiah (Matt. 16:14), and John saw two prophets returning before the end (Rev. 11:3–13). Some stories tell of Jesus talking to Moses and Elijah (Mark 9:2–13 and the parallel accounts in Matthew and Luke).

Some Christians identified Jesus as the new Moses (Acts 3:23, 7:37) or used extensive symbols associated with Moses to present Jesus (Matt. 1–7). The image of Jesus as the final prophet was widely used in later writings by Christians who were Jews (for example, the *Preachings of Peter,* see pp. 129–130). It had the advantage of emphasizing the message of Jesus, but failed to explain adequately his suffering and death. Nor did it address his ongoing relation to the community; for that another paradigm proved useful.

The Son of God

It is not clear just how and with what meaning this title was applied to Jesus. One of the earliest occurrences is the statement quoted by Paul and cited above: "designated Son of God . . . by his resurrection from the dead" (Rom. 1:3). Does this mean that Jesus was revealed to be the "Son of God" by his resurrection or that he was appointed to that status by virtue of the resurrection? Did he always hold that status or was it a new position he achieved? The original Greek is capable of both meanings.

The affirmation *Son of God* had different meanings for different people in the first century.

Generally speaking, the Greeks were more concerned with the category of *being* (and thus were likely to understand the Romans quote above in the first sense of "revealed"), while the Jews thought more in terms of *doing* (and were therefore apt to understand the quote in the second sense). To people of the Hellenistic world "Son of God" implied someone of divine descent, usually known through his teaching and wonder-working powers—a sort of divine man whose divinity was evident in his words and works of power.

To Jews, the title *Son of God* might mean something quite different. Often it was used as a designation for Israel as God's son (Exod. 4:22–23; Hos. 11:1; notice Matt. 2:15), or for the king as the representative of the people (Ps. 2:7; II Sam. 7:14). It was also used more broadly for the pious or righteous person (Sirach 4:10). In this regard we note that the expression "servant of God" (Greek *pais*) could also mean "son of God" (Acts 3:13, 26). For Jews the expression "son of" often carried the basic meaning of "having a resemblance to." Just as the "sons of thunder" are those with a thunderlike quality (Mark 3:17, with Luke 9:54), so son of God may describe someone with a godlike quality—a pious person.

The difficulty with such a title would be the different interpretations various communities would give it. Outside a Jewish milieu it could easily lose its connection with Jesus' life and come into conflict with Jewish monotheism.

No paradigm was perfect. None matched precisely what Jesus had actually done. Still such models were useful, for each explained something about Jesus. While a particular community may have emphasized one over the others or may have used one exclusively, most used them together, piling one on another:

ﻬ ﻬ ﻬ

*God **foretold** by the mouth of all the prophets, that his **Christ** should **suffer**. . . . **Moses** said, "The Lord God will raise up for you a **prophet*** *from your brethren as he raised me up. . . . God having raised up his **servant** [pais], sent him to you first, to bless you. . . . (Acts 3:17, 22, 26, emphasis added)*

The dynamic interaction of these various paradigms, along with other scriptural models and the remembered words and deeds of Jesus, constituted the vast body of oral Jesus tradition that would have been known to the hearers of the documents we are about to study. This tradition was never just a shapeless mass of data. Early on, it was organized into a story, though one with infinite variations.

THE BASIC STORY

We simply do not know the many ways these early believers told Jesus stories. We have only the hints of the speeches in Acts, the implications of Paul's practice drawn from his letters (which are not stories, but do presuppose stories), and the later development of the gospels. Thus, we cannot trace the precise stories of Jesus as they were told in this earliest period. Still we can do something more elemental: we can draw out the implications of how stories are told and apply them to what we know of the oral Jesus tradition. All stories, whether profound or trite, religious or secular, have certain basic elements in common.

What, then, are the elements of a story? Think about the story of Little Red Riding Hood. It starts with the straightforward task of our heroine trying to deliver lunch to her grandmother, but she is opposed by the wolf, who nearly subverts her mission. But victory is snatched from near defeat with the aid of the noble woodsman. We see here three pivots, or axes, on which the story turns:

There is the axis of purpose: a task is ordained to be done.

There is the axis of commitment: someone rises to the task.

There is the axis of conflict: adversaries and helpers intervene.

All stories revolve around these three axes. Think about the story of the Exodus from Egypt (Exod. 3–14). The purpose involves the freedom of the Hebrews from Egypt; the commitment is made by Moses; the conflict involves Pharaoh and his magicians on the one side and the assistance of Aaron and the plagues on the other.

Certain literary critics have further defined these three elemental axes in terms of pairs of "actants" or basic narrative roles. (We may consider the actants as the abstractions behind the actors in a story.) Basic to the axis of purpose are the *sender* and the *receiver* (Mother/Grandmother; God/Hebrews). Basic to the axis of commitment are the *subject* of the story and the *object* she or he is trying to obtain (Red Riding Hood/Lunch; Moses/Freedom). Basic to the axis of conflict are the *helpers* and *adversaries* who assist or resist the subject (Woodsman/Wolf; Plagues/Magicians). Visually, we can represent the elements of story as follows:

```
sender → object → receiver          (axis of purpose)
              ↑                      (axis of commitment)
helpers → subject ← adversaries      (axis of conflict)
```

Such a chart should be read along each of its three axes: a sender wishes to send an object to a receiver; a subject commits herself/himself to deliver the object; adversaries resist the accomplishment of this task while helpers provide assistance.

These basic elements may be found in all stories, though not usually as clearly as in *Little Red Riding Hood*. The actants may be characters, forces, or things, and may be portrayed or only implied. Nor do all subjects succeed in delivering the object to the receiver; they sometimes fail either through a lack of commitment or a lack of power. In any given story we may actually find a series of attempts to fulfill the purpose (delivering the object to the receiver). Now let us try to apply this model to a well-known story.

Reading and Reflection

Read, analyze, and chart the story of the Good Samaritan in Luke 10:29–37 according to this model. Who needs to receive something? Who delivers it? With what assistance or resistance?

We have here the failure of two subjects and the success of the third to deliver assistance to one in need. Adversaries and helpers are not other characters in the story but such elements as other commitments, laws of purity, racial prejudice, a donkey, money, and medicine.

This story contains three stages of development central to all stories: commitment, struggle, and accomplishment. First, each character is presented with the challenge to undertake the task. Two fail at this initial point and decline the commitment. Their stories end. One accepts the challenge, but must then perform the task, which leads to the second stage, the struggle (here, loading the man on the donkey, carrying him to the inn, providing for his keep). The stage of accomplishment or success (in this case, healing) is only implied in the story in Luke.

The model may be greatly expanded. Each of these stages may have several enactments of the model in a complex story, and the stage of performance may involve many tasks. In addition, the actants should not be identified with the actors in the story, for a given actor may fulfill different actantial roles at various points in the story. Yet however complex the story development may be, the basic narrative roles (actants) and the three stages are always implied in every story.

One basic difference between *Little Red Riding Hood* and the story of the Good Samaritan is necessary for our discussion. In the fairy tale, good overcomes evil by superior power and evil is destroyed; in the parable, good overcomes evil by love. We may refer to the former as a story of justice, in which people get what they deserve, and to the latter as a story of mercy.

If we chart the version of the Jesus story, which we discern in the proclamation of Peter (Acts 2), we find that it is basically a story of mercy. Thus:

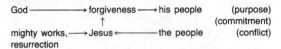

God wished to bestow forgiveness on his people; Jesus became the agent of that forgiveness; but he was resisted by his own people and killed. Nevertheless, through his mighty works and especially his resurrection they can know that God did triumph through him. Such seems to be the charter story implied in this synopsis.

Although we do not know what was actually said, we can make some inferences about the incidents used to tell this story. Given the axis of purpose, we can conjecture that the actual telling of the Jesus story implied in this brief synopsis would have contained incidents that demonstrated God's intention to redeem his people. It seems that citing Scripture was the primary means of showing this purpose, and we would expect incidents to be developed that show how Jesus' deeds corresponded to scriptural foretelling. Given the axis of commitment, we would expect incidents that show Jesus accepting the challenge, though he was tempted to turn aside. Finally, the axis of conflict implies many stories of Jesus' confrontation with the people and a strong emphasis on miracle.

Paul's letters, our earliest Christian literature, contain little that can be properly called a story of Jesus. That is not what the letters are about; they are not proclamation. They serve, rather, as instruction to those who have already heard and responded to the proclamation. Paul clearly presupposes his own version of that story, as is evident in passages like Galatians 3:23–28, Romans 3:21–26, or Philippians 2:5–11. Paul's version seems richly complex and our model can only hint at its shape, but we might chart it like this:

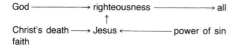

God wishes to send righteousness to all people; Jesus becomes the agent of that righteousness; he was resisted by the power of sin but triumphed through his death. This is very elementary, but even so we learn something by this exercise.

If we compare this pattern with the one from Acts given above, several conclusions may be drawn. This story about Jesus being God's agent to bring righteousness to all differs somewhat from the one we deduced from Peter's preaching. Paul has expanded the receiver beyond God's people to "all," and has refined the object from a general forgiveness to the attainment of righteousness. Apparently, not everyone told the story in the same way; there was a variety of understanding from the start.

In addition, the context in which the story is told seems to shape it. The Acts sermon, addressed to Jews, portrayed the receiver as "God's people," while Paul—the apostle to the Gentiles—expands God's purpose to include all.

Finally, there seem to be two events on which the storytellers focused. In one version the resurrection of Jesus is the supreme revelation; in the other, his death is paramount.

Different contexts and insights probably lie behind the various models or paradigms discussed earlier. Each represented a distinctive way of telling the Jesus story. Each would characterize him and his task in its unique way, providing great flexibility and variety in the verbal delivery. This variety alerts us to be constantly concerned, not only with the story but also with the tellers of the story and their historical and social settings. Their charter stories, community stories, and personal stories will exhibit strong correlations.

Now let us try to imagine how they told their stories. In the following pages we will meet first the great apostle, Paul, whose letters returned to his communities when he could not. Written to be read aloud in the assembly, these letters must be heard as well as seen. As we hear them, we must listen for the underlying story of Jesus in Paul's proclamation, and try to grasp the basic story of the world as he and his followers understood it (Chapters 3–5). For as these people heard the story of Jesus, they became participants in it, creating in turn a larger story that included their own lives. Next we will turn to the narrative literature, the gospels and the apocalypse, to see the many ways the Jesus story developed in the late first century (Chapters 6–11). Finally, we will listen for the echoes of other stories told by other voices—the minority reports (Chapter 12). To bring our discussion full circle, we will consider the story after the writings, studying the processes of collection and exclusion that produced the New Testament canon. At that point, we will step back from the immediacy of the individual writings to view their underlying unity. We will raise the question of history more abstractly, especially as it pertains to the historical Jesus, and discuss the relation of history to story (Chapter 13). This is a lengthy endeavor. Yet we may regard it not so much as work as a mystery to be explored, a story to be heard. All that follows is designed to help you hear the story more clearly than you otherwise might. Listen.

RESOURCES FOR FURTHER STUDY

A great deal of scholarly attention has been devoted to studying the materials about Jesus before the writing of the gospels. The method used to study this material was adapted from the study of literary and social forms in the Hebrew Scriptures and is thus called form criticism. Outstanding presentations of the method include:

Lofink, 1979, *The Bible: Now I Get It.*
McKnight, 1969, *What Is Form Criticism?*
Travis, "Form Criticism," in Marshall, 1977a.

The original works in form criticism will be of interest to more advanced students, especially:

Bultmann, 1931, *The History of the Synoptic Tradition.*
Dibelius, 1934, *From Tradition to Gospel.*
Taylor, 1935, *The Formation of the Gospel Tradition.*

The study of stories by an analysis of their abstract structures is explained in Patte, 1976, *What Is Structural Exegesis?*

Much of the work on the oral traditions about Jesus has been aimed at rediscovering what Jesus actually said and did, a topic known as "The problem of the historical Jesus." (See the discussion and resources for further study in Chapter 13.) The other issue, the question of how the Jesus traditions were actually used and understood in the early period, is addressed by tradition criticism. I know of no good introductory treatment. See the specific studies in tradition criticism by Fuller, 1980; and Hultgren, 1979.

The theory that the oral preaching of the early believers shaped the story of Jesus is argued by Dodd, 1951. Kelber, 1983, highlights the power of the oral gospel even while challenging the easy continuity between the oral and the written.

The developing understanding of Jesus is traced by Cullman, 1963; and Dunn, 1980. See also Hengel, 1983.

On expectations about the Messiah, see:

Klausner, 1955, *The Messianic Idea in Israel.*
Mowinckel, 1956, *He That Cometh.*
Nickelsburg and Collins, 1980, *Ideal Figures in Ancient Judaism,* trace a variety of paradigms.

One of the most readable treatments of the ancient world and its bearing on the New Testament is that of Freyne, 1980. See also Bruce, 1972; and Reicke, 1968. The standard reference treatment is that in Cook et al., eds., 1924, *The Cambridge Ancient History.*

On social conditions, see:

Casson, 1974, *Travel in the Ancient World.*
Carcopino, 1940, *Daily Life in Ancient Rome.*
Rostovtzeff, 1957, *The Social and Economic History of the Roman Empire.* More advanced level.
Watson, 1969, *The Roman Soldier.*

The major primary sources for the study of this era include:

Eusebius, *History of the Church.*
Josephus, *The Antiquities of the Jews.*
———, *Autobiography.*
———, *Jewish War.*
Philo, Collected works.
Suetonius, *The Lives of the Caesars.*
Tacitus, *Annals.*

All are available in convenient English translations in the Loeb Classical Library (Harvard University Press). Relevant extracts from these and other documents are conveniently available in:

Barrett, 1971a, *New Testament Background: Selected Documents.*
Kee, 1984, *New Testament in Context: Sources and Documents.*

On the Jewish sources, see Glatzer, 1969; and Montefiore and Loewe, 1974. For a brief description of the many, often obscure, Jewish sources from this era, see the appendix to Stone, 1980.

Major collections include:

The Dead Sea Scrolls (Dupont-Sommer, 1962; Vermes, 1968)
The New Testament Apocrypha (Hennecke and Schneemelcher, 1963; James, 1924)
The Pseudepigrapha (Charles, 1913; Charlesworth, 1983, 1985)

The Earliest Christian Literature

The Thessalonian Correspondence

A Literary Analysis of First Thessalonians
A Historical Analysis of First Thessalonians
A Comparative Analysis of Second Thessalonians
The Thessalonian Story
Resources for Further Study

2

Why no Christian literature from the first two decades after Jesus has come down to us remains a mystery. Perhaps none was written. Perhaps what was written was of inferior quality. Perhaps the oral tradition, discussed in Chapter 1, was so strongly felt that it seemed inappropriate to write. Perhaps some archaeologist will yet turn up something from that age. The literature that has survived began to appear around the year 50, when a traveling teacher, unable to return to some of his followers, wrote them a letter. We will examine that letter for its literary structure, its historical context, and its major teachings, and consider its relation to a second letter addressed to the same group but possibly written by someone else. This possibility will lead us to discuss the meaning of authorship in the ancient world.

The traveling teacher was Paul, who had been a follower of this new way for about fifteen years. Much of this time he traveled, building tents and spreading the word of this new faith. He had founded an assembly (as they called their meetings) in Thessalonica, a thriving seaport city in northern Greece (Macedonia). Paul felt uneasy about these new followers. He had not been able to spend as much time in Thessalonica as he had wanted to, and, even more serious, most of his converts had been Gentiles who lacked the Jewish background necessary to understand Paul's faith. Unable to return himself, he sent one of his assistants, Timothy, to check on the Thessalonians. When Timothy returned to Paul, probably in Corinth (about two hundred miles to the south), he was moved to write this letter, some-time in the late forties or very early fifties. (See I Thess. 2:17–3:10.)

A LITERARY ANALYSIS OF FIRST THESSALONIANS

Our study of Paul's first letter to the Thessalonians begins with a close look at its literary aspects. First we will examine its structure in relation to other ancient letters, then consider its rhetoric and listen for the story behind the words.

The Shape of the Letter

The general structure of a letter in antiquity was fairly fixed, though there was some variety in kinds of letters. Letters always began with the name of the sender, followed by the name of the receiver, and a greeting (often simply "health"). Then followed a personal section, often recalling some past association, and next the reason for the letter, usually a request of some sort. Letters regularly ended with salutations to mutual friends and a closing wish. Here are two typical examples of private letters: the first is written by a husband away from home on business and the other by a homesick recruit trying to reassure his mother that he is well.

&⁊ &⁊ &⁊

Damas, assistant, to Artemidora my sister [wife], greeting.
Before all else I make supplication for you every

Roman Legionary Stone Also known as a mile-stone, these six-foot pillars were the ancient equivalent of the billboard. They were set up by the legions in honor of the Emperor, extolling his greatness. This one, from Palestine, dates from the late second century and honors Julius Pertenax, whom the Syrian legions were putting forward as the next Emperor. The Romans built an awesome system of roads, connecting every part of their empire and greatly facilitating travel. (Middle East Archives, London.)

day. Please come up to the metropolis at the New Year, since I am coming up to the city. Salute your mother and your father. I pray for your health.

❧ ❧ ❧

Apollinarius to Taesis, his mother and lady, many greetings.

   Before all I pray for your health. I myself am well and make supplication for you before the gods of this place. I wish you to know, mother, that I arrived in Rome in good health on the 25th of the month Pachon and was posted to Misenum [to join the fleet], though I have not yet learned the name of my company; for I had not gone to Misenum at the time of writing this letter. I beg you then, mother, look after yourself and do not

worry about me; for I have come to a fine place. Please write me a letter about your welfare and that of my brothers and of all your folk. And whenever I find a messenger I will write to you; never will I be slow to write.

   Many salutations to my brothers and Apollinarius and his children and Karalas and his children. I salute Ptolemaeus and Ptolemais and her children and Heraclous and her children. I salute all who love you each by name.

   I pray for your health. (Hunt and Edgar: 333, 303)

Both letters follow a common pattern: there is a standard opening with the salutation "greeting." After alluding to praying for the recipient, the sender launches into the main reason for writing. A section of salutations to others precedes the formal closing, which concludes with another allusion to prayer. We can see a very similar pattern in I Thessalonians:

Paul began with the standard opening and greeted them (with "grace to you and peace" in place of "greetings"—1:1);

he alluded to praying for them;

he reminisced about their past association (1:2–3:13);

and then taught and exhorted them (4:1–5:22),

before closing with the wish for sanctity and grace (5:23–28).

The salutation to mutual friends, almost non-existent in I Thessalonians (5:26), will be expanded in later letters.

It is possible to sketch a "standard form" for Paul's letters (based on Doty, 1973:27):

> Opening
>   Sender
>   Receiver
>   Greeting
> Blessing/Thanksgiving
>   Often with a prayer

Main body
> Often begins with a formula ("I would not have you be ignorant" or "I appeal to you")
> Often ends with a reference to the near or ultimate future

Exhortations to good behavior

Closing
> Standard benediction ("The grace of the Lord Jesus be with you")
> Sometimes mentions the writing process.

Two conclusions are evident. First, Paul's letters were similar to ancient letters generally. The hearers of these letters would have known what to expect, what to listen for, and would have been guided by these expectations.

Second, there is a certain distinctiveness and innovation about Paul's letters. In addition to the specifically Christian wording introduced in the opening and closing, two major features stand out: the ethical exhortations at the end and the blessing at the beginning. This blessing is technically known as the thanksgiving, because it most often begins with the expression "I give thanks." Modern studies of these thanksgiving sections demonstrate that they are carefully crafted introductions to the main themes of the letters.

This thanksgiving section is especially important for understanding I Thessalonians, for it comprises over half the letter, a length unsurpassed in any of Paul's letters.

Reading and Reflection

Now try an initial reading of I Thessalonians, paying special attention to the way the thanksgiving (1:2–3:13) governs the whole letter.

1. For what does Paul give thanks?
2. What motifs from the thanksgiving recur in the body of the letter?

READING GUIDE TO FIRST THESSALONIANS

Opening   1:1
Thanksgiving with a long narrative extension   1:2–3:13
Main body   4:1–5:11
   Preliminary exhortation   4:1–12
   Teaching section   4:13–5:11
     with a formula ("I would not have you be ignorant"   4:13)
     with reference to the ultimate future   (5:1)
Exhortations to good behavior   5:12–22
Closing   5:23–28

The Rhetoric of the Letter

Timothy's report on the developments at Thessalonica after Paul left had been encouraging, and Paul was exuberant that these new followers were doing so well. The dominant note of the letter is joy and its primary literary feature is the thanksgiving. Paul gives thanks for three characteristics: their (1) work of faith, (2) labor of love, and (3) steadfastness of hope (1:3). Faith–love–hope is a triad we meet often in Paul. Here they provide the framework for the rest of the thanksgiving and the solution to two problems emerging at Thessalonica. Notice how they look to the past (faith), the present (love), and the future (hope), and how each of these joyful words has a companion of a different tone: Faith/work, love/labor, hope/steadfastness (or endurance). This interplay between work and joy provides the moving force of the letter.

Paul used two similes (metaphorical comparisons) to describe his relation to these Thessalonians; they echo this same duality and provide the dominant emotional orientation of the letter. On the one hand, he is "like a father with his children" (2:11). In Greek and Roman society a father was a stern taskmaster, who demanded that his children fulfill their duties, learn their lessons, live up to their station in life. On the other hand, Paul described himself as being "like a nurse taking care of her children" (2:7). The nurse was the loving, self-sacrificing, caretaker in this society. Paul sought to embody a gentle sternness and to elicit a labor of love.

This labor involves both the suffering with which the people embraced the faith (2:1–2, 14) and the physical labor required to earn one's keep (2:9 and 4:9–12). Paul bragged about the way they had accepted both his suffering and their own to attain this new faith. They had:

⁊ ⁊ ⁊

. . . turned to God from idols, to serve a living and true God, and to wait for his Son from heaven, whom he raised from the dead, Jesus who delivers us from the wrath to come. (1:9–10)

Notice again the three temporal references: they turned in the past, serve in the present, and wait for a future. But there is more than one way to wait, and some at Thessalonica were waiting in ways that Paul viewed as destructive. What their problems were is not completely clear to us, but they were basically of two kinds: a passive waiting for the end of the world that involved abandoning work and other normal activities (4:11; see also II Thess. 3:6), and something Paul refers to as ignorance—probably a faulty understanding of the End (4:13). Before we examine what that understanding was, we should consider the source of their information, the oral Jesus stories.

The Oral Tradition in the Letter

In responding to these concerns, Paul cited a fragment of the Jesus tradition about the coming end of the world. We can see how Paul used this tradition because another version of it has been recorded by another writer in the Gospel of Matthew. Writing much later than the time of Paul, Matthew included an extensive tradition, while Paul only alluded to a specific point. Yet we do find parallels:

I Thessalonians 4:15–17	Matthew 24:29–35
For this we declare to you by the word of the Lord, that we who are alive, who are left until the coming of the Lord, shall not precede those who have fallen asleep. For the Lord himself will descend from heaven with a cry of command, with the archangel's call, and the sound of the trumpet of God. And the dead in Christ will rise first; then we who are alive, who are left, shall be caught up together with them in the clouds to meet the Lord in the air; and so shall we always be with the Lord.	Immediately after the tribulation of those days the sun will be darkened and the moon will not give its light, and the stars will fall from heaven, and the powers of the heavens will be shaken; then will appear the sign of the Son of Man in heaven, and then all the tribes of the earth will mourn, and they will see the Son of Man coming on the clouds of heaven with power and great glory; and he will send out his angels with a loud trumpet call, and they will gather his elect from the four winds, from one end of heaven to the other.

Clouds, trumpet, angels, descent from heaven, gathering of the elect all point to a common, though not fixed, tradition. Paul's use of that tradition is free, citing not quoting. (Of course, quotation marks were not invented till the fifteenth century, and even Matthew may have used the tradition freely.) Both Paul and Matthew employ the same tradition of the unexpected coming, "like a thief in the night" (compare I Thess. 5:2 with Matt. 24:42–44).

We might note in passing that the Greek word Paul used here to refer to Jesus' coming has become a technical term in scholarly literature. The word *parousia* means "to be present," or more specifically to be present in an official way to exercise authority.

This comparison shows that aspects of the Jesus tradition were widely known in the world of Paul and his congregations, even if we cannot say in just what form. These traditions about the Parousia had probably been used in Paul's proclamation at Thessalonica and were now causing problems for them. What really was the problem?

One intriguing suggestion is that the issue at Thessalonica stemmed from this same oral tradition about the end. That tradition, as preserved in Matthew, includes the assertion: ". . . this generation will not pass away till all these things take place" (Matt. 24:34). This saying may have various interpretations, but might raise an important question: If the end were so near, why should one continue to work? Also, some may have understood it to mean that believers would not die before the return of Jesus and the end of the world. Perhaps they thought that those who died had fallen from the faith or committed secret sin.[1]

Further, these Gentiles would assume that those who die pass on to another life and thus would not participate in any events on earth. The Greeks generally considered humans as spirits or souls that escaped the body at death and went to a heaven or hell. The Jews, by contrast, understood humans as a living union of body and soul and did not originally believe in a life for the soul beyond death until it was reunited with the body.[2] Since this notion of resurrection was foreign to most Gentiles, they may have assumed that all who had died had missed out on the kingdom of God on earth.

Still, Paul had been gone from them less than a year, so it is unlikely that many had died or

that there was any disillusionment caused by the failure of the end to come. Their concern seems to have been with the fate of the departed rather than their own waiting. Thus, Paul started his explanation with the exhortation "that you may not grieve as others do who have no hope" (4:13).

It is worth asking how Paul established that hope, since it is unclear if the Jesus tradition itself said anything about the central problem, the fate of the dead. There is no such concern in the Matthean version available to us. Paul made three moves to apply the tradition to the problem. First, and most important, he interpreted the traditional saying of Jesus in the light of Jesus' own resurrection (4:14). As we will see, the early Christian conviction that Jesus rose from the dead often transformed how they understood his words and deeds. Here is a clear example of faith reevaluating tradition, for the tradition takes on a genuinely new meaning because of the conviction that Jesus rose from the dead. Second, Paul drew on the clear part of the tradition: Jesus' return would be a public and universal event in which he would gather all the elect (Matt. 24:31). Finally, Paul brought the word of the Lord up to date by adding an inference concerning the dead: they too will rise and join in this event (4:16). This follows inevitably from the other two: if all are to be gathered and if death has been overcome, then believers who have died must be raised. It was this living and dynamic character of the oral tradition that made it so valuable to the early church, and so problematic for the modern historian.

The Demands of the Future

Paul proceeded to build two further ideas on this oral tradition, both of which shift attention from speculations about the future to the more immediate concern of life in the present.

The first is a traditional idea, even commonplace. Since the day of the Lord will come unexpectedly, like a thief in the night, the people

1. Compare I Cor. 11:30, where Paul says that unworthy participation in the Lord's Supper can result in sickness and even death.
2. However, by Paul's time many Jews had been influenced by Greek ideas. For a full discussion of the issues involved see Cullmann, 1958, and Nicklesburg, 1972.

ought to be always prepared, living moral and faithful lives (5:1–3). This moral demand was common in writings about the coming end of the world (compare Matt. 24:42–51 and Rev. 3:3). It is a safe, if not inspiring, moral exhortation, resembling the warning to children that they had better be good because their parents may return from their errand at any moment.

The second idea is more daring and more inspiring (and, it turned out, more dangerous). Paul became captivated by his metaphor: the day of the Lord. He played with the ideas of night and day, darkness and light, boldly exhorting:

≈ ≈ ≈

But you are not in darkness brethren for that day to surprise you like a thief. For you are all sons of light and sons of the day; we are not of the night or of darkness. So then let us not sleep, as others do, but let us keep awake and be sober. For those who sleep sleep at night, and those who get drunk are drunk at night. But, since we belong to the day, let us be sober, and put on the breastplate of faith and love, and for a helmet the hope of salvation. (5:4–8)

Notice how the ethical enterprise depends now, not on some future event, but on the present event of a transformed life. People are no longer asked to be good just because they might get caught at it. Goodness is now based on the transformation that occurs in those who are already children of the day. That future day is already present in the transformed lives of these Thessalonians, according to Paul. This is Paul at his finest; imaginative, innovative, centrally concerned about ethics, blazing new trails, and saying more than he intended to. For if taken literally, his teaching implies that that day has already come. We will return to this passage when we discuss II Thessalonians.

This literary analysis has shown that Paul's letter has a two-part structure, reflected in the duality of ideas (work/faith, labor/love, endurance/hope), the duality of experience (present/ future, night/day, death/resurrection), and in the two basic aspects of the letter (thanksgiving/exhortation). Its theme is that of joy and "do so more and more" (4:1,10). There is little mention of controversy or of failure. The problems revolve around their expectations of the coming end. Paul responds to these concerns with a creative use of the Jesus tradition, then quickly moves on to practical concerns for the present life of his new congregation. We have also encountered several unusual ideas that are remote from our time. Now let us examine more closely the general and specific historical circumstances surrounding this letter.

A HISTORICAL ANALYSIS OF FIRST THESSALONIANS

We turn now from a consideration of the letter itself to an investigation of the life context in which it was written and read. Here we are trying to eavesdrop on the story of Paul and of his followers at Thessalonica. How much of their stories can we discern from a careful reading of this letter?

Paul's Relation to the Thessalonians

The most immediate context of this letter is that of a wandering teacher responding to the needs of one of his groups of followers when he is unable to return in person. Paul had two means of maintaining contact with (and control over) assemblies founded by him: personal emissaries and letters, both evident in I Thessalonians. Perhaps the primary purpose of the letter was to alleviate Paul's own anxiety about his new followers (2:17–3:5). They appear to have been primarily Gentiles (1:9), although Acts 17, which describes Paul's visit to Thessalonica, implies that the church there started in the synagogue, the Jewish house of prayer and study. How long Paul spent with his followers is uncertain. The letter implies that it was long enough to set up a business (or perhaps associate with a local tentmaker) and earn his own keep (2:9), while Acts implies a brief

The Grandeur That Was Rome   This artist's reconstruction shows something of the magnificence of Rome and, to a lesser degree, of all major cities. In the background is the Emperor Caligula's palace (about 40 CE). Directly in front of the palace (center) is the home of the vestal virgins, containing the altar and Temple of Vesta (the round building). This was the central "hearth" of the Roman people whose fire the vestals were never to let go out. To the right is a typical Roman temple to Castor and Pollux. The arch of Titus stands to the left (see detail on p. 169). Such enormous public buildings, each richly ornamented with statues and paintings, were the pride of ancient cities. (Alinari/Art Resource, New York.)

stay of two to four weeks (17:1–10). Acts is probably oversimplifying in the interest of a compact narrative.

Though we tend to imagine Paul as a modern pastor or missionary who devotes full time to his religious work, this was not the case. Like the Jewish synagogues, the earliest assemblies of Christians were organizations of laymen. Neither institution employed a professional clergy, and, even much later, rabbis worked at some trade to support themselves.

Paul seems to have been a tentmaker, which we should probably understand in the broader sense of leather worker (just as the modern term *cabinetmaker* means woodworker or carpenter). As a tradesman, Paul would have worked long hours, doing much of his teaching while at work at his bench: "We worked night and day . . . while we preached to you the gospel of God" (I Thess. 2:9).

The next context is the city itself. Thessalonica was a cosmopolitan city with a fair-sized Jewish community and a diversity of Greek, Roman, and local religious rites. Coins show a variety of deities: Apollo, Artemis, Athena, Heracles, Dionysus, Poseidon, Pan, Zeus, and Roma. This last indicates the existence of the imperial cult (worship of the Emperor) in the city. In Paul's day the temple of Roma would have contained images of Julius and Augustus. There was also a survival of an archaic fertility cult, whose formerly violent God was now transformed into

The Deified Augustus, about 25 CE The Emperor Augustus died in 14 CE and was deified that same year. This deification proclaimed that Augustus did not descend into the underworld, as all mortals did, but that he ascended into heaven where, like the other starry presences, he exerted his influence. The practice of Tiberias, and most later emperors, recognized such deification only for their deceased predecessors. (Hirmer Verlag, Munich.)

a protector of seamen. The diversity of this list reminds us that the religious experiences of Gentiles in that age was quite unlike our own. Rather than choosing one "best" religion, people usually combined elements from several religious systems, a process called syncretism. Generally, these deities provided only the public expression of religion; private religious needs were met in other ways, such as mystery religions, magic, and astrology. But all citizens would be expected to participate in these public rites.

The city possessed a good gulf, which made it an important seaport and, combined with its location on the Egnatian Way (the main road between Rome and the East), a prosperous trade center. Politically, Thessalonica was a free city and had its own popular assembly. In these ways it is typical of the kind of city to which Paul was

attracted and in which he proclaimed the Jesus story.

Now let us examine more closely what this letter reveals about Paul's telling of that story. In Chapter 1 we learned that the story of Jesus was expanded into the past, by seeing the Hebrew Scriptures as telling about Jesus, and into the future, by seeing Jesus as God's agent for the time of the end. First Thessalonians focuses on the latter, and to understand how Paul related Jesus to the coming end, we need to investigate what people thought about the end of the world in his day.

Paul's Version of the End of the Story

Some of Paul's descriptions of the future probably sounded a little odd, like science fiction or fantasy literature today. Heavenly trumpets, calls of archangels, resurrections, heavenly descents, meetings in the clouds—hardly the stuff of everyday reality. Actually, Paul culled these descriptions from a unique kind of literature, a genre as removed from the letter as science fiction is from normal life today.

Modern scholars have named this genre after its most popular representative, the Apocalypse of John (also called the Book of Revelation). The first word of that work is *Apocalypsis,* whose root meaning is "to take off the covering, to lay bare, to make naked," and thus by analogy to reveal, a revelation. An apocalypse is a written account intending to unveil the events of history, to see behind them to their true (spiritual) causes and effects. The apocalypses regularly achieved this unveiling by means of strange, often bizarre, symbolism: animals with multiple heads, angelic visitors, trips to heaven, and the use of symbolic numbers.[3] But apocalypticism was more than a way of writing; it was a total way of looking at life, what anthropologists call a worldview.

3. For a discussion of these elements of the genre, see Chapter 11.

The Worldview of Apocalypticism

This way of looking at life had been very influential in Jewish thought for two centuries before Paul; some elements of it were even older. The event that seems to have brought apocalyptic ideas to the forefront and made them compelling occurred in 168 BCE.

Antiochus the Fourth, a descendant of one of Alexander's generals and now the king of Syria, had been frustrated in his attempt to conquer Egypt and moved to solidify the territories he already controlled, including Palestine. Cooperating with certain elements in Jewish society who were extremely open to Greek culture, Antiochus sought to eliminate the most distinctive religious characteristics of the Jewish people: circumcision, dietary restrictions, Sabbath observance, and exclusive worship of one God. He made laws forbidding these practices, executing those who persisted. The Temple in Jerusalem was rededicated to Zeus, and a pig, a common Greek sacrifice (but considered an unclean animal by the Jews), was sacrificed on the high altar. To the faithful it seemed like the end of the world. They had been overtaken by a greater evil than they had ever known.

Yet the real problem of suffering is never the suffering itself, but rather how to explain it. The deepest anguish, even death itself, can be borne if one knows why one suffers. The traditional answer to the question of suffering was that Israel suffered because of sin: God was punishing and purifying the people. This had been a useful explanation, allowing the people of Israel to recover from the devastation of the Exile in 587 BCE when in one swoop they lost the kingship, the Temple, the land, and the prophets. This explanation was still given during the new suffering under Antiochus, and it was still effective, since few humans can claim to be without sin. Yet the explanation had one serious flaw: it did not explain why this suffering affected only certain people in Israel. Sin might cause suffering, but would that explain who was suffering? Precisely not the "sinners," since those willing to forsake

their ancestral faith and go along with these foreign ways were rewarded. Only the faithful suffered. How could one explain that?

The Source of Suffering

The history of the development of religion in Israel is a complicated and fascinating topic, well beyond our scope. But we should note a basic shift that occurred between the time of the kingdom (roughly 1000–600 BCE) and the time of Antiochus. In the four centuries since the end of the kingdom, Israel was in direct contact with other cultures, whose ideas of God and of the supernatural world influenced Israelite views. The most important of these contacts was with Persian culture. In Persia, the Jews encountered a form of monotheism that dealt with the problem of evil in a novel way.

Centuries earlier a religious reformer named Zarathustra, but known more commonly by the Greek form of his name Zoroaster, had rejected the ancient polytheism of his people for the worship of one God, Ahura Mazda. The Father of all, Ahura Mazda was said to have begotten twin spirits: one wholly good, the other wholly evil. These spirits struggle for control of the world and of humans; the one to whom we give our allegiance will prevail, according to this intensely ethical reformer. By the time of Israel's exposure to Zoroastrianism, the situation seems to have shifted; Ahura Mazda himself became identified with the good spirit and his opposite was known as Anra Mainyu, the evil one. Because it proposes two ultimate powers, this system of thought is called dualism.

This simple dualism of good and evil is a powerful and seemingly obvious conclusion to our human experience, but it could never be acceptable to many of the ancient Jews. Their idea of the absolute power and authority of their God, Yahweh, left no room for equal and opposite forces. This emphasis on the absoluteness of Yahweh is evident in a remarkable story in I Kings (22:1–23), in which God is portrayed as the real source of even the lies told by the false prophets:

the lying spirit is an underling in the heavenly court of Yahweh.

But this concept of God as absolute could not explain the suffering under Antiochus, at least not for some; so a compromise was reached. The latent notion of evil spirits—disobedient angels—was amplified by the contact with Persian dualism to account for the presence of a seemingly independent evil in the world. God, it was concluded, had an Adversary. Not at all an equal, this evil one was rebelling against his rightful role of subservience to Yahweh. The Hebrew word for adversary is Satan, though like many rebels he soon traveled under several aliases: Lucifer, the Devil, Beelzebub, the Evil One, the Prince of this Age. This last title suggests an explanation for the problem of the suffering of the righteous.

The Plot of the Apocalyptic Story

The explanation for suffering was grounded in the view that there are really two ages to the world: this age and the age to come. While the future age will be the time when God rules, when justice and righteousness prevail, the present is a time of great wickedness, ruled over by the Prince of Darkness. Because the Evil One is in control of the powers of this age, righteous people must expect to suffer: as the end of this age approaches, wickedness will exert itself with the desperation of someone drowning. Thus, the increase in wickedness is evidence that the end of the age is near. In this way we could say that for the apocalypticist the worse things became, the better they were: for when wickedness has reached its zenith, God will intervene, bring this age to an end, and establish divine rule on earth, the Kingdom of God. This sequence is shown in Figure 2.1.

While apocalypticists differed widely on how they envisioned the coming of God's kingdom, there was widespread agreement on the basic pattern: (1) there are two ages; (2) the new age is near; (3) evil will increase as that age approaches; and (4) God will suddenly and unex-

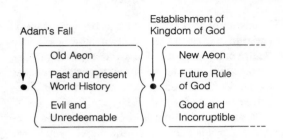

Figure 2 ▪ 1 Apocalyptic View of History This Age is under the control of Evil, but The Age to Come will be wholly Good. The Apocalypticist proclaimed that we stand at the end of the Present Age. (From *Interpretation: A Bible Commentary for Teaching and Preaching*, Vol. on Romans, by Paul J. Achtemeier, 1985. Used by permission of John Knox Press.)

pectedly intervene to overthrow evil. The details of how they told their stories of the end varied, but there was widespread agreement on this basic plot.

Paul's Revision of the Apocalyptic Story

Though Paul was no apocalypticist and his letters are far from apocalypses, he did share much of the apocalyptic worldview. Specifically, he agreed with the basic plot: Paul believed that this age would end soon and that he would be alive to see it.[4] Paul warned the Thessalonians that the end would be unexpected, and advised them how to live in this evil age (5:1–8). The role of the Evil One and the increase of evil are not clearly stated in this letter, but they were part of Paul's concept.[5]

But these apocalyptic motifs are not his central ideas; they are simply assumptions he makes about the world. Unlike the apocalypticists, Paul does not dwell on these last events but on their

4. I Thess. 4:17—"then we who are alive"; compare I Cor. 15:51–52 and 7:25–31.
5. Gal. 1:4; II Cor. 4:4; note, however, the emphasis on the suffering of the Thessalonians: 1:6; 2:9, 14.

implications: What manner of people ought they to be in view of the coming end? The strongest tendency of this letter is its diversion of concern about the end into concern for the present. But then, Paul did not make as strong a distinction between the two as was usual. Paul asserted that in some way the people already participated in that new day (5:4–5). Christ had delivered them from this present evil age, as Paul would remind the Galatians (Gal. 1:3). This meant that Paul could never abandon the world but was forced to live in and try to change it. For Paul future, past, and present all met in Christ. In his version of the story, the crucial act of divine intervention had already occurred in the death and resurrection of Christ. This meant that the new age had already begun. But it was not yet fully come. Paul lived in the gap between this *already* and *not yet* and developed his ideas about life and action accordingly.

In Summary

The notion of living in the world in love, with the faith that Christ has already been raised from the dead, and in the hope that he will soon return to establish God's kingdom is the letter's major theme. It is woven into the thanksgiving (1:3, 9–10; 2:2; 3:8, etc.) and underlies the seemingly random admonitions with which he closes (5:12–22).

This letter also reveals Paul's general strategy and method. He traveled continuously, spending only enough time in a city to establish an assembly; he was accompanied by companions who acted as his agents and shared his ministry; he used the Jesus tradition in an oral form and assumed that his followers were familiar with it; and he wrote letters, real letters for specific purposes to specific people, that are also well crafted and thematically integrated. We may illustrate this integration thus:

Thanksgiving (1:2–10) for their
  1. work of faith,
  2. labor of love, and

  3. steadfastness of hope,
elaborated in a narrative of past labors (2:1–3:10), and leading to instruction on:
  1. how to live in marriage and in community (4:1–12 = love/labor)
  2. knowledge about the fate of the dead and the nearness of the end (4:13–5:11 = hope/steadfastness)
  3. exhortations to respect workers and to work (5:12–22 = faith/work).

We see here not only Paul's rhetorical skill, but the needs of these men and women who so strongly anticipated that coming day that they encountered problems with their marriage vows and community love, misunderstanding about the fate of the dead, and a depreciation of work. Can we learn more from II Thessalonians?

A COMPARATIVE ANALYSIS OF SECOND THESSALONIANS

Second Thessalonians is most notable for its strong similarities and basic differences from First Thessalonians, which are so great that an increasing number of contemporary scholars conclude that Paul could not have written the second letter. We will use this question of the likelihood that Paul is its author to analyze the basic ideas of the work. First we will examine the understanding of "author" in Paul's world, then consider the arguments on both sides of the issue. This will allow us to wrestle with the meaning of the work, and will demonstrate the tentative nature of all interpretation.

At first glance it might seem peculiar to ask whether Paul wrote II Thessalonians, since the letter clearly lists Paul as its author (II Thess. 1:1); and in our time it would be unthinkable to write a letter in someone else's name. We would usually call that a forgery, and our copyright and libel laws are supposed to prevent such things. There are, however, some special circumstances in which we recognize the propriety of writing in someone else's name. Occasionally I am asked to write something for the Dean or Provost that they either sign and send on or deliver orally "as if" it were their own work. Also, on occasion, my secretary writes a letter for me, "as if" I were requesting a publication or some such thing—and even signs my name. And in my family, my wife and I each do half the Christmas cards which are sent from both of us. So there are a few cases in which we are not offended by pseudonymous ("falsely named") authorship even in the modern world. The ancients were still more accepting of such things.

The Question of Authorship

One of the more charming letters to come down to us from antiquity is known as Plato's Second Letter. In it Plato discussed his writings and his great debt to his teacher, Socrates. He felt, the letter tells us, so dependent on the master that he could only write in his name:

᪥   ᪥   ᪥

That is the reason why I have never written anything about these things, and why there is not and will not be any written work of Plato's own. What are now called his are the work of a Socrates embellished and modernized. (Letters II.314c)

Thus, it is no accident that Socrates does all the speaking in the *Dialogues*. Plato himself enters the dialogues only once: to ask a rather obvious question in the *Republic* and then fade into the background. This becomes even more remarkable when we consider how far beyond Socrates Plato actually went: he was certainly the greater thinker, and his later dialogues introduce ideas never hinted at in the early ones, which depend more on Socrates.

A disciple writing in the name of his master was a common and expected tradition in the ancient world. This practice may be observed in the Jewish tradition in the works of the prophets. Nearly all the writings of the prophets that we

possess contain later additions by their followers. This is quite clear in the case of Amos, whose oracles are wholly pessimistic: he believed it impossible that Israel would avoid God's judgment. Will God not rescue Israel? Yes, Amos declared, like a shepherd rescues a lamb from a lion: "two legs, or a piece of an ear" (3:12). Israel's doom is sure, like a man who runs away from a lion and directly into a bear. Or, if he should escape and reach home, he would lean against his wall only to have a serpent come out and bite him (5:19).

In contrast to this pervasive pessimism, the book of Amos ends on a very promising note: ". . . in that day I will raise up the booth of David that is fallen . . ." (9:11). Most scholars regard this as the work of a later hand; the tone is radically altered from the earlier pessimism, and even the presuppositions have changed. The rest of the book presumes that Israel is prosperous and mighty and does not realize the nearness of judgment, which was the situation in Amos' time. But the ending presumes that this prosperity has come to an end and that, in fact, the house of David has fallen (an event nearly two hundred years after the time of Amos). Thus, the ending to the book of Amos is thought to be written after the time of Amos not because it prophesied something later, but because it assumed that something much later had already occurred. The ending to the book was likely added by some follower of Amos more than two hundred years after Amos' time.

Such later additions are typical of the prophetic tradition and could be duplicated from nearly any of the writings of the prophets. The prophetic tradition was a living one and, as circumstances changed, the tradition was changed, expanded, adapted, and spoke to the new situation as if the prophet were still speaking.

An analogous situation exists with the Pentateuch, the first five books of the Bible, which are attributed to Moses, though one of them recounts his death (Deut. 34). Even more telling, these "words of Moses" discuss situations and institutions that did not arise until centuries after his death, such as the monarchy (Deut. 17). Further, when the monarchy did arise, there is evidence that the conservatives resisted the idea as an unnecessary innovation, apparently unaware of the "Mosaic" tradition in Deuteronomy (I Sam. 8). But how could someone writing so much later write in the name of Moses, or of Amos, or Socrates?

All three of these instances share something closely related to authorship: *author*ity. Plato saw himself acting with the authority of Socrates and therefore spoke in his name. The writer of Deuteronomy was drawing on genuinely Mosaic ideas and applying them to the new situation of his day and probably saw no difficulty in writing them in Moses' name. The schools of the prophets assumed a similar authority.

Not all pseudonymous writings stood on such authority. A whole class of writings, the *Pseudepigrapha* (sude-a-pig'-graf-a, false writings), were written in the names of ancient worthies without any valid claim to their authority: the *Books of Enoch,* the *Assumption of Isaiah,* the *Apocalypse of Adam and Eve,* and many more. Also, literary forgeries were widespread, though they usually took the form of plagiarizing someone else's writing. We must remember that there were no publishers in the modern sense. An author would read his work aloud, then have copies made to be sold at the local market. There was little to prevent someone from purchasing a copy and making unauthorized use of it. The Roman poet Martial regularly complained that much of the poetry sold in Rome was his, but most of the profits went to the pirates, who were selling it as theirs. A whole series of oracles, the *Sibylline Oracles,* written in the name of the Sibyl of Apollo at Delphi, are in fact Jewish religious propaganda. Nor were Christians above such forgery: there are gospels written in the names of nearly all the outstanding leaders of the first century. Some pious soul produced a whole series of correspondence between Paul and Seneca, the two great first-century letter writers (see Hennecke and Schneemelcher, II: 133). The range of possibilities concerning the meaning of authorship

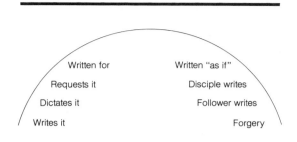

Figure 2 ▪ 2   The Meanings of Authorship

may be shown as a continuum (see Figure 2.2).

Paul himself did not "write" any of his letters in the sense of setting quill to parchment; he used a secretary to whom he dictated (for example, Rom. 16:22). A very useful system of shorthand that had been invented by Cicero's secretary about a century before Paul was widely used. The question of where on the continuum of authorship a given work ought to be placed can only be answered by a careful examination of that work.

Reading and Reflection

While the majority of scholars conclude that Paul really did write II Thessalonians, there are some good reasons for doubting it. Read II Thessalonians:

1. Note anything that reminds you of I Thessalonians.
2. What elements of the Parousia are definitely future?
3. How does the understanding of the Parousia in 2:1–12 differ from that in I Thessalonians?

Given the nature of authorship in that era, we must take seriously the possibility that II Thessalonians may have been written by a follower of Paul who used I Thessalonians as a model. If it does postdate Paul, it would be telling Paul's story in a new way.

Second Thessalonians as a New Story

Those who doubt Paul wrote both letters have three main concerns:

1. *II Thessalonians exhibits a strong dependence on I Thessalonians, repeating the same ideas and even the same words and phrases.* There is more overlap between these two letters than between any other two of Paul's letters—perhaps as much as a third of the letter repeats material from I Thessalonians. (For example, II Thess. 3:8 = I Thess. 2:9; II 3:10 = I 3:4; II 2:1 = I 5:12; II 3:7 = I 2:1.) This could indicate that someone was trying to imitate Paul, especially when we become aware that several of these repetitions use similar words but express different ideas. In the first letter, for example, they are admonished to stand firm "in the Lord" (3:8), while in the second they are to stand firm in the traditions taught in the word and letters of Paul (2:15). In a similar way, both I and II Thessalonians rationalize their suffering, but the first letter related it to past commitments and the near end (2:14; 1:6–

10), while the second relates it to future reward (1:5).

2. *The tone of this letter is too somber for it to have been written near the same time as the joyous first letter, unless some major disappointment had occurred.* Those who argue for a major change point to II Thess. 2:1–2, which may indicate that new opponents had come to Thessalonica, teaching that the end of the age had already arrived. On the other hand, the existence of forged letters implies that there actually were such letters, a phenomenon far more common in the late first century than during Paul's lifetime.

3. *The central issue, however, is that II Thessalonians seems to have a different understanding of the approaching end of the age (or eschatology, to use the technical term).* We saw that in I Thess. 5, Paul followed the common apocalyptic motif that the end would come "like a thief in the night," so one must be ready at any time. But in II Thess. 2:1–12, a detailed scheme of final events is spelled out, implying that the end is not at all near. A whole agenda of events must occur first, making it unlikely that the end will take anyone by surprise. This difference is so blatant that some who think the rest of the letter is from Paul suggest that 2:1–12 is an interpolation (a later insertion into the letter by someone else). If so, the most interesting part of the letter is an addition.

These three arguments cause many to regard it as a late work of the Pauline school, from a time when the expectation of a sudden end had waned but when there was a renewed interest in speculation about the end. On this reading, the letter is aimed at refuting enthusiasts concerned with the imminent end of the world, for such speculation was undermining the need to live responsibly in the world as it was (see Koester, 1983). This interpretation would be in line with the writing practices sketched above. On this reconstruction we encounter the story of the heirs of the Pauline tradition in a time when concern about the near end of the world had waned. To test this thesis, reread II Thessalonians after you have studied this later period (Chapter 5). But we should not understand too quickly. Other scholars continue to argue that Paul actually wrote this second letter.

Second Thessalonians as the Story of Paul

Instead of merely contrasting II Thessalonians with I Thessalonians, these scholars seek the relationship between them. The second letter implies three changes: persecution has increased (1:4, 6; 3:3); a new revelation has occurred, saying that the Day of the Lord has come (2:2); and someone has delivered this message by a word or letter purporting to be from Paul (2:2). Thus, the dramatic setting of the letter is that Paul has received word (though we are not told how) that his Thessalonian followers have been "shaken" in their faith and have come to believe that they already live in the new age, based on some word or forged letter claiming to be from him. This seems incredible, but we will encounter similar beliefs at Corinth (I Cor. 15) and Philippi (Phil. 3).

Given these changes, these scholars argue, we can explain the three concerns listed above. Paul might repeat the words and ideas of his first letter so that they could differentiate between a genuine and a forged work (point one). He would emphasize his teaching and letter rather than the oral tradition (II Thess. 2:15). Suffering might be better seen as a contrast with future reward (1:5) than as a part of the end of the age. The new situation could explain both the similarities and the differences between the two letters.

These aberrant ideas and the implication of fraudulent teachers working in Paul's name could also account for the more somber tone (point two).

The third point, concerning a different understanding of the end, is more complicated. This second letter provides a detailed schema of events that must occur *before* the coming of the Day of

the Lord, though with great ambiguity and no intention of providing a timetable:

The "man of sin" must come first (2:3).
"He who now restrains" will be removed (2:7).
"Jesus will slay him" when he comes (2:8).

Many question whether the person who reveled in the nearness of the End and its unexpected coming "like a thief" could also postulate such a series of prerequisites. The answer seems to be yes, for we find the two notions of immediacy and signs repeatedly coupled in apocalyptic writings, including the tradition Paul drew on in I Thessalonians (now found in Matt. 24, which includes both the thief metaphor and the detailed signs—24:43; 24:29–31). Consistent or not, apocalyptic literature regularly combined both the notion of the nearness and unexpectedness of the end with the idea of cosmic signs before the end. But is not such an agenda in tension Paul's sense of urgency, a sense so strong that he will advise other followers to abstain from marriage (I Cor. 7)? Perhaps. But Paul also sketches an agenda of events before the end in Romans (9–11), a section surely his own.

What Paul may have meant by these arcane references to a "lawless" man taking a seat in the Temple and the one "restraining" is very difficult to decipher. One suggestion is that this terminology grew out of the attempt of the Roman emperor Caligula to have his statue set up in the Temple in Jerusalem in 40 CE. Only the restraining influence of Petronius, the Roman governor of Syria, and a timely assassination, prevented this desecration. Surely such an event left an impression on people's imaginations and provided grist for the mills of apocalypticists.[6] (The other view, which concludes that the letter was written after Paul's time, often identifies this fig-

6. The story is told by Josephus, *Wars* 2.10, and an account is given by Philo who was part of an official delegation dispatched to Rome to persuade Caligula (officially named Gaius) not to complete his plan, *Embassy to Gaius*.

ure with the mysterious "Antichrist" mentioned in Revelation 13—a late first-century writing.)

But the new situation has another interesting feature: the Thessalonians claim to base their understanding on the teachings of Paul (2:2). Here the letter is emphatic: Paul denies he ever taught that the Day of the Lord had already come, and promises to sign his letters so there will be no future misunderstandings (3:17). But we have some evidence that Paul taught this, or at least something that could be understood in this way: In I Thessalonians (5) he boldly declared that Christians already live in "that day," so they should live like day people (see 5:5 and the discussion above; consider that 2:19 and 3:13 could also have been understood in a present sense). And this in a letter "purporting" to be from Paul!

Perhaps the Thessalonians so misunderstood Paul's metaphor about belonging to the day that when he heard a report of what they thought he had written to them, Paul no longer recognized it as his own letter. Thinking they had gotten a forgery instead, he wrote a new letter using many of the words and ideas of the previous letter which he had sent some months before.

We do not know whether this is what happened; it is merely a hypothesis that seems to explain the available data: the strong dependence on I Thessalonians, the new somber tone, and the emphasis on the future aspect of apocalyptic expectation, correcting a misunderstanding of the sense in which Paul thought they already lived in the coming Day of the Lord.

Those who argue that Paul wrote the letter raise other questions: Why would anyone address such a letter to Thessalonica? And why would someone writing a letter in Paul's name condemn such letters? Why the emphasis on authenticating the letter in his own hand? Why would a later writer risk being found out by such a ploy (especially if it could be checked against another letter like I Cor. 16:21)? All this is comprehensible if we imagine a scenario like the one described above.

In addition, a belief in salvation as entirely present experience, if held by some at Thessalonica before Paul wrote, would explain why they became concerned for those who had died: in dying they would be excluded from salvation. In I Thessalonians, Paul addressed the symptoms (concern for the dead); in II Thessalonians he dealt with the illness (a faulty understanding of the Day of the Lord). This is the argument of those who see Paul as the author of both letters. But again, we must avoid understanding too quickly.

Strong arguments on each side point to different aspects of the literature. Able scholars disagree on the issue. How, then, do we decide? First we must be sure we understand the arguments each side advances, and carefully examine the evidence each points to in the text of the letters. We must also exercise our imaginations and see the two quite different stories implied by the two different readings of II Thessalonians. One sees it as a continuation of the story of the first letter; the other sees it as a reflection of the story of the next generation. To test these two possibilities we need to become more familiar with both stories. It will be best to reserve judgment until we have completed our study of the Pauline literature. Ultimately, only a careful and imaginative reading of the letters themselves will lead to consent or disagreement.

THE THESSALONIAN STORY

We have now studied the earliest surviving Christian literature. In many ways it is what we might have expected. Its main concern is determining what it meant to live in relation to the Jesus story. There was no universal agreement, and considerable confusion, on how Jesus was to be understood.

In other ways this literature is perhaps surprising in the concern it shows for the end of the world. I Thessalonians reveals a Paul radically oriented toward the coming end; II Thessalonians (if from Paul) shows him intensely concerned about the end but more reserved about its present significance. In either case we encounter a worldview very different from the modern one. Our study of other letters will show that this future orientation to the coming of Jesus had profound impact on Paul's way of life, thought, and ethics.

We have also considered important issues of method. We have deliberately analyzed both the literary and historical issues involved in understanding these writings. We have raised the issues of context: both the context of the oral stories of Jesus and that of first-century culture. We have tried to get some feel for the shape of a letter in this ancient culture and for the expectations with which letters would be heard. These same issues will continue to occupy our attention as we examine the rest of Paul's letters.

RESOURCES FOR FURTHER STUDY

The best summary of research on ancient letters is Doty, 1973, *Letters in Primitive Christianity*. The classic studies of the thanksgiving in Paul's letters are O'Brien, 1977; and Shubert, 1939. More generally, see Malherbe, 1977; and White, 1982, 1984. On the social utility of Paul's letters, see Kee, 1980: 129–133; and Meeks, 1983: 109, 113–115.

On Paul's apocalyptic outlook, see the important studies of Beker, 1980, 1982. More broadly, see Minear, 1981, especially Ch.7.

On Paul's ethics, see Furnish, 1979; and J. Sanders, 1975. Special studies of Thessalonians include Best, 1972; and Marshall, 1983.

Significant chapters on Thessalonians are included in Beare, 1962b, Ellis, 1982; and Patte, 1983. See also Malbon, 1980.

For the case against Paul's writing II Thessalonians, see Bailey, 1978; Koester, 1982; and Perrin and Duling, 1982.

For the case for Paul's writing II Thessalonians, see Kümmel, 1966; and Marshall, 1983.

Paul's Letters to His Followers

ex ex ex

Philemon, Philippians, Galatians, Corinthians

Written from Prison

Written for Gentiles

Paul and His Followers

Resources for Further Study

3

In spite of all he wrote and all that has been written about him, Paul remains something of an enigma to us. In the earliest of his letters (Chapter 2) we saw him as a concerned teacher, writing endearingly to his former friends at Thessalonica—profoundly interested in the coming end of the age, yet cautiously shifting attention to the present as a time of hope and hard work. In this chapter we will see him in many moods: happy, confused, outraged, charming, professorial, bitter, witty.

As we read each of these letters, we will focus first on its literary and rhetorical design, for that will tell us what to expect from the letter. Then we will reconstruct, as carefully as we can, the historical setting in and for which it was written. Though we are rarely certain of the exact dates, all the letters considered here were probably written in the mid-fifties.

We begin with a study of two letters written while Paul was in prison, probably at Ephesus in 53 CE, but perhaps at Rome in 62. Whether or not they are early letters, these are marvelous examples of the intimate relationship between Paul and his followers.

WRITTEN FROM PRISON

Once, when Paul had been challenged by some other Christians who questioned his performance, he listed his "accomplishments" in this ironic way:

    ❧ ❧ ❧

[I have] far greater labors, far more imprisonments, with countless beatings, and often near death. Five times I have received at the hands of the Jews the forty lashes less one. Three times I have been beaten with rods; once I was stoned. (I Cor. 11:23–25)

The stoning referred to would have been an attempted execution, though not necessarily a legal proceeding (see Acts 14:19). The forty lashes was a disciplinary procedure connected with the synagogue; it was administered to troublemakers who could not be controlled in any other way. That Paul submitted to such a discipline indicates that he considered himself within the synagogue. (Only thirty-nine of the forty lashes were given, to insure staying within the limit prescribed in Deut. 25:3.)

Paul does not number his imprisonments, but implies that they were many. Prison in the ancient world was not, in itself, a form of punishment. There was nothing comparable to our prison system. Ancient prisons had two major functions: to detain the suspect for trial or punishment and to humiliate and intimidate unruly persons who aggravated the authorities. In either case, the stay would be short. In fact, accused persons were often left at large in the hope that they would flee into self-imposed exile, thus ridding the city of the problem. Banishment was one of the most severe punishments. Some of Paul's imprisonments resulted in the beatings he cited; at other times he was simply ordered out of the city; sometimes he was probably released unharmed. Acts 13–20 provides an authentic report of such encounters, though it is by no means complete according to Paul's own account.

At least two of Paul's letters, Philemon and Philippians, were written from such imprisonments. While it has been widely assumed that they were written from his imprisonment in Rome, that need not be the case. In fact, the extensive interaction assumed between Paul and Philippi, including trips by Epaphroditus [Ep-afro-dye'-tus] and Timothy, argue that Paul was not too far away (see 2:19–30), probably somewhere in Asia Minor. These two letters, though they are poles apart in their content and their reflections of Paul, may well have been written closely together.

The Whimsical Paul: Philemon

This is the shortest of Paul's letters and the last one in the collection. It is also the most personal, addressed to a particular person rather than to the whole community (but notice in verse 2 that the community is included). Still, the function of the letter—to represent Paul when he cannot be there in person—and its form follow Paul's standard practice.

Reading and Reflection

Read this short letter through quickly, and try to determine what has happened that caused Paul to write it. The letter is written for an unusual reason: something has happened in Paul's life that affects the community, rather than the other way around.

The Situation of Paul

While he was in prison, it seems, Paul met someone he recognized, a slave from the household of a wealthy friend. This slave, Onesimus [ohness'-eh-muss], had run away and had had a run-in with the law, although his captors have apparently not guessed his slave status. In the Greco-Roman world, slaves were not distin-

---

READING GUIDE TO PHILEMON

Opening (Sender/Receiver, Greeting) 1–3
Thanksgiving (with a prayer) 4–7
Main body 8–20
    The appeal for Onesimus 8–14
    No longer as a slave 15–20
Travel plans 21–22
    (Exhortations included in body)
Closing (with mutual greetings) 23–25
    (Writing process mentioned in 19)

---

guished by any physical or educational differences from the general population; they represented every strata of society, from the farmers and miners to medical doctors and tutors. Most were used in manufacturing and household maintenance. The most common route to slavery was lost wars; piracy was also a major source of slaves. Children of slaves remained slaves, and even free children were sometimes sold into slavery, especially females. One could also become a slave by failing to pay personal debts. Instead of filing claims against bankrupt assets, creditors had the right to sell the debtor to regain their investment. Such slavery was usually for a set term (perhaps seven years), and slaves were given a stipend that might be nurtured into the price of their freedom. The class of "freedmen" consisted of former slaves who did not have full rights as citizens, but were often economically better off than many citizens.

The addressee of the letter was a wealthy friend of Paul's, Philemon [fy-lee'-mun], whose spacious house was the meeting place of the assembly in that area (verse 2). He probably employed many slaves (for a large household in this era could employ hundreds, with perhaps twenty to thirty being common). Though the letter does not tell us his exact location, Colossae would be a reasonable guess, since the same names seem to be associated with both (see Col. 1:7, 4:10–14; Philem. 23). The two others joined with Phile-

House of Pompei This spacious interior courtyard marks the style of the grand Roman household. This *atrium* was sometimes partially roofed and might have been used for entertaining large groups. Public and private rooms surrounded the atrium, including dining, sleeping, and storage areas. Wealthy patrons provided early Christians with meeting places for worship and dining together, and housing for the traveling apostles, prophets, and other workers. For a floor plan, see page 91. (Alinari/Art Resource, New York.)

mon in the address, "Apphia our sister and Archippus our fellow soldier," are probably the two overseers of the congregation, perhaps a wife and husband team. Curiously, the whole church is included in the address.

Onesimus was probably as surprised to see Paul in prison as Paul was to see him. Their chance encounter led to Onesimus' conversion and Paul's dilemma: What to do with this runaway? Aiding an escaped slave was a serious offense, making one liable for any expenses the owner might in-cur as a result. Paul decided to send him back to his master and wrote this letter to explain the situation.

But what is Paul's purpose in writing? What does he want Philemon to do? The most common suggestion is that Paul wanted Philemon to accept Onesimus back as his slave without punishment, to be a good master. Runaway slaves were often subjected to severe punishment, including being branded with the letter "F" (for fugitive). Did Paul write to forestall such harsh treatment?

More recently, John Knox (1935) has argued just the opposite: that Paul was asking Philemon to free Onesimus and return him to Paul so that he could join Paul in his mission. This argument is possible because the letter never says what Philemon should do. It operates by implication and indirection—and not a little humor. Philemon may have had to read the letter several times to figure out what Paul wanted (and so may we), but in the end he would understand. This short letter is filled with puns, ironic statements, and double entendre, the implication of which is that Knox was right.

The Literary Devices of the Letter

First, we should know that Onesimus' name means "useful" or "profitable" in Greek. How inappropriate, for Onesimus had proven useless indeed. But Paul plays with the words, for now Onesimus is useful "to you and to me" (11). He goes on to pun on the name, "I want some benefit [*onaimen*] from you in the Lord" (20). In fact, it is just Onesimus that Paul wants, for he frankly confessed that he had "resolved with myself to retain [him] in order that he might minister on your behalf to me in the bonds of the gospel" (13, literal translation). Here Paul clearly states his preference, he would have kept Onesimus not in the bonds of slavery or of prison but in the bonds of the gospel. Instead, he sent him back, "sending my very heart" (12). Of course, Philemon has already been praised as one who refreshes the hearts of the saints (7), so that Paul can appeal directly: "Refresh my heart in Christ" (20).

Perhaps Paul was doing more than using a common expression when he said Philemon should receive Onesimus "no longer a slave . . . but as a beloved brother" (16). Perhaps he meant it literally. A literal reading of Paul's request to "receive him as you would receive me" (17) reveals Paul's true purpose. This would match the severe irony of Paul's promissory note, written in his own hand, to repay any debt Onesimus has, even

while reminding Philemon that he owes his very life to Paul (19). Paul does everything but command Philemon to free Onesimus to return to Paul (8). He appeals to him as an "old man and one in bonds" (9). But the bonds are those of the gospel, and the word for old man can also be understood as elder or ambassador. And so Paul concludes that he is confident of Philemon's obedience to the command he never issued, "knowing that you will do even more than I say" (21).

If the Onesimus later reported to be Paul's traveling companion (Col. 4:9) is the same fellow, Philemon was able to understand and to do more than Paul had requested. It is intriguing, hardly more, that the bishop of Ephesus at the end of the century was named Onesimus (Ignatius, *Ephesians* 1).

How did such a charming personal letter come to be included in Scripture? There is no clear answer. The importance of Paul, and possibly of Onesimus, might be a factor. Also, it has been observed that this is not entirely a private letter; it is addressed to the church as well (2). But none of these factors is sufficient to explain its preservation. We will see that some of Paul's other letters could be lost (I Cor. 5:9 refers to a previous letter now lost). Somehow this letter continued to be read long after the original problem had been solved. Knox went on to conjecture that it was Onesimus himself who collected and published the Pauline letters near the end of the century. That would explain the presence of this letter, but it remains no more than a guess.

Equally important, this letter provides us with insight into Paul's understanding of grace and ministry. In a basic and profound way the story of Onesimus—his failure, return, release, and ministry—mirrors the Christian experience. The story implied in this letter is one of freedom and partnership within a new community. These are, as we will see, basic themes of Paul's larger story. This letter also reveals an aspect of Paul we see only vaguely in the other letters. A deep sense of serious humor runs through Philemon, revealing a Paul whom we would be delighted to know, far removed from the bitter sarcasm we encounter in Galatians. Again, we are reminded of the need to interpret each letter in its historical context and to interpret Paul only in relation to all of his letters. He was far too complex a personality to be expressed in any one way.

The Reflective Paul: Philippians

This letter presents a couple of special problems, including the basic question of whether at least two letters might have been combined into one. We will consider this question as we first examine the organization of the letter, then turn to its historical setting and basic teachings.

The Literary Organization

The basic reason for questioning the unity of Philippians is the curious trick played on the reader about halfway through. The writer says, "Finally . . .", but then we are told that it is better to repeat a few things (3:1). But even that promise is not kept. Instead of repeating earlier topics, the letter moves on to new ones. And the whole tone of the letter changes at this point. While a mood of joy and even playfulness prevailed earlier, a new harsh note is introduced: "Look out for the dogs" (3:2).

There is also a problem with the assumptions made about a messenger sent from Philippi to Paul: in one reference he has been there some time, long enough for a report of his near-fatal illness to get back to Philippi (2:25–27); in another, he seems to have just arrived (4:18).

Possibly these are the remains of two or more of Paul's letters to the Philippians, joined together. But it is not essential that we decide, for if, in fact, they were originally two separate letters, they would still derive from essentially similar circumstances and times. And if they were originally one, the two distinct parts represent a basic division in the letter and should be considered separately. In either case, our interpretation will be little changed.

READING GUIDE TO PHILIPPIANS

Opening   1:1–2
Thanksgiving (with a prayer)   1:3–10
Main body   1:10–2:11
    "I want you to know"   1:10
Exhortations   2:12–18
Travel plans   2:18–30
Second teaching section   3:1–21
Further exhortations   4:1–9
Further personal plans   4:10–18
Closing
    Benediction   4:19–20
    Greetings   4:21–22
    Standard benediction   4:23

Reading and Reflection

As you read Philippians through, you will find some things discussed twice. Ask yourself:

1. What interactions existed between Paul and this community?
2. What sort of people opposed Paul, and how did he react to their opposition?

The Historical Setting

Again we find Paul in prison, and again we cannot be sure where. According to Acts (16), Paul was even in prison briefly at Philippi. The references to the Praetorian Guard (the emperor's personal bodyguard; 1:13) and to Caesar's household (4:22) may suggest Rome, but not necessarily so. The Praetorium could as well refer to the residence of the provincial governor (the King James version translated it "in all the palace"). Caesar's household probably refers to his slaves or to freedmen who were responsible for administering imperial affairs. Like bureaucrats in every age, they could be found everywhere.

It is difficult to imagine Rome as the source of the letter because of the frequent travels it mentions to and from Philippi. A location in Greece or Asia Minor seems more logical. There Paul would be accessible in a matter of weeks rather than months.

The Philippians had sent Epaphroditus to minister to Paul's needs while he was in prison. (In those days prisons did not provide meals or do laundry, so one depended on friends.) Paul was now sending him back (2:25). He planned to send Timothy soon (2:19), and hoped to follow not long after (2:24). In the meantime, word had already reached Philippi that Epaphroditus was ill (2:26), and Paul had learned about certain problems there (for example, 4:2), implying that the Philippians had communicated with him by letter or via another messenger.

The Relationship with Philippi

This extraordinary effort of the Philippians to provide for Paul's support while he was in prison points up the special relationship that existed between him and this congregation. Philippi, named after the father of Alexander the Great, was a coastal city located in northern Greece. It remained a relatively small city until Anthony chose to settle a colony of retired Roman soldiers there (about 40 BCE), causing it to flourish as a Roman colony. Its religion, like its population, was a mixture of ancient Thracian and Greek, with a strong overlay of Roman elements. We would expect such a city of Roman veterans to have a temple for the worship of Roma, the emperor, and such strong gods as Jupiter (king of the Gods) and Mars (God of War). They did, but there were also temples to the female deities: Athena, Isis, and the Thracian Cybele. The Jewish community there was small and was perhaps required to worship outside the boundary of the city proper (Acts 16:13). Acts indicates that Paul's primary contact in the city was with women, and the one convert named is Lydia, a businesswoman.

Apparently Paul had to leave Philippi and went on to Thessalonica, Corinth, Ephesus, and Gal-

atia (Acts 17–18). In this letter Paul thanks God for the "partnership in the gospel from the first day until now" (1:5), alluding to their continued financial support. Twice they sent him support in Thessalonica (4:16) and now they have sent Epaphroditus. All this implies an extensive mutual contact between Paul and his followers at Philippi. If we try to fill in the gaps, we may imagine the following sequence:

1. Paul visits Philippi.
2. His followers twice send emissaries after him with gifts (4:16).
3. He probably responds to these gifts; at least the returning emissaries bring news of him.
4. They learn that Paul is imprisoned, perhaps at Ephesus.
5. They send Epaphroditus with support (2:25, 30).
6. Paul likely sends thanks and a report that Epaphroditus is ill (2:26; 4:18 may be part of this letter).
7. His followers write Paul expressing concern for Epaphroditus and giving news of their own situation.
8. Paul writes the present letter and sends it with Epaphroditus (2:25).
9. He plans to send Timothy soon to assist them and then to bring a report back (2:19).
10. Paul plans to come himself as soon as he is released (2:24).

This foundation of mutual interaction makes Philippians one of the warmest and most personal of Paul's letters. Even the rebuke of his opponents is milder and more playful in Philippians, at least toward some of those opponents.

The Opposition at Philippi

In his first reference to opponents Paul seems more bemused than concerned. Some preach Christ out of envy and rivalry, he alleges, yet Christ is being proclaimed (1:15–18). But his tone shifts in his next reference: "Look out for the dogs, look out for the evil-workers, look out for those who mutilate the flesh" (3:2). It seems unlikely that these two references allude to the same opposition. This latter group may be further described as those "who live as enemies of the cross of Christ. Their end is destruction, their god is the belly, and they glory in their shame, with minds set on earthly things" (3:18–19). The first group could be considered partisans of Christ (apparently preaching a gospel oriented toward personalities), the latter as enemies of Christ.

These enemies urge circumcision, a practice usually associated with an antiworldly stance. Yet they seem more given to good food than to self-denial (3:19). Apparently they were more affected by Christ's resurrection than his death, and were perhaps already attempting to live a perfect life. This would account for Paul's assertion that he is not already perfect (3:12), and for his absolute emphasis on the cross of Christ (3:8–11). Their requirement of circumcision and Paul's emphasis on his Jewish past suggest that, like Paul, they were Jews.

Paul took pains to show that his rejection of circumcision was not due to some failure on his part to keep the Law. His autobiographical recital here is instructive for understanding his attitude toward things Jewish. He was, he says,

❧ ❧ ❧

circumcised on the eighth day,
   of the people of Israel,
   of the tribe of Benjamin,
a Hebrew born of Hebrews,
   as to the Law a Pharisee,
   as to zeal, a persecutor of the church,
   as to righteousness under the Law,
blameless. (3:5–6)

This self-portrait utterly shatters the common portrayal of Paul as one tormented by a failure to keep the Law. His own judgment on his guilt under the Law was sweeping, if unbelievable; he says he was "blameless." Whether his mother would have agreed or not, we must at least concur that Paul felt no dread before the Law. He was, as Krister Stendahl phrases it, one with a

"robust conscience" (1976:90). Further, it would be well to recall this positive evaluation of his Jewishness whenever we reflect on Paul's relationship with other Jews.

The other problem at Philippi concerned divisions in the church. Near the end of the letter Paul admonishes two women, Euodia [You-oh'-dee-ah] and Syntyche [Soon'-too-kay], "to agree in the Lord" (4:2). We are never told the basis of their disagreement, but they are described as significant people and we should, therefore, imagine a significant disagreement. These women had "labored side by side" with Paul in Christian ministry; they were his "fellow workers" (4:3). Whatever their disagreement and the nature of the partisan preaching Paul alluded to in Chapter 1, he does not seem too upset with them. If we sometimes get the impression that Paul insisted that people always agree with him, it is because his letters usually address problems he regarded as integral to the gospel. Incidents like this show that in other matters Paul recognized that differences were inevitable.

The Theme of the Letter

While Philippians may not be a unity of discourse, it is a unity of rhetorical images. The dominant image of the whole work is that of mutuality. There is a common sharing of a common life, a mutual participation by Paul in his followers' lives, by them in his, and by both in Christ's life.

Reading and Reflection

Reread Philippians, noting all the images used to express this mutual participation. What relationship is assumed between the Philippians, Paul, Christ, and God?

They are partners, partakers, fellow workers, fellow soldiers, imitators, having the same mind, the same love: counting others better than themselves. All these images of reciprocity and mutual service reach a climax in the central poetic section of the letter. Having given his own case as an example of his suffering on their behalf, by his imprisonment and his release (1:12–26), Paul urges them to engage in the same conflict (1:29–30). He grounds this appeal in the work of Christ, citing what was probably a hymn chanted in their worship:

る　る　る

Who,
　though he was in the form of God,
　Did not count equality with God a thing to be
　　grasped,
But emptied himself,
　taking the form of a servant,
　being born in the likeness of men.
And being found in human form
　He humbled himself
　And became obedient unto death,
　　even death on a cross.
Therefore
　God has highly exalted him
　And bestowed on him the name which is above
　　every name,
　　That at the name of Jesus
　　　every knee should bow,
　　　　in heaven, and on earth and under the
　　　　　earth,
　　　and every tongue confess that Jesus Christ
　　　　is Lord,
　　　　　to the glory of God the Father.   (2:6–11)

The poetic language, the regularity of the words, and the lack of any of Paul's usual vocabulary all indicate that this is most likely a hymn that Paul is quoting. Two questions arise: Why did Paul use this poem in this letter? What did these early Christians understand when they heard/sang it? The most common interpretation of the original meaning of the poem understands it as a reflection on the incarnation, the process of God becoming human in Jesus of Nazareth. In this view the poem is about the preexistent divinity of Christ (form of God), which he laid aside

("emptied himself") when he took on human form. This is an ancient and very influential interpretation, of great beauty and intellectual daring.

But some scholars have difficulty seeing this as the poem's original interpretation, for such explicit talk about preexistence was not common in Pauline circles. It became widespread, they think, only after the Gospel of John, late in the first century. These interpreters suggest another understanding of the hymn.

There was a popular ancient view that all life existed along a great "chain of being," which stretched from the divine to the lowest form of animal life. The universe would be harmonious when each creature kept its proper place, neither grasping for a higher place (pride) nor sinking to a lower one (corruption). Humanity, however, was thought to occupy an ambiguous middle ground, sharing not only the divine nature ("made in the image of God"), but also an animal nature, being bodily creatures. If we suppose such a context, the poem takes on a new meaning. Christ now appears as the true example of humanity, who, resisting the temptation of Adam to "be like God," became the obedient servant. On this reading Christ is like a second, but obedient, Adam.

We should not be surprised that the poem is capable of more than one interpretation, for that is the real wonder of poetry. But whether we understand it as talking about incarnation or about a second Adam, it is important that we see why Paul used it.

For Paul, this poem also reflected the mutual service that he found between himself and the Philippians, which was a reflection of the mutuality of the gospel: even as Christ served them, so they serve each other. They are to have the same mind as Christ (2:5). This theme of mutual service and sharing is the keynote of Philippians.

Philippians also shows how Paul's own life story reflected the larger Jesus story. In fact, Paul saw his own preaching, suffering, and labor as an imitation of Jesus' giving himself for the world (3:17–22; I Cor. 11:1). Paul, imitating Jesus, gave himself for the Gentiles. There is a direct correspondence between the sacred story of Jesus and the life story of Paul. That is why the sacred story is also a charter story, for it gives warrant to the lesser story. Thus these two stories are merely aspects of the same reality.

Let us proceed now to the other letters, considering some of the problems faced by these Gentiles as they sought to be followers of Paul and of Christ.

WRITTEN FOR GENTILES

The place of the Gentiles (all the non-Jewish peoples) in Paul's self-understanding is central. His mission is to persuade the Gentiles (Rom. 1:13; Gal. 2:9). Many others of that time undertook a similar task, so Paul was not unique. He was simply a traveling Jewish tradesman and philosopher, who spread the word of his faith to the people among whom he traveled: Gentiles.

The status of the Gentiles who adopted this new faith was not clear. Some of Paul's followers in Galatia became confused about their new obligations and turned to other teachers for answers, prompting one of his most scathing letters. But before turning to that letter, we need to understand the general context of this problem with Gentiles. Many other Jews, men and women, were successfully engaged in similar travel, business, and witness, attracting a multitude of Gentiles to the Jewish way. One such success story is related by Josephus, a Jewish historian living in Rome in the late first century.

The Outreach to Gentiles

It seems that a traveling Jewish merchant by the name of Ananias, probably in the process of selling his goods, had been teaching Jewish religion to the women in the household of Izates, the son of the king of the small country of Adiabene [ah-dee-ab'-en-ee] in northern Mesopotamia (north and far to the west of Palestine). Ananias succeeded in convincing many of these women of the su-

periority of the Jewish way. Through their intercession he was introduced to Izates, whom he also persuaded to embrace the Jewish faith.

Meanwhile, in the king's household, his mother Helena had also been instructed in and attracted to the Jewish faith. When Izates succeeded to his father's throne, and saw his mother's approval of the Jewish customs, he decided to make a full conversion by being circumcised and joining the Jewish people. However, his mother advised against this, fearing it could lead to insurrection among his people. (He had an older brother who would have liked to be king.) Partly convinced, Izates sought the counsel of Ananias, the Jew who had first instructed him. Ananias made an eloquent appeal for him to remain uncircumcised, citing not only the practical reasons that the queen mother had given, but also arguing that he could worship God without being circumcised and that such worship was superior to circumcision.

This situation did not change until another traveling Jew, Eleazar, arrived from Galilee. Eleazar was a scholar and when he found Izates reading the Torah accused him of hypocrisy, of pretending to follow the Law but breaking the principal law by refusing circumcision.[1] Convinced of his impiety, Izates immediately sent for a surgeon. His mother and Ananias were alarmed, but apparently the feared rebellion did not take place. (For the full story, see Josephus, *Antiquities* 20.2.)

This rare glimpse into Jewish missionary activity in the first century reveals several important clues for understanding Paul. First, we get the impression that this kind of appeal to Gentiles was widespread and reasonably successful. Despite a good deal of anti-Jewish sentiment among Gentiles, there was also a strong attraction to this ancient, monotheistic, and highly ethical religion. Second, the story reveals two major obstacles to the conversion of Gentile men:

---

1. *Torah* refers to the "Books of the Law," that is, the Bible, and also the law contained in those books, both the ritual law of circumcision and the moral law of the Ten Commandments.

social stigma and circumcision. The need for circumcision was a great barrier; the thought of cutting off that excess skin elicited deep fears (as Freud explained) and struck those who had embraced Greek culture as barbaric. The Greeks were deeply fascinated by the beauty of the body, especially the male body, and this deliberate mutilation appealed to them about as much as the incision rites of Australian aborigines appeal to us. Civilized people, they felt, did not do such things.

However, and third, the uncircumcised convert is placed in the untenable situation of confessing the truth of the Torah, the Law, and denying one of its obvious demands. Fourth, we can see the role of women, who would be unaffected by these concerns, in the success of the Jewish mission. Finally, it is obvious that there were various opinions among Jews regarding Gentile circumcision without any reference to Christianity. The man of the world, Ananias, did not think it was very important; the scholar Eleazar deemed this ritual to be the most important of the laws, without which the pretense of keeping the others would be impiety.

A more subtle aspect of the argument is worth noting. The new convert has to remain uncircumcised day by day, a condition that can always be changed. Thus, though Ananias would have to win the argument repeatedly, Eleazar only had to win it once.

Jewish Responses to Gentiles

The difference between Ananias and Eleazar was not only that between the pious merchant and the scholar but also that between the Palestinian and the diaspora Jew. Eleazar was from Galilee, from the homeland. Though the contrast between Jews in the Land and those outside (in the *Diaspora*) can be exaggerated, significant differences in experience existed in the two groups. Jew had lived abroad in large numbers at least since the time of the Exile (587 BCE) when military conquerors had carried many of the Jewish leaders off to Babylon, and probably even earlier.

By the time of Paul, these diaspora Jews outnumbered those in the Land by at least two to one. Literally millions of Jews lived in Egypt, Asia Minor, Mesopotamia, Greece, Italy, and farther north. Ties were closest between the Jews of Babylon and Palestine; both spoke Aramaic. Everywhere else the Jews spoke Greek, the common language of the day. The Scriptures had been translated into Greek since at least 150 BCE, parts of it much earlier. Paul regularly cited Scripture from the *Septuagint,* a Greek translation that originated in Alexandria in Egypt. Diaspora Jews regarded it as just as authoritative as the Hebrew original.

These diaspora Jews not only spoke Greek, but also they gave their children Greek names, dressed like Greeks, and observed Greek customs. They became Greek in every aspect of their lives except religion, and some even abandoned that to some extent. Thus, we should not imagine that only two distinct classes of people existed in Paul's world (Jews and Gentiles). There was a whole continuum of experience, with pilgrimages in both directions. At one extreme you might have strongly nationalistic Jews who tried to avoid all Gentile influence, like the Essenes who withdrew from society to live a holy, separated life; at the other, you would have Gentiles who were anti-Jewish, some viciously so. But between these extremes the more frequent experience was a great deal of mutual influence and accommodation. Jews in Alexandria enrolled in the Gymnasium and sought full citizenship in this Greek city, which would surely involve some token honor to the gods. Many Gentiles were attracted to, and no small number affiliated with the Jewish worship of God, as the story from Josephus illustrates. Conversion to Judaism was so common that the Roman satirist Juvenal mocked it as one cause of Rome's decline. Here he reveals the probable process by which a Gentile family would come to be incorporated into Israel:

🍃 🍃 🍃

Some who have had a father who reveres the Sabbath, worship nothing but the clouds, and the divinity of the heavens, and see no difference between eating swine's flesh, from which their father abstained, and that of man; and in time they take to circumcision. Having been wont to flout the laws of Rome, they learn and practice and revere the Jewish law, and all that Moses handed down in his secret tome, forbidding to point out the way to any not worshipping the same rites, and conducting none but the circumcised to the desired fountain. For all which the father was to blame, who gave up every seventh day to idleness, keeping it apart from all the concerns of life. (Juvenal, Satire *14.96–106; Loeb edition)*

From Juvenal's jaundiced perspective, it all starts with a father who keeps the Sabbath and abstains from eating pork. The son moves on to study the Torah, neglecting Roman law, and is soon circumcised. Juvenal's contempt for circumcision, for the dietary laws, for worshipping an unseen God, for anything not Roman, is obvious and typical of the Roman upper class—yet obviously not typical of all Romans, or he would not have been moved to mock them.

Perhaps the most famous incident of conversion is the report by Dio Cassius that Flavius Clemens, cousin and heir to the Emperor Domitian, was executed in 96 CE on the charge of atheism, along with "many others who were drifting into Jewish ways" (*History* 67.14.1–3).

Religion among the Gentiles

That Gentiles were open to Jewish proselytizing should not surprise us. The ancient world had changed dramatically in the three centuries before Paul. In the classical age of Greece the basic unit of civilization was the city, whose people, politics, gods, and laws were at the center of life. But Alexander and his empire changed all that. The city became far less important, and only rarely autonomous. The forces controlling life had shifted to faraway places. Though local customs and deities were still honored, they no longer held sway. The religious writings of this period show a longing for salvation and deliverance from sin, a search for immortality and, above all, freedom from Fate.

Fate (to which even Zeus was bound) bound all. One senses an overwhelming feeling of powerlessness. As one writer lamented:

⁊ ⁊ ⁊

We are so much at the mercy of chance that Chance herself, by whom God is proved uncertain, takes the place of God. (Pliny the Elder, Natural History *2.5.22)*

Various religious impulses emerged to deal with these feelings. In the *folk traditions* there was strong emphasis on ways to understand and manipulate the fates: magic and astrology flourished. These were probably the primary religious experience of the masses of this age, but they were by no means limited to the masses. The Emperor Tiberius never went anywhere without his personal astrologer, who continually cast his horoscope. Generals would not march into battle without consulting oracles and priests, who examined the entrails of sacrificial animals for favorable signs. Even a secular historian like Seutonius could not resist describing to the reader all the signs that foretold the death of each emperor.

Elixirs, charms, or prophecies were available for everything from love potions to poisons, curses to healings, fortune telling to business ventures. One old folk spell, for example, was supposed to cure sore feet: "I think of you; heal my feet. Let the earth retain the illness and let health remain here." This was to be recited nine times, touching the earth and spitting, and would only work if one was sober (Varro *On Agriculture* 1.2.27). But magic was also believed to have power to subjugate others, even to kill them. When Germanicus, the adopted son of the Emperor Tiberius, died mysteriously, his home was excavated and magical paraphernalia were found: human body parts, curses on lead tablets, blood, ashes (Tacitus, *Annals,* 2.69). Nearly everyone believed in magic, and most people probably practiced it to some extent. Its influence among the people was very strong.

Among the more well-to-do, the *mystery religions* offered the hope of salvation from such fates. Unfortunately for our study, the mysteries were just that: mysterious and secret. Their essence was some saving rite through which the initiated found enlightenment and salvation, usually involving a personal experience with a particular deity. In this rite the initiate would reenact the saving story of the God or Goddess and thereby gain freedom. One of the most moving descriptions of this process is found in a semicomical novel written in the middle of the second century by Apuleius, a Roman aristocrat from North Africa. The novel was titled *Metamorphoses,* more commonly known as *The Golden Ass*. Both comic and symbolic, it is the tale of a young man pursuing love and magic who is inadvertently turned into an ass. In the final book of this lengthy work, the ass regains his human form by devotion to Isis, the great Egyptian Goddess whose mystery rites flourished in this period. The themes of victory over death, new birth, and freedom from fate appear repeatedly in this last book and the prayer to Isis includes the following:

🐦 🐦 🐦

Most holy and everlasting Redeemer of the human race. . . . You protect men on land and sea. You chase the storms of life and stretch out the hand of succour to the dejected. You can untwine the hopelessly tangled threads of the Fates. You can mitigate the tempests of Fortune and check the stars in the courses of their malice. (11.75; Lindsay's translation)

Statue of Isis Combining Oriental mystery and Greek beauty, Isis captured the imagination of many. She was portrayed in a great variety of forms, but this lovely statue shows her in typical Greek guise, far from her Egyptian origins. Her worship was widespread, established even in Rome despite its hostility to foreign cults. She was commonly portrayed on jewelry and grave monuments and was worshipped in the Roman world into the sixth century. (Alinari/Art Resource, New York.)

Though such religious experience was highly prized, few could hope to attain it. The initiation process was a rigorous affair requiring both study and moral purity. In the various mysteries it involved rituals as diverse as bathing in milk to being showered by the blood of a bull slain on a grating above the initiate. It was also a lengthy and expensive endeavor, eventually costing the equivalent of many thousands of dollars. The masses could worship and experience the initiation from a distance but could never hope to be initiated themselves.

Beyond even the mysteries lay philosophy, which was a religious movement rather than an academic discipline in this age. There were a variety of philosophical schools, each pursuing its own vision of truth. What they shared was the conviction that such truth would liberate them from the mundane world. Whether by reason (Stoicism), self-denial (Epicureanism), mystical practices (Neo-Pythagoreanism), nonconformity (Cynicism), or some other means, the philosopher rose above the common experience.

A strong movement in philosophy during this period, typified by Stoicism, was toward understanding the divine as one rather than many. Stoicism used a method of symbolic interpretation by which the various gods and goddesses represented various aspects of the one God. While being a philosopher was nearly a full-time pursuit followed by only the intellectual elite, all cultured persons studied philosophy and were influenced by it.

These options were not mutually exclusive. Typically, a person would continue to participate in the traditional religious rites of the various gods and goddesses, perhaps worship especially Isis or one of the other saviors of the mysteries, learn as much philosophy as permitted by his or her station in life, and not neglect to heed omens and astrology. The dominant experience of that age was syncretism, combining elements from various religious systems in a pragmatic or useful fashion. After Alexander the Great had conquered the East, Greek culture spread and mixed with the cultures of Egypt, Persia, Babylon, Palestine, Syria, and the rest. The new civilization that arose is called the Hellenistic Age, a blend of East and West. Their religions, too, were blended so that the various national divinities were identified with each other and we find names like "Apollo-Helios-Mithras-Hermes" and "Zeus-Ahura Mazda." The hallmark of the Hellenistic age was the conviction that the Gods of all the nations were just different names for the same divinity.

Against such a diverse background we must read Paul's letter to the Galatians. Some Jews were exclusivists; many more were active and successful missioners, who demanded varying degrees of conformity to Jewish ways from their converts. Gentiles were sometimes anti-Jewish, especially the Roman upper classes. Many more were attracted to the Jewish faith to some extent, some recognizing it as an honorable and ancient tradition, others converting to it, and many not actually converting but adopting Jewish ways to some degree. The Jewish tradition spoke to the deepest needs of the age. Its one God promised freedom from sin and fate and life beyond death.

Gentiles Who Keep the Law: Galatians

Unlike the letters studied so far, this one is addressed to many churches in a broad geographical region known as Galatia. Unfortunately, two distinct areas were known by this name, so we cannot be entirely certain which place is meant. Yet the controversy dealt with in the letter had a far greater scope than a single city. Paul clearly felt threatened by this controversy: Galatians is one of his most vigorous letters, harsh and insulting. First let us review the harsh language, clarify the rhetorical structure, and then examine the historical setting and meaning of this letter.

Rhetorical Insults

If this letter were all we had of Paul's work we could only regard him as a rather uncharitable radical. When he launches the main part of his argument, he addresses his hearers as "O anoetoi Galatai," which J. B. Phillips translated as "O you dear idiots of Galatia" (3:1). Paul frankly admits that his tone is unpleasant, but explains that he is perplexed by what they have done (4:20).

This is the only letter in which Paul found nothing flattering to say about his readers in an opening thanksgiving. There is no thanksgiving. In its place we read:

⁊ ⁊ ⁊

I am astonished that you are so quickly deserting him who called you in the grace of Christ and turning to a different gospel—not that there is another gospel, but there are some who trouble you and want to pervert the gospel of Christ. (1:6–7)

There is some debate about whether the "him" they are said to desert is Christ or Paul, but it may be an intentional ambiguity. Clearly Paul, under personal attack by some group of opponents, was forced to defend himself as well as his message. Also, in the rhetoric of that time, no clear distinction was made between speaker and message. A primary task of the rhetorician was to present his own character to the audience.

Paul bows to no human authority. Repeatedly he refers to the Jerusalem leadership as "those who were of repute" (2:2; 2:6; 2:9), and cannot resist adding: ". . . what they were makes no difference to me." He calls Peter a hypocrite, perhaps even a sinner (2:14–17). His rhetoric is extreme: "Now I, Paul, say to you that if you receive circumcision, Christ will be of no advantage to you" (5:2). In a bitter metaphor he describes circumcision as being "severed" from Christ (5:4), and adds that he wishes that those who insist on circumcision would "mutilate themselves" (5:12). (One of the more repulsive forms of religion in Galatia involved the Galli, devotees of the Goddess Cybele who, in a frenzied rite of devotion, castrated themselves.) He attributes the desire to circumcise to a desire to "glory in your flesh" (6:12–13), as if they were making little trophies or collecting scalps. He curtly compared their scars to his (6:17).

The Rhetorical Structure

These insults, hyperbole, and ferocity give the impression of a passionate letter, dashed off in a moment of anger. Occasionally, the letter lends itself to this interpretation: Paul begins a sentence in 2:4, which progresses through verse 5 but never actually goes anywhere: it never reaches a main clause. That Galatians has often been interpreted as a passionate letter is a tribute to Paul's rhetorical skill, for it can be shown that it is a carefully organized, systematic work.

Yet its organization is not that of the standard Pauline letter. Though we can still find many of the formal sections we have observed in other letters, that pattern does not seem to determine the logic of Galatians. Consider the following:

Opening   1:1–5
Thanksgiving   (none in Galatians)
Main body (no formulas or future plans)   1:6–5:25
Exhortations to good behavior   5:25–6:10
Closing   6:11–18
    Standard benediction   6:18
    Writing process   6:11

Recent interpreters have suggested another approach to the structure of Galatians, viewing it as a judicial argument. Ancient rhetoricians had several ways to organize an argument, but the preferred scheme in Paul's day was a five-part appeal (see Clarke, 1953:23–37). The form of the rhetorical defense was deeply influenced by its origin in the law courts. Various Greek and Latin technical terms were applied to the different parts of the speech. Rough English equivalents would be:

1. *Introduction*—primarily to state the case, but to get the listeners' attention as well. The normal means for gaining the allegiance of the audience were appeals to the character of the speaker, the lack of character of opponents, the nature of the audience, or the facts of the case.
2. *Narrative*—to review the facts of the case and put them within the proper historical context. While this narrative would be generally agreed to by both sides, each presented it in a way that would support his later argument.

3. *Argument*—to clarify the issues by showing the points agreed on by the two parties and those that separate them.

4. *Proof*—to establish the truth of the speaker's point of view by a series of arguments, usually proceeding from the strongest to the weakest. This would be the longest and most important part of the speech. Sometimes combined with this, occasionally as a separate point, and sometimes even omitted was the refutation of the proofs offered by the opposing side.

5. *Conclusion*—to sum up the earlier argument and make an impassioned plea to persuade the listeners to accept the speaker's point of view.

The ancient listener, whether trained in the schools that taught such skills or not, had heard enough defense speeches to know what to listen for and what to expect. If we use this general pattern as a model, the course of Paul's argument will become clear.

Reading and Reflection

Using the rhetorical pattern sketched above, and the reading guide, try to answer the following:

1. Why does Paul tell these stories about himself?
2. On which points do he and his opponents agree? What is their central disagreement?

This narrative section is the most autobiographical passage in all of Paul's writings, but we must be cautious in interpreting it. Rather than being an attempt to tell his life story, it rehearses events so that the story supports his later argument. There is, for example, a direct contradiction in the sequence of events listed here and that given in Acts (contrast 1:17 with Acts 9:22–26). The point is not that either is wrong or that one or the other must be considered unreliable as a result of this

---

READING GUIDE TO GALATIANS

Introduction   1:1–11
    The salutation   1:1–5
    The charges   1:6–11
Narrative   1:12–2:14
Summary of case   2:15–21
Arguments   3:1–6:10
    Proofs   3:1–4:31
    Refutations   5:1–6:10
Conclusion   6:11–18
    Writing   6:11
    Summary   6:12–17
    Benediction   6:18

---

discovery. Instead, both are telling their stories in order to prove a certain point. Both are arguing a case. Within the literary conventions of their day, both might actually be correct. As we will see, Luke's case in Acts rests on his connecting Paul closely with Jerusalem; Paul's case is based on asserting his autonomy. Thus, we must expect that each will tell the story differently.

A rhetorically constructed argument required that every part of it contribute to the final purpose. Even the introduction lays the groundwork for Paul's later arguments. Notice especially the apocalyptic note of "the present evil age" and the *deliverance* already accomplished by Christ's death (1:3). This note of freedom will become the keynote of the letter. Notice too, the concise statement of the charges against Paul, charges related to the basic meaning of the gospel (1:6–7), implying that his gospel lacks divine sanction (1:11).

Even more revealing is the way Paul states the case in summary. He and his opponents agree on basic issues, including the key idea that being right with God does not originate in good works (2:15–16). Yet they disagree about what this means for the Gentiles. For Paul it meant that Gentiles were free from the Law (2:17–21).

The lengthy section of proofs fall into positive assertions, which prove Paul's case (3–4), and refutations of the implications of his opponents' position (5–6). He concludes with a recapitulation and an ironic comparison of scars (6:11–18). A final blessing (6:16) balances the opening curse (1:8). Before we analyze Paul's reasoning in detail, we must probe more deeply into the actual historical situation he confronted.

The Situation in Galatia

In the first century the term *Galatia* referred to two different but related areas. Broadly, it referred to the Roman province that stretched across central Asia Minor, but more precisely it referred to the northern part of this province where the "Galatians" (a relatively primitive people related to the Gauls) lived. The people in the southern part of the province were mostly Greeks; to call them Galatians (primitives) was not very nice; to call them mindless Galatians was even more insulting. But that is the point: Paul is not being especially pleasant in this letter. Though it is not impossible, there is no real reason to suppose that Paul traveled to this northern region. Ancient commentators who assumed he did were probably more influenced by the changes of the second century, which redrew this district and limited the name Galatia to the northern part. Thus, we should probably read the references to "Galatians" as light sarcasm. The obvious similarity between the circumcised "Galatai" and the castrated "Galli" surely produced its rhetorical effect.

The Opponents as Reactionaries

A more serious question concerns the nature of the opponents confronted in this letter. In general it seems clear that some "Eleazars" have come along behind Paul and persuaded these new converts that circumcision was as necessary for Christians as for Jews (for example, 5:2–10). It was, after all, demanded in the Bible. Who might have done such a thing? One possibility is that they were simply other Jews, like Eleazar, with no connection to Paul or to the Christian mis-

sion. It is not unlikely that if a man like Eleazar came on a Christian assembly reading the Torah and claiming to follow it he would have admonished them for not following its principal precept: circumcision. This may have happened, but it does not explain Galatians. The phenomenon was too widespread, affecting the whole province, and the agreement between Paul and his opponents was too specific (2:15–16). They were Christians; they preached "another gospel" (1:6).

This leads to the inference that they were Christian "Eleazars." We meet such people in one of the stories Paul told in the narrative section. In fact we meet an interesting variety of people in his stories.

Reading and Reflection

Reread the four stories: 1:11–17; 1:18–24; 2:1–10; and 2:11–14. How many different attitudes toward Gentiles can you discern in these stories?

The first story is that of Paul's "revelation" that turned him from an opponent of the church to a proponent of the Gentiles. Notice the intimate connection between the revelation and the mission to Gentiles (1:16). This link leads many to speak of it as Paul's *call* (a divine summons to a new mission) rather than his *conversion* (a changed religion). (He speaks of it in a manner similar to the prophetic calls in Isa. 6 and Jer. 1.) Paul completely isolates this event from Jerusalem because he wants to emphasize its divine origin.

The second story recounts Paul's trip to Jerusalem to visit with Peter for fifteen days. The verb "to visit" (*historeo*) means to become acquainted with or to get information from, and indicates that Paul was conscious of depending on Peter for information, but not for his gospel.

The third story involved an official trip to Jerusalem "by revelation," to present his gospel to the authorities there and gain their approval. This is probably (though not certainly) the same trip reported in Acts 15, where many additional details are provided. In the Acts version the explicit purpose is to decide the issue of circumcision, and Peter is the primary defender of Gentile liberty. Acts says the authorities decided to exempt the Gentiles from circumcision but imposed certain dietary regulations (Acts 15:19–20). This may be so, though Paul nowhere indicates that he knows of such dietary restrictions for Gentiles. Paul's account clearly shows that there was no absolute victory for his position at this conference. The most he can report is a kind of compromise, an agreement to disagree, in which Paul goes one way and Peter another (2:7–10).

This leads to the final story, in which Peter visits Paul's mission in Antioch. Apparently these Gentiles were not keeping the basic dietary laws, for when "certain men from James" came to investigate the situation at Antioch (2:12), Peter drew back from eating with the Gentiles. Paul confronted him. The skill with which Paul tells this story, causing the reader to cheer for Paul and to assume the correctness of his position, must not blind us to the probable outcome. For he never says he persuaded Peter. Barnabas, Paul's partner, actually went over to the other side (2:13) and no longer traveled with Paul (see Acts 15, especially verses 36–41).

A full spectrum of attitudes toward Gentiles is evident in these stories: from the "false brethren" who insist on circumcision on one side to Paul on the other. The "men from James" (and probably James himself) seem far more insistent on Gentile observance than Paul, and Peter and Barnabas seem to occupy a half-way position between James and Paul.

Do the opponents in Galatia fit on this same spectrum? Perhaps they are like the "men from James," Palestinian missioners claiming to represent the more authentic Jesus tradition of the Jerusalem church. Or perhaps they resembled those Paul labeled "false brethren," Christian Jews who insisted on Gentile circumcision. They may well have set out deliberately to follow up Paul's preaching, which they would have considered flawed and incomplete. After all, the very same Law (Torah) that Paul cites to support his gospel explicitly demands circumcision of God's people. One can almost hear them urging these Gentiles: "You have made a good start with your faith, but now let's go on to perfection. Keep the whole Law of God" (3:3 and Acts 15:5).

One difficulty with thinking that his opponents are connected with Jerusalem is that Paul takes pains to deny that he depends on Jerusalem for his authority (1:17–2:7). Is their argument that Paul ought to be dependent on Jerusalem, but is not, and therefore that his gospel has only his own, human authority? Or do they accuse him of having to depend on Jerusalem while they have some higher authority?

The Opponents as Radicals

The latter possibility is argued by those who regard these opponents not as more conservative than Paul, but as more radical. In this view, the opponents were promising a cosmic freedom to the Galatians. Freedom is the dominant theme of this letter. Such freedom was the purpose of Christ's death (1:3). Many of Paul's metaphors contrast with freedom: bondage (2:4, 4:8), confinement (3:23), custodianship (3:24), minor child (4:1), slavery (4:22). More particularly, Paul speaks of a bondage to "the elemental spirits of the universe" (4:3) and to "beings that by nature are no gods" (4:8). Such language seems characteristic of Hellenistic philosophical speculation rather than of conservative Palestinian Jews.

In the Hellenistic view, the universe consisted of a few basic elements, "which are not simply material substances, but demonic entities of cosmic proportions and astral powers which were hostile" to humanity (Betz, 205). These elements controlled human destiny for they worked within the individual and within the cosmos (hence, astrology). The purpose of magic, prayers, rituals, and rites (or "laws") was to control and contain these forces to prevent harm. If this was the thinking in Galatia, then circumcision would be a sort of talisman to protect one from the powers of the elements (which Hellenistic Jews often identified with angels).

Whether the opponents were Jews or Gentiles, the Galatians probably understood them in this Hellenistic fashion and saw their rites and laws as a means of triumphing over the limitations of Fate. In this kind of situation Paul stood out as the great apostle of liberty.

The Reasoning of the Letter

The lengthy section of proof and rebuttal begins in 3:1 and runs on to 6:10; basically, Chapters 3 and 4 are the positive proofs, and 5 and 6 the rebuttal. Betz's analysis of this section maintains that six major proofs are offered by Paul (19–21, 128–252). Use these summaries to reread Paul's arguments.

1. *The argument from past experience: the Spirit (3:1–5).* Paul makes good use of rhetorical questions: Did you begin by lawkeeping or by the experience of the Spirit? Are miracles worked among you by lawkeeping or by the Spirit?
2. *The argument from Scripture: Abraham (3:6–14).* Scripture attributes righteousness to Abraham on the basis of faith (*believe* and *faith* share the same root in Greek), and further promises to bless the Gentiles through him (that is, through a similar faith). Other passages are quoted (some out of context) to show that Law and faith are opposites.
3. *The argument from common human experience: Wills (3:15–22).* Just as a will cannot be altered once it has been put into effect, so God's promise to Abraham cannot be altered by the giving of the Law 430 years later. (Digression: why, then, the Law? It was a temporary restraining order until the coming of the Messiah.)
4. *The argument from Christian tradition: Baptism (3:23–4:11).* Paul compares the situation before the Messiah to that of minor children who, although they are heirs to the estate, are controlled by slaves. Baptism makes all children of God, but those children must not now turn back to "the weak and beggarly elemental spirits" of the universe who ruled through the Law. The sign of adoption is possession of the Spirit.
5. *The argument from friendship: Love (4:12–20).* Paul defends his character, reminding them of the exalted reception they gave him, "as an angel of God, as Christ Jesus" (14). He presents himself as a model for imitation (12), and compares himself to a mother in childbirth (19).
6. *The argument from story: Allegory (4:21–31).* Strictly speaking, neither this nor the previous point is an argument. It is a convincing story designed to move the feelings of the audience already (it is hoped) persuaded by the earlier arguments. Paul reads the story of Abraham's two wives as symbolic of two ways of serving God: by relying on the Law (Hagar, whose son did not inherit) or by relying on the promise (Sarah, whose son became heir). The implications for Paul's argument are obvious.

One final word on this section. Paul admonished his hearers with the Scripture, "Cast out the slave and her son" (4:30). Though this has been a text of many anti-Semitic preachers through the centuries, it has nothing to do with Jews. In the context of Paul's letter, it meant something like "reject the way of trying to please God by relying on the Law" (with perhaps the additional sense of rejecting those Christian opponents of Paul who preach otherwise). Its meaning is captured in Paul's closing maxim:

᳓ ᳓ ᳓

For freedom Christ has set us free; stand fast therefore, and do not submit again to a yoke of slavery. (5:1)

These arguments are designed to deny the usefulness of lawkeeping, be the opponents conservative Jewish Christians or liberal Hellenistic

Christians. Now Paul deals with their counter-arguments. Against whatever positive arguments they might muster, Paul launches a tirade on the dangers of depending on the Law (5:1–12). Against their logical arguments that his position leads to lawlessness he warns about "the flesh" (5:13–24), building an ethical exhortation on the contrast between flesh and spirit. Finally, he combines the idea of Spirit and of obligation in an appeal for mutual spiritual freedom and sharing, now obedient to the "law of Christ" (5:25–6:10).

In summary, Galatians represents Paul's attempt to present the gospel of Christ to Gentiles who felt constrained by fate, bound by powers beyond their control. For these Gentiles to be circumcised in an effort to protect themselves from such powers was, Paul felt, to miss the essential point of the gospel, namely, that Christ has already delivered his own from the powers of this age (1:3). This case is presented in an elaborately organized rhetorical argument, appealing to experience, Scripture (Law!), ritual, life, and story.

All together, Galatians is a grand argument for freedom that retains its persuasive powers nearly two thousand years later. But it was also a dangerous argument, as his opponents no doubt pointed out, since moral behavior left to spiritual promptings could lead to some strange aberrations. In fact, certain followers of Paul at Corinth who experimented with the limits of Christian freedom soon discovered another side to Paul.

Gentiles Who Ignore the Law: Corinthians

The ancient city of Corinth, strategically located on the narrow midsection of Greece, had been an important and prosperous city in the ancient world—a center of industry, trade, and vice. However, Corinth made the mistake of trying to stand up to Roman power and was completely destroyed in 146 BCE. The city lay desolate for a hundred years before Julius Caesar reestablished it as a Roman colony in 44 BCE.

Like Philippi, it was a place for army veterans who had served their twenty years and received a grant of land as part of their discharge. Officially, veterans were entitled to a grant of three thousand denarii (the equivalent of about ten years' pay) at retirement, but they often received a grant of land of equal value. In addition, about half their pay was withheld during their service as a kind of forced saving. Thus these men, in their early forties, approached their new life with a sizable endowment. It did not always work out well because the land was sometimes not the most desirable. But the settlement at Corinth was a success.

A thriving seaport city, Corinth attracted many other settlers as well. Situated on the isthmus and possessing two good harbors (one facing east and one west), the new Corinth became as prosperous as the old. It was a much more diversified city than most, attracting inhabitants from all quarters and all ethnic groups. A strong Jewish settlement existed there, though we know little about it. Corinth was a meeting place of East and West where one could hear half a dozen languages in addition to the dominant Greek and Latin.

This diversity was stimulated even further by the great athletic contests, the Isthmian Games, which Corinth sponsored every two years. Ranking only below the Olympic Games, these contests attracted competitors from all over the Greek world. The huge crowds were a stimulus to the local economy (including tentmaking, since many of the visitors stayed in tents). We get some impression of what Paul would have experienced from this somewhat dour description by a late first-century observer:

æ æ æ

That was the time [the time for the Isthmian Games] when one could hear crowds of wretched sophists [philosophers] around Poseidon's temple shouting and reviling one another, and their disciples as they were called, fighting with one another, many writers reading aloud their stupid works, many poets reciting their poems while others applauded them, many jugglers showing their

Sports Stadium, Aphrodisias The Greek stadium was essentially a race track, typically 200 yards long, with seating all around. This well-preserved example in modern-day Turkey would seat about 30,000 spectators. The Roman amphitheater was larger and devoted to more diverse entertainments, including gladiatorial combat and animal fights. (Photo by author.)

tricks, many fortune-tellers interpreting fortunes, lawyers innumerable perverting judgement, and peddlers not a few peddling whatever they happened to have. (Dio Chrysostomus, Discourses *8:9; Loeb)*

This mixture of peoples brought a multitude of religions into Corinth. The classical Greek deities were all worshipped in various shrines and temples, with Poseidon, God of the Sea, taking first place in this sailors' town. A major temple to the Goddess Roma and devotion to the emperor would be expected in a city founded by former legionnaires. Greek and oriental rites were combined in the worship of Asclepius (Greek God of Healing), Isis (Egyptian Goddess of Life), and Aphrodite (Greek Goddess of Love), who had major temples here. (See Figure 3.1.) Aphrodite was also the patroness of prostitutes. Strabo claims that her temple at Corinth employed a thousand sacred prostitutes (probably slaves), but whether he was referring to the old Corinth or the new is unclear (*Geography,* 378). Sacred prostitution, common in the East, derived from prehistoric fertility rites whereby union with the priestess of

the goddess would make the land fertile. It remained popular for other reasons. Corinth is the only city in the Greek world where we hear of such a temple, casting some doubt on the accuracy of Strabo's report. Accurate or not, it illustrates Corinth's reputation.

Paul's Contacts with Corinth

According to Acts 18, Paul's visit to Corinth was turbulent. He went into business with two other traveling Jews and stayed in the city a year and a half. He became so contentious in the synagogue that he was forced to leave it and meet in the house next door, which was owned by "Titius Justus, a worshiper of God," obviously one of those Gentile men who were almost converted to Jewish religion. Just as obviously, he was wealthy, since only the wealthy owned homes. Although a few Jews joined Paul in his withdrawal, his major success was with these Gentiles (Acts 18:1–11).

Reconstructing the further course of Paul's interaction with the Corinthians is not simple, but it reveals how Paul operated. What follows is hy-

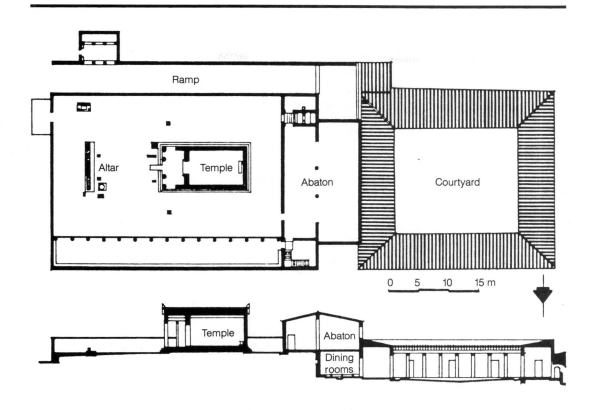

Figure 3 ▪ 1 Temple Complex of Asclepius at Corinth A floor plan (top) and a side view of the Asclepion. The temple and its altar were enclosed and would accommodate large crowds of worshipers. People sought healing from Asclepius, often spending nights here hoping for a healing vision. The dining rooms and courtyard, with its fresh spring, would have been used for religious and private purposes (guild meetings, family celebrations, parties). We can imagine the dilemma of a recently converted Corinthian invited to a family gathering in such a place (see I Cor. 10:14–11:1). (From *St. Paul's Corinth* by Jerome Murphy-O'Connor [Michael Glazier, 1983:163], used by permission.)

pothetical, having the merit of explaining the data available in Paul's letters to Corinth.

The evidence of First Corinthians First Corinthians reveals an ongoing relationship between Paul and Corinth, as we might expect. Not only has he sent his assistant Timothy back to Corinth (4:17), but he has also received a report from Chloe's people about the situation in Corinth (1:11). We know nothing else about Chloe. This

reference to her people indicates that she was a woman of some importance, perhaps a wealthy member of the church whose business required some travel (in which case her "people" would be her employees). Or possibly she was a local teacher (in which case they would be her disciples; see verse 12). This report alone might have prompted Paul to write, but he had also received a letter from Corinth asking his advice on a number of topics (7:1). Even more surprising, we learn that this is not his first letter to the Corinthians. For Paul declares, "I wrote to you in my letter not to associate with immoral" people (I Cor. 5:9). This reference to an earlier letter means that Paul wrote them sometime before "First" Corinthians. We no longer have this first letter, but a fragment of it may be preserved in what we call Second Corinthians, for a careful reading of that letter reveals that it is probably a composite of several separate letters.

The evidence of Second Corinthians   The hypothesis that II Corinthians is a composite letter has been increasingly accepted since it was proposed about a century ago. This assertion is based on a problem in the text of the letter: at two points the thought breaks off sharply, jumps to an unrelated topic, then abruptly shifts back to the original thought. The suggestion is that the intruding material originally belonged to a separate discourse.

Reading and Reflection

Try reading the following verses: 6:13 and 6:14, then 6:13 and 7:2; read 2:13 and 2:14, then 2:13 and 7:5.

The ideas in 7:2 seem to belong to those in 6:13, while all the discussion about separation from evil (6:14–7:2) seems to be spliced into the middle of a completely unrelated topic. This fragment on separation is not easy to relate to anything else in II Corinthians. Some have noted that this topic is similar to Paul's lost first letter (see I Cor. 5:9), but others point out that it calls for the precise kind of separation Paul says he did not advocate: separation from the world.

So too, Paul's anxious search for Titus in 2:13 is interrupted without warning and resumed without cause in 7:5. All the intervening material is irrelevant to this quest. It seems more likely that

the narrative about meeting Titus in Macedonia was originally connected and that this is another fragment from yet another letter.

Paul also referred to a painful letter that he had written out of much affliction (II Cor. 2:4), one that he initially regretted writing (7:8). This does not accurately describe I Corinthians or either of the fragments. There seems to be yet another lost letter, though again some argue that it is partially preserved in II Corinthians.

Chapters 10 to 13 match this description rather well. The tone of these three chapters is far harsher than the rest: in them Paul directly confronts his opposition and rails at the Corinthians for listening to them. After bragging "as a fool," he says they will have no trouble accepting him, "for you gladly bear with fools" (11:17–18). He chides them: "I robbed other churches . . . to serve you" (11:8). He threatens: "I fear that perhaps I may come and find you not what I wish, and that you may find me not what you wish" (12:20). "If I come again I will not spare them" (13:2). The most obvious point of these chapters is that the conflict has not been settled; the outcome is still in doubt, which explains their painful tone.

Yet the early part of the letter is relatively tranquil and presumes that the crisis is past. Titus has already returned with the comforting news of reconciliation (7:6). Paul even asks mercy for the offending party (2:5–9). Either chapters 10 to 13 were written before these comforting words, or we are to imagine that the conflict raged again at Corinth and that Paul learned of it while writing the letter, then dramatically shifted his tone at chapter 10.

A more logical hypothesis seems to be that there are three basic letters in II Corinthians, each of a somewhat different kind: there is the letter before the crisis (2:14–7:4, minus the addition on separation); there is the letter during the crisis (10–13), written in the genre of the fool's discourse; and there is the letter of reconciliation after the crisis (1:1–2:13 and 7:5–16). Chapters 8 and 9, both dealing with the collection, may have been attached to this last letter, or they may have been a separate letter or two (since 9:1 seems to reintroduce the idea of a collection as if it had not been mentioned earlier).

Thus the Corinthian correspondence seems to have been extensive, comprising a whole series of letters over several years' time. These letters also contain references to three visits by Paul himself and others by his associates, Timothy and Titus. A possible reconstruction of the course of events follows.

1. He establishes the church and spends more than eighteen months there (Acts 18).
2. He writes his first, now lost, letter regarding church discipline (I Cor. 5:9; perhaps = II Cor. 6:14–7:1).
3. He sends Timothy to visit them (I Cor. 4:17).
4. He receives reports from Chloe's people of divisions and immorality (I Cor. 1:11).
5. He receives a letter from the Corinthians concerning questions they need to have answered (I Cor. 7:1).
6. He writes another letter to answer them and to respond to Chloe's report. (= I Cor.).
7. He sends Timothy on another visit (I Cor. 16:10).
8. He hears of opposition at Corinth from outsiders with letters of reference. He is concerned, but does not yet realize how serious the situation will become (II Cor. 3:1).
9. He writes a third letter to warn and admonish them (= II Cor. 2:14–7:4, minus 6:14–7:1).
10. This letter is used against him and real danger to his leadership emerges (II Cor. 10:10).
11. Contrary to earlier plans (I Cor. 16:7), he pays a brief visit to Corinth, where he finds open rebellion and insult (II Cor. 2:5, 7:12).
12. He writes an angry letter (II Cor. 7:12, 2:4; = II Cor 10–13).
13. He sends Titus to check on affairs (II Cor. 12:17).
14. He learns from Titus of the success of his letter and of Titus' visit (II Cor. 1:13, 7:5–6).
15. He writes a letter of reconciliation (= II Cor. 1:1–2:13, 7:5–16).
16. He arranges for a "gift" (II Cor. 8–9).
17. He visits a third time (proposed in II Cor. 12:14, 13:1).
18. He writes Romans from Corinth (Rom. 15:25–27; I Cor. 16:3).

If this is an accurate reconstruction of the events (and I must stress again that it is a hypothesis), we can readily understand Paul's anxiety about meeting Titus in Macedonia (see item 13 above), and much more about these writings. Paul's letters are not the reflections of an armchair philosopher; they are very specific, forged from conflict and controversy. Paul honed the letter into one of his most important tools. Let us proceed to examine the contents of these two letters more closely.

Problems of Gentile Converts: First Corinthians

From the lost first letter we learn that the assembly at Corinth was having difficulty with moral issues; for Paul admonished them to keep themselves separate from the immoral members of their assembly (I Cor. 5:9–12). Although Corinth was well known for its vices, so that to "corinthianize" became an expression for debauchery, the moral standards at Corinth were probably not far different from those elsewhere in the Greco-Roman world. Most of the bad reputation really belonged to the old Corinth, which had been destroyed two centuries earlier. Like other places, the moral standards of Corinth were mixed. Generalization is dangerous, but necessary.

Morality among the Gentiles In this era, Gentiles asserted all sorts of moral standards from the Cynic's lack of concern with morality to the Stoic's moral seriousness. The mystery religions generally demanded a strict moral standard from the would-be initiate. At the heart of Gentile morality was the idea of purity, though there was no consensus as to what made one impure. One clear example of the lack of moral depth in the traditional religions is an inscription from a temple to Athena at Pergamum (just north of Ephesus, where Paul was when he wrote to the Corinthians):

æ æ æ

Whoever wishes to visit the temple of the goddess, whether a resident of the city or anyone else, must refrain from intercourse with his wife (or husband) that day, from intercourse with another than his wife (or husband) for the preceding two days, and must complete the required lustrations. (Grant, 1953:6)

Gentile ethics do not show the Jewish concern for the absolute demand of God. The Jewish God forbad all adultery, not simply because it made one impure but because it displeased him. As long as the new Christian message was proclaimed in a context dominated by this Jewish idea, there was no need to develop a theory of ethics. But when the proclamation was primarily successful with Gentiles, so that a split developed between this new way and the Jewish community (as was apparently the case at Corinth), the issue of ethics had to be addressed directly.

Reading and Reflection

Using the reading guide, read through I Corinthians and list Paul's responses to their questions. Are all these rules consistent with the freedom Paul advocated in Galatians?

Morality at Corinth   While the answers to their questions may seem obvious to us, we must try to imagine the situation at Corinth in which these were considered pressing issues. What could have created the dilemma that forced the Corinthians to write Paul for answers to just these questions? And why did they apparently fail to ask about the problems he addressed in the first six chapters? How are we to understand that they had

scruples about sexual relations between husbands and wives, yet saw no problem with visiting prostitutes? Not only did they not have a question about the case of incest, they were proud of it (5:1–2: literally, "you are ones who have become proud of it." See 5:6).

As background for this incident, we may imagine a case in which an older man had taken a far younger wife, probably because his first wife died. This was a very common occurrence: the new wife could well be younger than his own children, perhaps only thirteen or fourteen years old. When the man died, one of his sons married the wife, his legal mother—which the ancients considered incest. This cannot be attributed to a supposed low morality among Gentiles. It was absolutely forbidden in both Jewish and Greek culture. The Greek story of Oedipus, who inadvertently married his mother and suffered extreme humiliation as a result, gives some sense of the Greek abhorrence of marrying one's mother (whether natural or legal). Paul himself was shocked by this situation, and contrasted it with even pagan morality (5:1).

If we could discover the logic by which the Corinthians could be proud of this situation we might have the key to understanding what was happening at Corinth. By what logic could these Gentile Christians feel proud of incest, free to visit prostitutes, be dubious of sex in marriage, and uncertain of the Resurrection (to cite only the more obvious questions)? Of course, the existence of factions could mean that various people had problems with only some of these issues.

The problem behind the problems   One thread that ties nearly all these problems together is the question of the relationship between the physical and the spiritual. Only the issues of the collection and the lawsuits do not have an obvious connection with this question of body and spirit. The question of whether women should lead in worship without a head covering, for example, is not a question of style, but a question about the nature of being men and women in the created order (11:2–16). A hierarchy of beings was uni-

READING GUIDE TO FIRST CORINTHIANS

Salutation   1:1–3
Thanksgiving   1:4–9
Body: responses to problems   1:10–16:4

Paul's Problems with Them   1:10–6:20

Factions   1:1–4:20
Four distinct groups had emerged in the assembly, each attached to the person who had baptized them; the Paul party, the Apollos party, the Peter party, and the Christ party.
Incest   5:1–13
A man is living with his father's wife.
Lawsuits   6:1–8
The public courts rather than the church are being used to settle disputes between believers.
Prostitutes   6:9–20
Some believers are continuing to visit prostitutes.

Paul's Answers to Their Questions   7:1–16:4

Marriage   7:1–40
Should one marry?
Should married people have sexual relations?

Should widows remarry?
Should a believer divorce an unbeliever?
Food   8:1–11:1
Should a believer eat meat sacrificed to the Gods?
Is one free to eat even if it offends others?
Is it permitted to eat what is sold in the market?
Is it permitted to eat in the home of an idolater?
Conduct of worship   11:2–14:40
Should women pray and preach without a head covering?
How should the Lord's supper be eaten?
Should spiritual gifts be regulated?
Resurrection   15:1–58
Will there be a resurrection?
With what sort of body are the dead raised?
Collection   16:1–4
How should it be taken up?
When will Paul come for it?

Travel plans   16:5–9
Exhortations   16:10–18
Mutual greetings   16:19–23
Handwritten greeting   16:21
Blessing   16:22–23

---

versally assumed in Paul's world, and he seems to have accepted the traditional order that proceeded downward from God to angels, to men, to women. But women too had received the spirit of prophecy. They too addressed the congregation, including the angels. The question is really one of the proper understanding of the relation between body (the created order) and spirit (their ministry).

To be obedient to the Spirit, yet not offend the higher order of angels, Paul argued that women should veil their heads: the veil hid their status in creation and gave them authority to address the congregation. Nevertheless, he quickly adds: "In the Lord woman is not independent of man nor man of woman" (11:11).

As he does so often, Paul finds a middle ground between those who argue for dependence and those who argue for independence: he argues for mutual dependence. But, he asks: How ought people to understand themselves as human beings? Are they essentially spiritual, or is the physical an essential aspect? There was no agreement on such questions in Paul's world. It would be wrong to speak of a Greek view. As they did on most things, the Greeks differed in their understanding of human nature. Yet certain widespread tendencies in Greek culture help us to make sense of these problems.

Hundreds of years before Paul, in the dialogue recounting the death of Socrates, Plato reported this interesting interchange. Socrates speaks first:

ﻼ ﻼ ﻼ

"Do we think there is such a thing as death?"
"Certainly," replied Simmias.
"We believe, do we not, that death is the separation of the soul from the body, and the state of being dead is the state in which the body is separated from the soul and exists alone by itself and the soul is separated from the body and exists alone by itself? Is death anything other than this?"
"No, it is this," he said.
"Now, my friend, see if you agree with me; for if you do I think we shall get more light on our subject. Do you think a philosopher would be likely to care much about the so-called pleasures, such as eating and drinking?"
"By no means, Socrates," said Simmias.
"How about the pleasures of love?"
"Certainly not."
"Well do you think such a man would think much of the other cares of the body. . . ?"
"I think the true philosopher would despise them," he said.   (Phaedo 64c-e; Loeb)

Paul was not the first to have to explain the relation of the body to the pursuits of the spirit. But he took a very different tack than Socrates. To understand this difference, we need to explore the different interpretations of being human evident in the Greek and Jewish cultures.

The essential difference between the two can be seen by going back to the archaic period in each tradition. Several scenes in the *Iliad* and the *Odyssey* depict the hero descending into the Underworld to gain some information from the dead. Here he meets disembodied spirits, "souls of the departed dead flocked up from Erebos—brides, god-like youths, old men who had endured much,

innocent maidens who had only just put on grief, and many wearing the wounds of bronze spears, men slain of Ares [God of War], with armor all gory" (*Odyssey* XI: 40–50). In a very primitive fashion, these souls need the offerings of the living, especially blood, and can foretell the future. By contrast, no concern for life after death appears in the writings of the Jewish classical period. (For a late and pessimistic view, see Eccles. 9:10.) There is only the grave to which all go. Only once do we find a medium conjuring a ghost (I Sam. 28:3–20). When the ghost of Samuel appears before Saul, he says: "Why have you disturbed me by bringing me up?" Here the dead are gone; they no longer need the living.

When a concern for life after death did develop in Israel, especially during the religious persecutions, it was conceived of as a resurrection of the body. Thus, a dying martyr addressing the pagan king, who is having him killed because he refuses to worship his gods, says: "You accursed wretch, you dismiss us from this present life, but the King of the universe will raise us up to an everlasting renewal of life, because we have died for his laws" (II Macc. 7:9). Even Paul, a Jew who had been deeply influenced by Greek ideas, equated the ideas of a bodiless afterlife with the idea of nakedness (II Cor. 5:1–4).

But among the Greeks, beginning with Socrates (died 399 BCE), there is a clearly articulated belief in a bodiless afterlife, with separate destinies for the good and the evil. For Socrates the soul was not only deathless, it was birthless, preexistent–immortal (*Phaedo* 70–77, 105e). Thus the soul returns to its true abode after death:

ﻼ ﻼ ﻼ

But those who are found to have excelled in holy living are freed from these regions within the earth and are released from prisons; they mount upward into their pure abode and dwell upon the earth. And of these all who have duly purified themselves by philosophy live henceforth altogether without bodies, and pass to still more

*beautiful abodes which it is not easy to describe.
. . . (Phaedo 114c; Loeb)*

We must notice the condition, "such as have purified themselves sufficiently by philosophy." Earlier in the same dialogue we are told that the task of the philosopher "consists in separating the soul as much as possible from the body" (67c). In fact it had become a pun in Greek philosophical thought that the body was the tomb of the soul. (In Greek: Soma estin sema. Perhaps the closest we can come in English would be to say the womb is a tomb.)

Certain conclusions follow from this basic dualism. If we are essentially spiritual beings, we have somehow "fallen" and become entrapped into materiality, into body. But surely the first step in transcending the body and gaining our rightful place is to recognize the truth of our condition, to know our true natures. As the philosophers put it: know yourself—and your true self is spiritual.

While these ideas were widespread, there developed about this time a distinctive way of answering them: gnosticism (from the Greek word for knowledge, *gnosis*). There were countless forms of gnosticism, but all were based on this idea of an absolute dualism between matter and spirit. All sought the saving knowledge by which we could be freed from bondage to matter, usually through the secret revelations of a divine man who would descend into the world and reveal these truths. Many Gnostics were Christians who regarded Jesus to be that heavenly revealer. The problems at Corinth could have sprung from a gnostic-like interpretation of Christianity.

For example, if one takes as a starting point the absolute separation of matter and spirit, marriage—and especially sexuality—becomes a problem. One should be above the body. Even what to eat becomes a problem; by far the largest number of Gnostics were ascetics, often vegetarians. Other Gnostics argued, with equal logic, that if the body is ever and always evil it does not matter what we do with it. Thus, it is no more evil to visit a prostitute than it is to eat; both are bodily, and therefore irrelevant, activities. Nor should one put any emphasis on the differences between men and women, since this is purely a bodily matter. Thus the Gnostics were more apt than most to insist on absolute equality between men and women. Certainly the Gnostic would favor spiritual gifts, since they regarded themselves as the truly spiritual ones. Much of what Paul said about the wise and spiritual in I Corinthians (1–4) seems appropriate to a Gnostic view of the world.

But what about incest? What about being proud of incest? This is not in itself a Gnostic trait, but it is readily explainable in terms of a Gnostic worldview. Freed from materiality, the Gnostics believed themselves to be "born again." They would heartily endorse Paul's declaration that "if anyone is in Christ, he is a new creation; the old has passed away, behold, the new has come" (II Cor. 5:17). The Gnostic would understand this in a radical fashion: if the old has passed away, then the old relationships no longer apply. As a spiritual participant in the new order, one is freed from all the constraints of the old order, including family ties. The Corinthians were proud of their new freedom; so proud and so free that they endorsed this incestuous marriage.

Paul, the law, and the Gentiles Paul was deeply shocked when he heard this interpretation of his teaching; he could scarcely believe it. He demanded a solemn handing over of the person to Satan, presuming he would die as a result (I Cor. 5:5). Faced with a group that took his radical call to freedom literally, Paul quickly retreats. He even declares: "Neither circumcision counts for anything nor uncircumcision, but keeping the commandments of God" (7:19), striking a different note from that in Galatians, where he declares: "For neither circumcision counts for anything, nor uncircumcision, but a new creation" (6:15). Precisely such talk about freedom and new creation had caused the problem at Corinth. In the background at Corinth we do not yet see gnosticism, but the development of a gnosticizing and spiritualizing interpretation of Christianity. This Greek mistrust of the body and fascination with the spirit will eventually lead to daring new interpretations of Paul and Jesus (which we will examine in Chapter 5).

Evidently Paul adapted his teaching to his circumstances. In Galatia, faced with a challenge to freedom by those who insist on using the Law as a means to control their fates, Paul sounds like one who would abolish the Law. In Corinth, confronted by those who would abolish the Law in their new freedom, Paul sounds like one who lived according to God's demands. As interpreters of Paul, we must always remember that we are hearing only part of the story at any one time and must seek to know the whole story before interpreting its parts.

The Rhetoric of Controversy: Second Corinthians

We have seen earlier that II Corinthians is probably a collection of parts of several letters. Yet these letters focus primarily on one problem: opponents have appeared at Corinth and have succeeded in turning many of Paul's followers away.

Reading and Reflection

Use the reading guide to read through II Corinthians.
1. What charges did the opponents bring against Paul?
2. What means did they use to commend themselves?
3. How does Paul reclaim the allegiance of the Corinthians?

> ### READING GUIDE TO SECOND CORINTHIANS
>
> The letter before the controversy   2:14–6:13, 7:2–4
>   A thanksgiving   2:14–17
>   Living proof   3:1–6
>   Two dispensations   3:7–17
>   Paul's ministry   4:1–15
>   Not disheartened by death   4:16–5:10
>   Representatives of Christ   5:11–21
>   Plea for openness   6:1–13, 7:2–4
> The letter during the controversy   10–13
>   Plea not to force his hand   10:1–6
>   He will not be put to shame   10:7–18
>   Boasting like a fool   11:1–12:13
>   They accept fools   11:1–6
>   Admits his mistake: too meek   11:7–11
>   Comparisons with opponents   11:12–21
>   Boasting in his weakness   11:22–12:13
>   Plans for a third visit   12:14–13:4
>   Examine yourselves . . .   13:5–11
>   Greetings and blessing   13:12–14
> The letter after the controversy   1:1–2:13, 7:5–16
>   Salutation   1:1–2
>   Blessing   1:3–7
>   Main discourse   1:8–2:13, 7:5–16
>   Perils in Asia   1:8–11
>   Paul's boast   1:12–14
>   Narrative of events   1:15–2:13, 7:5–12
>   Resulting comfort   7:13–16
>
> Addenda on the collection   8–9
> A fragment of a letter   6:14–7:1

Clearly new missioners have come to Corinth. They claim to be servants of Christ (11:23), possess written testimonials to their excellence (3:1), claim to be superior apostles (11:5, 13), and have attacked Paul directly (10:10). He is charged with weakness (10:10), inferiority (10:7; 11:5), lack of good speaking skills (11:6), and perhaps with irregular handling of his finances (11:7, 9; 12:17). They probably also claim miraculous powers (12:12), visions (12:1), and a Jewish heritage (11:22). Eventually they succeed so well in alienating the Corinthians from Paul that when he hurriedly visits them, he is put to public shame (2:5 with 7:12 and 13:1–2).

We can learn much about Paul and his handling of controversy by comparing these three writings. In the first letter, when the controversy is discovered, the dominant metaphor is hiddenness, and there is an implicit contrast between insiders and outsiders. Whether it involves discerning the right fragrance (2:15), having intimate letters of recommendation (3:1), seeing the veil on Moses' face (3:13), finding treasure in clay pots (4:7), discerning the heavenly building behind the earthly tent (5:1), or knowing Christ from a human or a spiritual point of view (5:16), Paul continually implies that he is on the inside. He seduces the hearer.

The last letter, when the controversy was settled, is marked by contrasts between joy and sorrow, affliction and comfort, repentance and stubbornness. What is rhetorically enacted is the shift from stubbornness to repentance, with the corresponding shifts from affliction to comfort and from sorrow to joy. This is one of Paul's most gracious works, asking mercy even on the one responsible for the insult to him on his hurried second visit to Corinth (2:5–11).

The middle letter, written in the heat of controversy, after the insult but before the apology, is the most dramatic. Here we find the ironic Paul. Here we see him mocking his opponents (11:5), his audience (11:19–21), and especially himself (10:8, 18; 11:1, 16, 21–33; most of chapter 12). Paul readily admits all the charges brought against him, and in so doing he ironically turns their charges into badges of honor. His sufferings actually identify him as the servant of Christ (11:23 and following). This whole section is a delight to read if we remember that here Paul is writing "like a madman" (11:23) and do not take him literally. Paul offers us another glimpse of his sense of humor, moderating to some extent the harsh reflection of him in Galatians.

The Corinthian correspondence displays some of the problems Gentiles had with the new faith Paul preached. Corinth itself was a prosperous city which, despite its bad reputation, was prob-

ably no more wicked than any other large city. Paul had spent a year and a half there and exchanged numerous letters and several visits.

While these letters deal with a host of individual problems, two stand out: the difficulty of translating Jewish ethics into a Gentile context, a context that deprecated the body, and the issue of loyalty to Paul in the face of opponents who were probably more at home in the Gentile world than he was. These are the major themes of the two letters we know as I and II Corinthians. Taken together, they illustrate the range of issues Paul confronted in his mission as apostle to the Gentiles.

PAUL AND HIS FOLLOWERS

There is a great danger for those of us who deal with Paul from these texts alone, since his world was infinitely larger. Because the text is all we have left, the danger is that we will let it fill our whole canvas. But how much our image of Paul must shift from letter to letter. How distinctive is the image in Galatians from that in Philemon. How different his teaching seems in I Corinthians from that in Galatians. How little continuity we discern between I and II Corinthians. What tantalizing hints we come across: near death in Asia (II Cor. 1:8), frequent opposition, dramatic adventure (II Cor. 11). Yet we know almost nothing else about these events.

Still, the letters are a treasure mine, and it has been truly said that one meets Paul face to face in the reading of these letters. They are some of the most intense and personal writings we have from the Greco-Roman era, presenting us with an enormous range of feelings: rage to humor, endearment to sarcasm, poetry to incomplete prose. Strikingly well organized, according to the intended purpose, they are works of rhetoric and imagination as well as of spirit and idea. They are well worth many readings.

The letters reveal little about the men and women who became Paul's followers and friends. They seem to have been mostly Gentiles with strong sympathies for the Jewish tradition—many were more attracted to it than Paul thought wise. He forged strong emotional ties with these people, but spent surprisingly little time with them. Brief visits had to be reinforced by sending emissaries and, especially, letters—both of which substituted for Paul and represented (re-presented) him to the community.

Paul's central metaphor for this community is the family—the extended Hellenistic family of parents, children, slaves, and business partners. His most common salutation is "Brothers." Fellow believers are to be treated as brothers even if they are rebellious (II Thess. 3:15; see I Cor. 5:11, 6:1). A female coworker is addressed as a sister (Rom. 16:1). At other times Paul assumes a more parental tone, addressing them as his children (I Cor. 4:14 and II Cor. 12:14). Twice he describes himself as the father: he became father of Onesimus in prison (Philem. 10) and exhorts the Thessalonians like a father with his children (I Thess. 2:11). But he is also gentle among them, "like a nurse taking care of her children" (I Thess. 2:7). Once he describes himself as a mother giving birth to her children again (Gal. 4:19). Once he describes a congregation as his virgin daughter, for whom he has arranged a desirable marriage (II Cor. 11:2).

Two other family metaphors are more remote from us: the slave and the partner (for example, I Cor. 4:1, 9:19; Phil. 1:5). As Paul is the slave of Christ, he becomes the slave of all (I Cor. 9:19). And each is to serve the other (Gal. 5:13, literally "be a slave to"). This metaphor of the household slave whose task it is to serve the needs of others captured for Paul some of the meaning of the cross of Christ, who himself became a slave to serve others (Phil. 2:7). The terminology of redemption and of purchase price (I Cor. 1:30, 6:20) derive from the slave trade. There is, of course, some tension between these images and Paul's metaphor of freedom. But that tension is partly resolved by another image, that of voluntary association in mutual contractual obligation: partnership.

Partnership in Roman law created, in effect, an extended family; the earliest partnerships were those of brothers who inherited their father's estate but were not allowed to divide it. Paul Sampley has examined Paul's partnership imagery and found four distinct uses:

1. Paul understood himself to be in partnership with the church at Jerusalem, and in response undertook to collect an offering for their support (Gal. 2:1–10).
2. Paul entered into a unique partnership with the church at Philippi, the only church from which he received financial support (Phil. 4:10–20, 1:5).
3. Paul used his partnership relation to Philemon to induce him to treat Onesimus as he would treat Paul (verse 17).
4. Paul regularly used the terminology of the partnership even when formal aspects of support were lacking. "Be of one mind," "agree with one another," "fellowship," and, on the negative side, "fraud" were drawn from the partners' relation of mutual obligation (1980:103–108).

These obligations exist between Paul and his congregations and between members in their congregations. It is one more way of expressing their familial relationship, respecting both their absolute freedom and their absolute obligation to each other. Imaging his communities as a family allowed Paul to tread a narrow path between the mutual responsibilities he saw as necessary and dependence on the Law that he saw as dangerous.

One problem we face in interpreting Paul in these letters is that since they are written to his friends, he could assume they knew many things. But one letter that we will study was not addressed to his friends; it was written to a community with which he had not had previous contact. This is his most elaborate letter, presenting a long and carefully organized argument. With it, we conclude our study of Paul.

RESOURCES FOR FURTHER STUDY

Brief introductions of Paul and his thought include:

Beker, 1982, *Paul's Apocalyptic Gospel*.
Hooker, 1980, *A Preface to Paul*.
Scroggs, 1977, *Paul for a New Day*.
Ziesler, 1983, *Pauline Christianity*.

More substantive studies include:

Beker, 1980, *Paul the Apostle*.
Bornkamm, 1971, *Paul, Paulus*.
Bruce, 1977, *Paul*.
Davies, 1980, *Paul and Rabbinic Judaism*.

The problems of Pauline chronology are treated in different ways by Jewett, 1979; Knox, 1939; and Ludemann, 1984.

For discussion of Paul's metaphors for the communities, see:

Banks, 1980, *Paul's Idea of Community*.
Schweizer, 1965, *The Church as the Body of Christ*.

The most useful discussion of Paul's occupation is Hock, 1980.

Good introductions to his letters include Ellis, 1982; Keck, 1979; Keck and Furnish, 1984; Meeks, 1972; and Roetzel, 1982. Patte, 1983, is an advanced study, analyzing the letters with a structuralist methodology.

Works on specific letters include:

Philemon: Bruce, 1984; Getty, 1980; Lohse, 1971; Patzia, 1984; and Petersen, 1985.
Philippians: Getty, 1980; and Hubbard and Hawthorne, 1983.
Galatians: The recent commentary of Betz is now the standard work, 1979; it is especially provocative on the rhetoric of Galatians. See also Brinsmead, 1982, and the challenge by Kennedy, 1984: 144–152. Other commentaries include Conzelmann, 1979; Ebeling, 1985; Guthrie, 1981; and Osiek, 1980. Hays, 1984, seeks to discover the story implied in Galatians. Howard, 1979, explores the nature of the crisis in Galatia.
Corinthians: Barrett, 1974, 1975c; Conzelmann, 1975; and Furnish, 1984. On the nature of the opponents at Corinth, see Barrett, 1971; and Georgi,

1985. Two special studies on the social setting at Corinth have appeared: Murphy-O'Connor, 1984, *St. Paul's Corinth*, is a valuable, comprehensive collection and interpretation of ancient writers and a review of archaeology relating to Corinth; and Theissen, 1982, *The Social Setting of Pauline Christianity*.

On a broader scale, several writers have explored aspects of the social world of Paul: Grant, 1977; Hengel, 1974b; Judge, 1982; Malherbe, 1983; and Meeks, 1983.

More generally, Rose, 1959, *Religion in Greece and Rome*, is a good introduction to Greco-Roman religion.

A number of useful collections of primary sources include:

Ferguson, 1980, *Greek and Roman Religion: A Source Book*.
Grant, F.C., 1953, *Hellenistic Religions: The Age of Syncretism*.
Jonas, 1963, *The Gnostic Religion*.
Luck, 1985, is an excellent collection on magic and the occult in antiquity.
Rice and Stambaugh, 1979, *Sources for the Study of Greek Religion*.
The role of religion in everyday life is displayed in the novel by Apuleius, *The Golden Ass*, and the essay by Lucretius, *On the Nature of the Universe*.

The texture of Greco-Roman religion is explored in a more systematic way by:

Ferguson, 1970, *The Religions of the Roman Empire*.
Helgeland, 1975, "Roman Army Religion."
MacMullen, 1981, *Paganism in the Roman Empire*.
Teixidor, 1977, *Pagan God: Popular Religion in the Greco-Roman Near East*.
An adequate introduction to the philosophies of the period is Warner, 1958, *The Greek Philosophers*.

On the relation between Jews and Gentiles, see the balanced account of Gager, 1983, and the older work of Sevenster. On the Roman view of Christians, see Wilken, 1984.

Paul's Address to Those outside His Circle

ᔥ ᔥ ᔥ

Romans

Literary Analysis of Romans

Historical Analysis of the Context

The Theme of Romans: Two Views

In Conclusion: Imagining Paul's Story

Resources for Further Study

4

When we begin to read Romans, we soon sense that this is a different kind of work. It is unlike Paul's other letters, though explaining how it varies is not an easy task. Our first impression perhaps is that it is longer. It is the longest of Paul's letters (which may be why it was placed first in the collection of those letters). But it is not that much longer than I Corinthians. The standard Greek text of Romans is thirty-four pages; I Corinthians is thirty. But while I Corinthians is a virtual list of topics to which Paul needed to respond, Romans covers one topic. No other letter even approaches this length for one sustained argument.

The next thing we may notice is that the argument is hard to locate. Just what is the point? Paul never attacks anyone in Romans, never says any particular point of view is wrong, never indulges in name-calling. Though it seems to be one long argument, it is not easy to discover the major concern of that argument. This is due to a third difference. Nothing in the letter explains why Paul wrote it.

Certainly, he is planning a trip to Rome (15: 22–29), but to write such a letter simply to warn the Romans that he is coming is somewhat like using field artillery to swat flies—effective perhaps, but excessive. Also, Paul is evidently trying to drum up support for his trip to Spain. Some have suggested that gaining such support is the real purpose of Romans (which might make it the earliest surviving example of proposal writing). Other scholars make two telling points against this idea: first, if Paul were trying to gain support he could have done so much more directly and simply. But, second, it is unlikely that such was his purpose. We have seen that Paul was very reluctant to accept financial support even from the churches he founded (excepting only Philippi). How much less likely would he be to solicit support from a church founded by someone else. We should consider, then, that Romans differs to some extent from the other letters we have examined. Its length, determined pursuit of a single argument, and lack of a clear historical purpose all point away from the letter toward the essay as its genre.

First let us examine the literary features of this letter-essay, then explore its historical context, before turning directly to its possible meaning.

LITERARY ANALYSIS OF ROMANS

Reading and Reflection

Quickly read through Romans and try to discover the main contours of Paul's argument. I have found it useful to pay special attention to:

1. Paul's point of view. (When does he speak about "them," about "us," or about "you?")
2. Paul's introduction of a "dissenting voice." (When does Paul imagine someone might raise an objection or infer a conclusion?)
3. Paul's use of explicit logical indicators. (When does he use words like "therefore," "but," "so," "then," or "however"?)

The Form of the Argument:
The Points of View

Any writer finds it necessary to address the reader occasionally, usually by saying "you" or "we." Though Paul does this in Romans, he also does something else. At two points in the argument he shifts his basic point of view. After a lengthy introduction, he begins to discuss the "wickedness of men" (1:18) and continues in the third person for some time. Even when he addresses the reader and hearers as "you" (as in 2:1 and 2:17), it is still clear that he is talking about "them." He is talking about mankind, the human species and its specific manifestations as Jew and Gentile. Not until chapter 5 do we encounter a different point of view. Beginning at 5:1, Paul shifts his stance from considering "them" to talking about "us." It is "we" who are justified; "we" who were sinners; "we" who are baptized; nothing can separate "us" from the love of God. This way of speaking continues through chapter 8 and surely represents a new stage of the argument. In the next three chapters (9–11) Paul seems to revert to the third person. But while the "them" in chapters 1–4 referred to the universal them of humanity, here it refers to the Jewish people. Chapter 12 marks the beginning of another shift; this time to the second person, "you." The mood also changes. The address is now in the imperative: a demand.

Whatever the topic of this argument, then, its form seems clear enough. It begins with the universal, focuses on the particular instances of Paul and the Roman community and the people of Israel, and proceeds to the demands that such understanding brings to the hearers.

The Nature of the Argument

For us, the argument of Romans seems long, convoluted, and difficult to follow because we rarely encounter anything written in this style. But it was a popular style in the ancient world, especially among the philosophical schools where it served as a teaching technique. Actually, it may be considered an extension of the Platonic Dialogue. In a dialogue a philosopher enters into formal exchange of ideas with students and adversaries. Consequently, the argument takes many turns, and even detours, before it reaches its conclusion. But in the writing style we see in Romans the formal partner in the dialogue has disappeared, leaving his questions and objections behind. This style is called the *diatribe*. Primarily it was a style of speaking, in which the lecturer would raise questions or implications of the argument, which would then be pursued. Thus it would wander into alleys and byways rather than proceeding straight to a conclusion.

The writer of a diatribe imagines that his or her hearers are present, deals with any objections they might raise, and suggests related ideas to pursue. One objection might lead to another, and the argument detour through much unexpected terrain before returning to the main point. The purpose of this method is to form a bond between speaker and hearer and lead them to a common conclusion.

In reading or hearing a diatribe, pay very careful attention to the specific topic at hand, and watch closely for the turns and returns of the argument. It is crucial in reading Romans to be always clear about exactly what question Paul thinks he is answering at any given point in the work. We must be careful to avoid the old party game, in which an unsuspecting person is asked a series of questions, the answers are duly recorded, and new questions inserted so that the old answers become amusing and perhaps embarrassing. We must keep Paul's answers and questions together, for we understand an answer only when we understand the question for which it was intended.

In the best discussion of the diatribe and Romans known to me, Stowers (1981) explores the nature of this kind of writing and the features of Romans that correspond to it. He notes especially: (1) the use of an imaginary partner in conversation, (2) the raising of objections, and (3) the inferring of false conclusions. Watch for these devices as we read; they are used repeatedly. Examples of addressing an imaginary hearer include:

જ જ જ

Therefore you have no excuse, O man. . . . (2:1)
But if you call yourself a Jew . . . (2:17)
You will say to me then . . . (9:19)
Who are you to pass judgment. . . . (14:4)

Numerous objections raised to the argument include:

Then what advantage has the Jew? (3:1)
Are Jews any better off? (3:9)

The objections raised usually result from drawing a false conclusion from Paul's argument, such as:

Do we then overthrow the Law? . . . (3:31)
Are we to continue in sin? . . . (6:1)
Is the Law sin? . . . (7:7)
Is there injustice on God's part? . . . (9:14)
Has God rejected His people? . . . (11:1)

These rhetorical indicators, and other factors such as the use of "therefore," "but," "so," "for," and so on, must be carefully mapped for the modern reader to follow Paul's meandering argument.

A Comparison of the Argument

Another valid impression you may have had while reading Romans is that you have read some of these things before in the earlier letters. The lengthy discussion of eating food offered to idols (Rom. 14–15) echoes the earlier advice to the Corinthians (I Cor. 8–10). Why has Paul chosen to introduce this topic again? Were the Romans having the same kinds of problems that caused the Corinthians to inquire about this subject? Yet we miss in Romans any sense that they have asked for Paul's advice. Other parallels have also been noticed (Bornkamm, 1971:93–94). You may wish to compare the following:

Topic	Romans	Other
Justification by Faith	1–4	Gal. 3–4
Abraham as example	4	Gal. 3
Adam/Christ analogy	5	I Cor. 15
Slave of sin	7	I Cor. 15
Flesh and spirit	8	Gal. 4
Body of Christ and gifts	12	I Cor. 12
Food to idols	14–15	I Cor. 8–10

An obvious gap is in chapters 9–11, which discuss a topic unparalleled in the earlier letters. Nevertheless, such extensive parallels imply a sense of summing up, a synthesizing of Paul's earlier ideas—perhaps another reason why Romans was put first in the collection of his letters.

Though the most extensive parallels are between Romans and Galatians, significant differences exist in both the tone and the specific arguments of the two letters. While Romans defends much the same ground staked out in Galatians—that only faith makes one right with God—a sympathetic reader might well wonder what has happened to Paul in the interim. Gone is the sarcasm, coarse humor, and ironic belittling of his opponents. Here Paul is conciliatory, entreating rather than demanding, disagreeing without being disagreeable. The very style of the diatribe is meant to include and to persuade. And not only the tone has changed.

The substance of the argument in Romans represents a refinement of the ideas presented in Galatians. In Galatians the dying with Christ was left undefined (for example, 2:19–20; 5:24); in Romans, Paul defines this death by the ritual of baptism (6:3–4). In Galatians Paul left his hearers with a paradoxical sense of self—the "I" died with Christ (2:20)—but in Romans he differentiates this "I" into an I slain by sin and an inner self that lives and wishes to please God (7:9, 22). In Galatians the example of Abraham is asserted without any demonstration of the priority of faith over Law (3:6); in Romans Paul develops an elaborate argument based on the priority of time, the lack of boasting, and the effect of promise/grace (4:1–16). Clearly, Paul has continued to reflect on these ideas. (For a discussion of these and other points see Betz, 1979:123–124; 140–141.)

The most important difference between Romans and earlier works is the shift in attitude on Paul's part. He now goes out of his way to stress his continuity with the past, with things Jewish; he even defends the validity of the Law. Compare these two essentially similar passages:

Galatians 3:19–25	Romans 7:7–13
Why then the law? It was added because of transgressions, till the offspring should come to whom the promise had been made; and it was ordained by angels through an intermediary. Now an intermediary implies more than one; but God is one.	
Is the law then against the promises of God? Certainly not; for if a law had been given which could make alive, then righteousness would indeed be by the law. But the scripture consigned all things to sin, that what was promised to faith in Jesus Christ might be given to those who believe. Now before faith came we were confined under the law, kept under restraint until faith should be revealed. So that the law was our custodian	*What then shall we say? That the law is sin?* By no means! Yet if it had not been for the law I should not have known sin. I should not have known what it is to covet if the law had not said, "You shall not covet." But sin, finding opportunity in the commandment, wrought in me all kinds of covetousness. Apart from the law sin lies dead. I was once alive apart from the law, but when the commandment came, sin revived and I died; the very commandment which prom-
until Christ came, that we might be justified by faith. *But now that faith has come, we are no longer under a custodian,* for in Christ Jesus you are all sons of God, through faith.	ised life proved to be death to me. For sin, finding opportunity in the commandment, deceived me and by it killed me. *So the law is holy, and the commandment is holy and just and good.*

Both excerpts are struggling to make sense out of one facet of the old story, the story of God giving the Law to his people, in light of the new story in which God has acted to bring redemption to all people through Jesus. But the passage in Romans portrays the Law in a far more positive light. No longer do we hear about its transitory use. It is not now the Law that restrains, but sin. The Law indeed had promised life, even though the power of sin overruled it.

These, and many similar changes, show us that Paul has taken a different approach in Romans: he is far more intent on proving his case. He is more careful in his argument, more tolerant of other points of view, and less inclined to dismiss those who differ from the fellowship. To understand these changes, and to find a basis for interpreting the work as a whole, let us consider the historical situation of Paul and the Roman church.

HISTORICAL ANALYSIS OF THE CONTEXT

All the letters of Paul we have studied thus far were written to assemblies located in the eastern Roman Empire, in Asia Minor (modern Turkey) and Greece. This letter is addressed to "all God's beloved in Rome" (1:7), the center of power and influence over the Mediterranean world. Since there were probably several assemblies in so large a city, we need not visualize one central church. In this regard, Romans resembles an area letter (as is Galatians) more than one addressed to a particular local congregation. But unlike all Paul's other letters, this one is addressed to assemblies he had no hand in founding. Rome was not in Paul's mission territory. He had probably never been there (1:13). Surely he must have felt some reserve in addressing those who owed their existence to others (see 15:20; I Cor. 3:10). This basic situation would certainly shape Paul's rhetoric and purpose.

The Setting at Rome

It is one of history's little ironies that the origins of what was to become the most important church in Christendom are lost to us. Later generations, anxious to enhance the status of this center, could only boast of the ministry there of Paul and Peter, even claiming that the latter eventually became head of that church. Even then they could make no claims to a grand beginning. The likely inference is that the beginning was not grand.

Christianity Comes to Rome

The one clue we have to the origins of Christianity at Rome comes from the *Lives of the Caesars,* by the Roman historian Suetonius. However, he tells us more about the private lives of the Caesars than about their public accomplishments, and his anecdotal style often lumps important points together into mere lists. One such list occurs in his *Life of Claudius,* who ruled from 41 to 54 CE. After telling us that Claudius made it illegal for foreigners to adopt the names of Roman families and that he granted the Trojans exemption from taxation because they were founders of the Roman race, he adds:

≈ ≈ ≈

Because the Jews at Rome caused continuous disturbances at the instigation of Chrestos, he expelled them from the City. When the German envoys first visited the Theatre . . . (25.2)

And so he continues on a wholly different topic. That one sentence about the Jews is our clue.

There are two possibilities for interpreting it. Perhaps it means just what it says: riots in the Jewish community led by someone named Chrestos led to a decree of expulsion. Or perhaps Suetonius, or his source, has garbled the account. One possibility is that *Chrestos* should be read *Christos* (Christ). Though Chrestos was a common Greek name (meaning something like Goodfellow, it was often given to slaves), Christos (the Greek equivalent of Messiah, meaning the anointed one) would be wholly unknown and unintelligible to a Roman unfamiliar with Jewish lore. Serious outbreaks of trouble may have occurred in the Jewish community at Rome in the late forties, caused by the arrival of representatives of this Christos—trouble serious enough for some sort of expulsion to be the result.

On this reading, Claudius expelled Jews from Rome because of unrest in the Jewish community caused by the appearance of Christian missionaries in the late forties, about a decade before Paul wrote. An incidental support of such a reading is found in Acts 18:2, which reports that Paul encountered Christian Jews at Corinth who had been expelled from Rome by Claudius. Such an expulsion so early in the development of the church there would have serious consequences. It would mean that in the crucial early years the church at Rome was entirely Gentile, and that even later Jews and Gentiles probably formed separate assemblies in different homes at Rome—raising the specter of division and alienation.

The Jewish Community at Rome

Our first reference to the Jewish community at Rome is from 139 BCE, when Jews and followers of other oriental religions were expelled from Rome. But the first significant increase in the size of the Jewish community there seems to have occurred in the time of Pompey, a general who brought many Jewish slaves back to Rome around 60 BCE. They attracted Roman attention both by the peculiarity of their religion (especially Sabbath observance which seemed to the ancient Roman to be a terrible waste of valuable time) and by their otherwise industrious behavior. Their rapid establishment can be seen in Seutonius' special mention that Jews came in great numbers to the grave of Julius Caesar in 27 BCE for several nights in a row (84). This was probably more an organized show of support than a spontaneous response of grief.

It reveals a large and free Jewish community in Rome. More than a dozen synagogues from the imperial period have been found all over the city, indicating that the Jews there were not confined to one quarter. The serious anti-Jewish feelings manifested by Juvenal in the next generation (see pp.62–63) shows that not all Romans welcomed these foreigners—other grounds for possible antagonism between Jews and Gentiles at Rome. Would Paul have been aware of these possible problems?

Paul's Relation to Rome

One puzzling feature of Romans is the number of individuals Paul salutes by name in chapter 16—so many in fact that some argue that chapter 16 must be a fragment of a separate letter, perhaps to Ephesus (MacDonald, 1969: 369–372). In support of this view, these scholars point out that some manuscripts of Romans do not include chapter 16 and that 15:33 would be a suitable ending ("Now the God of peace be with you all. Amen."). Nevertheless, most scholars do agree that it makes good sense to regard 16 as part of the original letter. Paul's extensive greetings section is matched by his extensive travel plans in chapter 15, the most detailed of all his surviving letters. The omission of chapter 16 from some manuscripts probably indicates that the letter was circulated in a more universal form (without these salutations and without the address to Rome) as a summary of Pauline theology. If Romans was widely circulated as a general letter, this would have produced some confusion in the arrangement of the ending. The only real reason we have to doubt the authenticity of chapter 16 is the unlikelihood that Paul would have known so many Roman Christians.

Yet we must remember that first-century Jews were a truly international people who traveled widely and established relations with other Jews in the cities to which they went. The arrival and acceptance of Prisca and Aquila at Corinth reflects this interconnectedness, as does Paul's own travels. Acts (18:2) tells us that Aquila was a native of Pontus (in northeastern Asia Minor) who had been living in Rome when forced out by Claudius' decree. We could imagine that Prisca and Aquila returned to Rome when Claudius died in 54, a couple of years before Paul wrote. Such a return may explain other names in the list, while the presence of Epaenetus and Andronicus, who were associated with Asia Minor, remind us that there was probably a good bit of traffic from the provinces to the capital.

If the people addressed in chapter 16 are at Rome, indicating that many Christian Jews did return there after the death of Claudius, it may have created some problems for those Gentile Christians who had remained in the city. They would now have to work through the meaning of their faith in relation to a significantly different community. In fact, chapter 16 seems to reflect several different groups at Rome, probably different assemblies meeting in different homes, perhaps five (notice how several greetings include a group: 16:5, 10, 11, 14, 15). The private homes of this period were spacious, including both public and private quarters. (See Figure 4.1.) Yet a typical home could accommodate only thirty to thirty-five guests, especially if a meal were involved. Inevitably then, the believers in a given city would soon be divided into different groups and would tend to evolve in somewhat different ways (recall the divisions at Corinth discussed in Chapter 3). It is remarkable, but not impossible, that Paul knew the leaders of several such assemblies.

It is also likely that officials from these Roman congregations traveled to other places, since being the capital implied having influence beyond Rome. The people greeted in chapter 16 were leaders, most of them having some sort of title (servant, apostle, kinsman, fellow worker,

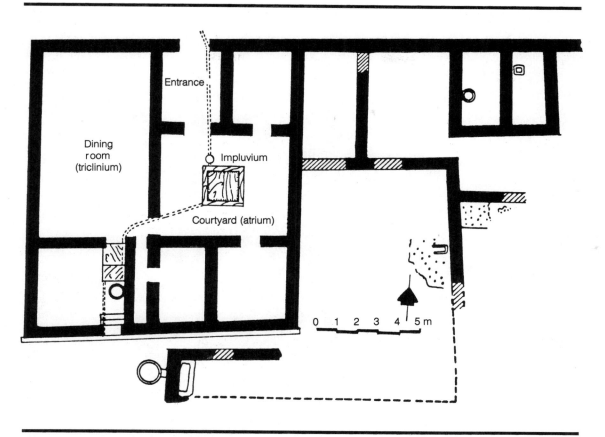

Entrance

Dining
room
(triclinium)

Impluvium

Courtyard (atrium)

0 1 2 3 4 5 m

Figure 4 ▪ 1 Roman Villa at Anaploga This floor plan shows the layout of a typical Roman house (for a related photograph, see pp. 90–92). One entered through a vestibule, on the floor of which were inscribed sentiments such as *havetis intro* (greetings to the arrivals) or perhaps *cave canem* (beware of the dog). This led directly to the atrium (courtyard) from which one could enter the public parts of the house, including the dining room and the washroom (the Romans had indoor plumbing and central heat). The atrium itself was a sacred space containing the hearth and the altar to the family gods. The impluvium (pool) in the center of the atrium held rain water brought to it by a system of channels from the roof. It was adorned with statues and fountains. A kitchen, wine room, plant room, and various bedrooms completed the building, which would be surrounded by solid, high walls. Houses differed in some details. In some, the part facing the street might contain small shops. Larger houses had two or three courtyards and perhaps four dining rooms. (From *St Paul's Corinth* by Jerome Murphy-O'Connor [Michael Glazier, 1983:154], used by permission.)

and so on). The presence of a significant number of women in this list, including Junia, who is listed as an apostle, and Phoebe, who is listed as a "diakonos" (literally servant or minister) of the

church at Cenchrea (a "suburb" of Corinth, where Paul was when he wrote this letter) reminds us of the contribution of women to this early period. Phoebe was the carrier and thus the first reader

Roman Apartment House   Only the very wealthy could afford the grand homes of the Roman period. Most people lived in apartment houses resembling this reconstruction from Ostia. The Hellenistic era was a time of rapid growth for cities, and an expanding population confined by city walls could only go up. As in our own time, living conditions in apartments might range from comfortable to squalid. (Alinari/Art Resource, New York.)

of this letter. Like Paul, these leaders were mobile people; Paul may well have met them without ever visiting Rome. This extensive greeting, if a part of the original letter, would mean that Paul was aware of the problems between Jew and Gentile that had arisen in Rome when the Jews returned after the death of Claudius. Part of the explanation of Romans lies in this situation of Jewish and Gentile controversy at Rome.

The Setting in Paul's Life

An additional explanation may be found by shifting our attention from the Roman scene to the immediate situation in Paul's own life. The most obvious reason for trying to build bridges to Rome was Paul's plan to visit there and, perhaps, use it as a base for missions to the West (15:24–32). This would certainly be a reason to write to Rome, but not a sufficient reason for the letter we actually have. This is too magnificent a work to be explained as a letter of self-introduction to prepare for a brief visit after celebrating Passover in Jerusalem.

As the plan to go west indicates, Paul regarded his work in the East nearly finished. He had planted assemblies in all the major cities and was looking for new territory. Having fought desperately to regain the confidence of his followers in Corinth, Paul had returned there to wait for a ship to take him to Jerusalem for Passover. In this precise situation, he wrote Romans (compare Rom. 15:25–27 with I Cor. 16:3–6).

The Politics of Paul's Mission

Paul described the purpose of this trip: "to minister to the saints" (15:25), by which he meant he was going to deliver a substantial relief offering to the Jerusalem church from the churches of "Macedonia and Achaia," his Gentile congregations in Europe. This was an event of greater significance than appears on the surface. We saw earlier that two chapters of II Corinthians (8 and 9; perhaps originally separate letters) concerned this collection and Paul's trip to Jerusalem. Paul worked diligently to collect this money, taking more than a year to do so (II Cor. 9:2; I Cor. 16:1–2). He sent special messengers to collect it and arranged for envoys from each congregation to accompany him on the trip to Jerusalem (I Cor. 16:3–4).

The significance of this offering may be seen in the logic by which Paul explains:

🙠 🙠 🙠

If the Gentiles have come to share in their [the Jews'] spiritual blessings, they [Gentiles] ought also to be of service to them [the Jews] in material blessings. (15:27)

Although this logic has been exploited by many who would profit from their spiritual ministry, for Paul the meaning of the statement worked backward: it was the monetary contributions of the Gentiles that would demonstrate to the Jerusalem church that they had become partakers of the spirit: if spiritual blessing, then material blessing. But the reverse must also be valid: since there is material blessing, there must be spiritual blessing. This collection is far more than a charitable deed; it is a political act. Paul was fully aware of its political nature, for he asked the Romans to pray ". . . that I may be delivered from the unbelievers in Judea and that my service for Jerusalem may be acceptable to the saints . . ." (15:31).

In fact, Paul is on his way to Jerusalem to confront the church there with a serious challenge: Do they accept the validity of the Gentile churches and of Paul's mission? On one hand,

such acceptance had already been granted at some sort of meeting in Jerusalem. According to Paul's report, the leaders there had given Paul "the right hand of fellowship" (Gal. 2:9), apparently a rite of association. But it is important to notice the limitation they placed on this association: Paul would go to Gentiles while Peter would go to Jews. In other words, they envisioned a "separate but equal" situation that proved unworkable. For as Paul went on to recount in Galatians, the agreement broke down when Peter visited Antioch (see discussion on p. 69). In the actual lives of Jews and Gentiles in the Diaspora it was impossible to be separate and, consequently, equality was threatened. In refusing to eat with the Gentiles at Corinth, Peter implicitly denied their equality (Gal. 2:11–13). The acceptance of the offering will confront the Jerusalem church with the acceptance of the equality of the Gentile churches of Paul.

The Church at Jerusalem

The situation of the Jerusalem church is not well documented, probably due to the destruction of Jerusalem in 70 CE and again in 135. What evidence we do have indicates that a rather conservative, law-observing tradition predominated there. Jesus' brother, James, soon became head of the community and, according to tradition, was followed by another relative, Symeon, a cousin of Jesus (Eusebius, *Church History* 3.11). James was known in Jewish Christian tradition as "James the righteous," and various legends developed about his piety and law observance (for example, that he was permitted to enter the Temple because of his extraordinary holiness; Eusebius, 2.23.4). While such claims are surely not historical, they reflect the attitude of those who held James in high regard. More directly relevant is the description the author of Acts attributes to James when he welcomes Paul to Jerusalem:

🙠 🙠 🙠

You see, brother, how many thousands there are among the Jews of those who have believed; they are all zealous for the law, and they have been told about you that you teach all the Jews who are among the Gentiles to forsake Moses, telling them not to circumcise their children or observe the customs. (Acts 21:20–21)

Notice the deep suspicion of Paul and the description of Jerusalem Christians as "zealous for the law." When he wrote Galatians, Paul seemed little concerned with what they thought of him at Jerusalem. (See p. 66.) There is even a slight mockery in his description of the leaders as those "reputed to be something" (Gal. 2:6). Yet even there we see the seed planted which is now being harvested. For Paul also reported that the Jerusalem conference had urged him to "remember the poor, which very thing I was eager to do" (Gal. 2:10). Perhaps this collection would have been nothing more than an act of charity had not subsequent events cast a shadow over the legitimacy of Paul's ministry and of the inclusion of the Gentiles. Or perhaps it was always intended to be what it now became: a symbolic statement of the unity of Jews and Gentiles in the new movement.

Just as the Gentile assemblies dramatize their dependence on Jerusalem by delivering the offering to Jerusalem, the Jerusalem church will dramatize its acceptance of Gentiles when it accepts the offering. To receive this gift from the Gentiles will be to recognize the unity of the church and the place of Gentiles as Gentiles in that church. In the process, they will be forced to validate Paul's apostolate to the Gentiles— something at least some of them were not anxious to do.

In contemplation of this approaching crisis, Paul sits in Corinth, writing Romans, and preparing to sail to Jerusalem with the offering from his Gentile churches. Uncertain of the outcome, he asks those at Rome to pray "that I may be delivered from the unbelievers in Judea, and that my service for Jerusalem may be acceptable to the saints" (Rom. 15:31). Notice how strikingly different is the attitude toward Jerusalem implied here from that of Galatians.

As we turn to the actual interpretation of the letter, both these contexts must be kept in mind, the life of the Roman assemblies and the life of Paul.

THE THEME OF ROMANS: TWO VIEWS

The theme of a work of literature is the total impression it makes, the sum of all its images, characters, plot, and structure (or, in nonnarrative literature, its images, rhetoric, and structure). We have considered the literary features of Romans and examined its historical setting. Let us turn now to the central question: What is it actually about? The many different interpretations of Romans may be divided into two basic approaches, suggesting very different themes for the work. The standard interpretation of Romans argues that its theme is the salvation of the individual. Another view, advanced by certain Scandinavian scholars, but having some precedent in the earliest interpretations of Romans, argues that its theme is the salvation of the world. Before examining these two themes more closely, we will briefly trace the major contours of Paul's discussion.

The Line of Argument

Earlier we saw that the argument of Romans is a diatribe rather than a simple logical progression. We observed further that the viewpoint of the argument shifts from third to first to third to second person, giving us the following major sections:

Chapters 1–4:   they
Chapters 5–8:   we
Chapters 9–11:   they
Chapters 12–16:   you

Reading and Reflection

Reread Romans, using the reading guide and the following very brief summaries of each major section. Compare your own reading of each section with that given in the summaries, trying to get a clear grasp of the logic of each section and of the logic that connects the sections to each other.

Understanding the Human Situation

Paul's conclusion, that all are sinful, has given him a reputation as a pessimist, but we should not miss the happy note on which he begins:

æ æ æ

For I am not ashamed of the gospel: it is the power of God for salvation to everyone who has faith, to the Jew first and also to the Greek. (1:16)

It is crucial for us in all that follows to remember that Paul's purpose is to explain how all may find salvation. Now we will trace the contours of this lengthy and involved argument.

Idolatry leads to pervasive sinfulness (1:18–32) Paul demonstrates that the wrath of God falls on all by means of two arguments that are very nearly syllogisms (a logical statement consisting of a major premise, a minor premise, and a conclusion). The first, stated in 1:19–23, should be carefully studied. The argument here is both simple and profound: something of God can be known through nature, namely his awesome power and his hiddenness. In other words, nature reveals only the mystery of God. Yet the human race has perversely persisted in resolving the mystery, reducing God to an image of the visible world, worshipping the creation rather than the creator. The logic here is straightforward:

Since the divine power and majesty can be known from nature;

and since people persist in worshipping nature instead of the divine;

therefore, they are without excuse.

Ironically, Paul locates the root cause of human

READING GUIDE TO ROMANS

Salutation 1:1–7
Thanksgiving 1:8–15
The argument 1:15–11:36
    Understanding human sinfulness and Divine salvation 1:16–4:25
    Understanding "our" salvation in Christ 5:1–8:39
    Understanding Israel's salvation 9:1–11:33
The exhortations 12:1–15:13
    To humility and unity 12:3–13
    To love of persecutors 12:14–21
    To obedience to government 13:1–7
    To love and good conduct 13:8–14
    To support both weak and strong 14:1–15:13
Travel plans 15:14–33
Greetings 16:1–23
Benediction 16:25–27

---

sinfulness in religion, or more precisely in a religious error.

Then Paul illustrates how this perversion affects every aspect of human life: perversion of the "heart" (what we would call the spiritual) results in idolatry; perversion of the "passions" (what we refer to as desires or drives) results in homosexuality; perversion of the "mind" (the will) results in evil behavior ranging from murder to disobeying one's parents (1:24–32). The logic of all these conclusions is that of a natural order. Thus, the natural order of worship is revealed in creation; that of sex is revealed in procreation; and the natural order of behavior is revealed in culture. Each of these "deviations" have one thing in common: each inverts the norm. Idolatry, homosexuality, and disobedience to parents become paradigms for the lostness of the human race. How different Paul's observation is here from that of the modern world, where one rarely hears homosexuality discussed in tandem with the other two. The homosexuality Paul refers to is actually a surface manifestation of a far deeper problem: failure to honor God. The homosexuality of Greco-Roman culture was not the exclusive and psychologically conditioned behavior that the modern world struggles to understand. It was voluntary and widely practiced, especially between older married men and teenage boys. (See the recent study by Scroggs, 1983.) It is crucial to understand that to Paul sin is a spiritual power operating within the human race, not simply a few bad deeds that might be listed and overcome.

All who judge stand under judgment (2:1–29)   Having condemned the perversities of the world, Paul's next sentence is shocking: "Therefore you have no excuse. . ." (2:1). Certain people can claim exemption from the first argument, namely those who live by the proper order (by the Law). The Jews, in particular, whose rejection of idolatry is evident, seem to be acquitted in this argument. But now Paul raises a second point. Even good people stand guilty, convicted by the very evidence that they find others guilty. Though much more rhetorically developed, the essence of this second argument is that all people set standards of behavior that they fail to live up to. Hence, in judging others, each condemns himself or herself as well.

These two points constitute a radical indictment and raise serious objections: Are moral Jews really no better off than immoral Gentiles (3:1)? Has God failed in his plan to create a holy people (3:5)? If all are wicked, is there any sense in trying to do good (3:8)? These are the first detours through which the diatribe style leads the reader, but we shall bypass them to follow the main road.

Scripture declares all to be under the power of sin (3:9–20)   Paul brings his argument for universal sinfulness to a dramatic conclusion by citing a medley of Psalms: none is righteous; all have turned aside. The curious thing is that we sense no sadness here in Paul's argument, no lamenting. In fact, his argument rushes on to new conclusions.

Righteousness now comes through faith in Christ (3:21–31)   Soon we realize that this argument about universal sinfulness was only the prelude; Paul's real thrust is to show that righteousness for all has appeared through faith in Jesus Christ (3:21–26). Paul spends very little time developing this argument; clearly it is something he expects his hearers will agree with. Yet it raises new objections: Is there no basis for boasting (3:27)? Are Gentiles really included (3:29)? Does this faith overthrow the Law (3:31)? Then what about Abraham (4:1)? The story of Abraham is found in the Law and helps Paul show the degree to which his own understanding of salvation can be supported by the Law.

The law itself teaches salvation by faith (4:1–25)   This last question leads Paul into a lengthy discussion of the relationship between faithful trusting and faithful acting (usually referred to as faith versus works). The point here is that the election of Israel rests on the promise of God, not on the Law or on circumcision, both of which are later than Abraham's faith—the Law centuries later. As he has done earlier (3:10), Paul clinches his case by quoting Scripture: that is why his faith was "reckoned to him as righteousness." Just so, he argues, "It will be reckoned to us who believe in him that raised from the dead Jesus our Lord" (4:22–25). Faith counts as righteousness. In Greek the words "faith" (pistis) and "to believe" (pisteuein) both mean primarily trusting in someone. Trusting in God through Christ now counts as righteousness in the same way as did Abraham's trusting. Paul now shifts his argument to "us who believe."

Understanding "Our" Salvation

In chapters 5–8, Paul explores the implications for himself and the Roman believers ("we") of this new situation, which has revealed both the wrath and the righteousness of God (1:17–18). We have peace (5:1). "We are now justified by his blood" and will "be saved by him from the wrath of God" (5:9). Paul explains how this comes about by an extensive analogy between Adam and Christ. Read 5:12–21, noticing the parallels Paul draws between the two. We can diagram the ideas:

Adam→ Disobeyed→ Sin→   Death→ All→ Condemnation
Christ→ Obeyed→   Righteousness→ Life→   All→ Acquittal

This daring comparison reveals why Paul thinks that a new situation now pertains. God has worked to reverse the disobedience of Adam; Christ as the "second Adam" begins the process of the new creation. This is the closest we come in any of Paul's letters to what his actual proclamation may have been, for we see here the outline of a charter story in which the primeval deed of Adam is repeated and perfected in the cosmic work of the Christ. The obedience of Christ, as we have seen in earlier letters, was his death.

New questions and objections are raised: If God overcomes sin with grace, are we to continue in sin that grace may abound (6:1)? If we are not under Law, can we sin without fear (6:15)? Is the Law sin (7:7)? If sin is only counted where there is a Law, did the Law bring death (7:13)? All are answered with an emphatic negative. If they remind us of the things his opponents in Galatia may have said that is probably appropriate. They reveal just how agonizing is the line between "freedom" and "anarchy" on the one side and between "obedience" and "legalism" on the other.

The argument resumes in chapter 8 with an extensive contrast between life "in the flesh" and life "in the spirit." This is not a contrast between body and spirit (see verse 10), as some of Paul's followers assumed, but between life under "Adam" and life under "Christ." This section ends with one of the most moving assertions of faith (trust) in all literature (8:31–39).

Paul now shifts his attention from the "us" to another group, his "brothers" according to physical relationship. The argument here is partly a return to the objection raised in 3:1, now dealt with more fully, and partly a response to the previous assertion of trust: Can God be trusted to keep his word to his people? It is also a continuation of the main line of the argument: What

are the implications of the revelation of God's wrath and grace? Paul struggles mightily, though perhaps unsuccessfully, for answers. None of the earlier letters have any parallel to this section.

Understanding the Salvation of Israel (9–11)

Paul first responds to the question of whether God has failed. This question is at the heart of Paul's dilemma, for his assertion that God now justifies all through faith in Christ seems to imply that God's covenant with Israel was worthless. The faithfulness of God in Christ seems to imply his unfaithfulness to his own people. Paul answers that God is absolutely free to do whatever he wishes to do. But when he recognizes that this raises more questions than it answers (9:14, 19), he modifies his answer, asserting that the present situation is not unique; it has always been only a "remnant" who were faithful (9:27). So too, there is now a remnant, to which Paul himself claims to belong (11:1). The intervening material, chapter 10, is really an anguished rehearsal of Israel's "zeal for God" (10:2) coupled with their rejection of the gospel (16). Realizing perhaps that the ideas of election and of a remnant do not deal with the real issues, Paul tackles the question of Israel's salvation directly (11:11).

His solution, which proved to be romantic and unrealistic, displays the strength of heart that made Paul a great human being: Israel's trespass has resulted in the inclusion of the Gentiles; the inclusion of the Gentiles will make Israel jealous; the return of Israel and their full inclusion will usher in the kingdom of God (11:11–12). Paul describes all this vividly, with an intricate analogy to an olive tree that is well worth careful study (11:17–24). His rapt conclusion declares God's ways to be a mystery: " . . . a hardening has come upon part of Israel, until the full number of Gentiles come in, and so all Israel will be saved" (11:25–26). This is Paul's ultimate hope.

We must also note here the audience Paul is addressing. His speaking of Jews in the third person (they) and his explicit address ("I speak to you Gentiles," 11:13) reveal his underlying purpose: these Gentiles must feel no superiority to the Jews, not even to those Jews who do not receive Paul's proclamation (11:18). Had later Christians heeded this admonition, much human suffering could have been avoided. Paul's conviction was that ultimately both Jew and Gentile would be redeemed.

Unfortunately, later Christians have only heard the first half of Paul's paradoxical assertion about the Jews and have used it as a basis for repeated persecution. But we must hear the whole of the mystery:

❧ ❧ ❧

As regards the gospel
  they are enemies of God,
    for your sake;
but as regards the election
  they are beloved
    for the sake of their forefathers.
For the gifts and the call of God are
  irrevocable. (11:28–29)

Paul admits he does not understand this but is willing to leave it to the judgment of God (11:33). Paul's understanding of God's grace forced him to embrace more than one paradox. We glimpse the absolute position of God's mercy in Paul's understanding of life by his almost Zen-like declaration that even universal sinfulness leads to life, "For God has enclosed all in disobedience, that he may have mercy upon all" (11:32, literal translation).

Ethical Exhortations   (12:1–15:13)

This brings Paul to the final phase of his extended argument: "I appeal to you therefore, brethren, by the mercies of God, to present your bodies as a living sacrifice. . ." (12:1). The rhetorical "therefore" points back to the entire preceding argument. Paul based his ethical demands on his understanding that God has already worked to accomplish salvation. This is what Rudolf Bultmann meant when he declared that for Paul

the imperative rests on the indicative: the demand rests on what God has done. There is nothing original about the ethical instruction offered here. Such actions were the common property of all persons of good will. What is original is the "therefore": the basis of ethics rests in the charter story of what God had done through Jesus. Now let us consider more carefully what "therefore" suggests: how ought we to interpret Paul's argument?

Two Interpretations

The process of interpretation is always circular. We begin with some general notion of what a piece of literature is about and modify that notion in the reading of the literature. Our general notion shapes the way we perceive the details and the details in turn shape the general notion. At its best, this is an ongoing process that continually refines our understanding and brings us closer to the full meaning of a text. At worst, a basic mistake will cause us to misread completely the original meaning of a work (as when one fails to realize that a certain article in the student newspaper is a satire). Most of our reading of literature falls between these two extremes, with varying degrees of correct interpretation. For Romans, two general notions are proposed as the correct context for interpreting the work.

Romans and the Salvation of the Individual

The traditional view, going back at least to Martin Luther and the Protestant Reformation of the sixteenth century, is that Romans concerns the salvation of the individual. According to this view the question Paul addresses deals with how a person is saved. Generally, those who hold this view see Paul as presenting his basic gospel to the Roman church to gain its support for his mission to the West.

The question, "What must I do to be saved?" (Acts 16:30), is one that all religions and all philosophies must answer, though many would phrase it differently. It is a version of the more general question: How does one achieve the highest possible good in life? This question raises others: Why do we not now possess the good? What is wrong? What is our true nature? What is the true nature of the Ultimate Reality? How can the individual apprehend this Ultimate Reality? According to the traditional view of Romans, Paul is addressing questions like these.

Martin Luther (1483–1546), father of the Protestant Reformation, established this reading of Romans. Luther was a man extremely oppressed by the notion of his guilt before God. Much to his father's dismay, he forsook his pursuit of law to enter an Augustinian monastery. There he prayed, fasted, and performed penance, but derived no satisfaction. He could not feel anything but God's wrath. But Luther was a scholar-monk, a professor of Old Testament. His study of Romans convinced him that since all are sinners, it is only the unconditional grace of God that brings forgiveness and salvation. He expressed it in Latin as "sola gratia," only grace. This interpretation of Romans, coupled with Luther's experience and great skill, certainly changed the face of Christendom.

The influence of this traditional view may be seen in the various outlines of Romans, nearly all of which divide the first section (1–4) into two; the first dealing with the problem (sin), the second with the answer (justification by faith). This leads logically to the next section (5–8), seen as a discussion of life in the spirit that culminates in the final section (12–15): practical instruction in living. The traditional view tends to neglect chapters 9–11, regarding them as a kind of parenthesis or diatribal detour.

Some modern interpreters go even further. Gunther Bornkamm, for example, argues that chapters 9–11 relate to the earlier discussion as problem to answer. Following the general line of Protestant interpretation, Bornkamm argues that Romans is written to refute all those who depend on good works for their salvation. He views the Jews as Paul's opponents, for they taught the keeping of the Law whereas Paul taught salvation by God's grace alone. He goes so far as to pronounce:

❧ ❧ ❧

In a way the Jew symbolizes man in his highest potentialities; he represents the "religious man" whom the Law tells what God requires of him, who appeals to the special statute granted him in the plan of salvation, and who refuses to admit that he has failed to measure up to God's claim on him and is in consequence abandoned to sin and death. (1971:95).

According to this reading, the law-observant Jews are worse off than the immoral Gentiles, for they refuse to admit their sinfulness. These anti-Semitic implications of the traditional interpretation have caused some modern interpreters to question this approach.

Romans and the Salvation of the World

Their uneasiness with the traditional interpretation has other bases, too. Such a strong emphasis on the individual seems anachronistic, they argue, for overwhelming concern with the inner self is uncharacteristic of Paul. So too, they point out, in Romans Paul is trying to build bridges between Jewish and Gentile Christians, not to divide them. He faces the need to explain his mission in terms acceptable to the conservatives in Jerusalem and is, therefore, unlikely to be thinking of contrasts. These interpreters point out that Paul does not speak of the forgiveness of sins in Romans, but rather of justification by faith—an objective and historical fact rather than an inner, subjective experience. The theme of Romans, they assert, is not the salvation of the individual but the salvation of the world. In Romans, Paul is sketching God's plan for the ages and thus validating his mission to Gentiles.

On this reading, Romans 1–4 is designed to show that something new has occurred in history: in the present time, God is both the just one and the one who makes just (3:26). This means that both Jews and Gentiles may be found acceptable to God: there is no distinction between them (3:22), both sin, both find salvation. The next section (5–8) addresses this newness by the contrast between Christ and Adam and by the new experience of being "in Christ," that is, in the Spirit.

Rather than receding into the background, chapters 9–11 stand out as the central section of the letter, its climax (Stendahl, 1976:4). In these chapters Paul deals with the relationship between two communities of faith. He forbids Christians to feel superior to Jews (11:17–18) and predicts salvation for "all Israel" (11:26). He does not say, Krister Stendahl observes, that they all become Christians.

Both interpretations view the final section (12–16) as ethical exhortation based on the whole preceding argument.

Patterns of Salvation

It is impossible here to reconcile these two interpretations of Romans, or even to choose between them. Each offers insights into Paul; each interprets portions of the text as more important than others; and each must in turn be tested by reading Romans. To what extent does each interpretation explain the specific data found in Paul's letter? Only you, as an informed and careful reader, can answer that question.

We can, however, ask a related question: To what extent do the descriptions of Jewish life presupposed by these two views correspond to first-century realities? In the first view Judaism is seen as the paradigm of legalism and self-justification; in the second view, Judaism is quite similar to Christianity. What was early Judaism like? How did other Jews in Paul's day imagine they were saved?

It is not a simple question to answer because we have very few contemporary sources to turn to for information. The primary Jewish evidence is derived from the Rabbis, whose works are not separate writings by specific individuals but comprise instead a vast collection of material—rather several collections, the earliest dating from a century and a half after Paul (the *Mishnah*, about 200 CE)—that has been combined and synthesized. Another body of Jewish material was preserved by Christians, though not without change. This material consists of individual works, though dating them is extremely difficult because many pretend they were written by the pious ones of ancient Israel. These works, the *Apocrypha* ("hidden works") and the *Pseudepigrapha* ("false writings"), were actually written over the course of centuries, some as early as two hundred years before Paul, many much later. All were continually revised by later hands.

This puts the historian in the uncomfortable position of depending on writings that are later in time and filtered by the concerns of later Christians and Jews (both of whom wanted to remember the first century in their own way). There is, however, one exception: we now have access to a body of literature that was unaffected by these later concerns. It was put into a sort of time capsule shortly after the time of Paul and was not opened until the twentieth century.

The time capsule in this case consisted of huge stoneware jars, sealed and hidden in caves in the nearly inaccessible hills along the Dead Sea in southern Palestine. A group of Jewish holy men, living in a commune in the area, apparently hid their sacred writings when the Roman army was invading the land to put down the rebellion of 66 CE. Why they never reclaimed them we do not know, but they were only rediscovered in 1947, when a bedouin goatherd threw a stone into one of the caves while looking for a lost animal. The breaking jar prompted further exploration and, years later, the discovery of many more scrolls in several caves. (The full story of this fascinating discovery is recounted by Vermes, 1977.)

These *Dead Sea Scrolls* reveal one type of first-century Jewish religion in its original form, uncensored by later Christian or Jewish concerns. Consequently, they are a suitable place to begin if we want to learn how some other Jews dealt with the issues that concerned Paul in Romans.

A Scroll from the Caves of Qumran Now known as the Dead Sea Scrolls, these writings were originally the library of a strict, ascetic Jewish sect. Containing both biblical writings and sectarian documents, they reveal much about first-century Jewish life. They were stored in large earthen jars, apparently hidden when the site was abandoned during the Roman invasion in 66 CE; and were preserved unmolested until the twentieth century. (Middle East Archives, London.)

A word of caution is necessary, however: these were surely untypical Jews who had forsaken society and family in their quest for holiness.

Rather than comparing the specific ideas of Paul and these other Jews on this or that subject, we wish to evaluate the general pattern of their religious conviction. The most fruitful comparison to date has been that of E. P. Sanders (1977), whose analysis is extensive and systematic (and highly recommended). What follows is indebted to his analysis, but is considerably simplified. Here we will address only two aspects of their system: What did they believe God was doing to redeem his people? And how did one become part of (and stay part of) what God was doing?

For those men (women were not allowed) in the community at Qumran who produced the Dead Sea Scrolls, the great thing God was doing in their day was creating and sustaining their community. They understood themselves to be a community of the End Time, those whom God had called out to inaugurate the Kingdom of God.

They understood themselves to be those prophesied by Isaiah who would "in the wilderness
prepare the way of the Lord" (40:3).

What they were doing in the wilderness was
keeping the Law as perfectly as they could. This
is only logical. Since the Kingdom of God and
the rule of God are the same thing, the way one
actualizes his kingdom is to obey his rules. Thus,
we are not surprised to find an extraordinary emphasis on rules at Qumran. One stayed in this
community by obeying these rules. Even minor
infractions resulted in disciplinary action (usually exclusion from the common ritual meal and
a reduction in rations). Major infractions resulted
in expulsion from the community. Consider the
following:

☙ ☙ ☙

*If one of them has lied deliberately in matters of
property, he shall be excluded from the pure
Meal of the Congregation for one year and shall
do penance with respect to one quarter of his
food.*

*Whoever has answered his companion with ob-
stinacy, or has addressed him impatiently, going
so far as to take no account of the dignity of his
fellow by disobeying the order of a brother inscribed before him, he has taken the law into his
own hand; therefore he shall do penance for one
year [and shall be excluded].*

*If any man has uttered the [Most] Venerable
Name even though frivolously, or as a result of
shock or for any other reason whatever, while
reading the Book or praying, he shall be dismissed and shall return to the Council of the
Community no more.*

After several more serious offenses, it continues:

Whoever has spoken foolishly: three months.
*Whoever has interrupted his companion while
   speaking: ten days.*
*Whoever has lain down to sleep during an Assem-
   bly of the Congregation: thirty days.*
(From the Community Rule VI *and* VII; *quoted
   from Vermes, 1968, 82–83)*

There are many more such rules, but these suffice to show that the community regulated every
aspect of the life of its members, including a
pledge of obedience to all who had entered the
community before him.

Getting into such a community was equally
difficult: "Every man, born of Israel, who freely
pledges himself to join the Council of the Community, shall be examined by the Guardian at the
head of the Congregation concerning his understanding and his deeds" (VI; Vermes, p. 81). Only
males, only native-born Jews, only those with
proper understanding and proper deeds could join,
and then only by examination. First they lived in
the community for a year (but without partici-
pating in the central meal); then, if they passed
muster, they were admitted. At this point they
gave all their property to the community. However, they spent another year on probation before
they were fully accepted and their property merged
with that of the community, and then only if they
passed further examination. All of this suggests
a very legalistic community, of the kind the traditional interpretation of Romans presumes for
Jews of this period. Yet it is not quite that simple.

If we also look at the hymns and liturgies of
the community we find that in their self-understanding they did not think of these laws in a
legalistic way. They did not understand them as
earning their salvation. They saw themselves as
redeemed by the mercy of God, despite their sins.
Consider:

☙ ☙ ☙

*As for me,
   my justification is with God.
In his hand are the perfection of my way
   and the uprightness of my heart.
He will wipe out my transgressions.
As for me,
if I stumble, the mercies of God
   shall be my eternal salvation.
If I stagger because of the sin of flesh,
   my justification shall be
   by the righteousness of God which endures for-
      ever.* (Community Rule XI)

Righteousness, I know, is not of man,
   nor is perfection of way of the son of man:
to the Most High God belong all righteous deeds.
The way of man is not established
   except by the spirit which God created for him
   to make perfect a way for the children
   of man. . . .
I lean on Thy grace
   and on the multitude of Thy mercies,
for Thou will pardon iniquity,
   and through Thy righteousness
   [Thou will purify man] of his sin. (Hymn 7)
      (Both quoted from Vermes, 1968: 92–93 and
      163–164)

Thus it seems fair to say that while the Qumran community placed great stress on keeping the Law, the men gathered there understood that their ability to keep the Law depended on the grace of God. God would create in them a spirit that would enable them to become obedient to his entire will. Sanders has shown that a similar pattern obtained in rabbinic circles, which later became mainstream Judaism, and in the more esoteric circles that produced the *Apocrypha* and *Pseudepigrapha* (1977:419–428).

This means that structurally, there was a strong resemblance between Paul and the Qumran community, even while they disagreed on nearly every particular point of content. This structural similarity may be portrayed thus:

Grace→ Spirit→ Obedience to God→ Kingdom of God

God's grace has resulted in his granting his Spirit to those who would be faithful, and this Spirit enables them to be obedient to God and leads the faithful into God's Kingdom.

Certainly, the two understood the nature of that Kingdom, the kind of obedience required, the experience of that spirit, the basis of that grace in radically different, perhaps antithetical, terms. Only the pattern is similar.

If this understanding of God's grace was shared in some way by other Jews, then we would expect Paul's argument to focus on showing the way God works for the salvation of the world rather than combating a legalism. The great issue that Paul needed to address, especially in light of his approach to Jerusalem with the collection, was the place of his Gentile congregations in the divine plan. If we add to this the special problems that the Roman congregations had with the proper relation between Jews and Gentiles, it appears likely that the central theme of the letter concerns the divine plan for the salvation of the world.

But again, we must be careful. Surely some, even many, would have failed to grasp this pattern and would see their lawkeeping as a legal transaction earning God's favor. One can point to such misunderstandings in the later literature of the Rabbis (and of the Christians), even as one can find this same pattern at work. Perhaps we must conclude that Paul is responding to both concerns to some extent, to the ultimate question of how God is at work in the world to bring about his Kingdom and to the immediate question of how one joins in that work. For these first-century Jews, to know what God is doing in the world would be to know what one must do to be saved.

Summary of Romans Discussion

The Letter to the Romans represents a new venture on Paul's part. Although it is deeply rooted in the life setting of the Roman Christians (and their conflicts between Jew and Gentile) and in Paul's own life (especially his approaching visit to Jerusalem, where he will have to defend his mission to Gentiles), it does not grow out of a specific crisis. In fact it is not addressed to one of his communities, but to a community founded by others. In Romans Paul transcends the letter genre and produces a letter-essay in the style of a diatribe. The hallmark of a diatribe is its dialogue-like style, in which an invisible listener is made to pose various questions and objections— usually as a result of a misunderstanding of the argument. The purpose of this style is to persuade the hearer to adopt the same conclusions as the speaker.

Paul in Romans is at his most congenial, even

as he summarizes and refines arguments presented in a heated way in earlier letters. It contains the longest sustained argument of any of Paul's writings as it wrestles with this issue of salvation, both the salvation of the world and the salvation of the individual.

This ends our discussion of those letters that are indisputably written by Paul, his central letters. Before we proceed to consider other letters, whose authorship is disputed, we must pause to explore the possibility of hearing Paul's own story as it echoes through these central writings.

IN CONCLUSION:
Imagining Paul's Story

My ten-year-old is fond of telling my eight-year-old, "You remind me of a ranch-style house. Nothing upstairs." In quite a different sense, this is an apt metaphor for the age in which we live: the upstairs (God and company) is no longer an integral part of the structure. While individuals continue to worship God, the structures of modern life (politics, education, labor, the economy, and so on) operate solely on one level: the human. The ancients, and not so ancient, lived in trilevels: there was not only an upstairs but also a downstairs (for example, Phil. 2:10). Each level was thickly inhabited with various beings, and each penetrated and influenced the other. In the general literature of this period we encounter a multitude of nonhuman characters, not only gods and goddesses, but witches, demons, ghosts, and a multitude of minor divinities, such as the God Laughter and the Goddess Sleep. When the ancients told their stories, they portrayed far more characters than we are apt to have in our stories.

Paul did this too. In the story in which Paul lived it made sense to order one's behavior with regard to those who lived upstairs: Women were to cover their heads because of the angels (I Cor. 11:10; see also 4:9). One could act on behalf of the dead (baptism for the dead is mentioned in I Cor. 15:29). Paul even claimed a journey into "the third heaven," though he admitted he was

unsure whether this was a bodily or visionary experience (II Cor. 12:2).

More universal than these references, the presence of the Spirit pervaded Paul's story. The Spirit "sealed" the believer, providing a "down payment" on the experience of God's kingdom (II Cor. 1:22; Rom. 8:16; Gal. 4:6). The Spirit manifested itself in various gifts, from the mysterious to the mundane (I Cor. 12–14). This presence of the Spirit was not just a private experience for Paul; it was visible evidence of the dawning of a new age.

But Paul never tells us his story, not even his version of the Jesus story. We must infer those stories from what he does tell us in his letters. In what follows we will try to identify the basic images and metaphors used in the letters when Paul speaks of the universal order, then examine the metaphors for the community and, finally, consider how Paul pictured himself.

Images of the World

Two powerful images Paul used to describe life are "waiting" (for example, I Thess. 1:10; Phil. 3:20) and "freedom" (for example, Gal. 2:4, 3:23, 5:1). These two ideas are related, although they are in some tension with each other; they reveal Paul's basic story. Paul understood himself to live in the mysterious gap between two antithetical epochs. (For a general discussion of the understanding of these two epochs in apocalyptic thought see the discussion of Thessalonians on pp. 42–45.) The old age was passing away; the powers of evil had been defeated; those in Christ had been liberated from the powers of that evil age. Yet the new age was not fully here; it had begun with Christ's resurrection; Paul daily awaited its consummation.

Consider:

🙢 🙢 🙢

Formerly when you did not know God, you were in bondage to beings that by nature are not gods. . . For freedom Christ has set us free. . .

You turned to God from idols to serve a living and true God, and to wait for his Son from heaven, whom he raised from the dead. . . .
But our commonwealth is in heaven, and from it we await a Savior, the Lord Jesus Christ, who will change our lowly body to be like his glorious body, by the power which enables him even to subject all things to himself.
I consider the sufferings of this present time are not worth comparing with the glory that is to be revealed to us. For the creation waits with eager longing for the revealing of the sons of God; for the creation was subjected to futility, not of its own will but by the will of him who subjected it in hope; because the creation itself will be set free from its bondage to decay and obtain the glorious liberty of the children of God. We know that the whole creation has been groaning in travail together until now; and not only the creation, but we ourselves, who have the first fruits of the Spirit, groan inwardly as we wait the adoption of sons, the redemption of our bodies. (Respectively Gal. 4:8, 5:1; I Thess. 1:10; Phil. 3:20–21; Rom. 8:18–23)

"Groaning in travail" was a common, but wonderful metaphor for the birth of the new age out of the old. Like the onset of labor, the beginning of the distress would be mild, but constantly increasing until—just before the birth—the intensity would seem unbearable. Then, release! Paul lived very near this end. He lived in the time of the distress (I Cor. 7:26 and Rom. 8:18–23, quoted above). This brief period of affliction was the preparation for the eternal kingdom (II Cor. 4:17; Rom. 8:18). Twice in his letters he describes the end and assumes he will be alive when it occurs (I Thess. 4:17; I Cor. 15:51). He advised the Corinthians not to marry because there was so little time left in this age (I Cor. 7:25–31).

This age is still the age of sin and death, still ruled by hostile powers (I Cor. 2:8; II Cor. 4:4; Gal. 1:4). But all those in Christ have been liberated from these powers (Gal. 4:8, 5:1, quoted above); they have been made a new creation (II Cor. 5:17). This new creation began with the res-

urrection of Christ, who is the "first fruits" of a general resurrection, which will be consummated at his coming, for which Paul waits (I Cor. 15:20–23). But this waiting is in hope, for Paul already possessed a foretaste of this new creation in the Spirit.

As we have seen from the Thessalonian and Corinthian correspondence, this "already" and "not yet" of Paul was hard for his followers to grasp. They easily overemphasized one side or the other. Later followers of Paul also had this problem. But in Paul's story the basic nature of the world had been changed by the death of Christ, whose obedient death had reversed the disobedience of Adam. Those "in Christ" are freed from the power of sin and the power of this evil age.

Images of the Community

Paul's images of the community are naturally drawn from this story, but seldom in an obvious way. Thus the community is the perfume of the new age, the fragrance of life to those being saved, the scent of death to those perishing (II Cor. 2:14–16). We see here the dual experience of the community: living in this evil age and living beyond it.

Another metaphor drawn from this story represents the community as the "body of Christ." Paul backed into this image. He began with the general metaphor of an organization as a collective body whose various members fulfill various functions (I Cor. 12:14–26), but concluded with the declaration, "you are the body of Christ" (I Cor. 12:27). Paul never developed the potential of this image the way his later followers would; for him its primary significance remained the interconnectedness of the various members of the assembly (so Romans 8:3–8, the only other use of this image in Paul's letters). Yet it had a wonderful potential, reflecting as it did the two experiences of the community: suffering and resurrection. It was an image that would profoundly affect future generations. (For a discussion of a related metaphor of the community as a family, see pp. 81–82.)

More revealing is a metaphoric image, which Paul shared with another group of his time, that of the believers as the Temple of God:

☙ ☙ ☙

Do you not know that you are God's temple, and that God's Spirit dwells in you? If any one destroys God's temple, God will destroy him. For God's temple is holy, and that temple you are. (I Cor. 3:16f)

On the surface this idea is remarkably parallel to what we find in a Stoic writer of the late first century:

☙ ☙ ☙

But you are a being of primary importance; you are a fragment of God; you have within you a part of Him. Why then are you ignorant of your own kinship? Why do you not know the source from which you have sprung? Will you not bear in mind, whenever you eat, who you are that eat, and whom you are nourishing? Whenever you indulge in intercourse with women, who you are that do this? Whenever you mix in society, whenever you take physical exercise, whenever you converse, do you not know that you are nourishing God, exercising God? You are bearing God about with you, poor wretch, and know it not. Do you suppose I am speaking of some external God, made of silver or gold? It is within yourself that you bear Him, and do not perceive that you are defiling him with impure thoughts and filthy actions. Yet in the presence of even an image of God you would not dare to do anything of the things you are now doing. But when God himself is present within you, seeing and hearing everything, you are not ashamed to be thinking and doing such things as these, O insensible of your own nature, and object of God's wrath! (Epictetus, Discourses 2.8.9–14; Loeb)

Ethically, these two declarations are very much alike. Both Paul and Epictetus admonish their hearers to certain forms of behavior based on the conviction that God is within them. Paul may even have heard such Stoic preachers as he grew up, since they had a major school in his native Tarsus and conducted all their classes outdoors. (The name Stoic is derived from the *stoa,* the porch, at Athens where they got their start when they were not allowed inside the Platonic Academy. After that, the Stoics never conducted their affairs indoors.)

But we must probe beyond the surface resemblance and ask what each writer meant by having "God within." In the Stoic story, God was an elemental part of the universe itself and therefore part of human nature. Their favorite word for God was *Logos,* which they understood to mean Reason, manifested in the world as natural order and in the individual as the intellectual life. Thus the reason we each carry within ourselves is the divine, in the Stoic view.

Just how far this is from the Pauline view will be clear if we pursue the ethical implications of this way of understanding the divine. For the Stoics, the moral life is a life lived according to this divine reason, and ethics becomes a matter of the power of will. Even happiness must be attained by willpower.

What is happiness? One of the simplest observations is that we are happy when we get what we want. But the weakness of such an approach is immediately evident: we never get all we want. As soon as we have one thing, we want another. Reason then dictates that we stop trying to get all we want (an impossibility) and learn instead to want what we get (the Stoic answer). This demands an absolute mastery of the will, a lonely enterprise far removed from Paul's community of the Spirit.

In the quotation from Paul above, the community rather than the individual is the temple of the Spirit (all the "you" pronouns in this quotation are plural), because it experiences the indwelling of the Spirit. Having "God within" is not a natural condition of the human species, as in the Stoic story; it is a new creation of a new community in a new age, which is just now dawning in the resurrection of Jesus and the gathering of his elect. For Paul, the community is central; it is no accident that all his letters (including even Philemon) are addressed to communities.

It is important to see what is original about Paul's ethics; both the basis (God within) and many of the practical details can be found in Stoicism. The originality lies in his story: the new community of the new age, living in the freedom of Christ's victory over the powers of sin and death. But then, the difficulty is not knowing what is right but having the resources to do it. (For more details on Stoicism and the nature of the Logos, see the introduction to John's Gospel in Chapter 10.)

Self-Images

Our earlier discussion of the Pauline community has already pointed up several of Paul's images for himself: father, mother, nurse, brother, partner (see p. 82). These highlight the ways that Paul participated in the lives of these communities. Here we will consider three other images that point not to relationships but to identity: weakness, the cross, and correspondence.

Paul was not a weak person in any sense. There is a popular though ill-founded tradition that he was habitually ill; yet his rapid and wide travels belie this notion. No one in poor physical shape could have survived the perils listed in II Corinthians 10, including being adrift in the sea for twenty-four hours. Nor would anyone who has read Galatians think his personality weak. Intellectually, socially, religiously, Paul had great strength. More than once he mocks this strength in his mad boasting (II Cor. 11:21–30; Phil. 3:4–11).

In spite of (and maybe partly because of) this strength, Paul portrayed himself with the image of weakness: To the weak I became weak, that I might win the weak (I Cor. 9:22). But the real reason for his weakness is that he saw himself in contrast to Christ: I will . . . boast of my weakness, that the power of Christ may rest upon me

(II Cor. 12:9). Paul used a happy metaphor to describe this contrast, that of holding a treasure in a clay pot (II Cor. 4:7).

Paul's central metaphor for understanding himself derived from his identification with Christ:

🖜 🖜 🖜

I have been crucified with Christ; it is no longer I who live, but Christ who lives in me; and the life I now live in the flesh I live by faith in the Son of God, who loved me and gave himself for me. (Gal. 2:20)

This extravagant metaphor is hard to decipher, but it affected all that Paul did. It provided the framework for his understanding of Christian initiation (Rom. 6:1–4). It provided his definition of the Christian community as the community of those "in Christ" (I Cor. 12:13; Gal. 3:27). It even provided the context for his understanding of his own suffering: "we share abundantly in Christ's suffering" (II Cor. 1:5; Phil. 1:29). Paul lived his life under the image of the cross (I Cor. 1:23, 2:2, 4:9; II Cor. 11:24; Phil. 1:21) and participated in the story of Christ: even as Christ's suffering was redemptive for the world, so Paul's suffering was redemptive for his communities. And their suffering would in turn redeem their cities.

To this process Paul gave the names *example* (Greek *typos*, designating a sculptor's creation of a likeness) and *imitation* (Greek *mimetes*, from *mimesis*, designating a poetic creation). Both images point to a quality of correspondence between art and reality. For Paul they indicated the correspondence between human life and the divine world, between his story and the charter story. Paul and his congregations lived in, and helped shape, the cosmic story of redemption in which God was overthrowing the powers of evil and bringing his kingdom into existence in this world.

The initial phase of the story was a failure. God wished Adam to communicate his love and joy to the creation, but Adam failed because of the power of sin and the weakness of the flesh. Using the model of story relationships discussed in Chapter 1 (pp. 29–31), we can diagram this part of the story as follows:

Adam, the subject of this story, had the task of nurturing God's creation; but because his opponents were stronger than he, he failed to carry out the divine contract. That story aborted and a new need arose. Something had to be done about Adam's failure, for now all creation stood under the power of Sin and Death. Thus the Christ has come to fulfill a new contract to communicate God's gift of righteousness to humanity:

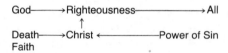

Unlike Adam, Christ proved obedient, and through his obedience all may be made righteous (Rom. 5, especially 15–21). But that is not the end of the story. A new contract remains to be fulfilled: this salvation must be communicated to those for whom it is intended. God's love must be delivered to the creation. The agents of this new action are Paul and his hearers:

God——→Love/Joy————————————→All creation
                    ↑
Spirit——→ Those in Christ ←————————Power of sin
                (Paul)   Weakness of the flesh
                (His communities)

For Paul, apparently, Christ's story is the crucial middle phase between the story of humanity in Adam and the story of Paul's own life and ministry. Given these interlocking story structures, we can perhaps better appreciate Paul's shocking declarations: "I have been crucified with Christ," "Christ . . . lives in me," "I live by faith" (Gal. 2:20). Paul's story does not merely follow the story of Christ; they overlap. Paul is in Christ, and Christ is in Paul.

The details necessary to give substance to this story are lacking; at least our present methods of analysis are not sufficient to discover them. Yet this kind of story is the basis for the letters, and we must endeavor to hear it whenever the letters are read.

RESOURCES FOR FURTHER STUDY

A variety of scholarly opinions on various facets of Romans is admirably covered in Donfried, 1977, which is an excellent place to begin further study.

Those who wish to pursue the question of the theme of Romans could begin with the short discussion of Stendahl, 1976. More comprehensive treatments of Paul's relation to the Jews are found in the classic work by Davies, 1980, and in the magisterial work by Sanders, 1977, 1983. Sanders' strength is his mastery of the Jewish sources, although his discussion of Paul must be read in conjunction with Davies, especially Davies' discussion of Christ as the new Torah (Law). Paul's Jewish background is also explored by Schoeps, 1961, though with less positive conclusions.

On the other side, the works of Bornkamm, 1971, and Kasemann, 1971, convincingly present the traditional view of Romans, which centers on the doctrine of justification by faith.

The special study of the collection by Nickle, 1966, provides useful insights into Paul's mission strategy.

On the diatribe style, see Stowers, 1981.

There are a few good introductory commentaries.

Achtemeier, 1985, is perhaps the best; but see also Maly, 1979; Smart, 1975; and Throckmorton, 1961.

Other standard commentaries include:

Barrett, 1957; Best, 1967; Black, 1973; and Bruce, 1963. Kasemann, 1980, will benefit those who know Greek.

Of the few works that take the narrative element in Paul seriously, see Hays, 1983; *The Faith of Jesus Christ;* and Petersen, 1985, *Rediscovering Paul.*

Paul for a New Day

‌⁊⧫ ⁊⧫ ⁊⧫

Colossians, Ephesians, Timothy, Titus

5

It has never been much of a secret that a great deal of early Christian literature was written in the names of people who did not actually put the words on paper. Even a glance at the great body of apocryphal literature—written in the names of Peter, Paul, Thomas, Mary, Andrew, and even Judas—makes it obvious that literature continued to be produced under their names long after these people were dead. But most of these works represent an esoteric kind of Christianity, and it has been generally assumed that they had fewer reservations about such false claims than their more mainline counterparts. Most ancient scholars accepted the authorship stated for the New Testament documents, although questions were raised about some (such as Second Peter) well into the fourth century.

But when the criterion developed that to be considered canonical a writing had to be written by an apostle, or at least by one of his associates, to question the authorship of a work was also to question its validity. Consequently, it became necessary to attribute even anonymous works to apostolic authorship, so that the gospels were each attributed to a disciple or a disciple's companion, Hebrews to Paul, and the Apocalypse to John the Apostle, even though none of these works claims such authorship.

The modern study of the Bible has recognized the fallacy of identifying validity with authorship. Not everything Paul wrote proved to be of enduring value; some of his letters were lost. Hebrews is no less powerful a writing simply because it was not written by Paul. Thus, modern scholars have been able to approach the question of authorship in a more neutral fashion; disputing the authorship of a work no longer means to dispute its teaching. Still, many people have trouble when scholars suggest that a biblical work was not written by the person it says wrote it. Deceiving about authorship seems to imply that the writer would deceive about other things as well. But such a conclusion represents a great misunderstanding of the ancient world, imposing our modern concepts of authorship and copyright most inappropriately.

As discussed earlier (pp. 45–47), the ancients viewed authorship in terms of authority rather than production. In ancient books there was no such thing as a title page listing the author; only the invention of printing and commercial publishing led to such status for authors. Considering the various possible meanings of the claim that a book is "from Paul" (see Figure 2.2, p. 47), we realize that no deception need be intended when a work was not actually written by the person it claims as "author(ity)." It is worth noting that of all the letters of Paul we have studied so far, only Galatians is written exclusively in his name. In each of the others he is joined by Timothy, Sosthenes, or Silvanus. And Galatians is largely a defense of Paul's authority.

The modern quest to define more precisely the authorship of these works is undertaken not to undermine their value but to describe more accurately the historical development of early Christianity.

EVALUATING CLAIMS TO AUTHORSHIP

Since the ancient concept of authorship as authority is so much broader than ours, criteria must be developed to distinguish the various levels of contribution by the person listed as the author. One way of stating this problem would be to ask:

When Paul and Timothy are listed as the authors of I Thessalonians or Colossians, how can we estimate the contribution of Paul to each? Or: How can we determine if a letter written in the name of Paul was actually written by one of his disciples after his death? Or: How can we prove if a letter claiming to be written by Paul was actually a forgery?

Sometimes evidence *external* to the letters helps to locate their origin. The latest possible date for a letter would be the first instance of direct citation by another author, and if that author is located some distance from the destination of the letter, we must also allow some time for its circulation. Further, if it has been widely distributed (especially in Rome, Antioch, and Alexandria), we know it has been circulating for some years.

Another external factor is the judgment of earlier investigators. About 150 a Christian leader in Rome, Marcion, established a canon that contained only the letters of Paul and one gospel. That list contained ten of the thirteen letters now in the New Testament (omitting I and II Tim. and Titus); it also contained one or two other letters that were eventually rejected from the New Testament. A later canon list from Rome, now called the Muratorian Canon (because it was discovered by a Renaissance scholar by the name of Muratori), includes the same Pauline letters as the New Testament. Another source of information is the fourth-century church historian, Eusebius, who included the debates about the canon in his history of the development of Christianity. Somewhat earlier, a Christian philosopher in Alexandria, Clement, had analyzed the question of authorship.

Yet we should not rely too heavily on these external testimonies. They often reached decisions on grounds that seem to us inadequate, and as often their decisions were influenced by their endorsement of, or antipathy toward, the ideas contained in the letters. All such external evidence is secondary. Of primary importance is the evidence that can be drawn from the letters themselves.

Three different kinds of *internal* evidence are useful in answering the questions about authorship: literary, intellectual, and historical. *Literary* evidence includes the style and typical vocabulary of a known author. In Paul's case this involves comparing the disputed letters with those that are clearly from Paul in a direct sense. His style may be characterized as intense and dialogical, personal and hyperbolic. While we must admit that different situations may elicit different styles (as Galatians and Philemon illustrate), Paul's letters are always vigorous expressions of his person. In the same way, vocabulary varies but exhibits a remarkable continuity from letter to letter. Not all topics are covered in all letters, but when a particular topic is broached, Paul uses a certain vocabulary to talk about it. Thus, in the undisputed letters, Paul always calls Peter "Cephas"; the Evil One is always "Satan" and never the "Devil" (*Satanas* rather than *Diabolos* in Greek); he speaks of Christ's "appearing" but never of his "epiphany" (*parousia* rather than *epiphaneia*). This consistency in Paul does not extend to some of the disputed letters. Obviously, the passage of time, moving into a new social context, and even employing a new secretary may all affect style and vocabulary.

Every writer has the privilege of changing his mind, but when we find evidence of *changed ideas* we may have a clue to authorship. Three kinds of changes are interesting: omissions of characteristic ideas of the writer; development of ideas beyond their earlier formulations; and contradictions of earlier ideas. None of these would automatically resolve the issue of authorship or of Paul's actual participation in the writing. Evolution of an idea may suggest primary authorship by a disciple, especially if the extent of change is considerable, but it may simply mean that Paul continued to think about an issue (as his thinking about the Law evolved between Galatians and Romans).

The final kind of evidence useful for determining authorship is *historical*. Unfortunately, the disputed letters are not laden with historical references; this is part of the reason they are disputed. Still, we may glean two kinds of historical data to help determine the kind of authorship.

First, we seek evidence of historical change in the situation and institutionalization of the church. Although we have no detailed information about the development of early Christian organizational structures, we can presume that they evolved from simple to more complex and that it became increasingly clear that the Christian assembly was not just another kind of synagogue. Thus we can ask: What is the relationship envisioned between Jews and Gentiles? What degree of organization has been achieved? Are there independent, paid pastors? Is there someone with authority over several churches (a proto-bishop)?

Second (and perhaps most useful) we ask: What are the historical presuppositions of the writer? It would be easy for one well acquainted with Paul to imagine himself in Paul's place and say what Paul would say if confronted by this new situation. But it is very difficult to do so without presupposing the new situation. A crucial question to ask about the disputed letters is whether they presuppose a historical situation that did not exist in Paul's time.

In applying these criteria to certain letters written in Paul's name, we discover why their authorship has been disputed and gain richer insights into the development of early Christianity. The writings left to us in Paul's name, or in which Paul plays a major role, allow us to reconstruct several trajectories of Pauline influence in the late first and early second centuries. Each trajectory lays valid claim to some facet of Paul; each ignores other aspects of this complex person. All testify to his significance.

THE TRAJECTORY OF THE NEW COMMUNITY

Colossians and Ephesians share much, including their concern for the relation between Jews and Gentiles in the new community. This was, as we saw in the last chapter, a genuine concern for Paul. Yet there are things about these letters that seem unlike Paul. Let's consider the evidence.

The Authorship of Colossians and Ephesians

Reading and Reflection

Read through Colossians and Ephesians looking for evidence of their historical settings. Do you notice anything about these letters that seems unlike the Paul you have encountered in the earlier ones?

Both of these works have strong external support. They were regarded as Paul's letters by Marcion (about 150) and were included in the Muratorian Canon (about 200). They were not questioned by any of the ancients. Similar language, though not direct quotation, appears in the letter of Clement of Rome to the Corinthians (about 95). The modern concern about their authorship arises only from data within the letters themselves.

Much of the *literary* evidence points away from direct authorship by Paul, though more so in the case of Ephesians than of Colossians. Forty words in Ephesians are not found in the rest of Paul's works, though many appear in late New Testament writings; the Evil One is referred to as the Devil, unlike Paul but like late works; the uncharacteristic phrase "in the heavenlies" occurs repeatedly. Certain prepositions (*en* and *kata*) are used much more frequently than in the other letters. Unlike Paul, the author of the thanksgiving did not pursue a single theme; unlike Paul, the author adopts a solemn liturgical style.

Whether either Colossians or Ephesians was directly written by Paul may be questioned, but Colossians resembles his style more closely. In fact, it can be argued that the author of Ephesians must have regarded Colossians as "from Paul," since he (or she) depended on it heavily. Fully a third of Colossians is found in Ephesians (73 of the 155 verses have parallels in Colossians). Parallels are also apparent between Ephesians and I Peter, Acts, and John. The literary evidence suggests that Colossians probably derives in some direct way from Paul, but Ephesians goes further afield, deriving from Colossians and other sources.

A similar result follows an examination of the *ideas* of the letters. Paul's ideas are everywhere, but with significant development and omissions. When Paul discussed the church in his other letters, he referred primarily to individual local assemblies (as in Col. 4:16). In Ephesians, however, the church is a universal entity: one church over the whole world (for example, 5:23). While Paul considered his work to be built on the one foundation of Christ (I Cor. 3:11), it is now said to be based on the foundation of the apostles and prophets (Eph. 2:5), and the apostles are regarded as "holy" figures from the past (3:5). While the divine mystery in Colossians is Christ, who reconciled Jews and Gentiles (1:27), in Ephesians the reconciliation itself is the mystery—the church rather than Christ (3:3–6). This emerging concern for the church is characteristic of Christianity from the late first century on.

On the other hand, the writer of Ephesians has a more fully developed understanding of Christ and more nearly equates him with God. In Colossians (1:20) God reconciles the world; in Ephesians (2:16) Christ is said to do so. While Paul said that God appoints officials in the church (I Cor. 12:28), in Ephesians (4:11) Christ is said to do so. Paul's earlier writings dwell on the death of Christ; the author of Ephesians, however, is more concerned with his resurrection (see 1:15–2:10). This writer actually declares that Christians have already been "raised with Christ" (2:6), which Paul carefully avoided saying in Romans (6:4). None of these ideas is foreign to Paul, but each is developed in ways that are not typical of the earlier letters; and the development in Ephesians goes beyond that of Colossians.

We find no problem imagining the *historical situation* in Colossians. Its close ties with Philemon seem to be good evidence of Pauline authorship (both associate Timothy with Paul in the address; both send greetings from Aristarchus, Mark, Epaphras, Luke, and Demas [4:10–14 and Philem. 23–24]; both call Archippus a minister [4:7 and Philem. 2]; both mention Onesimus [4:9]). While Colossians addresses no obvious crisis, the situation assumed is realistic. Epaphras, it seems, had preached the gospel in Colossae, an interior city in southwest Asia Minor (1:7) where Paul was unknown (2:1). Yet Epaphras apparently acted as Paul's deputy (1:7; most manuscripts read "on our behalf"). The purpose of this letter seems to have been to report on Paul's situation, which would be described more fully by Tychicus, the implied carrier of the letter (4:8). In the process a vague warning is given not to let anyone deceive them or judge them for their religious observances (2:8–23). This warning is not sharp enough to demand that we think of it as the primary reason for the letter, yet something definite seems to be envisioned, involving the occult (2:8—"philosophy"), questions of diet and Sabbath (2:16), self-abasement (2:18), and asceticism (2:21). These practices were so widespread that it may well be impossible to clearly identify the nature of the opponents. Though there are strong parallels to the Dead Sea Scrolls and to later gnosticism, the cosmic allusions and asceticism rejected here were typical of astrological speculations widely practiced throughout the Greco-Roman world. We cannot even be certain if the dangers warned against stem from within or outside the church at Colossae. Though the historical setting is not as clear as in other letters, it is not vague enough as to make it difficult to imagine as possible for Paul's time.

For Ephesians, on the other hand, we cannot easily imagine the historical context. First, there is an almost complete lack of historical references. There is no evidence in this letter that it was written to a concrete situation or with any specific problem in mind. More an essay than a real letter, it lacks even a formal addressee (the older manuscripts omit the words "who are at Ephesus" from verse 1). While we cannot deduce much concerning its assumptions about the institution of the church, we can see the letter assumes that the controversy about the status of Gentiles in the church has been settled: The unity of Jew and Gentile in the church is a given rather than a present struggle. This probably reflects a situation beyond Paul's lifetime.

All in all, Colossians is an ambiguous letter on the boundary of Pauline authorship. It was written either by Paul to a congregation he had not founded but which belonged to his circle or tradition (having been established by one of his disciples), or by one of his disciples to clarify what the great apostle would have taught. In either case this letter is less personal, less idiosyncratic, less surely stamped with Paul's own hand. It has moved some distance from the kind of discourse we have become accustomed to in Paul, but not so far as to make it impossible to imagine Paul making the journey—perhaps with a little assistance from Timothy, whose name is also on the letter. The ties with Philemon may indicate that it was written during the same imprisonment as that letter (about 56), though we miss dearly any sign of the humor and irony evident in Philemon.

Thus, it seems reasonable to conclude that while Colossians stands on the boundary of Pauline authorship, Ephesians passes beyond the boundary into the territory of the Pauline school after the death of the apostle. There is genuine continuity, but a new agenda. The purpose of Ephesians seems to have been to present a summary of Paul's teaching, perhaps to assert that here (and not with other interpreters) lies Paul's true heritage. As we will see, others were making similar claims.

While the majority of scholars today seem to regard Colossians as a work of Paul, only a minority think Paul actually wrote Ephesians. Years ago, Edgar Goodspeed conjectured that Ephesians may have been written as a sort of cover letter when Paul's letters were published as a collection, perhaps a decade or two after his death. While that was and remains a guess, it does express something about the kind of writing we have in Ephesians.

Wrestlers This stylized view of Greek wrestling is from the inside of a drinking bowl. The purpose of ancient wrestling was merely to throw one's opponent to the ground. Greco-Roman culture was pervaded with athletics, celebrated in various games. The best known were the Olympic Games, held every four years; second in importance were the Isthmian Games held every two years near Corinth. The Greeks showed no embarrassment over the nude male body, though such displays were an offense to many Jews. Paul may have witnessed the games at Corinth and used an athletic metaphor from racing to stress his point to the Corinthians (I Cor. 9:24; see also Eph. 6:12). (Alinari/Art Resource, New York.)

Reading and Reflection

Reread Colossians and Ephesians with the aid of the reading guides. If time does not permit a complete rereading, choose similar parts of both letters to read. Pay particular attention to the way the author uses the metaphor of the body.

The Ruling Metaphors: Body and Family

To a remarkable degree these letters have essentially the same pattern. Both begin with the stan-

READING GUIDES

Colossians		Ephesians
1:1–2	Salutation	1:1–2
1:3–12	Thanksgiving and prayer/praise	1:3–23
1:13–2:5	Message of rescue and release	2:1–3:21
1:13–20	The work of Christ	2:1–10
1:21–23	The work of the church	2:11–22
1:24–2:5	The work of Paul	3:1–13
1:24–25	The suffering	3:1–3
1:26–27	The secret	3:4–13
1:28–2:5	The labor	
	The prayer	3:14–21
2:6–3:17	Exhortations based on union with Christ	4:1–5:20
2:6–8	General principles	4:1–7
2:9–15	Christ as a cosmic conqueror	4:8–16
2:16–19	Implications for life	4:17–5:20
2:20–23	Christ's death and freedom	
3:1–11	Christ's resurrection and freedom	
3:12–17	General exhortations	
3:18–4:1	Exhortations to household duties	5:21–6:9
3:18	Wives	5:22–24
3:19	Husbands	5:25–33
3:20	Children	6:1–3
3:21	Fathers	6:4
3:22–25	Slaves	6:5–8
4:1	Masters	6:9
4:2–6	Final exhortations	6:10–20
4:7–9	Travel plans	6:21–22
4:10–17	Greetings	
4:18	Benedictions	6:23–24
4:18	Written with his own hand	

dard opening and thanksgiving, with poetic descriptions of Christ as the head of the cosmos and, especially, of the church. Both then draw out the implications of this headship for the lives of the hearers (in the exhortations) and close with salutations and travel plans. Colossians alone has a realistic discussion of some actual problems with food, drink, festival days, and worship practices (2:16–23). Both letters depend on standard rhetorical devices: lists of vices, lists of virtues, and instruction to the household, all built on the root metaphor of the congregation as a body.

This general organization and dependence on lists reveal a new kind of rhetoric, different from the judicial and deliberative rhetoric of the earlier letters. Here the rhetoric is demonstrative, seeking to show the wisdom of a particular point of view in the present. (See the discussion and chart on pp. 8–9). It seeks to move the hearer away from vice and toward virtue. That we have not encountered such rhetoric in Paul earlier can be evaluated two ways: it may be evidence that Paul did not write these letters, or it may help explain why these letters differ to such an extent from the others. However we explain it, there is no denying that these devices are rare in Paul's letters. The household instruction is unparalleled: Paul has shown no interest in children and his advice against marrying (I Cor. 7) would surely not win him any awards as an ardent supporter of the traditional family. Paul's earlier use of family imagery has been limited to the assembly as the household of faith (see p. 82).

In addition to this use of lists, both works repeatedly employ the metaphor of the body. In Colossians Christ is the head of the body (1:18); as his body, the church bears his suffering (1:24); the contrasting body of the flesh has been buried in baptism (2:11–12), a new body having been raised with Christ (2:12); they must not now submit to other heads (2:18–23). Works of the earthly body are to be put to death (3:5), but the new body is to be dressed in virtue (3:12). This hierarchical view of the church carries over into family relationships: as Christ/church, so husband/wife and father/children and master/slave. The metaphor reinforces the social world of traditional Greco-Roman society.

Ephesians shares this metaphor and draws these same lessons, even expanding them. Not only are believers raised with Christ, they are seated with him in the "heavenlies" (2:6). The notion of one body becomes a call to unity (4:4) and portrays dramatically the union of Jew and Gentile in the covenant and commonwealth of Israel (2:11–16). This genuine concern of Paul achieves new eloquence here.

Such concerns indicate one path the traditions of Paul followed, a path we might define as the creation of a new community. They carry forward Paul's concern for the one people of God, including both Jews and Gentiles. The Paul remembered here shares several traits with the Paul portrayed in Acts.

The Paul of Acts

We will reserve our study of Acts until Chapter 9 when we can treat it with its other half, the Gospel of Luke. Here we consider only the characterization of Paul in the story. Paul is a (perhaps *the*) central figure of Acts. He is introduced in chapter 8, and becomes the sole focus of attention by chapter 13. Peter, whose action predominates in the early chapters, is gotten off stage with the rather lame, "he departed and went to another place" (12:17). If character is revealed by actions and choices, as Aristotle taught, Paul is the one who carried the new way to the Gentiles while remaining a faithful Jew, trying to maintain the unity of the church.

Paul's Jewishness is highlighted. He is a Pharisee (regarded as the most important of the Jewish parties—23:6). He studied in Jerusalem (22:3). He always goes first to the synagogue (17:1–2). He circumcises Timothy (16:3). He takes vows and offers sacrifice in the Temple (21:26). The author even has him return to Jerusalem immediately after his experience of the risen Christ on the way to Damascus (9:19–26), something Paul himself denied (Gal. 1:17).

The portrayal of the unity of the church in Acts is a major theme. The believers shared everything in common (4:32); they grew and prospered in this unity (2:46–47). Paul himself promotes it by accepting the compromise concerning food regulations for the Gentiles (15:19–29), and he himself is Law observant (21:24).

The Paul of Acts is an obedient servant of the church, its representative to the Gentiles.

The Domesticated Apostle

While it is impossible for us to be sure that Paul did not write Colossians and Ephesians, we can be certain that the Paul personified there is far tamer than the Paul of the early letters. No longer do we find the demand for absolute freedom, the intense expectation of the near end of the age, the fiery enthusiasm of the Spirit. The Christian life is rationalized and moralized. Visions are distrusted (Col. 2:18). Faith itself becomes less a passionate commitment than a designation for proper Christian thought and practice (Col. 2:7; Eph. 4:13; but contrast Eph. 2:8). Christians should conduct themselves with respect to the impressions they make on outsiders (Col. 4:5). There is no felt discrepancy between the demands of the gospel and the demands of the family (Col. 3:18–4:6; Eph. 5:21–6:9). There is even the admonition to obedience based on the Law (Eph. 6:2). This tendency toward cultural accommodation and moral accomplishment represents one of the dominant directions in which the traditions of Paul were carried by many of his followers.

THE TRAJECTORY OF THE EMERGING INSTITUTION

We have seen that Paul had numerous associates, some intimate enough to join him in his authorship (Timothy, Silas, and Sosthenes). Out of the lengthy list of associates two merit special attention, having had letters addressed to them in the name of Paul. Obviously this presumes that they are no longer traveling with him; he has left them as settled overseers in Asia Minor and Crete according to the perspective of these letters. Apparently, he neglected to instruct them in the details of church operation, for he writes them letters on the subject. Yet, it is far more likely that Timothy and Titus knew all about Paul's practice of church organization. Most scholars today conclude that these letters represent a later generation putting into writing the teachings of the great apostle as they understood them to apply to their own time. They present Paul's pastoral advice for the care of the church and are thus called the Pastoral Letters. First we will consider the question of authorship, then examine more closely the portrait they paint of the emerging church and Paul's role in the development of that church.

The Authorship of Timothy and Titus

Sections of these letters, especially II Timothy, read like fragments of real letters from Paul. The last part of II Timothy 4, beginning at verse 6, contains either words from a letter of Paul or the work of an extraordinary imitator. The reference to the books (scrolls) and parchments (*codices,* more like our books) is perhaps too clever for an imitator (4:13). The end of chapter 1 and the first part of chapter 2 may also be from Paul. Some have guessed that a real letter stands behind these three compositions, providing a sort of model and inspiration, and that some late first-century or early second-century follower of Paul used Pauline tradition to create a kind of "last testament" of Paul (II Tim.) and then a sort of handbook of church order (I Tim. and Titus). This hypothesis remains a guess. Had we a similar handbook among the undisputed letters, or even specific information on how Paul organized his churches, comparison would reveal much about the development of early Christianity. Lacking such information, the best we can do is carefully read these letters and try to reconstruct the situation and the story behind them.

Reading and Reflection

Beginning with II Timothy, read through these three letters, making a list of the various church regulations they propound. Pay particular attention to regulations for the clergy, attitudes toward differing points of view, and the role envisioned for women.

It is sometimes said that whether Paul wrote these letters makes no difference, for the letters remain the same and are powerful writings in their own right. Though this is true to some extent, whether these letters come from the apostle himself or from a later disciple makes a great deal of difference in our understanding of the devel-

---

READING GUIDES TO
THE PASTORALS

II Timothy

Salutation   1:1–2
Thanksgiving   1:3–5
Admonition to courage   1:6–10
Paul's example and situation   1:11–19
Exhortations   2:1–4:5
   Take strength
   Remember Christ
   Remind people
   Turn from wayward impulses
   Know that the last days are evil
   Stand by the truth
   Proclaim the message
Paul's plight   4:6–18
Greetings   4:19–21
Blessing   4:22

Titus

Salutation   1:1–4
Titus' commission   1:5–16
Instructions for others   2:1–14
   Men, women, slaves

Instructions for Titus   2:15–3:11
   His themes, treatment of heretics
Travel plans   3:12–14
Greetings   3:15
   And blessing

I Timothy

Salutation   1:1–2
Timothy's commission: guard against
heresy   1:3–20
   with a thanksgiving   1:12–14
Instructions for church order   2:1–6:2
   Prayer, with roles for men and
   women   2:1–15
   Leader's qualities   3:1–13
      Bishops—deacons
Purpose of the letter   3:14–16
Warnings about heresy in the last days   4:1–10
Instructions to be passed on   4:11–6:2
   Men, women, widows, elders, slaves
Concluding admonitions   6:3–21
   Instructions to the rich   6:17–19
   Blessing

---

opment of the early church and our interpretation of Paul. For example: if what the pastorals teach about the role of women is the same as Paul taught, then we have badly misconstrued the evidence of the other letters. Before pursuing these differences, we need to consider the question of their authorship.

The evidence for authorship consists of many separate observations, and no single observation is compelling. Each could be explained in some way as a conceivable deviation from the Pauline norm. After a while, however, the process of explaining away the evidence becomes self-defeating, since everywhere we look something requires an explanation. Each of the separate kinds

of evidence challenges the conclusion that Paul actually wrote these letters.

Even the *external evidence* raises doubts. They were not included in the canon of Marcion, an ardent second-century follower of Paul. This implies that either he did not know of them or did not regard them as authentic. In either case, we are warned that their status is ambiguous. (They were included in the later, more orthodox, Muratorian canon and in third-century canons of later Marcionites.) But the really challenging evidence is in the letters themselves.

Except for the few passages referred to above, which echo Paul, the *literary evidence* points to someone other than Paul behind these letters. Over one third of the vocabulary of the Pastorals is not shared by the earlier letters. Those who count such things claim that of the 848 words used, 306 are not found in the other ten letters (36%). Most of these unique words, 211 of them, are part of the general vocabulary of second-century writers. Further, of the 542 words shared between Paul and the Pastorals, only 50 are not shared by other writers in the New Testament (these statistics are taken from IDB 3:670). Even the shared vocabulary raises problems, for words Paul used in one way are used differently by our author. "Righteousness" (*dikaios*), for example, is here used in the sense of being upright and moral rather than in the sense of justification, characteristic of Paul (compare Rom. 3:21–28 and I Tim. 1:9). The most striking similarities in vocabulary are not between the Pastorals and Paul, but between the Pastorals and Polycarp, an early second-century follower of Paul. Some have even suggested Polycarp wrote them in Paul's name. (There are many interesting parallels of words and ideas in Polycarp's *Letter to the Philippians,* probably written about 110.)

Style is a rather abstract concept, but those who point to stylistic differences call attention to a basic dissimilarity between our writer and Paul. Paul's style may be characterized as passionate, argumentative, involved. One always has the sense that Paul is there, face to face. Our writer, in contrast, is cool, dictatorial, above the battle. His distance from the reader is all the more shocking in light of Paul's personal relationship to Timothy.

Those who would discount this evidence usually point to the lapse in time, attributing this new style to the aging Paul waiting in prison for his appointed end (as II Tim. implies, but not I Tim. or Titus). They also suggest that the new subject matter would dictate a new vocabulary, or that Paul's secretary was given unusual latitude in the writing of these documents. It is not impossible.

The *ideas* of these letters are also not typical of Paul. As noted above, some of the altered vocabulary seems to be based on changed ideas: righteousness no longer means justification; faith no longer means trust, but a position to be held (I Tim. 3:9, 4:1). Christ is interpreted in terms of his epiphany, a common Hellenistic idea, rather than in terms of his death (II Tim. 1:10; also used for Christ's coming, I Tim. 6:14; Titus 2:13; Paul would have said *parousia*). The attitude toward the Law lacks the dynamic yes-and-no of Paul (I Tim. 1:9; contrast Rom. 7). Young widows are now urged to marry (I Tim. 5:14; contrast I Cor. 7:8). In fact, our writer completely reverses Paul's advice and insists that candidates for church office be married (I Tim. 3:2). Women are forbidden to speak in church (I Tim. 1:9; contrast I Cor. 11:5). Further, in the earlier letters Paul never spoke of special requirements for church office; he expected all to live up to the same standards. Nothing in Paul's letters indicates that he expected more from the leaders than from the followers.

Those who dissent argue that these changes are not so great; they are more a matter of degree. Other sentences can be quoted from the Pastorals that are more in accord with what we find in the other letters. Besides, they point out, Paul was not always perfectly consistent—even in the undisputed letters. Or perhaps the situation had changed sufficiently to account for these changed ideas. It is not impossible.

There is universal agreement that the *historical situation* has changed. The question is has it changed so much that it reflects the next generation after Paul? The whole issue of the acceptance of the Gentiles, for example, seems a moot point. There is no struggle with keeping the Law, nor even reference to those issues that so preoccupied Paul, except for mention of a "circumcision party" which "must be silenced" (Titus 1:10–11). The struggle with opponents also seems different. While Paul struggled with others in his own assemblies, there seems now to be a clear line between the faithful insiders and dangerous outsiders. And the danger of these unacceptable views now seems acute (for example, 4:1–5).

But the greatest change is in the organization of the church. A regular ministry, with specific qualifications, has been established. There is probably a paid clergy, to judge by the warnings against bishops and deacons being fond of money (I Tim. 3:3, 8; Titus 1:7). The requirement that the bishop be "not a recent convert" (I Tim. 3:6) seems quite out of place in Paul's time, when everyone was a recent convert. While our author does not regard this bishop as holding the monarchic authority that Ignatius claimed in the early second century (Ignatius demanded obedience to the bishop as to the Lord), still the concept of a ruler over the congregations in a city or region is evident. In fact, Timothy and Titus are imagined to be such regional superintendents, acting as apostolic delegates (Titus 1:5; I Tim. 1:3). The bishops they appoint will soon claim a similar authority. The requirements for bishop and deacons are also revealing: they are not specific to the office, but are very general and overlap considerably. Actually, little about them is specifically Christian; these are the traits expected of good upstanding leaders, traits that will make them respected by outsiders. Compare the requirements given in I Timothy (3:1–13) and Titus (1:5–9) with the similar list of characteristics set down for the good general by Onasander, a writer in the time of Paul:

ð ð ð

We must choose a general, not because of noble birth as priests are chosen, nor because of wealth as the superintendents of the gymnasia [schools], but because he is temperate, self-restrained, vigilant, frugal, hardened to labor, alert, free from avarice, neither too young nor too old, indeed a father of children if possible, a ready speaker, and a man with a good reputation. (Strategikos 1.1, Loeb)

Also revealing are some of the assumptions our author makes. He assumes gospels are *written,* citing a Jesus tradition from the Gospel of Luke as a writing rather than in the manner of Paul (I Tim. 5:18; contrast I Cor. 9:3–14 and the discussion on pp. 142–143). He has Paul include himself with the Gentiles, "we" who were once

disobedient (Titus 3:3); Paul always said "you." A pervasive assumption throughout these writings is that the church must settle down and be at home in the world, appoint respectable leaders, be above reproach, be well thought of by those outside, support the traditional family, not allow women too much authority.

Those who remain unconvinced point out that our knowledge of church organization in Paul's day is scant, but both bishops and deacons were known (Phil. 1:1; I Thess. 5:12). The bishop is not yet the one ruler of the church, as in Ignatius. The situation regarding heresy (deviant views) may have changed quickly. Perhaps on his return from his intended trip to Spain, Paul found he had to deal with a new situation. Perhaps he cited an earlier written gospel than Luke, containing the same tradition. None of this evidence is strong enough to demand we abandon belief in Paul's authorship, these scholars claim.

They are right. It is, as is every historical judgment, a matter of probability; the likelihood that Paul could not have changed in any one of these ways is not great. But the probability that he changed in all of them simultaneously is much greater. Not only are we confronted with a myriad of details that seem dubious for Paul, but a different story underlies these works.

The New Story of the Pastoral Letters

When we think back to Paul's story (sketched on pp. 104–108), we wonder: Where is the sense of the Spirit? Where is the sense of waiting for the near end? Where is the sense of freedom? Where is the sense of suffering that redeems the world? Where is the body of Christ? Where is the community as a family of brothers and sisters, slaves and partners? Where is the Paul who lived only "in Christ," who suffered, as Christ had, to redeem his communities? Paul lived at the end of the age, so intensely that he could advise against marriage so that full time might be devoted to the great task at hand. The time was short.

How different is the story of the author of the

Pastorals. Attention to the present has eclipsed concern for the future kingdom. Church as organization is replacing church as family. The desire to be well thought of by those outside has eroded freedom. Women have to be reassigned to the roles traditional in their culture: wives and mothers (how, we might wonder in passing, would those women Paul advised not to marry be saved by bearing children? I Tim. 2:15). Concern about the cosmic conflict that heralds the end of the age has been replaced by concern for proper church organization. The angels have gone.

The Authoritative Apostle

The great issues dealt with in the Pastorals concern order:

ordered teaching (I Tim. 1:3–20; Titus 1:10–16)
ordered worship (I Tim. 2:1–15)
ordered leaders (I Tim. 3; Titus 1:5–9)
ordered teachers (I Tim. 4:1–10; Titus 3:8–11)
ordered lives (I Tim. 4:11–6:19; Titus 2:1–3:7)

These issues imply divergence: there must be those who teach falsely; those whose worship is not orderly; whose lives are a scandal; women who are not submissive. Our writer represents that trajectory of the Pauline tradition that chose order over ardor. He (almost certainly a he) drew on that aspect of Paul that also strove for order. He gives us Paul the apostle, preacher, and teacher (II Tim. 2:11). He gives us a Paul created in the image of the bishop, pointing ahead to the church as an hierarchical organization. It is a compelling portrayal, perhaps the dominant picture of Paul in Western consciousness. Yet it is not the only way Paul was remembered.

If the two trajectories we have examined represent the taming and the harnessing of the apostle for the work of the church, the next three represent the highlighting of the impetuosity and the radicalness of Paul. Some of his followers emphasized Paul's rejection of normal worldly pur-

suits (especially the family); others emphasized his intense spirituality. We will explore these two approaches to Paul and then consider a trajectory that saw nothing worthwhile in the traditions of Paul.

THE TRAJECTORY OF WORLD DENIAL

A Christian work written in the middle of the second century contains the following story about Paul and a young woman by the name of Thecla:

While Paul was speaking to the assembly in the house of Onesiphorus, a virgin named Thecla, daughter of Theocleia and fiancee to a man named Thamyris, sat at a nearby window and listened day and night as Paul spoke the word and extolled the virgin life. She never left the window but pressed on by faith, with extreme joy. When she saw many women and virgins going in, she too desired to be counted worthy to stand before Paul's face and hear the word of Christ. For she had only heard Paul's words and had not yet seen him. After three days her mother sent for Thamyris, hoping to break the spell. When he arrived she reported what had happened, adding, "I wonder how a maiden of such modesty can be so troubled. Thamyris, this man is upsetting the whole city, for besides your Thecla all the women and young people go to him and are taught that they must fear only one God and live chastely. And my daughter, like a spider at the window, is bound by his words and is taken captive. Go and speak to her." Thamyris went to her both loving her and also fearing her fascination with this stranger. He chided her for her behavior and begged her to come to him. But she never moved. Her mother added her reproach, but she never turned from listening to Paul.
Thamyris left in great despair. He bribed two companions of Paul to learn more about this man who deceives young men and women into renouncing marriage, discovering that Paul forbids marriage and demands complete chastity. Thamyris succeeds in having Paul imprisoned, but Thecla bribes her way in to see him. Finally meeting

him she comes to complete faith. When her family learns of this, both she and Paul are brought before the governor. The governor demands to know why she will not honor her marriage contract. When she does not answer, but only stares at Paul, her own mother calls for her condemnation as an example to all brides who would forsake their sacred duty. Greatly moved, the governor consigns Paul to be beaten and banished from the city, but Thecla is condemned to be burned. She is carried off to the theater where the execution is to take place. Like a lost lamb looking for the shepherd she looks about for Paul and is comforted to see not Paul but the Lord sitting in the form of Paul. The place of execution is prepared, wood is gathered, Thecla is brought in naked, causing even the governor to marvel at the power that was in her. When told to mount the pyre, she makes the sign of the cross and climbs up on the wood. They light the fire and a great flame blazes up, but does not harm her. God caused a sudden rainstorm to extinguish the fire and Thecla is saved. She leaves the city and finds Paul, who is praying for her rescue. She becomes, like Paul, one who travels and spreads the word of Christ.

The Legendary Acts of Paul

There is much more to the story of Paul and Thecla that this summary omits. (You can read the full account in Hennecke II, 1965:352–364, or James, 1924:272–281.) But this sample of this mid-second-century work shows that some of Paul's followers remembered him in a way markedly different from that of the Pastorals. In fact, some of the views of those regarded as false teachers in the Pastorals correspond rather closely to the Paul of this story: forbidding young people to marry (I Tim. 4:3), encouraging unsubmissive women (I Tim. 2:11), telling strange and marvelous tales (I Tim. 4:7). People "who make their way into households and capture weak women, burdened with sins and swayed by various impulses, who will listen to anybody and can never arrive at a knowledge of the truth" (II Tim. 3:6–7) sounds like something Thamyris might say

about Paul. Curiously, one of the companions who betrayed Paul to Thamyris is named Hermogenes, who is also known from the Pastorals as among those in Asia, the westernmost province of Asia Minor, turning away from Paul (II Tim. 1:15). (This story, by the way, is set in Iconium in Galatia, the next province east of the province of Asia.) Onesiphorus is also mentioned in both (II Tim. 1:16). If we studied the whole story of Thecla, numerous other parallels and contrasts could be drawn.

It has even been argued that the Pastorals were written, at least in part, in reaction to the developing picture of Paul that came to fruition in the Thecla story: Paul as a social radical (MacDonald, 1983). This Paul rejects the ways of the world: virginity is the highest virtue; married people should refrain from sexual activity; only the continent will hear the voice of God; only the chaste will participate in the resurrection (*Acts of Paul* 3:5, 12). The social dynamics of this way of thinking imply freedom for women and a challenge to the traditional family and social order.

Women in antiquity were usually married in their early teens and could expect to be raising a family until they passed childbearing age. Very little birth control was practiced, although abortion and infanticide were widespread among Gentiles. The newborn would be laid at its father's feet. If the father picked it up, it was welcomed into the family. If not, the baby would be exposed and left to die.

Not only the enormous distraction of having a family would have limited the ministry of women. While generalization is difficult, since the status of women differed considerably among classes and times, in Greek society women were never autonomous. They *belonged* to their fathers (or if the father died, to their brother or some other male protector). The father would give his daughter to her husband (a vestige of this custom is still a part of the traditional wedding ceremony). In classical Athens, the wife was expected to stay almost entirely at home: her tasks were to raise children and produce clothing. Roman women had more freedom, including the right to own property, but they were also expected to be submissive to their husbands.

One of the many slanders Octavian (later called Augustus) alleged against Anthony, who had fled to Egypt and married Cleopatra, was that he allowed a woman "to make herself equal to a man" (Dio Cassius, *Roman History* 50.28.3). Women remained under the control of men throughout their lives; even widows were controlled by their sons. In the Roman period numerous advances were made toward some basic equality for women, especially in the philosophical schools. Educated women were not uncommon; Juvenal mocks their "masculine pretensions" in his derisive *Sixth Satire.* Yet the lot of most women was marriage and subordination to men. A philosopher of the Pythagorean movement (one most open to women) declared:

⋙ ⋙ ⋙

A woman must live for her husband according to the law and in actuality thinking no private thoughts of her own. . . . And she must endure her husband's temper, stinginess, complaining, jealousy, abuse, and anything else peculiar to his nature. (Thesleff, 1965:142–145; quoted from Pomeroy: 134–136)

In the earliest communities, however, there were orders of widows who moved beyond these social constraints (Acts 6:1, 9:36–42). It is a short step from an order of widows to an order of virgins, especially if leaders are encouraged not to marry. The requirement of the Pastorals that only "real widows" be enrolled (I Tim. 5:5) is probably meant to exclude virgins from this emerging order.

This freedom for women would be purchased at the price of radically challenging the central social institution of the Hellenistic world, the family. So sacred was this institution that it was considered a sacrilege not to marry, and in fact marriage was required by law in many cities. Augustus issued several marriage laws to prevent the decline of the Roman population. This tension between family and woman's freedom may

be seen in the provision of one of his laws: a freeborn woman who bore three children was freed from her dependence on the man (Balsdon, 1969: 83). Women were seeking such freedom, and some versions of Christianity promised to provide it.

It was possible to understand Paul's admonition to remain single, his attitude toward women, and his elaboration of the church as a "family" as an attack on the traditional family. Guarding against this implication, the author of the Pastorals advises:

⋙ ⋙ ⋙

Train the young women to love their husbands and children, to be sensible, chaste, domestic, kind, and submissive to their husbands, that the word of God may not be discredited. (Titus 2:3–4)

One of the common charges against Christians by Hellenistic writers is that they divide and disrupt the household. In fact, Christians created alternative households, as the practice of looking after widows already implies. The writer of the Pastorals saw such charges as a discredit to the gospel. The author of the *Acts of Paul and Thecla* thought such charges valid. For her (perhaps), Christ challenged the very foundations of sinful human culture.

The Radical Apostle

The story of Paul and Thecla is part of a larger work, *The Acts of Paul,* written late in the second century but based on oral traditions and legends that probably go back to the first century. It commemorates the more radical aspects of Paul, the side that advocated singleness in light of the approaching end (I Cor. 7:25–26, but notice 27). These stories extend Paul's logic that in Christ there is neither slave nor free, neither male nor female (Gal. 3:27–28). The Paul portrayed here is the passionate Paul, who prays for and receives miracles, who prophesies in the Spirit. Such stories pursue the implications of the assembly of believers as the new household, living outside the social conventions of the day. The tellers of these stories stood in opposition to Greco-Roman culture. They would have understood the Jesus tradition that declares: "I have come to set a man against his father, and a daughter against her mother" (Matt. 10:35). In these ways, they are truly heirs of Paul.

But our story has also resolved the tension in Paul. Paul did not deny sexuality, as the full discussion in I Corinthians 7 shows. Though Paul lived in light of the coming end, he was too Jewish to neglect the goodness of the creation: "For the earth is the Lord's and everything in it. . . . eat whatever is set before you without raising any questions on the grounds of conscience" (I Cor. 10:26–27; also Rom. 14:14). Paul lived a rigorous life, but he was no ascetic. Whereas Paul represented the invasion of the larger world by the message of Christ, the *Acts of Paul* represents a withdrawal from that world in the name of purity. It is a world-denying and culture-denying asceticism that loses the dynamic of Paul's yes and no. It solves the paradox of Paul by turning him into a social radical.

This portrait of Paul was widespread in the second century, and even much later. The *Acts of Paul* was used as scripture in some Christian circles, known as Manicheans. Thecla was eventually made a saint, as the church harnessed the energies of the virgins in monastic orders. Great Paulinists like Marcion and Irenaeus, and later Augustine, were profoundly influenced by the portrait of Paul as the model ascetic.

THE TRAJECTORY OF MYSTICAL EXPERIENCE

Other followers of Paul remembered him not so much for his universalism, or his authority, or his asceticism, as for his religious sensibility. Paul's great emphasis on the Spirit and his understanding of his life in Christ suggest his intense, inner aspect. There is no doubt that Paul underwent profound religious experiences. He reports being caught up to heaven (II Cor. 12:3), claims to speak in tongues more often than all the enthusiasts at Corinth (I Cor. 14:18), and, above all, reports that he encountered the risen Christ (Gal. 1:16). In his own account Paul equates this latter experience with that of the earlier resurrection appearances to Peter and the others (I Cor. 15:3–8). The author of Acts portrayed it as a visionary experience, but then the author of Acts believed that the risen Jesus ceased to appear to his followers forty days after the resurrection, when he ascended to heaven (Acts 1:3–9). We know that some Christians claimed to encounter the risen Christ very late in the second century. This claim seems to have been made particularly by the Gnostics.

From Mystical Experience to Gnosticism

We have encountered incipient forms of gnosticism in Paul's letters, especially at Corinth and possibly at Colossae. These early experiments may be considered a gnosticizing trend in Pauline Christianity, often abetted by things Paul said but often resisted by Paul himself. (See the discussion on pp. 76–79.) This trend will eventually achieve the status of a self-conscious movement in the second century.

We should say movements, for literally dozens of different Gnostic systems were invented; one writer listed sixty different movements. Some of them found their primary inspiration in the Gospel of John; many looked to Paul. Valentinus, a major Gnostic thinker who came to Rome from Egypt about 150, claimed that his teacher Theudas had been a disciple of Paul. Marcion, a Syrian deeply influenced by Gnostic thought, who came to Rome at about the same time as Valentinus, was so impressed with Paul that he excluded all non-Pauline writings from his canon. Other Paulinists violently rejected their claims to Paul, but that is a polemical and not a historical judgment.

Like Paul, the Gnostics were overwhelmed by

the experience of the Spirit. They believed that in their spiritual rapture they transcended their bodies and their senses and experienced union with the divine. Like Paul too, they sought to live in the Spirit not in the flesh. They could appeal to Paul's rejection of the authority of the church in favor of private experience (Gal. 1:12–16), to his claim to speak a secret wisdom to the mature (I Cor. 2:6), to his distinction between law and grace (II Cor. 3:6), to his teaching that Jesus' resurrected body was a "spiritual body" rather than a physical one (I Cor. 15:44–46)—he actually said that flesh and blood could not inherit the kingdom of God (I Cor. 15:50) and even Jesus took only the "likeness of flesh" (Rom. 8:3). In all these ways, and especially in the emphasis on spiritual experience, the Gnostics saw in Paul their true source.

This mysticism of experience was attuned to the spirit of the age. We have seen that the mystery religions sought to achieve transformation through mythic enactments. It was a mysticism of ritual. Philosophy sought the transformation of life and the attainment of enlightenment. It was a mysticism of the mind. Gnosticism, deeply influenced by both, was ultimately a mysticism of experience. Traces of all three are found in Paul. But the Gnostics went far beyond Paul.

They created a new story, or rather, they incorporated the story of Jesus into a larger one derived from Greek philosophical speculation. Even as the mythic speculation of the Greeks derived the universe from the primeval pair, Heaven and Earth, so philosophic speculation saw the world as a dualism of spirit and matter. Gnosticism viewed the material world as real but deceptive. Humans are really spiritual beings, created in God's image (which they understood to mean that the primal human was the mirror image of God). We are all deceived into thinking we are material creatures; we identify ourselves with our bodies. This is because we lack knowledge. Gnostics understood the old Greek proverb, "Know Thyself," to mean know your true spiritual nature. But this knowledge (gnosis) is not intellectual attainment. One had to know in

the depths of one's being, that is, experientially. This required a revelation, a revealer—Jesus.

The Gnostic understanding of Jesus was different from the traditional view: Jesus is the heavenly Man, the second Adam, of whom Paul spoke in Romans 5. He is humanity in its true state, now descended into the world to reveal the truth to those ready to receive it. Not all are ready. And to those not ready, the common people, he speaks in parables that point toward the truth and might eventually make them ready. But to the elect he imparts a secret knowledge. Typical of the Gnostic approach is the scene reported by an anti-Gnostic writer; Jesus explains the Parable of the Sower to his disciples:

🙠 🙠 🙠

[*The Gnostics claim that the sower in the parable*] *was not a good sower, asserting that if he had been good he would not have been neglectful, or cast seed 'by the wayside' or 'on stony places' or 'in untilled soil;' wishing it to be understood that the sower is he who scatters captive souls in diverse bodies as he wills. In which book also many things are said about the prince of dampness and the prince of fire, which is meant to signify that it is by art and not by the power of God that all good things are done in this world. For it says that there is a certain virgin light whom God, when he wishes to give rain to men, shows to the prince of dampness, who since he desires to take possession of her perspires in his excitement and makes rain, and when he is deprived of her causes peals of thunder by his roaring. (Paulus Orosius,* Consultatio *154.4–18; quoted from Hennecke I, 1963:266)*

The secrecy, the playful mythology, and the notion of souls captive to bodies are all typically Gnostic. Here we glimpse the radical novelty of their approach. Consider:

🙠 🙠 🙠

Jesus said: If those who lead you say unto you: Behold the Kingdom is in heaven, then the birds of the heaven will be before you. If they say unto you: It is in the sea, then the fish will be before you. But the Kingdom is within you, and it is out-side of you. When you know yourselves, then shall you be known, and you shall know that you are the sons of the living Father. But if you do not know yourselves, then you are in poverty, and you are poverty. (Gospel of Thomas *3*)

The Gospel of Truth is joy for those who have received from the Father of Truth the grace of knowing him through the power of the Logos which has come forth . . . which is he whom men call the Redeemer, since that is the name of the work which he must do for the redemption of those who knew not the Father, since the name of the Gospel is the revelation of hope, since it is a discovery for those who seek him. (Gospel of Truth, *quoted from Hennecke I, 1963:236, 511*)

How like Paul this sounds; how unlike Paul it is. That Jesus has come forth to redeem the world sounds like Paul. But now you must understand the hidden meaning. You must make the discovery.

Gnosticism plunges below the surface mean-ing to ever deeper meanings. "But it came to pass, after Jesus was risen from the dead that he spent 11 years discoursing with his disciples and taught them only as far as the places of the first com-mandment and as far as the places of the first mystery" (*Pistis Sophia;* quoted from Hennecke I, 1963:253). So much more remains to be re-vealed. In the quote above, from the *Gospel of Truth,* I used three dots to avoid some of the technical language which has the Logos (Word, Message, or Reason) coming forth from the Full-ness which is the Thought and Mind of God. In the system of Valentinus, perhaps the author of this work, the universe is a very complex place, with layer upon layer of realities. Each level is overseen by a pair of Rulers.

First you must understand that the world as you commonly experience it is a delusion. Val-entinians explained the origin of the world and of humanity by means of a very complicated story, in which redemption by Christ is the final phase. All derives from the primal pair: the Deep and

Silence, which was the Thought of the Deep. From them proceeded Mind and Truth, Word and Life, Humanity and Church, and numerous pairs of Rulers making up the Fullness of thirty. The youngest of these generations, Wisdom, desired to know the Deep itself. But acting without her proper consort, Willed, she strove upward to-ward him, with disastrous results: she conceived the monster Fancy, with whom she nearly per-ished in labor. The original pairs acted to save her by producing a single Ruler, Limit (also called Cross), who delivered her of the monster and re-stored the primal harmony. This Monstrous Form of Wisdom lay outside this harmony in places of shadow and void.

Mind and Truth then produce a new pair, Christ and Holy Spirit, who pity the Monstrous Form of Wisdom and descend to her through the Cross. Receiving form from them, she is then called Wisdom after her mother or Spirit after the com-panion of Christ who formed her. She becomes a Ruler of the lowest sphere, and Christ and Holy Spirit return to the Fullness.

Aware of her marginal position between the lowest and the highest, Wisdom (or Spirit) al-ternates between grief and joy. In her grief she brings forth Body; then aspiring toward higher things she brings forth Soul. Finally, having been touched by Christ and Holy Spirit, she brings forth Spirit. Now imitating the action of the Fullness, she sets out to create a world that imitates that cosmic world. As an image of the Deep, the First Father, she produces the Creator out of Soul. He then creates Heaven and Earth and all therein.

But the Creator worked blindly, imagining himself to be the agent rather than just the tool of Wisdom. Out of Body he created Humanity and breathed into it Soul. Unknown to him his mother, Wisdom, created other beings out of Spirit so that these three now are mingled. Some, dom-inated by Body, are so bound up with this per-ishable world that they can never be saved. The spiritual, in contrast, are so attuned to the Full-ness that they need no salvation. They ascend to the Fullness. But the rest, dominated by Soul, are capable of salvation; it was for these that

Jesus finally came from heaven. (This summary is based on the excellent discussion in Dodd, 1953: 97–114.)

These Souls may be saved by knowledge (gnosis) of their true being. Jesus came to reveal this knowledge, and it can now be learned from those he taught. But it lies not on the surface of his teaching, such as the common people think, but in the secret depths. When the common Christians call Jesus "Son of man" they do not understand what they say: Son of Man, indeed, Image of that Primal Humanity. (For examples of other Gnostic myths see the discussion of John's Gospel on pp. 260–263.)

A Gnostic work from a different school summarized the revelation of Jesus as a kind of password one must know to reascend safely through the spheres of the Rulers to the Father. When challenged by these Powers, one should reply:

🙠 🙠 🙠

I have recognized myself and gathered myself together from all sides and have not sown children to the Archon [Ruler] but have uprooted his roots and have gathered the scattered members, and I know thee who thou art; for I belong to those from above. (Fragment of the Gospel of Philip; *quoted from Hennecke I, 1963:273)*

Knowing oneself, gathering oneself, rooting out the bodily: by such means the Gnostic ascended. In practice these would involve asceticism (or, in a few cases, bodily indulgence), prayer and meditation, and attention to Gnostic stories and interpretations. These techniques were widely practiced in many diverse systems. The formula above is nearly the same as that given by the neo-Platonic philosopher, Porphyry, a century later in a letter to his wife: "Study to ascend into thyself, gathering from the body all thy scattered members which have been scattered into a multitude from the unity which up to a point held sway" (quoted from Hennecke I, 275). Porphyry was a strikingly unoriginal philosopher

and represents here only what would be typical of the philosophical enterprise.

The Apostle of Knowledge

Gnosticism represented a serious attempt to bridge the gap between Christian preaching and the philosophical tradition, trying to integrate Christianity into the best intellectual endeavors of their time. In so doing the Gnostics reused many of the elements of Paul's tradition, claiming especially his experience. But in recasting Paul as the man of knowledge, they distorted major elements of his self-identity as a Jew. Marcion, who shared much with the Gnostics, went so far as to deny any connection whatsoever between Christianity and Judaism, even rejecting the Hebrew Scriptures and the God they portray. He was convinced that the God revealed by Jesus and preached by Paul was the antithesis of the Jewish Creator. (All who are deeply influenced by Gnostic ideas will have trouble with the notion of God as Creator, as the Valentinian hierarchy shows.) For Marcion, Paul was the one true apostle. His canon consisted of the ten letters of Paul and a gospel, probably an abridged form of Luke who was thought to be a traveling companion of Paul. That one could exalt the authority of a tradition this much while altering its meaning so extensively is a remarkable accomplishment of the human imagination, one that should caution all readers.

THE TRAJECTORY THAT REJECTED PAUL

When Augustine allegorized the Parable of the Good Samaritan, he imagined that the Samaritan was symbolic of Christ, descending to help fallen Adam, providing the oil and wine of the sacraments, setting him on his beast—his body—and carrying him to the inn—the church. The innkeeper, he thought, was Paul. By the 400s Paul had clearly become the dominant voice in the church. It was not always so.

The Early Opponents

We know little about the opponents of Paul who constantly flit about in the background of the letters. They have been the subject of much study, but the available information is slight. We know them only through the charges Paul leveled against them, and who among us would wish to be known by the word of our adversaries? Worse, Paul never treats them in an organized way. He presumed that he and they and his audience already knew these opponents; there was no need to explain. One confusing factor is that from city to city and, sometimes even within one city, the nature of the opposition to Paul seems to shift. The opponents of I Corinthians seem to have little in common with those of Galatians or of II Corinthians. We must not suppose that Paul's opponents were a homogeneous group. Some, perhaps most, were more conservative than he and reluctant to depart from the Jewish traditions. Some were more liberal and eager to do away with all law, as they seemed to do at Corinth.

Paul confronted both and stirred controversy wherever he went. Even Peter and Barnabas, his traveling companion, opposed him at one point (Gal. 2). We presume Paul and Peter made up, but we are not told this. Barnabas never rejoined him, and Paul ceased to use Antioch as a base of operations after this incident. We can be certain that many of his contemporaries disagreed with him on one or more points at one or more times.

Ongoing Opposition

Tracing Paul's influence in the decades following his death (probably around 64) is not an easy task. None of the literature that can be dated with reasonable certainty between 65 and 95 refers to him until we come to Acts. None of the gospel writers seems indebted to him. But after 100, or perhaps we should say after the publication of Acts, Paul's increasing status is easily documented. He is quoted extensively, and some begin to consider his writings equivalent to Scripture (I Pet. 3:16), or as the only Scripture (Marcion). We have seen that many diverse groups laid claim to the authority of Paul.

A revealing scene near the end of Acts probably portrays the attitude of one group of Christians toward Paul at the time Acts was written (perhaps around 90). In this scene Paul has come to Jerusalem and made a report to the leadership on his mission to the Gentiles. Their response is to warn him: "You see, brother, how many thousands there are among the Jews of those who have believed; they are all zealous for the law, and they have been told about you that you teach all the Jews who are among the Gentiles to forsake Moses, telling them not to circumcise their children or observe the customs" (Acts 21:20–21). This is a false charge, as the author of Acts makes clear. There is no evidence in any of the letters that Paul thought Jews should not keep their customs; his concern was that Gentiles not be compelled to observe them.

By the end of the first century, however, we find followers of Paul asserting what Paul is accused of in Acts: teaching that Jews ought not to keep the Law. Ignatius of Antioch, in a letter to the Christians of Magnesia (a city about 50 miles north of Ephesus), declared: "It is an abomination to follow Jesus Christ and to practice Jewish ways" (10:3). For Ignatius, the form of Christianity dominant in Paul's time had become unacceptable. This trajectory will culminate in Marcion's rejection of all things Jewish, even their Scriptures and their God.

When we find Paulinists adopting this attitude toward Christians who are Jewish, we must expect to find those Jewish Christians adopting negative attitudes toward Paul.

The development of Jewish Christianity is very difficult to trace, for they were the losers in the struggle; and the history of the losers is usually obscured by the winners who write the history. The movement to be both Christian and law-observant did not die out with the first generation, nor even with the destruction of Jerusalem in 70. References to such groups in and around Palestine can be found into the seventh century, when this whole area was overrun by the Arabs and eventually converted to Islam. In the fourth century, Epiphanius discusses Jewish Christians of his day, telling us: "They break with Paul because he does not accept circumcision" (*Parnarion* 28.5.3).

Actually, there was diversity within the movement we call Jewish Christianity. Around 150, a Gentile Christian living in Palestine wrote an imaginary dialogue between himself and a Jew named Trypho. It is a stimulating debate, leading only to an agreement to talk further. The author, a philosopher named Justin, identifies several alternative views held by Jewish Christians: some keep the Law themselves, but do not believe Gentiles need to do so; some insist on Gentile observance; some do not insist that the Gentiles observe the laws but will not eat with them unless they do (and thus cannot share the eucharist); some have ceased to observe the Law themselves (*Dialogue with Trypho* 47). Surely the last and probably the first group would have had little difficulty with Paul. The other two probably, as Epiphanius says, broke with Paul.

Some went much further than simply not following Paul; they regarded him as the perverter of Christianity. We have a letter, probably written around 200, pretending to be from Peter to James, which discusses someone called "Simon." The allusion is to Simon Magus, mentioned in Acts (8:9–24), who was later regarded as the father of all errors. But in reading the letter it becomes obvious that Simon is a thinly veiled way of referring to Paul. Thus Simon is described as "going to the Gentiles" and as failing to present his gospel to James and receive the direction of the Jerusalem church, both of which apply to Paul but not to Simon. In this letter Paul is portrayed as Peter's direct enemy.

ð‌ð‌ð

For some from among the Gentiles have rejected my lawful preaching and have preferred a lawless and absurd doctrine of the man who is my enemy. And indeed some have attempted, whilst I am still alive, to distort my words by interpretations of many sorts, as if I taught the dissolution of the law and, although I was of this opinion, did not express it openly [see Gal. 2:11–14]. But that may God forbid! For to do such a thing means to act contrary to the law of God which was made known by Moses and was confirmed by our Lord. . . . (Letter of Peter 2:3–5; quoted from Hennecke II, 1963:112)

Later writings in this same tradition are even more pointed. There are several direct encounters between Peter and "Simon," always to the latter's disadvantage. Even the legitimacy of Paul's encounter with the risen Jesus is questioned, first by suggesting that even the pagans have such visions, perhaps prompted by demons, but then more ingeniously:

ð‌ð‌ð

So even if our Jesus did appear in a dream to you, making himself known and conversing with you, he did so in anger, speaking to an opponent [see Acts 9:4–5]. That is why he spoke to you through visions and dreams—through revelations which are external. But can anyone be qualified by a vision to become a teacher? And if you say it is possible, then why did the Teacher remain for a whole year conversing with those who were awake? (Pseudoclementine Homilies 19:1; quoted from Meeks, 1972:182)

Here we see Christians claiming Peter but opposing and rejecting Paul. It is worth noting what they reject: there is no discussion of Paul's highly nuanced understanding of the Law nor of his concern for Gentiles. What we find is a rejection of those Christians who laid claim to the Pauline heritage. *The battle we see reflected here is not over the ideas of Paul; it is a struggle between two communities and two different visions of the*

Christian life. If people like Marcion claim Paul, the only option Jewish Christians have is to reject him.

The Continuing Influence of Paul

No one was able to capture Paul. Neither his enemies nor his friends seem to have understood his dynamic and paradoxical message. No one pays attention to the careful argument of Romans with its forceful no, and equally forceful yes, to the Law. No one asks how in one place Paul can declare: "Circumcision is nothing; uncircumcision is nothing; the only thing that counts is new creation" (Gal. 6:15), while in another he writes: "Circumcision or uncircumcision is neither here nor there; what matters is to keep God's commands" (I Cor. 7:19). The paradox of Paul remained unexplored; no one attempted a historical interpretation of Paul.

Yet each of these communities found Paul an important influence and all but the last drew significant inspiration from his work. At the very least this ability of Paul to appeal to very diverse elements insured his continued influence. He became the most significant influence in the development of Christianity—the keeper of the Inn.

CHRISTIANITY AFTER PAUL

We may now draw some preliminary conclusions about the developments within Pauline Christianity in the next generation. Four trends appear significant:

1. *A new emphasis on the church emerges in these writings*. The church is coming to be regarded as a hierarchical institution with an ordained ministry tracing its roots back to Paul or to other apostles such as Peter or James. A primary concern of this institution is to preserve the "true teaching" of the apostles.

2. *There is a definite "settling in" and becoming acculturated*. The intense concern with the near end of the age seems to have faded, and with it the indifference to culture. There is a strong concern for what outsiders might think of the behavior of Christians, a longing to be respectable. This results in a certain moralistic element, extolling virtues and condemning vices, both common in the general literature of this era. Coupled with this concern is an increasing accommodation to cultural expectations, especially in regard to the family and the place of women. To be respectable the community must restrict the freedoms women gained in the early charismatic communities. When people spoke because they believed the Spirit inspired them, who was to prevent a woman from praying or prophesying? Only the fading of the charismatic experience and the increasing routinization of these tasks could lead to the silencing of half the assembly.

3. *Related to this new attitude toward culture was an increasingly direct attempt to interpret Christ and Christian experience in terms of the religious experience of Gentiles*. The earlier generation adapted the Hebrew Scriptures to interpret Christ; this generation begins to appeal to the Gentile traditions, such as the epiphany of the God, and to the ideas of the philosophers. Gentiles are playing the dominant role. This results in the development of many new ideas, prompting a very dynamic era in Christian thought.

4. *There is an increasingly clear demarcation between the various kinds of Christians*. No longer is there any question about the legitimacy of the faith of the Gentile Christians; quite the opposite. Jewish Christians are being relegated to the fringes; Gnostics are being driven out; ascetics are challenged. A large group emerges, still diverse but sharing much, that regards itself as the orthodox tradition: the guardians of the teachings of the Apostles. The authority of the Apostles escalates the value placed on their writings, resulting in an increase in the number of writings attributed to apostles and in the beginning of

the process to establish the true corpus of their works: a canon.

Finally, we have one small item of unfinished business left over from our study of the Thessalonian letters in Chapter 2. Now that we have a clearer idea of the developments among Paul's followers in the next generation, it would be appropriate to reread II Thessalonians and ask whether it is more closely related to these developments or to the Paul revealed in the earlier letters.

RESOURCES FOR FURTHER STUDY

On the general question of Paul's influence, see:

Dunn, 1977, *Unity and Diversity in the New Testament.*
Gamble, 1975, "The Redaction of the Pauline Letters."
Munro, 1983, *Authority in Paul and Peter.*

Extracts from many sources in the Pauline and anti-Pauline traditions, from the first to the twentieth centuries, can be found in Meeks, 1972, *The Writings of Paul*: 149–444.
Theological developments are traced by Ziesler, 1983:122–139.
The evolution of church order is traced by Schweizer, 1961.

The changing role of women in ministry is traced by Fiorenza, 1983, *In Memory of Her,* especially Part 3. The roles of women in society are treated by Pomeroy, 1975, *Goddesses, Whores, Wives, and Slaves.*
The concept of "trajectories" was introduced into New Testament studies by Robinson and Koester, 1971, *Trajectories through Early Christianity,* especially 1–19.
On the error at Colossae, see Francis, 1973, *Conflicts at Colossae.*
Second-century movements drawing on Paul are treated by:

Hoffman, 1984, *Marcion.*
Howe, 1980, "Interpretations of Paul in the Acts of Paul and Theca."
Knox, 1942, *Marcion and the New Testament.*

MacDonald, 1982, *The Legend and the Apostle.*
Pagels, 1975, *The Gnostic Paul.*
Verner, 1982, *The Household of God: The Social World of the Pastoral Epistles.*

The question of authorship is addressed by Aland, 1961, "The problem of Anonymity and Pseudonymity in Christian Literature of the First Two Centuries;" Cannon, 1983; and Koch, in IDB 5:712–714.
For a conservative defense of Paul's writing the Pastorals, see:

Barker et al., 1969, *The New Testament Speaks.*
Ellis, 1961, "The Authorship of the Pastorals," 49–57.
Guthrie, 1975, *New Testament Introduction.*

The nature of the opposition to Paul is treated extensively, with a large bibliography, in Gunther, 1973, *St. Paul's Opponents and Their Background.*
An excellent brief description of the variety and interconnection between various forms of Judaism in this era is given by Stone, 1980, *Scriptures, Sects, and Visions.*
For a brief treatment of each of the disputed letters, see Sampley et al., 1978.
Commentaries include:

Colossians and Ephesians: Barth, 1974; Bruce, 1984; Houlden, 1970; Lohse, 1971; Martin, 1973b; Mitton, 1976; Patzia, 1984; and Swain, 1980.
Pastorals: Barrett, 1963; Dibelius and Conzelmann, 1972 (technical); Fee, 1984 (argues that Paul wrote the Pastorals); and Hanson, 1982.

Stories Told

⁊⁊ ⁊⁊ ⁊⁊

Approaches to Understanding the Gospels

A Case in Point: The Empty Tomb Stories

Gospel Interpretation: A Review

Resources for Further Study

6

In those days Jesus came from Nazareth of Galilee and was baptized by John in the Jordan. And when he came up out of the water. . . .

This short, vivid scene comes at the beginning of the Gospel according to Mark. Immediately we recognize that it represents a different kind of writing from the letters we have studied so far. In this chapter we will explore the methods of study appropriate to this new kind of writing called gospel. One clue is found in the name itself. *Gospel* is from the Old English *godspel* (good spell). While spell implies a magical power, its root meaning is story. A gospel, then, is a good story. Certainly the most important characteristic of these writings is that they are stories.

This clue will provide further insight if we consider the Greek term that gospel intends to translate: *euangellion* (or *evangellion*). The stem, *angellion,* means an announcement or a proclamation (thus an *angelos,* an angel, is one who delivers a message). The prefix of this word, *eu-,* means good, happy, or well off. We meet this same prefix in English words like euphoric (a feeling of well-being), euphonic (a pleasing sound), and eulogy (good words spoken at a funeral). When used with a noun *eu-* implies greatness or abundance. *Euangellion,* then, indicates an announcement of something favorable, an extremely happy event.

One use of this word in the Greco-Roman world was for the news of victory brought back from the battlefront (TDNT, 2:722). Such announcements were the occasion of great celebrations and festivals. While the Christian usage probably does not derive from this secular usage, it does share

some of the same connotations and feelings, connotations hardly evident in our word "gospel."

Since gospels are stories about great good news of victory and triumph, we must endeavor to read them with some of the sense of expectation such a name implies. Our task is to hear them as they were originally heard, which also implies that we will hear them in the context of other ancient literature of a similar kind.

On the one hand, no ancient literature is exactly like the gospels, which seem to be a distinctive literary form invented by early Christian storytellers. On the other hand, they do resemble other kinds of ancient writings. Probably the strongest parallels can be traced to the form known as a *bios,* the story of a famous statesman, philosopher, or religious leader. There are also similar traits in various histories, more in Hebrew history than in Greek, and even in the *Dialogues* of Plato, especially the early ones that tell the story of Socrates' trial and death. There are also numerous similarities to the stories about the lives of the prophets found in the Hebrew Scriptures. Different readers probably heard in them echoes of, and expectations from, these various contexts. Thus, our second clue for finding appropriate methods for studying the gospels is that we must be conscious of the need to try to hear them within the literary context of antiquity. Striving to listen to them "as gospels" will require a new kind of listening on our part, different from the kind of attention we have given them as documents of our age, different even from the hearing we gave to the Pauline letters.

A third and final clue is the simple observation that there are four gospels—all very much alike—telling much the same story, though with significant differences between them. Thus our study must be comparative, involving careful observation of their points of agreement and their differences.

Before reviewing the various methods that scholars have developed for interpreting the gospels, we must become more familiar with what actually happens in a gospel story. Familiarity with the specific details of an actual story will help us appreciate the issues involved and the strengths and weaknesses of the various proposals for interpreting the gospels. For our purposes, the following exercise will suffice.

A CASE IN POINT:
The Empty Tomb Stories

Reading and Reflection

Carefully study all four accounts of the women coming to Jesus' tomb: Matt. 28:1–10; Mark 16:1–8; Luke 23:1–11; and John 20:1–18. Answer these questions for each version of the story.

1. Who went to the tomb?
2. What did they see when they arrived?
3. Whom did they meet?
4. What were they told about Jesus?
5. What was their response?
6. Who first saw the risen Jesus?

(This task, and all your study of the gospels, will be greatly aided by a study tool called a *Synopsis of the Gospels.* Two of the best are the *Synopsis of the Four Gospels* (hereafter, SFG) published by the American Bible Society and the *Gospel Parallels* (hereafter, GP) published by Thomas Nelson. The former is more complete and less expensive; but the latter is somewhat better arranged. Each is divided into a series of individual stories, though they are numbered differently. I shall regularly give the number of the section in each version. For the empty tomb story, see SFG #352 or GP #253.)

The differences between these accounts are so vast that some have been tempted to argue that

they do not refer to the same incident. Yet because they share a number of common elements, including the presence of Mary Magdalene, we are left with the task of making sense of them as different versions of the same incident.

The differences between the versions are stark: while in Mark the women approach the tomb "when the sun had risen" and find the stone already removed, in Matthew they witness an earthquake and an angelic descent (both lacking in the other accounts), and in John's version Mary arrived "while it was still dark and saw that the stone had been taken away from the tomb." The number of women is variously identified as one, two, four, or more, though Mary Magdalene is always included. In one set of traditions they are told to return to Galilee (and in Matthew they do), while Luke (aware of the Galilee tradition), keeps them in Jerusalem where they encounter the risen Jesus. Only in Mark do they flee in fear and say "nothing to anyone, for they were afraid." (The rest of Mark 16 after verse 8 is not in our oldest texts of Mark's gospel and probably was composed from the accounts in Matthew and Luke. For a discussion, see pp. 164–166.) In Matthew's version, the women encounter the risen Jesus as they leave the tomb; in John he appears after two male disciples come and go; in Luke he does not appear to the women, but to two unnamed male disciples far from the tomb; and in Mark he does not appear at all.

It is inappropriate to try to explain these differences here. When we finish our study of each gospel, the reasons for their differences will be obvious. Here our issue is the proper approach to dealing with such diversity. How should we proceed?

GOSPEL INTERPRETATION:
A Review

From earliest times the diversity of the gospels and the differences—some would say contradictions—between them have been a problem for serious interpreters. First I will sketch some of the ancient ways of dealing with this diversity, and then review the development of the modern study of the gospels.

The Ancient Approach: Reduction

The ancient interpreters who became keenly aware of the differences between the gospels usually chose one of three solutions to the problem: elimination, combination, or harmonization.

Various groups sought to achieve unity by eliminating all but one gospel. Some of Paul's second-century followers accepted only the Gospel of Luke, because they thought Luke had been Paul's traveling companion (see the discussion of Marcion on pp. 125, 127). Others kept only the Gospel of Mark because they felt more comfortable with a gospel that did not show Jesus being born as a baby. Still others attempted to maintain a thoroughly Jewish Christianity, recognizing only Matthew. The Gospel of John also had its champions, as did other gospels, which exist today only as fragments: the *Gospel of the Egyptians* was favored by Gentiles in Egypt while the *Gospel of the Hebrews* was used by Egyptian Jewish Christians.

Obviously each of these groups solved the problem of differences between the various gospels. By choosing to accept only one gospel as authoritative, that version of the gospel became the correct one; the others were simply ignored. Although these reductive attempts to achieve unity by rejecting multiple gospels never gained wide support in the churches, another kind of attempt did gain a wide following.

Sometime around 170 a church leader in eastern Syria set about to solve the problem of the disagreements between the gospels by combining the four gospels into one blended account. Tatian did this by carefully extracting sentences from the various gospels and weaving them together to produce one harmonious account of the words and deeds of Jesus. This monumental work of patience and ingenuity was called the *Diatessaron,* which might be translated "Through the

Four." Notice how cleverly he solves the problems of the empty tomb stories:

Matt. 28:1a	Now on the evening of the sabbath which is the dawn of the first day, at very early dawn, behind the rest
Matt. 28:1b	came Mary Magdalene and the other Mary and the other women to see
Luke 24:1c	the sepulchre, carrying with them the spices which they had prepared.
Mark 16:3	And they said among themselves, Who shall remove for us the stone from the door of the tomb? for it was
Mark 16:4b	exceeding great. And when they said
Matt. 28:2b	so, a great earthquake took place; and an angel descended from heaven, and came and rolled away the stone
Luke 24:2	from the door. And they came and found the stone removed from the
Matt. 28:2b	tomb, and the angel sitting upon the
3	stone. And his appearance was as lightning, and his raiment white as
4	snow: and for fear of him the guards were terrified; and became as dead
Luke 24:3	men. And when he was gone away, the women entered the tomb, and
Mark 16:5b	found not the body of Jesus: but they saw there a young man sitting on the right side, arrayed in a white robe;
Matt. 28:5	and they were amazed. And the angel answered, and said unto the women, Fear not ye: for I know that ye seek Jesus of Nazareth, which
6	hath been crucified. He is not here; for he is risen, even as he said. Come and see the place where our Lord
Luke 24:4	was laid. And while they were perplexed thereabout, behold, two men stood above them in dazzling apparel; and as they were seized with
5	terror, and bowed down their faces to the earth, they said unto them, Why seek ye the living one among
6	the dead? He is not here; he is risen: remember what he spake unto you
7	when he was yet in Galilee, saying, The Son of man is going to be delivered up into the hands of sinners, and to be crucified, and to rise again
Matt. 28:7a	the third day. But go quickly, and

Mark 16:7b

Matt. 28:7c
Luke 24:8
Matt. 28:8

Mark 16:8b

John 20:2

3

tell his disciples and Cephas, that he is risen from the dead; and lo, he goeth before you into Galilee; and there shall ye see him, where he said unto you; lo, I have told you. And they remembered his words; and they departed quickly from the tomb with joy and great fear, and hastened and went their way running; for perplexity and quaking had come upon them: and they said nothing to anyone; for they were afraid. But Mary ran, and came to Simon Cephas, and to that other disciple, whom Jesus loved, and said unto them, They have taken away our Lord out of the tomb, and I know not where they have laid him. Simon therefore went forth and that other disciple. . . .

(The only English edition of the *Diatessaron* is that of Hill, 1894, from which this is quoted: 253–254. But a number of modern works take essentially the same approach; for example, Thomas and Gundry, 1978.)

Amazingly Tatian achieved this agreement by omitting very little, changing only one word (the "but" before John 20:2, which in the original was a "so") and adding a couple of transitions (for example, the "when they said so" to Matt. 28:2).

Still, the effort is not as successful as might first appear. He hides the problems: the Lukan motivation of coming to anoint the body ignores the Matthean version that they come only "to see the sepulchre" (28:1) and is in some tension with the Johannine version in which the anointing was done before burial (John 19:40). Tatian is forced to blend what in his sources are alternatives: When and how to move the stone? Angels or men? Return to Galilee? To tell or not to tell? While he eliminated the discrepancies, and the enormous historical difficulties they present, Tatian distorted the meanings of the individual gospels.

It is easy to see why the *Diatessaron* became a very popular work. In some areas it seems actually to have displaced the four gospels in public reading in the churches. It continued to be used throughout the Middle Ages, though its popularity declined somewhat when Tatian, on other grounds, came to be considered heretical (deviant from the true faith).

A third approach sought to eliminate the contradictions and still preserve the autonomy of the four gospels. Near the end of the second century the bishop of Lyons, Irenaeus, argued that there must be four gospels—no more, no less. Although his arguments strike us today as less than convincing (for example, that the number four is divine), there is also a higher side to Irenaeus' argument, in which he speaks not of four gospels but of a fourfold gospel, the concept that prevailed in Christian thinking (*Against Heresies* III, 11.8). It is reflected in the way early canons were divided: the first section was never called "gospels," but "gospel," with each work being called "the gospel according to . . ." Thus, the church's intellectual solution to the problem of having four gospels is to speak of a gospel within the gospels, a unity in diversity, or as we might say, four versions of one gospel.

Believing in the unity of the gospel took several forms. At one extreme, it involved only the affirmation that a common faith in Jesus underlies all four; at the other there were those who sought to eliminate all discrepancies and harmonize the four on every point.

The most noteworthy of the many practitioners of this art is the fifth-century theologian and bishop, Augustine of Hippo, in North Africa. His *Harmony of the Gospels* was a comprehensive treatment that attempted to eliminate all inconsistencies. His favored solution was to imagine that the discrepancies stem from separate incidents, one not mentioned by either writer. Thus Mark's "young man" in the tomb was just a second angel not mentioned by Matthew, while Mark in turn failed to mention the angel on the oustide (3.24.63). An alternative strategy was to ignore certain differences, as Augustine ignored the problem of when the stone was moved. Some modern harmonizers adopt a similar approach, proposing additional incidents to account for discrepancies. (Lindsell, for example, gives us a sixfold denial for Peter; 1976:175f.)

TRAVELER SAFETY TIPS

American Hotel & Motel Association

1. Don't answer the door in a hotel or motel room without verifying who it is. If a person claims to be an employee, call the front desk and ask if someone from their staff is supposed to have access to your room and for what purpose.

2. When returning to your hotel or motel late in the evening, use the main entrance of the hotel. Be observant and look around before entering parking lots.

3. Close the door securely whenever you are in your room and use all of the locking devices provided.

4. Don't needlessly display guest room keys in public or carelessly leave them on restaurant tables, at the swimming pool, or other places where they can be easily stolen.

5. Do not draw attention to yourself by displaying large amounts of cash or expensive jewelry.

6. Don't invite strangers to your room.

7. Place all valuables in the hotel or motel's safe deposit box.

8. Do not leave valuables in your vehicle.

9. Check to see that any sliding glass doors or windows and any connecting room doors are locked.

10. If you see any suspicious activity, please report your observations to the management.

We Support the National Citizens' Crime Prevention Campaign.
TAKE A BITE OUT OF CRIME®

The difficulty with such harmonization is not that it is impossible, for if one is clever enough, and willing to make enough assumptions, any item of gospel tradition can be harmonized with the rest. The difficulty is the violence that such an approach does to the text. In order to harmonize Luke's version of the resurrection appearances, which happen only in Jerusalem, with Matthew's version, which happens in Galilee, one must seriously distort the story Luke intended to tell. Since we assume that each gospel writer told the story in a particular way for a purpose, our method must attempt to find that purpose. Certainly, these differences complicate our understanding of Jesus and of early Christians, but such complexity is more true to what actually happened. Our task, then, is to explain the differences between the gospels, without explaining them away.

The Modern Approach: Criticism

The words *critic* and *criticism* have negative connotations in our society, but they are not negative endeavors. Critic is from the Greek word *kritikos,* one who is able to discern, to make distinctions. Thus a critic is a person of discernment. Criticism is essentially the positive endeavor to understand literature, or anything else for that matter, by asking disciplined questions designed to elicit the information we want to know. It is analogous to what happens in a court: the judge does not simply let the witness talk; specific questions designed to bring out specific evidence must be answered. So too, the literary critic brings disciplined questions to bear on the literature.

If you are intent on just listening to the story, it can be annoying to have someone always interrupting to ask a question; yet we learn things by asking questions that we could not learn by just listening. And a good critic should be polite enough not to interrupt the story at an inappropriate time.

Unfortunately, biblical critics have not always been so polite. In fact, many of the earliest critics were adamantly opposed to the established Christianity of their time. They experienced this Christianity as a dogmatic restraint on their reason and worked to undermine it. Historically, the modern study of the gospels may be traced back to the Enlightenment in the eighteenth century and is intertwined with the nineteenth-century discovery of history. Both movements presented profound intellectual challenges to the traditional understanding of Christianity. Most regrettably, these controversies have colored the general perception of modern gospel studies. When stripped of all negative presuppositions and intentions, however, nineteenth-century scholars were confronted with a fact of enormous significance: there are discrepancies among the gospels. Critics did not invent the various accounts of the empty tomb; they seek only to explain the great variety of such accounts. Their attempts may be traced through four distinct stages. Though these stages are chronologically successive, with later stages displacing earlier, each successive stage adopts and refines the conclusions of the earlier ones.

Variety from the Use of Different Sources

As children, most of us assumed that the gospel writers simply recorded what happened. When we began to think historically, considering that one gospel must have been written first and that the other gospel writers may have read it before they wrote, we likely assumed that the gospels were written in the order in which they occur in the Bible. Augustine proposed this view in the fifth century and it remained the standard explanation until the rise of critical studies.

Later scholars examined the gospels intently, trying every conceivable combination of interdependence. One thing became clear: three of the gospels were so much alike they must be related in some way, being either directly dependent on each other or all dependent on an earlier gospel. The fourth gospel, John, was remarkably different—in the order of events portrayed, in the selection of events included, and in the interpretation of those events—so different that its dependence on any of the other three was considered doubtful. (These relationships can be seen in miniature by reflecting on the empty tomb narratives examined earlier.) Since three of the gospels seemed to view things in the same way, scholars soon coined the term Synoptic Gospels (from the Greek *opsis,* view, and *syn,* together) to refer to them. The problem of their interrelation became the Synoptic Problem.

But which of the three was written first? While each gospel attracted some champions, the primary battle was fought between proponents of the priority of Matthew (the traditional view) and the proponents of Mark, with Mark soon claiming a near-universal consensus. This consensus is questioned by some critics (notably Farmer, 1976, and his former students), and some scholars feel a need to reexamine the problem. Still, it would be an exaggeration to suggest that the critical consensus has been shaken; the case for this agreement seems well founded.

To examine the problem in detail would lead us out of our way; readers desiring a greater familiarity with the arguments that attempt to prove Mark was written first are invited to read the following digression. Others may safely skip it. Though no one argument by itself is conclusive, taken together they convince most people of the priority of Mark.

Excursus on the Priority of Mark

1. The subject matter of Mark is more extensively found in Matthew and Luke than either of them is found in Mark. While Matthew contains over 90% of Mark, Mark only contains 50% of Matthew. While Luke contains over 50% of Mark, Mark only contains 30% of Luke. In all but three cases, when a Markan passage is missing in Matthew or Luke it is found in the other one. This implies that Mark is the common element for both Matthew and Luke. (See Figure 6.1.)

2. The order of Mark is more clearly reflected in Matthew and Luke than the order of either of them is reflected in Mark. In most instances when either Matthew or Luke di-

verges from the Markan order, the other does not. More important, Matthew and Luke never share a common sequence unless it is shared by Mark. This is seen most dramatically in their beginnings and endings: neither the birth stories nor the resurrection appearances (both lacking in Mark) show any common order in Matthew and Luke. This also suggests that neither Matthew nor Luke had access to the other's gospel.

3. Certain awkward expressions in Mark are either lacking altogether in the other gospels or given in a form that is smoother or less troublesome. In Mark 10:17–18, for example, Jesus seems to draw back from attribution of divinity to himself, whereas in the same story in Matthew 19:16–17 the problem is avoided. Matthew (20:20–28) also reduces the disgrace of James and John by having their mother ask Jesus for their preeminence in the kingdom; in Mark (10:34–45) they ask for themselves. Yet Matthew leaves Jesus' reply in the second person plural, which is appropriate only in the Markan form of the narrative. Numerous minor problems could be cited, but two stand out: Mark attributed a quotation from Malachi to Isaiah (Mark 1:2) and cited the wrong high priest (Mark 2:26, compare I Sam. 21), whereas Matthew was more precise in both instances. (Even some of the manuscripts have attempted to correct Mark's faulty citation.) Mark may well have been working from a list of prophetic "testimonies," which had already combined the words of Malachi with those of Isaiah. Such lists, called *Testimonia,* were relatively common. In regard to the high priest, Mark located the David incident in the time of Abiathar, but Abiathar's father, Ahimelech, was high priest when this incident occurred (I Sam. 21:1–6). Abiathar became high priest before David's reign ended (II Sam. 15:35). David's son Solomon later deposed Abiathar because he had backed his rival to the throne Adonijah (I Kings 2:35). Other such difficulties in Mark

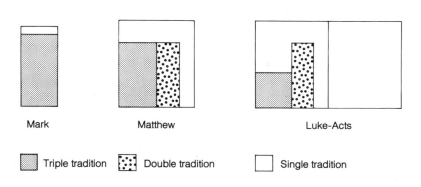

Figure 6 ▪ 1 Shared Traditions This figure shows what the gospels share without regard to the source of the shared material. Mark shares most of its material with the other two; Matthew shares about half its material with the other two plus a sizable portion with Luke alone; Luke shares less than half the material in the gospel with the other two, a large segment with Matthew, and an even larger segment with neither, having more unique material than either Mark or Matthew (including the whole of Acts). John is omitted from this comparison because his gospel has so little in common with the others.

do not appear in Matthew or Luke (for a recent list, see Kee, 1977b:14–16. A complete examination was made by Hawkins, 1909:114–153.) While we must also ask if Mark gained anything by these deviations, they have generally been viewed as primary evidence of Markan priority.

4. It is simply easier to imagine Matthew as an expansion of Mark than vice versa. If Mark were abbreviating Matthew, we would not expect him to omit completely such major Matthean features as the birth stories, the great blocks of teaching material (5–7, 10, 13, 18, 23–25), and the resurrection appearances. Nor would we expect him actually to lengthen many stories by adding incidental details; yet Mark's version of many stories is actually longer than Matthew's (compare Mark 2:1–12 with Matt. 9:1–9). We face even greater problems if we imagine Mark abbreviating Luke or combining it with Matthew when we consider how much of Luke's work is missing in Mark—including the whole of

Acts and the second half of Luke's gospel (discussed in Chapter 9).

Other arguments are often made, but they are usually technical, often obscure, and always inconclusive. These are sufficient for our purpose: to understand the development of the modern study of the gospels. While conclusions of this kind must remain forever tentative, working hypotheses, still conclusions are called for. The evidence adduced by scholars so far supports the view that Mark is the earliest of the gospels, with Matthew and Luke depending directly on Mark.

Once the priority of Mark gained acceptance and Matthew and Luke could be printed in parallel columns, with Mark in the middle, a remarkable discovery emerged: the middle column was often empty. Matthew and Luke share quite a bit of material not found in Mark. Since this other material does not occur in the same order or context in Matthew and Luke, it did not seem probable that one simply copied it from the other.

(Compare Matt. 7:7–11 with Luke 11:9–13.) Thus *Q* was born.

Q is the symbol (from the German *Quelle,* meaning source) that scholars use to designate the material shared by Matthew and Luke alone. It is generally believed to have been a separate written source to which they both had access. Remarkably, however, there is no other trace of its existence: not a single reference to such a document, let alone a copy, has come down to us. Those who do not see Q as a written document usually argue that it represents a widespread oral tradition, available to both Matthew and Luke, though perhaps not as a connected series. On the other hand, it is argued, Q can be reconstructed as an intelligible document.

In addition to the material found in all three synoptic gospels (the triple tradition), and the material found in both Matthew and Luke but not in Mark (Q, or the double tradition) we also find material unique to each gospel. That found in Matthew is generally labeled M, denoting Matthew's private source or sources; that found in Luke is labeled L. There is also material unique to Mark, but scholars to date have taken little account of it.

The general conclusions of source criticism can be clearly represented in Figure 6.2.

One of the least convincing conclusions of source criticism was that the older the source, the more reliable. Scholars in this period had a tendency to prefer the Synoptics to John, to prefer Mark to Matthew and Luke, and to value Q very highly. It was, of course, very congenial to nineteenth-century opinion that Mark made so little of the resurrection: no angels, no earthquakes, no appearances. And Q contains mostly sayings of Jesus, with only one miracle mentioned. We have learned, however, that the historical question is not so simple as to find the earliest source.

The historical question led scholars to the next stage of gospel criticism. For there was a great gap between the time of the events portrayed (before 30) and the earliest possible written source (Q was dated after 50, Mark after 65). Scholars now sought to explore this gap.

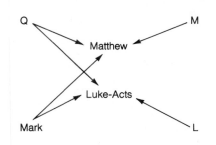

Figure 6 ▪ 2   Gospel Sources The dominant view of the sources of our present gospels is known as the four-source theory. In this scheme, Mark is taken to be the oldest complete gospel and one of the sources for both Matthew and Luke. Matthew and Luke also had access to a common source, Q (from the German *Quelle,* source), and to at least one other source unique to each, called M (for Matthew) and L (for Luke).

Variety from the Oral Transmission of the Tradition

A technique had been elaborated by Old Testament scholars to deal with the tremendous time lapse between events like the Exodus and the recording of those events centuries later. These scholars sought to determine the oral "form" and the typical social setting in which that form would be used for telling each story. Thus, the method is twofold: to determine the form of the tradition (legend, hymn, curse, lament, myth, example story, and so on) and to determine the typical situation in which that form would have been used (hymns would be used in worship, example stories in education). For example, the story of Abraham relinquishing Sarah to Pharaoh in order to protect his life can be shown to fit an early, nomadic situation, probably as a campfire tale (see Koch, 1969:111–132).

This method became known as Form Criticism (in German, *Formgeschichte,* the history of the form). New Testament scholars attempted to apply a similar method to the study of the gospel traditions. Their goals were to determine the source of each tradition and how and why it was preserved (or created) in the period between Jesus and the gospels. Again we notice an attempt to overcome the plurality of traditions and to get back to one "best" tradition.

We have seen that the gospels came into being in an oral, storytelling culture and that traces of the oral tradition are clearly discernible in Paul's letters (pp. 19–23 and 38–39). Obviously, the story of the Last Supper already existed as a narrative within the context of the church's celebration of the Lord's Supper before it was written down in any gospel (see I Cor. 11:23–34).

Other typical situations proposed for the transmission of the oral Jesus traditions include: missionary activity, instruction of new converts, polemics against other Christians or other Jews, the need for church order and discipline, and—above all—proclaiming the good news.

What we must imagine, then, is a rather complex process of transmission of the traditions about Jesus in a variety of forms. It is reasonable to assume that after 30 CE this material existed as a mass of stories and sayings that were used in a variety of contexts (sermons, debates, worship, and so on). This material would be selected and shaped to fit the contexts which transmitted it. Also, given the seeming lack of contact between the gospel of John and the Synoptic Gospels, we should probably posit at least two main channels of transmission: one flowing into the Synoptic Gospels, the other into John. The emerging picture of the history of the traditions behind the gospels may be shown in chart form (Figure 6.3).

Form critics sought to explain the diversity in the gospels by tracing the history of each tradition. Thus the German scholar, Joachim Jeremias, argued that in order to interpret the parables the interpreter must be conscious of the three different situations in which they have been used: the situation of the gospel writer, the situation of the early church and the oral transmitters, and the situation of Jesus. He warned that the meaning of a parable could be different as it moved from one situation to another (1963). Form critics sought to transcend this diversity by uncovering the earliest and most reliable form of the tradition, even as Jeremias sought to discover the meaning of the "parables of Jesus."

In the process, however, they discovered something about the gospels that led in the opposite direction, not back toward a primal unity but forward toward increasing diversity. For the form critics discovered that when they isolated the various units of traditions and constructed their histories, there were things still left: editorial connections, expansions, and conclusions—what one scholar labeled "the framework of the story of Jesus" (Schmidt, 1919). A new method then evolved to deal with this framework.

Variety from the Editing Process

At the end of his monumental volume, suggestively titled *The History of the Synoptic Tradition,* form critic Rudolf Bultmann presented a brief sketch of each gospel. He had begun to see that each writer was doing something unique with the gospel traditions, though he still maintained that "Mark is not sufficiently master of his material to be able to venture on a systematic construction himself" (350).

But as the attention of critics shifted from the tradition before the gospels to the way each gospel writer dealt with that tradition, a new method emerged to analyze the editorial activity of the gospel writers—Redaction Criticism (*Redaktion* being the German word for editing). By means of this analysis of editorial and compositional techniques, these critics hoped to arrive at the specific theological perspective of each writer.

Building on the priority of Mark as established by source criticism and alerted to the existence of editorial activity in the transitions, scholars began to examine the details of the stories and sayings more attentively. It became clear that each writer had a design that shaped the story of Jesus. This movement reached fruition in a brilliant and influential commentary on Luke's gospel by Hans Conzelmann, in which he demonstrated the editorial process at work (1953). Conzelmann showed, for example, that the change

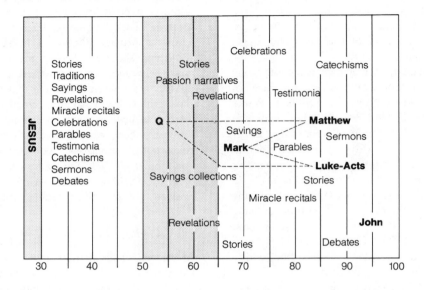

Figure 6 ▪ 3   The Gospels and Oral Traditions   After the death of Jesus the traditions about him passed through three distinct stages. First was the stage of oral traditions, when the stories and sayings of Jesus were transmitted by those who retold them in sermons, debates, and liturgies. The second stage was the collection of similar stories and sayings into longer units. Probably the earliest was the Passion Narrative (stories about Jesus' death), but there were also collections of miracle stories and sayings collections. Some of these collections may have been written down during this stage; scholars believe this was the case with Q. In the third stage written gospels appear, probably beginning with Mark.

Luke made in the geographical reference in the empty tomb narrative (from an appearance in Galilee to a saying in Galilee that he would appear—compare Luke 24:6f with Mark 16:7) is a deliberate reworking of the Markan tradition to fit the geographical scheme that Luke had followed from the beginning. Conzelmann argued that for Luke the culmination of God's saving activity centered in Jerusalem and that it was theologically impossible to shift back to Galilee at this point in his narrative (Conzelmann, 1961:93).

The excitement that many of us felt on our first exposure to redaction criticism is due to the ability of this method to take seriously the dif-

ferences between the gospels, to explain the differences without explaining them away. As scholarly attention to detail increased, so did appreciation of the abilities of the gospel writers. Soon it became evident that the gospel writers were doing more than editing: they were creative authors.[1] As one scholar wrote:

1. To regard the gospel writers as authors is not to suggest that the evangelists made these stories up. Though such complete fiction was possible in the ancient world, it was in fact rarely accomplished. The gospel authors worked with a vast body of tradition, largely fixed, which they molded to their purposes, as did Homer, Aeschylus, Sophocles, and Euripides in varying degree: the stories

ᔬ ᔬ ᔬ

At an earlier period in the history of New Testament scholarship the synoptic gospels (Matthew, Mark and Luke) were thought to be relatively uncomplicated documents which had been put together without careful planning and which told a rather straightforward story. Today the synoptics are understood to be enormously intricate products containing subtle and ingenious literary patterns and highly developed theological interpretations. (Dan O. Via, in Perrin, 1969:v)

Even those who moved beyond redaction criticism regarded it as a great advance over earlier methods, for it called attention to the specific purposes of each gospel writer. Its scope, however, soon seemed limited. The redaction critic concentrated on what was unique to each gospel, what had been edited. But it is possible that the material a writer adopted without change was as important as that which was changed. The attempt to understand the gospels as unified stories has led gospel critics to explore a variety of methods commonly called literary criticism.

Variety from the Writing of Literature

Literary criticism attempts to explore the meaning of the gospels as narrative entities, each with its own organic unity. Narratives differ in fundamental ways from other kinds of literature, creating worlds into which we must enter even before we understand them or decide whether we like them. They do not say; they show. They insist we meet them on their territory on their terms. Narratives involve characters and actions, not discussions of abstract ideas. To understand a narrative, we must discover the unity of its action, the nature of its world, the significance of its characters, and much more.

The means that gospel critics have used to explore the narrative nature of the gospels are extremely rich and diverse. It is not too much to say that every approach of general literary criticism has been applied to the gospels in recent years, often with surprisingly insightful results. Rather than explore these approaches here (many of which will be illustrated in the following chapters) we must consider the central concern of this chapter: How does a literary method address the problem of diversity among the gospels?

While accepting much of the results of earlier kinds of criticism, the literary critic is not content to explain the different versions of the empty tomb story as deriving merely from various sources, different channels of transmission, or different ideas. While each of these may account for some of the variations, there are larger considerations. There is a story at work. Angels and earthquakes, for example, may appear quite natural in some kinds of stories but seem entirely out of place in others. The narrative role fulfilled by the women or the disciples may vary greatly among the different gospels, and this would demand that they respond to the risen Jesus in ways appropriate to their character in a specific story. The logic of one plot may demand a return to the beginning ("Galilee"), while another plot requires continual movement forward. These are the issues raised by literary criticism.

We expect variety in literature, and differences between the Gospels are thus not surprising. Aristotle (384–322 BCE) carefully distinguished between what he called "history" and "poetry," which is approximately what we mean when we distinguish between ordinary writing and literature:

ᔬ ᔬ ᔬ

Poetry, therefore, is more philosophical and more significant than history, for poetry is more concerned with the universal, and history more with the individual. By the universal I mean what sort of man turns out to say or do what sort of thing. . . . By the individual I mean a statement telling, for example, "what Alcibiades did or experienced." (Poetics 1451b, Golden's translation)

---

and myths of classical literature were well known in Greek tradition. We would be wrong to limit literature to the modern notion of fiction.

This, of course, is the basic distinction between art and life: art interprets; life simply is.[2]

It is partly this effort of literature to go beyond the mere telling of an event to an interpretation of its meaning that accounts for differences among the gospels. Since the gospel writers sought to show the meaning of Jesus for their own communities, we must expect them to tell that story differently. In fact, a given writer might vary the telling of a story within a given work. For example, in Euripides' play *Ion,* the rape of Creusa is recounted five times, but each time it is told differently so as to shape the audience's reactions. Closer to our concerns, the story of Paul's inaugural religious experience is recounted in Acts not once but three times—and in three different ways.

Reading and Reflection

Carefully compare the stories given in Acts 9:1–30; 22:1–21; and 26:12–20, noticing all the differences between the accounts. A major thrust of this story is the commissioning of Paul to go to the Gentiles. How does this commission come to Paul in each case?

It seems incredible that when these variations were first noticed they were attributed to the use of different sources, as if even the clumsiest of editors could not have made them agree. But Luke was not a clumsy editor; he was a creative author who introduced these changes for his own reasons.

We will understand those reasons better when we observe how the author has made the mandate to go to the Gentiles fit the audience for whom the story is told. In the first telling, in chapter 9, the telling that the reader automatically regards as the authoritative version, the divine commission comes to Ananias in a voice from God (verse 15). This is probably the normal means by which people were called to service in the Lukan community (see 13:1–3). In the second telling, in chapter 22, the Jewish listeners hear that the divine commissioning came directly to Paul while he was praying in the Temple in Jerusalem, the central holy place of the Jews. In the third telling, in chapter 26, the secular ruler listens to a very abbreviated version of the story in which the divine commission is given in the inaugural vision itself by the epiphany of the risen Jesus (verses 16–18).

We have learned to speak of such changes as "literary license," for we recognize they are necessary for telling a story. In a sense each is true, for it does not change the basic meaning of the event; each is also appropriate for the place where it appears in the overall narrative. Unlike history, art does not need exact correspondence. As an ancient critic observed:

❧ ❧ ❧

Now I am well aware that the greatest natures are least immaculate. Perfect precision runs the risk of triviality, whereas in great writing as in great wealth there must needs be something overlooked. (Longinus, On The Sublime *33:1)*

Thus, in great art we must expect to find some imprecision, some disorder. If we refuse to "overlook" some of these inconsistencies, we will actually overlook a good deal of what the gospels have to tell us. Luke's writing would be the poorer if he flatly repeated exactly the same story each time; just as our understanding will be the poorer if we refuse to accept the different versions of the story in their variety, insisting that they be harmonized. Instead, being aware of their differences leads us to a more fruitful interpretation of the intention and meaning of the writer. Careful study of the discrepancies between the gospels, coupled with a literary analysis, will likewise lead us into a fresh understanding of what each writer was trying to say to the community for which he wrote.

---

2. It must be noted that the distinction cannot be taken at face value with regard to modern history writing. Modern historians aim to present meaningful history, an interpretation of the past, and not simply a chronicle of what happened.

Our Approach

In the chapters that follow, the four gospels will be studied using the results of these several forms of criticism. Each has something valuable to contribute to our understanding as long as we are aware of what each is capable of doing. Like tools, we must use the various methods to accomplish the ends for which each was designed. Here we will make only modest use of **source criticism,** since we will not focus on the origins of the gospel traditions. In general, I accept the conclusions of source criticism, though I am not convinced that later writers necessarily used earlier written sources. The oral gospel was a potent source throughout the first century and all the gospel writers had some access to it. While the hypothesis of Markan priority will be recognized when it reveals something interesting about the narratives studied, the basic analysis that follows is not dependent on that or any other source theory.

Form criticism asks two kinds of questions: What is the literary form of a particular unit of gospel tradition and what is the pre-Gospel history of such a unit. Again, we will devote only scant attention to the history of the traditions, but will often be interested in the literary form of a given tradition. The insights such analysis provides into the units of tradition will assist in our larger task: understanding the gospels as a whole.

More useful for our purposes are the questions asked by **redaction criticism**—questions that concentrate on what each writer has done to shape the traditions used. Often we will study the individual gospel traditions in detail, revealing (and trying to explain) their differences. However, our approach differs in two important ways from traditional redaction criticism. We are not primarily concerned with the ideas of the writers, since we do not view the gospels as ideas presented in the form of stories. We are interested in the stories themselves. Second, we do not depend on the conclusions of source criticism as confidently as many redaction critics. It is not necessary, for example, to believe that Mark is the source of Matthew in order to be instructed by their differences. This demonstrates how redaction criticism shades off into literary criticism.

For the variations among the gospel accounts of a given incident reveal, at the least, different ways of telling the story. Viewed this way, Mark's differences from Matthew are just as significant as Matthew's differences from Mark, or from John's for that matter. It is not a question of sources and their modification, but rather of a close reading of the texts in comparison with other ways of recounting the incident.

Primarily, our approach will pursue the questions raised by **literary criticism**—the plots of the stories, their ways of portraying characters, their images, devices, and points of view. Our chief concern is to understand these writings as unified narratives. Thus, we will begin in each instance with the question of how each is structured, including the nature of its plot. Here, it will be useful to clarify some of the terms used to describe how the gospels are organized. Some writers speak of outlines, others of structures or plots or narratives or stories.

The definitions of these terms vary somewhat from writer to writer. In general, an *outline* represents the formal ordering of ideas to show their logic and relationships. We use an outline when we write an essay or theme. One might outline a speech or sermon, but one would never outline a joke or a story, not in the formal sense of the concept at least. Thus, when the gospels were viewed primarily as sermons or theological treatises it seemed appropriate to outline them, but if the gospels are stories, an outline is inadequate for grasping their significance.

A *story* refers to a sequence of events, usually chronological, which form a pattern—an imitation of life as it is or might be. A story is told in a *narrative,* which recounts a story in a specific set of circumstances. This means that the narrative world is limited to the specific events narrated, while the story world is the larger reality that includes all the narrative implies. Hence, a narrative that ends "and they lived happily ever after" implies a story world of indefinite duration and bliss that goes beyond the narrative itself. A narrative represents the plotting of the specific incidents of the story. A story is distinct from a plot, though it will always have a plot when it is narrated. The same story may be told through a variety of plots, each subtly shaping its meaning.

Plot refers to the sequence of events in a narrative, the movement of the action. Aristotle defined plot as the relationship between the incidents (*Poetics* 1450a 51), the cause-and-effect logic that binds the incidents together and mandates that one follow the other. As one literary critic has suggested, the sequence: "the king died and then the queen died" is a story that lacks a plot. "The king died and then the queen died of grief" represents a story with a plot (Forster, 1962: 87). Now a causal relationship exists between the incidents.

A plot, again according to Aristotle, is marked by a beginning, a middle, and an end (1450b:27–32). The beginning is what we might consider an appropriate place to start, one that does not seem random or in need of justification. Middle incidents must then proceed in logical fashion from one to another, each growing out of the one before, until the plot reaches a conclusion—an appropriate place to stop. An end is a satisfying final incident that follows logically from what went before, but that needs no further incident to be understood.

Structure is related to the concept of plot, since it too deals with the ordering principle of a work. Yet it is a deeper sort of order than plot—the underlying pattern by which we intuit the meaning of a plot. One of the fascinating hypotheses of modern scholarship in several disciplines—from anthropology to literature, from history to linguistics—is that all human activity is structured.

Thus linguists talk of a structure to language that is deeper than word order, a grammar that allows us to make sense of words and sentences. So too, it will be argued here, a series of structures or patterns underlie the gospels' narratives and help shape their meanings. Our approach to comprehending these structures will be indirect, using the correlative concept of plot. The goal

for us is not to outline topics found in a given gospel, but rather to understand the organizing principles that shape and inform each of the Jesus stories.

Following the contours of their structures, we will examine each narrative in detail, focusing especially on those topics and concerns that scholars have raised in dealing with each work. Finally, we will try to place each writing in the social and historical context of the community for which it was written.

A word of caution is in order: the movement from narrative to history is a complicated one and not easily negotiated. We must attempt to speak historically about the gospels without committing the historicist error of assuming they are merely telling us "what happened." Though Jesus, Peter, Mary, and the others were real people with real personalities, we must be clear that we are not encountering these real people in the stories. Rather, we encounter characters shaped and defined by the various authors. The Jesus of Mark's Gospel may accurately reflect the Jesus of history (a topic we will address in the final chapter), but the two are certainly not identical. The gospels present us not with candid snapshots but with artistic portraits, each characterizing Jesus in ways deemed revealing to the community for which it was written.

Similarly, we must not assume that the disciples in the stories are simply the historical disciples; nor should we readily identify the Jews portrayed in these stories with the historical community of Jesus' time, or even of the time of the author. To do so would be to allegorize the stories, interpreting them as if they were about something outside the story. These stories are not windows on the real world; they are mirrors reflecting both that world and the author and audience they imply. These two views of the gospels may be graphically represented (Figure 6.4).

Now let us turn to the stories. We will study them in the order in which they were probably written, which is also a logical order, moving from the more simple narrative of Mark to the increasingly complex narratives of the other writings.

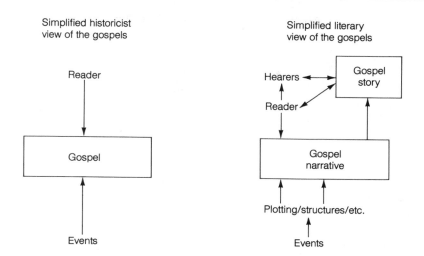

Figure 6 ▪ 4 Gospels and History A historicist reading of the Gospels imagines that the reader has direct access to the events of history by merely reading the gospels: the gospels are a window on the world. A literary reading of the gospels imagines a number of intermediate stages. While real events stand behind the gospel narratives, literary factors like plotting, and structures of story and perception determine how those events will be used in the gospel narratives. On the other side, a reader would recite these narratives to hearers, in part shaping their perception. This reader and the hearers would also be influenced by their general understanding of the gospel story, the overall story of Jesus with which they were familiar. Viewed this way, we should not be too quick to assume that what these hearers heard can be equated with the actual events.

RESOURCES FOR FURTHER STUDY

An excellent introductory survey of the methods of biblical interpretation is Harrington, 1979, *Interpreting the New Testament*. There is also a series of fine introductory works published by Fortress Press:

McKnight, 1969, *What Is Form Criticism?*
Perrin, 1969, *What Is Redaction Criticism?*
Petersen, 1978, *Literary Criticism for New Testament Critics*.

The standard reference work, a virtual history of New Testament scholarship, is Kümmel, 1972. An explanation and evaluation of these methods by religiously conservative scholars is the collection edited by Marshall, 1977a.

More advanced students will want to consult some of the seminal works:

Source criticism: Streeter, 1924; and Farmer, 1976a (the minority report).
Form criticism: Bultmann, 1931; and Dibelius, 1935.
Redaction criticism: Bornkamm et al., 1963; and Conzelmann, 1961.

For works on literary criticism, see the resources following the Introduction.

The standard collection of "other" gospels, those that did not become a part of the canon, is Hennecke and Schneemelcher, 1963, vol. 1. A paperback collection is now available in Cameron, 1982.

God's Kingdom in a Tragic World

ॐ ॐ ॐ

The Gospel according to Mark

7

The Gospel according to Mark, the shortest and simplest of the gospels, is also probably the earliest. Thus it is a suitable work for beginning our analysis of this new kind of literature. But Mark's Gospel is also carefully crafted and engagingly written. Here we will first consider the organization of the work, especially its plot and structure, then turn our attention to its portrayal of the meaning of Jesus and of the Kingdom of God. Finally, we will attempt to relate that picture to the historical and social setting of its first hearers.

THE STRUCTURE OF MARK'S GOSPEL

The gospel we know as Mark is really an anonymous work; nowhere does it reveal the slightest clue to the identity of its author. When it became necessary to associate each canonical writing with a specific apostle, church leaders in the second century attributed this gospel to John Mark, declaring him to be a companion of Peter, the ultimate source of the gospel. Peter and Mark are associated in Acts (12:25), II Timothy (4:11), and I Peter (5:13). But the evidence connecting either of them to this gospel is late.

The fourth-century historian Eusebius summarizes the tradition that Mark wrote this gospel after Peter's death to preserve the tradition (*The History of the Church* 3.39.15). Unfortunately he also implies that Mark died "in the eighth year of Nero's reign" (64 CE), which would mean that he died before Peter (*Hist.* 2.24.1). We simply do not know how soundly based these conclu-

sions are, and nothing in the gospel itself would suggest a connection with Mark or Peter. It might be more fruitful to consider why the gospel makes no claim to authorship than to try to prove that it was or was not written by Mark. If I continue to call the author Mark, I mean no more than the anonymous author of the gospel called Mark.

Whoever this Mark was, he had neither a good command of Greek nor a polished style, but he did create one of the most powerful literary works of the Roman era, in the process molding a new literary form, the gospel.

Seeking Mark's Pattern and Organization

One trait of gospel literature, as opposed to a Greek tragedy for instance, is the diversity of incidents included. Yet these incidents are arranged in a meaningful order. A device I have found useful on first approaching a gospel is to try to ascertain the characteristic themes or motifs of that writer keeping track of how those themes are used.

Reading and Reflection

Read the entire Gospel of Mark, making some sort of chart that will enable you to keep track of at least these four themes:

1. *Miracles* of healing, exorcism, or mastery of nature performed by Jesus.
2. *Popularity* attributed to Jesus.

3. *Opposition* to Jesus by his antagonists (foe or friend!).
4. *Suffering* by Jesus, either predicted or experienced.

Having read the gospel and recorded your results, try to ascertain the pattern which underlies Mark's use of these themes. The following is my analysis; compare it with yours.

———————

Mark's version of Jesus' "life" has shaped our general understanding of Jesus: his miracles led to his popularity. At first glance, the dynamic of the story is relatively simple:

miracles →   popularity →   opposition →   suffering

Notice that the two ends are opposites: miracles imply power, while suffering implies weakness. Eventually we must seek the logic by which the "man of power" becomes the "man of suffering," but for now let's examine more closely the actual arrangement of the incidents.

The way Mark uses the motif of Jesus' suffering is perhaps clearest. The first explicit reference to suffering occurs at 8:31, and is labeled as a new development ("Jesus *began* to teach . . ."). From then on references to suffering multiply, climaxing in the agony of the crucifixion.

In contrast, nearly all the miracles happen before this reference at 8:31. The three that occur afterward are strikingly different in character from the earlier ones: they do not promote Jesus' popularity. Those that take place before 8:31, however, produce an ever-increasing adulation of Jesus. At 1:22 they are astonished at his teaching; at 1:27f his exorcism miracle "amazes" them, raising the question of his authority and spreading his fame (demonstrated in a vignette in 1:32–34). After healing a leper, Jesus is so popular that he "could no longer openly enter a town" (1:45). At 2:12, after he heals a paralytic, the people exclaim, "We never saw anything like this." His next miracle produces the first opposition (3:6), but a great multitude follows him (3:7)—so great that he cannot even eat (3:20). A nature miracle prompts them to ask: "Who then is this that even the wind and the sea obey him" (4:41). More and more astounding miracles occur, coupled with increasing popularity (5:20, 42; 6:51, 55), until we learn: "They were astonished beyond measure, saying 'He has done all things well'" (7:37). This, the strongest expression of Jesus' popularity in this gospel, marks the climax of the first movement of the plot.

If the work ended here, it would be a sufficiently interesting story, not unlike many others written to praise famous men. But Mark now turns the plot completely around: the undercurrent of opposition (2:7; 3:6, 21f; 6:4f; 7:5f; 8:15) swells to a torrent; the guiding motifs of miracle and popularity ebb to nothing.

The turning point of the plot is reached in a marvelous scene that answers the question raised earlier: Who then is this? The scene itself is bracketed by Jesus' question, "Do you not yet understand?" (8:21), and by his ironic declaration: "There are some standing here who will not taste death till they see the kingdom of God come with power" (9:1).

Reading and Reflection

Reread this section (8:21–9:1) several times, considering the following questions:

1. How does Mark characterize the understanding of "man?"
2. Is Peter's understanding any better? Contrast the portrayal in Matthew 16:13–28, paragraph 122 in *Gospel Parallels* and 158 in *Synopsis of the Four Gospels*.
3. What does Mark suggest is the true understanding of Jesus' identity?
4. What is the connection of the very odd healing episode that forms the preface to this scene (8:22–26)?

———————

A standard scene in literature reveals the true identity of the hero, followed by a reversal of the action. Such a scene occurs in *Oedipus the King,* when the shocking news is delivered: Oedipus is the son of the king he has slain and of the queen he has wed. His identity precipitates his fate. So too, in Mark Jesus' identity engenders his fate. And a new understanding of Jesus as well as a new action begins in this crucial scene. But who achieves this new insight? It is not, as we often find, the hero himself. Mark portrays Jesus as already knowing (see 1:11, where the voice addresses Jesus directly). Nor is it the disciples, as Peter's subsequent rebuke shows (8:32). Instead, the hearers of the gospel story, who have witnessed Jesus' power and must now see his weakness, must realize that the Jesus who worked miracles was the Jesus who suffered and died. Like the blind man, the hearer achieves this "sight" in two stages.

Let us reflect for a moment on the privileged position of the hearer. In the opening scene, at Jesus' baptism (1:9–11), the hearer is offered special insight into Jesus that no one else in the story shares: this Jesus is the Son of God. In Mark's telling, only Jesus and the reader/hearers know what the heavenly voice reveals.

At the same time, the character with which the hearer most closely identifies is surely that of the disciples. While the crowds marvel, the disciples' response to Jesus shapes the first half of the narrative, which begins with their call (1:16), moves to the special appointment of the Twelve (3:12–19), and then to their special mission (6:7–13). We have learned to identify with this group and it is a little disconcerting that they fail to adjust to this new revelation about Jesus' suffering. Their confusion helps the hearer gain clarity and causes us to wonder if we really understand. Let us now examine the second stage, after which we should see clearly.

This second stage of the plot itself has two movements: a cycle of three predictions of Jesus' death (8:31; 9:31; 10:33), each followed by an interchange with the disciples showing they do not yet understand (8:32f; 9:32–34; 10:43–45). The whole section concludes with another blind man receiving his sight, this time with immediate results, including following Jesus (10:52). These two stories of blind men thus serve to frame this section, which focuses on understanding Jesus' death.

The second movement concentrates on the death itself, including the events leading to the crucifixion. The death scene, portrayed in the starkest possible terms, is not overshadowed by a resurrection appearance, for the original text of Mark does not seem to have included an appearance of the risen Jesus (see discussion on pp. 164–166). This stark crucifixion scene allows the hearer to grasp the implications of the last part of the scene of recognition, since after predicting his own death, we are told that Jesus

❧ ❧ ❧

called to him the multitude with his disciples, and said to them, "If any man would come after me, let him deny himself and take up his cross and follow me. For whoever would save his life will lose it; and whoever loses his life for my sake and the gospel's will save it. For what does it profit a man, to gain the whole world and forfeit his life? For what can a man give in return for his life?" (8:34–37)

This call to follow Jesus to a cross contrasts sharply with the portrayal of Jesus as the miracle worker that dominates the first half of Mark's gospel. Now we must ask: How exactly are these incidents linked? How are they plotted?

Plot and Structure

To summarize our preliminary observations, this gospel is structured into two halves: the first half dominated by miracle, the second by suffering. They hinge on the declaration that Jesus, and thus his followers, advances toward a cross. What then, is the relationship between these two halves of the gospel?

Perhaps our best indication of the relation between the portrayal of Jesus as the powerful healer and the portrayal of Jesus as the sufferer is found in the short, almost humorous, scene of the blind man whom Jesus had trouble healing. For the first half of the gospel reminds us of Jesus' first attempt to heal this hapless fellow. Jesus' use of physical means produces some sight, albeit distorted. Just so, the miraculous deeds of Jesus can lead to faith in him. But, like Peter's confession, such faith remains incomplete.

Only in the second half, the portrayal of Jesus' death, will everything become "clear," and then only by looking intently (8:25). Only careful scrutiny will reveal what it means to be a follower of the Jesus who suffers and dies.

Mark has highlighted this structure by his use of four declarations that Jesus is the "Son of God"—a title often associated with wonder workers in Mark's time. The first declaration is made by Mark in the opening sentence:

☙ ☙ ☙

The beginning of the gospel of Jesus Christ, The Son of God. (1:1)

The second declaration inaugurates Jesus' public ministry and is addressed to Jesus:

And a voice came from heaven, "Thou art my beloved Son, with thee I am well pleased." (1:11)

This voice dramatically confirms Mark's own declaration and takes the hearers into the story by revealing to us a secret not known to any of the characters in the story except Jesus. The hearers know who Jesus really is. Mark gives no indication that any of the other characters in the story have heard the voice: notice that, unlike some other portrayals of this scene, it is addressed only to Jesus.

But what might the earliest audience of this gospel have understood when they heard Jesus was the "Son of God?" We cannot be entirely sure, but one likely context was the very popular understanding that certain men were in some way

divine. They were usually great philosophers (Pythagoras) or great miracle workers (Asclepius)—perhaps both (Apollonias of Tyana). The miracle worker would, obviously, show his divinity by the mighty deeds he performed. The wise man demonstrated his divinity by his extraordinary competence, both in debate and in the strength and moral courage he displayed during trials. A Jewish writer contemporary with Mark, Josephus, portrayed Moses as a divine man (*Against Apion* 1.31).

Mark's characterization of Jesus in the first half of this gospel shares much with the conception of the divine man as miracle worker. Surely some in Mark's community were inclined to view him that way. Mark frustrates this inclination when he introduces the idea that Jesus will suffer and die, an idea the disciples cannot hear because they have already concluded that Jesus' power to work miracles precludes such a fate. The third assertion of Jesus' divine status addresses this tension.

This declaration comes at the end of the miracle section, following the scene of reversal in which Jesus declares he must suffer. It is addressed to the disciples:

☙ ☙ ☙

A voice came out of the cloud,
"This is my beloved Son;
listen to him." (9:7)

This command to listen should be understood in relation to what Jesus has just said about his suffering and the nature of being a disciple (8:31–9:1), but it becomes painfully obvious that the disciples have not listened. Will anyone?

The fourth declaration, that Jesus is son of God, occurs at the end of the crucifixion scene. It is spoken, not by a voice from heaven, but by an outsider, the one who supervised Jesus' death:

☙ ☙ ☙

and when the centurion who stood facing him saw that he thus breathed his last, he said, "Truly this man was the Son of God." (15:39)

This is Mark's bold assertion that only when one sees how Jesus suffered and died can one truly understand who he is. The incidents of his gospel are plotted to make this evident to the hearer.

Thus, the hearer has been assured by the narrator, by the divine voice, and by the action of the story itself that Jesus is the son of God. By this structural device Mark crafts his plot and reveals the shape of his gospel as a gospel of suffering. The way Mark shapes his material is meant to show that Jesus' real divinity must be seen in the manner of his death. The form of Mark's Gospel may be visually represented as follows:

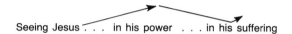

Seeing Jesus . . . in his power . . . in his suffering

With some reluctance, but with a sense of necessity, I suggest the following guide to Mark's structure. My reluctance springs from the way such a guide will inevitably distort the dynamic of a narrative like Mark's. Yet, I have found it necessary to find some pattern by which I can hold the whole of the narrative in my mind as I read parts of it. You may wish to refer to it as

you read more of Mark's story. Notice that this is not an outline and its intention is not to divide the writing into parts. Instead, it aims to reveal the connections between the parts. Thus the scene of recognition and reversal actually overlaps both the first and second movements of the action. Keeping in mind this structure of the gospel as a whole, let us now examine some of its parts in more detail.

THE PRESENCE OF GOD:
Kingdom and Power

The story opens with "the voice of one crying in the wilderness prepare the way of the Lord." Since there was no punctuation in Greek in Mark's time, we may wonder whether Mark intended "in the wilderness" to describe where the voice was crying or where the way of the Lord was to be prepared. The logic of the rest of the scene will favor the latter, but in either case, we learn that preparations are under way for the coming of the Lord.

That God would one day come to his people and rule over them, establishing the Kingdom of

---

READING GUIDE TO MARK

The time of preparation: in the wilderness 1:1–15
The first movement: power and popularity 1:16–9:8
   The call of disciples and the popularity of Jesus 1:16–3:11
   The twelve appointed: insiders and outsiders 3:12–6:6
   The mission of the twelve: power and astonishment 6:7–8:30
The scene recognition and reversal 8:21–9:8
   The healing 8:22–26
   The confession 8:27–30
   The prediction and rebuke 8:31–33

The demand 8:34–9:1
The revelation 9:2–8
The second movement: suffering and abandonment 8:31–15:47
   The three predictions: The disciples failure 8:22–10:52
   The death of Jesus: not to be served 11:1–15:47
      Controversy in Jerusalem 11:1–12:44
      Discourse on the end 13
      The betrayal and crucifixion 14:1–15:47
The time of preparation: at the tomb 16:1–8

God on earth, was a dream of many from ancient times. That idea took on added significance in the centuries after the Exile (587 BCE) when there were no more kings to sit on the throne of David. That kingdom was longed for and dreamed of as a time when universal peace and brotherhood would prevail (for example, Isa. 43, 49).

Although Jewish notions of both the nature of the kingdom and the means of its coming varied widely, from those who withdrew into the wilderness to quietly await God's time to those who took up arms in open rebellion, one main strand of tradition centered on the coming "anointed one" (*Messiah* in Hebrew, *Christ* in Greek). This Messiah was often seen as a second David, who would act with the power of God to establish justice and peace among the nations. Mark's use of the title Christ and his portrayal of Jesus' immense power raise the question of his view of the nature and coming of the kingdom.

A Closer Look at the Opening

"The beginning of the gospel of Jesus Christ, the Son of God." So the story begins, with an incomplete sentence that functions as a title to the work. This identification of Jesus as the Christ and the Son of God warns us to expect no mere history of "just what happened." Clearly this is history seen through the eyes of faith. It is history presented as "gospel," though what Mark meant by that term is not completely clear.[1] It had connotations of a victory pronouncement and of a story of happy news about a favorable event (pp. 135–136).

The beginning that Mark chooses is itself curious, for the story starts neither with Jesus' birth nor background (though the writer knew at least some background information—see 6:3). Instead, it begins in the middle of things, not with Jesus but with John the Baptist. To understand this, we need to study Mark's opening scene in

1. He also used the term at 1:14, 15; 8:35; 10:29; 13:10; 14:9.

relation to some of the expectations held by people at that time.

Reading and Reflection

Carefully study Mark 1:1–15 and try to answer the following:

1. Where do these events take place? Why?
2. How does Mark differentiate between Jesus and John?
3. Exactly what does Jesus preach?

James Robinson noticed a curious shift in Mark's language: though the beginning of the gospel is announced in 1:1, the gospel is not *preached* until after John is put in prison (1:14). Whereas verse 2 is cast in the future tense (what will happen), verse 15 uses the perfect tense to declare that the kingdom "has come." (Or perhaps, "has drawn near"—in either case something has taken place. See Robinson, 1957:24).

On the basis of this language, the events portrayed in verses 2–13 seem to be highly significant for understanding Mark's view of the kingdom of God. The events narrated here allow the kingdom to be proclaimed as an experience, not merely as a future expectation. Mark has carefully structured these events into a dynamic unit with its own logic, which reveals the basic purpose of his story.

The pattern that Mark adopts here is known as *inclusion* or *framing:* notice how the references to the gospel in verses 1 and 15 frame the whole incident. Another obviously balanced pair concerns John: his appearance (4) and his arrest/disappearance (14). In fact, each successive unit is matched with another so that the pairs form successive frames around a middle unit. You might visualize it as a series of parentheses: ((((⌢)))); or as an "X," where the lines converge on a midpoint. In fact, the ancients called this "an X-like pattern." The Greek letter "chi" looks like an X, so the pattern was called a *chiasmus* (pronounced kee-as'-muss). The passage could be visualized thus:

Beginning of the Gospel (1)
  Description of the messenger and his message (2–3)
    Beginning of John's ministry (4–6)
    John proclaims a stronger one is coming (7–8)
      Axial scene: Jesus' baptism (9–11)
    Jesus withstands Satan (12–13)
    End of John; beginning of Jesus' ministry (14)
  The message of Jesus (14–5)
Proclaiming of the gospel (15)

More simply, we can visualize three scenes: the first dominated by John, the last by Jesus, and the middle involving them both.

Now we must ask the crucial question: What logic binds these units together? What is their plot? Let us work from the middle out, as a chiasmus implies. The central scene may be taken as the empowerment of Jesus for his divine task, his inauguration. The Psalm quoted here was one used in the coronation of the king in ancient Israel (Ps. 2). This empowerment grows out of John's previous assertion that one stronger is coming who will "baptize with Holy Spirit." It leads directly to Jesus' encounter with Satan "in the wilderness." We must not let our familiarity with other versions of this incident influence our interpretation of Mark. He says nothing of the nature of this "temptation" nor does he say Jesus fasted. He does not describe it as a temptation to sin or weakness. Instead, he associates the experience with wild beasts and angels. The word translated "tempted" can equally well mean "tested," and it is no accident that this encounter is paired with the reference to Jesus as one "stronger." That Mark intended this scene to show Jesus' conquest of the power of Satan is made clear by an incident occurring a little later in Mark's story.

Jesus' mastery over demonic forces will lead to a severe charge being leveled against him by his opponents: he can expel demons because he is in league with their master. Jesus will reply to this charge with a little parable that also represents what Mark thinks happened in the wilderness encounter. The parable tells us no one can enter a strong man's house and spoil his possessions unless he is stronger and overpowers the strong man first (3:27). That Jesus is now freeing the demon possessed means that he has overcome the power of Satan: hence the "victory pronouncement," the gospel, with which Jesus returned from the wilderness (1:14).

Now we can also see why Mark began with the quotation from Scripture, for this is the time of prophetic fulfillment:

≥a   ≥a   ≥a

As it is written in Isaiah the prophet,
Behold, I send my messenger before thy face,
who shall prepare thy way;
The voice of one crying
in the wilderness prepare the way of the Lord,
make his paths straight. (1:2–3)

While Mark appears to be quoting Isaiah, he has actually crafted three separate references from the Scriptures into one saying: the part about sending a messenger is from Malachi (3:1); the part about "before thy face" is from Exodus (23:20); and the part about the voice and the preparation is from Isaiah (40:3). It was not unusual for writers in Mark's time to combine such sayings in a creative way, for they believed that each revealed the words of God and therefore need not be read in terms of the original context. It was unusual to attribute the combined quote to one source (Isaiah); more often the author would write "in the prophets" or some such general heading (some late manuscripts of Mark actually make this correction). Possibly, the three quotes were already combined before Mark and he recognized the Isaiah reference. Or maybe he wanted to emphasize the Isaiah aspect of the quotation. For each of these three sources contributes something unique to the effect of the combined saying.

The Malachi prophecy in its original setting eventually identified the messenger with Elijah (Mal. 4:5). As we saw in Chapter 1, it was generally expected that Elijah would return as a final prophet who would prepare God's people for his coming to them.

The Exodus passage shows the messenger to be both a guide and a protector who would bring the people to the promised land, the kingdom. It implies that the messenger leads the people, preparing their way.

The Isaiah passage, which Mark emphasizes, locates the place where salvation begins: in the wilderness. Though Jesus is already in the wilderness (1:4), he is driven "into the wilderness" by the coming of the Spirit (1:12f). And for good meaure, Mark adds, "And he was in the wilderness forty days, tested by Satan." As Scripture predicted, salvation has begun in the wilderness, a place traditionally associated with the demonic, and now the victory announcement can be made.

Further reading bears out this conclusion. The exorcisms, for example, are not "struggles," but a mere extension of the power of God's kingdom. When Jesus encounters the demons, their response is fear, even worship, and instantaneous obedience (1:24; 5:6–7). While we should not make too much of these exorcisms—there are, after all, only two—they do reveal the kind of world Mark's story creates.

The World of Apocalyptic Expectation

Exorcisms are not, in themselves, unique to the gospels, or even to Jewish and Christian literature. A Roman writing about a Greek wonder-working philosopher includes an exorcism, and comparing the way this tale is told with the Markan exorcisms will highlight the way in which Mark viewed the world:

≈   ≈   ≈

And when he told them to have handles on the cup and to pour over the handles—this being a purer part of the cup since no one's mouth touched that part—a young boy began laughing coarsely, scattering his discourse to the winds. Apollonius stopped and, looking up at him, said, "It is not you that does this arrogant thing, but the demon who drives you unwittingly," for, unknown to everyone, the youth was actually possessed by a demon, for he used to laugh at things no one else did and would fall to weeping for no reason and would talk and sing to himself. Most people thought it was the jumpiness of youth which brought him to do such things, and at this point he seemed carried away by drunkenness, but it was really a demon which spoke through him. Thus, when Apollonius began staring at it, the phantom in the boy let out horrible cries of fear and rage sounding like someone being burned alive or stretched on the rack, and he began to promise that he would leave the young boy and never possess anyone else among men. But Apollonius spoke to him angrily such as a master might to a cunning and shameless slave, and he commanded him to come out of him, giving definite proof of it. "I will knock down that statue there," it said, pointing toward one of those around the porch of the King. And when the statue tottered and then fell over, who can describe the shout of amazement that went up and how everyone clapped their hands from astonishment. But the young boy opened his eyes, as if from sleep, and looked at the rays of the sun [i.e., at Zeus, who had delivered him]. Now all those observing these events revered the boy, for he no longer appeared to be as coarse as he was, nor did he look disorderly, but had come back to his own nature nothing less than if he had drunk some medicine. He threw aside his fancy soft clothes and stripping off the rest of his luxuriousness, he came to love poverty and the thread-bare cloak and the customs of Apollonius. (The Life of Apollonius of Tyana, IV, 20 by Flavius Philostratus; quoted from Cartlidge and Dungan, 1972)

Apollonius was roughly contemporary with Mark, though this work was not written until about 200 CE. Some influence from the gospel tradition cannot be entirely discounted. Such tales were common in that century, but we must also notice some crucial differences between this and Mark's accounts.

This account of Apollonius lacks any sense of two antithetical worlds, any cosmic conflict between the Spirit and Satan, any notion of the impending end of the old order now invaded by some outside force—all of which are primary themes in Mark. Apollonius's mastery over the demon is even compared to that of a master over his slave, the very charge leveled against Jesus in Mark's story (3:22).

In contrast, Mark's story is embedded in that view of the world we now call apocalypticism, the origin and basic notions of which we have already explored (see pp. 43–45). Apocalypticism rests on the notion of a cosmic struggle between God and Satan, who, as the prince of this world (or this age), is seen to be in control of life. However, Satan's time is short and his actions will grow increasingly desperate. Thus the catastrophic events of "the present time"—sometimes called the "birth pangs" of the new age (13:8)—indicate the imminent arrival of the end.

Apocalypticism took many forms and displayed an amazing array of ideas. One form was Christian; for apocalyptic thought forms were useful to some Christians to interpret what was happening in Jesus of Nazareth. The opening scene of Mark's gospel presupposes an apocalyptic view of the world, but with one decided difference: it shows Jesus as already having overcome Satan. The "good news" is news of present victory. Thus Jesus already possesses power and authority over demons (6:7), over disease (3:15), even the authority to forgive sins (2:10).

All this is fairly easy to grasp. It is all played out by the time we reach chapter eight. Some such insight, as this, we must imagine, is what Peter had grasped when he saw that Jesus was the Christ (8:29). Why, then, does Jesus respond with the demand that Peter not tell anyone (8:30)?

The Great Secret

When scholars first saw that Mark was doing far more than reporting the facts about Jesus, they noticed especially his editing of the material to introduce a theme of secrecy. Initially this was interpreted as a fault: Mark could no longer be considered a good historical source (Wrede, 1901). But this was to ask Mark to do what he never intended; he did not write history. He wrote a gospel.

Scholars now realize that our primary concern must be to find how the theme of secrecy functions in Mark's narrative. When we ask the question this way, we gain some insight into the meaning of the gospel.

Two kinds of secrecy material first catch the readers' attention. Jesus enjoins strict silence on the demons and unclean spirits he exorcised (3:11–12; also 1:25; 1:34; but not 5:6–13), and he also regularly demands silence from those he has healed (1:44; 5:43; 7:36; 8:26; perhaps 5:19; but not 9:14–29 or 10:46–52). A third kind of material is soon evident: Jesus repeatedly attempts to hide (7:24; 1:35; 3:7; 6:31; 10:1).

Mark seems to be trying to conceal the fact that Jesus is the Messiah, thus Wrede originally called this the "Messianic secret." He supposed Mark was trying to explain why Jesus had not been recognized as the Messiah: Jesus hid. But is that a Markan concern? Probably not. Mark is writing for an audience that has no difficulty in recognizing Jesus as the Christ; his concern is how they understand that confession.

Some progress is possible if we ask from whom is the secret kept? Certainly not from the audience. We are let in on the secret from the opening words (1:1) and opening action (1:11). Nor does Jesus hide from the disciples; they are even privileged to a special divine revelation when Elijah, with Moses, appears to Jesus on a mountain (9:2–8). Jesus even tells them directly:

🙚 🙚 🙚

To you has been given the secret of the kingdom of God, but for those outside everything is in parables. (4:11)

So the secret is kept from "those outside."

On two separate occasions Jesus cautions the disciples not to tell: just after Peter's confession and again, when they are coming down from the mountain on which Jesus talked with Elijah and Moses, he admonishes them "to tell no one what they had seen until the Son of man should have risen from the dead" (9:9).

But why should they not tell? One answer in the story derives from the "until" in that last admonition: there is a time before which it is not appropriate to tell. There is a secret time during which God's Rule has entered the world incognito, so to speak. Another answer in the story is that the disciples do not yet understand. If Mark's Gospel ended at chapter 8 with the recital of Jesus' mighty deeds, there would be no reason not to tell. But this is not the end; a recital of Jesus' suffering and death follows. In fact, the secrecy motif is not abandoned until the very telling of the secret seals Jesus' fate: when he is on trial and is asked, "Are you the Christ the son of the Blessed?" he answers directly: "I am." (Neither Matthew nor Luke is so direct.) They then decide to kill him.

This aspect of the plot leads us to another answer to the meaning of the secrecy, an answer outside the story. Jesus' identity led to his death. This is true "before the story," that is, as a historical event that Mark had to reckon with; and it was true "after the story," as an experience of the Markan community. For Mark, Jesus simply cannot be understood as the man of power. The secrecy motif is one way of showing the inadequacy of the miracle tradition for revealing Jesus; he must be known as the man of suffering.

THE ABSENCE OF GOD:
Kingdom and Suffering

To be sure, the once popular dictum that *the gospels are passion narratives with extended introductions*[2] fails dismally to see the great

2. The phrase was coined by Martin Kahler in 1896 in a work translated into English as *The So-Called Historical Jesus and the Historic Biblical Christ,* 1964: 80, n. 11, and is widely quoted.

complexity of these works, but it does point to a worthwhile consideration: the large percentage of space devoted to the passion (suffering and death) of Jesus in each of the gospels, but especially in Mark.

This emphasis is not unexpected, given the prominence of the theme of Jesus' death in early Christian preaching. (See Paul's radical statement in I Cor. 2:1–2.) We have seen that form criticism traces the Jesus tradition back to the oral preaching of the church, and it is only logical that a great deal of tradition about his death would be preserved. Many scholars think that all the stories connected with the death of Jesus (most of Mark 14 and 15) existed as a connected narrative long before Mark wrote. Certainly, the telling of the stories of Jesus' death was a central Christian concern long before Mark.

The Desertion and Death of Jesus

Yet Mark went still further. As we saw above, after the reversal scene in Mark 8 everything converges on the suffering and death of Jesus. Thus, over half his gospel is oriented toward the passion.

Reading and Reflection

As you reread 8:31–16:8, consider:

1. How does Mark portray the disciples?
2. Why do the Pharisees oppose Jesus?
3. What is the meaning of Jesus' death?
4. Is 16:8 a suitable ending?

There are two sections to this final movement of the gospel. The first (8:22–10:52) is an artfully arranged series of three passion predictions (8:31; 9:31; 10:33), each responded to by the uncomprehending disciples, and each followed with a speech by Jesus that attempts to set forth a true understanding of discipleship. The whole section is framed by two miracles of sight that contrast with the lack of insight demonstrated by the disciples (8:22–26 and 10:46–52). Only after carefully preparing the hearer does Mark move to the events of the last week in Jerusalem portrayed in the second section (11:1–16:8).

This section is divided into two lengthy and two shorter segments:

11:1–12:44	The confrontation with the Jerusalem authorities
13:1–37	The discourse about the end
14:1–15:47	The betrayal, arrest, and crucifixion
16:1–8	The empty tomb

Abandoned by the Jewish Leaders

A new level of action emerges in chapters 11 and 12, as Jerusalem becomes the arena for a contest between Jesus and the Jewish leaders. Much of Jesus' action centers in the Temple, the traditional place where God encountered his people. But, as we will see in Mark's story, God is not there.

The first group whom Jesus encounters is, not surprisingly, those Jewish leaders associated with the Temple, the Sadducees, a sort of priestly aristocracy in Jesus' day. Wealthy, conservative in both politics and religion, the Sadducees prided themselves on faithfulness to the Law of Moses. They were the sort of folk who demanded to see it in the Bible before they would believe it. Thus they did not believe in resurrection, since there is no teaching about a resurrection in the Books of Moses. Their lack of concern about the afterlife probably indicates that they were unaffected by the persecutions of Antiochus Epiphanes, when the deaths of righteous Jews demanded some explanation and vindication. (For an example of such vindication, see II Macc. 7. To review the persecution of Antiochus see the discussion on p. 43.)

Not surprisingly, they challenge Jesus to de-

fend the idea of a resurrection by proposing a riddle (12:18–27); but he offers a subtle argument which, though it seems strange to us, was quite compelling in his time. Jesus shows that his own orientation is much closer to the Pharisees than to the Sadducees.

The Pharisees were mostly laymen, not priests, primarily middle class rather than wealthy, scholars rather than administrators. But their primary difference from the Sadducees concerned their view of the Law (or better, the Torah). While having the highest possible respect for its authority, they did not regard the Torah as a closed book. *Torah* really means something closer to instruction than law, and the Pharisees believed that God's instruction of his people was an ongoing process. Their duty was to take the Torah and use it to develop a life pleasing to God. A Pharisaic story about Torah goes like this:

ॐ ॐ ॐ

Both [oral and written Torah] were given at Sinai, as a king presents a gift to faithful servants. Once there were two servants, a wise one and a foolish one, and both received from their king a measure of wheat and a bundle of flax. The foolish one put them away in a chest, that they remain forever unchanged; the wise servant spun the flax into a cloth and made precious bread out of the wheat. Placing the bread on the cloth, he invited the king to be his honored guest. (Seder Eliyahu Suta 82. Quoted from Trepp, 1982: 219)

This adaptation of the Torah, which the Pharisees called Oral Torah, amounted to an oral expansion of the Torah by applying it to the new problems that arose from living. As we see in the story above, Oral Torah also was "given at Sinai"—a way of saying that it is as authoritative as the written word.

An example of this expansion of Torah may be seen in the Sabbath regulations. The Torah said to keep the Sabbath day holy, but what did this mean in daily living? Eventually, the heirs of the Pharisees spelled out thirty-nine different classes of work that would violate the Sabbath. The goal of this sort of expansion was "to build a fence around Torah" (*Aboth* 1.5), that is, to protect the central commandment by numerous smaller commandments all around it. In the hands of some this could become a stern legalism, but the majority of Pharisees seem to have been open to debate, aware of different interpretations, and humane in their conclusions. We meet one such appealing character in Mark (12:28–34).

We know little about the other group, the Herodians, with whom Mark here allies the Pharisees (12:13). Herod was a client king of Rome, not well liked by the Pharisees.

Jesus meets each of these groups in debate and defeats them all, reducing his opponents to silence (12:34). But it is the silence before the storm.

Forsaken: A New Apocalyptic Insight

As Jesus withdraws from the Temple, the scene of his conflict with his enemies, his disciples turn back, fascinated by the Temple's beauty (13:1). Once again, Jesus rebukes them, by prophesying that not one stone will be left on another; all will be thrown down.

This leads to the private inquiry of the disciples about "when" this will happen. Jesus' lengthy answer, cast in the form of an apocalyptic discourse, is a surprising blend of traditional apocalyptic images and novel, even contradictory, warnings.

Some confusing problems exist with this chapter, but several clear points may be observed.

1. Two countervailing tendencies run throughout the chapter. Though the final end is near (14, 26, 29, 30, 35), the time of the end is unknown (esp. 32, but also 7, 21). The first tendency is clearly apocalyptic, as is the birth pangs metaphor in verse 8. The desolating sacrilege expression of verse 14 is drawn directly from Daniel (9:27; 11:31) though we cannot be sure what Mark understood by it, despite the tantalizing parenthetical remark. Verses 24ff use standard apocalyptic im-

ages. The second tendency represents an effort to transcend mere speculation about the end and transform it into ethical seriousness. Our writer is most concerned to answer not the question of when the end will occur, but to declare how his community ought to live in light of the coming end. (The same attempt was made by Paul in I Thess. 4, 5.)

2. Here is a clear indication of the future status of the kingdom. Some apparently believed the kingdom had already fully come, and the thrust of verses 6–8 and 21–27 seem clearly designed to blunt a view of Christ's kingdom as present experience—even if accompanied by miracles (verse 22). Again, those at Thessalonica faced a similar problem (II Thess. 2). Yet not everything is future.

3. Mark lived in a time between the times. He believed that the Messiah had already come, but he knew the world was not yet made perfect. Thus Mark rejects an understanding of life in which Christians may expect to triumph over evil in any simple or naive way—not even in a charismatic, miracle-working enthusiasm (verses 22–23). The present reality is one of suffering (9–13).

Yet it is not simply suffering, not even suffering in the apocalyptic hope that the end is near. This suffering involves the faith that the new beginning has already been made, made not in triumph, but in suffering and the experience of Jesus. The suffering of the Markan community is to be taken up into the suffering of Jesus; like him, they suffer according to the plan and foreknowledge of God (13:23—"I have told you all things beforehand"). Thus Jesus closed his first major speech on suffering, in which a disciple is required to take up his cross and follow Jesus, by declaring:

❧   ❧   ❧

Truly, I say to you, there are some standing here who will not taste death before they see that the kingdom of God has come with power. (9:1)

So too, the apocalyptic discourse contains the promise: "this generation will not pass away before all these things take place" (13:30). These words from Jesus imply that our writer thought he was living in the last generation of the old age, not simply because he expected an imminent end of the world, but because Jesus' death had ended the old order.

This end may be seen in the Temple motif with which the discourse begins. Jesus has predicted the destruction of the Temple complex (13:2). Later he will be condemned on the charge that he has blasphemed by speaking against the Temple (14:58); and at the moment of his death the veil in the Temple is shown to be torn apart (15:38). But there is to be another Temple, one "not made with hands" (14:58). This new Temple was probably understood to be the community itself, the cornerstone of the new age (Juel, 1977).

Yet Jesus cautions his followers to "watch." This is the "watch for" of traditional apocalyptic expectation: watching for the Parousia, the second coming. But also, and possibly more so, it is the "watch out for" false, miracle-working messiahs (13:5, 22). The way ahead is one of tribulation (19). In Mark, the power of the coming kingdom lies in suffering (15:39), not in miraculous signs and wonders (13:22).

Abandoned by the Disciples

Jesus' relationship to his disciples now changes, or perhaps more accurately the separate courses on which they have been set now diverge widely. They become his opponents: one of them betrays him; his three intimates fail him; all forsake him at the climactic hour, even as he prophesied they would (14:27). It is astonishing that this betrayal scene is the last we see of the disciples in Mark, their shadowy forms disappearing over a far hill— or, perhaps not so shadowy, as the humorous appendage to their desertion makes its impact (14:51–52). Mark's failure to rehabilitate the disciples, along with his consistent portrait of them as uncomprehending has led to a great deal of speculation about his motives.

Perhaps the most extreme view is that advanced by Theodore Weeden, who argues that Mark was trying to undermine the authority of the disciples in the church of his time (1971:23–51; see also, Samuel Sandmel, 1970:52–54). These scholars point to the great ambiguity with which Mark treats the disciples. While Jesus makes positive predictions about their future, the reader is never convinced they are paying attention. They never seem to understand what Jesus is really saying. Even the final promise to the women, that Jesus would meet his disciples in Galilee (16:7), is made indeterminate by Mark's closing words: they did not tell the message (16:8). Thus, the reader cannot be absolutely sure that the disciples ever understood and obeyed.

Yet neither can the reader be certain that they did not. While we owe Weeden a debt for noticing the ambiguity, we must be careful not to overstate the case. If Mark had wanted to overthrow the authority of the disciples, he would not have left the reader so uncertain. The disciples, also, play a positive role in Mark (for example, 1:18, 20; 2:14; 3:14; 4:11, 33; 6:1, 7; etc.), and more importantly, the two-stage plot, coupled with the actual healing of the blind man after the second effort (8:25) and the candid reference to postresurrection understanding in the transfiguration scene (9:4), implies their eventual insight (as do 14:28 and 16:7). Also, the very act of reading the gospel implies that we cannot take the remark about the women's silence too literally. Had they not told, Mark could not relate their story.

Another scholar, Howard Clark Kee, argues that the reason for the ambiguity toward the disciples is that within Mark's story they are surrogates for his own community (Kee, 1977:43, 87–97). Their failure to understand merely illustrates the impossibility of grasping the meaning of Jesus' death until after God vindicated him in resurrection (96; Mark 9:9). While this approach probably fails to take their negative image seriously enough, it is surely closer to the truth than the other suggestion. The more balanced view of James Robinson seems to consider both kinds of evidence: the real foe of Jesus is not the disciples but Satan (8:33). Yet the disciples are tempted by the Satanic suggestion that the kingdom can be had without suffering; to that degree they betray Jesus:

🙠 🙠 🙠

Their opposition to Jesus' idea of suffering corresponds to their own unwillingness to suffer, and this in turn blocks their participation in the eschatological history which awaits Jesus in Gethsemane in definitive fashion. The sharpness of the debates of Jesus with the disciples is due to the fact that the issue at stake is Mark's eschatological understanding of history, which he sees advocated and exemplified by Jesus, but opposed in word and deed by the disciples. (Robinson, 1957:52)

Perhaps we may say that it is not so much the historical disciples whom Mark rejects as the notion they dramatically personify: a rejection of suffering discipleship. (See also Best, 1977, 1981; Tannehill, 1977.)

Abandoned by God: The Death of Jesus

Once again we must face the centrality of suffering for this gospel. Let us examine the crucial scene and see how Mark molds the story of the crucifixion, paying special attention to the action and characterization of Jesus (15:6–9).

It is startling that the last words spoken by Jesus in the gospel of Mark are, "My God, My God, why have you forsaken me?" Mark does nothing to relieve the stark realism of the crucifixion. Yet, Mark asserts, it is precisely the way Jesus died that leads to his recognition as God's son. There is no need for us to speculate what a Roman centurion might have meant by such an appellation. Mark is interested in the title for its own sake. (Luke felt free to report the centurion's statement quite differently, 23:47). How can Jesus' death lead to such a confession of his divine sonship?

The answer seems to lie in the three incidents given earlier, in which Jesus predicts his end. There he indicates it is a divine necessity (8:31—*must* suffer), a necessity also laid on the disciples, who live in a "wicked and godless age" (8:38, as the New English Bible translates it). Here we must recall the apocalyptic concept of two ages, the present age being under the control of the powers of evil. Still, we may question why it is necessary for him to suffer, since he has already successfully overcome Satan in the wilderness (3:22–27). The closest we come to an answer in Mark is after the third prediction, where Jesus declares:

🙠 🙠 🙠

The Son of Man also came not to be served, but to serve, and to give his life as a ransom for many. (10:45)

An implicit contrast is revealed here between two concepts of God's Kingdom: the King who would be served, a person of power and authority, and the servant messiah whose suffering brings life to many. For Mark, Jesus is the one who suffers.

It is also worth noting that each of the passion predictions foretells the resurrection (8:31; 9:31; 10:34). While not emphasizing the resurrection (there are no resurrection appearances), the ending clearly shows that a resurrection has taken place.

The Sense of an Ending

This ending requires closer examination. First of all, we have a textual problem. There are four different endings extant in the manuscripts of Mark. In addition to the ending that became a part of the received text (printed in many Bibles as verses 9–20), there is a short ending, which reads:

꒰ ꒰ ꒰

But they reported briefly to Peter and to those
with him all that they had been told. And after
this Jesus himself sent out by means of them,
from East to West, the sacred and imperishable
proclamation of eternal salvation.

This rather colorless, generalized ending seems
designed simply to relieve the tension in 16:8.
Its rhetorical tone and vocabulary are quite unlike Mark.

A third ending consists of an expansion of
verses 9 to 20, by the insertion of the following
between verses 14 and 15.

꒰ ꒰ ꒰

And they excused themselves, saying, "This age
of lawlessness and unbelief is under Satan, who
does not allow the truth and power of God to
prevail over the unclean things of the spirits [or,
does not allow what lies under the unclean spirits
to understand the truth and power of God].
Therefore reveal thy righteousness now"—thus
they spoke to Christ. And Christ replied to them,
"The term of years of Satan's power has been
fulfilled, but other terrible things draw near. And
for those who have sinned I was delivered over to
death, that they may return to the truth and sin
no more, in order that they may inherit the spiritu-
al and incorruptible glory of righteousness which
is in heaven."

While this ending shares something of the apocalyptic tenor of Mark, it is clearly more esoteric,
with a novel vocabulary and non-Markan tone that
separates it from the gospel itself. It also has scant
manuscript support. Bruce Metzger's summary
seems appropriate: "It probably is the work of a
second or third century scribe who wished to soften
the severe condemnation of the Eleven in 16:14"
(p. 125).

A fourth ending is no addition at all; there is
good manuscript evidence for regarding 16:8 as
the ending of Mark's gospel. The two oldest Greek
manuscripts we have end here, as do numerous

old Latin and Syriac translations. Several early
church fathers, such as Eusebius and Jerome, say
that their best manuscripts end at verse 8. And
many of the manuscripts that have additional
verses (9–20) indicate by some sign that they were
not part of the original gospel. In addition, analysis of the passage itself indicates that these verses
do not fit well. Eleven of the words and expressions are not found in Mark, and the sudden
change in subject from verse 8 (the women) to
verse 9 (Jesus, but simply "he" in the text) is
awkward. In addition, the existence of the shorter
endings is an argument against the authenticity
of the longer. What scribe would substitute the
shorter for the longer unless he regarded the longer
as unoriginal or (more likely) did not know of its
existence?

Almost all textual critics agree: either 16:8 is
the original ending of the gospel or the original
ending is lost. Those who argue for a lost ending
do so for the same reasons Mark has three spurious endings: 16:8 is a hard saying: Can a gospel
end with fear and silence? A more proper question would be: Does it make sense for Mark's
Gospel to end this way? One writer goes so far
as to exclaim:

꒰ ꒰ ꒰

Considered from the viewpoint of dramatic com-
position, the conclusion *of the Gospel at 16:8 is*
not only perfectly appropriate but also a stroke of
genius. (Bilezikian, 1977:134)

Gilbert Bilezikian stresses the dramatic appropriateness of such an ending. The story is told;
now the author must end it. Above all, he must
not introduce further ideas that will detract from
the impact of his story; to narrate resurrection appearances would do just that. (Mark clearly knows
such appearance stories, as his references to Galilee indicate: 16:7, 14:28).

Paul Achtemeier points to another important
element of this ending, ambiguity (1975:109ff).
The resurrection has taken place, but suffering
remains (13:9–13). The Kingdom has begun, but

has not come to completion. Even as Jesus' actions of power remained mysterious and fearful, so do his suffering and resurrection (for example, 4:35–41).[3]

This leads me to suggest a third point: the action of the faithful women is appropriate for anyone who understands this story. Jesus had three times predicted his death and resurrection; each time his disciples demurred. Each time Jesus added that his death would imply their own. Even the good news of the resurrection is now ominous, for as surely as it points to the death of Jesus, his death implies their own:

❧   ❧   ❧

And they went out and fled from the tomb, for trembling and astonishment had come upon them; and they said nothing to anyone, for they were afraid.

Such ambiguity characterized the situation of Mark's community.

THE SITUATION OF MARK AND HIS COMMUNITY

Intuitively, we all know that the context in which a conversation occurs shapes what is said and helps determine its meaning. Thus, the opinions expressed in the faculty lounge are likely to be more pointed than those heard in the classroom, and neither is encumbered with the footnotes of a scholarly article.

The same applies to literature, which must be read in the context in which it was written. To know what an author is trying to say, we must first know what questions he is addressing. Unfortunately, Mark gives us no direct information.

3. The expression "they were filled with awe" in verse 41 is more literally translated, "they feared with a great fear." It is the same verb as in 16:8. We find an interesting parallel just before the third prediction of Jesus' death: "They were amazed, and those who followed feared" (10:32), though the word "feared" here is not the same as that in 16:8.

Seeking the Historical Context

Mark's gospel is anonymous, undated, and makes no direct mention of its social, historical, or religious setting. Scholars have played a sort of detective game, discovering clues in the gospel and in early references to it and then trying to deduce the time and place in which it was written. Such an enterprise is not an exact science, so it is not surprising that no consensus has been reached to date. However, after briefly sketching the major suggestions advanced for situating Mark historically, we will be able to draw certain implications for its interpretation.

Perhaps around Seventy

There is general agreement among scholars that Mark was probably written sometime between 65 and 75, but they are divided on whether the balance of evidence favors a time before or after the year 70, when the Romans destroyed Jerusalem and the Temple.

The evidence is not decisive. Inferences rest primarily on the way Mark presents the apocalyptic material in chapter 13. Those who favor an early date allege that the way Mark develops this material shows that he expects serious trouble in the near future; but unlike Luke (21:20), Mark does not know the details. Those who favor a later date allege that the prophecy of the Temple's destruction indicates that Mark already knew it had happened.

While my own guess is that Mark was written during the war, perhaps nearer the end than the beginning, I also think he clearly perceived the disastrous end to which that war would lead. Consequently, it would make very little difference whether he wrote soon before or soon after the disaster of 70. And the war dragged on for another four years before the Romans conquered Masada in 74.

Perhaps in Rome

The traditional view, going back at least to the second Christian century, is that Mark wrote at

Rome under the influence of Peter. But that tradition is far from certain; it comes to us from Eusebius (writing around 325) who was quoting an earlier writer, Papias (c. 120) whose work is now lost and who depended on a report he had heard from "the presbyters" (apparently his name for people who had known the apostles). But Papias seems to have sometimes embroidered his accounts, and even Eusebius had some doubts about his abilities. (*History* 3.39.15f, Eusebius remarks: "He seems to have been a man of very small intelligence, to judge from his books.") In another place, Eusebius preserved a tradition that implies Mark's death occurred before Peter's (*History* 2.24.1). The tradition that Mark depended on Peter for his gospel grew over the years from a mere acquaintance without any consultation to direct supervision of the project by Peter (the growth of this legend is traced by Kalin, 1975).

Nevertheless, the case for a Roman origin of Mark's Gospel cannot be dismissed lightly; we have other evidence. Ralph Martin presents the case as follows:

1. Both Clement (died 215) and Irenaeus (died 202) support Rome as the place of origin, as does an old prologue to the gospel.
2. The book seems directed to a non-Jewish audience because (a) Jewish customs are explained (for example 7:3–4) and because (b) the Aramaic expressions found in the text are always translated (for example, 14:36; 5:41).
3. There are a series of Latinisms, loan words from Latin to Greek, which indicate a Roman provenance (for example, modius in 4:21, legio in 9:15, speculator in 6:27, quadrans in 12:42, and several others).
4. Mark's method of reckoning time is Roman, dividing the night into four watches, rather than three (6:48; 13:35). (Martin, 1975:214–217 and 202–203. The fourth point is drawn from Barker, Lane and Michaels, 1969:253.)

Thus there is some reason to relate Mark to Rome, and the sixties were an ominous time for Christians in Rome. In 64 a great fire in that city destroyed a substantial part of it. Living conditions in ancient Rome were poor for the majority of the population, who lived in the huge tenements. The emperor Nero had wanted to tear down many of these tenements and build a more glorious city. Thus, when many of them burned down in the fire, and the fire department was the emperor's personal responsibility, rumors spread that he had started the fire. To allay these rumors, Nero needed someone to blame. He hit on the Christians.

Though short-lived (Nero committed suicide in 68), this persecution was intense. Tacitus, writing nearly fifty years later, described the events thus:

᚛ ᚛ ᚛

But neither human help nor imperial munificence, nor all the modes of placating Heaven, could stifle scandal or dispel the belief that the fire had taken place by order. Therefore, to scotch the rumor, Nero substituted as culprits, and punished with the utmost refinements of cruelty, a class of men loathed for their vices, whom the crowd styled Christians. . . . First, then, the confessed members of the sect were arrested; next, on their disclosures, vast numbers were convicted, not so much on the count of arson as for hatred of the human race. And derision accompanied their end: they were covered with wild beasts' skins and torn to death by dogs; or they were fastened on crosses, and when daylight failed were burned to serve as lamps by night. Nero had offered his Gardens for the spectacle, and gave an exhibition in his Circus, mixing with the crowd in the habit of a charioteer, or mounted on his car. Hence, in spite of a guilt which had earned the most exemplary punishment, there arose a sentiment of pity, due to the impression that they were being sacrificed not for the welfare of the state but to the ferocity of a single man. (Annals 15.44, quoted from the Loeb edition. Also see Suetonius, "Nero," 16.2)

Three observations seem necessary here: first, Tacitus did not believe the Christians had any connection with the fire. Second, however, he

had a very low opinion of Christians, deeming
them deserving of "exemplary punishment."
Third, the actual charges on which they were
condemned varied from the specific charge of arson to a very general charge of "hatred of the
human race" (often leveled against Jews in the
ancient world because of their tendency to keep
to themselves). We notice that Christianity itself
is not a crime; the criminals (as the Romans
thought) simply happened to be Christians.

If Mark wrote his gospel at Rome, it was written during these events, when taking up a cross
and following Jesus was no metaphor (8:34). Jesus' word, unique to Mark, "Everyone will be
salted with fire" (9:49), and the odd reference in
Jesus' temptation scene, "And he was with the
wild beasts" (1:13), would take on new significance. If Mark wrote in Rome in the mid-sixties,
his assertion that discipleship constitutes more than
recognizing Jesus as the Christ, that it involves
inevitable suffering, was experienced by many in
his community. Those who favor this view believe Mark was written precisely to make sense
out of this "senseless" slaughter.

Perhaps in Galilee

Much of the evidence gathered to support a Roman origin for Mark's gospel can be under-
mined, and the rest is not very convincing in itself. The Papias tradition is unsure, and Irenaeus
and Clement may well depend on it. The Latinisms seem to be mostly in the traditional material, which Mark received, rather than in the
editorial connections. And, of course, Roman influence spread far beyond the city of Rome. Numerous cities in Asia Minor had large Roman
populations.

At least one modern interpreter has closely
examined Mark's geographical references, especially the return-to-Galilee motif of 14:28 and
16:7, and argues that Galilee was the home of
the community. The call to return to Galilee,
however, is for the final *appearance* of Jesus—
not a resurrection appearance, but the Parousia,
the second coming (Marxsen, 1969:54–95, es-

pecially 78–85). His evidence is difficult to sum-
marize, being drawn chiefly from inferences of
Mark's editorial activity on the supposed pre-
Markan traditions.

In Marxsen's view, Mark writes in the face of
the Jewish-Roman war during which Christian
Jews faced rejection and endured suffering from
both sides: from Gentiles because of their Jewishness and from Jews because they (apparently)
did not support the rebellion. In the midst of this
suffering, Marxsen believes, Mark called for them
to withdraw to Galilee and await the Parousia,
which Mark (wrongly) expected in the near future. Though we know very little about the church
in Galilee, the area was not culturally advanced
and there was a strong Gentile element in the
population (perhaps 50 percent). Inscriptional
evidence shows that Greek was widely used (Kee,
1977b:102). We do know that the war of 66–
74 was a time of intense suffering for the Jewish
people. One of the Jewish military leaders who
was captured by the Romans, then defected and
became an advisor to the Roman side, later wrote
an account of the war that has come down to us.
The man was Josephus and the work is called
The Jewish War. Written in the late seventies,
this work is an invaluable source for this period.
Josephus describes the beginning of Vespasian's
conquest of Galilee as follows:

❧ ❧ ❧

*Vespasian's first objective was the city of Ga-
bara, which he carried at the first assault, finding it deprived of effective combatants. Entering
the city he slew all males who were of age, the
Romans showing no mercy to old or young, so
bitter was their hatred of the nation and their
memory of the affront which had been done to
Cestius [whose leniency had allowed the revolt to
spread]. Not content with setting fire to the city,
Vespasian burnt all the villages and country
towns in the neighborhood; some he found completely deserted, in others he reduced the inhabitants to slavery. (III.7.1. [132ff]; Loeb)*

The conquest of Galilee did not take long, but
the Jews there suffered before and after the ac-

Arch of Titus, Detail of Menorah The great triumphal arch of Titus, still standing in Rome, shows many scenes from the conquest of Judea, including the deportation of slaves and (here) the removal of the treasures of the Temple. This is the only surviving representation of the great seven-branched lamp (Menorah) that stood in the interior chamber of the Temple. (Alinari/Art Resource, New York.)

tual invasion. The war dragged on for another seven years.

If Mark wrote his gospel in Galilee, it was written during this momentous struggle (so Marxsen interprets 13:7–8; p. 174). This theory proposes that Mark viewed these events as the last act of the apocalyptic drama, signaling the nearness of the end (Marxsen, p. 189). The duty of a disciple of Jesus was to persevere. The danger of false messiahs (13:6, 21) was the danger of those who took the simple road of revolution. Mark summoned his community to suffer as Je-

sus suffered and await his triumph. The major virtue of this view is the seriousness with which it considers the Markan theme of suffering.

Perhaps in Rural Syria

One of the recent interpreters of Mark takes issue with both the traditional view and with Marxsen's view. For Howard Clark Kee, the rural character of Mark, revealed in its knowledge of agriculture, housing, employment, and land ownership and taxation, speaks against a Roman origin, as does its "clear antipathy toward the city" (1977b: 102–104). Kee is more impressed by the preservation of Semitic style and, especially, actual Aramaic expressions than by the Latinisms (for example, 5:41; 14:36; 15:34). "The most plausible explanation for this would be that his readers in some way identified with the Semitic language background" (p. 101). Kee recognizes that another explanation would be the "originally Semitic tradition," but dismisses that as an explanation. However, one difficulty in thinking that the audience was presumed to know Aramaic is the redundancy at 10:46, since *Bartimaeus* actually means "son of Timaeus" in Aramaic.

While Galilee would certainly have provided an audience that knew Aramaic, Kee is not persuaded by Marxsen's argument, precisely because Mark's references to geography indicate "that he does not know Galilean topography accurately" (p. 103). The itinerary sketched in 7:31 is a little like going from New York City to Washington, D.C. by way of Boston. (See also 8:10 and 5:1.) Kee argues that this data is more suitably explained if we posit the location of the Markan community "in rural and small-town southern Syria" (p. 105).

He pictures the Markan community as that of the New Israel, whose people believed they participated in the inauguration of God's kingdom, opposed by demonic powers, severed from family ties (10:28ff), rejecting worldly security (10:23ff), but loving and forgiving within the community.

Again, we know little about church development in these areas. We can readily understand how such a community as Kee envisions would lead a difficult life. Surprisingly, Kee has no major treatment of suffering in his book, being content with a vague reference: "When obeying God conflicts with the demands of the state, the result will be martyrdom" (p. 147). He views the basic antagonism to be with the religious authorities (148ff), by which he apparently means Jewish religious authorities, though he fails to explain further what relation he sees between Mark's community and Jewish authorities. This is es-

pecially difficult to comprehend for the location and time of writing Kee suggests: rural Syria during or immediately after the Jewish-Roman war. We do, however, know from Josephus that Jews (and probably Christians) in Syria suffered a good deal from anti-Jewish sentiment both during and immediately after the war.[4]

A Gentile Christian, especially, who had identified with this "Jewish" movement might be tempted to "save his life" (8:35). More broadly, however, these were disruptive and trying times, so we may well imagine that there were those who longed for the Christ of power and miracle to circumvent the tedious process of "enduring to the end" (13:13). Those who adopt this view may believe Mark was written to advocate a deeper insight into the meaning of Jesus as one who also suffered.

Understanding the Social Situation

One thing seems clear: it is easier to propose some particular locale as the origin of Mark if part of the available evidence is ignored, but that is probably not very helpful. However, some conclusions may be drawn. There is remarkably little disagreement over date: 65–75 seems to fit the existing data—perhaps closer to 70. Second, there is strong agreement that Mark intended his community to identify with his portrayal of Jesus and thus gain insight into their suffering. It seems fairly certain that Mark's community is in the midst of persecution.

Wherever the community behind this gospel was located, the late sixties were an ominous time for Christians. Apparently both Peter and Paul had been caught up in the mass slaughter of Christians at Rome between 64 and 68. While there is no evidence that this persecution spread beyond the city of Rome, it would not be too encouraging to learn that the official policy of one's government was to exterminate Christians,

---

4. *Jewish War* II. 20.2 (599ff); VII. 5.2 102, (108ff). See also Gaston, 1970.

however far away one might be. Rumor had probably also carried the news that James, brother of Jesus and head of the mother church in Jerusalem, had been killed because of Sadducean instigation in 62. Christians were, after all, part of a close-knit, mobile group. Add to this, the Roman invasion of Palestine and their fear that Jews in other provinces might join the rebellion, and we can sense the danger that the community might be overwhelmed by the forces of evil.

The question that his community must answer, then, is how to respond to that evil. Robert Tannehill's fascinating study of the disciples' role in Mark suggests that Mark's portrayal of them is meant to elicit identification and sympathy from the reader (1977). Yet this sympathy is increasingly complicated by the disciples' failure. While the reader hopes for a "happy ending" and a reconciliation of the disciples, Mark refuses to provide it, leaving their final choice as open and ambiguous as the real choices of Mark's audience. (See also Best, 1977, 1981.)

Third, it does not seem that any of these solutions to Mark's place of origin takes seriously enough Mark's need to explain Jewish customs and interpret Jewish expressions while at the same time making extensive and subtle use of the Jewish Scriptures. It seems reasonable to conclude then, that no firm determination may be made about the place of writing without better evidence than is presently available.

Mark is far more than a simple retelling of the story of Jesus. Mark is a work of literature that attempts to portray Jesus, to illustrate his significance and meaning, to tell his story. To be sure this portrayal must be grounded in the Jesus who left footprints in the sand in Galilee, but Mark's intention is to make this Jesus understood by his own community. He achieves this mimesis, this representation, by the way he structures his material, by shaping his characterization of the disciples, by his development of the kingdom idea, by narrating Jesus' suffering in certain ways (and not others), and by many other devices. He did all this, it is argued here, because he lived in a certain situation to which (and from which) he spoke. We may be tempted to ask how someone in a different time and place might have told it differently. Fortunately, there is no need for speculation: we have four gospels.

RESOURCES FOR FURTHER STUDY

Useful introductory works on Mark include Achtemeier, 1975; W. Harrington, 1979; Hurtado, 1983; Kelber, 1979; and Stock, 1984.

Classic treatments include Lane, 1974 (more conservative); Lightfoot, 1950; Marxsen, 1969; Nineham, 1964; and Schweizer, 1970.

Special studies on Mark have been made by:

Belo, 1981, *A Materialist Reading of the Gospel of Mark*.
Burkill, 1963, *Mysterious Revelation*.
Kee, 1977, *Community of the New Age*.
Weeden, 1971, *Mark: Traditions in Conflict*. Two recent works contest Weeden's view of the disciples: Best, 1981; and Tannehill, 1977.

Excellent new works examining the literary nature of Mark have begun to appear. They include:

Best, 1983, *Mark: The Gospel as Story*.
Kelber, 1979, *Mark's Story of Jesus*.
Rhoads and Michie, 1982, *Mark as Story*. (Perhaps the best.)

On a more advanced level:

Dewey, 1980, *Markan Public Debate*.
Fowler, 1981, *Loaves and Fishes*.
———, 1985, "The Rhetoric of Indirection in the Gospel of Mark."
Petersen, 1980, is a special issue of *Semeia* devoted to literary approaches to Mark. See also vol. 32

of the journal *Interpretation*, which is likewise devoted to Mark.
Robbins, 1984, *Jesus the Teacher*.

Advanced works on special topics of importance include:

Achtemeier, 1970, on miracle stories.
Bilezikian, 1977, and Via, 1975, present contrasting views about the relation of Mark to ancient comedy and tragedy.
Donahue, 1973, on the trial narrative in Mark.
Juel, 1977, *Messiah and Temple*.
Keck, 1966, "The Introduction to St. Mark's Gospel."
Kelber, ed., 1976, *The Passion in Mark*.
Kelber, 1983, *The Oral and the Written Gospel*.
Kingsbury, 1983, *The Christology of Mark's Gospel*.
Malbon, 1983, "Fallible Followers: Women and Men . . ."
Robinson, 1957, *The Problem of History*.
Tuckett, 1983, *The Messianic Secret*.

A seminal study of "divine men" in ancient writing is that of Hadas and Smith, 1965. For a critique of this view, see Kee, 1973b, "Aretalogy and Gospel." A thorough study has been made by Tiede, 1972.

The history of the Kingdom idea is traced by Bright, 1953. For a general survey and a symbolist interpretation of the Kingdom in the gospels, see Perrin, 1976.

One of the most fruitful analyses of the temptation in Mark is that of E. Best, 1965; see also Keck, 1966. The traditional view that the passion narrative existed before Mark (Bultmann, 1972:275) has been recently contested by Donahue, in Kelber, 1976:1–20.

The best source for analyzing the evidence for the various endings to Mark, and other textual problems, is Metzger, 1971, *A Textual Commentary on the Greek New Testament*. For his discussion of the ending to Mark, see pp. 122–128. In this instance, Metzger's discussion can be followed by anyone, though usually some knowledge of Greek is necessary.

Few contemporary scholars would regard 16:9–20 as from Mark, although such a view is taken by Farmer, 1974, *The Last Twelve Verses of Mark*. He suggests that the non-Markan features of these verses could be explained by positing a pre-Markan narrative, which Mark edited to his gospel. Farmer is also one of the few who argue that Mark depends on Matthew and not vice versa, thus making the abrupt ending of Mark problematic. For major discussions of the issues, see R. P. Meye, 1969, "Mark 16:8: The Ending of Mark's Gospel;" and Reedy, 1972, who argues for a lost ending.

The Book of the New Community

❧ ❧ ❧

The Gospel according to Matthew

8

The author of this gospel said that a good scribe had to be like a person in charge of a large household, able to go into the storeroom and bring out things both old and new (13:52). By this definition, our author was a good scribe. We will find in this book many old things—some we have already found in Mark—but they are also new things, for they are used in new ways. In this chapter we will first consider some of the similarities to Mark, but we will use these observations to discover what is unique to Matthew, attempting to achieve some sense of the whole. Then we will turn to specific incidents in the story, giving them a close reading. Finally, we will investigate the probable situation from which and to which this book is addressed.

AN OVERVIEW OF THE WHOLE

It is remarkable that the Gospel according to Matthew contains over 90 percent of the material in Mark and yet is a dramatically different work. Whether Matthew actually used Mark as his source and consciously modified the text (as most New Testament scholars think), or whether he was simply heir to the same traditions, Matthew has approached those traditions in his own way. Our insight into this gospel will be increased by considering the similarities and differences between the two.

Reminders of Mark

Perhaps the easiest way to become aware of these similarities and differences is to compare a common scene. The scene of Jesus' baptism is important to both. Let us examine it closely.

Reading and Reflection

Compare Matthew 3:1–17 with Mark 1:1–11 (GP #s 1–6; SFG #s 13–18). Consider:

1. What variations in the telling of the story does Matthew exhibit when compared with Mark?
2. What new material does Matthew add?
3. How does Matthew show that he does not regard this as "the beginning"?

Let me note in passing that the two blocks of material shared by Matthew and Luke but missing in Mark (Matt. 3:7–10, 12) represent what scholars call Q, a common source shared by Matthew and Luke (discussed on p. 142). The extensive verbal agreement between Matthew and Luke argues for a common origin. The portrayals of Jesus' temptation are also so similar that they probably stem from a common source, but their genealogies differ substantially, making a common source unlikely.

The expression Matthew uses for a transition into this story is remarkable: "In those days came

John." But Matthew has just finished what we usually call the *infancy narrative*. In those days? This expression allows Matthew to achieve two goals: first it is an echo of a standard phrase in prophetic speech, for "in those days" God would establish his kingdom on earth (for example, Jeremiah 3:15–18). Second, the expression establishes a tie to the earlier stories by implying that both belong to the same period. It is not that this happens in the time of Jesus' infancy, but that the birth of Jesus is the beginning of a new time.

This conclusion is reinforced when we notice that John is already preaching the impending arrival of the kingdom (3:2), something that Mark reserved for Jesus after his baptism and after John's imprisonment (Mark 1:14–15). For Matthew the crucial event for the inauguration of the kingdom had already occurred before John appeared in the wilderness. The baptism of Jesus is *not* the beginning of the action in Matthew. Before the baptism scene we hear of Jesus' birth, the visit of the magi, the attack of Herod, and the flight into Egypt. Unless we disregard these early narratives as mere decoration (and such has often been their fate), we must consider that the scope and structure of Matthew's action will be quite un-Markan. We must consider seriously that, for Matthew, the story began when "Abraham became the father of Isaac" (1:2), and that its first significant event is the birth of Jesus.

Matthew also introduced a new dialogue between John and Jesus, explaining why it was appropriate for John to baptize Jesus (one expects ordinarily that the greater will baptize the lesser). His explanation is short and ambiguous: the baptism is "to fulfill all righteousness" (3:15). Though John is convinced, I am not so sure the reader is. But this answer allows Matthew to anticipate what follows.

For in the next scene Jesus reveals his righteousness in the now-detailed temptation scene. He does so by continual reference to Scripture, which Matthew has labored to show is being fulfilled in Jesus (five such fulfillments have already been indicated—1:22; 2:5; 15; 17f; and 23). But Matthew becomes even more direct, soon

explaining just what he means by the two important terms, *fulfill* and *righteousness,* combining them with a third idea, the Jewish understanding of the Law. His explanation follows:

ॐ ॐ ॐ

Think not that I have come to abolish the law and the prophets; I have come not to abolish them, but to fulfill them. . . . For I tell you, unless your righteousness exceeds that of the scribes and pharisees, you will never enter the kingdom of heaven. (Matt. 5:17–20)

These statements provide the theme for what follows in Matthew, a long speech usually called the *Sermon on the Mount* (Matt. 5–7). The substance of that speech is an examination of the categories of "righteousness," showing how they are "fulfilled" (brought to completion or perfection) in the teaching of Jesus. We will investigate these ideas presently, but first we must consider the close connection between this speech and the action of the narrative as a clue to the structure of Matthew's gospel. It is not the only such speech in Matthew.

Beyond Mark: The Five Speeches

The Sermon on the Mount is not found in Mark; it is Matthew's creation. Apparently he has gathered sayings of Jesus and composed them into a continuous speech.[1] Matthew has actually composed five such speeches, only one of which significantly parallels Mark.

That Matthew intended for each of these speeches to be seen as a special collection is indicated by the stereotyped expression with which he concludes them: "And it came to pass when

---

1. The reason for thinking that Matthew composed this speech is that much of the material in it is found in a variety of other settings in Luke and, in the case of three sayings, in Mark. You can see this at a glance by examining the indexes to the *Gospel Parallels* or the *Synopsis of the Four Gospels.*

Jesus had finished these sayings. . . ."[2] In addition, each speech is set off from the preceding context by references to "the crowds" or by the phrase "the disciples came to him"—usually by both. The disciples are mentioned at the beginning of each speech, four times by the stereotyped expression noted; the crowds are mentioned at the beginning of all but the fourth speech, where their presence would be inappropriate, since it is addressed to the disciples.

Thus, on the purely formal level, in considering the structure of the work, five long blocks of teaching material segment Matthew's gospel: roughly chapters 5–7, 10, 13, 18, and 23–25. Further, each of these speeches grows out of a narrative context and is followed by a narrative. The formal arrangement of Matthew's gospel, then, is an alternating sequence of narrative (N) and speech (S) sections in the pattern: N-S-N-S-N-S-N-S-N-S-N. It has been suggested above that the first speech served to explain and interpret the action of the first narrative by explaining the meaning of the phrase "to fulfill all righteousness." There are, in fact, numerous interconnections between the narrative and speech sections. When these speeches were first discovered, they were viewed as comments on the prior narrative section. They are also comments on the succeeding narratives. The Sermon on the Mount, for example, demonstrates Jesus' authority in word (7:28–29), while the next section shows his authority in deed (8–9). It is worth noting that the phrase concluding each discourse ("And it came to pass when Jesus had finished these sayings") is a half sentence leading into the next narrative. Thus we should not see the speeches as dividers but as connectors. Matthew's challenge was not to divide his narrative, but to find ways to connect the diverse incidents. These speeches allow Matthew to reflect on the significance of Jesus' action in the preceding section and to prepare the reader for the action that follows.

2. See 7:28; 11:1; 13:53; 19:1; 26:1. In the Greek it is a six-word sequence: *Kai egenito hote etelesen ho Iesous.*

The Structure of the Book

As we saw in Mark, any particular incident in a work must be read in light of its place in the structure of that work and the shape of the narrative. Thus, any analysis of miracles in Mark should consider how Mark transforms that theme in the second half of his work. Any serious study of the disciples must inquire about their narrative role in the work as a whole. The same holds true for Matthew, but its structure is far more complex.

Reading and Reflection

Read through the Gospel of Matthew paying particular attention to the flow of the action and to the interplay between action and speech. Notice especially the interconnections that Matthew has woven into his art (see Tables 8.1 and 8.2.) and compare your observations with those below.

The Plot of the Story

The analysis above implies that a significant component of the development of Matthew's action is the discourse material. In this sense Matthew is a much less dramatic gospel than Mark. In Matthew, the gospel has been rationalized more, made more didactic. Yet it is still a story and we can trace the relationship between the incidents, which determines the intention of the gospel as a whole. The following brief summary should be compared with the content of each section to see how adequately it expresses the action of the gospel.

The relationship between the first narrative section (1–4: the stories connected with the birth and baptism) and the second (8–9: the stories of miracles and discipleship) rests on the identity of Jesus and the nature of his authority. The opening genealogy locates Jesus as the culmination of God's ancient work with Israel. The stories of Joseph, John, and Jesus underscore their obedience to God, with Jesus being introduced as the one who fulfills all righteousness (3:15; 4:1–11). He calls disciples, then explains the nature of his work in the first speech (5–7), which has been recognized as a literary masterpiece in its own right. But it is even more, since it serves to interpret the previous narrative and to prepare for the next. The word of Jesus clarifies the deed of Jesus: he repeats and transcends the past, fulfilling it (5:17). He is not only the supremely obedient one ("to every word," 4:4), but the one to whom supreme obedience is due (7:24ff). No wonder the crowds were astonished by his authority (7:28). In short, this discourse defines the righteousness that must be fulfilled (7:20 with 3:15) and defines Jesus as the authoritative source of this righteousness (5:21ff).

The second narrative section demonstrates this authority and shows that not all will accept this new work of God-with-us. Chapters 8–9 are a series of three miracle cycles containing three miracles each. Each miracle includes some response to Jesus, often faith in him, and the first two cycles are each followed by two questions: on discipleship (8:18–22) and on obedience to tradition (9:10–17). This section concludes with an ominous dichotomy (reminiscent of the concluding "two ways" of the first speech): the crowds marvel but the Pharisees accuse Jesus of alliance with the prince of demons (9:33). This second narrative section is linked to the first by a nearly identical summary statement (9:35, 4:23). The speech of chapter 10 also reaches backward. The disciples are invested with the authority of Jesus to preach—the same message as John and Jesus—and to heal (compare 10:7 with 4:17 and 3:2) and points the way to their coming rejection and persecution in Jewish synagogues and Gentile courts.

The narrative section in 11 and 12 opens with an incident that ties it to the previous narrative by showing that the deeds recounted in 8–9 were the works expected of the one the prophets promised would come (11:2–5), then looks forward by declaring: "Blessed is he who takes no offense at me" (11:6). The narrative proceeds with a virtual listing of Jesus giving repeated cause for offense—so antagonizing the Pharisees that they seek to destroy him (12:14). But Jesus prevails, refuting the "alliance with demons," a charge now repeated from the close of the previous narrative section, and condemning "this evil generation"—those who do not recognize Jesus' identity, in contrast to his "brothers," the disciples (12:50; 28:10).

The third speech binds together two similar narrative sections in which the Pharisees are increasingly offended while the disciples understand. (The contrast with Mark at this point is striking.) Using seven parables, the third speech explains why the sowing of the word of the Kingdom should produce such divergent results and warns not to try to separate the good and the bad.

The fourth narrative section (13:53–17:27) begins with an explicit reference to Jesus' fellow countrymen being offended by him (13:57), then proceeds to show the disciples' ultimate recognition of Jesus' nature—they worship him (14:33). The Pharisees and Scribes continue to be offended (15:12; only in Matthew). But now we have a new issue: What about the Gentiles? A Canaanite woman is not offended, though one could hardly have blamed her if she had been (15:21–28). The rest of the section centers on the disciples who struggle to understand—again confessing Jesus to be Son of God (16:16) and beginning to see what this implies for their own sonship (17:24ff—"then the sons are free").

The fourth speech (chapter 18) now focuses on the requirements incumbent on the disciples as "brothers" of Jesus, sons of God, and citizens of the Kingdom of Heaven. Matthew anachronistically sets forth laws for the "church," focusing on the forgiving nature of the community. There is a deliberate reference both backward (compare 18:18 with 16:19, regarding the power

Table 8.1 Verbal Correlations within Matthew's Gospel (Interlocking Quotes)

	N_1(1–4)	S_1(5–7)	N_2(8–9)	S_2(10)	N_3(11–12)	S_3(13)	N_4(14–17)	S_4(18)	N_5(19–22)	S_5(23–25)	N_6(26–28)
Jesus traveled/teaching	4:23		9:35								
Kingdom at hand	3:2, 4:17			10:7							
Good tree/fruit	3:10	7:19			12:33ff						
Fame—brought sick	4:24						14:35				
Voice: Beloved Son	3:17						17:5				
Right eye/pluck out		5:29						18:9			
Divorce/adultery		5:32							19:9		
Heaven/word pass away		5:18								24:35	
And when he had finished. . . .		7:28		11:1		13:53		19:1		26:1	
Mercy/not sacrifice			9:13		12:7						
Alliance with demons			9:34	10:25	12:24						
Touch fringe/made well			9:20				14:36				
To lost sheep . . . Israel				10:6			15:24				
Take cross/follow				10:38f			16:24f				
Hated/for my names sake				10:22						24:9	
Endure to end/saved				10:22						24:13	
Receive X/receive me				10:40ff				18:5		25:40	
Sign of Jonah					12:38f		16:1ff				
Who has/more given						13:12				25:29	
Bind/loose							16:19	18:18			
Faith/move mountains							17:20		21:21		
Great/servant								18:1	20:26f	23:11	
First/last									19:30 20:16		
Blessed/he who comes									21:9	23:39	
Held John/Jesus to be prophet									21:26, 46		

Table 8.2 Thematic Correlations within Matthew's Gospel (Interlocking Ideas)

	N₁(1–4)	S₁(5–7)	N₂(8–9)	S₂(10)	N₃(11–12)	S₃(13)	N₄(14–17)	S₄(18)	N₅(19–22)	S₅(23–25)	N₆(26–28)
Fulfill all righteousness	3:15										
Dual responses		5:20	9:33f			13:8,24,47					28:18
Authority		7:28f 7:29	8:9 9:6f	10:1					21:23	24:9f	
Suffer for Christ's sake		5:11		10:18		13:21					
Prophecy of Isaiah	3:3 4:14		8:17		12:17 (11:2f)	13:14	15:17				
Take offense					11:6	13:57 (13:21)	17:27 (15:12)	18:6		24:10	26:31
Faith			8:10 9:2,22,29				17:20		21:21	23:23	
Gentiles in Kingdom			8:11f		12:18f		15:27f		21:43		28:19f
Pharisees condemned	3:7	5:20			12:7		15:3 16:12		21:45	23	
Brood of vipers	3:7				12:34					23:33	
Acts of obedience	1:24 3:15 4:19f	7:21	9:9		12:50		14:29				26:39f
Gospel of the Kingdom	4:23		9:35							24:14	(26:13)
Imminence of Kingdom							16:28			24:34	
John the Baptist	3:1 4:12		9:14		11:2f		14:2f 16:14f		21:25f		
Forgive to be forgiven		6:14f						18:35			
Correlations between N₁ and N₆											
Worship/kneel before Jesus	2:2,8,11 (4:10)		8:2 9:18 (9:6)				14:33 15:25		20:20		28:17 28:9
To save from sins	1:21										26:28
Son of God	1:23 3:17						17:5 (18:20)				27:54
To be "with" his people	1:23										28:20
King of the Jews	2:2f										27:11,37
Plot to kill Jesus	2:3f										26:4
Return to Galilee	4:12f						17:22				28:10,16
Three temptations	4:1f										26:38f 27:39f
To make disciples	4:18f										28:19

to bind and loose) and forward (compare 18:1 with 20:26–27 and 23:11, concerning greatness in the kingdom; see also the recurring theme of childlikeness in 19:13–15).

The fifth narrative section (19–22) brings to a climax the tension introduced in the second narrative: the Pharisees as the leaders of Israel are decisively rejected and the kingdom of God is removed from them and "given to a nation poducing the fruit of it." (This fruit metaphor recurs through Matthew; see 3:10; 7:14; 12:33–35.) All Jesus' foes are reduced to silence (22:46),

while Matthew continues to sketch the nature of the Kingdom and to establish laws for the new community.

The final speech section gathers together the preceding judgment of the Pharisees (23) and foretells the coming suffering of the followers of Jesus in the time before the final judgment of all (24–25).

The last narrative section first foreshadows Jesus' burial (26:6ff) and death (26:26ff) carefully explaining their meaning ("for the forgiveness of sins"—26:28). Matthew follows Mark's

---

READING GUIDE TO MATTHEW

The Revelation of Jesus Christ (1–10)

First Narrative: Jesus, son of Abraham, is shown to be the one who fulfills Scripture's promises by the manner of his birth and by his actions. (1–4)

First Speech: Jesus reveals his authority to redefine righteousness. (5–7)

Second Narrative: Jesus reveals his authority in three cycles of three miracles each. (8–9:35)

Second Speech: Jesus communicates his authority to the disciples and sends them on their mission as an extension of his. (9:36–10:42)

The Responses to Jesus (11–17)

Third Narrative: Jesus is shown to be the "One Who Is To Come" because he performs "the deeds of the Christ." (11–12)

Third Speech: Jesus uses parables to show that the Kingdom of God is mysterious and contains both faithful and unfaithful. (13:1–52)

Fourth Narrative: Various characters respond to Jesus: Herod thinks he is John; the crowds are baffled; the disciples twice confess; the Pharisees and Scribes question and are offended; the Canaanite woman persists

in her confession; Gentiles glorify the God of Israel; Pharisees and Sadducees test him; Peter confesses him to be the "Christ the Son of God," witnesses the events on the mountain, and pays the Temple tax. (13:53–17:27)

The Response of Jesus (18–25)

Fourth Speech: Jesus explains the compassion and forgiveness required for the Kingdom. (18)

Fifth Narrative: Jesus debates his opponents and shows that one's status in the Kingdom depends on how well one obeys God. (19–22)

Fifth Speech: Jesus pronounces judgment on the Pharisees and Scribes and on the whole world. (23–25)

The Righteousness of Jesus Vindicated (26–28)

Sixth Narrative: The obedient and righteous Jesus, betrayed by his disciples to the schemes of his opponents, dies as the Son of God and is raised from the dead to inherit the universal authority by which he commissions his disciples to make disciples of all the nations.

story of Jesus' betrayal, desolation, and crucifixion, with editorial touches and additions to carry forward the themes of Jesus' radical obedience (see 26:42), the completion of the divine plan (26:52–54), and the fulfilling of all righteousness (see 27:24–25, 51–54). Unlike Mark, Matthew concludes with a resurrection appearance of Jesus in Galilee. The plot comes full circle with Jesus claiming "all authority" and granting his eternal presence as the disciples are commissioned to "disciple" the nations. The story that began with Abraham now includes all.

Read this way, Matthew's story depicts Jesus as the creator of a new community, founded on his righteous words and deeds. Among the gospels, only Matthew calls this new community a "church" (16:18; 18:17). It is connected with the earliest call of God to Abraham (1:2) in the distant past; this community will persist to the end of the age (28:20). The Reading Guide provides a simplified chart of these basic ideas and shows the dramatic structure of this gospel.

Let us now focus on a few of the more important incidents.

THE DEEDS OF THE CHRIST (1–10)

It is perhaps more difficult for the modern reader to appreciate the opening of Matthew's gospel than that of any other work in the New Testament. For us it is a list of hard-to-pronounce names, even meaningless words. Yet Matthew's genealogy takes on real life for those who know something about the people mentioned. He leads us through the whole history of Israel, and our appreciation of Matthew's work grows as we become more familiar with that history. Matthew consciously connects his story with the story of God's past dealings with Israel. These ties to the Old Testament probably secured first place for Matthew in the New Testament when the canon was constructed. Let us now examine the genealogy more closely.

The Ancestors of Jesus

Matthew does not recite the history of Israel in a monotonous fashion but varies his presentation to emphasize certain points. The following exercise reveals these highlights.

Reading and Reflection

Read Matthew 1:1–17 aloud, trying to be conscious of the rhythm and movement of the words. You may also wish to compare this genealogy with that in Luke 3:23–38 (GP #7; also p. 1 and SFG # 19).

Matthew uses two literary devices to guide the listener's understanding of this genealogy: numerical symmetry and rhythmic interruption. The symmetry is first hinted at in the title sentence:

🐦 🐦 🐦

The book of the genealogy of Jesus Christ, the son of David, the son of Abraham. (1:1)

Unlike Mark, there is no declaration of divine sonship, nor is the proclamation called a "gospel." Instead it is a "book," a term as vague in Greek as it is in English. The word translated as "genealogy" is really a broad term for origin, source, generation, descent, and so on. The same expression is used in the Greek version of Genesis 5:1: "This is the book of the generation of Adam" (as the Revised Standard Version translates it). But it could also be translated as "the book of the origin of man." Matthew's phrase could bear a similar meaning, "the book of the origin of Jesus Christ." Matthew uses the same Greek word again in 1:18, translated "birth" in the Revised Standard Version. In addition, the verb translated "was the father of" in the genealogy is a related word. Perhaps we could get a similar (though more awkward) impression in English by using *genesis* in verses 1 and 18 and *generated* in the genealogy.

This emphasis on genesis recalls Mark's focus on the new beginning. Matthew's book also offers a new beginning, and it is quite possible that we should understand this opening phrase as a title for the whole work. By singling out David (the founder of the nation) and Abraham (the founder of the people), Matthew already implies a structure in his genealogy. He makes this structure explicit in verse 17, where he asserts that the genealogy consists of three sets of fourteen generations each.

Historically speaking, this presents a few problems, as even a general knowledge of the timespans involved would indicate: from Abraham to David was about 750 years, from David to the Exile about 400 years, and from the Exile to Jesus about 600 years. In fact, Matthew has had to omit several kings known from the genealogies in the Hebrew Scriptures (compare I Chron. 3:10–16 with Matt. 1:7–11), and the only way one arrives at fourteen in the last section is to count Jechoniah again though he was already counted in the previous section.

For a long time these historical difficulties were the main focus of scholarly investigation, but recently a new approach has emerged. Without glossing over the problems, this approach asks why such material was made a part of this gospel, a far more interesting question. Some indication of Matthew's intention can be seen in his arrhythmical arrangement of the names.[3]

The rhythmic pattern of the names is simple: A was the father of B; B was the father of C, and so on. This is the pattern of at least one of Matthew's sources (Ruth 4:18–22). But Matthew interrupts this smooth flow by the addition

of nongenealogical material: mention of brothers, naming of mothers, and references to events. The events noted correspond to the major divisions of Matthew's genealogy: the kingship of David and the deportation to Babylon. Clearly, Matthew's understanding of the history of God's people moves in three epochs, marked by these two events.

At both points there was a radical shift in the self-understanding of Israel. With a king, Israel became a nation "like the other nations," no longer simply God's people under his direct rule (I Sam. 8:4–9.) With the exile, all the major supports of Israel's faith were threatened or eliminated, including the monarchy (although they thought it would last forever: II Sam. 7), the land, the Temple, even God's action in history seemed questionable. (For a discussion of the meaning of these events in Israel's life see Bright, 1959:202–208, 328–331.) When we now see Matthew narrate other events about the genesis of Jesus Christ (1:18), the expectation of another such crucial event occurring naturally arises and the hearer is prepared for another radically new orientation to the meaning of being Israel.

References to "and his brothers" occur at two places in the genealogy, to differentiate the chosen line of Judah from the other sons of Jacob (the "fathers" of the other eleven tribes) and to call attention to Jechoniah, though in the Hebrew Scriptures Jechoniah (the birth name of King Jehoiachin) is not said to have had brothers. His father, Jehoiakim, had two brothers who also ruled. Matthew has apparently conflated the two similar names and probably used the expression to contrast with Judah and his brothers: just as the former inherited the kingly promise (Genesis 49:5–12), so the latter lost it in exile among the Gentiles.

References to mothers, normally not included in Jewish genealogies, occur at four places, plus the ending reference to Mary. The four share several features worth mentioning. First, they all have reputations that were in their times less than honorable: Tamar pretended to be a prostitute and

3. This suggestion is from Davis, 1973:520–535. Though my analysis differs somewhat, it is largely indebted to his work.

became pregnant by her father-in-law (Genesis 38); Rahab was a prostitute (Joshua 2 and 6:22–25); the wife of Uriah, Bathsheba, committed adultery with King David while her husband was away with the army (II Sam. 11); and Ruth spent the night in the granary, after which Boaz proposed marriage (Ruth 3).

Second, each incident relates a striking act of loyalty to God and his Law. Tamar rebuked the refusal of Judah to raise up a child for her dead husband as the law in her day decreed. Rahab became faithful to Israel at the cost of her own city. Uriah (and notice that Bathsheba is not really mentioned) was ultimately killed by David because he refused to violate the rules of Holy War by going home to his wife, as David had planned. Ruth forsook her people to follow her mother-in-law back to Israel.

Finally, all these faithful keepers of the Law were Gentiles! For the first time, we encounter an interesting tension that will pervade Matthew's gospel: in the midst of his history of Israel, Matthew underscores the presence of faithful Gentiles.

The presence of Mary in verse 16 may also indicate an apologetic attempt to show that immediate reputations are no gauge of God's work, since the other four women were all vindicated in later Jewish tradition. This should not be pressed too far, however, for the focus of Matthew's account is on Joseph rather than Mary.

In discussing Jesus' birth, Matthew carefully shifts the verb into the passive to exclude all human agency. To explain this mysterious construction Matthew elaborates on the "birth" (genesis) of Jesus, omitting entirely any incident properly called a birth story.

Fulfilling the Promises: A New Beginning

What is recounted instead of a birth story is the story of Joseph, "a righteous man" who is confronted by an awful dilemma: to obey the Law or to obey God. This is a radical way to state the issue, but I believe it is essentially correct. The Law demanded at least divorce under such circumstances, but instead the dream-messenger commanded marriage (Deut. 22:21). A book written a couple of centuries earlier, variously called *Sirach* or *Ecclesiasticus,* warned against trusting such ephemeral messengers: "Dreams give wings to fools," "Dreams are folly," and "Dreams have deceived many" (*Sirach* 34:1, 5, 7; compare also 15:1). After all, how could God contravene his own Law? But Matthew does not yet allow these questions to emerge. The dream messenger is obeyed, culminating in the fulfillment of an ancient prophecy and the birth of *Emmanuel,* God with us.

The story vindicates Joseph's decision by repeatedly showing that this birth inaugurates the time when all the ancient promises are being fulfilled. The manner of birth (1:22), the place of birth (2:5), the place of safety (2:15), the new residence in Nazareth (2:23), even the horror of Herod's slaughter (2:17), are all seen as fulfilling prophetic promises.

The birth immediately elicits a response, or more precisely two responses: Gentile Magi come to worship him, but Herod "and all Jerusalem" are troubled (2:1–3). While the Magi bring precious gifts to Jesus, Herod seeks to take his life. There is no real explanation of these responses; Matthew himself can only see in them the hand of God, fulfilling prophecy. There is some doubt about whether the historical Herod actually initiated such a massacre: he was certainly capable of it, but no other record exists of such an event. He was ruthless enough to kill three of his own sons, which led to the pun: "It's better to be Herod's pig (*hus* in Greek) than his son (*huios*)," since he attempted to keep the Jewish law which forbade eating pork.

Certainly, Matthew's audience would have had no difficulty believing such a thing, but we must ask a further question: Why include this kind of story in the gospel? Only now does Matthew reach the point where Mark began, the stories of John and the baptism of Jesus. Why has Matthew found it necessary to go behind the beginning that Mark had found appropriate?

Raymond Brown's analysis of this new beginning is instructive. He shows that the writing of a gospel such as Mark represented an advance over earlier Christian thinking about Jesus. Both Paul (in the mid-fifties) and Luke's report of the earliest Christian preaching understood the resurrection as the event in which Jesus' divine sonship was manifested. "Designated son of God . . . by his resurrection," is probably an early creedal form which Paul quoted in Romans (1:4; see also Acts 2:32). Mark, however, recognizing that the deeds of Jesus' ministry already revealed his divine sonship, located the recognition of that sonship at the baptism. But Matthew saw that such a formulation could be misleading, that it might seem like an attainment by Jesus, a sort of divine adoption, so he portrayed the divine sonship as already inherent in Jesus' conception (Brown, 1975:579f). It is not so surprising, then, that the birth of Jesus provoked the same responses as his life, death, and resurrection, for in Matthew his birth is just as surely a revelation of his divine status.

Jesus' birth, no less than his death/resurrection (Paul) and his deeds (Mark), evokes acceptance and rejection. We might be tempted to say that the Jews rejected him and the Gentiles accepted him, but that is too simple. More precisely, certain leaders among the Jews rejected him. We must remember that in Matthew's story the pious ordinary Jew, one obedient to the Law, recognized this new work of God. This Jew is portrayed by Joseph and by John.

Matthew's gospel has sometimes been considered anti-Semitic, a charge we will investigate fully at the end of this chapter. But we note in passing that Matthew used these stories to deal with a problem encountered only when addressing other Jews: How can Jesus of Nazareth be the Messiah, when the Messiah must come from Bethlehem? Matthew claimed that Jesus moved to Nazareth only because of the rejection at Jerusalem. This is an image worth pondering. Certainly, from this beginning, it is obvious Matthew had a complex relationship with both Jews and Gentiles.

Fulfilling Righteousness in Deed and Word

The early part of Matthew's gospel reads like a meditation on themes from the Exodus. Like Israel of old, Jesus has been called from Egypt, crossed through the water, and led through the wilderness.

Matthew has carefully molded the wilderness scenes to emphasize the faithfulness of Jesus, which contrasts sharply with the unfaithfulness of Israel during the Exodus led by Moses. Matthew adds both dialogue (3:14–15) and drama (4:1–11); the dialogue declares his intention to "fulfill all righteousness," and the drama actually shows him resisting the temptations of the devil.

Another Matthean addition to the baptism story also alerts the reader to a dominant concern of this work, the role of the Pharisees. Matthew alone portrays Pharisees and Sadducees coming to John for baptism (3:7). This is Matthew's first mention of them; they played no role in the Herod episode (2:4), but Matthew's antipathy toward them is deep and is manifested here at their first appearance. We will explore the reasons for this hostility in the section on Matthew's situation at the end of this chapter. (For a preliminary discussion of these groups, see pp. 161–162.)

The general thrust of Matthew's new material in the baptism and temptation stories is to present Jesus as eminently righteous, obedient to "every word that proceeds from the mouth of God" (4:4). The greatly expanded temptation story should be carefully read (chapter 4), especially noting the motifs of "son" and "obedience." It is noteworthy that worship is said to be due only to God, yet the Magi came to worship Jesus (4:10, 2:2). This unprecedented claim to authority, seen in the call of the disciples, is explained and demonstrated in the first of Matthew's five long speeches.

Reading and Reflection

Study Matthew 5–7, and try to outline the material. Look for thematic or verbal ties to chapters 1–4.

Matthew has set the stage for this mountain-top instruction in two ways. First, there are the many echoes of the Moses-Exodus stories. Though the category "new Moses" proved inadequate to interpret Jesus, Matthew used it to good effect in this early section. We have seen that the idea of genesis dominates chapter 1, that Joseph echoes the patriarch of the same name, and that the baptism and temptation sequence include Exodus themes. Now, like Israel of old, we come to the mountain of revelation, where God is present and the Law (Torah, instruction) is given (see Exodus 19–24 and Matt. 5:1, 21).

The second way Matthew has set the stage for this discourse is by the movement of the plot. The incidents of fulfillment, obedience, and righteousness narrated in chapters 1–4 require further explanation. These two terms, *fulfill* and *righteousness,* provide the keynote of the speech which could be titled "The Meaning of Righteousness Fulfilled."

The discourse is a unified speech (though there is little connection between the various sayings in 6:19–7:12). W. D. Davies has suggested that the organization of the discourse corresponds to the sayings of a teacher called Samuel the Just, who taught a century or so before Matthew:

ðð   ðð   ðð

By three things the world is sustained:
  by the Law,
  by the (temple) service,
  and by deeds of loving kindness
(1966: 305ff; see Mishnah Aboth 1.2)

It is attractive to see Matthew's speech as structured by this pattern; we could paraphrase it as follows:

Introductory considerations (5:1–20)
  a new understanding of the Law (5:21–48)
  a new understanding of worship (6:1–18)
  a new understanding of deeds of loving kindness (6:19–7:12)
Concluding considerations (7:13–27).

Under this arrangement, each of the major sections ends with an appropriate summary statement (5:48; 6:18b; 7:12). Each represents what Matthew has earlier demanded, a righteousness that surpasses·that of the Pharisees because the time of fulfillment has come (5:20, 17). It is crucial to see that this speech sets forth extraordinary demands, which make sense only in light of the conviction that the old promises are being fulfilled in the present time.

A comparison may be made to an extraordinary community of Jews who lived a monastic life at a wilderness place called Qumran, the community which produced the Dead Sea Scrolls. These scrolls reveal a people (usually identified as Essenes) that had a strict and radical ethic, so strict that they had to withdraw from contact with even the Pharisees lest they be polluted. (You may wish to read the scroll known as "the Community Rule," sometimes called "the Manual of Discipline"; a good English translation is Vermes, 1968:71–94.) Like Matthew, these people believed they lived in the time of fulfillment.

One of the primary ways they dealt with their Hebrew Scriptures was by writing a kind of commentary called a *pesher* (Hebrew for *interpretation*). In a pesher the interpreter moved directly from the scriptural sentences to their meaning for his community, believing that these ancient books were written to explain his own situation. The typical method was to cite a verse, then give its application to the community by the expression: "interpreted this means. . . ." Thus the comment on Habakkuk 1:6, which originally referred to the coming Chaldean invasion, reads: "Interpreted, this concerns the Kittim (the Romans)" (Vermes, 236). Because they believed they lived in the time of fulfillment, the Jews of Qumran

Qumran—Source of the Dead Sea Scrolls During the course of more than a century, around the time of Jesus, men sat at low tables in this room (the scriptorium) and patiently copied their sacred writings, both the scriptures and the special writings of their brother-hood. Eventually, when danger threatened, they hid their scrolls in the nearby caves, which served as their homes and libraries. Given the nearly inaccessible nature of the caves, it is not surprising that the scrolls remained hidden for almost two thousand years—until 1947. The cave pictured here, which is directly across from the scriptorium, seems to have been the central library of this austere religious community, usually identified with the Essenes. For a photograph of one of the scrolls, see page 101. (Both photos by author.)

developed an unprecedented community of celibate men who believed their prayers and holiness were bringing the kingdom of God. This radical community was based on an equally radical understanding of the Law, which they interpreted as requiring the life-style they had developed. (For more discussion of this community, see pp. 100–103.)

This conviction that the Scriptures were fulfilled in his own day motivated Matthew, with similar results: a radical reinterpretation of the Law. Because they believed that they were living in this time of fulfillment, Matthew's church had to know how to apply the Law to their situation. As we shall see, a parallel development occurred in other movements within Jewish religion in Matthew's time. But unlike other Jews, Matthew set Jesus, rather than the Torah, at the center of life. This should not surprise the reader of chapters 1–7.

In these first seven chapters the reader meets a Jesus who fulfills both Scripture and righteousness, one who teaches with an authority that amazed the crowds (7:28). Matthew next presents a new display of Jesus authority, in miracles (8–9). Nor will it surprise us that the author who painstakingly organized Jesus' teaching into a carefully crafted speech (5–7) now presents his deeds in an ordered series (8–9).

The next narrative section contains three cycles of three miracles each. Of these nine miracles, eight have parallels in Mark but only four are found in the same sequence as here. In addition, the cycles are separated by two short stories, each raising two questions about discipleship. This artfully arranged unit may be displayed in a diagram:

Cycle I

A. Healing a leper   (8:1–4)
B. Healing a paralyzed servant of a centurion   (8:5–13)
C. Healing Peter's mother-in-law (8:14–17)
      Two questions on discipleship: a radical forsaking of home and family   (8:18–22)

Cycle II

A. Rebuking a great storm   (8:23–27)
B. Expelling demons from two men into swine   (8:28–34)
C. Healing and forgiving a paralytic (9:1–8)
      Two questions on discipleship: fellowship with sinners and proper fasting (9:9–17)

Cycle III

A. Raising a dead girl and healing a woman of hemorrhage (conflated)   (9:18–26)
B. Healing two blind men   (9:27–31)
C. Expelling a demon from a mute (9:32–34)
      Summary passage repeated from 4:23 (9:35)

Finding New Meaning in the Miracles

A comparison with other versions of these stories in Mark and Luke will help us appreciate Matthew's accomplishment the more. If we examine this section in a synopsis (GP #s 45–57 or SFG #s 84–98), we notice first that Matthew has arranged the material in his own way. Only IA and IIC (in the diagram above) follow the same context as in Mark. The sequence of miracles recounted in chapter 8 occur in a different order in Luke, where they come, respectively, in chapters 5, 7, 4, 9, and 8. This should caution those who wish to produce a sequential account of Jesus' ministry. Apparently the gospel sequence relied more on the author's intention than on chronology.

Second, Matthew's version of every one of these stories is shorter than Mark's, often considerably so. This is prime evidence against the idea that Mark abridged Matthew. Several of Matthew's changes are made for stylistic and dramatic reasons, and perhaps for economy of space—a scroll could, conveniently, be only so long.

Third, one consistent difference is Matthew's elimination of all third parties, creating a direct encounter between Jesus and the one healed. (Compare Matthew 8:5–13 with Luke 7:1–10, GP #46, or SFG #85; Matthew 9:1–8 with Mark 2:1–12, GP; #52, or SFG 92; or Matthew 9:18–26 with Mark 5:21–43, GP #107, or SFG 95.)

Fourth, Matthew's sequence does not build to a climax of adulation as does Mark's. His miracles do occasionally spread Jesus' fame (9:26, 31), but they also result in a request to leave (8:34). Even in the miracles there emerges an opposition to Jesus: the crowds marvel, but the Pharisees grumble (9:34). This dual response at the close of the miracle section recalls the dual response to Jesus' teaching in the previous section: some will hear but not do, but such build houses that cannot stand (7:27).

Fifth, Matthew has a more direct statement to make about Christ than Mark. Miracles for Mark remain ambiguous, an inadequate means to correctly perceive who Jesus is; for Matthew they reveal his true identity. Matthew is able to venture this new interpretation of the miracles because his hearers seem to operate more fully within a Jewish sphere of reference. Mark's community seems to have been tempted to (mis)understand the miracles as the work of a "divine man." This community apparently faces no such danger; rather, the miracles show Jesus to be the promised deliverer: they fulfill the prophecy of Isaiah: "He took our infirmities and bore our diseases" (8:17, end of the first cycle). For Matthew the miracles are not the opposite of Jesus' suffering; Isaiah's prophecy enabled Matthew to interpret the miracles as already a part of that suffering.

Finally, this grouping of miracles serves a dramatic purpose in Matthew's story: they reveal the authority of Jesus. The previous section closed by noting the authority with which Jesus taught (7:28); in the middle of the miracle stories, at the end of cycle two, the crowds "glorified God who had given such authority to men" (9:8, unique to Matthew; see also 8:8ff). At the beginning of the next section Jesus invests his disciples with authority to heal (10:1). Matthew has presented the reader with an explanation of who Jesus is (1–4), showing both his authoritative word (5–7) and his authoritative deed (8–9), and now turns his attention to the way Jesus' disciples (and possibly Matthew's community) share in his authority. It would be fruitful at this point to study one of these miracles in detail as a concrete example of how Matthew worked.

At the end of this miracle cycle Matthew repeats the summary with which he closed the first narrative section (9:35 = 4:23). There it concluded the first calling of the disciples, here it precedes the special calling of the twelve. Together they frame the authoritative word and the authoritative deed of Jesus. Matthew is ready to stop and draw some conclusions, giving us his second major discourse.

Instructing the Leaders of the New Community

Like the Sermon on the Mount, this discourse is Matthew's own creation, drawn from a variety of sources and contexts. An examination of a synopsis will show the dexterity with which Matthew has adapted material. (See also Beare, 1962: 80f.) His main sources seem to have been: (1) the two accounts Mark used to tell of the naming of the twelve (3:13–19) and of their instruction (6:7–11), which Matthew has combined; (2) the Q version of a charge to "seventy others" (Luke 10:1–2) plus other Q material (Luke 12:2–9, 51–53; 14:26–27; 17:33); (3) material Mark used in his apocalyptic discourse (13), and (4) other material not found in any other gospel (Matthew 10:23, 40–42).

As before, this material is carefully arranged, though in a novel way. It is arranged in the "X-like" pattern called a chiasmus (discussed on pp. 156–157), in which the first and last items correspond, the second and next to last, and so on in the pattern A B C D C′ B′ A′. Notice how this speech follows the pattern:

The setting of the discourse (9:35–10:4)

A   Instructions for a mixed reception (10:5–15)

B   Description of persecutions (10:16–23)

C   Disciple treated as his master (10:24–25)

D   Do not fear—God knows (10:26–31)

C'   Discipleship is acknowledging Je-
        sus   (10:32–33)
B'   Descriptions of persecutions   (10:34–
        39)
A'   Reception of disciples is reception of
     Jesus   (10:40–42)
     (Adapted from Gaechter: 41)

By this scheme, the turning point is reached
in verses 26–31, an exhortation to courage. It is
striking that everything following this midpoint
has a direct relationship to Jesus. Everything before the midpoint referred to an abstract master-
disciple relationship; afterward it is the relation
of Jesus to his disciples. Earlier, general persecution was described; now it is persecution because of Jesus. Earlier this reception was seen as
a general response to a message; now it is a reception of Jesus. This second half of the discourse is clearly "Christian": it depends on the
post-Easter reflection on the meaning of Jesus for
the church. It is written for Matthew's own community. This does not mean that Matthew created it himself. He relied on traditions found in
his sources (Q and the traditions in Mark), but
used them in a new way.

Some suggest that even the first half (5–25)
was written for the church, especially since the
persecutions envisioned there do not seem to have
originated during Jesus' lifetime. (See the special
study of Hare, 1967.) The early Christians did
not preserve everything Jesus said, only those
sayings and stories that they found useful in their
daily lives. Therefore these instructions are probably no more limited to the twelve than was the
Sermon on the Mount: they are in use in Matthew's community and not simply an antiquarian
recollection.

But this conclusion creates other problems.
Matthew certainly did not support an exclusive
mission to Israel (10:5, but contrast 28:19–20)
nor did he seem to believe that the end would
come before the gospel was preached throughout
Israel (10:23, but contrast 24:14). Various solutions have been proposed for this complex
problem. Perhaps the most common is to view

the charge to go only to Jews as an early, conservative tradition that Matthew rejected in favor
of a universal mission. But an equally important
issue is how Matthew bridges the gap between
the two. Does Matthew motivate the change in
instruction so that the reader is convinced the
mission is now a universal one?

Several scholars have pointed to a scene where
such a change seems to occur: Jesus encounters
a Gentile and is persuaded that his initial reluctance to minister to her is mistaken (15:21–28).
In that scene Jesus echoes the saying in 10:5: "I
was sent only to the lost sheep of the house of
Israel" (15:24, only in Matthew). The woman
insists on her place at "the Lord's table," even
if inferior (15:27) and Jesus immediately changes
his mind (Brown, S., 1978).

What, then, has Matthew gained by portraying this series of events? First, he has justified
the outreach to Gentiles by showing that Jesus
himself made the shift. Immediately after the episode with the woman in chapter 15, Jesus goes
into Gentile territory, where they responded to
him and "glorified the God of Israel" (15:31).
Second, it enabled Matthew to assert that Israel
remained at the center; Gentiles were now admitted into Israel. As the Gentiles in the genealogy already implied, there was a place among
God's people for faithful Gentiles. (Curiously,
Matthew called the woman a "Canaanite" rather
than a "Greek" as Mark referred to her in 7:24.
The Canaanites were an ancient Gentile people
who were eventually allowed to live in Israel.)
Thus, we may interpret all of the instruction in
chapter 10 as applying to Matthew's church, since
their bearing witness to Gentiles (10:18) is part
of their mission to Israel (10:5), and Gentiles are
now included in Israel.

This discourse interprets the previous sections
in two ways: it establishes the continuity between
John, Jesus, and the early church by investing
them all with the same message (3:2; 4:17; 10:7),
and it extends the authority of Jesus to his disciples (7:29; 9:8; 10:1). Thus, as the second half
of the discourse shows, the disciples stand in the
same relation to the world as Jesus did. The ref-

erences to suffering and rejection look forward to the next section.

THE RESPONSES TO JESUS (11–17)

To comprehend the various responses to Jesus in Matthew, we need to understand more about the expectations of people in that time. It was an age of expectation, even among Gentiles. The Roman poet, Virgil (in 40 BCE), had proclaimed the beginning of a new era, a golden age of justice and men "sent down from heaven" (*Eclogue* IV). But the expectation among Jews was older and more highly developed. The centuries before Matthew wrote had seen many variations on the theme of God's coming deliverance of his people. Before considering more directly how Matthew portrays Jesus as Messiah, we will review some of the expectations of his contemporaries.

He Who Is to Come: The Variety of Messianic Expectations

The task of reconstructing the types of Messianic expectation at that time is enormously difficult. Since the proclamation that Jesus was Messiah changed the situation in dramatic ways for Christianity and for Judaism, it is difficult to determine the situation before that time. To make matters worse, nearly all the available data are filtered through subsequent Christian interpretations or through later rabbinic conclusions, evolving partly in response to Christian proclamation. Certainly, there was great variety. It is erroneous to speak simply of Jews expecting a conquering king like David; that was only one strand in a tapestry of ideas not yet woven into a coherent pattern.

One of the exciting things about the Dead Sea Scrolls discovered in caves around the Dead Sea in 1947 and later, is that they preserve a stratum of Jewish thought uncensored by either Christian or Rabbinic interpretations. And the concept of "Messiah" in the scrolls is certainly different from

any we might imagine on the basis of Rabbinic and Christian formulations. At Qumran they seem to have expected two messiahs, one priestly and one royal, but neither was expected to play any significant redemptive role. God himself would bring in the new age; the messiahs would merely preside at the inaugural banquet.[4]

Several other messianic categories survive in the literature of this era, but we cannot always be sure how they were applied by the various groups. For example, a popularly expected person was the Final Prophet (see pp. 27–28). He was usually thought of as Elijah or Moses, but Matthew seems to know a tradition that included the reappearance of Jeremiah (16:14). Insofar as the Samaritans (a half-Jewish people living between Judea and Galilee) had a messianic expectation, they probably expected a new Moses. For they rejected the Davidic monarchy and included only the Pentateuch (the first five books of the Bible) in their Scriptures.

In whatever way they conceived of the coming of the kingdom of God, and through whatever agent, most Jews looked forward to its appearance. We may perhaps generalize: the Zealots strove most ardently for its coming, the Sadducees the least, with Essenes and Pharisees somewhere in between. The Zealots, an activist group who believed in a literal kingdom immediately, apparently also believed they could bring it about. They stirred up several active rebellions, with disastrous conclusions (see Acts 5:36f). Content with the status quo, the wealthy priestly aristocracy, chiefly Sadducees, apparently had little interest in such notions.

The response attributed to Gamaliel in Acts (5:34–38) represents the attitude of the Pharisees: only God can bring about the kingdom. The Pharisees banded together in religious brotherhoods, eating their meals in priestly purity, while waiting and praying for the coming of God's

---

4. See the introduction to Vermes 1968:47–52, the "Messianic Rule," p. 121, and "The Community Rule," p. 87. The brevity of these references indicates their lack of functional significance. The evidence is discussed by LaSor, 1956; Priest, 1963; and Higgins, 1967.

kingdom. The Essenes adopted a similar strategy, but engaged in a more radical quest for purity—abandoning normal society to live a communal existence in mutual holiness. Their task was to wait, in patience and purity, for God to inaugurate the new age. But whether these groups imagined the kingdom coming through bloody battle or by God's own decree, none imagined a messiah who would suffer.

The only place in the Hebrew Scriptures where an ideal figure is said to suffer is in the "Servant songs" of Isaiah of Babylon. Isaiah had to explain why Israel had suffered so, deprived of the homeland, living in captivity. He held out the hope of restoration in a grand new Exodus (Isa. 40:1–11; 45:1–13), but also idealized and glorified the suffering: through exile, a witness to God was being made to the nations. He portrayed Israel's suffering as redemptive:

🙢 🙢 🙢

For he grew up before him like a young plant,
*　　and like a root out of dry ground;*
he had no form or comeliness that we should look
*　　at him, and no beauty that we should desire*
*　　him.*
He was despised and rejected by men; a man of
*　　sorrows, and acquainted with grief;*
and as one from whom men hid their faces he
*　　was despised, and we esteemed him not.*
Surely he has borne our griefs and carried our
*　　sorrows;*
yet we esteemed him stricken, smitten by God,
*　　and afflicted.*
But he was wounded for our transgressions, he
*　　was bruised for our iniquities;*
upon him was the chastisement that made us
*　　whole, and with his stripes we are healed.*
All we like sheep have gone astray; we have
*　　turned every one to his own way;*
and the Lord has laid on him the iniquity of us
*　　all.[5]*

Certainly, early Christians saw in these words a marvelous reference to the fate of Jesus. It became perfectly clear after his death. Yet, as we have seen in Mark, no one—not even the disciples of Jesus—expected a suffering Messiah.

A very interesting interpretation of this Servant passage is known as the *Targum of Jonathan* on Isaiah 53.[6] What is remarkable about this interpretation is that it identifies the Servant with the Messiah, but studiously avoids any notion that the Messiah would suffer: a challenging interpretative feat. It reads:

🙢 🙢 🙢

. . . The righteous will grow up before him, yea,
like blooming shoots, and like a tree which sends
forth its roots to streams of water will they in-
crease—a holy generation in the land that was in
need of him: his countenance no profane counte-
nance, and the terror at him not the terror at an
ordinary man; his complexion shall be a holy
complexion, and all who see him will look wist-
fully upon him. Then he will become despised,
and will cut off the glory of all the kingdoms;
they will be prostrate and mourning, like a man
of pains and like one destined for sicknesses; and
as though the presence of the Shekhinah [God's
glory] had been withdrawn from us, they will be
despised, and esteemed not. Then for our sins he
will pray, and our iniquities will for his sake be
forgiven, although we were accounted stricken,
smitten from before the Lord, and afflicted. But
he will build up the Holy Place, which has been
polluted for our sins, and delivered to the enemy
for our iniquities; and by his instruction peace
shall be increased upon us, and by devotion to
his words, our sins will be forgiven us. All we
like sheep had been scattered, we had each wan-

---

5. The whole song is worth reading, Isa. 52:13–53:12. The other servant songs in Isaiah are: 42:1–4; 49:1–6; and 50:4–9. For a discussion of their original intention,

see Lindbloom, 1972:267ff and 428ff; Heschel, 1962:146–151; Von Rad, 1965:221ff; McKenzie, 1968:xl–xlvii. See also the general discussion in Chapter 1, p. 27, above.
6. A Targum was an Aramaic interpretive translation of the Hebrew Scriptures that was used in synagogue worship. Originally this was an oral response to the Scripture read in Hebrew. Its roots are ancient, though it was not put into written form until well into the Christian era.

dered off on his own way; but it was the Lord's good pleasure to forgive the sins of all of us for his sake. (Neubauer and Driver, II, 1969:5f)

The logic of these changes seems to follow this pattern: since this figure does some of the things Messiah is to do, he can be identified with the Messiah. But then we have to understand the suffering referred to as applying to someone else. For Messiah will conquer evil, not suffer.

Other than this negative generalization (Messiah would not suffer), there was little agreement as to what God would do when he established his kingdom. But with this confusing swirl of Messianic ideas as a background, the thrust of Matthew's third narrative section (11–12) becomes clear: although the Pharisees—offended at his lack of purity—do not understand (12:14), Jesus does the works of the Messiah (11:3–6; 8:17). It is all as Scripture foretold (12:17–21; note the emphasis on Gentiles). This section contains a kaleidoscope of responses to Jesus, of which Peter's confession is the highlight (notice 13:54, 57; 14:1–2, 33; 15:12, 27, 31; 16:1; 16:13–20; and 17:4, 6). This confession now takes on the aura of an extraordinary accomplishment, quite unlike the Markan portrayal (GP #122 or SFG #158). This is a beautifully wrought section, interweaving the defense of Jesus, the antagonism of the Pharisees, and the inevitable rejection. It should be studied as a unit, noting especially the materials unique to Matthew.

The Kingdom in a New Community

We should expect Matthew's concept of the kingdom to share much with Mark's, since he uses a great deal of the same material. Both were strongly influenced by an apocalyptic worldview, looking forward to the imminent arrival of God's rule. (See discussion in Chapters 2 and 7.) Yet we have already seen one way that Matthew deliberately digresses from Mark, by having the kingdom announced by John the Baptist (3:2).

Matthew also includes a striking addition to the narrative concerning the charge of an alliance with Beelzebul.[7] Matthew allows the charge to be made three times (9:34; 10:25; 12:24), choosing to answer only on the third occasion. To the answer we have already heard in Mark, he adds Jesus' declaration of the meaning of the exorcisms:

ᴥ ᴥ ᴥ

But if it is by the Spirit of God that I cast out demons, then the Kingdom of God has come upon you. (12:28)

The expression "Kingdom of God" is unusual for Matthew; he regularly uses only "Kingdom" or "Kingdom of the Heavens" (32 times, but see 19:24 and 21:31, 43). This probably indicates his use of a traditional formulation (or possibly he used "God" in parallel with "Spirit of God" in line 1). Even more important, the verb tense is the past, and in the Greek a special kind of action is involved that indicates a completed action (an aorist tense). The coming of the kingdom, at least, is placed in the past. The presence of the kingdom should be seen in the exorcisms, because there the enemy Satan is overcome. The apocalyptic cast of this concept should not be overlooked.

This kingdom concept is explained in the next speech, the seven parables of chapter 13. Parables are both easy and difficult to interpret: they speak directly to the reader, but they come to us preceded by a history of interpretations, including those of the gospel writers.

Joachim Jeremias, in a masterful study of the parables, shows that the church sought to apply and reinterpret the parables chiefly by allegorization (Jeremias, 1963:66–89), that is, by imagining that each item in the parable represented

---

7. Compare Matt. 12:25–37 with Mark 3:23–30; GP #86 or SFG 17–118. The same addition is made by Luke, implying that it had already attained this form in Q. Yet it signifies a major concern of Matthew.

something else. Unlike a real story, an allegory does not make sense by itself; the reader must know the "key," that is, what each part of the story really refers to. (See the first chapter of Via, 1967.) A true parable, on the other hand, is a self-contained story that makes an impact on its hearers by the insight it provides. While we must expect that Jesus may have also used allegories, many of the allegorizations that we find in the gospels seem designed to fit the situation of the church. Similarly, the allegorizations of the parable of the Sower and the parable of the Weeds seem to fit the situation of the church more closely than that of Jesus.

Reading and Reflection

Carefully study Matthew 13 and consider:

1. What is Matthew's understanding of the nature and function of the parables?
2. What are the characteristics of the kingdom?
3. What is the relationship between the present and the future?

A radical tension between present and future is evident throughout Matthew's gospel (Bornkamm, 1963:15–51). Such tension is evident in these parables as the contrast between sowing and reaping, between present experience and final expectation. At every turn, the unexpected is found in the midst of the everyday. The long tradition of interpreting the mustard seed and leaven parables as the gradual growth of the kingdom should not blind us to Matthew's own view, which does not mention growth (the process) but shocking result (the outcome).

Clearly these parables refer to something already begun, already planted. Of the evangelists, Matthew alone shows Jesus consciously building a church (16:18), but he does not simply equate the kingdom and the church (for example, the Parable of the Tares).

Matthew presents a much more positive picture of the disciples than Mark (for example, compare 14:32 with Mark 6:51). Or to put it another way, the disciples fulfill a different narrative role in this gospel: they are the legitimate successors of Jesus, a common theme in biographies of philosophers in Matthew's time (Talbert, 1977:105ff). Matthew's legitimation of the disciples may be seen in the commission in chapter ten and traced in the subtle variations in the material included in the next section (14–17). In the two feeding episodes, for example, the disciples clearly duplicate Jesus' own action, and the feeding itself becomes typical of the eucharistic meal. Now they understand Jesus' teaching (16:12). This new emphasis on the disciples is also evident in Matthew's recasting of Mark's central scene, Peter's confession (16:13–23, GP #122, SFG #158).

While Matthew does not delete the rebuke to Peter (as Luke will), he certainly emphasizes his preeminence (see also 14:22–33; 17:24–27; 18:21f). Only in Matthew is Peter given extraordinary power "to bind and to loose." (A power later extended to all the disciples—18:18.) In Rabbinic literature this expression is used in connection with the rabbi ruling on a point of law, meaning to forbid or allow, but it also has a broader legal meaning to find guilty (or excommunicate), or to acquit (or forgive). (See Jeremias, TDNT, iii: 751; Green, 1975: 153.) The declaration given here views the judgment of Peter/the church as being ratified by God. (See a similar bestowing of authority in John 20:23.) Such extraordinary power is in some tension with the faulty judgment immediately shown by Peter (16:22–23), a scene that Matthew expands.

Clearly, then, Matthew avoids an overidealized image of his community, never simply identifying it with the kingdom of God. Yet he does show that that kingdom has already appeared in the words and deeds of Jesus and has now become shockingly obvious in the community that seeks to follow Jesus. Hence, the closest possible connection between Jesus and the church.

THE CHARACTERIZATION OF JESUS (18–28)

In the following discourse (chapter 18), Matthew qualifies the church's authority to pass judgment in two ways: by introducing specific church laws that act as a sort of constitution and by placing the whole discussion of judgment in a context of forgiveness.

Reading and Reflection

Read chapter 18, making a list of the laws Matthew lays down. What are the characteristics of true citizens of the Kingdom of Heaven?

The arrogance to which Matthew's argument could lead (not unknown in the church) is here nipped in the bud. The closing parable (18:23–35) especially—a real parable, not to be allegorized—establishes the basis of church discipline by recognizing the universal need for forgiveness (see 6:4f).

Jesus as the Righteous Judge

This parable provides the transition into Matthew's next section (19–22) with its theme of judgment, which is explained in the final discourse (23–25). Although this is often believed to be a judgment of the Jews, or the Pharisees, or of "false Israel," the scope of the final discourse is a judgment on all the nations (25:32). This section differentiates true and false discipleship. It is, as H. B. Green suggests, a recapitulation and exemplification of some aspects of the Sermon on the Mount (1975:166); both disciples and Pharisees stand under judgment (19:25ff).

This echoes an earlier motif, that the kingdom contains true sons and sons of the evil one (13:38, 48) and that situation must persist until the "close of the age" (13:30, 40). Matthew takes a parable from Q and reworks it to introduce this theme of inclusion/exclusion (compare 22:1–14 with Luke 14:16–24, GP #205, SFG #279). Here we see the two aspects, the inclusion of "both bad and good" (22:10, only in Matthew) as well as the final judgment (22:11–13). Being in the church is no protection against the coming judgment. Matthew's account of the story of the man who sought eternal life sets forth the requirements (19:16–30 = Mark 10:17–31, GP #189, SFG #254). Besides moderating the theological difficulty raised by Mark's introduction (which seemed to question Jesus' divine status), Matthew's story differs in three important ways from the earlier telling: (1) He includes the radical summary of the law characteristic of his community, "love your neighbor as yourself" (19:19, 22:36–40). (2) He changes the subsequent question to show that even this standard is not enough (19:20). (3) In Jesus' answer, he says, "if you would be perfect" (5:48) go, sell all, and follow me (19:21). This brings us to the crux of Matthew's argument with his fellow Jews (the topic of the next major section): obedience consists in more than keeping the Law; it consists in following Jesus. But this "following Jesus" is not simply identifying with him: Matthew thought that many would be turned away at the last judgment even though they preached and worked miracles in Jesus' name (7:21–23). Matthew calls them "evildoers" or, literally, "lawless ones." The "higher righteousness" (5:20) does not demand less than the scribes and Pharisees; it demands more. Disciples will fail unless they keep the Law as revealed in Jesus (24:35; 5:18). The Pharisees fail because they refuse to recognize the true heir to the vineyard (21:33–46, especially 43).

What, then, is the relationship between the church and the kingdom? In one sense the church is the kingdom, the seed planted in the earth, the leaven hidden in the lump. Yet it stands in paradoxical tension with the kingdom: the catch must be sorted; the weeds discarded. It is the maidens, wise and foolish, waiting for the wedding for which only some of them are prepared (25:1–13). Between the church and the kingdom stands the judgment.

An examination of the final discourse (23–25) will show how Matthew developed this concept of judgment. Over half the material in 23–25 is unique to Matthew, revealing the importance of this theme for his work as a whole. Discussion of chapter 23 will be reserved to the next section, but its context as a message of judgment is to be emphasized. It is a judgment Matthew had seen fulfilled in the destruction of Jerusalem in 70 CE. If this chapter has a bitter tone, it is the bitterness of one who has seen the awful judgment.

The rest of the discourse shifts location (as did the third and fourth discourses—13:36; 18:21) but continues the theme of judgment, by using material from the apocalyptic discourse (Mark 13) and by adding Q and other materials concerning the coming end. The climactic scene is reached in a prophetic vision of the last judgment (25:31–46, only in Matthew). This important scene should be read and considered carefully.

If Matthew has written his book well and if we have read it well, there should be no need to elaborate on his judgment here. We ought to recognize his portrayals as easily as a shepherd recognizes a sheep or a goat. People are included on the basis of their fulfilling the Law of Love of Neighbor, now focused as a response to Jesus. The crucial factor is not naming Jesus, but responding to his demand for "higher righteousness." The one new twist is the innocence with which the righteous act, but even that was foreshadowed (19:13–15).

If we ask further how this parable influences the understanding of the nature of the church and its relation to the kingdom, one final note may be added. Those gathered for judgment are called "all the nations" (25:32), yet the judgment itself is clearly an individual event. Several commentators have interpreted "all the nations" in Matthew to mean "the Gentiles," thus excluding Is-

rael as a separate identity.[8] It is true that the term "nations" in the plural often means Gentiles (6:7, 6:32, 20:19). But this would present us with a concept of the kingdom foreign to the rest of the gospel. The point here does not seem to be the modern liberal notion that a pagan can be a "Christian" unwittingly, but rather that true righteousness is required even of those who call Jesus the Lord. It is therefore a judgment on the church, which Matthew has already designated as "nation" (21:43). (See the treatment of *ethne* by Schmidt in TDNT, ii: 364–372.) We may also note that if Matthew had meant the nations as opposed to Israel he had no reason to add *all*.

This parable confirms our earlier picture of the tension between the present of the church and the future of the kingdom. Matthew's church is in the process of coming to terms with living "between the times"; the kingdom has been inaugurated but it has not been consummated. The church's task in this interim is to be faithful in doing the will of God, keeping the Law, following Jesus (see 7:21; 12:50; 19:17). In the final narrative section Matthew portrays the paradigm of such a life: the ultimate obedience of Jesus.

Jesus as the Example of Righteousness

Jesus is the source of the higher righteousness that Matthew demands in two realms: he is its authoritative teacher (5:20) and its model (4:1–11). Now Matthew turns his attention to the latter, reworking the passion story to emphasize the themes of obedience and surpassing righteousness. The passion narrative was the most fixed part of the Jesus tradition, and Matthew's version is very similar to Mark's. Yet this also suggests that even minor variations may be important for Matthew. Before examining in detail the trial and crucifixion, notice how Matthew foreshadows both

8. See Green, 1975:206; see also Hare and Harrington, pp. 359–369. For an opposite view, see Meier, 1977:94–102.

Jesus' burial (26:6–13) and death (26:20–29), carefully explaining their meaning: for the forgiveness of sins (26:28, only in Matthew). Matthew offers no fuller explanation, but he is sure that these are not accidental or unfortunate events. Jesus is deliberately fulfilling the will of God (26:52–54, only in Matthew). This is described in what may be called the climactic scene of the gospel, the submission of Jesus to the Father's will in Gethsemane (26:36–46), a scene portrayed more intensely in Matthew than in Mark or Luke. The real struggle is not an agony in the face of death (as in Mark) but a struggle of the will; that accomplished, true obedience follows.

Reading and Reflection

Carefully study Matthew 27, in relation to Mark's account and as a unified narrative.

1. Does Matthew emphasize the same points as Mark?
2. How does Matthew show that this is a cosmic event?
3. What is the role of the Pharisees in this event? Of the Jewish leaders?

Of the many observations possible, I shall limit myself to two that show how Matthew's interpretation of this event presents a radical new interpretation of Mark's notion that Jesus' death revealed his divine sonship (Mark 15:39). First, Matthew introduces cosmic phenomena into the text so that the centurion sees far more than the manner of Jesus' death (Matt. 27:51–54). Second, Matthew introduces the title Son of God into the crucifixion scene itself, in the form of a threefold taunt that is really a temptation to abandon the cross (27:40–44). This recalls the earlier threefold temptation (4:3, 6, 8) and perhaps echoes the threefold prayer in Gethsemane. In each of these scenes, the obedience of Jesus keeps him in the path of righteousness. By means of these

and other modifications, Matthew transforms the story from one of suffering to one of obedience. Thus, Jesus fulfills all righteousness (3:15).

In Matthew's version there need be no reluctance to portray the resurrection, for it vindicates this obedience. At this point we may reflect back to the analysis of the four accounts of the empty tomb (p. 136). Perhaps the variations noted between Matthew and Mark are now more intelligible. Matthew's portrait of Jesus causes him to represent this scene differently. Thus in his closing episode, which takes us back to the beginning and the promise of Emmanuel, Jesus appears to his disciples in Galilee and declares:

🐦 🐦 🐦

All authority in heaven and on earth has been given to me. Go therefore and make disciples of all nations, baptizing them in the name of the Father and of the Son and of the Holy Spirit, teaching them observe all that I have commanded you; and lo, I am with you always, to the close of the age.

The Matthean Portrayal of Jesus

The narrator in Mark announced Jesus as Christ, son of God. In contrast, the narrator in Matthew announces Jesus as Christ, son of David, son of Abraham. Though Matthew also describes Jesus as son of God (3:17), even as "God with us" (1:23), the difference in nuance is worth considering.

An author may use several methods to reveal character: the responses of other characters, the evaluative point of view of the narrator, the titles and attributes assigned to a character, and—most importantly—the deeds and words of the character. Without doubt, the Matthean Jesus is a complex character: the magi approach him as king of the Jews (2:2); John calls him the "one mightier" (3:11); the voice from heaven declares him to be "my son" (3:17); the centurion recognizes him as a person of authority (8:8); Jesus calls himself "son of man," an expression that meant roughly "a human being" (8:20; 12:8; 16:28). This list could be extended.

But if we focus our attention on what Jesus does and says, two characteristics seem to predominate: Jesus is one endowed with great authority, and, conversely, he is the supremely obedient one. While Jesus is introduced with the quotation from Isaiah that points to "God with us" (1:23), he is depicted as the one whose every action is oriented toward doing the will of God. Thus, his first deed and first word are explicitly to fulfill all righteousness (3:15 and 5:17–20). His final act, in Gethsemane, is to choose the divine will.

This tension between authority and obedience is a central facet of Matthew's characterization of Jesus. Matthew's new telling of the temptation scene highlights this tension: Jesus, as son of God, is tempted to act with independent authority—a temptation echoed in Gethsemane and on the cross. Because he is supremely obedient, he is given supreme authority (28:18). In this way Jesus becomes the leader of a new community and its chief model. The people too can now be sons of God (5:9; 45; 13:38) and address God as "our Father" (6:9). Now let us investigate more directly the nature of that community.

THE SITUATION OF MATTHEW AND HIS COMMUNITY

Once again, we have a writing that is thoroughly anonymous—with no attempt to identify author, place, or time of writing—and again, we have little hope of recapturing these particulars. We must explore the document for clues to its social and historical setting, but the clues point in two different directions. As one writer lamented nearly a half-century ago:

❧ ❧ ❧

The Gospel seems to contain so many contradictions, and to wear a double face. It is at once

'Jewish' and anti-Jewish, 'legal' and anti-legal, narrow and anti-Gentile and also catholic and universalist. (Montefiore, I, 1927: lxxiii)

Thus, for example, Matthew has Jesus declare "The scribes and Pharisees sit on Moses' seat, so practice and observe whatever they tell you" (23:2–3). The Seat of Moses indicates their teaching authority and implies Matthew's acceptance of the Oral Torah. But he immediately goes on to condemn them in the most stringent terms, calling them "blind guides" (23:16; 16:6, 12). Both of these declarations are found only in Matthew; the other gospels are neither so positive nor so negative.

We may summarize by saying that some clues point to a "Jewish Matthew," a writer at home in the Jewish tradition. Our study of Paul revealed that many early Christians continued to worship within the synagogue, considering themselves Jews, and being so regarded by other Jews. They probably considered themselves Jews who belonged to the brotherhood of Christ as other Jews belonged to the brotherhood of the Pharisees or Essenes. This was not simply an early phenomenon; some Christians continued in this fashion for hundreds of years (Pines, 1966). Was Matthew such a Christian?

Or was he opposed to such a way of being Christian, as other clues in the book might indicate? We do know that some Christians, especially Gentile Christians, rejected a "Jewish" understanding of Christianity. Early in the second century, a Gentile Christian writer declares: "It is an abomination to follow Jesus Christ and to practice Jewish ways" (Ignatius, *To the Magnesians* 10). By the middle of the second century Marcion, that ardent follower of Paul, declares that there are only contradictions between Jewish and Christian traditions (pp. 125–128).

We must review the relations between Jews and Gentiles in Matthew's time and try to discover the emerging consciousness of Judaism and Christianity as two separate movements. Only then will we be prepared to address Matthew's relationship to the Jewish people. First, let me address two logical, but faulty assumptions: that people in Matthew's day were either Jews or Gentiles, and that Judaism in Matthew's time was a standard, stable religious movement to which all Jews adhered. Neither is correct.

Jewish Gentiles; Gentilized Jews

In Matthew's day the Jews were a populous and far-ranging people, sometimes estimated to comprise as much as 10 percent of the population of the Roman Empire, though this figure seems too high. Jews had lived outside their homeland at least since the Exile (587 BCE) and, by Matthew's time, there were Jewish synagogues in every major city in the empire. In Egypt the Jews were said to number one million (Philo, *In Flaccum* 43), with the largest settlement in Alexandria—the leading intellectual and cultural center of that era. Two of the five sections of Alexandria were Jewish, though Jews lived and had synagogues in the other quarters as well (*In Flaccum* 55). Large Jewish communities also existed in Syria, Asia Minor, Italy, and even Parthia.

Several factors contributed to an increasingly large Jewish population. First, the Jews were nearly the only ancient people who did not practice infanticide, the killing of unwanted infants. More important, many Jews in this period sought to convert Gentiles, and many Gentiles were receptive (pp. 61–65). Many Gentiles converted to Jewish religion (became proselytes), but others resisted full conversion. A fairly large contingent of such people gathered around the synagogue and became known as a special class: the devout or the God-fearers (Grant, 1962: 105; Luke 7:1–5, Acts 10:1f; 14:1).

Even as some Gentiles in Matthew's world had already moved toward becoming "Jewish," many Jews had become "Gentile" in all but their religion. The majority of Jews lived in the Diaspora, among Gentiles: they spoke Greek, read their Bible in Greek, adopted Greek names and dress—in many important ways they began to think like

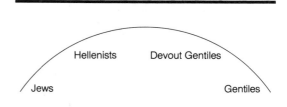

Figure 8 ▪ 1

Greeks. This group is usually referred to as the Hellenists (from *Hellas*, the name for Greece). So instead of two antithetical groups, Jews and Gentiles, it is more accurate to speak of a continuum of identification with four recognizable concentrations (see Figure 8.1).

As might be expected, the middle groups had the most in common and early Christianity apparently made its strongest appeal to them.

The Diversity of Judaism in the First Christian Century

The other faulty assumption would be to think there was one major form of Judaism in Matthew's time. This might be true by 150 CE, but it was not the case when Matthew wrote. We need some sense of the historical development in this pivotal period.

The nature of the major religious sects of Jesus' time have been briefly characterized in the discussion above and in Chapter 7 (pp. 161–163). Let us examine these groups more closely, since the history of all four was profoundly influenced by the political events that touched Israel.

Since the fall of the monarchy in 587 BCE, Israel had enjoyed only one century of virtual independence—the period of the Maccabees. This independence was brought to an end by the visit of Pompey to Jerusalem in 63 BCE. On the pretext of settling a dispute between two rival claimants to power, Pompey effectively asserted Rome's hegemony over Palestine. At first Rome was content to rule through the appointed priest, then through puppet kings, the Herods, but eventually, in 6 CE, a Roman governor was appointed. This direct rule, coupled with a census to determine taxes, led to the first Jewish revolt and the founding of the new sect, the *Zealots*. These Zealots should not be viewed primarily as a political or nationalistic group; their first motive was religious. They considered recognition of Caesar as Lord and the payment of taxes with coins bearing Caesar's image to be violations of the first commandment (Exod. 20:2). They were strictly observant Jews, as recent excavations of their mountain stronghold have shown (Yadin, 1966:164ff). They shared much with the Pharisees; they have even been referred to as leftwing Pharisees (Herford, 1952:51). But they differed on one essential point: for the Zealots faithfulness demanded active resistance to Rome and the overthrow of the government. Consequently, they were hostile to the ruling aristocracy (the Sadducees) but immensely popular with the people. So popular, in fact, that in 66 CE they precipitated a war with Rome that lasted more than seven years. According to Luke, one of Jesus' disciples was a Zealot (6:15; Acts 1:13). Barabbas is characterized as a Zealot (Mark 15:7) and his popularity with the people is entirely believable.

Firmly opposed to this zealotry were the *Sadducees*, a wealthy priestly aristocracy that ran the domestic affairs of the Jewish people under the Roman governors (Reicke, 1968:155ff). Like all rulers, the Sadducees were in no great hurry for the kingdom of God to come. They had little concern or respect for the common people, a feeling that was duly reciprocated.

A third sect, the *Essenes*, responded to Rome in yet another way. Like the Zealots, they believed that the foreigners polluted the land. So polluted had Israel become that even the Temple had been desecrated by unworthy priests appointed by Gentile kings. But unlike the Zealots, the Essenes adopted a completely quietistic attitude: they withdrew from society to form a new holy society worthy to be called Israel. They followed a strict discipline and mingled only with each other, since even fellow Jews were deemed polluted. Apparently one group of these quietists withdrew to Qumran near the Dead Sea and produced the scrolls discovered at midcentury (the Dead Sea Scrolls). Other Essenes formed enclaves within various villages. They maintained the strictest discipline of any of the Jewish sects. Some even refused to marry, since contact with women might contaminate them. Although Essenes are not mentioned in the gospels, probably because of their seclusion, they represented one of the major religious options in first-century Jewish religion. Apparently, numerous other small sectarian groups of various kinds also existed, but we know little about them (Simon, 1967).

A moderate approach to Rome characterized the most influential of the groups, the *Pharisees*, who have the worst reputation of any of these groups—due in no small part to Matthew's writing. In English today "to be a Pharisee" means to be a hypocrite. Precisely Matthew's opinion (23:13, 23, 25). There probably were Pharisees who were hypocrites, even as there were Christians who were hypocrites. But that is obviously not what they intended to be. The Pharisaic party of Jesus' time was in its period of growth and diversity, organized into local fellowships or brotherhoods that served both social and religious ends. Their attempt to keep the ancient laws of purity caused them to avoid possibly polluting contact not only with Gentiles and Samaritans, but also with less observant Jews. However, these brotherhoods were not rigid, closed communities; a great deal of variety of interpretation was allowed and a consensus emerged only after prolonged debate. The leaders of the Pharisees seem to have developed the understanding of Jewish tradition that became standard: Rabbinic Judaism.

The Emergence of Rabbinic Judaism

The two formative teachers of Pharisaism before the time of Jesus were Hillel and Shammai, contemporaries whose dates are uncertain, though they probably both died between 10 and 20 CE. They represented divergent tendencies. For Hillel, the heart of the Law was love of neighbor, so he continually endeavored to adjust Torah to life. For example, the provision of Torah that required debts of fellow Israelites to be remitted in the seventh year (Deut. 15:1–6) had become a hardship for the poor because it was nearly impossible to obtain loans as the seventh year approached. Hillel created a new provision, whereby the law of release of debts could be expressly waived in a formal legal proceeding before the loan was made (Bruce, 1969:80). The common sense of this solution should not blind us to its radical nature: it effectively annulled the biblical law. We should also notice its intent: to serve the poor, the same intent as the original law.

Shammai represented a stricter interpretation of the Law, a more literal understanding. Against Hillel he argued that the Shema (a part of the daily prayer) must be recited while reclining in the evening but while standing in the morning, since the Scripture says to pray "when you lie down and when you rise" (Deut. 6:7; *TB Berakoth* 11a; Davies, 1966:264). Such literalism characterized much of his teaching. F. F. Bruce considers it "probable" that the lawyers who "load men with burdens hard to bear" are Shammaites (Luke 11:46; Bruce, 1972:80). It is also worth noting that Shammai was from a wealthy family, while Hillel was more of a commoner and oriented more to the needs of the people. Their respective attitudes may be seen clearly in a famous rabbinic story:

❧ ❧ ❧

A gentile once came to Shammai and offered to convert to the Jewish way but on a condition. It seems he found the Torah too complex and insisted that it be taught him "while standing on one foot." Shammai chased him away with a stick. The would-be convert went to Hillel with the same request. Hillel responded, "Whatever is hateful to you, do not do to your neighbor. That is the entire Torah. The rest is commentary; go and learn it." (See TB. Shabbat, *31a)*

The striking similarity between Hillel's reply and Matthew's report of Jesus' summary of the Law (7:12) should not be overlooked.

Many similar stories illustrate the differences between Hillel and Shammai, and their personal antagonism was perpetuated by their disciples for at least the next century, and thus during the period of Matthew. Many of their differences are remembered even after a deliberate attempt to impose unity, and we must suspect that there was a good deal more diversity than just these two schools in the early period. The very nature of the Pharisaic approach would produce diversity, for although it drew upon an authoritative revelation, it depended on argument and analogy to prove new applications. It would take many years to achieve consensus by these means.

Just when the majority of the Jewish people began to regard themselves as "heirs of the Pharisees" is difficult to determine. Eventually one group, the rabbis, emerged as the intellectual and religious leaders of the Jewish people. The most decisive event in the evolution of rabbinic leadership was the publication of the *Mishnah*, a vast collection of rabbinic lore combined over many decades and published in final form about 200 CE. Certainly the rabbis, and Pharisaic leaders like Hillel, were influential long before then. But they were not the only influences. In the long period between the time of Herod and the Second Jewish War (that is between 6 CE and 135) the Zealots rivalled, and often surpassed, the Pharisees in popular support, leading the people in two wars of national liberation against Rome. Also, many sectarian movements (including Christianity) struggled for recognition. Although the Pharisees, or their heirs the rabbis, were eventually able to piece together a consensus which held and molded Judaism into its classical form, Matthew's gospel was written during the struggle.

One of the most dramatic events of this long struggle occurred in 70 CE: the Roman conquest of Jerusalem and the destruction of the Temple. According to Josephus, Zealot activity rose sharply under the procuratorship of Felix (52–60; *Antiquities* xx. 185f). This sect harassed the Roman authorities and all who cooperated with them. This tumultuous period, marked by the ineffectiveness of Felix and the inattention of the new young emperor, Nero, culminated in open rebellion in 66. The war, surprisingly, lasted more than seven years and left the Jewish people in a chaotic state. Soon after the war a few far-sighted Pharisees under the leadership of Yohanan ben Zakkai gathered at Yavneh (also called Jabneh and Jamnia) to form a school for the study of Torah. From this center Pharisaic leadership eventually established its hegemony over Judaism, but not automatically. The Sadducees, like any wealthy aristocracy, did not lie down and play dead just because the Temple was destroyed. In fact, private sacrifices—though not the great public festivals—continued to be offered in the Temple ruins, and some pilgrimages were still made (Safrai and Sterns, I, 1974:211; Gaston, 1970:3; Clark, 1960:269–280). But their aristocratic policies were ill-suited to the new situation after 70.

The Zealots were temporarily discredited by the failure of the war. And the Essenes were ill-equipped by their withdrawal to assume leadership. For the Pharisees, however, the time seemed ripe to inaugurate policies long believed in but heretofore blocked.

With the Temple at least temporarily removed, the Jewish people needed a new center. The answer was obvious to the Pharisees. Years earlier, Yohanan ben Zakkai had declared that Torah was the source and end of life (*Aboth* 2.8). A story told about him reveals the ambiguous attitude of the Pharisees to the destruction of the Temple: both to mourn it and to surpass it with Torah.

❧ ❧ ❧

When a fellow rabbi mourned the loss of the Temple, lamenting that there was no longer a place to make atonement for Israel's sins, Rabban Yohanan ben Zakkai is said to have comforted him by saying there was another atonement as effective as the Temple, namely, deeds of kindness. "For it is said, I desire mercy and not sacrifice." (see Avoth de Rabbi Nathan, A, *ch. 4; and* Hosea 6:6)

Later rabbinic opinion would declare: that whoever busies himself with Torah—it is as one who offered a burnt offering (Neusner, 1975:84; see *TB Menahot,* 110a). As W. D. Davies notes, the Pharisees accepted the priesthood in principle but opposed it in fact (1966:258).

One problem confronting these postwar Pharisees was reconciling differences of opinion within their own ranks and refuting the opinion of those outside. They told an amusing story about the suppression of Shammaite opinion:

❧ ❧ ❧

*Rabbi Abba said that Samuel told him that for three years the debate raged between the disciples of Shammai and the disciples of Hillel, both claiming their interpretation of the Law was the correct one. The debate did not end until it was interrupted by a voice from heaven, declaring: Both Shammai and Hillel teach the words of the living God, but the laws must be fixed according to the rulings of the disciples of Hillel. (*TB Erubin *13b)*

Such overcoming by incorporation seems to have been the preferred way of the rabbis. However, they were not adverse to outright condemnation of opposing groups:

❧ ❧ ❧

*All Israel will share in the world to come. For it is written, "Your people shall all be righteous. . . ." But these do not have a share in the world to come: anyone who says there is no resurrection of the dead prescribed in the Law [a teaching of the Sadducees], and anyone who says that the Law is not from heaven and an Epicurean. Rabbi Akiba [c. 140] says: in addition, anyone who reads the heretical books. . . . (*Sanhedrin 10.1)*

More to our point was the direct move that was made to exclude Jewish Christians from the synagogue. Around 90 CE a member of the Yavneh school known as Samuel the Small reworded one of the blessings recited daily in the synagogue, to make it impossible for Jewish Christians (and perhaps others who refused to follow the Pharisaic line) to continue to worship there. The new prayer went:

🙣 🙣 🙣

Let there be no hope for renegades, And wipe out the kingdom of pride speedily in our days, and may all Nazarenes [Christians] and heretics perish instantly, May their names be erased from the Book of Life and not be inscribed with those of the righteous. Blessed be Thou, O God, Who humblest the proud.[9]

Matthew versus the Pharisees

Matthew must have been written before this liturgical innovation became widespread (otherwise he could not have counseled obedience to the Pharisees, 23:2–3), but probably not much earlier. If, as is most likely, he used Mark as a source, sufficient time must have elapsed for that gospel to have become popular and authoritative. There are also indications that Matthew knew the historical details of the fall of Jerusalem (21:43; 23:34ff; 27:35). Therefore it is reasonable to date the writing of the Gospel according to Matthew to around the year 85 CE.

It is also reasonable to see Matthew's community engaged in an activity similar to that of the Pharisees at Yavneh—a reinterpretation of the meaning of being Israel in a time of dissolution—but with this difference: Matthew believed the coming of the Messiah had inaugurated a new situation which, like the monarchy and the Exile, must transform Israel's self-understanding. The essential difference of Matthew's community lies in its understanding of Jesus as "God with us," actually involving worship

of him (2:2; 8:2; 9:18; 14:33; 20:20; 28:9, 17; contrast 4:10. See Kilpatrick, 1946:107f; Kingsbury, 1975:40–83).

Matthew's vision of Israel tried to include the best from the past, especially the Law (5:17–19), and even much of the Oral Torah (23:2–3). He saw a continued Jewish piety (23:23), payment of the Temple tax (17:24, 27), performances of private sacrifice (5:22), observance of the dietary laws (15:20; contrast Mark 7:19), and even the continued importance of the Sabbath (24:20). But he did not wish to understand all these as they were being defined at Yavneh. At Yavneh, Rabbi (teacher) was developing into the central title of authority, but Matthew explicitly rejected this title (23:5–10). This rivalry with the rabbis at Yavneh produced Matthew's references to "their" synagogues (4:23; 9:35; 10:17; but see 6:2, 5; 23:6). But he never spoke of their Law (contrast John 15:25). (See Kilpatrick, 1946:110f; Davies, 1966:271.)

Matthew's strong endorsement of Gentiles probably marks him as a Hellenist, a Jew of the Diaspora who saw his congregation as the proper continuation of historic Israel. So too, his concern with ethics rather than purity and his writing in Greek from Greek sources (Mark and Q) are evidence of a Hellenistic rather than a Palestinian orientation (Stendahl, 1968:xiff).

An automatic authority of the rabbis over Hellenistic Judaism should not be assumed too readily (Goodenough, I, 1956:llff). Synagogues were autonomous and independent institutions which varied greatly in different cities. If we imagine Matthew in the context of Diaspora Judaism, rejecting the emerging authority of the rabbis of Yavneh, both the "Jewish" and the "anti-Jewish" material in the book makes sense. Matthew had not, as many suggest, converted from Judaism to Christianity. He saw himself as a Jew who was convinced the Messiah had come, thus changing the meaning of being one of God's people. What greatly disturbed him was that others claimed the same Jewish heritage, guiding the Jewish people in ways that seemed blind to him. The argument (one side of which we hear in

---

9. The Twelfth Benediction of the great official prayer, *The Shemoneh Esreh*, which consists in 18 benedictions, most more positive than this. All 18 are in Schürer, 1979:460–461 or Bonsirven, 1964:131ff.

Matthew) concerns the legitimate continuation of the heritage of Israel. Ironically, the very success Matthew's church had with the Gentiles insured that his vision of things would never come to pass. The more Gentiles the movement attracted, the less firmly it retained its Jewish roots.

Thus W. D. Davies was essentially correct when he called the Sermon on the Mount "the Christian answer to Jamnia [Yavneh]" (1966:315). But we should not consider this a formal dialogue. Rather, it was the response of one living in the Diaspora to something happening far away, something he did not entirely understand, which affected the Jews among whom he lived, worked, and worshipped. The purpose of Matthew's "Book of the Origin of Jesus the Messiah" (1:1) was to tell the story of how the coming of the Messiah has inaugurated a new phase in the history of God's people and to explain how they were expected to live in that new age.

Matthew may have lived in a large city, a city with many synagogues. Some were Christian; others were Pharisaic; still others were probably neither. Matthew wrote for his own people, showing them what he saw as their real heritage and differentiating them from the Pharisees. This seems to be a reasonable picture of the historical and social location of Matthew's gospel. It is probably not possible to be more precise on his geographical location, but understanding his social and historical situation casts new light on the meaning of his gospel.

RESOURCES FOR FURTHER STUDY

Introductory works include Edwards, 1985; P. Ellis, 1974; Mounce, 1986. And on a more advanced level, Kingsbury, 1986; Meier, 1979; Stanton, 1983; Waetjen, 1976.

Standard commentaries include Beare, 1982; Fenton, 1963; Filson, 1960; Green, 1975; Hill, 1972; Schweizer, 1975. The conservative work of Gundry, 1982, is very provocative. The volume by Albright and Mann in the Anchor Bible Series is somewhat idiosyncratic.

On the structure of the Gospel: The first to notice the structural significance of the five speeches and to elaborate an interconnection was B. W. Bacon (1930) who argued that Matthew attempted to arrange his gospel into "five books," imitating the five books of Moses (the Torah or Law). W. D. Davies, 1964:14–108, offers a thorough analysis and critique of Bacon's work. See also Rolland, 1972, Kingsbury, 1975, and Barr, 1976. Because he associated the speeches only with the narratives that precede them, Bacon designated the passion and resurrection narratives as an "Epilogue"—hardly an adequate understanding of their role in the story.

For an excellent discussion, complete with charts, of the historical problems of the birth narratives, see Raymond E. Brown, 1977: 74–94, 225–228. Matthew's account of the birth of Jesus is remarkably like Jewish expansions of the events around the birth of Moses, as seen in Philo's Life of Moses I, 8–22, and especially Josephus, Antiquities of the Jews, II, 9.2. An excellent discussion of the purpose of these birth stories in Matthew is Stendahl, 1964:94–105. For a feminist interpretation, see Schaberg, 1985. On the genealogies see Johnson, 1969; and Davis, 1973. The place of Jesus' birth was also a problem for John (7:40–44), though he dealt with it in a radically different way. A succinct history of Herod's reign can be found in Schürer, 1973:287–329.

On the theme of Moses in Matthew see Bacon, 1930:165–186; Davies, 1964, chapter 2; Green, 1975:18f.

On the variety of sectarian groups of Jews in the first century see Simon, 1967:85–107. See also Stone, 1980; the evidence from Josephus is well summarized by Rhoads, 1976:32–42, 97–122 (though Josephus mentions other groups as well, for example the Life, 11). Part One of Glatzer, 1969, provides a good collection of primary sources. See also Montefiore and Loewe, 1974, and Lipman, 1974.

An excellent study of this period is Jacob Neusner's *First Century Judaism in Crisis*, 1975a. More substantial treatments include Bruce, 1972; and the newly revised reference volumes by Schürer, 1973 and 1979. Other useful discussions of the politics and parties of this period include Davies, 1966; Herford, 1952; and Lohse, 1976. On the significance of Rabbinic Judaism see Moore, 1927, and, from a somewhat different perspective, Urbach, 1975.

While both Matthew and Qumran believed that the Law was fulfilled in their community, what they actually did with the Law was quite different: the Qumran community practiced a radical legalism; Matthew radically transcended the laws. For a complete discussion of this pesher method in Matthew see Stendahl, 1968:182–303. A very readable introduction to the life, history, and ideas of the Qumran community is Vermes, 1978. An excellent bibliographical guide to the Qumran literature is Fitzmyer, 1977.

A nice survey of the messianic views of various Jewish groups is found in chapter one of *The Servant Messiah* by T. W. Manson, 1966:1–35. See also Klausner, 1955; and Mowinkel, 1956.

On the effects of Hellenism on the Jews, see the excellent summary chapter, "Hellenism and the Jews" in *Hellenistic Civilization* by W. W. Tarn (World, 1952):210–238 and Safrai and Stern, I, 1974:117–83. The classical treatment is Hengel, 1974a.

A detailed exposition of the Jewish aspects of this gospel (though not sufficiently attentive to the negative elements) is Kilpatrick, 1946. See also Montefiore, 1927, and the excellent treatment of the setting of the Sermon on the Mount by Davies, 1966.

Specialized studies of various aspects of the social and historical context of Matthew include: Able, 1971b; S. Brown, 1978; Cope, 1976; Farmer, 1976a; Flusser, 1975; Hare, 1967; Isaac, 1984; Riches, 1983; Thompson, 1970; van Tilborg, 1972.

Special studies of various themes in Matthew include:

On miracle stories—Held in Bornkamm, 1963:165–299.
On use of scripture—Gundry, 1967; Goulder, 1974.
On use of the Law and righteousness—Meier, 1976; Przybylski, 1980.
On use of Wisdom ideas—Suggs, 1970.
On the genre of Matthew—Shuler, 1982.
On the Theology of Matthew—Donaldson, 1985; Kingsbury, 1975.

On the parables in chapter 13, see Kingsbury, 1969; for a discussion of Matthew's method of interpretation and a comparison with rabbinic parables see M. D. Goulder, 1974:47–69. On parables generally see Jeremias, 1963; Lambrecht, 1981; Perkins, 1981; or Stein, 1981. For a bibliography: Kissinger, 1979.

There is considerable debate whether the sayings regarding Peter and the church's divine authority (16:19; 18:18) stem from Jesus or whether they were created by the post-Easter church. For a positive evaluation of their historicity, see Cullmann, 1962:182ff, 217; a negative judgment is registered by Bornkamm, 1970:37–50. See also Kingsbury, 1979. For further bibliography on Peter see Chapter 12.

The Gospel as Heroic Narrative

৵ ৵ ৵

The Story of Luke-Acts

9

Mark began by announcing "good news" and Matthew spoke of a "book" for a new generation, but Luke acknowledges that he has constructed a narrative and provides some information concerning how he went about it:

❧ ❧ ❧

Inasmuch as many have undertaken to compile a narrative of the things which have been accomplished among us, just as they were delivered to us by those who from the beginning were eyewitnesses and ministers of the word, it seemed good to me also, having followed all things closely for some time past, to write an orderly account for you, most excellent Theophilus, that you may know the truth concerning the things of which you have been informed. (1:1–4)

A great deal can be learned about Luke's situation, purpose, and procedure from a careful reading of this preface to his work, and we shall return to it repeatedly in our discussion.

In this chapter we will explore the shape and extent of Luke's narrative, showing that it includes both the Gospel and the book known as the Acts of the Apostles. We will trace the narrative through its major phases, from the birth of John the Baptist to the imprisonment of Paul in Rome, then explore the historical and cultural setting implied in the writing.

UNDERSTANDING LUKE'S NARRATIVE

The most striking thing about Luke's narrative is that, unlike Mark and Matthew, he does not limit it to the time of Jesus. Matthew implied that the story goes on (with Jesus' promise to be with the disciples "till the close of the age"), and envisioned a period of churchly ministry before the end (compare Matt. 24:14 and Mark 13:10). Luke actually continues the story into a second volume, a sequel to his story of Jesus, which we know as the Acts of the Apostles. This is surely the most important observation we can make about the shape of Luke's narrative.

The Significance of Acts for Understanding Luke

That Luke-Acts is a two-volume work seems beyond dispute. This is one of those rare conclusions of biblical scholarship that commands near-universal acceptance. The evidence for common authorship is clear and convincing, even though we cannot be entirely sure *who* this author was because both volumes are anonymous. The two volumes share a common understanding of Christian life, a common literary structure, style, and vocabulary; both are addressed to the same person, both open with a distinct prologue—the second making explicit reference to the first—and the second volume takes up exactly where the first leaves off.

But the two do not merely come from the same author, they form a literary unity: one work in two volumes. H. J. Cadbury has shown that this unity is implicit in the prologues (1958:8ff). The second prologue begins: "In the first book, O Theophilus, I have dealt with all that Jesus began to do and teach . . ." (Acts 1:1), surely a reference to the Gospel. This corresponds exactly to the literary conventions of Luke's time. Josephus, for example, wrote a two-volume work *Against Apion,* the second of which begins: "In the first book, my most honored Epaphroditus, I have shown. . . ." And Philo's essay, *That Every Good Person is Free,* refers to a preceding volume (now lost) with the words: "Our first book, O Theodotus, was on the thesis that every base person is a slave." (Both quoted in Cadbury, 1958: 9.) Thus, Luke makes exactly the sort of connection one should expect for a single work in two volumes.

This conclusion is strengthened if we compare Luke's second prologue with the first (Luke 1:1–4, quoted above). While the second prologue explicitly labels the content of the first volume as "what Jesus began to do," the first prologue does not limit the narrative to Jesus' work. It refers to "the things which have been accomplished among us" (Luke 1:1), thereby including the action of Acts. We have reason to suppose, then, that from the outset Luke envisioned the whole of Luke and Acts as a literary unity. This work is now usually referred to as Luke-Acts.

Luke consistently reshapes the telling of the story of Jesus so that it anticipates the story of the church in Acts. Notice, for example, how the story of Jesus' baptism is told.

Reading and Reflection

Carefully compare Luke's version of Jesus' baptism (3:20–23) with Mark's version (1:9–11) (GP #6 or SFG #18), then compare it with Acts 2:1–4 and 1:14.

1. When does Jesus experience the divine voice in the two accounts?
2. How much emphasis does Luke give to John the Baptist?
3. What about this incident anticipates the story in Acts?

Although Luke's version of the baptism is recognizably the same event, even down to exact verbal correlations at certain points, he has dramatically transformed its significance. Its dramatic function in Luke concerns the reception of the Holy Spirit and the inauguration of ministry. (Note also how the correlation of Spirit and ministry is reemphasized at Luke 4:1.) The coming of the Spirit is connected with prayer rather than baptism, and Luke makes several changes to separate this event from any expectation of the coming of the kingdom. Not only does he omit any mention of the kingdom in Jesus' subsequent preaching (compare Luke 4:14–15 with Mark 1:1–14–15), he also separates the baptism from the temptation scene by interjecting a genealogy 3:23–38). Thus, unlike Mark, the baptism does not function as the prelude to Jesus' conquest of Satan (contrast "immediately" in Mark 1:12).

Luke's attitude toward the coming of the kingdom will be considered when we come to Acts; for now it is sufficient to observe his method. These changes illustrate what we might call Luke's proleptic view of Jesus, that is, his story of Jesus anticipates and foreshadows his story of the church. Thus the account of the coming of the Spirit upon the early church in response to prayer has cast its shadow before it in the account of Jesus' baptism.

Luke's Literary Methods

These observations about Luke's handling of the baptism scene causes us to raise three related questions about Luke's way of writing: How does the writing of Acts influence and shape the writing of the Gospel? Are Luke's methods comparable to those of the ancient historians? How dependent is Luke on his sources? We will consider these in reverse order.

One clue often used to identify various sources in Luke's writing is the varieties of style. Luke's Greek style varies from very good Greek to a thoroughly "Hebrew-like" Greek (usually called

Semitic Greek, which uses grammatical constructions similar to those in the Semitic languages such as Hebrew and Aramaic rather than the normal constructions expected by a native Greek speaker). For example, the finest Greek in Luke–Acts is the opening prologue (Luke 1:1–4), consisting of a forty-two-word Greek sentence with one principle clause, one relative clause, three adverbial clauses, and three participial phrases. Delightful. (Contrast Mark's opening "sentence," consisting of five Greek words without a verb.) However, as a Greek reader would move from Luke's first sentence to his second, his stylistic sense would be jarred. This second sentence is one of the most Semitic constructions in the book, reading almost like a sentence out of the Septuagint, a rather literal Greek translation of the Hebrew Scriptures. (An impression of this style change is possible if you read Luke 1:1–4 in the New English Bible, and proceed with verse 5 from the King James version.) How can we explain this change in style?

One possibility, often advocated in the past, is that this variation stems from Luke's use of different sources: either the prologue was Luke's own composition, whereas in verse 5 he followed a Semitic source that he translated rather literally, or perhaps the opposite was true. Since prologues were rather easy, and could even be purchased, perhaps Luke's real style emerges only in verse 5.

Today, however, scholars are more apt to see this change of style as a conscious literary technique. This view, which goes back at least to Adolf von Harnack (1906), argues that the switch from the high style of the prologue to the Semitic style in verse 5 represents a conscious imitation of Septuagintal Greek (for example, Leaney, 1958: 79; Creed, 1930:6f).

This phenomenon is widespread in Luke–Acts, for Luke seems to make a deliberate effort to suit his language to the topic. Cadbury studied Luke's style extensively and drew these generalizations: Luke's most biblical language is found in the birth stories. The body of the Gospel is somewhat better Greek, yet Luke introduces Semitic constructions where there were none in his sources. The first part of Acts is similar, but with improved Greek, and as the book progresses the style becomes increasingly secular, climaxing in Paul's speech before Agrippa which contains a half dozen classical Greek idioms in grammar alone (1958:223–225). Haenchen noted: "Luke is at his most literary in the four scenes where his subject matter demands it: 17:16–34 (Paul's speech at Athens), 19:21–40 (the riot and speech at Ephesus), 24:1–23 (Paul's accusation and defense before Felix), and chapter 26 (Paul's defense before Agrippa)" (1971:75).

Luke's pattern, then, seems to be to use Semitic Greek when Jews are involved and a more formal Hellenistic Greek when speaking to or for Greeks. Luke follows this pattern even in small things: in Acts 15 he calls Peter by his Greek name, "Peter" (15:14), but has the Jerusalemite James refer to him by the Hebrew counterpart, Symeon (15:14). Before Acts 13:9, he always uses Paul's Semitic name Saul; at 13:9 he says, "Saul who is also Paul," and from then on he is always Paul—a good Greek name. It is, Cadbury remarked: "When Paul's career is fairly started among Gentiles" (1958:225ff). Numerous other examples could be cited (see Creed, 1930:lxxvi–lxxxiv). This effort to fit the language to the character reveals a kind of conscious literary artistry not usually associated with the gospel writers. A careful study of Luke's style does not support the view that he was merely reporting what he found in his sources. Luke worked hard to find language appropriate to the narrative.

This attempt on Luke's part to be (or at least appear) authentic extends to other details as well. The city officials of Thessalonica, for example, are referred to by the unusual term "politarchs" (17:6), a designation confirmed by inscriptions found there. Numerous other local designations as well as navigational terms and cultural practices have been proved accurate (Cadbury, 1958: 242ff). Such verisimilitude would have been appreciated by persons of culture in antiquity.

At least one school of ancient historiography allowed a writer great freedom of invention as long as what he invented was appropriate to the situation. Thus, Cicero (in 56 BCE) urged Lucceius, his would-be biographer, to embellish his accomplishments while giving the essential truth about his consulship. (*Letter to Lucceius* found in his *Basic Works,* Modern Library edition, 1951: 399–402). A more germane example may be cited from the historian of the Peloponnesian War (431–404 BCE), Thucydides, who made extensive use of speeches by his major characters. He explains his procedure:

& & &

With references to the speeches in this history, some were delivered before the war began, others while it was going on; some I heard myself, others I got from various quarters; it was in all cases difficult to carry them word for word in one's memory, so my habit has been to make the speakers say what was in my opinion demanded of them by the various occasions, of course adhering as closely as possible to the general sense of what they really said. (i.22; also cited in Cadbury, 1958:185)

Such a procedure was still being commended to the would-be historian a century after Luke's time. Lucian in his essay *How to Write History* advises:

& & &

If a person has to be introduced to make a speech, above all let his language suit his person and his subject. (58)

Something very similar to this is what Luke may be doing in Acts, a supposition that is supported by examining the speeches themselves. Each of the speeches follows a basic pattern, with the specific content changed to fit the dramatic situation (Dibelius, 1956:165; Haenchen, 1971:185; Kennedy, 1972:433).

Reading and Reflection

Compare the two very different speeches of Peter (2:14–41) and Paul (17:22–34); then answer the following questions.

1. How does each speech begin?
2. What authorities are quoted?
3. What is the main focus of the speech? (Note that Paul's speech is cut off before he can develop his main point.)

It is true that some of the more objective historians of Luke's time rejected such free invention, partly because it was not always as carefully used as Thucydides claimed, but Luke was not an objective historian. He was, instead, what Haenchen calls a "dramatic historian" (1971, 103ff). He did not simply report what happened; he showed it happening, conjuring up scenes and speakers to make his history live.

Such dramatic art fits well with the two recognized purposes of historical writing: to furnish pleasure to the reader and to make the subject intelligible. (See Cicero, *Letter to Lucceius;* Lucian, *How to Write History,* 53.) Lucian is often quoted as opposing the goal of giving pleasure. Indeed he says, "history has one task and one end—what is useful—and that comes from truth alone" (10). But that statement appears in a context in which he condemns an overdose of fictitiousness in history. He saw the task of the historian as resembling the task of a great sculptor: a sculptor does not manufacture his own gold, but fashions and arranges it.

& & &

The task of the historian is similar: to give a fine arrangement to events and illuminate them as vividly as possible. (51)

The material to be shaped is the "bare record of events," which must be formed by a "historian of taste and ability" (16). History should "delight and instruct," as Horace (died 8 BCE) demanded of all poets (*On the Art of Poetry*, 337). To learn in what Luke intended to instruct, we need only consult his preface.

Finally, these observations on Luke's literary methods, combined with the results of our study of the baptism scene, imply that Luke consciously molds the story of Jesus to the story of his earliest followers, and in turn he carefully crafts the story of his followers to reflect the story of Jesus. Thus we find a dynamic interaction between Gospel and Acts. This interaction is evident in the structure of the work.

The Structure of Luke-Acts

The structure of Luke's gospel is perhaps more universally recognized than that of the other gospels because his order of events differs markedly from the order in Mark and Matthew. The device Luke uses in this rearrangement is obvious to every careful reader of the gospel: he has transformed Jesus' journey to Jerusalem into a major event. Thus he notes in 9:51 that Jesus set his face to go to Jerusalem, and everything that happens from then till 19:28 is portrayed as part of this journey. This is a uniquely Lukan idea. (See index to the *Gospel Parallels:* xxiii or *Synopsis of the Four Gospels:* 347–351.)

This supposed journey easily divides Luke's gospel into three sections: before the journal in Galilee, the journey, and after the journey in Jerusalem. Even a casual acquaintance with Acts reveals that journeying—the missionary journeys of Paul—is a major motif of that work. It seems reasonable, then, to ask if they perform a similar structural function.

A preliminary objection might be raised by those who find the structure of Acts indicated in 1:8 ("You will be my witnesses in Jerusalem, in all Judea and Samaria, and to the end of the earth"). While there is some validity in this observation, 1:8 describes the progress and intention of the Christian witness, it does not seem adequate as a summary of the structure of Acts. First, Rome (where Acts ends) is not the end of the earth but its center. In addition, all these goals

are accomplished by chapter 12, at least in a preliminary way (see 11:19–21).

On the other hand, there seem to be clear markers in the narrative that identify the various stages of the story. In the Gospel, Jesus indicates his resolve to go to Jerusalem (9:51); Paul in Acts also indicates his resolve to go to Rome (19:21). No less clear than the notion of Jesus' arrival at Jerusalem (Luke 19:28) is the indication in Acts that a new kind of ministry involving journeys must be initiated (13:1–3). Other divisions in Acts represent subdivisions of these major sections, in my judgment.

Paul's journeys are the watershed of the action in Acts. Before the journeys (reported in Acts 13:1–19:20), the center of action is the Jerusalem church; afterward the entire focus is on Rome (see 19:21). Add to this the observation above about the parallels between the inauguration of Jesus' ministry and that of the church, plus the fact that each opens with a formal prologue, and a nearly perfect parallelism is evident between these two volumes. This structure may then be represented as follows.

READING GUIDE TO LUKE–ACTS

Introduction to the two volumes   1:1–4
  The origin and spirit-indwelling of Jesus   1:5–4:13
    The gathering of witnesses in Galilee   4:14–9:50
      The instructing of the witnesses on the journey to Jerusalem   9:51–19:27
      The witnessing of the events in Jerusalem   19:28–24:53
Introduction to the second volume   1:1–5
  The origin and spirit-indwelling of the church   1:6–2:47
    The witness to Jesus in Jerusalem and beyond   3:1–12:25
      The journeys that carry the witness to the nations   13:1–19:20
      The progress of the witness to Rome   19:21–28:31

The striking thing is that this structure involves neither chronological development nor a certain idea; its basis is geography. Though the tradition found in Mark already contained the notion of a Galilean ministry followed by removal to Judea and Jerusalem, Luke has used it in a new and radical way. Thus the "journey" in Mark (10:1) consists of the statement that he left there and went to Judea; in Luke this takes ten chapters. In these chapters Luke has gathered material found in different contexts in the other gospels (plus some material not found in the others), carefully changing or omitting any geographical notations that do not fit his journey scheme.

This geographical structure will cause Luke problems, notably the location of the resurrection appearances, which we observed at the very beginning of our study of the gospels (see p. 136). It will also force him to be inconsistent about the route Jesus followed to Jerusalem, whether he took the shorter route through Samaria (9:53) or followed the alternate one through Jericho (18:35): the roads did not permit traveling both routes on the same trip. Thus some have questioned whether Luke knew Palestinian geography (Pritchard, 1972:116).

But Luke is not trying to teach us geography, and we do him an injustice if we fail to see the literary importance of this structure. The journey is a literary device, the meaning of which is found in the declaration: "It cannot be that a prophet should perish away from Jerusalem" (13:33). It is not portrayed realistically and contains little that could properly be called a travel narrative. It is content to remind the reader repeatedly that Jesus is on his way to Jerusalem (9:53; 13:22; 17:11; 18:31; 19:11). Let us now consider how Luke uses geography to interpret history.

Luke's View of History

Surprisingly, Luke's gospel also begins in Jerusalem, despite the fact that Jesus is associated with Nazareth (or Bethlehem) and John with the wilderness in the rest of the tradition. Luke's first action occurs in the Temple in Jerusalem (1:9); even more shocking, the first appearance of Jesus is also in the Temple in Jerusalem (2:43, 46). The Gospel closes with a command to stay in Jerusalem and in its very last words portrays the disciples as "continually in the Temple blessing God" (Luke 4:44–52). This concentration on Jerusalem and the Temple certainly shows Luke's positive appreciation of Israel and the Jews.

More than appreciation, however, Luke manifests a certain understanding of history, involving the centrality of Jerusalem in the plan of God. At its simplest level, Luke's scheme of history moves in two directions: in the Gospel everything moves toward Jerusalem; in the Acts everything moves away from Jerusalem. This was no easy task, given the fact that Paul, the major figure of Acts, was firmly associated with Antioch in the tradition. Notice Luke's attempts to tie Paul to Jerusalem (8:1–3; 9:26; 12:25; especially 22:17) in spite of Paul's own reluctance to be so tied (contrast Galatians 1:15–23). This geography is Luke's literary means of asserting the sovereignty of God in the development of Christianity. In Luke's view, God is active in the affairs of history to bring about salvation. Thus, Luke is concerned in a way the other gospel writers are not to interrelate his special history with general human history (Luke 2:1–3; 3:1–2; and so on).

This is a very ambitious goal and Luke–Acts is a very ambitious work. Some thirty or forty years after Jesus every major city in Asia Minor, Greece, and Italy had one or more Christian congregations. In his remarkably readable story of the expansion of Christianity Luke mentions 95 different people, 54 cities, 32 countries, and 9 Mediterranean islands. Perhaps such rapid spread suggested to Luke the geographical concept that is the cornerstone of his work. He structured his material according to geography, producing an "orderly account" (1:3), though hardly the kind of order a modern reader expects. Let us now pursue Luke's argument in more detail by considering each section of his work in turn.

GATHERING WITNESSES IN GALILEE

The first section of Luke's story contains two major parts: scenes concerning the origin of Jesus and scenes portraying his early ministry in Galilee. While we have encountered many of these scenes before, they are portrayed here in a rather novel way: in both cases Luke uses geography to interpret the meaning of the action.

Another Way to Begin

Mark (depending on Isaiah) portrayed the origin of salvation in the wilderness, but Luke places both the opening action of his gospel and the first action of Jesus in the Temple in Jerusalem. The birth stories of these opening chapters are artfully structured: a series of six scenes, each celebrated with a short poem or hymn, interweaves the events surrounding the births of John the Baptist and Jesus.

First	The Angel appearing to Zechariah in the Temple announces the coming birth of John including a hymn to John, which identifies him with Elijah.
Second	The angel appearing to Mary in Nazareth announces the coming birth of Jesus including a hymn to Jesus, which identifies him with David.
Third	Mary visits Elizabeth (Zechariah's wife) who announces that the babe has "leaped in her womb for joy," and Mary bursts into a hymn to the Lord who "has helped his servant Israel."
Fourth	The account of the Birth of John complete with a hymn by Zechariah to the Lord who "has raised up a horn of salvation . . . to give light to those who sit in darkness."
Fifth	The account of the Birth of Jesus complete with a hymn by the angels to Jesus who is "born this day in the city of David, a Savior. . . ."
Sixth	Jesus is presented in the Temple and

there a righteous man named Simeon is inspired and bursts into hymn declaring that he has seen salvation "a light for revelation to the Gentiles and glory to thy people Israel."

This arrangement implies a special status for John and suggests a comparison between John and Jesus. In terms of design, there seem to be two cycles of three scenes: the paired angelic announcements are synthesized in Mary's visit and the paired birth accounts are synthesized in the final Temple scene, which returns full circle to the Temple scene of the opening. The immense literary skill manifested here recalls Luke's promise of an "orderly account" (1:3).

Luke alone of the canonical writers depicts a scene from Jesus' childhood, though the pious fancy of later believers created many such stories, some charming, some grotesque. (See *Pseudo-Matthew*: 410ff, and the *Infancy Gospel of Thomas*: 392ff; both are in Hennecke and Schneemelcher, I, 1971.) Whatever the source of Luke's story, he used it for two purposes: to connect Jesus with the Temple at the very outset of the action and provide a transition to the inauguration of Jesus' ministry, which forms the second part of this introductory section.

Reading and Reflection

Carefully read 1:1–4:13, reflecting on these questions:

1. How does Luke use the motifs: Temple, Holy Spirit, prayer, and Gentiles?
2. What points of comparison and contrast are established between John and Jesus?
3. How does Luke modify the Markan tradition of Jesus' baptism and temptation?
4. Compare the births of Samuel (I Sam. 1–2) and Isaac (Gen. 18:1–15; 21:1–7) with those in Luke.

John the Baptist and Jesus

The figure of John remains somewhat shadowy in the gospels. However, he was not quite as unusual in his time as he may seem to us. There were apparently many such ascetics who withdrew into the wilderness to obtain purity, a quest that would require various kinds of ceremonial "washings." For example, Josephus, never modest, tells his readers of the great extremes to which he went to decide between the various Jewish sects, claiming to have, in turn, become a Pharisee, a Sadducee, and an Essene. Then he adds:

≥ε ≥ε ≥ε

Not content, however, with the experience thus gained, on hearing of one named Banus, who dwelt in the wilderness, using only such clothing as trees provided, and feeding of such things as grew of themselves, and using frequent ablutions [baths] of cold water, by day and night, for purity's sake, I became his devoted disciple. With him I lived for three years. . . . (Life 11; Loeb edition)

Admitting the substantial difference in the function of the washings (John's baptism seems to have been administered only once), the picture of Banus shares much with that of John, including the notion of gathering personal disciples (see John 1:35). John, at least, appears to have been the same type of person.

Josephus also seems to have known about John the Baptist; at least we find a reference to John in our text of Josephus. Some think that it may have been added by a later Christian copyist; if so, it is surprising that the image of John is so different from that in the gospels—especially in the relationship depicted between John and Herod. Josephus' reference to John is set within the context of a battle Herod lost to Arabia; some saw the loss as a divine retribution for his killing of John. He then describes Herod's handling of John:

≥ε ≥ε ≥ε

When others too joined the crowds about him, because they were aroused to the highest degree by his sermons, Herod became alarmed. Eloquence that had so great an effect on mankind might lead to some form of sedition, for it looked as if they would be guided by John in everything that they did. Herod decided therefore that it would be much better to strike first, and be rid of him before his work led to an uprising. . . . (Antiquities of the Jews xviii 5.2 [118]; Loeb edition)

The picture here is that of a charismatic leader, very popular with the common people, too popular for his own good.

Further clues about John may be gleaned from the gospels. There are indications that the relationship between John and Jesus (or at least between their respective disciples) was not always as smooth as we usually imagine (John 3:22–27, 4:1–3). We also find evidence that disciples of the Baptist remained active and independent of the early Christian movement (Acts 18:24f, 19:1–7). Some think that many of John's disciples regarded John as himself the redeemer, not simply the forerunner of Jesus. A small sect that believes this exists in present day Iraq, though it is debated whether they really derive from John. (See Kee, 1977a:248f, 63f; C. H. Kraeling, 1951; Drower, 1962.) Whatever the precise historical details, it seems clear that Luke strives to establish a proper understanding of the relationship between John and Jesus.

Hans Conzelmann argued that Luke intended to strictly separate John and Jesus. Leaning heavily on Luke 16:16 ("The law and the prophets were until John, since then the good news of the kingdom of God is preached"), Conzelmann argues that John represented the old era, the time of Israel, separated from the new era, the time of the church by the ministry of Jesus, which becomes the center of history (1963:18–27). His case is strengthened by careful observation of Luke's editing of material also found in Mark; for example, Luke edits John right out of the baptism scene (3:20–21).

Not all are convinced, however, and the case is considerably weakened if the birth stories are considered. (Conzelmann regarded them as irrelevant; p. 22 n.2; for a critique of Conzelmann on this point see Minear, 1966.) The birth stories intimately link John and Jesus, even as they repeatedly subordinate John to Jesus (for example, 1:32 vs. 1:76 and 1:17). Also, John is presented as "preaching the gospel" (3:18, only in Luke), and stressing the same repentance-forgiveness theme that characterizes the Lukan Jesus (compare 3:3; 5:32; 24:47). John even possessed the Holy Spirit (1:15, which is in some tension with the tradition behind 3:16).

Two tendencies seem evident in the way Luke handles the traditions about John and Jesus. Although he carefully intertwines their births and destinies, he just as carefully separates their work and mission. John is that "Elijah" who will "turn many of the sons of Israel to the Lord" (1:16–17). Thus, he is not only the precursor of Jesus, he preaches the "good news" and points to Christ (3:16, 18). He preaches repentance (3:3), even as does Peter and those who come after (Acts 3:19).

Using Tradition to His Own Ends

Luke's power to transform what he touches may be seen in the "baptism scene," which is actually no baptism at all. Luke has completely reinterpreted this event to display two of his dominant motifs: prayer and the Holy Spirit. As in Mark, the voice from heaven is addressed to Jesus. Now, however, this is not due to any secrecy but because the scene is depicted as one of prayer and the voice thus becomes the response to Jesus' prayer. Whereas Mark had portrayed the Baptism-Temptation as an eschatological event ushering in the kingdom (see pp. 156–158), Luke separates the temptation from the baptism by his summary (3:23) and by inserting the genealogy. (That this genealogy has little connection with Matthew's in either function or content would seem clear evidence that Luke did not know Matthew's gospel. For a discussion of the discrepancies, see Brown, 1977:74–94.) Dividing the baptism and the temptation enables Luke to link

the wilderness encounter with Satan to what follows, making it the foundation of Jesus' public ministry, rather than considering it a result of the baptism. Luke's own understanding of that encounter is revealed in 4:13: Satan is no longer able to touch Jesus, and departs "until an opportune time"—until he uses Judas to betray Jesus (22:3).

The last temptation returns us to the Temple once again, marking the end of the introductory section. Jesus returns "in the power of the Spirit into Galilee" (4:14), where he will stay until he "set his face to go to Jerusalem" (9:51).

Luke begins the narrative of Jesus' Galilean ministry with the story of his rejection at Nazareth, thereby causing a few logical problems. The story involves the charge that Jesus has been healing in Capernaum but not at Nazareth (4:23b); in Luke's account, Jesus has not yet been to Capernaum nor worked any miracles. (Mark used this episode in chapter 6, after a miracle section.) What, then, does Luke gain by placing this scene at the beginning of this part of the story?

Jesus' rejection at Nazareth is set in a synagogue and reflects what we know about synagogue worship in the first century, which apparently followed the pattern:

Recitation of the Shema ("the Lord is one"),

Saying the eighteen prayers,

Singing or recitation of Psalms,

Reading a fixed portion from the Law of Moses,

Reading a selected reading from the prophets,

An explanation of one or both passages, and

A closing blessing by a priest or a prayer by a layman.

There were no clergy, though various elders would be in charge of a given synagogue and a "head of the synagogue" would supervise the service. Various members of the congregation, or interesting visitors, might be asked to read and comment on the Scripture. According to later tradition, prayers were said standing and facing the

Temple in Jerusalem; Scripture was read while standing, but explained while sitting. (See Schürer, 1979:447–463; Herford, 1952:99f; Bouquet, 1953:209ff).

A similar scene is portrayed in the other gospels, but Luke has made major changes. (Read Luke 4:16–30, comparing it with the Markan and Matthean accounts; see GP #10 or SFG #33.) First, he tells us what the prophetic reading for the day was: The passage from Isaiah that says: "the Spirit of the Lord is upon me." Indeed! The reader who has followed Luke's narrative knows this full well. Second, Luke provides a synopsis of Jesus' sermon: the claim that the Scripture is fulfilled.

Third, Luke represents the people as responding favorably to this proclamation, which leaves Jesus' sharp reply less than cogently motivated. Apparently we are to understand that Jesus is resisting their acceptance of the implication of the Isaiah prophecy that he would work miracles. In fact, Luke is carefully crafting this story to prepare his audience for the accounts in Acts, for Luke saw in Jesus' further reply—"No prophet is acceptable in his own country"—an illustration of a major concern of his work, the mission's concentration on Gentiles.

This leads him to introduce a fourth change: Jesus continues his sermon by associating the Gentiles with the poor and lowly to whom the good news would be proclaimed, justifying this mission by reference to the works of Elijah and Elisha. "When they heard this, all in the synagogue were filled with wrath" (28). A mob action ensues, in which they nearly throw Jesus off the edge of a cliff. Here one might expect that Jesus would leave Israel and go on to preach to the Gentiles. Instead, this leads directly to a string of miracles and the call of the disciples. Not until the middle of the Acts is such a withdrawl suggested:

ર ર ર

It was necessary that the word of God should be spoken first to you (Jews). Since you thrust

it from you, and judge yourselves unworthy of eternal life, behold, we turn to the Gentiles. (13:46)

Luke reiterates this sentiment in the final scene of his work. When Paul is in prison at Rome, he tries to convince "the local leaders of the Jews" concerning Jesus. Only a few respond. Paul summarizes:

ર ર ર

Let it be known to you then that this salvation of God has been sent to the Gentiles; they will listen.   (28:28)

Luke's reason for transposing this pericope (selection) to the very beginning of Jesus' ministry is clear; he is able thereby to foreshadow the whole course of his narrative. We see here another indication that Acts is "the rest of the story" begun in the Gospel. This points to a major theme of Luke-Acts, the way in which the disciples of Jesus function as a bridge between Jesus and the church.

"Built upon the Foundation of the Apostles"

As we saw earlier, Matthew had no hesitation in portraying Jesus as the founder of the church (Matt. 16:18; 18:17), though one gets no such impression from Mark. Luke falls in the middle: implying more than Mark, without Matthew's anachronism. With a striking sense of appropriateness, he reserved the word church (Greek: *ekklesia*) until well into the story in Acts, first using it almost incidentally (5:11). Such precise and realistic use of terms is one of Luke's characteristics.

Rather than transporting the church back to the time of Jesus, he uses "the Apostles" as the vital link between Jesus and the church. Thus he is most careful to replace the fallen Judas and to note that the replacement must be: "one of the men who have accompanied us during all the time that the Lord Jesus went in and out among us, beginning from the baptism of John until the day when he was taken up from us" (Acts 1:21f). For Luke the church stands on the sure foundation of eyewitnesses (1:2). Luke alone of the evangelists asserts that the apostles are witnesses even to the crucifixion (23:49).

As we saw in our study of the period after Paul, this emphasis on the apostles seems to be a characteristic of the emerging orthodox consensus toward the end of the first century. (See pp. 131–132.) It became a keystone of defense against the Gnostic version of the faith in the mid and late second century. (On Gnostic interpretations of Christianity see pp. 179 and 125–128.) Thus, Irenaeus (c. 185) attacked the Gnostics who claimed to have a special private oral teaching from the apostles that justified their reinterpretations of Scripture. Irenaeus declared:

ॐ ॐ ॐ

We appeal to that tradition which is derived from the Apostles, and which is safeguarded in the churches through the succession of presbyters. . . . Those that wish to discern the truth may observe the apostolic tradition made manifest in every church throughout the world. We can enumerate those who were appointed bishops by the Apostles, and their successors down to our own day, who never taught, and never knew, absurdities such as these men produce. (Against Heresies, III.2.2, 3.1; from Richardson, 1953)

The apostles thus came to be regarded as the sure foundation on which a proper understanding of the Christian faith could be built. This is a clear example of the way Luke's new situation casts new light on the disciples, quite a different portrayal from that of Mark.

This concern for the disciples is evident in Luke's handling of their call to follow Jesus, which is much more clearly drawn and better motivated in Luke than in Mark or even Matthew. (Compare Luke 5:1–11 with Mark 1:16–20; SFG #41 or GP #17.) Luke picks up on the fishing image and turns the call into an allegory of the church

itself—with a great catch to be taken as it launches out into the deep (Conzelmann, 1961:41f).

But showing the call of fishermen is one thing, justifying why such people are called is another. Are these disciples really suitable people for the great task Luke attributes to them? Luke's apologetic here works on two fronts: showing why the better people are not suitable (5:7, 21; 6:7, 11; 7:29f), and showing the suitability of the lowly (5:27–32; 6:12–16; 6:30ff; 8:1–3). These two themes are brought together in Luke's version of the anointing of Jesus (7:36–50. Can you imagine this scene in Matthew?). This orientation toward the poor and the outcast will reappear throughout Luke–Acts.

The role of these disciples in the rest of this section is somewhat different from that in the corresponding section in Mark. Their task now is to be with Jesus. Though they still do not grasp what he means, they do not oppose him (compare 9:18–27 with Mark 8:27–9:1; GP #122–123 or SFG #158–160). Notice the subtle changes in this discourse on discipleship: it is now a daily cross; the contrast of this evil age is bypassed; they are promised to see the kingdom, but not with power. These changes reflect Luke's concern for the ongoing life and witness of the church and his neglect of ideas connected with the coming of the kingdom.

Here Luke has omitted a large section of material found in Mark (Mark 6:45–8:27 is not found in Luke), and commentators who believe Luke used Mark as a source are not in agreement as to whether it was intentional (Conzelmann, 1961:52ff) or simply because Luke had a defective copy of Mark (Kee, 1977a:198 n15). Three factors favor the former explanation: the omission alleviates the Markan duplication of feedings and water miracles; it solves several awkward geographical moves that do not suit Luke's scheme (notice he omits the place of Peter's confession, 9:18); it allows Luke to establish a close connection between three important events—the feeding, the confession, and the transfiguration—which now all point to Jesus' coming passion (see especially 9:30f). In addition, we might note that Luke has written a rather lengthy work. A scroll was a rather awkward device—it could, conveniently, only be of a certain length—and Luke was close to exceeding that limit (Cadbury, 1958:324).

By the end of this first section (9:50), the gathered disciples witness the coming of great events, yet they do not understand. They need instruction, which Luke will supply in the next section.

INSTRUCTING THE WITNESSES ON THE JOURNEY TO JERUSALEM

In his first section Luke softened the Markan theme of the disciples' misunderstanding (compare 8:25 with Mark 4:40; and 9:22 with Mark 8:31–34). At the close of the Galilee section, Luke deliberately introduces a reference to Jesus' passion into the healing-exorcism story, then adds:

ᘒ ᘒ ᘒ

They did not understand this saying; and it was concealed from them, that they should not perceive it; and they were afraid to ask him about this saying. (9:45)

Unlike the Markan ignorance, this is not natural or perverse. It is divinely ordained.

Now, in the second section of his narrative (9:51–19:27), Luke portrays a journey from Galilee to Jerusalem, the divinely appointed city, the city of suffering (13:33). In this Lukan portrayal, Jesus—by taking his disciples with him to Jerusalem—is performing a highly symbolic act, a movement toward understanding. Thus the primary activity of this section is the instruction of the witnesses, and the section properly closes with the declaration, "and when he had spoken these things" (19:28, literal). Luke focuses attention on these witnesses in the final words of the Galilee section, subtly modifying a traditional saying to read: he that is not against *you* is for *you* (9:50, emphasis added, in Mark it is *us; see also* 10:16).

Like the Galilee section, the Journey section opens with a scene of rejection. In an incident found only in Luke, the Samaritans reject Jesus "because his face was set toward Jerusalem" (9:51–55). More than mere regional rivalry is involved; Jesus is in danger of rejection by all because of what will happen in Jerusalem. Luke moves directly from this rejection to three radical sayings about following Jesus (9:57–62; Matthew used these in his miracle cycle, 8:19–22). In Luke, the movement toward Jerusalem is a movement toward understanding the mystery of Jesus' passion.

The Incredible Journey

This so-called journey has occasioned much scholarly debate, and with good reason. For one thing the trip from Galilee to Jerusalem was considered a three-day journey (about sixty miles), yet Luke implies a much longer time. There is time, for example, for the seventy "others" to go on a preaching tour (10:1–17); a tour, incidentally, which presupposes a fixed center to which they "return" (10:17, contrast 10:1. Conzelmann, 1961:67). And however often we are reminded that they are on their way to Jerusalem, we get no sense of progress, and are given no itinerary. There are other confusing points: in 17:11 the geography is odd, both in the order of reference (from south to north) and by supposing them to be close to Galilee even though the journey has been going on for seven chapters; the warning, to flee from "here" because of Herod, ignores the fact that Herod had no authority in Samaria where Jesus presumably was. Herod Antipas, son of Herod the Great, was Tetrarch only over Galilee and Perea in the north. Similarly, Luke suppresses the name of the "village" of Mary and Martha (10:38) since in the tradition recorded in John (11:1) their village is Bethany, a scant two miles from Jerusalem.

These and other geographical irregularities prompt most commentators to wonder about Luke's map of Palestine. (See Conzelmann's curious attempt to draw a map to Luke's specifications, 1961:69ff.) Most assert that he is confused in matters of geography. But I think not: confusing, perhaps, if we try to take him literally, but not confused. His suppression of place names is too deliberate, his use of Jerusalem too intentional to suppose it is mere incompetence. We must take more seriously the deliberate fictitiousness (or, to use a more positive expression: the creative artistry) of this journey, the literary purpose of which is to point to Jesus' death:

❧ ❧ ❧

It cannot be that a prophet should perish away from Jerusalem. (13:33; 19:11ff; 18:31)

If we understand the meaning of Jerusalem, it will be clear that Jesus journeys to Jerusalem whether he moves north or south, or whether he does not move at all.

Learning on the Way

There is a grave disparity within the Journey section between form and content: the form is that of a travel narrative, but the content has almost nothing to do with a trip, being mainly instructional. Yet in another sense, form and content are perfectly congruent. The primary task of the disciples in this section is to be "with" Jesus (see Acts 13:31), for only then are they prepared to be witnesses to him. Being with Jesus "on the way" is a favorite metaphor of Luke for what God is doing to redeem the world. (See Acts 9:2; 19:9, 23; 22:4; 24:14, 22.) The "way" to Jerusalem becomes the paradigm of the church as it seeks to follow the Way of God. Thus, teaching those who are with him on the way is a most appropriate activity.

You may wish to read through this section, using a synopsis to appreciate the methods Luke uses to develop this material to his own ends (beginning at GP #137 or SFG #174) and studying one or two units in some detail.

A favorite technique used to interpret the tra-

dition is the posing of questions that shape the reader's understanding of the teachings. For example, the final parable of this section, concerning the nobleman who went to a far country to receive kingly power, is expressly set in the two-fold context of nearness to Jerusalem and of the disciples' (false) expectation of the imminence of the kingdom (19:11). By providing such a context, Luke shapes the way the reader understands the parable. In this instance he is able to bring out one of his primary concerns, that Christians should not be surprised or concerned about the delay of the Parousia, the return of Jesus.[1]

By this device Luke is able to give a different impression of the meaning of these parables from that of the same parable in another context. Compare, for example, the parable of the Lost Sheep in Matthew (18:12–14) with that in Luke (15:1–7; GP #172 or SFG #219). Luke adds vividness, even a party, and shapes our understanding of the parable through two additions. He includes a specific setting in the life of Jesus (he is accused of attracting all the wrong kinds of persons, 15:2); and he adds two similar parables (the lost coin and the lost son). By these means a new value is placed on "lostness"; the lost recognize the salvation that has come to them, while the grumbling elder brother is unable to see the marvelous deed to which he might be witness. We see here, and throughout Luke-Acts, a striking concern for the marginal people of society: the sick, the poor, the powerless, and those regarded as sinful or unclean.

In this context, Luke's handling of the "Sign of Jonah" is instructive. Jesus' mere presence constitutes the sign, for one "greater than Jonah is here" (11:29–32; compare Matt. 12:38–42; GP #152 or SFG #191). For Luke, the great act is to be witness to Jesus. It is the one necessary thing, as the charming story of Mary and Martha asserts (10:38–42, only in Luke).

---

1. Examples of this technique of framing Jesus' teaching can be found at 10:25; 11:1; 12:13; 12:41; 13:1; 13:23; 14:1, 3, 7; 15:2f; 16:14; 17:20; 18:1; 18:9. All these settings are found only in Luke.

Learning about the Way

Luke's understanding of the Kingdom of God begins to come into focus in this section. The Pharisees are made to ask when the kingdom will come; to which Jesus replies that it is not coming with signs to be observed.

❧ ❧ ❧

For behold, the Kingdom of God is in the midst of you. (17:20f)

This, then, becomes an occasion for teaching the disciples about the kingdom.

Reading and Reflection

Carefully study the instructions concerning the Kingdom in Luke 17:20–37 (GP #183–184 or SFG #234–235), noting all the ways Luke's version differs from that found in Matthew 24:26–28, 37–41.

Commentators are divided on the translation of the last phrase in Jesus' reply to the Pharisees: the Greek could equally well mean the kingdom is "in your midst" or is "within you." It may be understood existentially (Perrin, 1967:74), or in an individualized and spiritualized sense (Perrin, 1976:43ff), or as a historical reference to the time of Jesus (Franklin, 1975:17). Whichever way we take it, it is important to realize that the saying is the positive side of a denial; it represents the reason there can be no signs: the kingdom is (already) among them/within them.

Even more interesting is the way Luke rewords the traditions about the "coming" of the Son of man in the ensuing teaching to the disciples. It is not at all clear here that Luke is anticipating a future, apocalyptic appearance of the Son of man. In fact, he explicitly links the suffering of the Son of man with his appearing—the only such association in the whole of the Synoptic tradition.

Luke's great reserve about the future coming of the kingdom is evident in the closing parable of this section, a parable for which Luke creates a context: they supposed that the kingdom of God was to appear immediately (19:11). While in Matthew's version of the parable (25:14–30) the emphasis was on the judgment through which the church must pass on its way to the kingdom, Luke emphasizes the duration of the present time (19:11–27). The present is a time of faithful witnessing to the kingdom already in our midst, inaugurated by the suffering of the Son of man. This brings Luke to journey's end: Jerusalem, the city of destiny.

THE WITNESSING OF THE EVENTS IN JERUSALEM

Sometimes a seemingly obscure argument can lead to very fruitful results. This is the case with a very technical argument about whether Luke used another account of Jesus' last days in addition to that of Mark, for there are very substantial differences between the two accounts (for the argument, see Taylor, 1926).

The counterargument may be put simply: if it is possible to explain all Luke's variations from Mark as matters of style or as matters directly reflecting Luke's purpose, there is no need to posit hypothetical sources. Hence, Conzelmann (1961: 73–94) has attempted to show that, viewed in the perspective of Luke's whole work, all his variations make sense. In so doing, Conzelmann offers a compelling interpretation of the meaning of Luke's narrative. Many of the following observations are indebted to Conzelmann's careful analysis.

In Comparison with Mark

Reading and Reflection

Read 19:28–24:53, noting any major ways that Luke's version of these incidents differs from Mark's version: 11:1–16:8 (GP #196 and following or SFG #269 and following).

1. Continue to notice Luke's emphases (especially Temple, prayer, Holy Spirit).
2. What aspects of Luke's narrative seem calculated to protect or defend Christianity in the eyes of the Roman authorities?
3. Characterize Luke's portrayal of Jesus' death.

———

Mark was careful to organize the time of Jesus in Jerusalem into a week, noting the passage of each day and night. Matthew followed the same scheme, though his own views of the Temple forced him to move the cleansing of the Temple story from Monday to Sunday (Matt. 21:10ff; Mark 11:11–15). Luke abandons this pattern. He speaks of Jesus preaching "one day" (20:1), of his teaching "every day" (21:37), and of his being "day after day in the Temple" (22:53). The Jerusalem ministry thus becomes one of indeterminate length; something comparable to the Galilean ministry or to the journey.

Nor does Jesus return to Bethany each night, as in Mark's version. Luke knows the Bethany tradition (19:29 and 24:50), but for him the significant place is the Mount of Olives (21:37), the place of prayer (22:39ff).[2] Without Bethany, there can be no anointing scene (Mark 14:3–9), but Luke has managed to use the scene earlier for his own purposes (7:36–50).

These modifications illustrate for us the reorientation of the whole story in accord with Luke's basic view of Jesus. It is not surprising that some have felt the need for another source, especially if they were not prepared to view the gospel writers as authors in their own right. Yet when we become aware of Luke's purpose, we can see the logic of his version of the story and will not be easily seduced by theories of other sources.

2. This symbolic use of space is evident in Luke's version of the "Sermon on the Mount," which no longer occurs on a mountain, the place of prayer, but "on a level place" (Luke 6:17; see Conzelmann, 44f).

Consider, for example, Luke's handling of Jesus' withdrawal for prayer just before his arrest. (Compare Luke 22:39–46 with Mark 14:26–31 and Matt. 26:30–46; GP #239 or SFG #330.) There are enough differences to make the hypothesis of an additional source possible; yet if we examine the nature of these changes they all make sense in light of Luke's purpose. What in Mark is a crisis of one facing death, and in Matthew a temptation to disobedience, becomes in Luke a routine withdrawal for prayer "as was his custom" (22:39; 21:37). And prayer here is answered, an angel comes (22:43; notice that Luke earlier transformed the two incidents in which a voice spoke from heaven into times of prayer: 3:21, 9:28). Thus also prayer is admonished at the outset (22:40). In Luke the disciples are exonerated of any fault; they sleep "for sorrow" (22:45). This is in keeping with Luke's general elevation of the disciples into the primal "eyewitnesses" of the faith. While such analysis does not prove that Luke did not use an additional source, it tends to make such a hypothesis redundant. Far more important than any theory of sources is the way such careful observation can contribute to our understanding of the purpose and intention of Luke's narrative.

He Entered the Temple

One who has followed Jesus on the long journey to Jerusalem may be surprised that he does not "enter" Jerusalem on his arrival. Luke omits the actual entry, saying only that he "entered the Temple" (19:45; compare Mark 11:11). Perhaps, as some suggest, Luke misunderstood and thought that one could enter the Temple without entering the city (Conzelmann, 1961:75 n. 1). But in light of what we have observed about Luke's method of using place as a metaphor, it seems more likely that he simply suppresses the city name to focus attention on the Temple, where Jesus spends all his time until the Last Supper, which does take place in the city. Jerusalem is the place of destiny, the place of Jesus' death (13:33); but the

Temple Inscription This partial inscription, now in the Rockefeller Museum, was a part of Herod's Temple in Jerusalem. Written in both Latin and Greek, it forbade Gentiles to enter the Temple. This physical barrier corresponded to the social barrier between Jew and Gentile in the first century. (Middle East Archives, London.)

Temple is the place of God's reaching out to his people.

Jesus' first act on arriving is to claim the Temple for his own, cleansing it to make it fit for prayer and teaching (19:45–48—a different scene from that of Mark—see GP #200 or SFG #273). Luke has prepared the reader for this situation by introducing Jesus as one whose natural home is the Temple, conducting his father's business (2:41–51). Jesus now spends all his time in the Temple (19:47; 20:1; 21:1; 21:37), and "all the people came to him in the Temple to hear him" (21:38). This is the great opportunity, when the whole people gather to hear Jesus—a theme to which Luke will return. Jesus' early followers,

also, will spend their days in the Temple (Acts 2:46; 3:1ff; 5:20).

Luke's abbreviated account of the cleansing lacks the air of impending crisis and imminent end that one finds in Mark, in accord with Luke's understanding of the postponement of the end. Even the great apocalyptic discourse is transformed by Luke: it no longer provides signs of the end time (compare Luke 21 with Mark 13; GP #216 or SFG #290). Luke sees the desolation of Jerusalem as an act of retribution (21:22); having rejected its time of visitation, Jerusalem must face the consequences (19:41–44).

Luke seems to have known the events of the seige and conquest of Jerusalem and projects the details back into the time of Jesus. This is not exactly a "prophecy after the event," since Luke is relying on what he regards as an authentic tradition about Jesus, but he recasts it to point up his own interpretation of that event. In Luke's view, Jerusalem was destined for destruction, hence the mission of the church must be traced beyond Jerusalem, even to Rome (the plot of the book of Acts).

But how could such a religion succeed in Rome? Founded by one crucified as an insurrectionist, and propagated by one who spent a lot of time in Roman chains, Christianity needed some defense.

This Man Is Innocent

That Jesus was innocent is a conviction shared by all the gospel writers. But Luke goes further; he shows that the Roman authorities themselves recognized his innocence. In fact, three separate Roman officials proclaim Jesus' innocence: Pilate, who pronounces the official verdict three times (23:4, 14, 22), Herod (23:11), and the centurion who supervised the crucifixion. The latter declares, "certainly this man was innocent" (23:47; compare Mark 15:39).[3] Luke offers an "expert"

3. In a similar fashion in Acts, Paul will be declared innocent by three separate officials: Claudius Lysius (23:29), Festus (25:25), and Agrippa (26:31).

witness: the thief on the cross is made to testify to Jesus' guiltlessness (23:41). At one point the reader is actually forced to admit that Jesus is falsely accused. For when Jesus is brought before Pilate, Luke is careful to give the exact charges:

る   る   る

We found this man perverting our nation, and forbidding to give tribute to Caesar, and saying that he himself is Christ the King. (23:2)

Yet the reader knows that Jesus did not forbid such tribute (20:19–26).

Such a miscarriage of justice raises another problem for Luke, since it seems to impugn the integrity of Roman officials. He deals with this by showing that they were largely at the mercy of their circumstances. In addition, much of the blame is laid on the Jews, who engineered Jesus' trial and constantly harassed Paul. In fact, in Luke's version one almost has the impression that the Jews crucified Jesus (see Luke 23:22–26).

On the other hand, Luke is careful to show Jesus, the early Christian community, and even Paul to be good, law-abiding Jews. Of the many examples, Cadbury summarizes:

る   る   る

. . . The circumcision of John, of Jesus, and of Timothy, the attendance at the temple by Jesus' parents and admirers and by the early Christians, and the regular participation in the synagogue services of Jesus, Paul and others, the ritual observances of shearing or shaving which Paul made in connection with vows—these are some of the points which would indicate that Christianity is not anti-Jewish. (Cadbury, 1958:306)

Cadbury also suggests one possible motive for this "Jewishness": if Christianity is really a form of Jewish religion, it would come under the legal protection of the Empire. The religion of the Jews enjoyed several important advantages including exemption from worship of the emperor, an issue that eventually became crucial for Christians. Jews were allowed to pray for the Emperor rather than to him. In addition, if Christianity were deemed a new religion it might be considered to have no legal standing and face official harassment. Yet our information on these matters is scanty, so it is difficult to say how seriously such distinctions as legal and nonlegal were taken or how perceptive Roman officials were about the (to their minds) subtle distinctions between these two faiths.

Earlier, however, we learned that Tacitus assumed the worst about Christians (pp. 167–168). In addition, we know that in the early years of the second century Christians could be brought to trial and even executed simply for being Christians. (See the full discussion on pp. 292–293.) Whatever the official status of Christians, Christianity had been considered subversive for some time. Luke's modifications of the trial narrative seem intended to dispel some of the basis for such a charge.

Jesus as Martyr and Hero

Reading and Reflection

Carefully compare Luke 23:26–49 and Mark 15:21–41 (GP #248–250 or SFG #243–248), and make a list of all the differences.

1. What new sayings are attributed to Jesus?
2. Who witnesses these things?

The contrast between Luke's account of the crucifixion and Mark's is striking because of their diametrically opposite tendencies. Mark sought to depict the starkness of the event, the reality of the suffering, while Luke sought to portray the death of the ideal martyr, a victor over evil. Mark's Jesus cries out: "My God, my God, why have you forsaken me." Luke's Jesus declares:

"Father into thy hands I commit my spirit." God's presence, not his absence, supports the death of the faithful. (Compare the death of Stephen in Acts 7:54–60.)

It has been suggested that there is something of a romance about Luke's work (Spivey and Smith, 1974:180). There is, as we say, a "happy ending," and without too much complication of the plot. There is not (as in Mark) a reversal of the action, but rather a steady growth from the birth stories to the resurrection. The action is an ever-ascending progression, ending in triumph and victory. The crucifixion is only one more stage in the upward progress of the story, an event that was necessary in the divine scheme of things revealed in the Scripture. When two disciples encountered the risen Jesus on the road to Emmaus, they lamented the seeming catastrophe of the crucifixion. Luke gives this response:

ૐ ૐ ૐ

O foolish men, and slow of heart to believe all that the prophets have spoken! Was it not necessary that the Christ should suffer these things and enter into his glory? And beginning with Moses and all the prophets, he interpreted to them in all the scriptures the things concerning himself. (24:25–27; compare Acts 28:23f)

Jesus' death was no catastrophe; it was arranged by God. Why God so arranged things Luke does not attempt to answer, but that all this happened according to God's will is clearly portrayed. Jesus thus becomes a model of Christian behavior (I Peter 2:21; 4:1), and through that lens Luke reinterprets the story of Jesus for his own community. Luke's Jesus is heroic in a classical sense. He faced many trials but overcame them all; he conquered even death. Like that great classical hero, Hercules, he was exalted on high after performing the works assigned to him. Luke alone portrays the scene of Jesus ascending, describes it twice, in fact. It is the closing scene of Luke and the opening scene of Acts.

WITNESSING TO THE EVENTS IN JERUSALEM

In passing from the Gospel of Luke to the Acts, we cross into new territory, since unlike the Gospel this writing is not limited by fixed and authoritative sources. Even if some sources were available for Acts, they had not attained the authoritative structure of the Jesus story or the likely status of Mark. Consequently, Luke is able to create more fully his own pattern and story and, in doing so, he creates a lively and interesting account. As F. J. Foakes-Jackson reflects:

ૐ ૐ ૐ

We are often blind to the excellences of St. Luke and Acts, because, like the Aeneid and the Odyssey, we read them in short portions, and examine their every word, forgetting that they are not school exercises or fields for expert ingenuity, but literary masterpieces. (1931:xix)

We must attempt a holistic approach to Acts, concerned not so much with the bits and pieces as with the movement of the whole action and the way that action influences our understanding of Luke's gospel.

The Beginning of Acts

Luke has chosen the difficult task of converting the closing scene of his gospel into the opening scene of Acts. To do so he has had to make certain changes. The two accounts may be laid out as follows:

Luke 24:44–53
 Acts 1:1–14
Same day (13. 36)
 40-day period of appearances (3)
To preach repentance/forgiveness (47)
 No parallel
Beginning at Jerusalem (47)
 In Jerusalem and . . . (8)

Stay in the city (49)
Do not depart from Jerusalem (4)

You are witnesses of these things (48)
You shall be my witnesses (8)

I will send power from on high (49)
You will receive power (8)

Led them to Bethany (50)
Return from Mt. Olivet (12)

Blesses them (50)
Questions and answers about Kingdom (6)

Carried up into heaven (51)
He was lifted up, a cloud received him (9)

Return to Jerusalem (52)
Returned to Jerusalem (12)

Were continually in the Temple (53)
Went to the Upper Room (13)

On the basis of the geographical contradiction, Conzelmann concludes that the gospel version is a secondary addition (94), and it must be admitted that Bethany is not the same place as the Mount of Olives. (See Kraeling's cautious discussion, 1964:396ff.)

But we have learned to tread lightly when considering Luke's use of geography: he may well be using these places with literary intent. And on his map they may be closer than on ours (Luke 19:29). Possibly, Mount Olivet has such a strong association with prayer in Luke's scheme of things that it would be inappropriate at the end of the Gospel but most appropriate at the beginning of Acts (1:14). This may also account for their return to an upper room, rather than to the Temple, or it may be part of the Pentecost tradition with which Luke must work. He takes them to the Temple immediately after Pentecost (2:46; 3:1).

Another major change in the way the scene is described in Acts is the inclusion of a short dialogue between Jesus and the disciples. They ask him if the Kingdom is to be restored at that time. Jesus' answer highlights another major Lukan theme and prepares the way for the story in Acts:

☙ ☙ ☙

It is not for you to know the time or seasons which the Father has fixed by his own authority. But you shall receive power when the Holy Spirit has come upon you; and you shall be my witnesses. . . . (1:6–8)

Thus Luke shifts our attention from the ultimate goal of the Parousia (the coming of Jesus) to the more immediate goal of being his witness; that is, from an ultimate idea of God's Kingdom to the intermediate idea of the church. Jesus' ascension into heaven and his enthronement at God's right hand (2:33) is the necessary prerequisite for this new idea of the church. Luke alone presents an ascension narrative, and Luke alone presents an account of the life of the church.

Crossing the Boundaries

Earlier we argued that, like Luke's gospel, Acts is structured into three parts: before the journey narrative, the journey, and after the journey (pp. 211–212). The first major section (Acts 1–12) shows the rapid and divinely led expansion of the witness "in Jerusalem and in all Judea and Samaria and to the ends of the earth" (1:8).

Reading and Reflection

Skim through Acts 1–12, noticing how the witness to Jesus is carried across the various boundaries mentioned in 1:8. What stages are used in this section to accomplish the incorporation of the Gentiles into the church?

The first stage, beginning in the Temple (as we have come to expect), could be labeled the struggle among the Jews. It culminates in the death of Stephen (chapter 7). The witness to Jesus is shown to be remarkably successful among the

Jews. Many join the new way (2:41; 4:4) and these form a unified community (4:32), though not entirely without problems (5:1–11; 6:1). A Pharisee even intercedes on behalf of Peter and John (5:34). The real hostility seems to come from the Sadducees (4:1; 5:17–18; also pp. 161 and 171).

We are also introduced in this section to a group whom our writer calls *Hellenists*. These are Jews who had adopted Greek ways, probably originally from the Diaspora, Jews who lived abroad. Like some Jews in our own time, these particular Hellenists felt the pull of the land and returned to live in it. Also, like some American Jews returning to Israel, they found they did not always see things in the same light as those already living in the land. Luke introduces the dispute between these Hellenists and the apostles as one of "serving tables"; yet this should be understood in the context of this earliest community, where sharing a common table was also sharing the Lord's Table (2:42, 46). The qualification of these servants points in the same direction: they were to be "of good repute, full of the Holy Spirit and wisdom" (6:3).

Following the controversy between the Hellenists and the Hebrews, another dispute breaks out between these Christian Hellenists and other Diaspora Jews who had returned to the land. In his typical concern for authentic detail Luke tells us the name of their synagogue: The Synagogue of the Freedmen. This is a likely indication that they had lived abroad as slaves, probably captives of some war. They now accuse Stephen, one of the Hellenists appointed to solve the earlier crisis, of blasphemy, speaking against "the holy place and the law" (6:13).

We should note that these two central aspects of Jewish life, Temple and Torah, would have had different meanings in the Diaspora and in the Land. The Temple could play little role in the daily round of Jews living in Egypt, Asia Minor, Rome, or points further west. The real center of Jewish life in the Diaspora had long been the synagogue, the house of prayer and study. Nor

would the Torah be understood in quite the same way abroad. For one thing, major aspects of the Law applied only to life in the Land, where issues of purity seem to have been paramount. Jews living among Gentiles could not possibly be so pure. Though we cannot be sure how many of these debates were already explicitly understood in the first century, we may be certain that Jews already disagreed about these things before the appearance of Christianity. Thus, some of the earliest divisions within the Christian movement were simply the extension of earlier divisions within the Jewish people.

Stephen, despite a brilliant defense, is killed, but not before Luke introduces his major character: "the witnesses laid down their garments at the feet of a young man named Saul" (7:58). Saul is introduced as an opponent, consenting to, and then actively perpetuating a persecution of the church (8:1). Many were forced to flee Jerusalem, especially the Hellenists (the phrase "except the apostles" in 8:3 seems to imply that the more orthodox Hebrew element remained unaffected by this persecution). As they fled, they preached. Luke later lets slip that they preached directly to Gentiles at this time (11:19–20); for now, however, he wished to hide that fact in order to portray a more orderly progression.

And the progress of the witness proceeds with vigor. First in Samaria, to people who were considered half-Jews (8:5). Then to an Ethiopian eunuch, a Gentile but a true worshipper of God, probably a full convert (8:27). Both categories were on the boundaries of Jewishness, but still incorporated in the broader concept of the people of God. The dictum of the rabbis was: "The usages of the Samaritans are at times like those of the heathens, at times like those of the Israelites, but most of the time like the Israelites" (*Tractate Kutim,* 1, 2; quoted from Baron and Blau, p. 68). Officially, Jews and Samaritans did not intermarry, but they were regarded equally in all civil law. A eunuch stood in a similar situation. Both Samaritans and eunuchs were forbidden to participate in the Jerusalem Temple. The social lo-

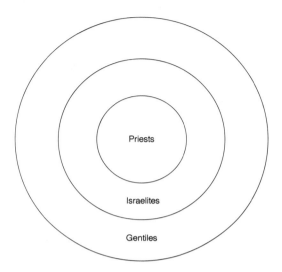

Figure 9 ▪ 1a Jewish Social Space Like most peoples, the Jews considered themselves above other peoples. To Greeks, the whole world was either Greek or barbarian; to Jews, the world was either Jew or Gentile. Gentiles were "those outside." For Jews this social distinction was also a religious one, and people were defined socially according to their status in the Temple. Only priests were allowed to enter the Temple's central shrine; Israelites could enter the surrounding court; Gentiles had to remain outside.

Figure 9 ▪ 1b Jewish Social Space: Boundaries Certain groups did not fit neatly into the categories of Jew or Gentile. Proselytes, for example, were former Gentiles who had become Jews. In most ways they were regarded as Jews but not in all: a priest, for example, was forbidden to marry a proselyte. Jewish eunuchs were another marginal group, with obvious marriage restrictions. Samaritans, natives of northern Israel, were treated like Gentiles in regard to marriage and social interaction but like Jews in business. The most marginal group of all included devout Gentiles, those who worshipped the God of Israel but who had not become proselytes. For the most part, they were treated like Gentiles.

cation of these groups is shown in Figures 9.1a and 9.1b.

Now, before we are taken beyond the boundary, we encounter the first of Luke's three portrayals of the transformation of Saul from an enemy to a follower of the way (9:1–19; see the earlier discussion of this scene, p. 146, and of Paul's account, p. 68). But it is not Saul who broaches the boundary; with delicate irony Luke reveals that it was Peter, the central apostle—a Hebrew not a Hellenist—known in other traditions as the apostle to the Jews (Gal. 2:9). Peter, having already validated the mission to the Samaritans (8:14–17), now becomes the agent for spreading the word to the Gentiles (10:1–48).

This carefully crafted story is divinely directed in every detail. Actually the story is told twice, once as it happens and again as Peter reports it to the Jerusalem church—not all of whom think it proper. In both versions, the decisive point is that the Gentiles too received the Holy Spirit (11:18). It is interesting to note that in the second telling, Luke subtly shifts this decisive action of the story from near the end of Peter's preaching (10:34–44) to the beginning: "As I began to speak the Holy Spirit fell on them" (11:15). Luke's repetition marks this as an important story, for if we accept it the rest of the book will naturally follow. In fact, Luke will tell it in summary one more time (15:7–9), when he confirms its meaning: God "has made no distinction between us (Jews) and them (the Gentiles)."

At one point, at least, the story is perfectly historical. Cornelius is just the sort of Gentile to which Christianity made its greatest appeal. "A devout man who feared God" (10:2) surely marks him as a would-be convert to Jewish faith who stopped short of full conversion because of the aversion to circumcision (see the discussion, pp. 61–62). He is marked as one who "gave alms liberally" and "prayed constantly." It is precisely at his afternoon prayers (10:2–3) that he receives the divine command to summon Peter, which results in his receiving the Holy Spirit. This comes as no surprise to the reader of Luke-Acts, for Luke has reinforced this connection between prayer and Spirit from his opening scene on. (See, for example, the reworking of the Baptism of Jesus, discussed on p. 215).

All that remains is for Luke to clear the stage so that he can tell the story of Paul's witness to the Gentiles. He does this with a story of Herod's persecution of the church (12:1), which resulted in Peter's flight: "he departed and went to another place." Admittedly not a very gracious exit, but it opens the way for the next stage of the story.

WITNESSING ON JOURNEYS INTO THE WHOLE WORLD

The journey section of Acts begins (13:3) and ends (19:21) as decisively as the journey section in Luke, even using the same technique of a resolve to go to the city of destiny: Jerusalem/Rome.

The theme of this section is vividly portrayed in the first two chapters: while there was some success among Jews, the overwhelming acceptance came from Gentiles. Chapter 13 closes with a scene that makes this explicit (13:46–48), and chapter 14 explores the acceptance among Gentiles.

In chapter 14 we have both high drama and comic relief, illustrating typical responses to the gospel. We join the story in the city of Lystra (14:8), to which Paul and Barnabas have fled as a result of disturbances at Iconium; their preaching there had divided the city and led to stiff Jewish opposition. At Lystra Paul performs a miracle, followed by a great celebration (compare the parallel miracle by Peter, 3:2–8). Only gradually does Paul realize that the people, speaking their native language rather than the common Greek, are about to offer a sacrifice to him and Barnabas, who they believe are manifestations of the ancient Gods Hermes and Zeus. Try as he might, Paul only "scarcely restrained the people from offering sacrifice to them" (14:8). At this point the scene is completely reversed. "But Jews came from Antioch and Iconium; and having persuaded the people, they stoned Paul and dragged him out of the city, supposing that he was dead" (14:19).

In this graphic fashion, Luke contrasts the typical response of Jews and Gentiles and justifies Paul's earlier resolve: "Behold, we turn to the Gentiles" (13:46). The Gentiles may not quite understand, but their openness and zeal are hard to match. Apparently, such Gentiles need someone to carefully tell them the full truth about the things of which they have been informed (Luke 1:4).

Luke mediates this simple dichotomy in two ways in the succeeding narrative: he shows that these new Gentile converts are closely tied to the Jerusalem church and to the traditions of the Jewish people (chapter 15) and that not all Gentiles warmly embrace this witness, especially the elite (chapter 17). This last reminds us of Luke's earlier theme: it is the lost who are chosen (Luke 15). So little did the philosophers understand the witness that they supposed that when Paul proclaimed Jesus and Resurrection he spoke of a new divine couple (resurrection being a feminine noun in Greek, 17:18). This is amusing to the reader, who knows more than these philosophers. In passing we must note that the way Luke's Paul uses the pagan tradition as a stepping stone to Jesus is more typical of the approach of the church in the late first century than it was of Paul (contrast Romans 1–3, where Paul's argument is from nature rather than pagan philosophers; see Vielhauer, 1966). This is one of many ways that Luke has used Paul for his own ends.

Another major way that Paul is made to fit the Lukan mold is the degree to which Paul is seen to depend on Jerusalem and adapt to the wishes of the more traditional Jews. In Acts, Paul immediately returned to Jerusalem after his experience at Damascus (9:26); Paul claimed otherwise (Gal. 1:17–18). So also the compromise struck by the Jerusalem Council, that Gentiles should keep only the most basic of the food laws, is unknown in the Pauline literature (Acts 15:19–21). These basic food and purity laws probably represent an application of a rabbinic notion that the whole law is only incumbent on Israel because it derives from the special covenant at Sinai, but the universal covenant that God made with Noah meant that even Gentiles had to adhere to certain demands (Gen. 9, Williams: 32). This effort to relate Christianity closely to the Jewish tradition is a consistent theme of Acts to which we shall return when we discuss the situation of the community.

The scenes of the journey section are richly textured and dramatic gems in the finest tradition of heroic narrative. They consistently portray Luke's major themes (such as prayer, Spirit, and the inclusion of the lowly). Overall, they dramatize the ever-expanding witness into the world. If we trace Paul's journeys on a map we will see that he went ever farther afield. While this has the ring of historical probability, it precisely matches Luke's literary intention of showing the gradual, divinely directed spread of the witness to Jesus to the whole world.

Ephesian Coin, about 50 CE On the reverse of this coin from the time of Paul we see a male and female figure in a temple, inscribed to Rome and Augustus. The male figure surely represents the Emperor; the female may be the Goddess Roma or, perhaps, a personification of the province of Asia. The Imperial cult seems to have been especially popular in this region. The front of this coin portrayed the famous statue of Diana (Artemis) found in the Temple at Ephesus. According to Acts (19:23–41), early Christian preaching adversely affected the local economy by reducing the market for reproductions of shrines of Artemis. For a picture of the statue see page 283. (Hirmer Verlag, Munich.)

This section closes with a scene at Ephesus depicting the conquest of Jesus over magic (19:11–20). Such magic, along with astrology and related practices, represented the primary religious experiences of the masses in the Hellenistic age. The dominant feeling of that age was powerlessness, lostness, and a sense of being at the mercy of Fate. The traditional religions were not able to deal with these feelings. Philosophy offered a way out for the cultured elite. The Mystery Religions promised new birth and freedom from fate for the initiate, but the enormous cost in initiation limited such liberation to the wealthy. Acts portrays, in a way that must have been very appealing to Gentiles of that time, the redemption of the common person who participates in the divine scheme of things. The ending note is appropriate:

ta   ta   ta

So the word of the Lord grew and prevailed mightily.

WITNESSING OPENLY IN ROME

The last section (19:21–28:31) of Luke's lengthy work opens on an ominous note: a near-riot in Ephesus led by the silversmiths, who are losing money because these new followers of the Way (as Luke calls it) are no longer buying their icons. While it may be unlikely that this economic impact would be felt as soon as Luke describes, there were economic implications for the Christian mission. A provincial administrator writing from this same region about three decades after Luke describes how he successfully repressed the Christian "superstition" and comments on the renewed economic activity:

ta   ta   ta

There is no shadow of doubt that the temples, which have been almost deserted are beginning to be frequented once more, that the sacred rites which have been long neglected, are being renewed, and that sacrificial victims are for sale everywhere, whereas until recently a buyer was rarely to be found. (Pliny's Letter to Trajan; *quoted from Bettenson: 5–7)*

We see from this quotation and the story in Acts that ancient civilization was holistic rather than segmented into different spheres (economic, political, educational, religious). All areas were intertwined. Religious rites and allegiances had economic and educational implications. (For a more detailed discussion of the ancient economy see Chapter 11.) The emergence of Christianity was not just the arrival of a new religion; it refused to blend into the rest of the culture and its success produced a serious challenge to that culture. The great opposition to Christianity manifested by the persecutions of the second, third, and fourth centuries represents a struggle to the death between two opposing views of reality. The economic roots of this conflict are clear in this first episode of the last section. Notice the implied exoneration of Christians. No wrong has been committed; the law is on their side; proper Roman officials protect them.

Some Daring Adventure

In a way more typical of the ancient novel than of a history, Luke has packed numerous scenes of adventure into this closing section: sea voyages, intrigues, riot, arrest, trials, mutiny, shipwreck, clairvoyant predictions, encounter with primitives. It is exciting reading. This technique is in keeping with Luke's heroic style, and Paul is always portrayed as completely in charge of each new situation.

One aspect of Luke's technique in this section has stirred great debate. Four times the narrative point of view suddenly shifts from the third person (He or they did. . . .) to the first person plural (We did. . . .). These four sections are: 16:10–17; 20:5–15; 21:1–18; and 27:1–28:16. In each case the shift to and from the first person plural point of view is abrupt and in each case it involves a sea journey. The most frequent explanation of these passages is that they represent the times when Luke was with Paul (leading one student to the definite conclusion that the author was a sea captain, since that is the only time he joins the narrative).

But another explanation appears more likely. Vernon Robbins has shown that a regular feature of sea-journey narratives in the Greco-Roman world was the use of a first person plural viewpoint, even in narratives written in the third person. The most exact parallel of the many he cites is from a second- or third-century (BCE) account of an expedition of one Hanno to found colonies:

ᘯ ᘯ ᘯ

And he set forth with sixty ships. . . . After passing through the Pillars we went on and sailed for two days' journey. . . . (Robbins, 1978:226)

Robbins concludes: "The evidence within contemporary Mediterranean literature suggests that the author of Luke–Acts used 'we' narration as a stylistic device" (229). It is a way of involving the reader in the intimacy and danger of the travel by ship rather than a claim that the author is present. It is perhaps not unrelated to the author's claim in the preface that he is narrating the things "accomplished among us," not implying thereby that he witnessed the gospel events. Many of the other features of these sea narratives are also typical of this genre, including the shipwreck.

Travel was more extensive and safer in the Roman world than it had been for centuries before (or would be for centuries after), but it still entailed considerable risk. Travel by boat was especially risky, and therefore also exciting. One ancient sage described it thus:

ᘯ ᘯ ᘯ

What is a boat? A sea-tossed affair, a house without foundations, a ready-made tomb, . . . a prison in winged flight, fate bound up in a package, the plaything of the winds, a floating death, a bird made of wood, a seagoing horse, an open weasel-trap, uncertain safety, death in prospect, a traveler amid the waves. (Secundus the Silent Philosopher, 14; quoted from Perry, 1964:87)

The End Is the Beginning

The question of the meaning of the ending of Acts is tied to the question of the date of Acts. Did Luke stop his narrative because he had reached his own historical present, or was there some other reason? The dramatic date of this last scene is about 60 CE: Paul is awaiting trial in Rome. If this could be shown to be the time of the composition of Acts, with the Gospel of Luke earlier and Mark earlier still, a whole new picture of the development of the gospels would emerge. But I do not believe this can be shown. In fact, there is good reason to believe that the Gospel of Luke must have been written subsequent to the events of 70 CE, moving the date of Acts at least into the mid-eighties. This will be discussed in the next section.

Yet this raises another question: If Luke knows the rest of the story, why does he stop here? There may be several reasons. First, as Haenchen says, the really fitting end of Acts would be the Parousia (1971:98). Failing that, some intermediate end must be devised. Second, this end has a certain dramatic appropriateness. As John Chrysostom, a fourth-century Christian commentator, remarked:

ᘯ ᘯ ᘯ

At this point the historian stops his account and leaves the reader thirsting so that thereafter he guesses for himself. This also the non-Christian writers do. For to know everything makes one sluggish and dull. (Homilies on Acts, 55; quoted in Cadbury, 1958:322)

Third, in all probability Paul died at the hands of the Roman government, either at the end of this imprisonment or during Nero's persecution of sixty-four as early legend has it. (Haenchen argues that Luke presupposes Paul would die in Rome, basing his argument on 27:24; 20:25, 38; 1971:731f.) But to recount Paul's death at the end of Acts would work against the interpretation of history Luke has built up in his story. It would collapse the whole upward movement of the action that Luke has so patiently built and establish a false parallel between the death of Paul and that of Jesus.

Finally, this *is* the rest of the story, if we but understand what story Luke is telling. It is the story of the progress of the gospel, or more precisely of the witness to Jesus, from the initial gathering in Galilee, through the climactic events of Jerusalem, to the heart of the civilized world. (Thus Luke has to suppress the pre-Pauline origins of Christianity in Rome.) The witness has now been established in Rome, in undeserved chains to be sure, but with the witness being given "quite openly and unhindered."

In one way the writing of a book of Acts, a narrative of the witness to Jesus, is only a logical extension of what Matthew had already implied, namely a long period of witness—of churchly ministry—unto the close of the age. Matthew's final scene promises Jesus' continued presence in this interim period, but it seems implicit that he is present in a new way, a way unlike the ministry or even the resurrection appearances.

Luke makes this explicit: first, by portraying the ascension of Jesus into heaven, from where he will return only at the end of time; and second, by continuing to narrate the story of the witnesses. But in adding Acts, Luke really goes far beyond Matthew and Mark, shifting the focus from the past to the present. It is possible now to speak of the story of the church as something distinct from (though completely dependent on) the story of Jesus. In this sense Luke really was the first church historian.

THE SITUATION OF LUKE AND HIS COMMUNITY

Like both Mark and Matthew, this gospel is anonymous, giving no explicit indication of its author's identity. Nor does it say where it was written or when. It is addressed to one Theophilus, but does not locate him in space or time. Once again, these matters can only be deduced from clues in the writing itself.

General Aspects of Luke's Situation

Several observations that bear on Luke's historical setting have been made in the course of this discussion. First, the one sure thing that many commentators are willing to make about Luke is that he is not from Palestine; his geography is too befuddled (Kümmel, 1966:105). Yet this geographical confusion serves a literary purpose and is not a firm basis for identifying Luke's locale. Still, it seems safe to assume that Luke did not expect his readers to be familiar with the fine points of Palestinian topography.

Second, Luke probably lived some distance in time from the fall of Jerusalem; far enough to view it dispassionately as a historical judgment of the nation, yet close enough to know some of the details. If so, Luke was probably written sometime in the late eighties or early nineties; either date would be in harmony with Luke's admission that he belongs to the second or third generation of Christians (depending on the "ministers of the word," who depended on the "eyewitnesses"—Luke 1:2).

Third, Luke's orientation is primarily toward Gentiles. He not only justifies their inclusion, but sees a deliberate turning from the mission to Israel to reach Gentiles (especially Acts 13:48, 28:28). In this sense it may be relevant that the name Theophilus (Luke 1:1; Acts 1:1) means "one who loves God," a name that would be entirely appropriate for one of the devout Gentiles who appear so often in the story. In any case, this attitude toward Gentiles seems again to indicate a time late in the first century.

Finally, we observed Luke's effort to make Christianity appear innocent of the slanders urged against it before the Roman authorities, and to present the Romans in a way that Christians could accept and admire. A concerted effort at the end of Acts attempts to show Paul's innocence, to such an extent that one commentator has called chapters 16–28 "a catalogue of Paul's acquittals" (Foakes-Jackson, 1931:xvii). Some have even imagined that the immediate purpose of Luke's work was as a brief for the defense at Paul's trial (Munck, 1967:LV–LXI). Such a proposal faces several difficulties, including the very "nonlegal" character of the work. The proposal also views Acts in isolation from Luke's gospel. Luke is just as concerned to show the innocence of Jesus as that of Paul, and there can be no question of influencing a judicial outcome in Jesus' case. Rather, the whole work is a general defense of the Christian cause before a Roman public with a decidedly poor opinion of Christians. (See Tacitus' malicious judgment, p. 167.) One aspect of this defense is to present Christianity as a legitimate form of Jewish religion, which Rome recognized and protected.

However, numerous first-century Christians had little use for Rome. The author of *Revelation,* for example, labeled her the Great Whore (17:1). And the repeated admonitions in the New Testament to obey the government and pay taxes (Romans 13:1–7; I Peter 2:13–17; 3:13), indicate that some at least were not so inclined. Luke apparently wanted to establish good relations between these two parties; he is, as Robert Grant notes, "the only evangelist who takes such responsibilities [as fall to citizens of the empire] with full seriousness" (1977:46).

In short, Luke was coming to terms with Rome without recourse to the apocalyptic notion of evil governments whose overthrow must precede the coming kingdom. Luke's positive attitude toward Rome was probably formed before the last years of Domitian (before 93–96 CE), who showed hostility to both Jews and Christians. Among other measures, he made it a crime for a Roman citizen to convert to Jewish religion, probably including Christianity (Dio Cassius, 67.14.1–3). During these years, the book of Revelation probably took its final form. Luke gives no indication of such upheaval; he reflects a community that realizes it is going to have to settle down and live in the world.

All this is in agreement with our impression of Luke as a man of some culture, who felt at home in the Greco-Roman civilization and wished to relate to it. Is it possible to be more definite on who he actually was?

Did Luke Write Luke-Acts?

The tradition that Luke-Acts was written by Luke, the physician and traveling companion of Paul,

can be traced to the Muratorian canon (c. 170) directly, and indirectly perhaps back another thirty or so years. This indirect proof stems from Marcion, a confirmed Paulinist, who chose only Luke's gospel for his canon probably because of Luke's association with Paul (Thompson, 1972: 4f). The question we cannot answer is: On what basis was this attribution made? Was it an older tradition or a learned deduction?

There are a couple of pieces of evidence from which such a deduction could be made. First, there are the "we" sections in Acts, discussed above. It is generally presumed that these prove the author of the book is with Paul at these times. Second, a reference in II Timothy, presumably written during Paul's Roman imprisonment, says that "only Luke is with me" (4:11). Since one of the we sections brings the author to Rome, Luke must be that author. If this is the basis for the ancient tradition of Lukan authorship, it rests on two tenuous presuppositions: that the presence of the first person plural pronoun indicates the author's presence and that Paul actually wrote II Timothy from Rome. Few modern scholars defend Pauline authorship of II Timothy, and the change to the first person plural may be for dramatic reasons rather than a personal account. (See discussion, pp. 121–122 and 230–231. On the latter point, see Cadbury, 1958:357; on the former, see Kümmel, 1966:261ff.)

Of course the strong interest in Paul, the claim to rely on the testimony of others, and the Gentile orientation are all consonant with Lukan authorship. A popular argument that has no real force is the alleged medical language of Luke. Cadbury has clearly shown that Luke shares his language with writers who are not physicians (1958: 358; 1920:39–72).

Still, of those I surveyed on the subject, the majority support Lukan authorship (Thompson, 1972; Creed, 1930; Williams, 1957; Manson, 1930; Munck, 1967), while one flatly denied it (Haenchen, 1971) and three believed it was not possible to reach a decision (Cadbury, 1958; Leaney, 1958; Foakes-Jackson, 1931). The grounds for rejecting Lukan authorship center on the differences perceived between Paul and our author.

In addition to many specific points of difference, there is a basic difference in attitude between our author and Paul: between one in the heat of battle and one reporting the battle after a victory has been secured and the bitterness forgotten. While Paul fights passionately for his apostolic authority and the freedom of his Gentile converts, for Luke these are matters long settled. Not only does he not fight for Paul's apostolic authority, he rather ignores it. In fact, Acts 1:21–25 implies that Paul would not be qualified to be an apostle. Again we must imagine the passage of a considerable length of time. Whether it would be possible for a personal acquaintance of the great apostle to so transform him some twenty-five years or so after his death is not within the scope of our debate. The evidence does not seem compelling on either side. Clearly, however, the world of Luke–Acts and the world of Paul are very different and the story of Paul is used for a different purpose than that for which Paul himself fought.

The Purpose of Luke-Acts

We should, perhaps, take Luke at his word when he says he writes to show the true significance of the facts about Jesus and his followers (1:1–4). The primary concern of Luke is not simply to present the facts of history (many of which Theophilus already knew) but to interpret history as well. What does it mean, Luke asks, that Jesus of Nazareth has lived, suffered, died and been raised from the dead and that a witness to him has gone out into all the world? His answer seems to be that it means a new era has dawned. He has no name for this new era. (Eventually it will be called the age of the church, but Luke cannot yet know that.) He knows it is not the eschatological kingdom. That kingdom will come in God's own time (1:6–8); in the interim, however, God has brought salvation to the Gentiles.

Writing late in the first century, some writer of great skill and quite at home in the Greco-Roman world has presented a remarkable story of the dawning of a new age. The hero of this story is Jesus, a man of great compassion and unconquerable power. Endowed with the Spirit, this man called together a group of disciples and instructed them on the Way. After his death, he was exalted to heaven, from whence he reigns and brings God's plan to completion. His work is carried on by his followers, themselves now endowed with the Spirit. This work of God had its focus in the Temple in Jerusalem, the ancient center of God's revelation. But from Jerusalem, a witness to God's work has spread throughout the whole world, even to the very center of political power, Rome itself—where it continues quite openly and unhindered.

RESOURCES FOR FURTHER STUDY

Good introductory works include:

Danker, 1976, *Luke*.
Edwards, 1981, *Luke's Story of Jesus*.
Juel, 1984, *Luke-Acts: The Promise of History*.
Talbert, 1982, *Reading Luke: A Literary and Theological Commentary*.

For detailed studies of the text consult one of the major commentaries on Luke's Gospel: Caird, 1963; Ellis, 1967; Fitzmyer, 1982, 1984; Leaney, 1958; or Marshal, 1978b.

Or on Luke's Acts: Bruce, 1954; Crowe, 1979; Haenchen, 1971; Hanson, 1967; Marshall, 1982; Munck, 1967; Talbert, 1984b; or Williams, 1957.

Important monographs on Luke-Acts that point in new directions include: Cadbury, 1958, 1920; Hengel, 1979; Jervell, 1972, 1977; Johnson, 1977; Talbert, 1974; and Tiede, 1980.

Three important collections of essays are: Keck

and Martyn, 1980; and Talbert, 1978, 1984b.

Gasque, 1975, has summarized the history of the interpretation of Acts.

The definitive study of Luke's view of history is Hans Conzelmann (1961); his understanding of Luke is clearly seen in the German title of his book, *Die Mitte der Zeit* (The Middle of Time or the Center of History). Conzelmann argued that Luke envisioned three historical epochs: from Adam to John, the time of Jesus, and from the founding of the church to the second coming. His argument relies heavily on Luke 16:16: "The law and the prophets were until John; since then the good news of the Kingdom of God is preached." There is much to be said for this view, though it ignores contrary evidence. For a summary critique with an excellent bibliography, see E. E. Ellis, 1972. Conzelmann's view is widely adopted: Barker et al., 1969, 281ff; Kee, 1977a, 189ff; Perrin, 1974, 200ff; Spivey and Smith, 1974, 151ff. Hengel defends the essential reliability of the Lukan history, 1980.

Luke's view of history is often called "salvation history" (from the German *Heilsgeschichte*) or the history of redemption. As generally used, it refers to a special "sacred history" distinct from the general history of the world. "These two run side by side, and at certain points they intersect, but salvation history is not exhausted in world history" (Perrin, 1974:201). On the other hand, salvation history is believed to reveal the true meaning of general history.

Luke's methods, techniques, and even goals are much like those of his near-contemporaries, for whom history was a branch of rhetoric, the art of persuasively presenting a case. (See Quintilian, *Institute* IX.4; X.1.3. For a good summary and comparison of the methods of ancient historians, see F. C. Grant, 1957:119ff. The most complete work on Luke's methods and purpose is still Cadbury, 1958; see also Drury, 1976.) Within this context of making a case, Luke has proven to be remarkably ac-curate in such things as use of political titles, navigational terminology, and local customs, as well as several incidents in Paul's life that can be confirmed from Paul's letters. On the other hand, there are a number of historical problems which do not fit well with our knowledge from Paul or other sources. (For a list, see Cadbury, 1958:366f; Haenchen, in Keck & Martyn, 1966.) Still, in standards of accuracy, he compares well with the better historians of his time.

Discussions of the genre of Luke-Acts have tended to focus either on the Gospel or the Acts, the former usually favoring biography, the latter history. Important works include Barr and Wentling, 1984; Barrett, 1961b; Callan, 1985; Hemer, 1977; Talbert, 1974. Praeder, 1981, relates it to the ancient novel or romance.

For a discussion of Luke's theology in comparison with Paul, see Vielhauer, 1966; the numerous ways Acts differs from Paul's letters are also traced by Bornkamm, 1971:xv–xx; Haenchen, 1971:112–116; Kummel, 1966:102–105.

On John's baptism, see Creed, 1930:309–313.

While Mark's references to the destruction of Jerusalem were vague, Luke's details correspond closely to those given by Josephus in his lengthy account of the destruction of Jerusalem (*The Jewish War*, V and VI). The siege, the bank works, the surrounding wall, and the terrible slaughter are all described: *Jewish War* V, 6.2 (262); V, 12.1–3 (491ff); V, 9.1–3 (408ff). Josephus claims that 1,100,000 people perished during the siege and 97,000 were taken captive, though those numbers seem to be inflated, VI, 9.3 (419). Josephus, too, regarded the destruction of the city as divine retribution; for example, VI, 6 8.4 (398).

Among the modern scholars who have recognized various parallels between the Gospel and the Acts, I am especially indebted to Talbert (1974), Perrin (1974:205), Spivey and Smith (1974:150, 167, 253), and Conzelmann (1961:17).

Irony and the Spirit

❧ ❧ ❧

The Gospel according to John

10

🙚 🙚 🙚

Last of all, aware that the physical facts about Jesus had been presented in the other gospels . . . , John wrote a spiritual gospel.

So an early writer justified John's substantial differences from the Synoptic Gospels (Clement of Alexandria, about 200, as preserved in Eusebius, *History of the Church* 6.14.7). While we may wonder just how much John knew of the other gospels, there is no disputing that his approach was markedly different from that of Mark, Matthew, or Luke. This Fourth Gospel, as it is frequently called, does not often include the same stories and sayings we have come to expect from the Synoptics (except for the stories of Jesus' death, which are remarkably similar). In addition, even when we find a parallel story or saying, the wording and the order of events vary considerably. Perhaps even more important, the general organization and story pattern of this gospel is unlike anything we have encountered so far.

THE STRUCTURE OF JOHN'S GOSPEL

In this chapter we will explore the action and structure of the gospel, undertake a close reading of major incidents in each section of the gospel, then reflect on how, why, and where such a gospel may have come into existence. During this last inquiry, we shall examine some other early Christian writings that are remarkably like this gospel, namely, the letters called First, Second, and Third John. First, let us try to trace the course of the action portrayed.

The Movement of the Action

A few peculiarities about the ordering of the incidents in this work might make us wonder whether the author has paid sufficient attention. For example, chapter six opens with Jesus going over to the other side of the Sea of Galilee, but chapter five had closed in Jerusalem—sixty miles away. (This awkwardness was already noted by Tatian, who placed chapter six before chapter five in his *Diatessaron*.) Another problem occurs at the end of chapter 14, in which Jesus admonishes his disciples to rise and go elsewhere (14:31); though he continues to speak for two more chapters and nobody moves until 18:1.

Chapter 21 presents a different kind of problem, for it clearly represents material added to the gospel by another hand. It presupposes the death of the original author (verse 23) and adds the additional testimony of his disciples to the trustworthiness of his word (verse 24: the "we" who know that "his" testimony is true). There is also good manuscript evidence that the story of the adulterous woman (7:53–8:11) was a later insertion into John's text. For we find it in different places in different manuscripts: sometimes after 7:36, other times after 7:44, sometimes after 21:25, and still other times after Luke 21:38 (see the evidence in Metzger, 1971:219–222). Apparently, this story was never included in a gospel, but was just too good to lose. John 5:4 is also an addition to the original, a sort of scribal comment on the story.

At the very least, these observations caution that the text of John's gospel has a history of revision and that it is not possible to speak convincingly of the original text. We may also conclude that the movement of the action will probably not hinge on incidental details of place or time.

Yet the real questions are: Does the material make sense as it stands? And is the arrangement of the material based on considerations other than geography? Do the geographical discrepancies add to or detract from this other sense? It is possible that, for John's plot, chapter five must precede chapter six however awkward the connection. We must try to discover John's own techniques for ordering the gospel material.

Reading and Reflection

On your preliminary reading of John's gospel, look for formal indications of order. I have found it especially useful to note:

1. What kind of material is being presented (narrative, dialogue, monologue, transitions), and when does the text shift from one to the other?
2. What means has the author used to order the material (explicit statements of order, repetitions of similar incidents, use of numbers, references to time or to earlier incidents)?

In spite of the seemingly loose ends mentioned above, the plot of John's gospel is more tightly organized than that of the other gospels. It contains fewer incidents, elaborates each more, and connects them in explicit ways. For example, John organized the opening incidents into a week by the expression "the next day" (1:29, 35, 43), and then "on the third day" (2:1). The wedding thus occurs on the "seventh" day of the narrative (and both a wedding feast and the seventh day were powerful symbols for the Kingdom of God). Jesus' action at this wedding is then labeled "the first of his signs" (2:11). But instead of a list of signs, as we might expect, only one more is numbered, "the second sign" (4:54), also performed at Cana. Because of this partial listing

Papyrus Fragment of John's Gospel This small fragment is the oldest portion of the New Testament known to us, perhaps written as early as 130—just a generation after the Gospel itself. Only about 2-1/2 by 3-1/2 inches, it is written on both sides, showing that it was part of a codex (book form) rather than a scroll. It contains what is now chapter 18 of John; the side shown represents verses 31–33, with verses 37–38 on the reverse. (John Rylands Library, Manchester, England.)

and because Jesus is reported to have performed other signs in Jerusalem (2:23), there has been considerable debate about whether John used a source that consisted of a collection of miracle stories, usually called the *Signs Source* (Fortna, 1970). He may well have used such a source, but we miss the more important point if we do not ask why these two incidents are linked by this numbering. They form a frame around one unit of material, marking one movement of the action: from Cana to Cana.

Besides these two signs, this section portrays one action of Jesus (cleansing the Temple) and two dialogue-monologues (with a Jewish ruler in chapter 3 and with a Samaritan woman in chapter 4). Responses of disbelief (2:18), wavering indecision (Nicodemus), and wholehearted belief (4:42) are described. The reader is thus forced to reflect on the identity of Jesus, an identity already presented in chapter 1 by direct testimony from the narrator, aided by the testimony of John the Baptist, Andrew, and Nathaniel.

Following the Cana section, Jesus returns to Jerusalem, where he heals a man on the Sabbath (5:1). It is not possible to get much of a sense of the time element in the following incidents, since they are identified only by the vague temporal reference "after this" (5:1; 6:1; 6:66; 7:1). Time within these incidents, however, is sometimes more explicit (6:22; 7:14, 37). The organization of each incident is similar: each begins with an action of Jesus, which leads to a dialogue with someone who misunderstands, and culminates in a monologue by Jesus. Thus the healing of the invalid (5:1–9), elicits a controversy about Jesus healing on the Sabbath (5:10 and following), which in turn becomes a speech by Jesus (5:19–47). A similar pattern is found in the narratives of the Feeding of the Five Thousand (6:1–58), of Jesus at the Feast of Tabernacles (7:1–8:59), and of the healing of the blind man (9:1–10:21). C. H. Dodd, in an excellent discussion of the organization of John, has shown this scheme of action–misunderstanding–monologue to be a characteristic pattern of this gospel (1953).

The healing of the blind man is remarkably like the healing of the invalid with which this section began (compare 5:1–15 with 9:1–38). They both involve healing of long-term illnesses, take place in Jerusalem, involve a pool, occur on the Sabbath and cause offense to the Jewish leaders, comment on the relation of sin to sickness, spring from the need and not the faith of the recipient, are misunderstood, and both end with a lengthy speech by Jesus. Yet they are different, especially in their portrayals of the response of the one healed. The second story (one might almost say second version of the story) carries us much

further than the first. Jesus is vindicated and the error of his opponents is clear, at least to the reader.

These signs of Jesus continue to reveal his identity, but the explanation of that identity is more fully developed in this section. Jesus is presented in the context of the great Jewish Holy Days: Sabbath (5 and 9), Passover (6), Tabernacles (7–8), and Dedication (10:22–42). The reader learns that Jesus is the True Bread, the Living Water, the True Light, the Good Shepherd. The contrast of these symbols with ordinary bread, water, light, and shepherds and Jesus' bold declaration: "You are from the below; I am from the above" (8:23, literal) reveal an important aspect of John's view of the world. Reality exists on two levels, an ordinary reality and another "true" or "good" reality. So far, all the action has been directed downward, initiated by the descent of the "Word" into the world (1:14). The action of these first two sections shows the impact the descent of that Word from above had on the world below. We may consider it a metaphor of descent. The next incident, the raising of Lazarus, continues to reveal this impact, but begins to reverse the metaphor as one from below is raised.

The Lazarus narratives are the climax of Jesus' earlier actions (his ultimate sign) and the foreshadowing of his ensuing passion (and his own resurrection). It is the last of the signs of glory (11:4 and 2:11) and the dramatic cause of Jesus' own death (11:46–53; 12:17–19). The section closes with a daring and isolated pronouncement of Jesus:

☙ ☙ ☙

I have come as light into the world. . . .
I say as the father has bidden me. (12:44–50)

While the prior narrative has shown the impact of that light on the world below, much of what follows focuses on what Jesus has to say. He speaks no more to the world, but concentrates all his energies on the disciples. Jesus' last meal with his disciples is turned into an occasion for extensive conversation that soon becomes a monologue (chapters 14–17). Dodd made the intriguing suggestion that John here reverses his normal pattern of action-discourse (1953:400). Whereas in the earlier narratives Jesus acted and then spoke to explain the action, now discourse precedes action and explains the ensuing passion narrative.

The passion narrative itself is the same story we have already encountered in three other versions: recognizably the same yet with a distinctive Johannine perspective. It is the strong similarities in the four passion accounts that convince us that this part of the Jesus tradition was the most fixed and probably the earliest to be told as a connected unit. After retelling the story of Jesus' death and resurrection, John's whole work reaches its climax in a general declaration of its content and purpose:

❧ ❧ ❧

Now Jesus did many other signs in the presence of the disciples, which are not written in this book; but these are written that you may believe that Jesus is the Christ, the Son of God, and that believing you may have life in his name. (20:30–31)

But instead of ending there, the narrative continues with an additional resurrection appearance and the testimony of the Johannine community to the veracity of the account (21), thus balancing the testimony of the narrator and of John the Baptist to Jesus of chapter 1. This balancing of the opening and closing leads us to ask whether the other units of John's narrative correspond. We have identified the basic units of John's narrative as the movement from Cana to Cana (2–4), the movement from Sabbath Healing to Sabbath Healing (5–10), the Raising of Lazarus (11–12), the Speeches to the Disciples (13–17), and the Passion Narrative (18–20). Actually, these seem to form a chiasmus, a series of concentric circles in the following pattern:

1	Testimony to the true identity of Jesus
2–4	The glory of God revealed in signs
5–10	The union of Jesus with God in action
11–12	The ultimate sign
13–17	The union of Jesus with God in word
18–20	Jesus is glorified in his passion
21	Testimony of the community to the truth

But there appears to be an even more basic underlying structure.

The Structure of the Gospel

These stages of John's narrative are also encompassed in a larger structural design, already hinted at in the above discussion—a design of descent and ascent. The underlying theme of the action in chapters 1–12 is the descent of the Word into the world (1:9). Beginning in chapter 13, when Jesus recognizes that his hour has come, the gospel reenacts the ascent of Jesus to the Father (13:1). Many scholars have recognized this theme of descent-ascent as the organizing principle of the gospel (Bultmann, 1971; Dodd, 1953; Brown, 1966; and others). This larger structural framework takes up and enhances the action sketched above.

The turning point between these two halves is a dramatic pronouncement by Jesus, unattached to any story; it begins:

❧ ❧ ❧

He who believes in me, believes not in me but in him who sent me. And he who sees me sees him who sent me. I have come as light into the world. . . . (12:44–50)

This is both a summary of the narrative to this point and the beginning of a new action. Several important changes occur now.

First, Jesus' orientation shifts from the world to his immediate followers: Jesus speaks no more to the crowds, but privately instructs his disciples (Dodd, 1953:390). His topic also changes. Earlier, Jesus had spoken of light and life; now he speaks of love. (By Dodd's count, the terms *light* and *life* are used 82 times in 1–12 but only 6 times thereafter; *love* is spoken of 31 times in 13–17, but only 6 times earlier; 1953:398.) Also, there are no more signs/miracles after chapter 12, even the word disappears until the final sum-

mary. Finally, and most significantly, what happens in 13–20 corresponds with what happens in 1–12 as answer to question or as fulfillment to promise. Although the signs of 1–12 anticipate what Jesus will do once he is glorified, the substance of 13–20 is his glorification (Brown, 1966:541). Thus, while Jesus had demurred in chapter 2: "My hour has not yet come" (2:4), chapter 13 opens: "And when Jesus knew that his hour had come. . . ."

We recognize, then, that the structural form that underlies John's narrative is like the basic Johannine worldview: a dualism. It is a going out from the Father (1–12) and a return to the Father

---

READING GUIDE TO THE GOSPEL OF JOHN

Coming Down from the Father 1–12

Testimony to the true identity of Jesus 1
  The narrator—the Baptist—the disciples
The glory of Jesus revealed in signs from Cana to Cana 2–4
  The wedding at Cana: first sign
  The sign of the temple cleansing
  The dialogue with Nicodemus: being born from above
  The controversy with John: the one from above
  The dialogue with the woman: living water/true worship
  The healing at Cana: second sign
The Union of Jesus with the Father: Sabbath Healing 5–10
  A healing in Jerusalem—controversy—explanation by Jesus: as the Father so the Son
  The sign of bread—controversy—explanation by Jesus: true bread from Heaven
  Teaching at the Feast of Tabernacles—controversy—explanation water and light from above

A healing in Jerusalem—controversy—explanation by Jesus: The good shepherd gives his life; I and the Father are one
The ultimate sign: death and resurrection 11–12
  The story of Lazarus: Jesus as life
                        One should die
                        for the people
  The approach of Passover
    The anointing of Jesus
    The world drawn to Jesus

    Jesus' pronouncement

Going Up to the Father 13–21

Jesus with His disciples 13–17
  The supper and service
  Jesus explains his glory
  Jesus prays for glory
Jesus performs his work 18–20
  The arrest
  The trials of Jesus and Peter
  The death of Jesus
  The appearances of the resurrected Jesus
The testimony of the community 21

(13–20)—a descent and an ascent. We may be tempted to view these as two antithetical movements, but their relationship is more subtle. Each contains a basic irony. The glory of Jesus is both manifested and hidden in his signs, and his ultimate glorification and return to the Father is his crucifixion.

The first movement of the book is concerned with signs. Narrowly defined, these signs are mighty works, miracles, which have the power to reveal God in Jesus. That is, they function as revelations no less than the discourses of the second movement. They reveal Jesus' glory (2:11), but only to those with eyes to see it (6:26). The second movement of the book is concerned with the fulfillment of these signs, the coming of the hour that at first was only signified in the giving of wine. The ironic enthronement of Jesus (19:19–22) fulfills his promise to be "lifted up" (3:14); it is his exaltation (17:1).

Let us examine these two movements in greater detail.

THE DESCENT:
The Word Became Flesh

Both Mark and Luke began directly with a dramatic incident that immediately involved the reader in the action. Matthew started with a genealogy, though that also had a dramatic impact as an interpretation of Israel's history. John does not open with a narrative incident of any kind. He starts outside historical time and space: "In the beginning. . . ."

The Prologue as a Literary Device

This opening section of John's gospel (usually called the prologue) is unlike anything we have encountered in the gospels so far.

Reading and Reflection

Read John 1:1–18 aloud.

1. What is the main theme of the passage?
2. What attributes and activities are portrayed for the Word?

This prologue, sometimes called a hymn, is very different from the psalmlike hymns of Luke 1–2: it is abstract, philosophical, esoteric. Most scholars believe John has constructed this prologue by combining an already existing poem with narrative material about John the Baptist.[1] Before discussing the ideas of the prologue we must raise the question of its literary significance.

The literary effect of the prologue is to distance the reader from the narrative; it inserts an interpretive overlay between the reader and the action. The effect is similar to that of allegorization, in which an author first tells the reader the real significance and identity of the characters and action that follow. The closest analogy in the Synoptic Gospels is Matthew's use of the speeches to interpret the actions of Jesus. The use of such material by Matthew and John represents a move away from the immediacy and drama of art toward the rational reflection of philosophy and theology. Yet John remains an imaginative work that skillfully interweaves narrative, dialogue, monologue, and a narrator's point of view into a readable unity.

The juxtaposition of abstract philosophical generalizations about the Word and concrete historical references to John the Baptist (1:6–8) exposes a basic paradox of this gospel: by its very approach it is ahistorical (that is, philosophical or theological; concerned with things outside space and time, things that happened "in the begin-

---

1. Notice how verses 6–8 and verse 15 interrupt the flow of the main declaration about the Word. Some translations even put verse 15 in parentheses.

ning"). At the same time, however, John is telling a historical story about historical persons. John's story, paradoxical at its very heart, is guided by the basic idea that the timeless entered time, the Word became flesh (1:14–18).

This is a more extreme form of the problem of all historical literature. Literature by its nature refers only to itself, not to external events. Yet the gospels are literature about such events. (This conflict between the demands of literature and history will be discussed in Chapter 13.) John addresses this tension between ultimate and historical realities by constantly speaking on two levels, which we may call the *apparent* reality of the visible, tangible world and the *true* reality of the unseen world. John designates these the Below and the Above (8:23). If these two worlds were perfectly congruent, the literary form would be allegory. But for John the two are anything but congruent; they are nearly the opposite. In John there is a paradoxical relation between these two worlds, and the literary form is irony.

The Irony of It All

Like all important concepts, irony means different things to different people. It is a form of comparison—an implied comparison, never stated. Irony forces the hearer or reader to consider a relationship between two dissimilar things. Were someone to say to you, "a fine friend you are," you would be forced to compare your action with that expected from a friend and—if meant ironically—see your failure as a friend. We may regard such sarcasm as an elementary form of irony, where the speaker says one thing but we know that the opposite is meant.

Literary studies often distinguish two forms of irony: verbal and dramatic. Verbal irony is expressed through the use of sarcasm, double entendre, and ambiguity, when the real meaning of the words contrasts with (and usually destroys) their literal meaning. John's gospel has examples of verbal irony that range from simple verbal ambiguities (such as 3:3ff, where "born anew" can

mean both "born again" or "born from above"; 4:10ff, where "living" water means also simply "flowing" water; 7:8, where "going up" to Jerusalem may refer to a simple journey or to his ascension to the Father—see 20:17 and 12:23) to profound interpretations of the meanings of Jesus' death (such as the "prophecy" of Caiaphas in 11:50–51 and the sign on the cross in 19:19–22).

Dramatic irony concerns the plot; it is a situational irony where the action portrayed forces the reader/hearer to understand the opposite of what is being portrayed. The real meaning is the tragic reverse of what the participants think. Dramatic irony was a common device in Greek tragedy. Thus, for example, Oedipus accuses the blind prophet of corruption, when in fact it is he who is blind and corrupt, having unknowingly killed his father and married his mother. We see him pronounce a curse on the murderer and pledge to avenge the dead king "as if he were my father"—all the while knowing what he does not know: that the king was his father and that he had killed him (Sophocles, *Oedipus the King*). Although Oedipus imagines that when he discovers the identity of the murderer all will be well in his land, the tragic opposite is true. Most of the irony of Oedipus turns on the audience knowing what Oedipus does not, the identity of his parents. So too, in John's gospel the irony depends on the hearers knowing the true identity of Jesus.

Such situational irony pervades John's gospel, especially the portrayal of Jesus' death, which really means the opposite of what it appears. And the irony of the release of Barabbas, who was an insurrectionist, while Jesus is crucified on a similar charge, has not escaped John's notice (18:39–40). Eventually we will see that nearly every incident in John has an ironic dimension. At the risk of overgeneralizing, we may say that John writes in an ironic mode.

In his somewhat overcomplicated theory of literary modes, Northrop Frye describes the ironic mode of thematic poets (such as T. S. Eliot,

Virginia Woolf, and Ezra Pound) as a "sense of contrast between the course of a whole civilization and the tiny flashes of significant moments which reveal its meaning" (1957:61). Without wishing to press the formula too literally, I suggest John is doing something similar. Consider, for example, John's use of the story of the cleansing of the Temple. (Compare John 2:13–25 with Mark 11:15–19, 27–33.) John saw in this "tiny flash" a far more profound meaning than any of the earlier writers. He saw an indication of Jesus' own death and resurrection. Such scenes with double meanings permeate this gospel, though they are not always so clearly delineated.

A correlative theme of this irony and double meaning is the misunderstanding of Jesus by persons in the story, such as Nicodemus in chapter 3. In part, at least, such misunderstanding is a deliberate literary device. It allows the author to have Jesus explain his meaning, hence the long speeches. All this (speeches, misunderstanding, irony) follows directly from the worldview of the prologue.

The Shape of John's Universe

Translating the prologue from Greek into English is one of the most difficult tasks to confront an interpreter of John. This difficulty arises from several causes, the most basic of which is that John is talking about things for which we have no English equivalents. Thus the dominant concept of this prologue is that of the *logos,* usually translated as word:

№ № №

In the beginning was the word (logos) and the word was with God and the word was God.

But logos means far more than the English term *word;* it can be used of any part of the process of communication or for the total act of communicating. It can mean: a word, a saying, a statement, a speech, a conversation, a story, language itself, the process of communication, or

reason as the presupposition of communication. We simply have no English equivalent—not even an adequate paraphrase. So it seems best to leave the word untranslated and force the reader to confront its alien character. A number of other ambiguities are evident in the prologue, which any good translation will seek to resolve. But part of John's effect stems from his lack of clarity. What follows, then, is not a good translation, but a rather literal transposition into English, trying to preserve some of the ambiguity of the original. You would do well to compare it with several of the standard English translations.

№ № №

When things began the Logos was; the Logos was with God; and as God was the Logos. That one was with God when things began. All things through that one came into being; and without that one nothing came into being; that which had come into being in that one was life and the life was the light of humanity. And the light shines in the darkness and the darkness has not mastered it. It was the perfect light, enlightening all humanity, coming into the world. In the world it was and the world through that one came into being and the world knew it not. To that akin to it it came and the kin were not receptive; But as many as received that one, to them he gave the prerogative to become children of God, to the ones trusting in the name of that one, the ones who, not from blood, nor from the desire of the flesh, nor from the desire of a man, but from God were born. And the Logos became flesh and pitched a tent among us, and we marveled at the glory of that one, glory as of a father's only child, full of grace and perfection. Out of the fullness of that one we all received, grace against grace. The Law through Moses was given, grace and perfection through Jesus Christ came into being.

At this point, the poem (if such it be) remains somewhat obscure to us, for we lack a sufficient context within which to interpret it. For starters, we must ask in what context a first-century hearer was likely to understand the meaning of logos. But it is not quite that simple, for logos was used in a variety of contexts, three of which deserve special consideration. (See the treatment of logos in TDNT, VI: 69–143, esp. 77ff.)

First, logos was used in the Greek translation of the Hebrew Scriptures, the Septuagint. To translate expressions such as the "word of God," the translators had the choice between two Greek words. But, especially in translating the prophets, they consistently chose *logos* rather than its Greek synonym *rhema*. Thus, Greek-speaking Jews were familiar with the expression the "logos of God" as a way of referring to the Scriptures. Logos here would refer to the revelation God gives to his people. It would be equivalent to the Torah, God's instruction to his people (Ps. 119). God's logos was the Law, but also the divine word that came to the prophets—the same word by which God had created the world ("And God said let there be. . . ."). Much of what John says about the logos makes perfectly good sense within this context. Reread the prologue above, imagining that the reader understood logos to be the divine revelation, the word of God.

A second and completely unrelated context in which logos had a specialized meaning was in Greek philosophical writing. The dominant philosophical movement of John's time was Stoicism, a philosophy that goes back to Zeno (died about 263 BCE), a materialistic philosopher whose works only survive in fragments. (For a discussion of the general purposes of Stoicism see pp. 106–107.) Basic to his understanding of things was the notion of an elemental order of the universe, which he called variously Destiny, Providence, Nature, or Logos. Zeno made a bold and successful move to reinterpret traditional Greek religion of external gods and goddesses in terms of this interior and immanent concept of the ultimate. He declared:

❧ ❧ ❧

The General Law, which is Right Reason (Logos), pervading everything is the same as Zeus, the Supreme Head of the government of the universe. (Fragment 162; found in Barrett, 1961a:62)

This move to identify God with Reason was successful in part because educated people in late antiquity had grown uncomfortable with the gods of Greek mythology. Zeus's penchant for seducing young maidens was hardly the sort of thing to inspire awe, yet by the Stoic reinterpretation even such antics were redeemed. If Zeus is now Reason, perhaps the maiden is our human understanding, which is to be seduced and made pliant to the will of Reason. Thus, by allegorization Stoicism transcended and rescued mythological religion for many. A prime example of this transformation is the widely quoted Hymn to Zeus by Cleanthes, which begins: "Thou, O Zeus, art praised above all gods," and includes the line "we are thy offspring," a version of which Luke has Paul quote at Acts 17:28. The hymn has been published in a number of works, including Barrett (1961a:63).

The basis of this allegorization is the identification of God with Reason (Logos), seen as the ordering principle inherent in the universe. We can know this Reason/Logos because we partake of it; we have reason/logos. "The Nature of the Universe ought to be apprehended by Reason (Logos), which is akin to it" (Posidonius, a Stoic thinker of the first century BCE; quoted in Barrett, 1961a:65). In the Stoic vision of things, the wise man knows reason (logos) and lives in accord with it. "You are," says Epictetus, the greatest of all Stoic philosophers, "a principal work, a fragment of God himself; you have in yourself a part of him [the logos]" (*Discourses* II, 8.9–14; Loeb). Now Stoic philosophy was not an academic exercise in John's time; it was a very aggressive popular movement preached by wandering philosophers in the marketplace. Thus we may presume that John's audience had already heard that they must live in accord with logos, believed to be both an expression of the divine will and even of divinity itself. (Reread 1:1–18, noting any ideas that may be illuminated by a Stoic context.)

The third context with a distinctive use of logos is an intermediate step between the first two. We may call it Jewish philosophy and see it most clearly in Philo of Alexandria (about 20 BCE–CE

45). By Philo's time, Alexandria had replaced Athens as the intellectual center of the world. It was a huge city with a strong and vital Jewish community, and the Septuagint was probably translated there. Alexandria also witnessed a lively interaction between Jewish and Greek thought: the primary Greek influences were Stoicism and Platonism, while the main Jewish influence was from the Wisdom movement. Already nearly a thousand years old by Philo's time, the Wisdom tradition sought to understand life by seeking wisdom from close observation of daily life. The classic text of the Wisdom tradition is the book of Proverbs. (A fuller account of this movement may be found in Anderson's chapter on wisdom, 1975:528–562, and von Rad, 1973, or Scott, 1965.) This practical approach was well suited for dialogue with Greek philosophy, yet it lacked the extensive "natural theology" of Greek thought. In Israel, God was the presupposition even of such practical wisdom, and metaphysics, or speculation about the divine was relatively unknown. The nearest approach to such speculation was the concept of wisdom itself. Wisdom was symbolized, idealized, and very nearly personified into a reality along side God. Thus in the book of Proverbs itself we have this exalted praise of wisdom:

🙚 🙚 🙚

I, Wisdom, dwell in prudence. . . . By me kings reign, and rulers decree what is just, by me princes rule, and nobles govern the earth. I love those who love me, and those who seek me diligently find me. The Lord created me at the beginning of his work, the first of his acts of old. Ages ago I was set up, at the first, before the beginning of the earth. When there were no depths I was brought forth, when there were no springs abounding with water. When he established the heavens, I was there; when he drew a circle on the face of the deep, when he made firm the skies above, when he established the fountains of the deep, when he assigned to the sea its limit, so that the waters might not transgress his command, When he marked out the foundations of the earth, then I was beside him like a master work-

man; And I was daily his delight rejoicing before him always. (Prov. 8:12, 15–17, 22–30)

Wisdom is here exalted to near-divine status as metaphor passes into mythology. A later work in this tradition, commonly known as *Sirach* (also as *Ecclesiasticus*) described wisdom thus:

I came forth from the mouth of the most high and covered the earth like a mist. I dwelt in high places . . . In every people and nation I have gotten a possession. Among all these I sought a resting place; I sought in whose territory I might lodge. Then the Creator of all things. . . . said, "Make your dwelling in Jacob, and in Israel receive your inheritance." (Sirach 24:3–8)

This theme of homeless wisdom is most poignantly portrayed in *First Enoch:*

Wisdom could not find a place in which she could dwell; but a place was found (for her) in the heavens. Then Wisdom went out to dwell with the children of the people, but she found no dwelling place. (So) Wisdom returned to her place, and she settled permanently among the angels. Then Iniquity went out from her rooms, and found whom she did not expect. And she dwelt with them, like rain in a desert like dew on a thirsty land. (42; quoted from Charlesworth, I: 33)

All of these ideas about wisdom had a long tradition in Israel before John wrote his prologue. Clearly he draws on them even though he speaks of Logos rather than Wisdom. Whether he made that leap himself or drew on a wider tradition is no longer certain. We do, however, see a similar shift in Philo.

For our purposes, Philo achieved two significant things with the wisdom concept. First, he developed it further so that wisdom actually appears as a separate identity, an intermediary between God and humanity. And second, he did not refer to it with the feminine name wisdom (*sophia* in Greek) but used the masculine term reason (logos), a concept marvelously suited to reflect also the divine revelation. (See for example, Ps. 118:89, "Forever, O Lord, thy word (logos) is firmly fixed in the heavens.") Philo was able to accept much that the Stoics taught about logos, but believed they erred in identifying logos with God; instead, logos proceeds from God and is his revelation. (See Dodd, 1953:54–73.)

Thus, Philo could write, all should "endeavor to know the Self-existent [God] or, if they cannot, at least to see It's image, the most sacred logos" (*On the Confusion of Languages* 97, in Loeb). And in another place he declares, "For the logos is the God of us imperfect men, but the Primal God is the God of the wise and perfect" (*Allegorical Interpretations* III: 207). This logos is God's agent in creation and his chief messenger:

⁂ ⁂ ⁂

To his Logos, his chief messenger [angelos], highest in age and honour, the Father of all has given the special prerogative, to stand on the border and separate the creature from the Creator. This same Logos both pleads with the immortal as suppliant for afflicted mortality and acts as ambassador of the ruler to the subject. . . . [He is] neither uncreated as God, nor created as you, but midway between the two extremes, a surety to both sides. (Loeb, Who Is the Heir of Divine Things: *205–206)*

Readers familiar with Philo's thought would have no trouble understanding and would surely approve of what John said in this prologue: the creative power and divine status of the Logos, its enlightening function, its being in but not accepted by the world, all this was shared. Now reread the prologue, imagining all three contexts.

One point of the prologue is not explained by these contexts. Although they all imagine that the Logos comes to the world, a world truly its own, accepted only by the few, yet only John dared draw the momentous conclusion:

⁂ ⁂ ⁂

And the Logos became flesh and pitched a tent among us. (1:14)

And that is why John wrote a gospel rather than a philosophical essay. He intended to show the outworking of this incarnation of the Logos by telling his story. As we might expect, the life of this Logos-become-flesh will be extraordinary, and remarkable things will occur in it.

And We Beheld His Glory

John recounts fewer miracles than the other gospels, but there is something unusual about them. They are sometimes called "more miraculous," an impossible expression that nonetheless captures the phenomenon. In John, the miracles of Jesus are spectacular: he turns water into wine (2:1ff), heals a boy "at the point of death" (4:46ff), heals a man "ill for thirty years" (5:2ff), feeds five thousand with five loaves and two fish (6:1ff), walks on the sea (6:16ff), heals a man "blind from birth" (9:1ff), and raises Lazarus from the dead (11:1ff). It would be difficult to imagine more awesome events.

We should find our major clue for interpreting these from John himself: he never calls them miracles or even wondrous works. They are always "signs." Sign is an ambiguous word. It could be used as a synonym for miracle, but John recognized the possibility of eliciting a deeper meaning. (See Rengstorf's lengthy article in TDNT, VII: 200–269.) John used the term sparingly, but it is a key term in his conclusion (20:30f), and he used it in connection with each miracle except the one in chapter 5 (2:11, 23; 4:48, 54; 6:14, 26; 9:16; 11:47; 12:18, 37; no further reference until 20:30f). Curiously, in chapter 5 he explains why the miracles are "signs."

Being challenged for healing on the Sabbath, Jesus replies, "My Father is working still, and I am working" (5:17). This response is probably part of a larger Jewish argument about God and the Sabbath. For although the biblical tradition that God rested on the Sabbath was clear, Jewish scholars were reasonably sure that God never took a day off. Births occurred on the Sabbath; people died on the Sabbath. Surely these were works that only God could do. John's Jesus adopts this conclusion and applies it in a new way: since Jesus is the one from above who does the works of God, he too works on the Sabbath. In fact, he works on the Sabbath precisely because he does the work of God (5:19–47).

This is ironic, since working on the Sabbath was generally considered a sign of low spiritual aspiration. John declares Jesus' Sabbath cure is just the opposite: a sign revealing his union with God. The meaning of these signs is not easy to grasp, because we look at them "from below." We confuse the event with its meaning. John expects his reader to be able to do more.

Consider the sign of Jesus feeding the five thousand. The people are so impressed that they want to make Jesus king. Nothing could better demonstrate that they failed to grasp the sign. When they eventually approach Jesus with the ironic question: "When did you come here?" he responds, "Truly, truly, I say to you, you seek me not because you saw signs, but because you ate your fill of the loaves" (6:26). Yet how could they have not seen the sign? It was not, as a student once suggested, because they were in the back of the crowd. They saw the miracle; they did not see the sign. They did not realize that it signified something quite beyond ordinary food. John has Jesus explain the sign by means of a typically Jewish gloss on Scripture. When the crowds cite the manna tradition from the Exodus story and imply that this was expected to occur again in the last days, when a new Moses would arise, Jesus challenges their reading of the text. They read: "He (Moses) gave them bread from Heaven." Jesus shifted both the subject and the verb. Since Hebrew was written without vowels, it could often be read in more than one way. Later rabbis would delight in finding new meanings in old texts by supplying unexpected vowels. So Jesus says the text should be read, "He (God) gives them bread from Heaven" (6:32). That bread from heaven is "true bread." It is Jesus himself. That is the significance of the sign (Borgen, 1963).

Simply put, the sign reveals that Jesus is doing the work of God. God multiplies the loaves every year in the harvest; he produces wine from water; he heals. For John the performance of these deeds should evoke faith not because they are spectacular, but because they are significant. To the one who can see (like the blind man in chapter 9) they reveal the wisdom of God. We know when the crowds ask Jesus when he came here, they are puzzled only about how he got to the other side of the lake after the last boat left without him. But in John's ironic fashion that is the real question. The reader who understands the prologue knows the true answer.

John is fond of such irony. The story in chapter 9 is laden with it, often to humorous effect.

Reading and Reflection

Read the story of the healing of the man born blind in John 9 and 10. Why do the Jewish leaders reject Jesus? What examples of irony or sarcasm do you find?

The Jewish leaders had rejected Jesus because he was from Nazareth (7:41; a problem also faced by Matthew and Luke). But instead of using the Bethlehem tradition John found an alternative one more suited to his purpose; he used a tradition about the hidden origin of the Messiah (7:27). Then, in chapter 9, he shows the Jewish leaders making just this confession about Jesus: they do not know where he comes from (9:29). How ironic, for they really do not know. They do not see the sign.

The final sign of Jesus is the climax of the signs—the ultimate work of God—and a sign of things to come. The ultimate work of God is to give life, and in chapter 11 Jesus raises Lazarus from the dead. This complex story is well worth our close study. It opens as Jesus is informed of Lazarus' illness. On one level, Jesus' response seems to be insensitive or even cruel: "This illness is not unto death; it is for the glory of God, so that the Son of God may be glorified by means of it" (11:4). Is Jesus saying that God would kill someone just so Jesus could be glorified by raising him up? Is this a publicity stunt? If the reader asks such a question he or she has progressed no further than Nicodemus (3:4). To see the sign of Lazarus the reader must understand that in John's scheme of things the Lazarus incident leads directly to Jesus' death (11:47–53) and that his death is his glorification (12:23). In a symbolic way Lazarus' death and resurrection are Jesus' death and resurrection; it is "for the glory of God."

On this note the first movement of John's story, the descent, is complete. The logos has become flesh and manifested the glory of God (1:14, 18). The reader must now witness his reascent to the Father.

ASCENT:
The Hour Has Come

One major purpose of this first movement of John's gospel has been to teach the reader how to read the story, how to see the signs. Jesus performs the works of God (5:30; 14:8–11). This is the descent of Logos into the world. Now the hour has come for the ascent (13:1). In the rest of the narrative, there are no more signs in the sense of miracles. Yet all Jesus does and says is sign. Jesus' whole action becomes a visible presentation of his true nature and glory (John 2:11). The writer has now set the stage for us to encounter the familiar events of the passion.

The Events before the Passion

Perhaps the most striking thing about Jesus' last supper with his disciples in this gospel is that there is no Last Supper, no eucharistic meal (13:1–30). The scene is familiar from the Synoptic Gospels: there is the final gathering on the night before the arrest; Judas is revealed as the betrayer (as in Luke, Satan entered him; Luke 22:3 = John 13:27); they eat together. But novelties appear (a foot-washing ceremony); familiar events disappear (no agony in Gethsemane); there are special Johannine touches ("He immediately went out, and it was night," 13:30; see 1:5; 9:4; 11:10; note also 20:1).

The omission of the Last Supper is variously explained. A daring school of interpretation believes John is deliberately antisacramental (recall that there was no baptism scene either). Those who argue this way must see certain passages as later additions (such as 3:5; 6:51–58), and, as Robert Kysar recognizes, ignore a basic aspect of John's thought: that faith may be mediated through sensory experience (1976:109). While radical, such a view must be given serious consideration in light of John's general divergence from the Synoptic tradition.

Another attempt to explain the omission of the eucharistic meal derives from the differences in chronology in John and the Synoptics. All four gospels connect Jesus' death to the Passover festival, a spring ritual that commemorated the Exodus from slavery in Egypt, a festival of freedom. A central aspect of the festival involved the killing of a lamb in the afternoon, which would be eaten at an evening communal meal involving at least ten people. In John, Jesus dies in the afternoon of the Day of Preparation, at about the time the Passover lambs were slain in preparation for the evening meal (John 19:31). In the Synoptics, Jesus eats the Passover meal with his disciples and is executed the next day, which by Jewish reckoning would be Passover day (see Mark, 14:12 and parallels; GP #234 or SFG #308). However, Mark also reports that Jesus died on "the day of preparation" (15:42). Let us deal first with the historical and then consider the literary issue.

Some of the confusion, but certainly not all, may stem from different ways of relating days to nights. Ancient practice varied widely. Pliny the Elder noted:

ﺰ ﺰ ﺰ

The Babylonians count the period between two sunrises, the Athenians that between two sunsets, the Umbrians from midday to midday, the common people everywhere from dawn to dark, the

Roman priests and the authorities who fixed the
official day, and also the Egyptians and Hippar-
chus, the period from midnight to midnight.
(Natural History *II.79.181)*

The official practice in Israel was like the
Greek, counting from sundown to sundown: the
evening is connected with the following daylight
rather than the preceding daylight. Thus, what
we call Monday night would, by Jewish and Greek
standards, be Tuesday night (the night that goes
with Tuesday). Similarly, "Passover evening"
would be what we would normally call the evening of the day before, rather like our Christmas
Eve. This may account for some of the confusion
in the texts, for Mark probably followed a Roman system (in 11:11–12 he seems to regard
evening and morning as representing two separate days; compare Matt. 21:17–18). In the Roman system, "Passover evening" would imply
the evening after Passover day, while under the
Jewish system it would mean the evening before
Passover day.

The historical question then becomes: Did Jesus die on the day before Passover or on Passover day itself? If Jesus died on the day before
Passover, as in John, and the next day was both
Passover and Sabbath (Saturday), then he would
have been crucified in either the year 30 or 33,
since in those years the two holy days coincided.
If Jesus died on Passover day and the next day
was Sabbath (Saturday), as in the Synoptics, Jesus was crucified in 27, since Passover fell on a
Friday in that year.

This leads us to the literary issue: How does
this chronology influence the way John told his
story? Clearly, if Jesus died before Passover Eve,
he could not have eaten the Passover meal with
his disciples since it was eaten that night. Consequently, John could not portray the Last Supper in its Synoptic form. This would not mean
that John's community did not celebrate the Eucharist (Communion). Jesus' death, understood
as the death of the Passover Lamb (1:29), would
naturally point to a commemoration of that death
in a Passover meal. Yet this would raise the seri-

ous question of whether it would then be possible
for John's church to celebrate the Eucharist in
anything like the Pauline form (see I Cor.
11:23–26).

A third explanation argues that sacramental
teaching permeates the whole gospel, but that John
does not portray the sacramental acts themselves
because he "will not divulge the Christian 'mystery'" (Dodd, 1953:393n1). As we learned earlier, the Mystery Religions were powerful and
popular religious movements in John's day and
each centered on some secret ritual, often involving bread, wine, and blood (pp. 64, 126).
We know from other sources that the unbaptized
(that is, the uninitiated) were not allowed to witness the Eucharist in some Christian circles (for
example, *Didache* 9:5). Perhaps John hides the
central rituals because they are too sacred to share
with the uninitiated. While the rituals are not
portrayed, wine and bread are certainly strong
symbols in the gospel: 2:1ff; 15:1ff; 6:32ff; 51ff;
19:34; Brown, 1966:CXIV.

We should notice how the same observation
that neither the baptism nor the Last Supper is
portrayed in John can lead to two opposite conclusions: John is antisacramental; John is wholly
sacramental. This problem does not lend itself to
a clear solution.

Whether we regard John as sacramental or antisacramental (or something in between) depends
on larger questions of interpretation, such as how
we understand the meaning of the signs and, especially, how we understand the meaning of Jesus' death.

The Words before the Passion

Nowhere is John's divergence from the Synoptic
tradition more radical than in chapters 14–17.
Nothing like this exists in the Synoptics; the final
apocalyptic speech (Mark 13 and parallels) is only
a remote reflection of a similar idea: the farewell
words of Jesus. But in both form and content
John's speeches are unique.

Reading and Reflection

Read John 13:31–17:26, and try to answer the following:

1. In his final hours with the disciples in the Synoptics, Jesus addressed such concerns as the betrayal, the denial of Peter, coming persecution, the need for service, and his return to them. Which of these themes are addressed here?
2. The events discussed here are future from the viewpoint of Jesus in the story; are they also future from the viewpoint of the narrator?
3. What is the Spirit called and what is it said to do?

We can readily demonstrate that these speeches are not "historical" in any simple sense, especially if we consider the Synoptic gospels as historically grounded (for example, Schnackenburg, 1968:21f). These ideas belong to a different thought world and it is the world of the author, for we encounter the same ideas and even the same vocabulary in the remarks of the narrator. (The prologue, for example, reveals an identical worldview.) Even more revealing, it is the same thought world seen in the letter called First John. Our author has not merely replayed the historical record, he has transposed the sayings and actions of Jesus into a new key; he has given us a new interpretation. This is, of course, also true of the Synoptics but less radically, in a way that long remained undetected. Whether John's interpretation is a legitimate one depends on several factors, including what is meant by legitimate.

John chose a new means of interpretation. While Matthew created speeches for Jesus by combining units of tradition into new patterns, John developed single ideas into long discourses. Most agree that these exact words were not spoken on the night before the passion, but there is no consensus on whether the words spoken then are truly represented here. John and his community claim that they never truly understood Je-

sus until after his death, when they experienced his resurrection presence, as Dodd correctly asserts these speeches would be more appropriate coming from the resurrected Jesus (1953:397). John apparently is not prepared to do that, though later writers will. (*The Gospel of Thomas,* for example, consists of sayings of the resurrected Jesus to Thomas; see Hennecke and Schneemelcher, I, 1963:511–522.)

But John's contention from the beginning has been that, for those who have eyes to see it, the real significance of Jesus' words and deeds reveal that he comes from above. The bare deeds themselves are meaningless, unless one sees the "sign" (6:26). We might say that these speeches are no less historical than the cleansing of the Temple. The event itself is probable, but John's interpretation is a claim that it means something specific. Certainly, Jesus said some things privately to his disciples. Dodd shows that the basic themes of these discourses are the same as those found in the Synoptic tradition (1953:390ff). Common to both are teachings on the disciples' mission, precepts for living in community, warnings of persecution, promises of assistance and of the Spirit, and predictions of death. Yet what John actually tells us about those themes diverges greatly from the Synoptics because he is interpreting Jesus for his own community—he narrates the meaning of these words, rather than merely repeating what Jesus said.

John undertakes such "revisionist history" confidently, as he explains in these speeches. Jesus' word is like a seed planted in the believer; it grows and bears fruit (15:3–7). More importantly, John's community knows the presence of the Spirit, who reminds believers of what Jesus taught (14:26) and leads them into all truth (16:13). He has shown earlier that the proper understanding of events was remembered only after Jesus' resurrection (2:22; 12:22ff). Now he speaks for Jesus just as Jesus spoke for God (16:14; 14:10), or perhaps, more accurately, "the risen Christ speaks through the evangelist" (Cullmann, 1976: 18). Thus, John shows Jesus speaking of the one who has ascended into heaven (3:13), introducing his own words and concepts into the time of Jesus. Only the scale is different, for we saw similar things in the Synoptics. An abiding feature of the gospel form is its blend of past and present. The gospels not only tell us what Jesus said to his disciples, they also relate what their authors believed Jesus was saying to their own communities.

One such revision is in an area we have been watching develop since Mark: the tension between the present and the future experience of God's kingdom (although kingdom of God is not an expression John uses much; it occurs only at 3:3, 5). To appreciate what John does here it is helpful to recall the story of Lazarus. When Jesus tells Martha, "Your brother will rise again," she replies, "I know that he will rise again in the resurrection at the last day." But Jesus declares:

🙚 🙚 🙚

I am the resurrection and the life, he who believes in me, though he dies yet shall he live, and whoever lives and believes in me shall never die. (11:25–26)

Here Jesus shifts from a future-oriented eschatology to a present-oriented fulfillment (Kysar, 1976:88). This is typical of the view of Christian existence expressed in these discourses and probably represents John's basic contribution. (See 20:31, noting its emphasis on the present.)

It will be helpful at this point to consider a few definitions widely used in writing about "last things" (eschatology). *Futurist Eschatology* is used to refer to a conception of the kingdom of God and related events as entirely or essentially in the future. *Realized Eschatology* refers to an understanding of the present as the time of fulfillment. In a fully realized eschatology there is no future element. *Inaugurated Eschatology* is used to express the belief that while the kingdom of God has already begun to appear, it is not yet fully realized. This idea involves a future expectation. The Synoptic Gospels present an inaugurated eschatology; which viewpoint does John represent?

Clearly, a few references appear to envision a future fulfillment: 6:40; 12:48; 14:3, 18, 28; 20:17. Apparently, however, these future elements are not very important to John. His casual way of handling them (for example, it is not always clear whether by "coming again" he means the second coming or the resurrection; see 16:66ff) and their relative scarcity in the text indicate that the balance has shifted dramatically from the imminent expectation of the end (as in Paul, and probably Mark) to the present life of the believer. John stops just short of the gnosticizing interpretation that Paul challenged at Corinth (I Cor. 15; see also pp. 76–79); the present does not wholly swallow up the future. Clearly, however, those Corinthians would be very pleased with much that John teaches (Pagels, 1973). In John's view, eternal life is something one has now (17:3).

This is not so much a contradiction of the Synoptic view as it is a novel approach. The Synoptics, and Jewish tradition generally, approach the kingdom with what we may call a horizontal metaphor: the kingdom stands out ahead of them, beckoning them forward. John understands life with a vertical metaphor: the kingdom exists in a world above this one and descends.

The final prayer of Jesus with which John ends this section fulfills several functions. It summarizes and concentrates many of the important ideas of the book (Käsemann, 1968), and carefully explains the meaning of Jesus' coming death as the Son of the Father. It also completes the final metaphor of ascent (17:11) and represents Jesus offering himself to the Father, an offering actualized and accepted in the death of Jesus, which follows (see Dodd, 1953:420ff). It should be read carefully.

Accomplishing His Passion

Although it is unlikely that John used any of the Synoptics as a source, it is revealing to compare his account with theirs for two reasons: first, since the passion narrative is the most fixed part of the

Jesus story, we might expect strong similarities even between independent accounts. And, second, John's emphases will generally stand out when compared with other accounts.

Reading and Reflection

Read John 18 and 19 and carefully compare selected incidents with the Synoptics' accounts, Mark 14:26–15:47, and parallels (the reading begins at SFG #330 or GP #238; revealing incidents include SFG #s 330–332, 343–347).

1. List ten specific ways that John's account of the suffering and death of Jesus differs from the other accounts.
2. Try to explain one or two of these differences in terms of what you already know about John's emphases and techniques.

There is an implicit irony in calling this "the Passion of Jesus," for passion (from *pathos,* something that befalls one; suffering) is essentially passive. As John tells the story, however, this is actually something Jesus does; even Simon of Cyrene is eliminated (19:17). The soldiers are powerless to arrest him (18:6); he sets the terms by which they take him (18:8). Jesus is the one from above (18:36; 19:9). He controls his own destiny and pronounces his own judgment on the affair: it is finished (19:30). This act of Jesus is a basic Johannine idea (12:27). The offering of himself to his Father is somehow an essential act—*the* essential act of Jesus (18:37). It represents no defeat; there is no power of darkness here (19:28; contrast Mark 15:33). This is the moment we have been waiting for (2:4), the exaltation of Jesus (3:14f). Irony.

Is Seeing Believing?

Like everything else in his gospel, John's account of the resurrection goes its own way (20:1–30). Much here is typical of John, but two aspects deserve our attention. First, John has an alternate tradition regarding the giving of the Holy Spirit (20:22). He wishes to tie the experience of the Spirit directly to the experience of Jesus (see 7:39). Second, John uses the resurrection appearances to further his meditation on the relation between seeing and believing which is basic to his idea of "signs."

The scene here is one of the famous scenes in literature. Thomas has missed the first appearance and expresses his doubts: "Unless I see . . ." (20:25). In the very next incident the risen Jesus appears and challenges Thomas to examine him and "not be faithless but believing" (20:27). "Thomas then answers: 'My Lord and my God.'"

What is the meaning of this? How is the reader to respond? John recognized that such evidence was no longer available, for he has Jesus say to Thomas: "Have you believed because you have seen me? Blessed are those who have not seen and yet believe" (20:29). Here John is employing the ultimate irony of his book: no amount of miracles can ever produce faith, yet he recounts a story full of miracles, precisely to produce faith. Like the crowds at the Feeding (chapter 6) one is always in danger of missing the sign—the insight produced by apprehending the meaning of Jesus, which points to faith.

In this sense, everything in John's gospel hinges on his characterization of Jesus. And the overwhelming trait of that characterization is that Jesus is the One from Above. He is, quite literally, "beyond us." He transcends the human situation in nearly every way. He is beyond time: "Before Abraham was, I am" (8:59); "In the beginning . . ." (1:1). His existence extends forward into the life of the community after his death, and he will be there at the last day (14:18–19; 5:28–29; 6:39–40). Thus, while John's narrative is occupied with what we may call the life of Jesus, the story time extends both backward and forward to previous and later history, and even beyond history. Some of these themes are implicit in the Synoptics, but John has attained a new clarity of expression.

John has quite abandoned the apocalyptic view

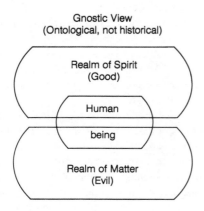

Gnostic View
(Ontological, not historical)

Realm of Spirit
(Good)

Human

being

Realm of Matter
(Evil)

Figure 10 ▪ 1 Gnostic View of History (From *Interpretation: A Bible Commentary for Teaching and Preaching*, Vol. on Romans, by Paul J. Achtemeier. Used by permission of John Knox Press.)

of history. He no longer stands poised between the past and the future (see the discussion and figure on p. 44). In fact, John shares much with the gnostic view of the world, which emphasizes being (ontology) not time (history). We might depict the gnostic view as in Figure 10.1. John shared much with this gnostic view of life, for, like the gnostics, John's Jesus is from beyond time.

This "beyondness" of John's Jesus raises acutely the question of his actual humanity. There are no birth stories; Jesus expresses few emotions; he is not surrounded by children; no one ever "touches" him (Culpepper, 1983:106–112). Only the profound assertion of the reality of his "becoming flesh" (1:14) and the reality of his death preserve his human quality. But precisely this other, divine dimension of Jesus points up Jesus' true identity: he is one with the Father (10:30). The question John posed to his hearers was whether they could "see" the real significance of all that Jesus had said and done. Such sight, he maintained, leads to eternal life. Even "those who have not seen" may attain such insight by hearing such a story as John has written (20:30–31).

The disciples clearly attain such insight, at least by the end of this story. They remain somewhat uncomprehending throughout, but only because they have not yet experienced the resurrection and the Spirit. Perhaps the most significant difference from the Synoptic versions is that the disciples do not abandon Jesus in Gethsemane (compare Mark, 15:50; Gp #240 or SFG #331). One of them, at least, stands at the cross and becomes the caretaker of Jesus' mother (20:26–27). This same disciple, sometimes called the one whom Jesus loved, attains insight within the story, before the resurrected Jesus appears (20:8). This brief study hardly does justice to this brilliant, witty, and ironic book, which merits many readings. Now let us proceed to inquire about the kind of community that provided the background for such a work.

THE SITUATION OF JOHN AND HIS COMMUNITY

Much energy has been devoted to the task of deciphering the kind of community to which, and from which, this gospel is addressed. This scholarly work enables us to consider the likely process by which the gospel came to be written, the supposed identity of the author, and the social and historical situation it presupposes. We seek to discover the kind of audience the author imagined. Before we turn to the audience, however, we must inquire about the author.

The Composition of the Gospel

Three questions about the author concern us here: Was the writer of this gospel acquainted with the other gospels? Was the writer of this gospel one of Jesus' immediate disciples? What else can be known about our writer from other early Christian writings also connected with the name of John? We will consider them in this order.

Did John Know the Synoptic Gospels? Outside the passion story and isolated sayings of Je-

Table 10.1

Reference in John	Number in GP and (SFG)	Title of Incident	Degree of Correlation
1:35–51	11/17 (21)	Call of Disciples	A variant tradition
2:13–22	200 (25)	Cleansing of Temple	Same action, different words and context
4:46–54	46 (85)	Healing Official's Son	Same location and action "Son" in John, child/servant in Matthew Slave in Luke
6:1–21	112/13 (146/47)	Feeding the 5,000 and Walking on Sea	Same action and sequence Different words and characters (a lad's lunch)
6:66–71	122 (159)	Peter's Confession	Different story
12:1–8	232 (267)	Anointing at Bethany	A variant tradition
12:12–19	196 (269)	Entry into Jerusalem	Different portrayal of the event
13:1–30	225 (309/10)	Last Supper	Foot-washing replaces meal

sus, John shares only eight major incidents with the Synoptic Gospels. These do not demonstrate the extensive verbal correlations that existed among the Synoptics themselves. For our purposes, Table 10.1 will prove a convenient tool for noting these similarities and differences.

There are few relatively insignificant, but striking, verbal correlations between John and either Mark or Luke in these stories. For example, both Mark and John estimate it would take more than 200 denarii to buy bread for the 5000, and they both appraise the perfume used in the anointing at 300 denarii. In the latter incident both use the unusual expression "perfume made from real Nard." These, and a few other details, convince some that John knew and drew upon Mark and Luke at least. (Kümmel concluded that such dependence was "indisputable" [1966:144]). But this ignores the real problem: the degree of difference shown in even these stories, which differ in far more details than they agree. We may add to this the number of incidents which John does not share with the Synoptics; some of the most notable of which include:

The wedding at Cana (2:1ff)

The story of Nicodemus (3)

The story of the Samaritan woman (4)

Several long disputes with the Jews (for example 5:10ff; 7:25ff; 8:30ff; etc.)

Healing miracles (5:1ff; 9:1ff)

The raising of Lazarus (11:1ff)

The extended farewell discourse (14–16)

The prayer for the disciples (17)

In addition, John omits several important Synoptic accounts:

Jesus' temptation (and perhaps his baptism)

Peter's confession of Jesus as the Christ

The transfiguration

The Lord's Supper

The agony in Gethsemane (contrast John 12:27ff)

All Jesus' parables

All the exorcism stories

Numerous healing stories

The situation may be seen in miniature by carefully comparing John with similar Synoptic material:

John 3:3	John 3:5	Matt. 18:3	Mark 10:15 Luke 18:17
Truly, truly I say to you, unless one is born anew, he cannot see the kingdom of God.	Truly, truly I say to you, unless one is born of water and the Spirit, he cannot enter the kingdom of God.	Truly I say to you, unless you turn and become like children, you will never enter the kingdom of heaven.	Truly, I say to you, whoever does not receive the kingdom of God like a child shall not enter it.

In this example we see that the similarities between the Synoptic traditions are great enough to posit a common source or mutual dependence, but the Johannine traditions are probably an independent reporting of what may have once been a common tradition. John has shaped the material to fit his own distinctive worldview and way of speaking. And, it must be added, it is rare for John to share even this much with the Synoptic tradition (I owe the example to Lindars, 1981).

We must also consider that in the overall portrayal of Jesus there are significant differences in historical detail. John describes several trips to Jerusalem, with most of the action taking place in Judea in a period of about three years; the Synoptics imply only one trip in one year. Also, the overall mythic pattern is that of the descent of the divine savior into the world, a pattern not found in the Synoptics (see Kümmel, 1966:142; Talbert, 1977, chapters 2, 3).

In short, it does not seem safe to presume that John relied on any of the Synoptic Gospels. Apparently, then, John represents a separate tradition, or rather a separate preservation of the same tradition. This would explain the presence of similar stories and even similar sequences (especially in the passion narrative), told differently, in different words and with varying emphases. Perhaps the few verbal correlations represent points at which the traditions had contact in the period of oral transmission, as Raymond Brown suggests (1966:XLVIf). We should probably imagine the process of transmission as illustrated in Figure 10.2.

In fact there are reasons to think that the process of composition of this gospel were more involved than this figure indicates. It seems probable that we can isolate various stages in the evolution of the gospel, based on observations of phenomena within the text.

The Process of Composition

Like the Synoptics, this gospel is anonymous, without explicit historical references, and surrounded by second-century traditions for which we lack convincing supporting evidence. Yet we have one advantage: chapter 21 is a very early postscript to the gospel.

Reading and Reflection

Read John 21.

1. Why was it added to the gospel?
2. What evidence does it provide concerning authorship and the process of composition?
3. Why do you suppose such attestation was necessary?

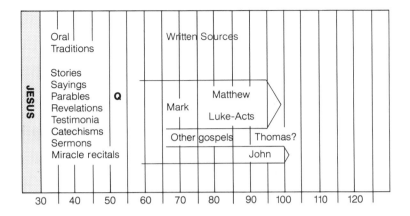

Figure 10 ▪ 2 Channels of Oral Tradition Although our knowledge of the process of oral transmission in the Jesus traditions is meager, it seems clear that one major strand of tradition feeds all three of the Synoptic Gospels. Paul also seems to have stood in this tradition. The Johannine traditions, however, seem to have followed a separate course for several decades before the writing of the Gospel of John. The similarities John manifests to particular Synoptic incidents are probably best explained by imagining some contact between the two strands of oral tradition. There were probably other strands as well, and it is difficult to prove whether gospels like Thomas and Peter depend on the canonical gospels or on similar oral traditions.

Although we have here an explicit claim that the authority of some never-named disciple of Jesus stands behind this gospel (21:24), the traditions in the gospel itself are anything but the simple recollections of an eyewitness. They represent thoroughly interpreted and highly developed reflections on the meaning of Jesus. Any adequate solution to the origin of this gospel must consider both factors.

One cautious but imaginative theory of the origin of John's gospel does just that. In his magisterial commentary in the Anchor Bible Series, Raymond E. Brown suggested that we can reconstruct five stages in the composition of John (1966:XXXVI–XL).

Stage one: The mere existence of a body of Jesus material, stories and sayings, in the life of some church. This is in an oral tradition, not dependent on the Synoptic tradition though perhaps having some contact with it. This material may depend on an original disciple (p. CII).

Stage two: The shaping and development of all this material into Johannine patterns of thought, probably under the influence of a dominant theologian-preacher, perhaps the same original disciple. Unified stories were developed at this stage (for example, chapter 9).

Stage three: The organization of much of this material into a consecutive gospel, the first edition of the Gospel of John, probably by the preacher-theologian who shaped stage two.

Stage four: The reediting of the gospel, primarily adding new material designed to meet new problems; the overwhelming problem seems to have been the effect of the Twelfth Benediction excluding Christians from synagogue worship (see p. 203). This experience seems to be reflected in 9:22–23.

Stage five: The final reediting of the gospel after the death of the evangelist, probably by one or more of his disciples. A primary motive of this editing is to preserve other material from stage two that had not been included in the earlier editions. This material produces the awkward junctures in the text, for example, 5:1 and 14:31 (the material in John 15 and 16 was probably an alternative version of that in 14, but is now simply added to it). Obviously, chapter 21 belongs to this stage.

At first glance such a theory may appear over-complicated, yet it does not differ greatly from the process proposed for the composition of works of the Hebrew prophets such as Jeremiah. It may be possible to combine stages four and five into one reediting by friends or disciples of the author, as Cullmann suggests (1976:9f), giving basically three phases to the material: collecting and shaping; an original gospel mainly like the present work; a final edition published after the death of the author.

If we now reexamine chapter 21, Brown's theory will help illuminate what is found there. Several purposes can be adduced for adding this material, including the desire to preserve a good story not included in the earlier version. But the overriding purpose seems to be to defend the work of the evangelist from a slander that had arisen: with the death of the author the validity of his gospel was questioned, since some apparently had believed that he would not die until Jesus returned (21:22f). The final editor seeks to squelch such a problem by carefully giving the "original" story. We might note in passing that this legend implies that the community originally expected the return of Jesus in the near future, within the lifetime of the author. We must now inquire about the identity of this author.

On Whose Authority? The Disciple Whom Jesus Loved

It is perhaps germane to inquire what kind of authority this gospel expects to rest on an anonymous disciple, since it consistently refuses to provide a name for him. Much effort has been expended in identifying him and we may gain a perspective on the problem by briefly reviewing those attempts. First, the evidence in the gospel itself must be examined.

The "beloved disciple" is first mentioned at 13:23ff in the context of the last supper, at which he reclined close to Jesus. He is next mentioned in the crucifixion scene where Jesus entrusts his mother to him (19:26). In the empty-tomb narrative he raced Peter to the tomb and arrived first, but entered last. Yet he "sees and believes" (20:2–9). In each of these incidents (as well as those in John 21) this disciple is paired with Peter, to Peter's disadvantage. (Peter is not mentioned in the crucifixion scene, but the faithfulness of this disciple implicitly highlights Peter's absence and contrasts with Peter's denial.)

Besides these direct references, Oscar Cullmann argues that there are two other references to this disciple (1976:71ff). In the scene of Jesus' arrest Peter and "another disciple" follow him (18:15ff). Both his anonymity and his relation to Peter suggest that he is the same character. There is one other point at which an unnamed disciple appears: in the opening section two of the disciples of John the Baptist follow Jesus, one unnamed and the other identified as Andrew, the brother of Peter (1:35–41). This would introduce our author at the very beginning, a handy device if the gospel is going to depend on him. The variation in terminology that is used to refer to him is probably not significant. Cullmann suggests that all the references were originally to the "other disciple" and that "the one whom Jesus loved" was added by the final editor. (See 20:2, where he is both the "other disciple" and "the one whom Jesus loved"; 1976:73. See also Brown, 1966:XLIV.)

But who was he? The Muratorian Canon, from late second-century Rome, identified him with John the son of Zebedee, as did Irenaeus (*Against Heresies* III.1.2). Eusebius followed Irenaeus (*Church History* III.23.1ff), but apparently had no Papias tradition regarding John (but see III.39.1f). Several modern commentators seem ready to accept this ancient tradition (Brown, 1966: LXXXVII–CII; apparently Dodd, 1953; and with modifications Schnackenburg, 1968:85–104; see Kysar's summary, 1975:83–101; though Brown has recently changed his mind, 1979:33). Others have suggested Mark (whose full name was John Mark), or even Lazarus (who is also said to be loved by Jesus in 11:3, 5, 36; discussion and bibliography in Cullmann, 1976:74ff). Two other possibilities of a different order are also proposed. Several German scholars have argued that he is a symbolic figure, sort of a narrator (or "implied author") invented by the collective authorship. In this view he represents the ideal disciple (Bultmann, 1971).

More recently, Cullmann has argued that he is an otherwise unknown disciple from outside the circle of the Twelve (1976:74–85). First, Cullmann points out that the Twelve play surprisingly little role in this gospel, being mentioned only at 6:67–71 and 20:24. They appear to be a separate group from "the disciples." In addition, this critic does not think the traditional identification with John, son of Zebedee is consistent with the otherwise uniform tendency to hide the identity of the author, for 21:2 lists the sons of Zebedee as present in that scene. Rather, one of the two "other" disciples present seems to be a more likely candidate. The contrast with Peter in this final scene is in line with this reasoning. At least this much can be said: the attempt to obscure the identity of the author has been successful. There seems to be no good reason to identify him with one of the Twelve.

A more important question now arises: Why was the author's identity hidden in the first place? Was it due to humility? (Brown, 1966:XCIV), fictitiousness? (Bultmann, 1972:484), or is it simply inexplicable? (Cullmann, 1976:84). We know that John's gospel was not easily accepted outside its own circle (Eusebius III.24.5ff; Muratorian Canon, 9–33). It is not quoted by the orthodox Fathers until near the end of the second century, and is rejected by some as late as the beginning of the third century (Kümmel, 1966:139). But does an attestation such as that found in chapter 21 really help? The editors apparently thought so, but we must be careful to note that they claim two kinds of authority: that of the anonymous disciple and that of the community in which he worked (21:24: we know).

Remember that all the other gospels were accepted without such internal attestation, mainly because they were used by the churches. The editors verge on introducing a novelty, making the gospel's reliability rest on the authority of its author. Clearly, by the middle of the second century such an idea was accepted. It actually became necessary to associate a specific apostle with each writing to gain acceptance of the work. John seems to represent the transition between the earlier anonymous tradition and the second-century tradition of apostolic authorship.

The Johannine Community

One factor we have not yet discussed is the existence of other Johannine literature; the New Testament contains three letters also attributed to John that clearly come from the same circle. After reading them, you will readily understand why they have long been identified with the gospel. These are relatively simple documents, as the following reading guides illustrate.

Actually, the reading guide to First John implies more order to the material than one senses while actually reading it. It is an extraordinarily free composition, more like a musical composition than a logical argument, themes and variations rather than thesis and proof. The following exercise should provide some insight into what was happening in the Johannine community.

READING GUIDES TO THE JOHANNINE LETTERS

First John

Prologue   1:1–4
Testimony to the message   1:5–10
Purpose of the letter   2:1–17
Warnings about Antichrist   2:18–27
The marks of God's children   2:28–4:21
    Do not commit sin   3:4–10
    Love one another   3:11–18
    Keep Jesus' word   3:19–24
    Confess Jesus came in the flesh
    4:1–12
    Possess the Spirit and love   4:13–21
    Summary and conclusion   5:1–21

Second John

Salutation: Elder to the Elect Lady   1–3
Plea for love   4–6
Warning about deceivers   7–11
    They deny Jesus "in the flesh"
    Do not receive them
Closing greetings   12–13

Third John

Salutation: Elder to beloved Gaius   1–4
Commendation for service to strangers
5–8
Condemnation of Diotrephes: not receiving the brethren   9–10
Testimony to Demetrius   11–12
Closing greetings   13–15

Reading and Reflection

Read I John, chapters 1 and 4.

1. How does the prologue in 1:1–4 resemble the prologue in John's gospel?
2. What images of good and evil are shared between this letter and the gospel?
3. Why does the writer urge the hearers to "test the spirits?" What is the test?

First John is just as insistent as the author of the gospel "that Jesus Christ has come in the flesh" (4:2). It fact, that now seems to be a major controversy in the community, for the letter declares that all who do not subscribe to this view are "antichrist" (4:3). This is strong language, indicating a serious breech within the community. Such a basic division is not evident in John's gospel; if the letter comes from the same group it probably represents a later development perhaps from about 100 (Brown, 1982:100–103).

The number of correlations in form, images, and ideas, including the basically dualistic worldview, convince most readers that the letters come from the same arena as the Gospel of John. It is not necessary to imagine they were written by the same person, though that is not impossible. A more likely hypothesis, carefully explored by Brown, Cullmann, and others, is the existence of a kind of Johannine community or "school." Attempts to reconstruct the nature and general character of this school must remain less than precise, but these writings contain traces of three distinct but overlapping spheres of influence: Jewish tradition, Greek tradition, and gnosticism.

First, the Johannine circle was related to Judaism. John's attempt to explore the meaning of Jesus in relation to the major Jewish holy days (Sabbath, Passover, Tabernacles, and Dedication are all discussed in 5–10) and his concern for the exclusion of Christian Jews from the synagogue (9:22; 12:42; 16:2) convince most commentators that this community had Jewish roots. Dodd, for example, examines the treatment of the Law in John and concludes: "Though no one but a Jew would be likely to possess such knowledge of the Torah, the evangelist clearly feels himself to be outside the Jewish system" (1953:82). Thus John consistently speaks of being put out of the synagogues (9:22; 16:2) and of "their law" (15:25;

10:34), referring to "the Jews" in a fashion that presumes psychological distance (Fuller, 1977; Barrett, 1975). So it seems that John's community is one further stage separated from Judaism than was Matthew's (pp. 203–204), but unlike Matthew (yet like Mark), John felt the need to explain Jewish customs (2:6; 4:9; 6:4; 9:7; 18:28). John's us/them mentality is similar to the notion of certain Jewish sectarians who regarded the main body of the people as deceived (or perverse). John shares other features with some of the sectarians, and in particular with the Qumran community, especially his dualism and opposition to the Temple. At the same time, W. G. Kümmel has pointed out decisive variations: their different attitudes toward the Law; the role of a messianic redeemer (virtually ignored at Qumran); and the apocalyptic expectation of the imminent end, so strong at Qumran but virtually ignored by John.

Second, the Johannine circle had been influenced by Hellenistic Jewish philosophy in the tradition of Philo of Alexandria. We have already seen some of the similarities of terminology and concept (pp. 245–246). Whether this influence was through direct contact with Alexandrian philosophy (Dodd, 1953:54ff) or whether it represented a sort of parallel expansion of the Biblical wisdom tradition (Brown, 1966:520ff), we surely must imagine a community in active dialogue with both its Hebrew and Greek heritages.

Third, the Johannine circle had some relationship to gnosticism. Kysar is probably correct that "appeals to gnostic, along with purely hellenistic, influences are on the decline" as explanations of John's intellectual milieu (1975:145). Surely some have moved too quickly from observed similarities, to supposed influences, to presumed origins. Nevertheless, there is sufficient correlation between this gospel and later Gnostic ways of speaking about Jesus to warrant the inference of some connection between Johannine and Gnostic Christianity (Bultmann, 1972, index on *Gnosticism* and *Archetypal Man*). Many complicated questions surround the origin and development of gnosticism, including the precise meaning of the term. (For a discussion, see Nock, 1964:xiii–xvii; Jonas, 1958; Yamauchi, 1973; Rudolph, 1983; R. M. Grant, 1961.)

Most scholars are convinced that gnosticism, as a self-conscious movement, did not emerge until the second century but that most of the Gnostic ideas existed much earlier. Christianity often proved to be the catalytic agent needed to synthesize these Gnostic ideas into a system. (Something like this seems to have happened at Corinth in the early fifties, causing Paul to write I Corinthians. See Chapter 3.) Briefly, Gnostic ideas include: the world is essentially a dualism of matter and spirit; only the spirit is really good; humans in their essence are spirit and must transcend the flesh to realize salvation; such transcendence is possible by special knowledge, mediated from above (see pp. 124–126). For a clearer understanding of gnosticism, consider this summary of a popular Gnostic story:

❧   ❧   ❧

There was once a young man sent by his father on a dangerous mission. He needed to go to Egypt and recover a magnificent pearl which had belonged to his father but had been stolen by a dragon. So the lad takes on a disguise: laying aside his royal robes, he dresses as an Egyptian and takes a room at an inn near the dragon's lair. But the Egyptians suspect him. They mix him intoxicating drinks, cloud his mind. He forgets his mission, forgets the pearl, forgets even who he is. Only a magical letter sent from his father rouses him from his drunken stupor and causes him to remember who he is, whence he came, and what he is about. Coming to his senses, he seizes the pearl and rushes for the border, re-ascends to his father. Shedding his filthy and impure rags, he regains his robe of glory and adores the glory of the father. (The complete "Hymn of the Pearl" can be read in the Acts of Thomas, *108–113, in Hennecke and Schneemelcher, II: 498–504 or in Jonas, 1958:113–114)*

Although there was a wide range of Gnostic systems, they usually shared a basic worldview.

Some of these basic points are clear in the story above. First, something has gone wrong; humanity has somehow "fallen"; we have forgotten who we really are. Our wrong is not something we do; it is a flaw in the nature of the universe itself, for the visible universe was a mistake from the beginning. Second, there is a secret knowledge that will redeem. This is not knowledge in the ordinary sense, not philosophic insight or a correct understanding of the Law—this knowledge is mystical. One writer described it as knowing

ð̳ ð̳ ð̳

Who we were; what we became;
Where we were; to where we have fallen;
Where we are going; from what we are redeemed;
What birth is, and what rebirth.
(Excerpts from Theodotus 78)

Line two is especially revealing, for it envisions a recollection of life before the fall. This is not the kind of knowledge one person can tell another; it must be personally achieved in an ecstatic experience. Third, there must be some way of mediating this knowledge to us, and that was usually accomplished through some divine savior who descended from that world above into this world below. In some Gnostic systems this savior is called Anthropos (Human), or sometimes Son of Man, and seems to represent a primordial humanity, eternal, unfallen, pre-existent, who now descends into the world to redeem his fallen counterpart (Dodd, 1953:109ff). These three factors are evident in the Gnostic-like story of the fall in a Jewish-Hellenistic work from the second century; I summarize:

ð̳ ð̳ ð̳

The Human is created in the image of God: so alike that it would be impossible to tell the difference between the Human and the Divine. This Human lives and rules alongside God. Like God, Human desires to create and so fashions the seven planetary spheres, each ever farther from

the Divine Mind. One day this Human descended through the spheres, desiring to rule all. Breaking through the vault of Harmony, he showed to Lower Nature the beautiful form of God. She, responding to that beauty, looked back in love. Passing over the water, he too sees the beautiful form of God reflected back to him. He could do nothing but love it and desire to dwell in it. And at once, with the wish came the reality, and so the Human came to inhabit the form devoid of reason. And Nature, having received into herself the beloved, embraced him wholly, and they mingled—inflamed with love. And this is why of all the creatures of earth, the Human is two-fold, holding both the mortality of the body and the immortality of the Human. (The Poimandres of Hermes Trismegistus, *12–15; a complete version can be read in Jonas, 1958:150–151 or Barrett, 1961a:84–85*)

This myth is mediated by Poimandres, a manifestation of the Absolute, and is meant to impart the saving gnosis, whereupon the soul reascends to the Father. Such mythic speculation was a regular feature of gnosticism, and Gnostics found it relatively easy to fit Jesus into this mythic framework, especially as Jesus is portrayed in the Fourth Gospel as the one from above, the Logos. (For a more elaborate Gnostic myth of origins, see pp. 125–126). The first two recorded commentators on the Gospel of John were Gnostics (Dodd, 1953:102), and this surely contributed to the work's slow acceptance by some orthodox Christians. That John's gospel is open to such gnosticizing interpretations is evidence that it was probably written before such thought was decisively rejected within the community, that is, before the letter called First John.

Some have even characterized John's presentation of Jesus as a kind of "naive docetism" (Käsemann, 1968:26). Docetism, from the Greek *dokeo*, "to seem, or appear to be," was a belief that Jesus only "appeared to be" a human being but was actually a spirit being descended into the world incognito. An interesting exercise is to read through the Gospel of John, searching specifically for signs of Jesus' humanity: How does John show (or fail to show) that Jesus is a real human being? While John may not be called a docetist, he (naively?) fails to present the human qualities of Jesus. Even so, by choosing to tell his story as a gospel John has chosen an inherently anti-Gnostic form, one never used by the Gnostics though they wrote many so-called "gospels."[2] The Gnostic gospels dwell on the resurrected Jesus and the teachings of Jesus; they do not portray the career of a real person. None of them could ever be mistaken for a biography or a historical account. Thus, even though the Gospel of John differs greatly from the Synoptics in content, its literary form is closer to them than to the Gnostic gospels.

This observation raises an interesting incidental point: John wrote a gospel that seems to be similar in form to Mark, for example, yet he offers no significant evidence of dependences on Mark. Did John, then, reinvent the gospel form? Perhaps, but there is no real reason to believe that John was unfamiliar with Mark, or Matthew or Luke, even though he was not dependent on them for his traditions.

A fourth and final point about the Johannine circle is obvious: this community is characterized by a selective syncretism, combining elements from diverse religious traditions into a new tradition. John's community is not afraid to appropriate key elements of alien religious movements, shape them according to its own faith, and produce a new synthesis. It is a strategy the church in late antiquity would make its own.

The Elusive Particulars:
Time, Place, and Purpose

If we reject the late second-century tradition that identified this gospel with the Apostle John and the city of Ephesus, then there is no way to locate the Fourth Gospel geographically. The above constellation of characteristics (Rabbinic Judaism, Jewish philosophy, gnosticizing philosophy, syncretism) probably existed in every major city in the Roman Empire, and in some not so major.

A bit more may be said about the date, or perhaps dates would be more accurate. The final edition of this gospel was probably produced toward the end of the first century, so that the tradition about the immortality of the beloved disciple (21:23f) was significant enough for his eventual death to cause a problem. This is supported by the traditions about expulsion from the synagogues, which probably occurred in the nineties. But the writing of the gospel cannot have been much later, since a fragment of John's gospel, discovered in Egypt, is generally dated between 135 and 150, and sometimes "at the beginning of the second century" (Brown, 1966: LXXXIIf). Known as P52, this is, ironically, the oldest surviving New Testament text. Thus the most likely date for the final edition of the Gospel according to John would be the late nineties. Unfortunately, there is no way to judge the time lapse between this final text and the earlier edition (or, in Brown's scheme, editions). We may equally well imagine a few months or a few decades. In the past, a frequent argument claimed that the high degree of Hellenization manifested by the gospel required a late (possibly even a second-century) date. But this ignores the extensive Hellenization of certain segments of Judaism even before the Christian era. Certainly the process of shaping this material to Johannine thought patterns (Brown's second stage) must go back several decades before the composition of the gospel. For John, surely, and probably for each of the other gospels as well, it is too simple to ask when it was written. The gospel was developed over a long period of time, achieving its final form near the end of the first century.

Finally, we might think it easy to agree about John's purpose, since he states it explicitly: "that you might believe that the Christ the Son of God is Jesus" (literal translation of 20:31). But it is

---

2. See Petersen, 1970; compare some of the apocryphal gospels in Hennecke and Schneemelcher, I, 1963; especially the *Gospel of Truth:* 523ff; and the *Gospel of Thomas:* 511ff; see also section VII:231ff.

debatable whether this means "might come to believe" or "might continue to believe," for the
various manuscripts are divided between the use
of future and present tenses for *believe*. Every
conceivable hypothesis has been argued by various scholars (see summary in Kümmel,
1966:161ff, and the discussion in Brown,
1966:LXVII–LXXIX).

The more serious purposes advanced for John
include: to appeal to a non-Christian public, to
refute Christian heretics (especially Gnostics), to
encourage and confirm believers in their faith,
to appeal to Jewish Christians in the diaspora
synagogues, to demonstrate the superiority of
Christian faith to Jewish piety, to appeal to
Jewish sectarians, especially the followers of
John the Baptist and the Samaritans, to interpret
Christianity more adequately than the Synoptics.

All these purposes are present to some degree
in the gospel, but not all are central. John lived
in a very complex situation, propounding a version of the faith that differed significantly from
other interpretations. Recent works by Raymond
Brown and J. Louis Martyn have attempted to
locate John's community more precisely. While
they differ on important details, a clearer picture
of John's community has emerged from their in-
vestigations. To the left of John's community
stood the gnosticizing Christians who viewed Jesus as the descending revealer who transcends the
bounds of an earthly and historical person. He is
known not so much by past traditions as by the
immediate experience of those who have the Spirit
(Woll, 1981). To the right stood a whole array
of more conservative systems of Christianity,
Jewish experience, and the Gentile world. Brown
(1979) identifies six distinct groups on this side
of the spectrum; three do not believe in Jesus:

The World: those who prefer darkness to light
(for example, 9:39; 12:35ff; 16:20).

The Jews: those within the synagogues who opposed and excluded the Johannine Christians (especially 9:22; 16:2).

The Baptists: those followers of John who did
not believe Jesus surpassed John (especially
3:22–26).

And three who claimed to believe in Jesus, but
whom John found to be inadequate:

The Secret Christians: those who quietly believed in Jesus but also desired to remain within
the synagogues (especially 12:42–43; 19:38–39).

The Jewish Christians: those who had left the
synagogue but who interpreted Jesus primarily
on the basis of his miracles (6:60–66; 7:3–5;
8:31–32).

The Apostolic Christians: those who followed
Peter and the Twelve but saw Jesus as the Davidic Messiah rather than the One from above
(6:67–69; 14:9; and the contrast between Peter
and the Beloved Disciple).

If we add the Gnostics, perhaps the Samaritan
Christians (4:39), probably apocalypticists, and
divisions within John's own community we
glimpse the tremendous diversity of late first-
century Christianity. Within this diversity, the
community that is reflected in this gospel struggles to identify itself and to proclaim its vision
of Jesus in contrast to these others. In this sense,
it is a sectarian vision. John's community stands
in conflict with its surrounding culture and not
in easy accommodation to it. This community
emphasizes love and prays for unity (17:20–21)
even while it vigorously rejects those outside. John
has drawn a portrait of Jesus that speaks to this
situation of diversity and attempts to assert the
truth of his own community's understanding of
Jesus against competing claims.

RESOURCES FOR FURTHER STUDY

Simple and competent introductions to John are Bruce, 1984b; Kysar, 1976; and Smith, 1976.

The finest commentary on this gospel is Brown, 1966, though the older works by Dodd, 1953, and Lightfoot, 1956, remain extremely useful. Bultmann's important commentary, 1971 (original, 1941), is both difficult and dated. Bultmann's source theories have been very influential, on which see: Smith, 1965. Also difficult are Barrett, 1978; Haenchen, 1984; and Schnackenburg, 1968 and 1980; but they contain a wealth of insight into the text.

A useful guide to the extensive literature on John is Kysar, 1975. Recent discussions of the setting and sources of John are admirably summarized and evaluated by Smith, 1984.

Important monographs include

Barrett, 1975a, *The Gospel of John and Judaism*.
Borgen, 1965, *Bread from Heaven*.
Brown, 1979, *The Community of the Beloved Disciple*.
Charlesworth, 1972, *John and Qumran*.
Cullmann, 1976, *The Johannine Circle*.
Dodd, 1963, *Historical Tradition in the Fourth Gospel*.
Fortna, 1970, *The Gospel of Signs*.
de Jonge, 1977, *Jesus: Stranger from Heaven and Son of God*.
Käsemann, 1968, *The Testament of Jesus*.
Martyn, 1979, *History and Theology in the Fourth Gospel*.
Nicholson, 1984, *Death as Departure*.

Provocative studies of the Farewell Discourse include Painter, 1981; and Woll, 1981. Both relate what is said to supposed happenings in the Johannine community.

On the chronology of Jesus' death and the Last Supper see Finegan, 1969:291–298; and Jeremias, 1955. Finegan treats a broad range of chronological issues in great detail, including the various calendars and ways of counting years. He generally takes a conservative approach to the ancient sources, trusting their literal meaning more than may be warranted.

Literary aspects of John are explored, in a rather technical fashion, by Culpepper, 1983. A careful discussion of the uses of irony in literature is Booth, 1974.

On John's use by Gnostics, see Pagels, 1973.

On the Johannine Epistles: The extensive commentary by Brown, 1982, not only explains the letters but shows their many relationships to the Gospel of John. The commentaries of Bultmann, 1973; and Dodd, 1946, are also useful, as is the conservative work of Marshall, 1978c.

The Dawn of a New Day

⁊ ⁊ ⁊

The Apocalypse of John

Theories of Interpretation

The Nature of the Genre

Symbols, Images, and Meanings

The Plot of the Apocalypse

Symbol, Story, and History: The Setting of Revelation

Resources for Further Study

11

The Apocalypse of John is also known as the Revelation of John (*apocalypsis* being the Greek word for revelation). Its dual name is perhaps evidence of its ambiguous position in Christianity. While it is very popular in some circles today, others rarely read it. Even those who are fascinated by this work rarely claim to understand it completely. Its history has oscillated between times of compelling concern and times of complete neglect. Already in the second century some considered it the ultimate revelation, while others condemned it utterly. It has had strong defenders, but many have even disputed its inclusion in the New Testament. As late as the time of Eusebius (about 325), debate still raged about whether it should be recognized.

In this chapter we will review three popular and scholarly approaches to interpreting Revelation, exploring its relationship to other ancient literature of a similar kind, then carefully study its symbolism and plot. Finally, we will see how this work fit the social and historical situation in which it was written and read. Since considerable background is necessary to read and appreciate Revelation, we will read only short excerpts from it until late in this chapter.

THEORIES OF INTERPRETATION

❧ ❧ ❧

And I saw a beast rising out of the sea. . . . It causes all, both small and great, both rich and poor, both free and slave, to be marked on the right hand or the forehead, so that no one can buy or sell unless he has the mark, that is, the name of the beast or the number of its name.

This calls for wisdom: let him who has understanding reckon the number of the beast, for it is a human number, its number is six hundred and sixty-six. (Rev. 13:1, 16–18)

Wisdom, indeed. This seems to call for more than wisdom—perhaps a crystal ball. How shall we interpret such an image? Can we ever understand what John was referring to? Such a scene raises acutely the issue of how we make an accurate interpretation. We should begin by admitting that there is no ultimate and final interpretation of any work of literature. All works of literature elicit varying interpretations, and no interpretation ever exhausts the meaning in a work of art.

But with the Apocalypse there are not only diverse interpretations, there are diverse strategies suggested for making interpretations. Three different theories are advocated for making sense out of this work. Some argue that it must be interpreted entirely in terms of events in the first century (historical views); some argue that it actually predicts the future (prophetic views); and still others insist that it is best seen as a book of timeless symbols (symbolist views). Without judging the adequacy of each approach, let us try to understand what their advocates mean.

Historical: The First Century in Code

The basic idea of the historical interpretation is that all the symbols in Revelation refer to people and events that existed in the first century. At first this may not seem very promising, but most of John's images may be interpreted as coded references to first-century events. That beast, for example, whose name/number is 666 may well have been a coded way of referring to Emperor Nero. To understand this we need to digress briefly to discuss ancient numbers.

Neither the ancient Greeks nor Hebrews had numbers; more precisely, neither had a separate system of symbols for indicating numeric values. Both used the letters of the alphabet for this purpose. One of the great contributions of Muslim civilization was the invention of our present number system (thus Arabic numbers). Before that, we used a system the Romans had invented which, although a great improvement on earlier practice, was still cumbersome. But imagine that we did not have a separate number system so that:

A =	1	H =	8	O =	60	V =	400
B =	2	I =	9	P =	70	W =	500
C =	3	J =	10	Q =	80	X =	600
D =	4	K =	20	R =	90	Y =	700
E =	5	L =	30	S =	100	Z =	800
F =	6	M =	40	T =	200		
G =	7	N =	50	U =	300		

While the Hebrews had only twenty-two letters and the Greeks only twenty-four, and they came in a different order, these equivalents are reasonably analogous to their systems. Notice this is not a digital system. Twenty is not two (B) with a zero; there was no zero. Imagine trying to add NOPE + SQE (two ways of writing 185!).

Now we can understand what it means to get the number of a name: simply add up the letters of the name. In the English above David would be 418; in Hebrew it was 14; in Greek 18. Thus, interesting possibilities develop. Scribbled on a wall at Pompeii, for example, was the less than bold declaration: "I love her whose number is 545," a cryptic reference only intelligible to the young man who wrote it and his circle. Another practice involved finding similarities between diverse things just because their names added up to the same value, a practice Jewish mystics called *gematria*. Similar to this is a political slogan that

Seutonius reports someone wrote on a wall in Rome:

☙ ☙ ☙

Count the values: Nero has the same number as "murdered his own mother." (Nero, *39.2*)

In this case both words add up to 1005. How then might Nero be the figure behind 666?

The process is a bit cumbersome: one takes the Greek form, *Kaisar Neron,* transposes the letters into Hebrew, and the sum is 666. Obviously, with such flexibility, other solutions are possible as well: some interpreters have suggested Gaius Caesar (Caligula), others Domitian. Clearly, no amount of wisdom would lead to a solution unless it was already known to the hearers, but this was probably the case. The historical interpretation insists that the sum referred to some first-century person whom John and his community regarded as the embodiment of evil, the beast from the sea.

Similarly, all the symbols and images of the book are interpreted to refer to events of the first century. The seven churches to which letters are written in chapters 2 and 3 are considered by historical interpreters to be real congregations in these specific cities. Various first-century disasters are referred to in the earthquakes and fire, such as the eruption of Mount Vesuvius. According to the historical interpretation, then, all the symbols and actions of Revelation are really coded ways of referring to first-century realities. Others take a wholly different approach.

Prophetic: Things That Are Yet to Be

Other interpreters assume that Revelation intends to tell about the future. Some believe it forecasts the whole future history of the church from John's day to the end of the age, others that it only predicts the events that will occur at the end of the world.

Those who take the more rigorous view believe that Revelation offers a kind of meta-chronology of the whole course of history. They view the work as being chronologically arranged from John's time (chapter 1) to the end of the age (chapter 22). Thus, the seven churches of chapters 2 and 3 are not individual congregations of the first century, but predictions of the seven "ages" or epochs through which the church would pass from the first century to the second coming. They point out that the first church, the apostolic church in this view, is relatively pure. Succeeding churches have both vices and virtues. The last church by contrast is neither hot nor cold and is in danger of complete repudiation (3:16). To these interpreters, this wealthy church that has lost its zeal seems typical of the mainline churches of contemporary America.

According to this view the figure referred to under the symbol 666 must, because it occurs late in the Apocalypse, refer to some future figure, an antichrist who will appear on earth at some point in the future. These interpreters imagine that one can trace the whole course of Western civilization in John's Apocalypse.

Most who hold a prophetic view do not go so far. In fact, the most popular approach (popular in the sense that one is apt to hear it on the radio) makes some compromise with the historical view—but only a modest one. They hold that the first three chapters of Revelation are historical and refer to events in the first century, but beginning at 4:1, where the angel tells John to "come up here," there is a great gap that includes all the time between the first century and the end of the age. These interpreters assert that all of Revelation after chapter 4 refers to events at the end of time.

Thus these interpreters agree with the historical view that the seven churches are real historical congregations, but insist that the figure represented by 666 is a future person, properly designated as the antichrist, who will appear in the last days. Like the other prophetic interpreters, they believe that our own times are those "just before" the end (otherwise the work would be meaningless to us).

Symbolist: Truth Not History

A third approach to Revelation argues that the two approaches discussed above are both right and wrong. The historical view is right in that these symbols represent first-century events; and the prophetic view is correct in applying them to future historical events; but both are wrong to believe that the symbols apply only to some specific event. In this third view, Revelation is a book of timeless truths in symbolic form. The symbols have no specific connection with historical events, though many such events may correlate with the symbols. The seven churches represent seven kinds of churches that exist in any age and any time. Some are pure; some are tepid; most are a mixture of success and failure.

Even more interesting is the symbolist interpretation of 666, now understood as a timeless truth, not a reference to some historical person. To begin, we might observe that the Greek text does not say it is the number of some particular person, but "it is a human number." Now we should see the number 666 as merely an intensification of the number 6, the number of the day of the creation of humanity and one short of the number of perfection, 7. Further, the symbolist can point to an early Christian tradition that found it significant that the numerical value of Jesus in Greek was 888 (*Sibylline Oracles* 1.324ff, in Hennecke, II: 710). Now 8 represents the beginning of the new week, the eighth day is the first day (and the day of resurrection). The symbolist interpreter, then, sees 666 as representing the arrogance of the human claiming the sovereignty that belongs only to Jesus as Lord of the new age. The antichrist, then, might well be Nero (or Hitler, or Mussolini, as certain prophetic interpreters have alleged) but he is all of us to the degree that we falsely claim to be ultimate. Thus, the symbolist approach attempts to uncover the timeless truths hidden in the symbols of the Apocalypse.

Our Approach

In one way our approach differs from all of these views, for they are ways of interpreting the meaning of Revelation for today, while our purpose is to discover what it meant to its first hearers. With this goal in mind, some interpretations of Revelation advocated by certain interpreters today are not possible.

For example, shortly before the 1984 presidential election a flyer proclaimed that 666 pointed to Ronald Wilson Reagan, the only American president with six letters in each of his names. Why is such an interpretation of Revelation 13 unconvincing? Does it merely depend on our political sympathies? No. This interpretation makes three basic mistakes.

First, this interpretation rests on certain assumptions about Revelation that are not at all likely. It assumes that Revelation was actually talking about our time rather than the time in which it was written. It also assumes that the United States is so important that only American presidents should be considered candidates.

Second, the author of the flyer was apparently unfamiliar with the relationship between numbers and names in the ancient world. Once we know that the ancients used letters for numbers, so that every name was also a number, we will see that the symbol 666 in Revelation has nothing to do with how many letters one has in one's name.

Third, such an interpretation would have meant nothing to the audience to which Revelation was addressed. They simply did not know Ronald Reagan. If we assume that the author was addressing a real message to real human beings in the first century, interpretations like this one become impossible. This does not mean that a prophetic interpretation is automatically ruled out, but it

would have to be a prophetic insight able to be understood by the original hearers.

In fact, all three modern approaches (historical, prophetic, and symbolic) are instructive, for they were also the three modes of interpretation available to the original audience. Certainly they heard in Revelation an interpretation of their own history (as the historical approach would insist); surely they regarded it as in some way predicting the near end of the world (a prophetic idea); surely they appreciated the symbolic nature of the book and applied these symbols to their lives. We can be sure of these things because Revelation was not the only book of this kind at that time. There were many others not included in the canon, and becoming familiar with them will help us know how to read Revelation. Once again, the question is one of genre, or kind of literature.

THE NATURE OF THE GENRE

We have already encountered shorter examples of this kind of writing in II Thessalonians 2 and Mark 13, with its parallels in Matthew 24–25 and Luke 21. And we have seen that the worldview underlying this kind of writing was widespread in first-century Jewish circles. (See the discussion on p. 43 and pp. 158–159.) Works of this kind take their name from the Greek title of Revelation; they are called apocalypses and the kind of literature is called apocalyptic literature. We can very briefly summarize our earlier discussion of the worldview of apocalypticism as a dualism: the heart and driving force of history is a cosmic struggle between God and Satan. It rested on the firm conviction that God would soon intervene, overthrow evil, and establish the new age of righteousness. This was the hope of the apocalyptic writers.

Yet this hope was rarely stated so directly, for apocalyptic literature is a literature of indirection. Let us now consider the literary features and typical characteristics of the various writings that are enough like Revelation to be called apocalypses.

The Literary Traits of Apocalyptic Literature

The best way to gain an impression of this kind of literature is to read as many different examples as you can. One that is universally accessible is the book of Daniel (7–12) in the Hebrew Scriptures. Another is IV Ezra (also called II Esdras), found in Roman Catholic Bibles or in a collection known as the Apocrypha. Other possibilities include *I Enoch* 14–15 and 17–36; *II Enoch; II Baruch* 53–74, the *War Scroll* from Qumran; the *Ascension of Isaiah;* the *Apocalypse of Peter.*[1] The genre was vigorously pursued in some early Christian circles, by reediting older apocalypses to make them explicitly Christian (IV Ezra) or by writing entirely new works (in addition to those attributed to John and Peter, there is also one of Paul, one of Thomas, and at least two of James, as well as several that used the names of earlier writers, such as the *Ascension of Isaiah,* roughly contemporaneous with Revelation).

This is just a sampling of the available literature, which is only a small surviving portion of the works written. This shows that the Book of Revelation was part of a major literary tradition in antiquity, the genre of apocalyptic writing. Two other conclusions may be drawn from even a glance at these writings. First, apocalypses traveled under many names. (And conversely, not all works called apocalypses are similar. Title is only one clue to genre.) Second, there was a great deal of variety exhibited within the genre. We can get an idea of the type of literature this was from the following excerpts:

⋙ ⋙ ⋙

A)   And after [one thousand] three hundred and thirty-two days the Lord will come with his angels and with the hosts of the saints from the seventh heaven with the glory of the seventh heaven, and will drag Beliar with his hosts into Gehenna, and he will bring rest to the pious who shall be found alive in the body in this world . . . and to all who through faith in him have cursed Beliar and his kings. (Ascension of Isaiah *4:14–16* quoted from Hennecke and Schneemelcher, II: 649)

B)   And these things shall come to pass in the day of judgment of those who have fallen away from faith in God and have committed sin: cataracts of fire shall be let loose; and obscurity and darkness shall come up and cover and veil the entire world, and the waters shall be changed and transformed into coals of fire . . . And the stars shall be melted by flames of fire. . . . (Apocalypse of Peter *5* quoted from Hennecke and Schneemelcher, II: 761)

C)   And it came about, when I had spoken to my sons, the men called me. And they took me up onto their wings, and carried me up to the first heaven. And they put me down there. They led before my face the elders, the rulers of the stellar orders. (Second Enoch *3:1–4:1* quoted from Charlesworth, I: 111).

D)   Then a great angel came forth having a golden trumpet in his hand, and he blew it three times over my head, saying, "Be courageous! O one who has triumphed. Prevail! O one who has prevailed. For you have triumphed over the accuser, and you have escaped from the abyss and Hades. You will now cross over the crossing place. For your name

1. The most convenient collection of Jewish apocalypses is Charlesworth, 1983; though the old collection of Charles, 1913, may be more widely available. For Christian apocalypses, see Hennecke and Schneemelcher, II. Other apocalypses, mainly with a Gnostic inclination, may be found in the collection of material from the library at Nag Hammadi, in Robinson, 1977.

is written in the Book of the Living. (Apocalypse of Zephaniah 9:1–3 quoted from Charlesworth, I: 514)

E)   *After this I saw in the night visions, and behold, a fourth beast, terrible and dreadful and exceedingly strong; and it had great iron teeth; it devoured and broke in pieces, and stamped the residue with its feet. It was different from all the beasts that were before it; and it had ten horns. I considered the horns, and behold, there came up among them another horn, a little one, before which three of the first horns were plucked up by the roots; and behold, on this horn were eyes like the eyes of a man, and a mouth speaking great things. (Daniel 7:7–8)*

Remember that we are considering a literary genre that lasted more than three centuries; variety should be expected. Nevertheless, certain typical features are found in many apocalypses:

1. The claim that a secret revelation has been given to some seer or prophet (as in all the examples above).
2. This revelation is imparted in a dream, a vision, or a transportation of the seer to heaven—often the three means are combined (see C above).
3. The revelation is usually mediated by some figure, such as an angel, who acts as guide and interpreter to the seer (C and D).
4. The revelation is usually not self-explanatory, but consists of a variety of arcane symbols involving cosmic upheavals, animals (often composites of different animals, with multiple heads), mythological figures, and numbers (E).
5. The reception of the revelation is often attributed to some figure from the past: Moses, Enoch, Daniel, Adam, and so on. This practice of pseudonymity gives the name to the major collection of these works: they are called the pseudepigrapha [sood-eh-pig′-gra-fa] (all of the above).

An awareness of these characteristic features will help us to read Revelation. But to understand the genre better, we need to add one more dimension to our analysis. The central impulse of the apocalypse brings together two diverse elements from the history of Israel: a concern for God's redemptive activity in history and a concern for the cosmic action of God in ritual and story.

The Prophetic Hope of Restoration

The rise, development, and decline of prophecy in Israel is a fascinating topic, but it would take us too far afield to pursue it here. In its heyday in the eighth to sixth centuries BCE, prophets in Israel acted as judges of the covenant, pronouncing divine blessings or curses on the people for their faithfulness or unfaithfulness to God's laws. These blessings and curses were to be carried out in history, which was considered to be under divine control. So intertwined were the prophets with history that they are often thought of as foretellers of the future; that was never their primary task. They looked to the future to explain the present. When Israel fell on hard times, when the divine judgment had fallen, the prophets began to look beyond the present distress to a time of restoration. They looked forward to a time when God would act to restore his people to their former glory. There would be a new Exodus (Isaiah 40). A new David would arise to sit on his father's throne (Jeremiah 23:5). God would make a new covenant with his people (Jeremiah 31). The prophets saw these as historical events that would bring back the "good old days," before Israel forsook God (Hosea 2:14–20).

However, things did not work out this way. As the years after the devastation of Israel in the exile grew into centuries, the prophetic hope waned. History seemed to have passed Israel by; all her energies were now directed inward. A few prophets persisted, also directing their attention to the inner life of the people (Malachi, for example). Soon even these ceased. There were no more prophets. The tradition arose that God had withdrawn the spirit of prophecy in the days of Haggai, Zechariah, and Malachi (about 400 BCE). (Thus the reappearance of the Spirit among early Christians was itself considered a significant event, marking the dawn of a new age—see Acts 2:15–17.) This prophetic consciousness is the ground from which apocalyptic expectation grew, feeding on the hope of renewal.

Mythic Enactments of Renewal

An even older pattern of renewal existed throughout the ancient Near East, from Babylon to Egypt, including Israel. This pattern also centered on the king, not now as a historical hope but as a divine agent. The Babylonian story of creation, enacted at the New Year's festival, is its clearest example. In this story the act of creation is God's victory over chaos, establishing the order of the world.

The story takes place in primeval time, before the creation of heaven and earth. Only the gods existed. But the gods have grown raucous and noisy and Tiamat (Chaos), mother of them all, was offended by their clamor. She makes plans to destroy them all. She creates monsters to fight on her side: serpents, dragons, the sphinx, and others, and she works other magic. The gods cower in terror. Finally Marduk is brought forward. Son of the Sun, God of the Storm and the Four Winds, wisest of the gods, he is made king. All the gods invest him with their powers to determine destiny, and his word becomes supreme. He and Tiamat meet in a raging battle. He drives a fierce wind into her open mouth, pierces her inflated torso with his arrow, and kills her. From her split carcass he creates heaven and earth. He fixes each of the gods in his own sphere, orders the heavens, and then, from the blood of Tiamat's consort, he creates humanity to be the servants of the gods. He makes his home in Babylon, where he becomes shepherd of the human race. (The complete story in translation is in Pritchard, 1955:60–72.)

Every year in Babylon they reenacted this story. Each year, as the old year wore out, Chaos reasserted herself. The king lost his throne, the family disintegrated, law ceased. Then once again the priest would enact the drama of God's conquest of Chaos (portrayed as a sea monster or dragon). This ritual battle between the divine warrior and the dragon and the ensuing victory resulted in the reestablishment of order and of marriage, the recoronation of the king, the preservation of society—or rather the creation of a new society in the truly new year.

In Israel this story was adapted and applied to their God (Isa. 51:9–11—notice how the victory over the dragon is associated with the theme of the Exodus, a cosmic event is linked to a historical event). This theme of the divine warrior seems to have been closely connected to the king and to worship at the Temple at Jerusalem. The power of the king to suppress chaos is his power to create a just society. These ideas also influenced the development of apocalypticism.

Apocalypticism as a Mytho-Prophetic View of History

Paul Hanson argues persuasively that the blending of these two visions of God's victory in the increasingly pessimistic atmosphere of Israel after the Exile resulted in the gradual dawning of apocalypticism (1979). The mythic story of God as the warrior who conquers Chaos provided the inner structure of apocalypticism that depicted the struggle between good and evil in cosmic dimensions. The prophetic hope of restoration was transferred to a cosmic redemption at the end of time. But the prophetic concern with real history always remained, and the triumph of God was always envisioned to include the historical situation of his people. As apocalyptic thought developed, it evolved a specific view of how history works, which we may summarize as follows:

1. God has appointed a time for the end of the present world order and that time is imminent (see excerpt A above).

2. This Age is under the control of the powers of Evil, so we must expect that the good will suffer and the wicked prosper. This represented a complete shift from the earlier optimistic tradition that proclaimed that good would prosper and evil be punished which is found, for example, in Proverbs (A and D).

3. This age will soon be replaced by another, the age to come, which will be the exact opposite of this one. The new age will be accompanied by the judgment of evil and the reward of the righteous (A, B, and D).

4. Between these two ages stands the decisive act of divine intervention. There was great variety in the ways they imagined this would take place. Some spoke of God sending the Messiah. Others spoke of two messiahs. In some visions, Michael would act as God's agent, perhaps alone or more often leading the armies of heaven. Others saw themselves as the human agents of the coming divine deliverance; some even advocated revolutionary violence. Others believed the final battle would be fought by God himself (A).

5. As the end of this age approaches there will be an increase in the activity of evil and a period of intense suffering for the righteous. Usually called the period of tribulation, its most common metaphor was the labor of a woman in childbirth—birth pangs of the new age (B).

The literary characteristics of apocalypses sketched earlier become logical once we understand the basic nature of apocalyptic thought. An apocalypse is symbolic because it claims to see behind the veil of ordinary experience, revealing this cosmic struggle between God and Satan. It is intended to transcend our common perceptions and reveal the ultimate causes of the events—a "revelation" of the cosmic processes underlying history. Only symbols could portray the interrelatedness of historical and cosmic events. The most commonly used images were numbers, an-imals, and heavenly signs (sun, stars, moon, etc.). Dreams, visions, and angels are the agents of this secret wisdom. And wisdom is required in the hearer to perceive the truth behind the symbol.

Even the pseudonymity of apocalyptic literature makes sense in this context, for the apocalypticist lived in a time after prophecy, yet believed that he (or she) had a message truly derived from the earlier prophets. One advantage of this pseudonymity was that it allowed the writer to be an extraordinarily accurate predicter of the future course of events from the time of the ancient worthy to their present, because of course it had all already happened. Often the fictional device employed was a "sealed book" that was revealed to the ancients but kept hidden until the last days, when it would be unsealed (Daniel 12:4). Here too the sense of unveiling what had been hidden is appropriate.

No one apocalyptic work contained all these literary and ideological characteristics; there was great variety. Examining these traits will help us experience Revelation as a typical example of a genre, and will help us to appreciate the unique contributions of that work. Our ability to appreciate this literature will depend to a great extent on our ability to deal with its strange symbols.

SYMBOLS, IMAGES, AND MEANINGS

When you drive down the road and see a diamond-shaped sign at the edge with an S-shaped line on it, you instinctively slow down. You know it means danger. The road curves ahead. This is part of the common knowledge of all drivers. But what might you make of such a sign if you were an alien? Watch out for esses? Scenic route? Snake crossing? We know such interpretations are ridiculous, yet no more so than some interpretations of Revelation. These three erroneous readings of the road sign symbol represent three types of errors commonly made in reading the symbolism of Revelation.

Mistaking curves for snakes is the kind of error that occurs when we lack the common knowledge of the original hearers, then imagine another context quite foreign to the original one—usually our own, modern context. Thus, for example, some interpreters will tell us that the symbol of the stars falling from heaven refers to nuclear missiles, for this is easy for us to imagine. But if you lived in a preelectric world, you would have seen hundreds of "falling stars" nearly every night of the year. We must always test our interpretations by asking if they would have made sense in the original context of Revelation. Since neither John nor his hearers could have conceived of nuclear missiles, we must conclude that this is not a possible interpretation for the original meaning of the work.

To mistake the curve sign for an "S" and then imagine it refers to a scenic route is the kind of mistake that results from a disregard of context altogether. The interpreter allows his or her own imagination to invent hidden meanings, which might be possible in the original context, but there is no evidence of that meaning in this particular case. Hence, we must seek a consistent, overall interpretation within which the individual symbols may be interpreted.

Imagining the "S" on the sign refers to real esses stems from a misreading of the genre. It results from taking literally what was meant to be symbolic. This is an especially common error in reading Revelation, a book filled with symbols. A general rule for Revelation might then be: never take the work at face value. Remember, it attempts to reveal a hidden reality, to produce insight. Revelation does not mean what it says; it means what it means. And to unravel what it means we must avoid taking symbols literally, keep a reign on our imaginations, and not ignore the historical context. We have to learn how to interpret the many symbols it uses.

A Guide to the Symbols

Many of the symbols used in Revelation were the common property of apocalypticists; they have a stylized meaning, which we have little difficulty interpreting. One example is the use of numbers, which the ancients generally regarded more mystically than we do. Numbers in Revelation must be read as symbolic statements instead of quantifiable amounts. The most obvious use of number symbolism is the number seven. The esoteric qualities of seven were widely discussed in the ancient world, especially among the neo-Pythagorean philosophers.

Pythagoras had sought to understand the harmony of the universe, pursuing his investigation through music and mathematics. He discovered the mathematical basis of harmony. In the Pythagorean system, certain numbers were considered masculine (3, 5, 7) and others feminine (2, 4, 6). For Pythagoras the great numbers were one, the foundation of all that is, and ten, a perfect number. Ten is the triangle of four: if one makes a triangle with four dots on each side, the dots total ten. (A square of a number originally meant the same thing, forming a square of dots.)

$$
\begin{matrix}
& & \bullet & & \\
& \bullet & & \bullet & \\
\bullet & & \bullet & & \bullet \\
\bullet & \bullet & & \bullet & \bullet
\end{matrix}
$$

Notice that our triangle is built on one, the root of all, and contains the three dimensions and the three harmonies (1:2; 2:3; 3:4). Any two adjacent lines create masculine numbers; any two alternate lines create feminine numbers. Four dots in three directions point to seven and result in ten, both numbers of great significance. Such are the mystical qualities of numbers.

Another writer, Philo of Alexandria, described the mysteries of seven as follows:

❧ ❧ ❧

So august is the dignity inherent by nature in the number 7, that it has a unique relation distinguishing it from all the other numbers within the decade [the first 10 numbers]: for of these some beget without being begotten, some are begotten but do not beget, some do both of these, both beget and are begotten: 7 alone is found in no such category. (On the Creation 99; Loeb)

By "beget" Philo means it generates another number from one to ten by being doubled or tripled; being "begotten" is to be produced in such a manner. So 1 through 5 all beget; 6, 8, 9, and 10 are all begotten. Seven alone remains ungenerated and ungenerating. Thus the Pythagoreans used it to symbolize the Unmoved Mover of Aristotle; the first cause which is itself uncaused. This is admittedly a strange way to view numbers; but it was popularly accepted as true at the time the Apocalypse was produced.

We have learned, then, that not all numbers are alike. Each has its special significance, though some (6, 8, and 9) were seldom felt to be symbolic. John only uses five or six numbers in a symbolic way. Briefly, here are John's more important numbers:

3   stands for the spiritual world.

4   stands for the created order.

7   stands for perfection (and also the sum of 3 and 4).

10 stands for totality.

12 stands for Israel, as the people of God (being also the product of 3 and 4).

John makes it appear that he has more numbers by using multiples of these numbers, especially squares. Such multiplication intensifies the meaning of the root number. Thus Christ rules 1,000 years: his full time (20:4). There are 144,000 redeemed (7:4) (that is, $12 \times 12 \times 10 \times 10 \times 10$): all God's people. The New Jerusalem lies "foursquare," with multiples of twelve (21:16–17). Another derived number is $3\frac{1}{2}$, which stands for the period of evil, being half of seven but neither three nor four. This $3\frac{1}{2}$-year period can also be called 42 months or 1,260 days.

John used colors in a similar fixed way:

White stands for victory (not purity).

Red is the color of war and strife.

Black the color of famine and suffering.

Pale (actually a grey-yellow, the color of rotting meat) is the color of death.

Animals too are used symbolically:

Beasts are always Satanic powers.

The Lamb is the animal of sacrifice.

The Lion is King.

Eagles and Oxen are the superior animals of their kind.

Horns point to power and thus to rulers.

Multiple heads point to multiple rulers.

These are all commonplace images that the first-century hearer would readily have known. We, however, will need to keep a scorecard.

In addition to these ordinary images, John helps the audience along by providing his own interpretations of several of his symbols. Revelation provides more than ten such explicit interpretations:

Reference	Symbol	Interpretation Given
1:8	Alpha/Omega	Who is/was/is to come
1:13	7 Stars/lamps	Angels/churches
8:3	Angel with censer	Prayers of saints
10:1–11	Little open book	Must prophesy again
11:7	Great city/Sodom	Where Lord was crucified
13:6	God's Tabernacle	Those dwelling on earth
13:18	666	Number of (a) man
14:14–20	Winepress	Wrath of God
17:9–15	7 Heads, 10 horns	7 Mountains/kings, 10 kings
18:21	Angel with millstone	Babylon cast down
19:11–16	One on a white horse	Word of God

The meanings of several other symbols are obvious: the Lion/Lamb of 5:6 is surely Jesus; the earthquake in 6:12 represents judgment; the birth in 12:1 is surely that of the Messiah. The descriptions of Jesus in chapter one are derived from Daniel and the appearance of the high priest. With a little effort, we can decipher most of John's symbols.

Three aspects of this correlation between symbol and interpretation need elaboration. First, the use of symbols forces the hearer to operate on two levels at the same time. On one level we move in a fantastic universe of angels and monsters, whores and virgins, stars and temples, dragons and warriors, Christ and antichrist. Yet on considering John's own interpretation, we find that we are also operating on the level of ordinary experience. We are not hearing about stars, but about churches (1:20). John is not really eating books, he is prophesying (10:9–11). It never would have occurred to me to picture a prayer meeting as an angel swinging a golden censer and throwing it upon the earth (8:3–5), but perhaps John's prayer meetings were more lively than those I have seen. And there is something maliciously appropriate in symbolizing the grandeur of Rome as a gaudy prostitute riding on a scarlet beast, at least from the provincial perspective of John (17:3–14). But late first-century Roman culture is under attack, not gaudy prostitutes. We must, then, learn to keep our heads as we travel through this esoteric terrain and exotic symbolism, most of which seems to refer to everyday realities. This does not imply that the book should be read like a code book. John's story is about monsters and whores, and we must experience these as real images to feel the power of his work. Premature translation will destroy the story. But to fail to make the interpretation will destroy its meaning.

There is another sense in which the hearer is forced to think on two levels, for reality itself exists on two levels in John's book. Notice, for example, the analogy between the stars and the lamps. Lamps are earthly analogues to stars; they represent below what the stars are above. As one

Roman Coin of Domitian, from about 83 CE   This naked infant seated on a globe with his hands extended into a field of seven stars is a tribute to Domitian's son who died in infancy. The inscription refers to "The Divine Caesar. . . ." John saw such tributes as Antichrist and pictured Christ holding the seven stars (see Rev. 1:12–20). (Hirmer Verlag, Munich.)

ancient observed about fortune telling by looking into a fire:

æ æ æ

It is not so very mysterious that this Flamelet, trivial as it is, and produced by human agency, should yet possess an awareness of that greater and celestial Flame as of its Sire, and that it should know and announce to us by divine intuition what the latter will be doing up on the crest of the sky. (The Golden Ass, quoted from Lindsay: 57)

Thus, there are connections between things below and things above. On the level of interpretation too, there are angels and churches, an analogy more compelling when we recall that in Greek the word *angelos* means messenger. In this story there is an above and a below to the world, and John has ascended into the above "in the spirit" (4:2), where he sees behind the veil of ordinary experience to the true causes. This notion of the world as consisting of an above and a below that correspond to each other in certain crucial ways was widely shared in John's world. Deriving from the mild and diverse Platonism of ancient culture, it was popularly assumed that this world was an imitation, a copy of that other world of truth and reality. (For more discussion of this point see pp. 254, 308–309.)

Closer inspection of John's use of symbols reveals a third, more shocking point. John has disarmed a number of his most powerful symbols. He has, in fact, transformed images of power into images of vulnerability, symbols of conquest into those of suffering. The Apocalypse portrays at least three such reversals of symbolic value. The first and most dramatic of these occurs in chapter 5. Let us consider the scene.

Reading and Reflection

Read 5:1–6.

1. What is the basic drama of this short scene?
2. Why does John cry?
3. Note the contrast between what John "heard" and what he "saw." What emotional impact does this change in symbols cause?

Reversing the Images

This is a very dramatic scene. John shapes the hearers' reaction to it by sharing his own: he wept when no one was found worthy to open the scroll (5:4). An angel comforts him with the news that "the Lion of the tribe of Judah, the Root of David" is able to open it. This is a standard prophetic symbol based on the description in Genesis 49:9–10, which depicted Judah as a lion and as ruler. It was elaborated in later traditions to show the

lion tearing his enemies to pieces. If this is what the hearers expected, they would have been greatly surprised. For instead of the bloodthirsty lion, what actually appears is a bloody lamb incongruously described as "standing as though it had been slain." What are we to make of this transformation of symbols?

On the one hand, this is simply creating images for historical events. Jesus just did not match up to the grand and regal messianic expectations commonly held; he was no second David. He did not overthrow the evil earthly powers. The pagans continued to dominate God's holy people. Instead of slaying the wicked, he was slain by them. This is history. But John also makes a more daring point. He asserts that the lamb *is* the lion. Jesus is the Messiah, a messiah who has conquered through suffering rather than by tearing his enemies to pieces. It is his suffering that enables him to open the scroll, for he has conquered and is worthy. Jesus does not conquer by overwhelming the enemy with superior force. Instead, he shows that the superior force overwhelming all is suffering. Hence, the sufferer is the conqueror; the victim is the victor.

There is a similar reversal of images in chapter 12, where we hear about a dark war in heaven, with Michael and his angels driving the dragon and his host out of heaven, casting them down to earth. In Jewish tradition, Michael was the "chief of the holy angels" (*Ascension of Isaiah* 3:16) and often performed messianic tasks (for example, Daniel 10:12; 12:1). Another apocalyptic work describes him as "the mediator between God and men for the peace of Israel. He shall stand in opposition to the kingdom of the enemy" (*Testament of Dan* 6:2). This image of cosmic warfare corresponds to the image of the lion and, like it, is immediately reversed. For when heaven celebrates this triumph, it is explained:

🌿 🌿 🌿

They have conquered him by the blood of the Lamb and by the word of their testimony, for they loved not their lives even unto death. (12:11)

Again conquest is attributed to suffering. But this time it is not only the death of the Lamb, but that of his followers who add their testimony to his. Not only does Jesus' suffering overthrow evil, so does that of his faithful followers. Once again, the victim is proclaimed the victor.

Another scene of cosmic war occurs later in the book with the appearance of the Divine Warrior, riding a white horse (19:11–21). Once again we have the traditional images of the eschatological battle, and again they are subverted. There is the battle setting, but no battle is ever portrayed. The narrative jumps directly to the victory pronouncement (19–20). We are told that the hosts of the wicked are all killed (the traditional image), but their deaths are attributed to one sword, "The sword of him who sits upon the horse, the sword that issues from his mouth" (21). They are undone by the word of Jesus, which is the Word of God (his title in verse 13) as well as the word of his testimony (verse 10; note his other titles in verse 11: the faithful and true, which point to his death). This symbol of "his testimony" is complex. The "testimony of Jesus" is his death, but it is also testimony about Jesus (see 1:9). This faithful witness about Jesus will lead to suffering: the *martys* (Greek for *witness*) will become the martyr. Again, the death of Jesus and the suffering of his followers bring about the overthrow of evil. This is even more evident when we observe that Jesus appears before the battle with his robe dipped in blood (19:13).[2] The blood is his.

Jesus conquers through his death and the death of his faithful followers. It is not that the wicked have killed him and now he returns to kill them; the Lamb is not transformed into a Lion. John's symbol is more radical: the Lamb is the Lion. The death of Jesus overthrows evil (compare John 12:31). "The blood of the saints and the martyrs of Jesus" has caused the fatal inebriation of the great harlot (17:6; 16:6). The victims are the victors.

Thus while John draws his images from the traditional apocalyptic stock, even using the central symbol of cosmic combat, his experience of Jesus has led him to radically reverse the value of these symbols in order to express the conviction that faithful witness brings salvation and judgment. But this conviction is not argued, or even stated; it is portrayed, enacted in a story. Let us turn our attention to that story and its action, plot, and structure.

THE PLOT OF THE APOCALYPSE

John seems to lead the hearer by the hand until about halfway through his work. He carefully tells us there are seven letters, seven seals, seven trumpets. Then he seems to abandon us near the end of chapter 11, and does not resume numbering his sequences again until chapter 16. This has produced a great variety of outlines for the work. Many interpreters have been unable to resist the urge to remedy John's deficient numbering, and various sequences of seven have been created out of the material John neglected to number. This does not seem wise. Before we proceed to help John in this way we should try to understand his own organization. Perhaps these sequences were not meant to be numbered. In part this urge to organize everything into a series of seven, perhaps even into seven such series, is the result of a rationalistic reading of the book. The modern urge has been to organize everything into an outline, hardly the best way to comprehend the structure of a narrative. The Apocalypse must be encountered as story, with imagination. We are almost ready to attempt such a reading. Having gained some perspective on the general kind of literature this represents and explored the way it uses symbols, we must now examine the general methods it employs to weave together the diverse material this work contains.

---

2. Note that in the earlier reference to Jesus treading the winepress, it occurred "outside the city," a traditional way of locating Calvary—14:20. The probable source, and a more traditional use, of this bloody robe-winepress imagery is Isa. 63:1–6.

Principles of Organization

Revelation is presented as one vast vision that John experienced on an island called Patmos, off the coast of Asia Minor, while he was "in the Spirit on the Lord's day" (1:10). Thus, it is a book of ecstasy. Since by its nature ecstasy transcends the senses, ecstatic literature must not be expected to conform completely to rational analysis. In Revelation, as one commentator suggested, "we must reckon with an element of incoherence" (Sweet, 1979:44). Similarly, John's grammar does not conform to the proper Greek usage. Numerous grammatical "mistakes" occur in Revelation, but not (as is often assumed) because John knew no better; a grammatical construction he misuses in one place is often correctly used in another. We must understand that ecstasy does not always follow the rules. These loose ends of grammar and event enhance the feeling of extraordinary experience. We must anticipate a bit of untamed order in this enthusiastic literature.

On the other hand, we should not assume too readily that John's narrative is incoherent simply because his organization is not immediately obvious to us. John employs two other principles that lend his work an aura of enthusiasm and complexity. One type of complexity results from John's practice of making later events and cycles mirror earlier ones and echo their meanings. Such *recapitulation* is not a matter of simple repetition, for the later symbols modify, intensify, and focus earlier ones. But the underlying meanings of the two are the same. Thus, for example, the relationship between prayer and judgment originally shown in seals five and six (6:10, 12) is recapitulated in the new image of the angel with the censer, full of the saints' prayers which, when thrown on the earth, brings judgment (8:3–5).

Understanding this principle solves many problems, for we do not have to imagine that the narrative is always moving on to new events: it may be reexplaining old events. Thus, for example, we hear the declaration in 11:15 that the Kingdom of God has come. Rather, it seems to come and go, for chapter 12 opens with a new vision of conflict carrying us back in time to the birth of Jesus, and further to the Exodus and the Garden of Eden. This flashback may be interpreted as John's attempt to reimage the coming of the kingdom. It is as if he were saying: now that you have seen the coming of the kingdom, let me show you how it happened. He is recapitulating the meaning of earlier images by showing what brought about the kingdom: the birth of the Messiah. Such recapitulation does not preclude the possibility of progress within the narrative, but the progress will be on the level of the images rather than their meaning.

Another type of complexity is achieved by mingling material from separate scenes to interlace the two scenes, a technique known as *intercalation*. John often interweaves material from one section of his book into another section to bind the two sections more closely together. Thus, if we imagine two cycles that we designate A B C and 1 2 3, intercalation might produce a combined sequence: A B 1 C 2 3. This sandwiching of outside material into the first sequence forces the hearer to imagine a relationship between them, thus creating a unity. Most of the material that seems out of place in the Apocalypse may be explained by this principle.

While recapitulation echoes earlier meanings in new symbols, intercalation echoes the symbols themselves. Thus, for example, the symbol of the 144,000 who are sealed in the middle of the series of seven seals (7:1–8) really belongs to the battle scene (14:1) and ties the two scenes together. Intercalation applies to the repetition of symbols, recapitulation to the repetition of their meaning. It is possible for a scene to be both a recapitulation and an intercalation (for example, 8:3–5).

The use of these techniques has produced a complex work. It is no wonder that commentators seeking a simple outline or a linear development have produced divergent results. We must expect to find symbolic material from one section intercalated into other sections, binding them together. We must anticipate recapitulations of similar ideas under very different symbolic images, producing a sense of repetition and explanation. We must also expect to find some material that seems wildly out of place, enhancing the ecstatic nature of the book (16:15). Now we are ready to read the Apocalypse itself.

Reading and Reflection

For your first reading of the Apocalypse (which should take about an hour) try to: (1) note all the formal elements that John uses to pattern his work (especially his numbering of series, or when he says "and another"); and (2) vividly picture the basic scenes with which you are presented, noting when the basic scene shifts.

Patterns of Numbers: 7-3-2

The first three chapters contain only one numbered sequence, that of the seven churches. It is universally agreed that these form a major segment of the work. The next numbered sequence occurs in chapter 6 and afterward: seven seals. This leads directly into another: seven trumpets. The last three trumpets are also separately numbered as a series of three woes. Closer examination shows that each series of seven is somehow marked by the author so that it consists of subsets of four and three. In the Seals, for example, there were four horsemen and three heavenly signs. Here the four seem to relate to earth and the three to the spiritual world. The seventh trumpet, the final work of God, brings the proclamation that the kingdom has come.

The next explicit numbering does not occur until chapter 16, where John reports seeing seven angels with seven plagues. How, then, are we to construe the material in 12–14? Notice that John introduces these seven angels by saying he saw "another sign" (15:1). If we look for earlier signs, we find two. Chapter 12 begins with a reference to the "great sign" which was seen in heaven—

READING GUIDE TO THE APOCALYPSE

Opening address to the audience   1:1–11
  with a literary address to the seven
  churches   1:4–7

The Letter Scroll

The vision: "in the spirit on the Lord's Day"
Jesus and his seven letters   1:12–3:22

The Sealed Scroll

The heavenly scroll—a closed book
4–11
  The heavenly liturgy of creation   4
    and redemption   5
  Unsealing the scroll   6–7
    Silence . . . trumpets   8–11
      Announcement: the kingdom of the
      world has become the kingdom of
      our Lord
Resumption of the heavenly liturgy

The Open Scroll

The scroll of the heavens—an open
book   12–22
  (Scroll introduced in 10:1–11—an intercalation)
  The first sign in heaven: a woman
  pursued   12–14
    Eve/Israel/Messiah/Christ   12
    Satan/Rome   13
    Lamb/Judgment   14
  The second sign in heaven: 7 final
  plagues   15–16
    The vision of the prostitute   17–18
      with scenes of judgment   19:1–21:8
    The vision of the Bride   21:9–22:5
      with scenes of restoration   21:22–
      22:5
Closing address to the audience   22:6–20
  with a literary farewell to the churches
  22:21

a woman clothed with the sun—then immediately shifts our attention to "another sign" (12:3). This material may be understood as a series of three signs or as a great sign with two other subordinate signs. To support the dualistic view we have the double vision of the open Temple (11:19 and 15:5). The triadic view would find evidence in the heavenly significance of the number three.

This last sign consists of seven angels pouring seven bowls of wine on the earth (the ancients drank their wine from bowls). The seventh is again climactic: "it is done" (16:17). Yet it is not done; the story continues. Now one of these seven angels presents John with two contrasting visions of two very different women: the Whore of Babylon (17:1) and the Virgin Bride of Jerusalem (21:9). There is no other numbered sequence in the rest of the revelation. Apparently the remaining scenes are to be construed with these two visions of the feminine. Even though one can easily find a series of seven visions, each marked by the construction "I saw," in the scenes from 19:11–21:8, John did not number them. Nor should we.

John's explicit use of numbers would have been valuable in listening to this work, even though the numbers do not solve all the problems of its structure. This general structure will become clearer if we now turn our attention to the action portrayed.

Three Dramas in One

Aristotle observed that the action of a story is defined by its beginning and end. But the beginning and end of this work seem to stand outside the story. Revelation begins and ends by directly addressing the reader in the guise of a letter, a most unusual form for an apocalyptic work. There is a word to the reader and advice to the hearers (1:3 and 22:18–19). The work begins and ends in the real world and draws the reader into the story. The end corresponds to the beginning.

Opening	Correspondence	Closing
1:1, 4, 9	John names himself	22:8
1:1	An angel sent	22:6
1:3	Reader blessed	22:7
1:3	The time is near	22:10
1:1	To soon take place	22:6
1:4	Grace to you	22:21
1:8	The Alpha and Omega	22:13
1:17	John falls at feet of someone	22:8

This technique of beginning and ending by directly addressing the reader serves as a bridge from the consciousness of the everyday reality to the consciousness of the reality created by this story. It is like the steward who greets you as you enter and exit an airplane, easing your transition. It resembles the writing on the screen at the beginning and end of a movie, leading you into and out of the story. These two sections frame the whole work and help shape its meaning.

The Drama of the Letters

John has welcomed the hearers aboard his craft and now launches into his first drama: the risen Christ appears to John and dictates seven letters to seven angels of seven churches. (The angels are to the churches as stars are to lamps—1:20.) This action, completed in 3:22, constitutes the first scene in John's drama.

Each letter follows the same pattern:

The Addressee is given.

The Sender is designated by referring to some of the symbolism used to describe the risen Christ in the earlier vision.

The works of the church are diagnosed.

The appropriate praise or blame is given.

The refrain occurs: the one having an ear should hear.

The promise of future reward is given.

The only variation is that in the last four letters the promise and the refrain occur in reverse order.

Statue of Artemis, Ephesus Museum This traditional statue of Artemis (called Diana by the Romans) shows her as a goddess of the wild, associated with the hunt. To the Greeks, she was the virgin sister of Apollo. Her sacrifices were birds and wild animals, and her priestess rode in a chariot drawn by stags. (Photo by author.)

Statue of Artemis Ephesia, Ephesus Museum How unlike the traditional Artemis is this statue from Ephesus. Hung with ripe fruit (variously interpreted as pomegranates, eggs, or breasts), she was a figure of fertility and life, far from the virgin huntress. Yet one of Artemis' traditional functions was to give and protect life, so that identification of this goddess with the Greek Artemis (and the Roman Diana) was possible. Her monumental temple at Ephesus was one of the Seven Wonders of the World. (Photo by author.)

Each letter is an integrated unity. The description of the Christ, the diagnosis, the promise all correspond. Thus, to Ephesus (the first church and closest to Patmos) the One who holds the seven stars complains of a star falling from its first position, and threatens to remove the lamp. Viewed historically, there is a certain sense of irony in this threat. The Ephesians had twice been forced to move their city because of the silting of the harbor (in 550 and 287 BCE). Further, they are praised for resisting the Nicolaitans (meaning "conquerors of people"), then offered a reward for conquering. There is further irony in their reward: to eat of the tree of life. Such a tree was a primary symbol for Artemis/Diana, whose great shrine was located at Ephesus. But the irony thrusts even deeper, since finally the tree of life is the cross of Christ.

Such thematic unity and historical irony mark each of the letters. The following information will help you to hear some of the original irony. Smyrna had itself died and been reborn: it had been destroyed in 600 and rebuilt in 290 BCE. A local mountain was associated with the worship of Niobe, whose rites included ten days of mourning. Pergamum was the earliest and greatest center of the Emperor cult in Asia Minor. Great temples to Zeus and Asclepius marked the city, both of whom were symbolized by the serpent. Little wonder that John believed Satan's throne was there. Like the Nicolaitans, Balaam and Balak are symbolic names: their amusing, yet devastating story is in Numbers (22–25). It includes a talking donkey, a charlatan prophet, magic curses, and disaster for Israel. Briefly, a greedy prophet almost succeeds in destroying Israel by a counsel of cooperation and intermarriage with pagan culture.

Thyatira was the least important city of the seven, but receives the longest, central letter. The opposite of Ephesus, it shows love but no discernment. A woman leader is apparently prominent in this city. John calls her Jezebel, another symbolic name. Jezebel was the ancient queen, wife of King Ahab and daughter of King Ethbaal, a Phoenician; she established the worship of Baal in Israel. Her story and great struggle with Elijah is told in I Kings (16:29–19:18). She is the archetype, the original model of one who seduces Israel to worship false gods. John's condemnation of his female opponent, who also claimed prophetic powers, could not be more complete. Curiously, in the one specific charge he makes against her (she teaches that Christians may eat things sacrificed to idols), she seems closer to Paul's position than does John (compare I Cor. 8 and Rom. 14). Sardis, a nearly impregnable city, had been captured twice in its history through surprise nighttime attacks. Its name was legendary for lost wealth. Philadelphia, like Smyrna, had a large Jewish community. John's bitterness toward Jews is extreme, bordering on hatred. Yet he seems to make a strong claim that he and his community represent the real Jews. To the degree that these letters represent real settings in these cities, we must presume a situation of rivalry between John and other Jews. Like the community behind the Gospel of John, this community probably has felt the sting of expulsion from the synagogue (see pp. 203–204, 257–258).

The last letter brings this first cycle to an end on an ominous note. He has nothing good to say about Laodicea, a city known for its tepid water piped in from a hot spring five miles distant, which is lamented for its tepid church. Specializing in the production of a rich black wool, its people are offered white garments. Renowned for ophthalmology (and invention of an eye salve), they are told to purchase salve for their spiritual eyes. At the same time, however, John shows Jesus coming to them, solemnly inviting them to the sacred supper.

This brings us to the close of the first act. The scene shifts, and a new action begins.

The Drama of Heavenly Worship

John is now transported into heaven where he observes the heavenly court at worship (4:1). Applying Aristotle's principle of beginning and end once again, we find that the worship begun in chapter 4 culminates in chapter 11, where the twenty-four elders resume their worship of God (11:16). We witness the heavenly liturgy, to which, we may suppose, the earthly liturgy of John's congregations would in some ways correspond.

The initial scene focuses entirely on God. John majestically describes the entire creation at worship before the creator. The four living creatures include wild and tame animals, the flying eagle, and humanity. Ezekiel had used similar images (Ezek. 1:4–14). In later Jewish tradition they were understood to represent the chief of their kind: each king paying homage to the king of kings. The twenty-four elders may represent the twenty-four priestly families (I Chronicles 24:4–6), or they may represent the twelve tribes and the twelve apostles (Rev. 21:12–14), or both at once.

But this scene of primal harmony is soon disrupted by an angel calling for someone worthy to open a sealed scroll. When no one is found, John weeps. Here we feel the loss of the world as it might have been: a world in need of redemption, sealed off from God's revelation.

The subsequent scene focuses on Jesus, the one worthy to open the scroll. This strange scroll requires some discussion. Three suggestions have been made concerning its symbolic significance. First, it may recall the common apocalyptic theme of the sealed book. Because the apocalyptic revelation was intended only for the last days the original book was sealed and hidden until the appropriate time (see Dan. 12:4 and compare Ezek. 2:8–10). To unseal such a scroll would then mean to reveal the message of the world's end. Judgment and salvation are at hand.

Second, a scroll with seven seals may reflect the Roman practice of sealing a will with the seals of seven witnesses. Only when the will was to be put into effect would it be unsealed. Thus, to unseal such a scroll would mean to put into effect the will of God.

Third, the scroll may reflect the scroll of the Torah, the revelation of God. We know of other early Christian traditions that spoke of the Law as "veiled" to those outside Christ (II Cor. 3:14) and of Christ "opening" the Law to new understandings (Luke 24:27). To unseal such a scroll would mean to reveal the true meaning of the Hebrew Scriptures. While John never quotes the Scriptures, he continually repeats their ideas and phrases. (The extent of his repetitions may be conveniently studied in the Jerusalem Bible, where they are put in italic type.) But we should be in

no hurry to make a choice between these three possibilities. All three images work; all three may be intended.

In any case, the meaning is much the same: Jesus as the Lamb slain worthily reveals and actualizes the will of God. He brings God's rule into reality (5:13). Or we may translate more fully: the harmony of creation has been disrupted. The will of God no longer prevails. Only the death of Jesus reestablishes the harmony. Of course, such a translation loses much of the force and delight of John's images and cannot quite capture his meaning.

We come now to our first apocalyptic cycle (6:1–8:2), a series of seals, each producing a small dramatic scene. We also encounter the first major intercalation (all of chapter 7), which puns on the seals by a sealing of the righteous. Logically, the symbol of those sealed relates to future action, to the following series of trumpets (9:4) and to the coming battle (14:1). To encounter them here is to feel that these actions are related to each other.

Let us examine more closely how this series works, the logic by which the various scenes succeed each other. The first four scenes are an obvious unit, showing four horses with their riders. Interpreters differ on the meaning of the first rider on a white horse. Because Christ later appears on such a mount (19:11), many have argued that Christ is symbolized here. But others contend nearly the opposite: noting that the figure lacks all the identifying iconography of the Christ given in chapter one, they propose that the rider of the white horse represents the conqueror, a military figure. More specifically, scholars have shown that the bow points to the Parthian warrior who made fearsome use of that instrument. Parthia was Rome's arch foe in this era, a constant threat to peace on the eastern frontier. Thus, the first rider is the harbinger of war. In a similar way these symbols can be directly related to Roman warfare. The god of the Roman army was Mithras, who was commonly symbolized as riding a white horse, carrying a bow, and crowned with the sun. Both interpretations view the first rider as conqueror, allowing us to make sense of the sequence. Each leads inevitably to the next:

conqueror⟶ war⟶ famine⟶ death

War inevitably led to famine in the ancient economy because it disrupted the planting or harvesting of crops in that overwhelmingly agrarian society. The famine envisioned here is serious; a day's worth of wheat is going for a day's wages.

The logic of the four horsemen is straightforward—the simple lesson of history. What, then, makes it a revelation? To answer this question we must consider the rest of the sequence. Seals five, six, and seven have no inherent connection to these four horsemen. Their logic lies in their breaking the logic of the first four. They answer the question, how shall we ever get free from the oppression of history? How can the awful work of the conqueror be arrested? The answer is wonderfully naive: by the prayers of the saints. For the prayers of the saints (seal five), sealed with their suffering, lead inevitably to the divine judgment portrayed as seal six. If the first four seals only reveal the logic of history, the last three pull aside the veil (apocalypsis) and reveal the hidden course of history in the divine will.

According to this logic, seal seven should reveal the kingdom of God. But it is far too early in the story for that. John delays (10:6). Instead of the end, seal seven opens out into a new sequence of seven trumpets. A short intercalation (8:3–5) recapitulates the power of the prayers of the saints to bring judgment to the earth. The new sequence of trumpets recapitulates the judgment allusively portrayed in seal six. A profusion of images portray the destruction of one third of the earth. Another major intercalation intrudes between the sixth and seventh members (10:1–11:13).

The intercalation has three visions. The first portrays a small open scroll that John is to consume. The imagery repeats that of Ezekiel (2:8–3:3). As Ezekiel's message was both sweet and bitter, so John proclaims both salvation and judg-

ment. The second shows John measuring the Temple, a symbol of preservation. Notice that the true Temple is to be preserved while the outward court is to be trampled by the Gentiles, just as John's communities will be preserved despite outward oppression. The third reimages this proclamation and preservation under the symbol of the two final witnesses, Moses and Elijah returned as the Jewish traditions anticipated. These two "lamps" (11:4) enact the mission of the church, whose suffering brings judgment and vindication.

With that judgment John hastens on to the final trumpet. Great voices signal: *the kingdom of the world has become the kingdom of our Lord and of his Christ, and he shall reign forever and ever* (11:15). Heavenly worship resumes. Surely the hearer expects the end of the tale. Creation is redeemed. But the story does not end. John sees into the heavenly Temple and startling new action follows.

The Drama of the Woman, the Dragon, and the Warrior

John's final scene retells one of the oldest and most enduring stories in literature, stretching back some two thousand years before his time but alive and still interesting today. In ancient times this was the story of Marduk defeating the dragon Tiamat; in Medieval legend it was the story of St. George and the dragon; today it thrives in fantasy literature and computer games. It provides the archetypal plot of many stories. And it is the most powerful part of Revelation. New characters are introduced. Woman holds center stage. Dragons, beasts, and warriors control the action. A decisive shift now occurs in the nature of the action, which to this point has been dominated by divine action. In Chapter 1 we discussed the basic structure of stories, involving a subject trying to deliver an object to a receiver (see pp. 29–31). Using this model, the basic story contracts of the first two acts may be simplified thus:

God→ salvation/judgment →world
        ↑
John→   Christ   ←unfaithful witnesses
angels

But in this third scene the action shifts, as the beasts become the subject of the action:

dragon→ war/destruction→woman/witnesses
          ↑
harlot→   beasts   ←warrior, faithful witness
kings

Now the dragon becomes the determiner of the action, waging terror and warfare on the woman, attempting to destroy her child, persecuting the faithful. The only hint we have had of this new action is in the scene of the two witnesses, an intercalation in which this story pattern was foreshadowed (the beast was mentioned at 11:7, even though not formally introduced until 13:1).

The story portrays a dragon attempting to destroy a woman and her son. The woman is a complex symbol: she is Israel, mother of the Messiah; she is Eve, whose promised seed would destroy the serpent (Genesis 3:15). We cannot know whether first-century readers would have also thought of her as Mary, nor can we be sure they would have recognized motifs from Greek and Roman mythology: the attempted destruction of the newborn Romulus and Remus, the founders of Rome; the Goddess Roma portrayed on coins as Queen of Heaven. A contrast with Roma may be intended here.

Failing in his attempts to destroy the child or the woman, the dragon turns his attention to the rest of her offspring. Like Tiamat of old, he conjures a beast from the sea and a beast from the earth who attempt to coerce all people to worship them and the dragon. The Lamb and his 144,000 stand against them. Multiple scenes of judgment follow and culminate in the seven angels with the seven final plagues. The plagues parallel the motifs of the trumpets, but now the destruction is complete. Like the trumpet series, they end with a proclamation: "it is done" (16:17).

Just what is done is portrayed in two visions of two women: a gaudy prostitute and a virgin bride, each with accompanying scenes of judgment and of redemption respectively. It is impossible to summarize adequately the action of the various scenes, but perhaps some clearer delineation of the characters and symbols will enable us to read them with greater understanding.

Ultimately, the image of the beast goes back to Daniel, where it contrasted the animal character of the nations with the human quality of Israel. The seven heads and ten horns are allegorically related to the various Roman rulers (17:9–10); the first head whose death stroke does not kill the beast alludes to the assassination of Julius Caesar, which did little to stop the Empire (13:3, in the Greek text it is not the head which is healed but the beast). For John the key to this conflict with the beast involves worship; the beast demands total allegiance. It is death to refuse such worship (13:15).

This demand of the beast is answered by the demand of the angel, flying in midheaven with eternal good news:

ð   ð   ð

Fear God and give him glory, for the hour of his judgment has come; and worship him who made heaven and earth, the sea and fountains of water. (14:7)

This is the central proclamation of the work. The essential struggle is for the hearts and minds of men and women. To worship the beast is to bruise the heal of the son; to worship Christ is to crush the head of the serpent (Genesis 3:15). Notice the nice word play on head. A Christian bishop writing to one of these same churches a couple of decades later admonished them:

ð   ð   ð

Seek, then, to come together more frequently to give thanks [that is, to celebrate the Eucharist] and glory to God. For when you gather together frequently the powers of Satan are destroyed, and his mischief is brought to nothing, by the concord of your faith. There is nothing better than peace, by which every war in heaven and earth is abolished. (Ignatius, to The Ephesians 13:1–2)

Thus, the real war of Revelation is a war to conquer the hearts and minds of the people of Asia Minor. Receiving the mark of the beast on the hand and forehead (13:17; 14:9) is probably a symbolic way of speaking about submitting to the economic (hand) and spiritual (head) domination of the Empire. To worship at the shrine of the emperor was one thing, but even to buy one's daily bread required using coins that testified to his deity. (See the coin on p. 42).

Two harvest images complete this first sign: the wheat and, especially, the grape harvest (14:14–20). The results of this harvest are bread and wine, and the wine/blood covers 1,600 measures: the whole earth. The eucharistic themes are clear.

The second sign recapitulates and greatly expands the portrayal of judgment. Enlarging on the wine metaphor, seven bowls of wrath are poured out on the earth. Those who poured out the saints' blood are given blood to drink (16:6). They are drunk with wine (17:2). The Babylonian whore is drunk with the blood of the saints and the witnesses of Jesus (17:6). The logic of these judgments is to show that evil ultimately defeats itself, even as the beast ultimately turns on the prostitute, strips her naked, and eats her flesh (17:16). John may be remembering what Rome did to Jerusalem.

There follows a lengthy lament and ironic liturgy over the fall of Babylon: kings, merchants, sailors, all weep for the departed glory (18), while the multitude rejoices (19). This liturgy follows the ancient mythic pattern:

The appearance of the divine warrior (19:11–16)

The cosmic warfare (19:19–21)

The coronation of the proper king (20:1–6)

The fixing of destinies (20:11–15)

The divine marriage (21)

The Deified Vespasian, about 80 CE We may see here an aspect of the ceremony of deification: the Emperor is enthroned on a quadriga, a chariot drawn by four elephants. He holds a septer and Victory. The inscription bears witness to "the Divine Vespasian." (Hirmer Verlag, Munich.)

John might be accused of mixing his metaphors in this wedding between a lamb and a city. The city is a combined idealization of Jerusalem, the dwelling place of God, and the Garden of Eden. It represents the redemption of Creation, now including the city, a human creation. In this magnificent vision of the end, the work of humanity is taken up into and perfected in the work of God.

Summary of the Plot

Three separate actions are recounted in Revelation. The risen Christ appears and dictates seven letters to his churches. The Lamb appears in the heavenly throne scene and opens a sealed scroll that reveals the will of God and the judgment of evil. The dragon makes war on the elect but is overcome by the divine warrior, resulting in the replacement of the whore by the bride. Each action has its own scroll (Reading Guide, p. 281). There is the scroll on which the seven letters are written (1:11), the sealed scroll that must be opened by Christ (5:1), and the small open scroll that John must consume (10:2). This open scroll is described in the intercalation that foreshadows the action of scene three, thus properly belonging to that final action. It may be that the open scroll represents the revelation of nature (which John sees by looking at the heavens—12:1), while the sealed scroll represents the special revelation of the Hebrew Scriptures, which must be opened by Jesus to be known. The letters would then represent the new revelation given in Jesus.

Each action shows the realization of the coming of salvation and judgment, with subsequent acts being recapitulations, elaborations, and clarifications of earlier ones. In the letters Jesus has promised to come to his churches in judgment (3:3) and salvation (3:20). The second act offers a fuller portrayal of this coming judgment (seal six and the six trumpets) and salvation (seal seven and trumpet seven). These are made possible by the "Lamb slain," by the death of Jesus. The relationship of the third act to the second is evident if we see the link between chapter 11 (the declaration that God's kingdom has come and the resumption of heavenly worship) and chapter 12 (the birth of the Messiah and the struggle with Evil). The new action of chapter 12 represents a recapitulation of the earlier action, explaining how the change of kingdoms has occurred historically.

These three acts do not represent one continuous action. The relationship between them is one of meaning, later acts expanding the meaning of earlier ones. The three scenes do not grow out of one another in the way we anticipate in a modern drama. They more closely resemble three one-act plays on a common theme, performed in succession within a common frame. Each scene reveals the hidden dimension of life in which the kingdom of God is realized: Jesus comes to his churches, enables the cosmic worship of God to persist, and overthrows the work of the evil one. These are three dimensions of the work of Christ, not three consecutive actions. Each reveals the meaning of Christ's death and resurrection. I am tempted to say they portray the work of Christ

in relation to the church, in relation to the cosmos, and in relation to history. But that is perhaps clearer than John would wish to be. The unity of this work is achieved by using a common set of symbols in all three scenes, by intercalating aspects of one scene in another, and by presenting all three in a common setting.

The Framework of a Letter

We saw above that the opening and closing of Revelation correspond, that they employ the device of a letter, and that they address the hearer directly as a person in the real world. Such letters were often read in public worship, as were apocalypses (I Cor. 14:26).

John's "letter" apocalypse certainly presupposes a liturgical context. The implication of the opening is a public assembly at which a reader presents a letter to the congregation (1:3–4); the experience takes place "on the Lord's day" (1:10); the work uses extensive liturgical material (for example, 1:5–6; 4–5; 7:12) with numerous allusions to the Lord's Supper. The closing invites the hearer to "come" and "take of the water of life" (22:17), having strictly separated insiders from outsiders (22:14–15), complete with a curse (18) and an invitation to "come Lord Jesus" (20). These elements are all associated with the Eucharist in other early Christian literature (for example, in I Cor. 16:20–22; *Didache* 10:6; and Justin, *First Apology* 66).

As we have seen earlier, the symbolism and the plot of Revelation both focus on the death of Christ, a death that proves to be his victory over the forces of evil. In the third major scene the focus on blood and wine is especially extensive. Overall, then, we may infer that the probable social setting of Revelation is an assembly for public worship, which culminated in the "coming" of Jesus to the communion table. On this reading, Revelation is a literary correlate to the worship service. It portrays, on a cosmic and symbolic level, what happens in the liturgy: in the spirit on the Lord's day, the risen Jesus comes to his congregation, examines their worthiness to receive him, reveals the will of the Father, and overthrows the powers of evil, thereby enabling the true worship of God and the coming of God's rule. The impact of such a reading of the Apocalypse is the topic of our next section.

SYMBOL, STORY, AND HISTORY: *The Setting of Revelation*

The Apocalypse tells us that it was written by John (1:1) during the reign of the sixth emperor in a series of seven (17:10). Unfortunately, none of this helps determine the precise historical setting of the work. We have at least four different ways to count the number of emperors. To make matters worse, John may not have intended this numbering to be taken literally, since the emperor is always a six claiming to be an eight in the symbolic way John used numbers.

Nor does the name John help; it was a common Jewish name and, without some further clue (like "son of . . .") it is impossible to establish his identity. Further, he does not claim to be John the apostle as later tradition assumed. (A living apostle would probably not have spoken of the apostles the way our author did in describing the heavenly Jerusalem—21:14.) Even if our author had claimed to be John the apostle, we would have to test the claim, for so much of apocalyptic literature claims authorship that is false. Hence, we will have to find a less direct way to John's historical setting.

We are no better off concerning the date of the work. One would think that the references to Nero would allow us to date it in his reign (the late sixties), but John also knew a legend of Nero's return (17:8), necessitating a date after his death. The two emperors after Nero neither persecuted Christians nor insisted on divine honors, according to the evidence available. The case is different, however, with the third emperor after Nero, Domitian. While he has traditionally been portrayed in darker hues than the historical record supports, there is little question that emperor worship, attributing divinity to the living emperor, bowing when coming into his presence, and addressing him as Lord and God increased under Domitian, especially in Asia Minor. In his reign, there was nothing equal to the persecutions under Nero, but it is likely that the general hostility toward the Christians as atheists—those who refuse to honor the Gods and thus threaten the well-being of the community—focused on their refusal to ascribe divine honors to the emperor. (In fact, five emperors before Domitian had been declared by the Senate to be gods, perhaps pointing to Domitian as the "sixth"—17:10.)

The earliest external reference to the date of the book comes from one who grew up in Asia Minor but became bishop of Lyons in Gaul (France) in 178. Irenaeus declared that John wrote the Apocalypse near the end of the reign of Domitian—about 95 CE. This is a reasonable date for the final composition of Revelation. Like other narrative works, such as the Gospel of John, it may have gone through several editions before it reached its final form. Its persistent popularity shows that Revelation continued to speak to the needs of the churches for decades. The situation envisioned in the Apocalypse existed from the middle of the first century into the fourth.

Christ against Culture

We saw in the reading of the letters (Rev. 2–3) that there were factions in the Johannine communities. John deliberately opposes those he calls Nicolaitans, as do some of the congregations. John seems to regard them as outsiders (2:6), although some within the church at Pergamum seem to hold Nicolaitan views (2:15). There was also the other prophetic voice accepted at Thyatira, whom John designates Jezebel (2:20). Although these may well have been a separate group from the Nicolaitans, John lumps them together as prophets such as Balaam, whose teachings about cultural assimilation to Canaanite ways led to divine judgment on Israel during the entrance into the promised land (Numbers 25:1–9; 31:16). John's opponents seemed to share a relaxed attitude toward Greco-Roman culture; for example, that Christians were permitted to eat meat sacrificed to idols (2:14, 20).

We must not let John's bitter condemnation blind us to the fact that this was a perfectly logical position for a Christian to hold. Paul held similar views, though with certain qualifications (I Cor. 10:14, 25–28). We do not know whether these other prophets also had built-in safeguards, and John would probably not have told us if they did. Obtaining meat would have been a real problem for urban, non-Jewish Christians. Nearly all the meat offered for sale in the marketplace would have been previously sacrificed to some deity. Unlike the Jews, the Greeks only burned a small portion of the sacrificial animal. An ancient story tells how Prometheus tricked Zeus into choosing the inedible portions of the animal for the Gods, leaving the rest for human consumption (Hesiod, *Theogony:* 535–557). Since most slaughtered animals would have been "sacrificed" in this way, those who ate the meat would have been understood to have communion with the deity to whom the sacrifice was made.

Jews avoided this problem by their strict dietary laws and by living in an extensive community that could provide its own meat. The Jerusalem church seems to have demanded that Gentile Christians avoid such pollution (Acts 15:20); John belonged to this stricter school. Avoiding such meat, and other contacts with the religious aspects of Greco-Roman culture, would have been possible only as long as Christians could find shelter in the Jewish community. The difficulty in John's day, however, was that a gulf of hostility had developed between the Jewish communities and the Christian communities of Asia Minor. John regarded them as a synagogue of Satan, no true Jews (2:9). They probably had a similar opinion of him.

This issue affected more than what one could eat. Nearly every aspect of ancient culture was permeated by religious observance. Education began with the reading of Homer. Medicine was practiced in the name of Asclepius, God of Heal-ing. Entertainment consisted of sporting events (both the bloody arena and the Olympic games) dedicated to the gods and the theater dedicated to Dionysus. Each performance began with a sacrifice to Dionysus whose altar stood at the front of every theater. To ply a trade meant to belong to a guild, but trade guilds were devoted to a patron deity regarded as the founder and protector of the craft. Mutual assistance societies (the ancient form of insurance) would gather in the name of some god or goddess. The very coins by which one bought and sold, and paid one's taxes, testified to these gods and goddesses. One could not live, it seemed, without the mark of the beast on the head and hand (13:16).

The Jews had dealt with these issues by constructing alternative institutions. Cut off from this alternative, John's communities were feeling their way forward. Some believed that culture could be redeemed by participation. The gods, they would have reasoned, are either nothing at all or faulty perceptions of the one true God. In either case, participation in occupations and meals carried out in their names was of no consequence to Christians. John disagreed and called for separation. Some, perhaps, began to create alternatives. We do know that the success of Christianity in Asia Minor had significant economic and social implications. Early in the second century a provincial governor from Asia Minor wrote to the emperor to clarify how he should proceed against the Christians. He concluded with the following assessment:

᪳ ᪳ ᪳

Persons of all ranks and ages, and of both sexes are, and will be, involved in the prosecution. For this contagious superstition is not confined to the cities only, but has spread through the villages and rural districts; it seems possible, however, to check and cure it. It is certain at least that the temples, which had been almost deserted, begin now to be frequented; and the sacred festivals, after a long intermission, are again revived; while there is a general demand for sacrificial animals, which for some time past have met with but few purchasers. (Pliny, Letters 10.96)

Here we see one concern of the new governor: Christianity had adversely affected the economic life of Asia Minor. This only added fuel to the Roman opposition. The churches of Asia Minor became locked in a bitter struggle not only with the Roman government but with the whole culture in which they lived as well. Thus, it became Christ against culture.

Culture against Christ

The history of Roman persecution of Christians in the first century is not easy to trace, for little evidence remains. The persecution by Nero in the mid-sixties, discussed earlier (pp. 167–168), seems to have been directly aimed at Christians, but was limited to Rome and to the last four years of Nero's reign. There is no evidence that the new line of emperors beginning with Vespasian actively persecuted Christians. There is widespread evidence of local harassment in various places but none of official, government-sponsored persecution. There is some evidence of Roman action against all philosophers and against all "eastern cults," which would have affected Christians as well as others. Actually, the first definite evidence we have of Roman suppression of Christianity as a policy derives from just such a situation. Interestingly enough, it comes from Asia Minor and is reflected in the letter of Pliny partially cited above (pp. 291–292).

In this letter we learn that Pliny had published an imperial edict forbidding all "political associations." Asia Minor had continually resisted Rome's conquest, but it was especially important to maintain order at that time because Trajan was preparing for war with Parthia and his supply lines would run right across this area. Pliny had been sent out as a special Imperial legate to insure the peace. The situation was considered so volatile that Trajan had forbidden Pliny to form a fire

brigade of 150 men for "that province and especially those towns have been troubled by bodies of this kind. Whatever name we give to those who are brought into association, and whatever the purpose, they soon become gangs" (Pliny, *Letters* 10.34). Not surprisingly, the edict forbade all private associations. When Christians continued their clandestine meetings, they attracted Pliny's attention. He had already arrested, interrogated, and executed a number of Christians before he appealed to the emperor for guidance. He was uncertain, he says in the letter, whether they should be punished for the mere profession of Christianity or only for the crimes associated with it. (Crimes of atheism, cannibalism, and arson were common charges. They denied the gods, said that they ate flesh and drank blood, and spoke of setting the world on fire.) He admits he has tortured a couple of deaconesses in order to learn more about their actions and that he has executed some because they refused to forsake their religion. He reasoned that whatever the nature of their belief, refusal to obey a direct order of the governor was sufficient grounds for execution. Those who recanted, cursed Christ, and offered adoration, wine, and incense to the image of the emperor were released.

The Emperor Trajan's reply commends Pliny for the enlightened way he has handled the inquiry. Though reluctant to lay down strict rules for such cases, Trajan offers the following policies:

🙟 🙟 🙟

No search should be made for these people; when they are denounced and found guilty they must be punished; with the restriction, however, that when the party denies himself to be a Christian, and shall give proof that he is not (that is, by adoring our Gods) he shall be pardoned on the ground of repentance. . . . (Pliny, Letters 10.97)

This is our first official word on Roman attitudes toward Christians, coming two or so decades after the traditional date of the writing of Revelation, but probably reflecting earlier practice. Pliny begins by saying he has never been present at any trials of Christians, implying that such trials were already in process. The great revival of religious and economic activity he cites implies a serious effort to turn people away from this new religion. He even notes that some had left the Christians "as many as 25 years ago." Actually Trajan's policy may represent an amelioration of earlier practice, since it leaves room for repentance and forbids active searches.

The evidence in Revelation indicates that the community was being persecuted (1:9; 2:10, 13; 6:9–11; 14:12; 17:6) though it only mentions the name of one martyr, Antipas (2:13). John himself had apparently been banished rather than executed, if that is how we are to understand his presence on Patmos (1:9). There is remarkable agreement between John's account and that of Pliny: the litmus test centered on ascribing divine honors to the emperor.

John had come to see this requirement as the embodiment of evil, a conspiracy between the demonic forces and the imperial government. How abhorrent he would have found Paul's earlier advice to honor the emperor (Romans 13:1–7). How convenient those other prophets may have found such advice.

The Johannine Circle

We may then conclude that these communities represented a distinctive type of early Christianity, at odds with the more conservative Jewish Christians and the more liberal Pauline type. Its worldview is separationist and sectarian. We saw a similar sectarian attitude behind the Gospel of John, though the issues seem to be different. We must ask whether these two works stem from the same circle.

Many scholars have concluded that they do, and there is considerable evidence to relate them. Both understand Jesus' death as his decisive victory over evil. Both have strongly negative attitudes toward Jews. Both speak of Christ in similar terms: logos, witness, lamb, shepherd, judge, temple, and so on. Both view the world as existing on two levels, above and below. Both acknowledge that some significant aspect of the End is already a present reality. Both use numbers symbolically. Both focus on worship, especially the Jewish festivals, to interpret Jesus.

Other scholars highlight the serious differences between them. A problem recognized as early as the third century is the vast difference in the quality of Greek in the two works. The Greek of John's gospel is excellent; that of Revelation is poor. Both are anti-Jewish, but Revelation seems more intent on claiming the title of true Jew; in John's gospel, Jew has become a term of derision. Both pronounce the climactic formula: it is finished/it is done, but they do so in words as different as these two English translations (John 19:30, Rev. 16:17). Revelation seems to delight in the traditional apocalyptic language of Jesus' coming and the eschatological battle; John's gospel rarely uses such language.

The thrust of these and similar observations gives us no reason to believe that the same person authored both works. It is unlikely that they even derive from the same circle, understood as a formal association of prophets. Yet there are too many correlations to believe that they originate from entirely separate arenas. Probably they do come from the same communities, but are separated either by time (say, ten to twenty years) or by having as their source different factions within the larger group. All the Johannine writings reveal a community with strong factions, ranging from Jewish Christians to Gnostics. From the view of Jesus as preexistent (John's gospel), it seems that some moved on to gnosticism and others rejected such a view, insisting on a Jesus "in the flesh" (First John). Others apparently assimilated to culture ("Jezebel"); and still others rejected that culture (the Apocalypse). Let us now consider how the Apocalypse functioned in the lives of men and women in first-century Asia Minor.

The Apocalypse in the Real World

Recent attempts to explain the social function of Revelation have turned to analogies such as what scholars of religion call myth and ritual. This is a difficult concept, made more so by the popular and pejorative meaning of myth in our culture. In popular usage, a myth is something that is not true (as in, the myth of free elections in the USSR). This is the opposite of what the term means in scholarly discussion.

By the term *myth* scholars understand a story so true that it determines the truth of other stories and events. It is a world-making story. Thus it would be more proper to speak of the myth of communism in Russia, meaning thereby that the communist interpretation of reality shapes the world in that country. In the United States, we might speak of the myth of democracy. These stories shape the perceptions of life held by those who live in the respective myths.

One function of myth as it is told and acted out in ritual is to allow the believer to experience the world as it ought to be and to reshape the lived world so that it makes sense in terms of the mythic world. It is a bridge from the world of ordinary experience to the world of ultimate reality, taking the everyday up into the cosmic by means of a participation in the mythic story.

If we look back to our analysis of Revelation, we can see an analogous process at work. The hearers are first encountered in the world of ordinary experience, then they are taken on a fantastic journey into another reality. First, they meet the risen Jesus, then they ascend into Heaven itself. Finally they witness the ultimate battle— the cosmic struggle between the Dragon and the Lamb—a more uneven match would be hard to imagine. But things are not as they seem. Slain, the Lamb destroys the Dragon and his beasts. In each cycle, symbolic expression is given to the coming of Jesus in salvation and judgment, but the images of violence are transformed into images of faithful suffering. The hearers experience a vision of life that makes the unintelligible

meaningful; they are transformed as they comprehend that it is their suffering witness that brings salvation and judgment to the world—just as the suffering of Jesus was really the overthrow of evil.

We must not underestimate this experience. It is a real experience of the community, not just a glimpse of some future day that might give them courage to endure present suffering. They actually experience the "coming" of Jesus *in the present*. He comes to them through his prophet; he comes to them through the recital of the apocalyptic vision; and he comes to them in the liturgy of the Eucharist, of which this recital is a part. This present experience *looks back* to the "coming" of Jesus, which brought salvation to the world through his testimony and faithful witness (1:2; 1:18). It also *looks forward* to the "coming" of Jesus, when "every eye shall see him" (1:7). Yet the real power of the Apocalypse is not this hope for a future coming of Jesus, but their present participation in that coming.

It is the nature of ritual not to be confined to a time. Ritual transcends time. It takes place on "the Lord's day." The (present) day, which celebrates Jesus' victory over death, but also that (past) day of triumph itself (Easter morning). Further, it is that (future) "day of the Lord," which will mark the end of all things. In worship, present, past, and future blend. The liturgical recital of the Apocalypse becomes a real experience of the Kingdom of God because the worship of the community actualizes the rule of God. This is why the central theme of the Apocalypse is true worship. The struggle of the Apocalypse is the struggle between the worship of God and the worship of the beast. To worship God is to experience his kingdom. To worship the beast is to fight against that kingdom.

We might think this experience would be short-lived. That when the people leave the service and return to the suffering of the real world they will be shocked back to their senses. Yet that is exactly the point: their "sense" has been changed. Having participated in the Apocalypse they no longer consider their suffering as weakness or as something to be avoided. Now they understand that suffering rules. Their suffering will result in the fatal inebriation of the whore of Babylon. They cannot be shocked back to "reality," for they live in a new reality in which lambs conquer and suffering rules. Thus, the victims have become the victors.

While such a vision of life led to the excesses of some of the martyrs who rushed to their appointed end, it also provided a meaning in life for those who suffered helplessly at the hands of Rome. They no longer suffered helplessly; they were now in charge of their own destiny. By their faithful witness, they participated in the overthrow of evil and the establishment of God's kingdom—perhaps a greater victory than most people achieved in Roman Asia Minor.

Reading and Reflection

You are now ready for your second complete reading of Revelation. I suggest you read it aloud. If possible get together with several others, divide it up into sections, parts, voices, and read it with as much dramatic flair as you can. If you are well prepared, this should take less than an hour and a half.

RESOURCES FOR FURTHER STUDY

Two very good introductory commentaries on Revelation are those of A. Y. Collins, 1979, and Schüssler Fiorenza, 1981.

More advanced, but still very readable, commentaries include those of Sweet, 1979, Beckwith, 1919, and Mounce, 1977. Students who know Greek will profit from Caird, 1966, and Charles, 1920.

Important monographs include:

Aune, 1983, *Prophecy in Early Christianity.*
A. Y. Collins, 1984, *Crisis and Catharsis.*
Schüssler Fiorenza, 1985, *The Book of Revelation.*

The genre of apocalyptic literature is discussed in:

A. Y. Collins, 1986, *Early Christian Apocalypticism.*
J. Collins, 1979, *Apocalypse: The Morphology of a Genre.*
Hanson, 1979, *The Dawn of Apocalyptic.*
Minear, 1981, *New Testament Apocalyptic.*
Russell, 1964, *The Method and Message of Jewish Apocalyptic.*

For the study of other apocalypses see J. Collins, 1984; Stone, 1984; and the resources cited on pp. 271.

Studies oriented toward a literary understanding include:

Efird, 1978, *Daniel and Revelation.*
Schick, 1977, *Revelation: The Last Book of the Bible.*

And on a more advanced level:

Farrer, 1949, *The Rebirth of Images,* and especially 1964, *The Revelation of St. John the Divine.*
Schüssler Fiorenza, 1977, explores a structuralist reading.
Kermode, 1967, *The Sense of an Ending.*
Wilder, 1971, *Early Christian Rhetoric.*

The phenomenon of myth and ritual and the social impact of Revelation can be pursued in:

Aune, 1972, *The Cultic Setting of Realized Eschatology.*
Berger and Luckmann, 1966, *The Social Construction of Reality.*
Cabannis, 1970, *Liturgy and Literature.*
A. Y. Collins, 1976, *The Combat Myth in the Book of Revelation.*
Court, 1979, *Myth and History in the Book of Revelation.*

Eliade, 1959, *Cosmos and History*.
Gager, 1975, *Kingdom and Community*.
Hooke, 1935, *Myth and Ritual*.
Levi-Strauss, 1967, "The Effectiveness of Symbols."
Rowland, 1982, *The Open Heaven*.
Shepherd, 1960, *The Pascal Liturgy and the Apocalypse*.

The question of Roman attitudes toward Christians is addressed in most of the commentaries and in many of the monographs mentioned above. The following are more specialized studies:

Frend, 1967, *Martyrdom and Persecution in the Early Church*.
Horbury and McNeil, 1981, *Suffering and Martyrdom in the New Testament*.
Plescia, 1971, "On the Persecution of Christians in the Roman Empire."
Wilken, 1984, *The Christians as the Romans Saw Them*.

Echoes of Other Stories

❧ ❧ ❧

James, Jude, Hebrews, Peter

The Family of Jesus: James and Jude
Traditions of a Hellenized Judaism: Hebrews
Traditions Associated with Peter
How Jewish Was Jewish Christianity?
Resources for Further Study

12

The New Testament is not a historically balanced document. More than one quarter of it is the work of one writer (Luke-Acts), a writer who exalts Paul. In addition, Paul's authority stands behind nearly half (thirteen) of the twenty-seven writings in the New Testament. This strong emphasis on the Pauline tradition means that many other traditions have been recorded less completely. Acts, for example, is often called the "Acts of the Apostles," but we learn little from it about most of the apostles: Judas' suicide, James' martyrdom, and Peter's early ministry. Nothing is said of their careers nor of their distinctive accomplishments or individual views. Concerning nine of the original twelve apostles we learn almost nothing. About dozens of others we know little more than their names: Matthias, Apollos, Nicanor, Nicholaus, Ananias, Aquila, Priscilla, Mary, Lydia, James, Archippus, Sosthenes, Onesimus. Their stories remain untold. Of countless others, we know not even their names.

From this silence a few voices do speak, briefly, hardly more than an echo of the living stories. Five short writings made their way into the canon, preserving vivid impressions of diverse kinds of early Christians. One of these works, Hebrews, is anonymous, but its very name reveals its close ties to Christians with Jewish roots. Another claims James, brother of Jesus and head of the church in Jerusalem, as its author. Again, clearly a Jewish orientation. A third, hardly one page long, is written in the name of Jude, another brother of Jesus. Finally two works are attributed to Peter, but they are themselves works of different orientations. We saw from our study of Paul that Peter was a mediating figure between the thoroughly Jewish Christianity of James

and the Gentile Christianity of Paul. In Acts he appears as Paul's ally, while in the anti-Pauline trajectory we saw him portrayed as the enemy of Paul. The two letters preserved in his name represent a more positive response to Paul.

These five writings are usually known as the General Epistles (because they are not addressed to a specific church) or the Catholic Epistles (Catholic means "universal," and they speak to the whole church). They could well be called the Jewish Epistles, since they stem from that segment of the early church we designate Jewish Christianity. They represent somewhat different versions of the Christian story than we have studied so far and will help us appreciate the diversity and commonality within early Christianity.

THE FAMILY OF JESUS:
James and Jude

We find real ambiguity toward Jesus' family in early Christian writings. As we learned earlier, Mark shows his family trying to suppress Jesus' activities (3:21, 31–35) and John explicitly states that they did not believe in him (7:1–5). Yet from Paul we learn that one of the resurrection appearances was said to be to James (I Cor. 15:7), who was considered one of the apostles and a leader of the Jerusalem assembly (Gal. 1:19, and Acts 1:14). Eusebius claims that James was the first bishop of Jerusalem, followed by Symeon, a cousin of Jesus (*Church History* 3.11.1).

According to the gospel traditions Jesus had four brothers, Jacobos (which nearly all English versions give as James), Joses, Judas, and Simon, and at least two sisters (Mark 6:3 and Matt. 13:55). Like the name Jesus, these are Greek

versions of traditional Jewish names: Jesus/
Joshua, Jacobos/Jacob, Joses/Joseph, Judas/
Judah, Simon/Simeon. In the early traditions they
are said to be brothers, with no further explanation, and one assumes the writers meant actual
brothers. However, in the middle of the second
century, clear traditions regard these brothers as
children of Joseph by a previous marriage (*Protoevangelium of James* 9:2, in Hennecke and
Schneemelcher, I: 379). These traditions coin-
cide with the increasing exaltation of Mary and
the understanding that she remained a virgin
throughout her life. In the fourth century Jerome
argued that they were really cousins of Jesus,
children of Mary's sister who was also, and con-
fusingly, named Mary. This rather unlikely hypothesis became the standard opinion in the Middle Ages.

While we lack the historical sources necessary
to trace these traditions, we may assume that Jesus' relatives, and especially his brothers, enjoyed significant authority within the early Christian movement, at least within those segments of
the movement that looked to Jerusalem for leadership. Writings in the names of these brothers
would have carried far more authority than we
might initially assume. Simon and Joses have left
little mark, Judas only a trace, but an extensive
tradition developed around James.

Traditions about James

Like Paul, James was not only a historical figure
but also a legendary one, and the hero of one
branch of the emerging Christian movement. In
Paul's time, "certain men from James" urged
stricter Jewish practice at Antioch (Gal. 2:12).
Acts identified him with those observant Jews who
did not insist on Gentile observance of the Law
(21:18–20; 15:13–21); others claimed him for
the stringent anti-Paulinists who insisted on complete observance of the commandments (the anti-
Pauline *Letter of Peter to James,* along with an
endorsement by James, can be found in Hennecke, II: 111–115; for the anti-Pauline tradition

and the various tendencies within Jewish Christianity, see p. 130). He is often called James the
Righteous, which implies his faithful observance
of the Law. The *Gospel of Thomas* refers to him
as "James the Just, for whose sake heaven and
earth came into being" (12). In the *Gospel of the
Hebrews,* and probably in the tradition behind I
Corinthians (15:7), he was the first to encounter
the resurrected Jesus (7; in Hennecke, I: 165).
Hegesippus, a Jewish Christian living in Palestine about 150, described James thus:

❢ ❢ ❢

*James, the Lord's brother, received control of
the Church, together with the apostles. He is
called James the Righteous by everyone from the
Lord's time till our own, for there were many
named James. This one was holy from his birth;
he drank no wine or intoxicating liquor and ate
no meat; no razor came near his head; he did not
smear himself with oil, and did not go to the
baths. This one alone was permitted to enter
the Temple sanctuary, for he did not wear wool
but linen. And alone he would enter the Temple and be found on his knees, praying for forgiveness for the people, so that his knees grew
hard like a camel's. . . . (quoted by Eusebius,*
Church History 2.23.4 *from a lost work of Hegesippus,* Memoirs)

How early this legendary portrait of James took
shape is not clear, but certainly those who preserved it regarded James as law-observant, veg-
etarian, teetotaling, ascetic, and so extraordinarily pious that he was allowed to dress in priestly
garments and enter the Temple. These are the extreme expression of motifs found throughout the
James traditions.

Five writings come down to us in the name
of James: two with the title *The Apocalypse of
James* and two letters, one in Coptic (Egyptian)
and one in Greek, and a *Book of James* more
commonly known today as the *Infancy Gospel of
James* or *The Protoevangelium of James.* This
last mentioned work recounts the birth of Mary
and has no connection with James other than the

use of his name (translation in Hennecke, I: 370–388). The two apocalypses and the Coptic letter are late works, perhaps from the third century. Though they contain many Jewish Christian themes, they have been deeply influenced by Gnostic ideas. Most of the texts of these three writings had been lost until the great discovery, in 1946, of a Gnostic Christian library from the fourth century at Nag Hammadi in Egypt. These texts have been published and an English translation is now available (Robinson, 1977). It is unlikely that any of these have a direct connection with James, though their incorporation of legendary material about James indicates they stem from one trajectory of the James tradition.

The Letter of James

The Greek Letter of James is that found in the New Testament. It stems from the first century, and although it may contain traditions derived from James, it was probably not actually written by him. At least it does not seem to have been so regarded until Origen, after 200 (Eusebius, *Church History* 2.23.24–25, 3.25.3). Jerome reports that it was thought to have been written by someone else in James' name but later gradually gained authority (IDB 2: 795). It is possible, however, that these negative opinions stemmed from its Jewishness and its non-Pauline character, since neither Origen nor Jerome had much sympathy for a Jewish version of Christianity. (On the meaning of authorship in antiquity, see pp. 45–47.)

The internal evidence for authorship is indeterminate, since we have no other James tradition against which to measure it. We could argue that its excellent Greek style would be beyond a Palestinian Jew like James, but that would surely indicate some prejudice on our part. Many Palestinian Jews were fluent in both Greek and Aramaic. Besides, a significant number of Hebraic expressions underlie the Greek (IDB 5: 469). For now, we will leave the question of authorship open as we read the letter. It may have been written by James (who died in 62) or by one claiming his traditions in the next three or four decades. Our only basis for deciding will be the content of the letter itself.

The Meaning of the Letter

As you read the Letter of James, you will notice that it is not a letter in our sense. It is not a communication sent on some specific occasion from one person to another. The concern of the letter is not some specific historical problem, but the general issue of ethical exhortation. It is a moral essay dressed up like a letter; such "letters on morality" were common in antiquity, as the letters of Cicero and Seneca show.

The organization of the letter is very loose, but again, typical of this kind of writing. Seeking to move the hearers to certain kinds of action in the present involved what the ancients called demonstrative rhetoric; it was not formally organized and consisted chiefly of an ordered series of topics. Rhetorical effect is achieved by repetition, amplification, comparison, and striking statement rather than by a well-ordered

---

READING GUIDE TO JAMES

Theme: the role of steadfastness   1:1–4
Wisdom and faith as sources of steadfastness   1:5–18
Good works as a result of steadfastness
1:19–2:26
   Expressed toward the powerless
   Faith is dead without works
Teachers must excel   3:1–4:12
   Control of the tongue
   Possession of wisdom
   Lead to peace
Rich often fail   4:13–5:6
Final advice   5:7–20
   Patience, truthfulness, prayer
   Rescue the wanderers

argument. (For a comparison with other types of rhetoric see the Introduction, pp. 8–9 and Chapter 5, p. 116.) Our reading guide to James only suggests the flow of the thought.

Reading and Reflection

Read the Letter of James, then make a list of the *specific* problems it addresses. Were such problems more likely to arise in a Jewish, Gentile, or mixed community?

The letter opens with a common rhetorical device, a chain of virtues: people should rejoice over their trials, for trials lead to patience and patience leads to perfection (1:2–4). Patience here signifies steadfastness or endurance; perfection might be better translated as completeness or maturity (*telos* in Greek). Such a chain, even these specific virtues, was commonly urged in Jewish, Stoic, and Christian writings. The basic impulse of Stoicism was to meet all life's developments with steadfastness, achieving that inner calm of the rational creature. Actually, little about this letter is distinctively Christian. Put another way, Christian morality for our author is not very different from any other kind of morality.

This exhortation also provides the foundation for all that follows in the letter; the remainder may be regarded as more specific instructions on how to achieve the steadfastness that leads to maturity. Within this basic framework of trials-steadfastness-maturity the author's mind seems to wander freely from topic to topic: wisdom, faith, and a grasp of one's mortality are the prerequisites for steadfastness (1:4–15); these come from God (1:16–18) and lead to a practical, moral doing of good deeds (1:19–27). This morality is most evident when expressed toward the poor and powerless (1:27–2:13). Faith without good works

is false (2:14–26). Even higher standards are demanded of teachers (3:1), who must be able to control their tongues (3:2–12) and possess the heavenly wisdom (3:13–18) that leads to peace rather than the passion that leads to strife (4:1–12). Merchants and the rich, especially, fail in such matters (4:13–5:6). Patience, truthfulness, and prayer are necessary as they await the coming of the Lord (5:7–18). Those who wander from the truth should be rescued (5:19–20). Surprisingly, the work has no formal conclusion, final summary, or letter characteristics to mark the end.

In these seemingly random exhortations, we find various rhetorical flourishes that indicate a keen ear for Greek, including repetition, rhyme, word play, puns, alliteration, sequences, parallelism, and the diatribe. Even in English the rhetorical polish of passages such as 5:7–11 and 2:14–26 is evident. The ability to use such devices suggests that our author knew Greek rather well.

James versus Paul?

Ethics is a dangerous enterprise. For, on the one hand, one can mistake the understanding of virtue for its accomplishment (like the person who is proud of achieving humility), and, on the other, the very struggle for ethical achievement may become an end in itself. This last is known as *legalism,* in which attaining the good is understood as a matter of keeping certain rules. Such rules bind the believer to lesser powers than God, according to Paul's argument in Galatians, but they also bind God: He, too, must play by the rules and duly reward those who are good. Thus one may, indeed must, earn one's salvation by performing good works. In our study of Romans (pp. 100–103), we learned that legalism was a constant temptation for early Christians and Jews.

Paul met the challenge of legalism by insisting on the absolute freedom of the Christian (Galatians) and by asserting the absolute priority of faith over good works (Romans). In Abraham he found a clear example of this priority. James saw the Abraham story differently.

Reading and Reflection

Compare Galatians 3:6–9, Romans 4:1–25, and James 2:14–26. Of what is Abraham an example? What is the relationship between faith and works?

The points of contact and the striking points of contrast between Paul and James have led some interpreters to think that James was attacking Paul. And, if taken in an abstract or absolute sense, they do contradict each other. Paul argued that Abraham was put right with God through faith (hence, keeping the Law was unnecessary), but James responds that Abraham was put right with God by his works (thus, faith alone is inadequate). Both claim Abraham as the model of righteousness, but they draw opposite conclusions. How, then, shall we understand the relationship between these two?

First, we find that they appeal to different aspects of the Abraham tradition. For Paul, Abraham's trust in God led him to leave his homeland and to seek an heir from Sarah. For James, his sacrifice of Isaac perfected his faith by his works. Paul focused on the inaugurating events while James looked to climactic events. Because they are speaking in different contexts, we naturally expect them to say different things.

Second, although they use the same words, they seem to have different definitions for them. In fact, if we probe beneath the words, their meanings are very much alike. James equates "faith" with believing in God (2:19), but Paul understands faith to be a solid trust in God that influences the course of one's life. In other words, Paul includes in "faith" what James defines as "faith and works." Both assert that only this life-changing response to God is adequate. Rather than attack Paul, James seems to be opposing someone using Paul's words with a different meaning than Paul attached to them.

Finally, however, we must not minimize the distance between James and Paul. The very fact that they emphasize different aspects of the Abraham story indicates that they themselves lived in different versions of the Christian story. Paul stood on the boundary of Israel, reaching out to the Gentiles, inaugurating a new event as surely as did his model Abraham. James stood within the establishment, observing the ongoing life of the community. James belonged to those who were more impressed with the continuity of Christianity with the past work of God in Israel than with the novelty of including the Gentiles. Thus, James represents a more Jewish Christianity.

The Context of James

Little can be said with certainty about the authorship or date of this moral tract. It could have been written by James, or by one of his disciples, or by someone who felt attached to that tradition. Arguments are possible on both sides: The very good command of Greek that our author displays might point to a setting in the Hellenistic world outside Palestine (thus, to an author other than James), but the number of underlying Semitic expressions probably indicate a native Hebrew speaker. On the one hand, the opening address ("To the twelve tribes in the Dispersion") indicates that the geographical sphere of the letter is the Hellenistic world, far beyond the influence of James in Jerusalem. Yet on the other, the assumption of this very address, its implied point of view, is that the writer is living in the homeland. The references to Jesus are so sparse and so general that it is hard to imagine this work was written by his brother, yet there are strong echoes of those teachings of Jesus now preserved in the Sermon on the Mount, widely regarded as his most characteristic (for example, 5:1–6, 12; 1:22; 2:8, 12; 3:18). James seems to demand rigorous keeping of the Law, even every point of the Law (2:10); yet he defines the Law by the very paradigm used by Paul: love your neighbor as yourself (2:8; Rom. 13:8).

The date of the writing remains elusive. The

crucial issue is: How does what is said here relate to Paul? The analysis above implies that James was directed not against Paul but against an oversimplification of Pauline tradition. But when did such an oversimplification arise? We know that some of Paul's followers in the late first century reduced the definition of faith to belief, which is the sort of faith James finds inadequate. We saw this precise use of faith as a noun rather than as a verb in the Pauline trajectory that led the Pastoral letters, for example (p. 120). This might mean James was written near the end of the first century, long after the death of the historical James in 62.

However, the rhetorical questions that Paul included in Romans (for example, 6:15) indicate that such oversimplification was possible in his lifetime, at least by his opponents. This might mean that James was directed against the same oversimplification of his teachings that Paul himself fought. If so, it is surprising that there is not even a mention of those aspects of the Law over which James and Paul struggled (circumcision and the dietary laws—Gal. 2:12). This omission probably, but not certainly, points to a controversy after the time of Paul and James. While we cannot be sure of either date or authorship, two other kinds of considerations will help us locate the situation of the letter more accurately.

First, we can observe the kinds of advice given, and ask who would need this sort of exhortation. We have already learned that a good deal of the letter has a Jewish cast. The work is so completely in the Jewish tradition that some argue that it was originally a Jewish tract, now rewritten to insert a few Christian references. Jesus is only referred to twice (1:1, 2:1). If we deleted these two references and change one or two other words, this letter would be wholly Jewish. The major concerns, such as the doing of the Law and the protecting of the weak, are typical of Jewish ethical exhortation. In addition, the designation of the assembly as "synagogue" (2:2, Greek), the appeal to "Abraham, our father" (2:21), and the appeals to the wisdom tradition (1:5; 3:13) point to a Jewish milieu. The primary

office in the church seems to be teacher (3:1) and there is little evidence of hierarchical organization—both are more typical of the synagogue than of the church.

The advice given in the letter also indicates that the community contains both the poor and the very wealthy: merchants are admonished (4:13–17); the rich are chastised (5:1–11); and the gold ring (2:2) marks the visitor as a member of the Roman aristocracy who alone were permitted to wear such rings in this period. It is, then, a mixed community in which our author is trying to instill some of the ideal of poverty. Such exhortation seems most appropriate to a Jewish community of the Diaspora that includes Gentiles.

Gentile influence may also be seen in the conviction that God gives wisdom "to all" people (1:5), the reference to God as the "Father of lights" (1:17), and the definition of faith as belief in God (2:19). Some refinement of this point may be achieved by a second strategy, comparing the advice given in James with another writing, known to be addressed to a Gentile audience.

There is an early second-century work known as the *Didache* (Did-da-kay'), or the *Teaching of the Twelve Apostles*. This essay is slightly longer than James and seems to have been used by the Syrian churches in the early second century. The first half is an ethical exhortation based on the Jewish Wisdom tradition of two ways: a way of life and a way of death. The last half gives instructions for baptism, celebration of the Eucharist, and the role of prophets. The *Didache* shares much with James, including the summary of the Law as the two great commandments (James 2:8; *Did*. 1:2) and multiple allusions to the Jesus tradition (*Did*. 1:3–6). But the specific exhortations differ markedly: the *Didache* admonishes against homosexuality with young boys and condemns abortion and infanticide (2:2); it forbids eating meat offered to idols (6:3). These are specific ethical problems Gentiles would bring to Christianity; they would not have been issues for Jews. Thus, the *Didache* is addressed explicitly as "the teaching of the Lord to the nations (Gentiles) through the twelve apostles (1:1).

None of this is characteristic of James. The community to which James is addressed probably included Gentiles, but Jews and Jewish ethics still predominated. Gentiles seem to have been incorporated into Israel, becoming a part of the twelve tribes of the Diaspora (1:1). James seems to represent a version of Christianity that was itself substantially Jewish. That there were such Jewish versions of Christianity, and that they were associated with the name of James, has become increasingly clear from recent research.

The Letter of Jude

Although the Greek text of this letter names the author as "Judas, the brother of Jacob," Christian tradition has regularly shortened the name to "Jude," probably because of the infamy of that disciple named Judas who betrayed Jesus. Judas was a common name of this period, being the Greek form of the Hebrew Judah. We know nothing else about the author other than his claim to be the brother of Jacob (James), and thus by implication the brother of Jesus. Whether he was so related, or merely claiming that tradition, is disputed.

Jude, like James, is a letter only in a formal sense; actually it is more of an exhortation. Its address could hardly be more general: "to those who are called." There may be some irony here, for among Gnostics the "called" were the common Christians as opposed to the "elect" Gnostic few. Lacking all the traits of an actual letter, Jude is a tract or sermon in letter form. It is a partic-

---

READING GUIDE TO JUDE

Letter opening   1–2
Purpose: to contend for the faith   3–4
   Exposition of Scripture   5–19
   Exhortation to faithfulness   20–23
Final blessing   24–25

---

ularly fine example of a type of an ancient rhetorical exercise known as invective, the dark side of demonstrative rhetoric, the opposite of eulogy. As eulogy intends to praise the worthy, so invective seeks to damn the unworthy (Matt. 23).

Jude is a very short work, having only one chapter, and its structure is straightforward.

Reading and Reflection

As you read Jude, notice all the forms of vilification used to attack those regarded as unworthy, usually called the heretics.

Our author uses three devices to discredit those believed to have abandoned apostolic faith; they range from simple name-calling (4, 11–12, 16, 19), to disparagement of their morality (4, 8, 10), to powerful comparisons with biblical and apocryphal examples (5, 6, 7, 9, 11, 15). The power of this condemnation stems from the vividness of the language and the tying together of the various techniques. Thus the "ungodly," who are said to be "licentious" and to "defile the flesh," are compared to "Sodom and Gomorrah" (4, 7, 8). The series of metaphors in 12–13 are powerful and provocative.

On the positive side, the hearers are exhorted to "contend for the faith which was once for all delivered to the saints" (3). While this appears to be a cogent appeal, we must realize that we are given no clue as to what this faith was thought to be. Instead, it is a general appeal to "apostolic tradition" (verse 17). Much the same can be said about the rejected tradition: we find only vague generalities. "They" are ungodly; "we" are apostolic. But the identity and the teachings of the *they* and the *we* are left undefined.

The social function of this kind of writing is not to define and expel the heretic, but to unify the group and make deviance from the norm less likely. This writing probably stems from a group of Christians conscious of their own identity and of their differences from other groups. The references to preserving the apostolic tradition (3, 17) probably place them in the late first or early second century. The claim to the Jude tradition and the citation of noncanonical writings like *Enoch* (14) and the *Assumption of Moses* (9) place them within the framework of Jewish Christianity. These writings were especially popular with the marginal movements among the Jews, such as those at Qumran.

Jude seems to represent a more sectarian spirit than James and gives no evidence of including Gentiles. They lived in a rich story world that not only looked to the angels as examples, but ascribed honors to them (8–9). They saw themselves as heirs to the Exodus (5), now awaiting their final deliverance. Their main task in the interim was to be holy (20–21). In this way too, they resembled the Jews of Qumran.

TRADITIONS OF A HELLENIZED JUDAISM: *Hebrews*

Though commonly known as the Letter to the Hebrews and often attributed to Paul, this work is neither Pauline nor is it a letter. It even departs from the form of a letter, at least until the very end. Even then the writer declares, "I exhort you, brethren, bear with my word of exhortation, for I have written unto you briefly" (13:22). We might well regard it as an exhortation discourse, though the writer must have smiled a little when he added the "briefly." Containing some twenty-five pages of closely connected argument, this is a lengthy work by ancient standards. Such exhortations were often connected with the explanation of a reading from Scripture (Acts 13:15).

The Structure of the Argument

Hebrews is a good example of deliberative rhetoric, a work that attempts to prove a case and move the hearers to a specific course of future action. Deliberative oratory did not adhere to strict organization; all that was required was an introduction and a conclusion, between which a proposition was stated and proven.

Reading and Reflection

Read Hebrews 1–2 and 12–13. What seems to be the thesis of this work? What do you take to be the thrust of the argument?

The basic structure of Hebrews consists of a series of passages alternating between the explanation of an idea and the elaboration of the implications of that idea. It begins by contrasting the former and current revelations of God, then draws the implications: therefore we must pay close attention (2:1). This is the constant pattern: first an idea is discussed, then there is the exhortation on the implications of neglecting this idea. The diagram shows the shape of the letter.

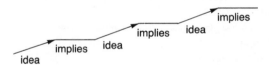

In effect, our writer has interwoven two presentations: a theoretical argument about the superiority of the new revelation to the old and an exhortation to greater moral accomplishment. The ideas lead to the implications, and the implications in turn lead on to new ideas that have further implications. The underlying logic is what we call *a fortiori:* if the lesser is true, then how much more true is the greater. (Put another way: if your dad was unhappy when you broke his lawn mower, how much more unhappy will he be when you wreck the car.) In Hebrews, the argument that the new way is superior to the old has implications that require more of the followers of that new way. The continual interaction between these two aspects of the argument, the superiority of the new way and the increased responsibility, gives the work a dynamic quality and an apparent complexity. The interaction is so pervasive that it is not always possible to be sure when the author passes from idea to implication, but the following scheme is widely adopted.

The major portion of the argument centers on Jesus as high priest (4:14–10:39), a startling idea. No other New Testament document calls Jesus a high priest, though certain priestly themes are associated with him (such as atoning for sins). In fact, the widespread tradition that Jesus is a descendant of David would seem to preclude any priestly service, since priests were from the tribe of Levi not from Judah. We will examine this priestly tradition more closely further on.

Preceding the major division is a short section arguing the superiority of Jesus to earlier mediators, the angels, the prophets, and Moses (chapters 1 and 2, with the accompanying exhortation). Following it, another short section portrays the great faith of the heroes of the earlier traditions (11, with the accompanying exhortations). Rhetorically speaking, these constitute the introduction and the conclusion to the main argument. In Hebrews, the main argument (4–10) concerns the establishment of Jesus' priestly service and the implications of that service for life and worship. Both the introduction and the conclusion center on the superiority of Jesus over the earlier heroes, and therefore the greater responsibility of those who would follow him (*a fortiori*). The priestly theme is introduced at 2:17 and culminates at 13:10–16. The basic line of the argument is given in the following verses: 1:1–4; 2:1; 3:1; 4:14; 5:7; 6:1–6; 8:1–2; 9:6–11, 15; 10:19–25; 12:1–2; 12:18–29, which provide a kind of synopsis of the book. Before we examine the argument more closely, we must devote some attention to the probable contexts of this work.

READING GUIDE TO HEBREWS

The Revelation of a Son is superior to that through angels or prophets   1:1–14
    Exhortation: pay more attention   2:1–4
As human, Jesus is superior not only to angels but also to Moses   2:5–3:5
    Exhortation: do not miss the promised rest   3:6–4:13
Jesus the Son of God is the great high priest   4:14–5:11
    Exhortation: go beyond the elementary   5:12–6:20
The high priest after the order of Melchizedek   7:1–10:18
    Exhortation: draw near to God   10:19–39
The witnesses of faith   11:1–40
    Exhortation: strive for holiness   12:1–10
        Miscellaneous exhortations   12:11–13:21
        Final exhortations in letter form   13:22–25

Imagining Contexts

"To the Hebrews" occurs as a title on the earliest manuscripts we possess but is not a part of the text. It would have been added when this work was included with others in a collection. It rests, in part, on the way the work identifies with the Jews (1:1; 2:11, 16, etc.). No author is indicated, nor can one be deduced. Some of the more interesting suggestions, in addition to Paul, include Barnabas, Apollos, and Priscilla—all are mere guesses. Although it was once attributed to Paul, it has nothing in common with the Pauline letters except an incidental reference to Timothy in the closing. That closing also contains the only geographical reference in the work: "They of Italy salute you" (13:24). This could mean the writing was sent from Italy, or it might only indicate people of Italian origin living elsewhere.

The only temporal reference in the work implies that the priests still minister at the altar in Jerusalem (8:4). If taken literally, this requires a date before 70 when the Temple was destroyed by the Romans. But perhaps we should not understand it this way, since our author never refers to the Temple but only to the tent or tabernacle, the portable shrine of the pre-Temple period in Israel. It is also possible that some priests continued to minister in the ruins of the Temple until it was utterly destroyed in 135. The case against an early date is that the leaders of the community claim apostolic descent and belong to the next generation (2:3).

The internal evidence for establishing the setting of Hebrews is scant. The best we can do is hazard a guess based on the general nature of the work and on our knowledge of similar works. Three possibilities have emerged, and each contributes something to our understanding of Hebrews.

The Alexandrian Judaism of Philo

Alexandria, in Egypt, was one of a hundred such cities that Alexander the Great had founded in his own honor when he conquered the world from Greece to India shortly before 300 BCE. But it became *the* Alexandria, the intellectual and cultural capital of the world. The library there surpassed all others, not only collecting but editing the texts of the classical authors and producing the first known critical editions. It was a spectacular city—its main east-west street was a hundred feet wide. Population figures are hard to come by, but it is estimated that one to two million people lived there in the first century. There were three main social groups: the Greeks, the native Egyptians, and the Jews. By the first century the upper classes in these separate communities had begun to intermarry. The Jews had the right to self-rule and constituted the largest concentration of Jews outside Palestine. This community translated the Hebrew Scriptures into Greek in the version known as the Septuagint (between 300 and 150 BCE).

From this community we know, especially, one man: Philo of Alexandria (about 20 BCE–45 CE). Born into a wealthy family, he received a thorough education in both Greek and Jewish culture, though he never learned Hebrew. Philo's immense scholarship (more than thirty-five of his

works have come down to us) was built on one central assumption: Judaism was a more perfect form of Greek philosophy. Both older and more precise than the philosophers, the Law contained all their central ideas. For example, philosophy taught the control of the passions through reason. So too did Moses, according to Philo, in the story of creation. For God first presented Adam with the animals (emotions), but found no suitable helper among them. Only the special creation of Eve (reason) produced a companion worthy of human creation (Gen. 2:15–24). Philo relied heavily on such allegorical interpretations of Scripture, always exploring what was taught by the philosophers, especially the Stoics. It was Philo's conviction that everything in Scripture had a symbolic meaning. Thus the Sabbath rest pointed to God the Unmoved Mover; Feast days symbolized gladness of the soul; circumcision portrayed the cutting off of excess pleasure and passions (*Migration of Abraham* 91–92).

Symbolic meanings are everywhere because this world itself is a reflection of the Eternal. Following Plato, Philo viewed the world as a copy of the eternal forms. The Tabernacle was a perfect example of the way this world is a copy of the Divine:

🙠 🙠 🙠

*When God willed to send down the image of divine excellence from heaven to earth in pity for our race, that it should not lose its share in the better lot, he constructs as a symbol of the truth the holy tabernacle and its contents to be a representation and copy of wisdom. (*Who Is the Heir of Divine Things? *112)*

Thus by studying the copy one could learn about the reality, for they correspond.

Philo went even further. He saw in the creation story and its declaration that God created humankind "after his image" not only a correspondence between divine and human wisdom, but the existence of an independent heavenly wisdom that was itself the image of God (*Who is the Heir?* 230–231). This divine image, the pattern from which humanity was made, Philo called the Logos, a term the Stoics used for Reason. This Logos stands on the boundary between God and creation, revealing the One to the many and "pleading with the immortal as suppliant for afflicted mortality" (*Who is Heir?* 205). (See discussion of Logos, pp. 244–247.)

This conception of the world as a reflection of the heavenly reality, as well as this vision of the heavenly mediator, helps clarify the meaning of Hebrews (see, especially, Hebrews 8).

The Ascetic Judaism of the Essenes

A general introduction to the Essenes accompanied our discussion of the various Jewish movements of the first century (pp. 62, 200). Two facets of the movement stand out in relation to Hebrews: their priestly nature and their strong asceticism. The Essene movement seems to have come into being over a struggle for the office of high priest. When the Maccabees were fighting against the religious suppression of Antiochus Epiphanes (shortly before 150 BCE) they were joined by many pious Jews who saw this as a struggle of light against darkness. But when the Maccabees eventually prevailed, they gravely disappointed many of their followers. For instead of purifying the Temple and reappointing the legitimate high priest, who traditionally had to be a descendant of Zadok, they assumed that office themselves. In the view of some, this completed the defiling of the Temple begun by Antiochus.

The historical sequence is vague, but many of these protesters seem to have retreated to Qumran, a monastic community in the hills around the Dead Sea.[1] At Qumran they established the true Israel and the true Temple, their community. Their spiritual worship and common meal became the true sacrifice. Within their community, the zadokite high priest ruled, and at the end of the age they expected both the princely messiah

of common tradition and a second, priestly messiah (*Community Rule 9* and the *Messianic Rule.*) The priestly messiah was to be the teacher of the community, even as the living priest was the current teacher.

This understanding of the community as the Temple resulted in a strong emphasis on purity— both ritual and moral. Since women were considered ritually unclean during their monthly cycles, they were not permitted in the community at Qumran. In a striking departure from Jewish practice, the men at Qumran were celibate. (Other Essenes married, but not those at Qumran.) They swore obedience to their superiors, all who had entered the order before them, and organized their day around work and worship so that some members of the community were always at prayer, day and night. They pledged themselves to keep the whole Law, as it was interpreted and expanded by the teacher of righteousness. Their interpretation of Scripture was literal and imaginative. They applied the laws directly to their own situation, but also engaged in highly symbolic interpretation to show that the Scriptures were fulfilled in the experience of their own community. They believed they lived in the time of fulfillment and that God had established with them the new covenant prophesied by Jeremiah (Jer. 31; see *Community Rule* 1, 5). Their goal was nothing less than perfection, both individual and communal.

Like the Essenes, the community behind Hebrews believed themselves to be the true Israel, who served God with purity and sacrifice (see, especially, Hebrews 13).

The Esoteric Judaism of the Mystics

The prevailing forms of Judaism and Christianity have been essentially rationalistic, and only scant attention has been paid to their more mystical aspects. This is especially true of Judaism, the tendency being abetted by the common Christian misconception of Judaism as a legalistic religion. More recently, especially because of the pioneering work of Gershom Sholem, it has become

---

1. Most of their history must be reconstructed from allusions in the *Damascus Rule* and the *Commentary on Habakkuk*. For a concise discussion, see Vermes, 1977:137–162.

evident that there was a mystical strand even among the rabbis. This mysticism centered on the vision of God, or of the throne or chariot of God, in which the mystic felt transported into paradise.

Many surviving Jewish writings show traces of such mysticism. Enoch describes the ascent into heaven in mystic imagery of fire and ice (*I Enoch* 14). The *Apocalypse of Abraham*, probably written about the same time as Hebrews, portrays Abraham's ascent to heaven where he sees the throne of God, a throne of fire, and the chariot of God. He attains this vision through worship and the repeated recitation of a heavenly song, taught him by an angel (15–18):

ぶ ぶ ぶ

You are he my soul has loved, my protector. Eternal, firey, shining, light-giving, thunder-voiced, lightning-visioned, many eyed, receiving the petitions of those who honor you and turning away from the petitions of those who restrain you by the restraint of their provocations, redeemer of those who dwell in the midst of the wicked ones, of those who are dispersed among the just of the world, in the corruptible age. . . . (17:14–17)

The goal of this sort of mysticism was to ascend through the various (usually seven) heavens by means of mystical experiences, so that one eventually beheld the exalted throne of God (compare II Cor. 12:1–4 and Rev. 4).

So too, the hearers of Hebrews were admonished to go beyond the elementary (6:1–8), to ascend to the throne of grace (4:16), and the worship at the Heavenly Zion (12:18–29). With these three contexts in mind, let us examine the meaning of Hebrews in more detail.

Understanding Hebrews

The general meaning of Hebrews centers on the superiority of Christ, the Son, to the various messengers of God. But the specific meaning of this theme for its first hearers demands closer ex-

amination. We will examine two important, but somewhat varied, passages in order to illustrate the various ways Hebrews corresponds to these contexts. The first selection, the opening, is replete with technical words; the second, chapter 9, presents us with a clear portrayal of the world-view that underlies this writing.

The Opening

The following translation attempts to capture something of the structure and meaning of this passage.

ぶ ぶ ぶ

In many parts and in many ways
*   having spoken long ago to the fathers in the*
*   prophets,*
God spoke in the last of these days to us in a
son,
*   whom he appointed heir of all things,*
*   through whom also he made the spheres*
*   who*
*   because he is the brightness of his glory*
*   and the stamp of his being,*
*   because he upholds all things in his pow-*
*   erful word,*
*   because he made himself a purification of*
*   sins,*
*   sat down on the right hand of the Majesty on*
*   High,*
*   having become so much superior to angels*
*   by as much as*
*   he has inherited a more excellent name*
*   than they.*
*   (Hebrews 1:1–4, original translation)*

This is a marvelous example of the kind of sentence favored by an educated Greek audience: complex, balanced, protracted. The basic point is made by the subject and verb in line three: God spoke. The contrast between his former speaking (partial and piecemeal) and his latter speaking is evident. The son is then described by three relative clauses (whom, through whom, who) each of which employs a vocabulary remarkably reminiscent of Philo of Alexandria. He is said to be the heir, maker of the spheres, the brightness, and the stamp. The heir may be understood in messianic terms (Ps. 2:8) and in wisdom terms (Prov. 3:35), which Philo developed by proclaiming wisdom to be the heir of the world and of all things (*Who is the Heir?* 98).

The word translated as "spheres" here is a distinctive Greek word sometimes translated as "ages" or "times." For Philo these spheres are the eternal counterparts of actual times (*On the Change of Names* 267). Philo adopted the basic Platonic notion of the universe as consisting of the visible world and a world of Reality above this world of appearances. This transcendent world contains the pattern and original form of all things. Whether or not our author shared this Platonic notion, the same basic vocabulary is shared.

The term *brightness* is an ambiguous word in Greek; it can be either active (a radiance that flashes forth) or passive (a reflection that flashes back). The *Wisdom of Solomon* uses the passive sense to describe Wisdom as the brightness of God, the "unspotted mirror" of his power and goodness (7:25–26). Philo used the term repeatedly. This world, he declared, is the "brightness of God's holiness," "a copy of the original" (*On Noah's Work as a Planter* 50). Here the sense is more active, with the world seen as a duplication of the original holiness of God. He also described the creation of Adam as the making of a copy, fragment, or "brightness" of God (*On the Creation* 146; see also *On Special Laws* 4.123). Again, the Platonic influence is evident.

The word translated as "stamp" is the Greek word *charakter,* which derived from the practice of minting coins. The coin is said to take on the *charakter* of the die used to stamp it. Philo used this metaphor to demonstrate the superiority of the Hebrew tradition over the Greek. While Greeks assert that human nature is akin to the "upper air," Moses clearly showed it "to be a genuine coinage of that great spirit . . . signed and impressed by the seal of God, the stamp of which is the eternal Word [Logos]" (*On Noah's Work as a Planter* 50). Philo repeatedly asserted this impress of the divine image on humanity through the Logos.

Like Philo, our author asserts that all things are upheld by the Word, but he uses another word for "Word." He uses *Rhema,* not *Logos.* This might indicate lack of contact with the Philonic tradition, or it might represent a deliberate disagreement. In a key passage describing the Logos, Philo places it among the angels:

❧ ❧ ❧

*If there be any as yet unfit to be called a Son of God, let him press to take his place under God's First-Born, the Word [Logos], who holds the eldership among the angels, their ruler as it were. (*On the Confusion of Tongues *146)*

But for our author, that one is far more than the first of the angels:

Having become so much superior to angels as he has inherited a more excellent name than they. (1:4)

While Philo saw the Logos as the chief of God's angelic creatures, our author painstakingly shows that the Son is superior to all angels.

Whoever composed this opening sentence of Hebrews was surely familiar with the popular Hellenistic philosophy, especially Stoicism and Platonism, which we see clearly reflected in Philo of Alexandria. Such familiarity can be demonstrated at many points in Hebrews. It can also be shown that the Septuagint, that Greek translation native to Alexandria, is the version of the Scriptures that is regularly quoted (for example, 2:7 quotes the Septuagint version of Psalm 8:5; the Hebrew is different). This does not mean our author depended on, or even knew of, Philo. But it does show that they lived in similar contexts.

The Priest

Hebrews represents both a radical reinterpretation of Jesus and a reinterpretation of the meaning of the priestly service. On the one hand, Christ is understood essentially as the high priest (rather than as the savior, Lord, servant, or Messiah of other traditions); yet the whole meaning of the priestly service is revised and interpreted so that it becomes a model for Jesus' life and death.

Reading and Reflection

Study chapter 9, especially verses 11–22. List at least five ways Christ is said to be superior to the ordinary priestly service.

This passage describes the ministry of Christ in the true heavenly sanctuary, of which the earthly one was but a copy. Like Philo, our author considers the earthly tabernacle a copy of the heavenly original. But he goes far beyond Philo with an extensive analogy between the services of the two.

Just as Moses had sanctified the former with the words "This is the blood of the covenant" so Christ shed his blood to form a new covenant (9:20, 15). More radical than Philo, our author declares that the new makes the old obsolete (8:13). Curiously, Philo had used the same observation of the correspondence between the earthly copy and the heavenly original to establish the opposite point, the validity of keeping the Law: keep the Law because it corresponds to ultimate reality.

In the ways that our author is more radical than Philo, this writing seems to share much with those from Qumran. They too believed that a new covenant had been given, making the old obsolete. They too believed that the actual service of priests in the sanctuary was inferior to the spiritual service of the community, a service of entering into the presence of God with the sacrifice of praise and obedience. If we add to this the shared concerns with angels, the contrast between the novice and the mature (5:12ff), the sense of Scripture as really applying to their history (for example, 3:5–6), the strong moral tone and the even stronger appeal to ascetic practice (7:26;

10:26–27), we get a strong sense of the affinity between Hebrews and Qumran. Even Melchizedek, an obscure figure in writings of this era, is known to have been a center of speculation at Qumran. In the *Melchizedek Scroll* he is portrayed as one who would proclaim release to the captives and atonement for their sins in the final year of release, known as a jubilee year. Many would turn to this context of sectarian and ascetic Judaism for the proper context within which to interpret Hebrews.

The Entering

In addition to these specific parallels to Qumran, Hebrews shares much with the more general traditions of Jewish mysticism, especially in the exhortation sections. The hearer is admonished to be bold enough to enter the holy place (10:19). As Jesus has "passed through the heavens," so must the hearers (4:14–16). They enter the heavenly Jerusalem and worship with angels (12:22). Perfection is possible (6:1). If we try to translate the general admonitions of Hebrews into concrete practice, the picture emerges of a community intensely dedicated to prayer and holy living (see, especially, 13:1–17).

Conclusions

Our knowledge of this entire period is limited, and our information about minor movements within Judaism and Christianity is scant. The community behind Hebrews seems to share the most with the community behind the Dead Sea Scrolls, but that may only be because we know more about that community than any other. The similarities with Philo, the mystical implications, and the vague Platonism, all point to a complex community of Hellenized Jews who interpret Jesus in the light of ideas and aspirations evident in these contexts. It is more likely that these factors were widely shared than that Hebrews should be related directly to one group or the other. Hebrews seems to represent a kind of Jewish Christianity quite at ease in the Hellenistic world.

TRADITIONS ASSOCIATED WITH PETER

We have encountered Peter many times in our study of other traditions. The earliest references to Peter are in the letters of Paul, in which he is regarded as a leader of the Jerusalem church whom Paul took special pains to get to know (Gal. 1:18); as someone opposed by Paul for his waffling stance on Jewish-Gentile relations (Gal. 2:11); and as the apostle to the Jews (Gal. 2:7). The author of Acts claims him for the Pauline school by portraying him as the predecessor of Paul and even as the originator of the mission to the Gentiles (Acts, especially 10–15). All the gospels portray him as the leader of the disciples, though they also show him opposed to Jesus and denying him. Much of Mark's portrayal shows him faltering and uncomprehending. The Johannine tradition seems to consciously compare him to the unnamed "beloved disciple" to Peter's consistent disadvantage (pp. 258–259).

We have seen that in some Jewish-Christian traditions Peter is portrayed as the true apostle opposed to Paul "the man who is my enemy" (p. 130). In later traditions, Peter is claimed as the founder of the church at Rome, where Constantine (in the fourth century) built St. Peter's Basilica, presumably over his tomb. The tradition of his death during Nero's persecution and his burial in Vatican Hill may be traced back to the late second century, though there are earlier allusions that may support the tradition. The earliest of these comes from *First Clement* (about 95 CE) implying that both Paul and Peter died in Rome (5:4).

In addition to the *Acts of Peter,* six other writings come down to us in the name of Peter: only two have been accepted into the canon, despite strong support for a third for a long time. We have already looked at the *Letter of Peter to James* and the accompanying *Preachings of Peter.* Both

are second-century documents from a community with a strong Jewish orientation. There is also a *Gospel of Peter,* of which we possess only a section dealing with the death and resurrection of Jesus. This story represents a pious elaboration of the accounts of the four canonical gospels. The Jews are treated rather poorly and the point of view is that of a Gentile (for example, the writer limits the Law to "them" at paragraph 5). It was probably written in the early second century by followers of Peter. Late in the second century it seems to have been connected with Gnostics, but the fragment we have lacks Gnostic traits.

The *Apocalypse of Peter* was very popular for several centuries and a strong candidate for inclusion in the canon. The Muratorian Canon accepted it, but with the warning that some opposed it. It exists today only in an Ethiopic translation, a partial translation in another language, and a couple of Greek fragments. A major portion of the work consists of a vision of the damned built on the framework of the Apocalyptic Discourse in the Synoptic Gospels (Mark 13 and parallels) and a vision of the blessed based on the transfiguration story (Mark 9 and parallels). These fanciful and sometimes grotesque scenes are designed to reinforce piety: blasphemers are hung by their tongues, women who seduce by their braided hair, men by their thighs; those who have had abortions or exposed their children stand in a horrifying pit and see their children happily playing in a place of delight; special tortures are described for those who did not honor their parents, those who engaged in premarital sex, and for disobedient slaves. There is no concern with the historical future or with the coming of Jesus, as we might expect in an apocalypse. This devotional work was probably composed in the early second century.

Finally, there are the two Letters of Peter in the New Testament. Neither was included in the Muratorian Canon, and Eusebius reports that First Peter was accepted in his day but Second Peter was still disputed. The two works present somewhat different views of Peter.

Peter as the Exhorting Elder: First Peter

This short letter is written to "the exiles of the dispersion" in the provinces of Asia Minor, which overlapped the area in which Paul worked. This address is very general, raising the question of whether it is a letter at all. Many other aspects of the work are also disputed, including authorship, date, and purpose. The only available evidence must come from the letter itself, since we have no other writings indisputably from Peter. External evidence is of little help. The letter was not cited by name until the late second century, although Polycarp seems to quote it without naming it in his *Letter to the Philippians* (about 135).

Reading and Reflection

I Peter is a practical letter, concerned with Christian action in worship and behavior.

1. What aspects of worship are discussed?
2. How many times are terms like *revelation* or *revealed* used? Through what does such revelation come?
3. Make a list of the kinds of behavior encouraged.
4. To what social classes is it addressed?

The Genre

"I have written briefly to you, exhorting and declaring that this is the true grace of God; stand fast in it" (5:12). So our author accurately describes his work. It is essentially a message of exhortation to patience, morality, and endurance in a time of persecution. More precisely, it is a message of confirmation, confirming the decision of the hearers to trust in God's grace. Most of the letter seems quite conscious of the new status of the hearers (for example, 1:2–4, 14, 18, 22; 2:10; 3:21; 4:3). They have recently passed from the licentiousness of the Gentiles into the way of Christ. The means of their passing was baptism (3:21). It is this grace that the writer aims to confirm.

READING GUIDE TO FIRST PETER

Salutation   1:1–2
Blessing on the newly born   1:3–9
Salvation revealed through the prophets 1:10–12
The exhortations   1:13–5:11
  To a new lifestyle   1:13–2:10
  Advice to aliens: good conduct   2:11–17
  Duties of the household   2:18–5:11
    Servants   2:18–25
    Wives   3:1–6
    Husbands   3:7
    All   3:8–12
    Baptism and suffering   3:13–4:11
    The present suffering   4:12–19
    Elders   5:1–11
Closing personal section   5:12–14

We do not know much about the liturgical rites of the early Christians, which probably varied a great deal from place to place. However, an interesting story in Acts 8:14–25 recounts that the Samaritans had received the word and the baptism of Jesus. Then the Jerusalem authorities sent Peter and John to confirm their conversion, pray for them and lay hands on them that they might receive the Holy Spirit. If this practice of baptism being followed by an apostolic confirmation represents a conviction of early Christianity, we have clear evidence of the genre of this work. For it seems to be an apostolic sermon confirming the newly baptized in their faith and admonishing them to moral behavior in the face of opposition. Much of the imagery of the letter makes sense within this context.

Baptism, Revelation, and Braided Hair

The imagery of I Peter is vivid and diverse, but overwhelmingly it portrays rebirth. Much of it is drawn directly from the ritual of baptism itself: new birth, resurrection, purification, and washing (1:3, 22, 23; 2:24; 3:21). Baptism is identified with the death and resurrection of Jesus (Rom. 6) and thus is an event of revelation. This revelation both looks back at the death of Christ (1:18–21) and forward to the final revelation (*Apocalypsis* in Greek) of Christ (1:7, 13). Both the past and present revelations exist in the baptismal rite; worship experience refuses to be bound by time, as we learned in our study of the Apocalypse of John.

This understanding of ritual as revelation was widely shared in the Hellenistic world, finding its most dramatic representation in the Mystery Religions. Each mystery had its own central act of initiation, ranging from the viewing of the grain in Demeter's rites, to the wine of Dionysus, to the killing of a bull in Mithraism. These were life-changing events. One of our clearest presentations of the mysteries comes from a comic novel, The *Metamorphosis*, better known as *The Golden Ass*. It is the story of how a young dandy makes an ass of himself, quite literally, in the pursuit of beautiful women and magic. Thus tragically transformed, he is forced to wander the world bearing other men's burdens, done in by fate. At the climax of the novel he returns to his human form as a result of his devotion to Isis, into whose mysteries he proceeds to be initiated. The process is complicated. Considerable time elapses, as he devotes himself to worship and to study. He is told that only the Goddess can select the time of initiation:

☙ ☙ ☙

The act of initiation had been compared to a voluntary death with a slight chance of redemption. Therefore the divine will of the Goddess was wont to choose men who had lived their life to the full, who were coming near the limits of waning light, and who yet could be safely trusted with the mighty secrets of her religion. These men by her divine providence she regenerated and restored to strength sufficient for their new careers. (Chapter 11; quoted from Lindsay, 247)

The initiation itself consisted of a ritual bath, worship in the temple of Isis, secret instruction,

a ten-day fast from meat and wine, vows, and a nighttime ritual that it was forbidden to reveal but which is described as visiting heaven and hell, followed by a morning revelation of the initiate to the congregation. He is dressed as the sun, carrying a torch and wearing a wreath of palm leaves on his head. He describes the ensuing celebration "as if it were a birthday."

We do not know if early Christian baptism was equally dramatic. But we do know that it re-presented the death and resurrection of Jesus, required serious moral preparation, resulted in a new birth, and demanded a transformed manner of life from the initiate. All this is evident from I Peter.

The moral instruction of I Peter takes a form we have met in the writings of the Pauline schools, the household code. The household here includes slaves (2:18), wives (3:1), husbands (3:7), "all of you" (3:8), and elders (5:1). This last is somewhat awkward after the "all of you" and is something of a novel category. Perhaps it was later appended to the other list. The instructions given are remarkable only for their conformity to the norms of the Greco-Roman world. They contain nothing radical and nothing specifically Christian. Slaves are to be submissive and suffer patiently; wives are to be submissive and not braid their hair or adorn themselves; husbands are to be considerate of their wives; all are to have unity and love and are not to retaliate. The death of Jesus provides the model for all this behavior: he suffered quietly (2:21).

The Theme of Suffering

The connection between suffering and the rite that commemorates Jesus' death and resurrection is perhaps automatic. Much of the talk about suffering in I Peter is of this rather expected sort. Yet near the end, the tone seems to change and the exhortation takes on a certain urgency. This change seems to occur at 4:12: "Beloved, do not be surprised at the fiery ordeal which comes upon you to prove you, as though something strange were happening to you." The present tense implies that this is a current experience of these communities. It is also described as religious persecution, not simply the general suffering that comes to all. It comes "for the name of Christ" and one is to "suffer as a Christian" (4:14, 16). Moreover it is an active persecution, for the adversary is said to prowl like a roaming lion "seeking someone to devour" (5:8). Unfortunately, the letter does not indicate who this adversary is (other than the Devil) or what form it has taken. Is it possible for us to reconstruct the social situation of the time?

The Social Implications

Some things we know. The setting is in the Christian communities of Roman Asia Minor, all except those on the Mediterranean coast. These northern provinces were less permeated by Hellenistic culture than the coastal cities that had occupied most of Paul's attention. Resentment against Roman rule ran strong in these provinces. Roman conquest had brought with it a certain prosperity, but it was largely limited to the upper class: the rich became richer and the poor became more hostile to the status quo. This hostility of the lower classes created an unstable political environment on Rome's eastern frontier. (For more details see the discussion of the setting of the Apocalypse, pp. 290–295.)

We may also be reasonably certain that the hearers of this letter were from the lower classes. Slaves are admonished, but not masters. There are no exhortations to the rich, as we found in James. They are addressed as exiles (1:1) and aliens (2:11), which may show they had marginal social status. The strong theme of submission implies a specific problem: the conversion of parts of a household, especially the women and slaves. A household was supposed to manifest harmony and to worship at a common altar. As Gentiles now affiliated with this new religion, their social situation probably deteriorated further (4:4).

Surprisingly, there is no hint of disaffection with Rome in the letter. Just the opposite occurs: they are admonished to be subject to the emperor and the governor (2:13). Admittedly, this implies some need to so exhort. Some probably were not in subjection. Nevertheless, there is no expressed hostility toward Rome such as we found in the Apocalypse (which was also addressed to Asia Minor, but only to the western and southern cities). If the "Babylon" of the closing refers to Rome, as is generally assumed, we may detect some underlying hostility. For the name associates Rome with that first destroyer of Israel. But we might also expect a more positive attitude toward Rome in a letter written from the capital.

The Author

This is the only Petrine work actually attributed to Peter by any substantial number of scholars. They relate it to the tradition that Peter traveled to Rome in the early sixties and died there during Nero's persecution (64–68 CE). Often they consider the last chapter and a half an addition based on the Neronian persecution. According to this hypothesis Peter would have written a general baptismal exhortation, which he then composed as a letter by adding the more specific admonitions about suffering, then sending the entire work to the Asia Minor churches. We know nothing else about the connection between Peter and these churches.

One problem with this view is the lack of evidence that Nero's persecution extended to the provinces. It seems to have been limited to Rome. It could be argued, of course, that with persecution of Christians as the official policy in the capital their situation would have deteriorated in the provinces even without official Roman persecution. Peter may also have assumed that it would spread there, since he would not have known that Nero would shortly lose the Emperorship.

Another problem is the excellent Greek style of our author. This is highly polished language with many constructions of a literary style (as opposed to the common style of spoken Greek). Yet Peter was a Galilean fisherman who, reportedly, could not even speak Aramaic without a northern accent (Matt. 26:73). He is described in another source as "uneducated" (Acts 4:13), an expression that actually means illiterate. That, of course, would have been more than thirty years earlier, but it is unlikely that such a man would have developed a fine Greek style so late in life. We would have to imagine that he used a very good scribe.

Those scholars who doubt that Peter actually wrote the letter point to a number of factors that seem to connect it with the late first century. Most notably, it seems to depend on some of the Pauline letters for its teaching. The advice on government (2:14–17), for example, seems based on Paul's teaching (Rom. 13:1–7). Strong echoes of Paul may also be heard in 1:18–19; 2:24; 3:16; 5:10, 14. The converse of this argument is that the letter reveals so little of Jesus; we expect more from the original disciple. Also, the teaching on female submission, the concern to live lives that outsiders will admire, and the development of the church as an institution all seem more in harmony with the late first century than with the time of Peter (see discussion, p. 131). Though Peter does not claim the authority of a bishop (5:1), he clearly acts like one. There is a paid clergy (5:2) and they can claim an absolute power, though our author urges them not to do so (5:3). The intellectual justification for hierarchy is already in place: Jesus as the chief shepherd with each pastor as an underling (5:4).

The issue of authorship may be clarified by a curious statement at 4:12, "By Silvanus, a faithful brother as I regard him, I have written briefly to you. . . ." This expression is vague; it could mean anything from Silvanus having written (composed) the letter for Peter, to his acting as a scribe, to his serving as the messenger to deliver it. Whether this Silvanus was the same one who traveled with Paul (I Thess. 1:1) remains a conjecture, but it would account for the strong orientation to Paul's thought. Also, the final greeting adds Mark and "she who is at Babylon" to the letter and may point to the existence of a Petrine group at Rome.

It seems best, then, to consider I Peter as derived from Peter through this group. One possibility is that the source of much of the first four chapters was a contemporary Petrine baptismal exhortation, a kind of confirmation sermon. When real persecution developed against the Christians of Asia Minor, this general exhortation may have been expanded with the additional material beginning at 4:12 to produce the unified letter we now have. That the letter is a unified composition is indicated by the device of inclusion: compare 1:6–7 with 5:10 and with 4:12–13. We are unable to date it precisely because we know little about the actual situation in Asia Minor. As we noted in our study of the Apocalypse (p. 293), Pliny found persecution in progress when he arrived there in 111. Some would relate I Peter to this event. Yet nothing in I Peter suggests that the persecution stems from the Imperial government. It may well have involved only the local administration, and local hostility to Christians was probably widespread from the time of Nero. Thus we must probably content ourselves with the late first century (perhaps 75–95) as a date for the letter.

Reading and Reflection

Reread I Peter aloud, imagining that you are a baptismal candidate ready to join this group, which finds itself harassed by neighbors and persecuted by the government.

Peter as the Apocalyptic Prophet: Second Peter

The Second Letter of Peter in the New Testament is quite unlike the First. It is too abrasive for modern sensibilities, too combative, too self-righteous, too gloomy in its detailing of the end of the world for our tastes. It is also a much neglected letter. Yet this is all the more reason to study it, for it will help us to see more clearly the contours of the world it shapes and of our modern world. In addition, II Peter is a mediating work, on the boundary between the Jewish milieu of James and, especially, Jude and the Gentile traditions of Paul.

This work contains numerous correlations with Jude, so many in fact that Jude is generally thought to be a source for our author. Consider these parallels:

Jude		II Peter
2	Greeting	1:2
3	Need to write	1:5
5	Remind, though know	1:12
5b–19	Extensive parallels	2:1–3:3
24	Without blemish	3:14

(Adapted from Reicke, 1964:189; see also
Sidebottom, 1967:65–67)

The extensive parallels in chapter 2, particularly, demand some explanation. Either Peter used Jude as a source, or vice versa, or both used a common source. Whichever way the dependence worked (and scholars generally favor the dependence of II Peter on Jude), two inferences may be drawn: First, the works have very different concerns. Jude shows no interest in the Parousia (central to II Peter); II Peter avoids the use of noncanonical Jewish writings so prevalent in Jude (omitting the citation of *I Enoch* and the traditions concerning Michael, Cain, and Korah). Second, this creative use of previously existing tradition was a hallmark of writers in antiquity, demonstrating clearly that the claim to authorship was not a claim about the origin of the material.

On the Pauline side, we find something equally significant: our author cites Paul as Scripture:

ea   ea   ea

So also our beloved brother Paul wrote to you. . . . There are some things in [his letters] hard to understand, which the ignorant and unstable twist to their own destruction, as they do the other scriptures. (3:15–16)

Paul's letters now exist as a collection, and are considered to be part of the canon of Scripture. Our author may actually know a two-part canon, for he speaks of "the predictions of the holy prophets and the commandments of the Lord and Savior through your apostles" (3:2). He is the first author to indicate that Paul is considered Scripture and the first to imply a twofold canon. In this endorsement of Paul, however, we should not overlook the implication that our writer claims for Peter the power to interpret correctly what Paul intended. The opponents also claimed Paul, but they "twisted" his meaning in our writer's judgment.

Second Peter represents an attempt to assert the authority of Peter in the face of other teachers with differing interpretations of Paul and different understandings of the coming end. This claim is embedded in a distinctive literary form.

Yet Another Genre

Second Peter is cast as a letter, addressed to no one in particular and consisting of general instructions and warnings. The letter form is part of its literary style, but it is not an actual letter. Written as if it were Peter's last words to his followers, it is a reminder of his lifelong teaching put forth on the eve of his death (1:12–15). In this regard it is similar to II Timothy, which claims to represent the last wishes of Paul, his testament. So too, II Peter claims to be the testament of Peter, a sort of farewell speech.

Such testamentary literature was widely known in the first century. The final speech of Jesus in the Gospel According to John (14–17) is rather like a testament. Our most extensive example, however, is an older Jewish work, which we know only in its Christian version, the *Testament of the Twelve Patriarchs*. Modeled on the deathbed speech of Jacob (Gen. 49), this work claims to give the final wishes of each of the twelve sons of Jacob, the ancestors of the nation. Each of the twelve sections follows the same basic pattern: the patriarch calls his family together, recounts his life, warns them of vice and exhorts to virtue, predicts their future course, and finally dies. In II Peter this narrative has been transposed into a letter and the biographical element is minimal. What remains is the notion of the last words of a great man of God who warns, exhorts, and predicts the future. Thus we may consider II Peter a testamentary letter.

Purity and the Parousia

To what does Peter testify? He testifies to the certain coming of the Day of the Lord, admonishing his hearers to live pure lives in view of that coming day. He bases this conviction on the knowledge (a favorite word) of the prophets and of the Christ, alluding to the experience of Peter on the Mount of Transfiguration (Mark 9:1–8).

Reading and Reflection

Read II Peter, noting the motifs of Purity, Knowledge, and Coming. How does this letter teach Christians to triumph over evil?

READING GUIDE TO SECOND PETER

Salutation   1:1–2
The testimony of Peter   1:3–21
  Peter's faith   3–11
  Peter's reminder   12–15
  Peter's experience of Christ's majesty
  16–21
Predictions of false teachers   2:1–22
  Their perversions   1–3
  Their coming foretold   4–10
  Their condemnations   11–22
Predictions of scoffers   3:1–10
  Denial of Jesus' coming   1–7
  Rebuttal: God's timetable   8–10
Exhortations: what sort of persons   3:11–18

Addressed to Gentiles (1:1), this work uses a Gentile vocabulary and focuses on Gentile concerns. The vocabulary is evident in the first clause of the elaborate, and somewhat bombastic, first sentence of the letter proper (in Greek, 1:3–7): "divine power" has granted the things that pertain to "piety" that we may escape the corruption of "passions" and become "partakers of the divine nature" (1:3–4). These words represent distinctive ideas of Gentile religious thought; one, the idea of sharing in the divine nature, is alien to Jewish circles and even to other Christian groups. It does not occur anywhere else in the New Testament but is frequently seen in Stoic thought, where human reason is considered a spark and fragment of divine Reason. In addition, Stoics would readily understand the corrupting influence of the passions, for they regarded them as the source of delusion. The chain of virtues recounted in 1:5–7 is a typical Stoic device.

Second Peter differs from Stoicism in its understanding of how one escapes such passions and how one partakes of the divine nature. The answer begins with baptism (1:9), involves the knowledge of Jesus (1:16) and a proper interpretation of Scripture (1:20–3:2), and culminates in the coming of the Lord and of the new earth (3:3–13). The understanding of this approaching end is also distinctive. Our writer refutes a static view of history (a commonsense view also rejected by Stoics) and advocates a view of history as three ages: the time from the Creation to the flood (when the world was destroyed by water); the time from the flood to the end (when the world will be destroyed by fire); and the time of the new heaven and the new earth (3:5–7, 13). Water and fire were two of the basic elements of Greek physics, the other two being air and earth (3:12). This notion of the earth destroyed by fire is not found in any other New Testament work, but was a common Greek expectation. In fact, the successive dissolution of the world by water and then by fire was part of the cyclical view of history typical of Greek thought. Our writer differs in seeing these dissolutions as part of a meaningful story: God's rescue of his creation.

This grand vision of baptism, Scripture, and history underlies the basic concern of the writer: "Since all these things are thus to be dissolved, what sort of persons ought you to be? . . ." (3:11; 3:14). The purity, patience, and peace required are derived from the divine nature itself and may only be acquired by overcoming the corrupting passions (1:4; 2:10). The vision of our writer is captured in a marvelous metaphor: the Scriptures are a lamp set in this dark world until that new day dawns (1:19).

In Peter's Name

Little about this rhetorically flamboyant and highly Hellenized letter convinces us that Peter actually wrote it. Given the practice of pseudonymity discussed earlier (pp. 46, 109), this work has all the earmarks of an imitator. It depends either on Jude or on the same source used by Jude. Its language and much of its thought are closer to Stoicism than to Palestinian Judaism. It presumes that the first generation of Christians has passed away (3:3) and responds to the loss of eschatological expectation common in the second and third generations. It even invokes the writings of Paul, now known as a collection and considered Scripture (3:15–16). Paul is used against other Paulinists, who are said to "twist" Paul. These are "lawless" people (3:17) who deny the coming of Jesus and, judging by chapter 2, have a false view of the Hebrew Scriptures. Though we cannot be sure, this reminds us of that Pauline trajectory that led to Marcion (p. 128). Add to this the late external attestation and the ancient debate about its authorship, and we may reasonably conclude that it was written between 100 and 125. There is no hint about its geographical setting, unless we interpret the conscious reference to I Peter (3:1) to mean it was addressed to the same area in Asia Minor. If we are right in relating II Peter to developing Marcionite ideas, the choice of Peter as the voice of the letter would represent a conscious attempt to assert the authority of another apostle alongside Paul, on whom the Marcionites depended exclusively. Certainly, II Peter was part of the great debate of the second century: Who is the rightful heir of the apostles?

Petrine Trajectories: Simeon, Simon, Cephas, Peter

We are not lacking in Petrine materials, but we are unable to demonstrate that any come directly from Peter. This is not unexpected. Peter was a Galilean fisherman and it is likely that his entire ministry was oral. His impression was made on the minds of those who heard him, not on sheets of parchment. His audience was surely diverse. Even his names indicate that he traveled in more than one circle. Given the highly patriotic name of Simeon, he was more commonly referred to by the Greek name Simon (Simeon occurs only in II Peter 1:1 and Acts 15:14). Jesus gave him the added name of Cephas ("Rock"). We have no evidence that this word was used as a personal name before. The Aramaic Cephas was then adapted to the Greek world by turning the Greek word for rock (*petra*) into a proper name, Peter. This represents an accommodation to a new cultural situation, and the dominance of this version of his name implies that Peter moved into the Greek world. (Paul's practice of referring to him as Cephas was probably conditioned by his understanding of Peter's ministry as limited to Jews —Gal. 2:7). The name Peter is also an invention, although it is close to the Greek "Petron" and Latin names like "Petreius" and "Petronius" were common. Peter continued to be claimed by different circles in the following generations. Let us examine two such claims.

The Jewish Peter

Both the *Acts of Peter* and that large body of material collected in the name of Clement (the *Pseudoclementine Homilies* and the *Pseudoclementine Recognitions*) make Peter the centerpiece of a Jewish version of Christianity. In both works Peter is the active opponent of Paul. He also opposes other understandings of being Jewish, for example, rejecting completely the notion of the Temple and various segments of the Old Testament that support sacrificial worship. These are regarded as false prophecies wrongly inserted into Scripture by false prophets. These works envision an active mission to Gentiles, but expect them to observe the Law and (it seems) be circumcised. Both works may be traced to sources from the middle of the second century and continued in active use for many centuries. While rejecting other forms of Judaism and Christianity, the Pseudoclementines are remarkably open to both. Jesus is presented as a prophet, a sort of second Moses, but then in a rather surprising move, Peter is portrayed as teaching:

☙ ☙ ☙

The Hebrews are not condemned because they did not know Jesus . . . provided only they act according to the instructions of Moses and do not injure him whom they did not know. And again the offspring of the Gentiles are not judged, who . . . have not known Moses, provided only they act according to the words of Jesus and thus do not injure him whom they did not know. . . . In all circumstances good works are needed; but if a man has been considered worthy to know both teachers as heralds of a single doctrine, then that man is counted rich in God. . . ." (Pseudoclementine Homilies 8.7.1–2, 5. Quoted from Hennecke, II: 564)

Jews may be saved by following Moses, Christians by following Jesus, but most blessed are those who follow both. Here we see the continuation of Peter's role as mediator, on the boundary between Jew and Gentile. To some degree this is a continuation of the portrayal of Peter in Matthew and in II Peter.

The Episcopal Peter

Perhaps because of this boundary position Peter was also vigorously claimed by Gentile Christians. This is seen most clearly in the traditions

incorporated into the *History of the Church* by Eusebius in the early fourth century. Peter is portrayed as the bearer of Christianity to Rome (2.14.6; 5.8.2), where he died as a martyr, having inaugurated the office of bishop (3.2). Thus, Peter is the one on whom Christ built his church (6.25.8).

This image of Peter as the rock on which the church is built derives from Matthew (16:18), but just what it meant in the Matthean situation, in which no one was to be called "father" or "master," or even "rabbi," is not entirely clear (23:8–10). It was, however, the image of Peter that became dominant. It owes something to First Peter (especially chapter 5) and was eventually taken up into the Medieval papacy.

Perhaps this very trait of Peter—to be "on the boundary" between Jew and Gentile, between Paul and James, between ruling elder and scriptural expositor—made him such a valuable symbol for the emerging Christian consensus that resulted in the early catholic church.

HOW JEWISH WAS JEWISH CHRISTIANITY?

Let us go back now and consider only the writings that were eventually included in the New Testament canon, making some general observations about Jewish Christians at the end of the first century. Admittedly this is only part of the picture. We have seen that many other associated writings originated in Jewish Christian circles. In general, they are more distinctively Jewish than those in the canon (which reveals something of the process of canonization, as we will see in the next chapter). Yet if we compare these writings with the literature associated with Paul we will learn something about the development of Christianity.

As suggested earlier (p. 131), the literary heirs of Paul exhibited four characteristics:

1. New emphasis on the church as a hierarchical institution.

2. Fading concern with the end of the age and an increased concern for reputation, resulting in a new moralism.
3. Use of Gentile religious thought to interpret Christ.
4. Clear separation between accepted and deviant interpretations and interpreters.

Similar tendencies may be found in this literature. Here too there is a clear separation between the acceptable and the deviant, and a strong urge to hold fast to the "faith once delivered" (Jude 3). Related to this concern for true faith is the claim to apostolic authority. Only Hebrews fails to claim the authority (authorship) of a holy figure of the first generation—and it claims to be heir to their traditions (2:3). This claim to apostolic authority largely replaces the need to argue a case: opponents are simply labeled false teachers, who are known by the immoral lives they lead. True Christians, in contrast, must live lives of moral excellence. This is typical of the kind of moralism and aspiration to social respectability that we saw in the Deutero-Pauline literature.

Nevertheless, real differences do emerge. There is less concern here than in the Pauline traditions with church organization and little evidence of a hierarchy (though some hierarchical focus may be discerned in the mediating work of I Peter).

While James and Hebrews share the general decline in eschatological expectations evident in the late first century, the coming end is a major theme of II Peter, and apocalyptic literature and ideas are evident in Jude. However, I Peter, Hebrews, and James share in the general move away from an apocalyptic worldview, a move characteristic of late first-century Christianity. Little attempt is made to interpret the world as a struggle between good and evil. And finally, the emphasis on the authority of Scripture is greater in these writings than in those of the Pauline schools. II Peter is especially concerned with the proper interpretation of Scripture, and Hebrews is essentially an exercise in scriptural interpretation. Jude seems to employ a broader canon, which included *I Enoch* and the *Assumption of Moses*. Only in II Timothy (3:16) do we find a similar concern in the Pauline heritage.

These writings also help dispel the false understanding that to be Jewish was the opposite of being Gentile. At least two of them (Hebrews and II Peter) are deeply influenced by the Hellenistic world, as were many Jews in this era. (Neither is as thoroughly Hellenized as Philo of Alexandria.) Jew and Gentile were not exclusive options, only poles of a continuum of experience. Both Judaism and Christianity were complex movements, and Jewish Christianity shared in the complexity of both.

RESOURCES FOR FURTHER STUDY

A general treatment of non-Pauline Christianity is Bruce, 1979, *Peter, Stephen, James, and John*.

Significant monographs on special topics include:

Balch, 1981, *Let Wives Be Submissive: The Domestic Code in I Peter*.
Brown, Donfried, and Reumann, 1973, *Peter in the New Testament*.
Elliott, 1981, *A Home for the Homeless: A Sociological Exegesis of I Peter, Its Situation and Strategy*.
Williamson, 1970, *Philo and the Epistle to the Hebrews*.
Yadin, 1958, "The Dead Sea Scrolls and the Epistle to the Hebrews."

Important commentaries have been written by:

Bauckman (Jude, II Peter)
Beare (I Peter)
Bruce (Hebrews)
Buchanan (Hebrews)
Davids (James)
Dibelius and Greeven (James; technical)
Reicke (James, Peter, and Jude)

Less technical works include:

Best (I Peter)
Jewett (Hebrews)
Kelly (Peter and Jude)
Laws (James)
Senior (I & II Peter)
Sidebottom (James, Jude, II Peter)

The Story after the Writings

੨੦ ੨੦ ੨੦

One Story in Many

The Making of the Canon
The Meaning of the Canon
Canon, Story, and History
Resources for Further Study

13

In our close study of the various writings that comprise the New Testament, we have savored the rich diversity and extraordinary variety of ideas, practices, literary genres, purposes, and abilities of the various writers. Now we must raise a new kind of literary question. The New Testament itself reaches us as one document—in a way it never appeared to its earliest hearers. Does it, then, make sense as a unified work? It hardly seems possible. Yet we have all seen pictures that seem to consist of innumerable and random dots and shapes which, on close inspection, appear to have little connection. Yet when we step back from these pictures hidden relationships appear. Suddenly they make a whole picture; we see it.

So too, the people who live in your city are extremely diverse; you may think they have nothing in common. Yet sociologists assure us that they do share many things. As Easterners, Southerners, Westerners, or whatever, they share certain tendencies. As speakers of English (or Spanish or German), they understand the world in certain ways. As Americans, they are committed to certain common values of freedom and democracy, however much they may disagree as Republicans or Democrats.

This final chapter will focus on the unity that can be found amid the diversity of the New Testament writings. First, let us consider how the writings of the New Testament were collected into a common canon, then sketch in broad strokes the Story that informs all the stories we have heard so far. Finally, we will consider the relation of the basic story—especially the stories of Jesus—to history.

THE MAKING OF THE CANON

It is not quite accurate to think that these early Christians set out to create a canon. No Christian writer even speaks of a "canon" in the sense of a list of sacred works until the fourth century. What is evident before then is a complicated, and often unconscious, process of excluding and including certain writings as reliable and authoritative witnesses to Jesus.

The Process of Exclusion

Not all early Christians' writings were included in the canon. We have seen that even some of Paul's writing was lost. The preface to the Gospel According to Luke claims that "many others" had constructed similar narratives; surely this suggests more writers than Mark and Matthew. What, then, happened to all the other writings?

Some works were not saved through mere neglect; they were simply not powerful enough to outwit the enormous forces of destruction in a world where writing was an extremely expensive and time-consuming process. This is true of all kinds of literature from antiquity. As with Greek and Roman writings generally, so with early Christian writings, only a small fraction of the original survives. Other writings, however, were deliberately and consciously excluded.

The major issue facing Christians in the second and third centuries was the increasingly sharp distinction between various versions of Christianity. Our study of the individual writings shows that Christianity was diverse from the beginning but, by the second century, this diversity was threatening to create essentially different faiths, each calling itself Christianity. For the sake of simplicity, we may speak of the emergence of an extreme right wing and extreme left wing.

On one side, then, we find those whose commitment to the biblical traditions of Israel was so strong that it shaped their understanding of the Christian faith, so that it appeared as a variety of Jewish experience. Generally we call these the Jewish Christians, though in fact Jews and Jewish influence appear all across the spectrum. The other extreme included those whose commitment to Greek learning and worldview was so strong that it shaped their understanding of their faith, so that Christianity appeared as a variety of Hellenistic philosophy. We generally call these the Gnostics. Yet a word of caution is appropriate here: Greek influence is evident even in the most conservative Jewish circles, and Jewish influence is strong among the Gnostics.

To name the "middle" group is not a simple task. They called themselves the "orthodox," a word made up of the Greek words for straight (as in *ortho*dontist) and praise, or worship (as in *dox*ology). They were the ones claiming to get God's worship straight, worshipping in the proper way. They also took the name "catholic," a term meaning universal, though in fact there was no universal version of Christianity. And in some places, such as Syria, it seems that these "catholics" were not even in the majority. Nevertheless, they emerged as the dominant body in the church and like all the victors in history got their choice of names. Here I will call them the orthodox and the catholics, framing them always with invisible quotation marks, indicating those toward the middle of the spectrum.

This middle group eventually ratified the canon. It is not surprising, then, that works that are clearly Gnostic works (such as the *Gospel of Truth*) or clearly Jewish Christian works (such as the *Gospel of the Hebrews*) are not to be found there. Further, works that tend toward gnosticism (such as the Gospel of John) or Jewish Christianity (such

as James) had the greatest difficulty being accepted into the canon. A primary criterion for inclusion in the canon was whether a writing manifested orthodox teaching. This will simplify our quest to discover some underlying unity in the whole, for certain works have been excluded.

The Process of Inclusion

On Easter in the year 367, a Christian bishop of Alexandria in Egypt, Athanasius by name, published a festal letter in which he listed the writings he deemed canonical. This is the first such list to include precisely the twenty-seven books we know as the New Testament. Others before him had drawn up lists, but they were always partial and always included other works that were eventually excluded. That it took over three hundred years for this list to appear should caution us that the process of canonization was a slow and ill-defined one. It does not seem to have occurred to anyone to draw up a canon list until about 150—a century after Paul began to write. The Bible of these early Christians was the Hebrew Scriptures, which they knew primarily in their Greek translation (the Septuagint), and these new writings were not automatically added to it.

Our earliest clue to the development of a new canon comes from II Peter (about 125). The writer refers to Paul's letters (showing that they had been collected) as being twisted by other interpreters, "as they do the other scriptures" (3:15–16). The "other" implies that Paul's letters are gaining scriptural status. In another place this writer reflects the beginnings of a two-part canon:

☙ ☙ ☙

You should remember
  the predictions of the holy prophets and
  the commandments of the Lord and Savior
    through your apostles. (3:2)

Notice that the parallelism is not complete: the writings of the holy prophets (Old Testament) are not set beside the writings of the apostles (New Testament). The new revelation is seen as the word of Jesus, to which the apostolic writings bear witness. This concept appears to have guided early Christian thinking before 150.

The practice of Jewish Christians seems to have reflected the practice of Jews generally; their primary authority was the Hebrew Scriptures, supplemented and interpreted by the oral tradition. But for these Christians the oral tradition consisted of the words and deeds of Jesus. Papias (about 125), for example, makes clear his preference for the oral tradition of Jesus; they are superior to the written word: "For I did not suppose that information from books would help me so much as the word of a living and surviving voice" (Eusebius, *Church History* 3.39.4). Yet writers like Papias used certain books as reliable sources of tradition about Jesus—one step on the long road to canonization.

The practice of Gentile Christians was not very different, though we have consistent evidence from II Peter, the letters of Ignatius and Polycarp, and others that they knew and used a collection of Paul's letters. They cite these letters as authoritative, but not in the way they cite the Hebrew Scriptures. The question for these second-century Christians was not so much whether a given writing was canonical, but whether it was helpful. Did it build up the church? Was it useful for public reading? The writings that eventually emerged in the canon were those that a large number of Christians in many places and over a long period continued to read in their public services.

Opinions differed widely about which books were worthy of such reading. But about 150 a crisis in the church at Rome gave a whole new impetus to the process of canonization. Marcion had concluded that the Hebrew Scriptures were incompatible with the new revelation of God in Jesus Christ. The loving (and always good) Father of Jesus was pure spirit; the just (and sometimes bad) Creator was tied to this material world (see p. 128). This wholesale rejection of the Hebrew Scriptures created a vacuum, which Mar-

cion filled by publishing a purified New Revelation in two parts: The Gospel and The Apostle. He purged both Luke's gospel and Paul's letters of all Jewish elements, creating a new Scripture that he used instead of the Hebrew Scriptures.

We are more certain of the Roman church's reaction to his discarding the Hebrew Scriptures (they condemned it) than we are of their reaction to his creation of a new Scripture. Yet it is probably no coincidence that the Roman church seems to have produced its own list of acceptable books sometime in the next generation after Marcion— perhaps around the year 190. This list is somewhat misleadingly entitled the *Muratorian Canon.* Both parts of the title are modern. L. A. Muratori discovered this badly preserved Latin manuscript from the eighth century in a monastery library at Milan in the early 1700s. Because the writing refers to a Roman bishop from the mid-second century as "recent," it is generally assumed that the original was written by the end of the second century. More importantly, it is an anachronism to call it a canon, since it is, as it states explicitly, a list of books recommended for public reading. Because it reveals so much about the thinking of these early Christians, I quote the entire document:

☙ ☙ ☙

. . . The third gospel book according to Luke. Since Paul had taken him in as a competent writer, the physician Luke wrote it down after the ascension of Christ under his own name (but) according to his (Paul's) views. Yet he himself did not see the Lord in the flesh either and therefore he too began his narrative, as far as he was able, with the birth of John. The fourth gospel is by John, one of the disciples. When his fellow-disciples and bishops urged him he said: Fast with me for three days from today and we shall tell each other what is revealed to each of us. That same night it was revealed to Andrew, one of the apostles, that John would write everything down under his name, and they were all to check it.

And therefore, although different prefaces (principles) are presented in the various gospel books, this still makes no difference for the faith of the believers, since everything is explained through the one leading Spirit in all of them: concerning the nativity, the passion, the resurrection, the association with his disciples, and concerning his twofold coming, the first time when, in lowliness, he was despised, which has taken place, the second time resplendent in regal power, which is to come. Is it surprising therefore if John so consistently brings the various things forward also in his letter, when he says of himself: what we have seen with our eyes and heard with our ears and touched with our hands, that we have written down for you. For thus he introduces himself not only as a spectator and hearer, but also as a describer of all the miracles of the Lord, in the (correct) order.

The Acts of all the apostles have been written in one book. Luke sums up for the excellent Theophilus what successively took place in his presence, as he makes clear by omitting Peter's martyrdom and also Paul's departure from the city for Spain.

The letters of Paul themselves make it clear, to anyone who wishes to know, what (they are), from where and for what reason they were sent. The first of them all to the Corinthians, forbidding the heresy of the schism; next to the Galatians, forbidding circumcision; then to the Romans, explaining that Christ is the rule of the Scriptures and their principle, he wrote rather extensively. It is necessary for us to discuss these one by one, since the blessed apostle Paul, following the rule of his predecessor John, wrote to only seven congregations mentioned by name, in this order: to the Corinthians, the first; to the Ephesians, the second; to the Philippians, the third; to the Colossians, the fourth; to the Galatians, the fifth; to the Thessalonians, the sixth; to the Romans, the seventh. For when (a letter is written) anew to the Corinthians and Thessalonians to reprove them, it is clear that there is one church scattered over the whole earth. For John also writes, in his Revelation, to seven churches, yet he speaks to all of them. But one to Philemon, one to Titus and two to Timothy (written) out of affection and love have been held sacred in honour of the catholic church for the regulation of ecclesiastic discipline. There is also in circulation a letter to the Laodiceans and another to

the Alexandrians, fakes in Paul's name for the sect of Marcion and still others that cannot be received in the catholic church: for gall cannot be mixed with honey. In addition a letter from Jude and two with John's subscription are preserved in the catholic church; and the Wisdom which was written by Solomon's friends in his honour.

We have also included the Revelations of John and Peter, although some of us will not let them be read in church. Recently in our time Hermas wrote the Pastor [or the Shepherd*] in the city of Rome, when his brother Pius was seated as bishop on the throne of the Church of the city of Rome. For this reason he should be read, but he cannot be read to the people in church, nor (be counted) among the prophets, whose number is complete, or among the apostles, until the end of time.*

We accept nothing at all by Arsinous, or Valentine, or Miltiades. They compiled a new book of psalms for Marcion, together with Basilides, of Asia Minor, the founder of the Cataphrygians. (Quoted from Klijn, 1980:218–221, who also includes the Latin text)

It would take a rather perverse logic not to think that the lost beginning talked about Matthew and Mark, meaning the four gospels were recognized at Rome. But there seems to have been serious questions about John, to judge by the obviously legendary story that supports not only its apostolic authorship but claims that the other apostles checked it. All Paul's letters are included, though arranged in a curious order and believed to be written later than the seven letters of John in Revelation. Some writings are missing: Hebrews, James, I and II Peter, and there are doubts about Revelation. Yet there is support for another Revelation, that attributed to Peter, along with the *Wisdom of Solomon*, which is recognized as pseudonymous. There is also a conscious rejection of works associated with Gnostic teachers and an explicit distinction between books that are merely sound and pious (such as the *Shepherd of Hermas*) and those that should be read aloud in the assembly.

Even a century later many of these problems

remained unresolved. Around 325, Eusebius provided a classification of these early writings, probably reflecting the discussion of the great school of Alexandria in Egypt. He writes:

ə ə ə

We must, of course, put first the holy quartet of the gospels, followed by the Acts of the Apostles. The next place in the list goes to Paul's epistles, and after them we must recognize the epistle called I John; likewise I Peter. To these may be added, if it is thought proper, the Revelation of John, the arguments about which I shall set out when the time comes. These are classed as Recognized Books. Those that are disputed, yet familiar to most, include the epistles known as James, Jude, and 2 Peter, and those called 2 and 3 John, the work of either the evangelist or of someone else with the same name.

Among the spurious books must be placed the "Acts" of Paul and the "Shepherd," and the "Revelation of John, if this seems the right place for it: as I said before, some reject it, others include it among the Recognized Books. Moreover, some have found a place in the list for the "Gospel of the Hebrews," a book which has a special appeal for those Hebrews who have accepted Christ. These would all be classed with the Disputed Books, but I have been obliged to list the latter separately, distinguishing those writings which according to the tradition of the Church are true, genuine, and recognized, from those in a different category, not canonical but disputed, yet familiar to most churchmen; for we must not confuse these with the writings published by heretics under the name of the apostles, as containing either Gospels of Peter, Thomas, Matthias, and several others besides these, or Acts of Andrew, John, and other apostles. To none of these has any churchman of any generation ever seen fit to refer in his writings. Again, nothing could be farther from apostolic usage than the type of phraseology employed, while the ideas and implications of their contents are so irreconcilable with true orthodoxy that they stand revealed as forgeries of heretics. It follows that so far from being classed even among Spurious Books, they must be thrown out as impious and beyond the pale.

(Church History 3.25. Quoted from Williamson, 1965:134–135)

We see here the slow, painful process of creating an agreed upon canon. It was not enough that a work was not heretical; it had to meet the test of usage. The process of inclusion was the process of incorporating diverse works into a common tradition.

We should remember that the physical means of book production contributed to this piecemeal approach. Books were written on papyrus, a paperlike material made from pounded reeds. Papyrus sheets were rather brittle so they were not folded; instead they were rolled up. A short writing, like Philemon, would fit on a single sheet about a foot square. It would be rolled and tied with a string. Longer works were made by sewing many sheet of papyrus together and rolling them from each end around long sticks. A work like Romans would form a scroll about eighteen feet long. The longest works, such as Matthew, Luke, or Acts, would run up to thirty-three or thirty-four feet, about the limit of what was manageable for this form. Longer works were divided into two scrolls (which is why there are two scrolls of Samuel and of Kings in the Hebrew Scriptures). A given congregation might possess a collection of these scrolls, but few would have a complete set of the writings available; they were very expensive.

A new technology came into use sometime in the first century. A very finely crafted leather, called *vellum,* was used for paper. This vellum was sewn together along one edge, producing what we think of as a book, then called a *codex.* Early codices reflected the scroll conventions in manner of writing, width of columns, and length of documents. Gradually, however, these elements changed, and by the beginning of the third century the codex had replaced the scroll. This new technology allowed the combination of numerous works into a common book, so that what we consider the New Testament became technologically possible.

The Process of Transmission

It is still a long way from the fourth century canon to the twentieth century New Testament that we read. All the New Testament documents were written in Greek, though many were soon translated into other languages. The Greek style used strikes us as odd: they wrote in all capital letters with no punctuation, not even spaces between words. Consider:

YOUMIGHTHAVESOMEDIFFICULTYREAD
INGTHESELINESFORALLTHEUSUALCLUE
SAREMISSINGANDITISPOSSIBLETODI
VIDEWORDSDIFFERENTLYANDPERH
APSYIELDVARIOUSMEANINGSEVEN
SHIFTINGACOMMATOADIFFERENTL
OCATIONMIGHTSIGNIFICANTLYALT
ERTHEMEANINGANDIMAGINEWHAT
AFEWMISSPELLINGSWOULDDOTOT
HESSENSE

About 900 cursive script replaced this style; and word separation and elementary punctuation were introduced.

In the West, Latin replaced Greek as the language of the Bible. Around 400, Jerome translated the Bible into Latin (the vulgar tongue, hence the *Vulgate*) and this translation became the standard Bible in the West for the next thousand years. Only during the Renaissance, with its call to go back to original sources, was Greek reintroduced in the West, and scholars imported from Greece to teach it. This led first to the effort to produce the most accurate Greek text possible. Erasmus of Rotterdam, the great humanist priest of the late Renaissance, produced the first modern Greek text of the New Testament. It was very primitive by modern standards, and based only on late manuscripts; the text was often "corrected" on the basis of the Vulgate. But it was a beginning.

There followed the long development of that discipline known as *textual criticism*, the effort to reconstruct, as precisely as possible, the original texts of these ancient writings. The first stage of text criticism was the publication of the Greek manuscripts currently available in cathedral and monastic libraries. These were generally late manuscripts from the tenth to fourteenth centuries. The next stage involved the discovery of much older manuscripts, usually from the libraries of ancient monasteries (though one was found in the Vatican library itself). As a result of this late nineteenth-century detective work, we now possess complete manuscripts from the 300s and numerous papyrus fragments going as far back as 135. These contain many variant readings, and modern textual criticism compares all the variants of all these manuscripts plus citations in early writers and early translations, eventually arriving at the most probable reading in each case. The standard Greek texts available today, based on more than five thousand sources, provide us with the most accurate texts available since the first century.

This return to the Greek text also sparked an interest in translating the Bible into the languages of various people. When the Vulgate was made, Latin was such a language, but it had long since become the language of the intellectual elite. The masses spoke the regional languages which evolved from Latin: Italian, French, English, and so on, and now various translations began to appear in these languages. The most significant English translation, made in 1611, is known as the King James Version. It remained the standard English version for three hundred years and is the direct ancestor of several twentieth-century translations, including the Revised Standard Version.

Only as a result of this long historical process are we able to study the New Testament as one document. Now let us explore how that document fits together and produces its own meaning.

THE MEANING OF THE CANON

The arrangement of the New Testament writings into their present order was itself a drawn-out affair, by no means agreed to by all. Some lists begin with Luke, others put John before Luke, allowing Luke and Acts to come together as they were certainly meant to do. Even the great Easter letter of Athanasius, the first to list the precise twenty-seven books we have in the canon, does not give them in the present order. He put the general letters before Paul and inserted Hebrews into the middle of the Pauline letters. What is the logic of the present order?

The Order

That Revelation should come last in the canon was perhaps inevitable: both its widely disputed status and its contemplation of last things dictate that it be placed at the end. So too, the general priority of Gospel over Apostle is logically necessary and is reflected in every list we possess. But in what kind of order are the gospels themselves listed?

We cannot be certain, for no early writer discusses the reasons, but a likely guess would be that Matthew was placed first because it made the best transition from the Hebrew Scriptures to the new writings. Both in style and content Matthew is the most "Jewish," continually quoting the Hebrew prophets to validate the story of Jesus. Mark and Luke seem to be grouped next because they are most like Matthew; John is put last because it deviates most from the common pattern of the others—and perhaps because it was the most disputed.

That this order obscured the connection between Luke and Acts was compensated for by the natural transition that Acts provided to the next major section, the writings of Paul. For Paul is the hero of the last half of Acts. His writings are arranged variously in different lists: Marcion began with Galatians, the letter in which Paul is most antithetical to Jewish tradition. The Muratorian Canon, quoted earlier, follows a curious order, attempting perhaps to be chronological or to counter Marcion's emphasis on Galatians and Romans.

The present order begins with Paul's most ex-

tensive argument (Romans), which seems like a systematic statement of his ideas; the rest are arranged in order of decreasing length (though first and second letters are always put together). Length seems to us a strange criterion, but the whole of the Quran is arranged according to length, beginning in Surah Two with the longest of Muhammad's recitations. Following the short note to Philemon, the general letters appear, again in basic order of length from Hebrews to Jude.

The Story

The New Testament does not tell a story, but it does imply one. It is a very optimistic story, an account that begins with Abraham (Matt. 1:1) and culminates in the coming of the New Jerusalem (Rev. 22). Put another way, it is the story of God's acting to redeem his people. Abraham is the father of the faithful, the one God called to forsake home and native gods for a new land. In this new story, that "new" land now comes down out of heaven as a gift from God because Jesus the servant and son of God has lived, died, and been raised to new life. There are various ways to understand his life and death, reflected in the various gospels, but the witness to him has spread throughout the world (Acts). The canon suggests that that witness is most fully presented in the teachings of Paul, but all the apostles bear witness to it. The final work shows that even now the risen Christ appears to his churches in these letters and he comes to them in the sacraments of baptism and eucharist. As they worship God through him, the powers of evil are overthrown and the kingdom of God arrives on earth.

This story has had profound influence on the history of Western civilization: it is the promise of the future, the new tomorrow, progress. From Augustine's *City of God* and the Christian culture of the Middle Ages, to the secularized versions of the story in the modern notions of progressive liberalism and Marxism, it has shaped the vision of untold millions of people.

At the center of the Christian story stands the

story of Jesus, or more accurately the stories of Jesus. We have seen that each gospel writer told that story in a unique way. They differed in countless details. Of course, if one is determined enough and clever enough all the differences between the gospels can be explained away. Since Augustine began this task nearly 1,500 years ago, in a work called *The Harmony of the Gospels,* more effort has been put into harmonizing them than in understanding them on their own terms. A literary approach, such as we have undertaken here, avoids such harmonization to avoid obscuring the meaning of each work. But these are important works with stories of more than passing interest, and few of us will be content not to probe behind the level of story to ask what actually happened. When we do, we raise the question of history.

CANON, STORY, AND HISTORY

☙ ☙ ☙

Measureless pours forth
   The creative wantonness of bards,
Nor trammels its utterance
   With history's truth.
   (Ovid, Amores 3.12.41)

Thus, did the great poet of love, Ovid, recognize that the truth of poetry was not always the truth of history. Not only must a little poetic license be taken from time to time, the very art of poetry and narrative requires the writer to deceive us. We must believe that these words, sparse and planned, represent real life. We are to think that the narrative writer is telling us what happened when in fact we are being told far more. As the English satirist, Jonathan Swift, quipped: "Poets are liars by profession."

Poets do lie or, as we prefer to say, they create fictions. Just as the visual artists deceive us

by portraying a three-dimensional object in two-dimensional space, so the verbal artists deceive us by making a highly selective and artfully arranged series of incidents seem real and natural. An essential feature of all art is to be artful, imaginative, fictional. We do not ask of a story whether it really happened; we ask what it means and how it achieves that meaning.

To extend this logic to the gospels, we may say that to the extent they are stories artfully told we have no right to demand that they tell us just what happened. This is readily recognizable in regard to the parables Jesus told: thus, we do not ask whether a man actually went down from Jerusalem to Jericho, and the story of the Good Samaritan is unaffected by such historical considerations. It is a true story whether or not it happened (Luke 10:29–37).

Yet the gospels are not simply parables; they concern a real flesh-and-blood person, Jesus of Nazareth. Nevertheless, we must admit that they disagree on scores of incidents from his genealogy to the stories of the empty tomb. These disagreements are all the more significant if we conclude, as do most scholars, that some of these writers had access to the works of the others. They felt free to change, rearrange, omit, and add. Apparently the gospel form did not restrict an author to simply the bare facts.

The gospels are not historical narratives; they are designed to reveal and proclaim Jesus as the Christ. Convinced that Jesus had risen from the dead and that he was still with them, these writers understood him in a dramatically different way than had his contemporaries. They did not, like history, record information about a dead figure from the past; they confronted the hearer with a living person in their time. The problem of the historicity of the New Testament is one of the most challenging issues raised by the modern study of the Bible. It is too complex to be resolved in a few pages. We can, however, clarify the true nature of the problem and show how some current scholars approach a solution, especially in regard to Jesus.

The Nature of History

Just what do we mean when we use the expression "the historical Jesus?" In a general way, we all understand that we are trying to discover the things that Jesus actually said and did. Yet this expression is extremely ambiguous, rooted as it is in the ambiguity of the concept "history" in English usage. We may use the word "history" to mean "what actually happened in the past." In asking: "Was the resurrection of Jesus reported in the gospels a historical event?" we usually mean: Did it actually happen? If we had been standing there that first Sunday morning, would we have seen it? Yet, we also use the word "history" to mean an account of what happened in the past. History is what historians write. Now if we ask whether the resurrection is a historical event, we mean: Would a historian writing about Jesus include such an event in the account?

Traditionally, historians encouraged us to view these two usages as meaning the same thing. For they were, they said, attempting to tell us just what happened. Modern historians have become more modest, recognizing the hypothetical nature of their enterprise, and a little reflection on the nature of that undertaking will further clarify the problem of a historical understanding of Jesus.

The most important limitation historians face is that they lack direct access to the subject they intend to study. The past is gone; only in comic strips and science fiction are people able to encounter the past directly. We have access only to certain "evidence" of the past. We assume that this evidence was caused by "events," although we can never directly bring back these supposed events. The historian, then, gathers and evaluates this evidence and infers what must have caused it.

Thus, the work of the historian is like that of the detective who gathers evidence to prove that someone did, or did not, commit some crime. The detective must, as Sherlock Holmes advised Watson, learn to think backward. Holmes's method, you will recall, was to gather all the evidence available. Once he had all of it he could solve the crime. As he explained it, his task was simply to deduce what event would have left all this evidence, and no other. Holmes would certainly have made a first-class historian, for just this deducing events from evidence, as cause from effect, is the historian's main task.

We may carry our analogy one step further. Like the detective, the historian must follow certain rules in gathering and evaluating evidence. Some kinds of evidence are worth more than others. Firsthand accounts are far more valuable than hearsay. In a courtroom one may only testify to what one has personally seen or heard; rumors are not considered valid testimony. Yet even here, legal procedure calls for caution. If the defense can show that the person who claims to be an eyewitness to the crime is unreliable or a notorious liar, the testimony is questioned. Children and others with limited intelligence are allowed to testify only under very strict guidelines. If it can be shown that the witness has a vested interest in the outcome of the trial, the jury will have correspondingly less faith in the testimony. The historian exercises similar restraint with the sources.

Primary sources are preferable to secondary ones, since the former come from the time and situation being investigated—rather like an eyewitness. Secondary sources, from a later time, may give information about the time and situation being investigated but that information is filtered through later concerns. For the study of Christianity between 50 and 60, Paul's letters are primary sources; Acts is a secondary source. The gospels are secondary sources for a history of Jesus but primary sources for a history of Christianity in the last third of the first century. Like the attorney, the historian raises questions about the reliability of the witnesses, about how well-informed they could have been, about the biases they show. Generally, modern historians are trained to be skeptical of their sources, to subject them to careful analysis, to prefer empirical and testable data, and to use only natural explanations. These factors raise problems for the ancient historian, whose sources are few and distant, but the last point raises special problems in investigating religions.

Religions generally claim not to have natural causes; they are the work of God, or the Gods. While the historian cannot deny this possibility, it is outside the scope of historical investigation. The Athenians believed that Athens prospered because it was favored by the Goddess Athena; the historian must seek other causes. Christians believed they grew and prospered because the Holy Spirit empowered them; the historian must look for more natural causes. In neither case does the historian assert that the supernatural hypothesis is wrong; it is merely outside the scope of historical investigation. To take a modern example: we all remember memorizing the three (or four or five) causes of the Civil War. They were natural phenomena—regional competition, industrialization, invention of machinery, and so on. But President Lincoln believed that the Civil War was God's punishment on this country for failing to include black people in the great Declaration of Freedom that led to the American Revolution. He may have been right, but it is not a historical explanation. It is well worth remembering that a historical explanation is only one kind of reckoning, one which plays according to the very strict rules of skepticism, criticism, empiricism, and naturalism.

Ideally then, the historian would prefer primary sources that stand up to rigorous and critical examination and provide data that can be tested. Rarely is this possible. But even having such a source would only be the beginning of the historian's task: an eyewitness provides the best evidence but not necessarily the best history. An eyewitness can provide facts, but history demands more.

The past becomes intelligible only when some historian makes sense out of the facts by producing a convincing interpretation of their significance. If we had an eyewitness account of the crucifixion of Jesus it would be of immense help to the historian, but would not itself be history,

because it would lack historical perspective. It would fail, most basically, to interpret the historic significance of this event. A historian must provide context, understand relationships, demonstrate significance. This is one reason why history will never be an exact science, however scientific it may become. It will always depend on the skill, the insight, and the imagination of the historian.

And, one must add, the biases and values of the historian play their part. It is reported that after World War II Winston Churchill declared: "History will be kind to us here. I know, for I will write it." He did, and it was. A Nazi history of that war might read somewhat differently. This subjective element in history cannot be ignored. The nineteenth-century goal of knowing only the facts is an illusion. History always remains a tentative reconstruction of the past based on the available evidence, which must then be rigorously tested. Such history will possess varying degrees of probability based on the quality of the evidence and the skill of the historian. Some reconstructions are only possible, others probable, still others highly certain or apparently established beyond all reasonable doubt. But the historian may never claim certainty—the past is gone and our reconstruction of it remains ever open to revision.

Given these conditions, we can readily understand why writing a history of early Christianity is so difficult. There are so few sources available, and those we do have are strongly biased. The very nature of history as a skeptical, empirical, and tentative investigation is at odds with the attitudes of many people toward the things told in these documents. Even more difficult is the problem of the historical Jesus, since there are no primary sources. And the late secondary sources, on critical examination, seem to differ in numerous chronological and factual details. Further, they are all pervaded by a supernatural event: the resurrection of Jesus from the dead. How to achieve a historical interpretation of Jesus is a complex and controversial question. What follows is an attempt to trace the main contours of that debate and to show how some contemporary historians interpret Jesus.

The Historical Jesus

A literary analysis of the gospels shows how Jesus was portrayed by four different authors in four different situations. They give us clear historical information about how Jesus was regarded in the last third of the first century. But can the historian also discover there the necessary evidence to reconstruct an historical portrait of what Jesus himself was like? Such a task may only be attempted after the kind of literary analysis we have already engaged in, for the historian must be aware of the nature and purpose of the sources. And our basic sources for a reconstruction of the historical Jesus are the four canonical gospels. Neither the noncanonical gospels nor the non-Christian writings that mention Jesus are of any significant help in historical reconstruction. Yet because the gospels are documents of faith, the question of the historical Jesus has been understood as: Can we get *behind* the gospels to Jesus?

There was a time when historians understood their goal to be to get back to the earliest and best sources, on the assumption that the earlier a source was the better. This was one of the chief motivations of both source and form criticism, but it proved faulty; the earlier sources as well as the later ones were documents of faith and imagination. This discovery resulted in an eclipse of historical-Jesus research, many asserting that it was impossible to reconstruct the life of Jesus. More recently, a "new quest" has emerged, or perhaps we should say several new quests, for so far there is no unanimity on the goals, methods, or results of such study. There is only the general agreement that each incident and each saying must be subjected to historical analysis to determine, on the basis of certain criteria, whether an incident or saying is more, or less, likely to be historical.

Scholars differ in their basic approach to this problem. Some assume that the gospel incidents are basically historical unless one can prove otherwise. Others assume that, given the creativity of the early church, only incidents or sayings that can be proven to be historical are to be accepted. Most take a middle position: they begin with aspects that can be fairly conclusively established and proceed from this base to more or less probable material, trying to establish a coherent portrait of Jesus.

Conservative critics, who tend to regard the gospel material as historical unless it can be shown to be nonhistorical, have developed what we may call negative criteria. As a practical matter, these criteria relate to only a small portion of the Jesus material, since only a few scenes can be shown to be nonhistorical. Three negative criteria are often cited.

First, material should be judged to be nonhistorical if it assumes a situation that did not exist at the time of Jesus. Thus the instructions for dealing with a wayward brother, including bringing him before "the church" (Matt. 18:15–20), would not seem to be historical, since there was no "church" in Jesus' time. Nor would the commissioning scene at the end of Matthew (28:18–20), since neither the trinitarian baptismal formula nor the universal mission seem to be known in the earliest church (compare Acts 2:38; 10:28; Gal. 2:7–9).

Second, material should be judged to be nonhistorical if it contradicts other established material. This has a limited applicability, but surely Jesus did not cleanse the Temple on both Palm Sunday (Matt. 21:10f) and Holy Monday (Mark 11:12–19) as well as at the beginning of his ministry (John 2:13ff).

Third, material should be judged historically suspect if it can be shown to be a development of material found in another gospel or in another place in the same gospel. Thus the allegorical explanations of the parables are suspect, and Luke's (21:20) more elaborate description of the destruction of Jerusalem is less likely to be historical than the very general Markan description (13:14). Of Mark's three passion predictions (8:31; 9:31; 10:33), the more detailed and specific references are more suspect than the brief and generalized reference (9:31), though this does not prove that 9:31 is historical.

These negative criteria eliminate the more obvious anachronisms, but do little to clarify who Jesus was, unless one is simply prepared to accept the rest. Modern historians with their premise of skepticism are not so prepared. Thus, positive criteria must be used to try to establish what is most probably historical. Five such criteria seem useful.

The first criterion which may appear a little odd and is widely misunderstood, is that material should be judged historical if it can be shown that it is distinctive from both Jewish *and* Christian thought. The logic here is impeccable and should be obvious: if an item cannot be easily traced to a time before or after Jesus, it is most reasonable to assume it comes from Jesus. Of course this is strange reasoning, since Jesus surely gained much from his Jewish heritage and passed much on to his followers. Admittedly, this criterion will not isolate what is most important about Jesus, nor does it imply that material that does not pass this test is questionable. It can only be used as a positive criterion. For this purpose it is extremely powerful: whatever this criterion reveals has the highest probability of being historical.

One example is Jesus' baptism by John, since baptism of fellow Jews is uncharacteristic of Judaism and since the early church did not believe Jesus needed such a baptism "for repentance." Therefore it is quite unlikely that either a general Jewish tradition was attributed to Jesus or that his followers later invented such a scene. It is likely historical.

Aspects of Jesus' teaching also pass this test, for example, the exhortation not to resist evil (Matt. 5:39ff) was uncharacteristic of both the early church and of Judaism. Similarly, the parables attributed to Jesus are often so startling, both in their teaching and their form, that there can be little doubt that he told parables and that we possess versions of many of them. There is, however, a major difficulty in applying this criterion

to very many incidents, since we are certain of very little about actual affairs in early Judaism or early Christianity. We must remember that we have no literary remains for the first two decades of the Christian movement and little from the Jewish side during this crucial period.

Second, there is a somewhat less rigorous variant of this criterion that is still helpful. Material should be judged to be historical if it contains elements that are awkward for, or contradictory to, early Christianity. The logic here is that people do not readily invent problems for themselves. By this criterion, too, the baptism of Jesus by John appears to be historical. Jesus coming to John for baptism is awkward because John's baptism is one of repentence and because the master usually baptized the disciple.[1] It would be too much to claim that Jesus actually became a disciple of John, but almost certainly he was baptized by him. Using a similar logic, the notion that Jesus was executed by the Romans on a charge of insurrection is almost certainly historical. It was a fact that early Christians were at some pains to explain away.

And consider the saying:

☙ ☙ ☙

But to what shall I compare this generation?
It is like children sitting in the market places
*   and calling to their playmates,*
"We piped to you, and you did not dance;
*   we wailed, and you did not mourn."*
For John came neither eating nor drinking,
*   and they say, "He has a demon;"*
*   the Son of man came eating and drinking, and*
*   they say,*
"Behold a glutton and a drunkard, a friend
*   of tax collectors and sinners!"*
(Matthew 11:16–19)

---

1. Thus, Matthew stops to explain it (3:14f), and the apocryphal *Gospel of the Nazaraeans* has Jesus explicitly disclaim, "wherein have I sinned that I should go and be baptized by him?" (Fragment 2, in Hennecke and Schneemelcher, I, 1963:147)

Again, notice the implicit equality between John and Jesus. We find nothing of the Christian tendency to subordinate John. But even more significantly, we see here an evaluation of Jesus no Christian would have made up. Not only did early Christians practice fasting like John and unlike Jesus (for example, Matt. 6:16 and 9:14–17), but it is impossible to think of them inventing a description of Jesus as a glutton and a drunkard. Surely, this is a real charge leveled by some of his enemies. Jesus was apparently not sufficiently ascetic to fit some people's idea of a man of God.

Using this criterion, we would attribute more historical weight to the version of the story in which Jesus shrinks back from being called "good" (Mark 10:18) than to the one in which it occasions no problem (Matt. 19:17). The saying that the kingdom of God is not coming with signs (Luke 17:20–21) seems in some tension with the general early Christian attitude toward the end, but quite in harmony with another saying that declares: "If it is by the finger of God that I cast out demons, then the kingdom of God has come upon you" (Luke 11:20). Both are probably historical sayings of Jesus.

Third, a variation on this test is: material should be judged to be probably historical if it contains elements that are awkward for, or contradictory to, the ideas of the gospel writer in whose work it is found. At the least, such material was firmly embedded in the tradition before the time of the evangelist. Again, the story of Jesus' baptism is instructive, for we see a progressive diminution of the role of John. Already in Mark, John is clearly labeled the inferior predecessor (1:7), yet Mark did not hesitate to say clearly, Jesus came and was baptized by John (1:9). He is the only gospel writer to be so explicit. Matthew introduced an explanatory dialogue justifying the event (3:14–15); Luke reported John's imprisonment before the baptism scene and never says John baptized him (3:20–21); John omits the baptism altogether (1:29–34). John even has the Baptist renounce any claim to messianic titles, not only Christ, but even Elijah or the Prophet (1:20–21).

We see then a tendency of the gospel writers to report only information that advances their own stories and convictions. When we find conflicting data, we may assume it is probably historical. The logic of historical reasoning here goes something like this: when we find people giving out information that they would rather not tell us, we can be confident that the material is trustworthy. If a colleague tells me she has not yet read a certain book, or a student tells me he has not read an assignment, I have no reason to doubt the report.

Thus the elements of futuristic eschatology found in John, Luke's locating Jesus' home in Nazareth, Matthew's saying about an exclusively Jewish mission (10:5) and his exemption of the Pharisees from an active role in Jesus' death all gain in their probable historicity by being found in sources that would like to deny such points. In both this and the previous criteria we might say that the historical probability is directly proportionate to the embarrassment factor: the more embarrassing the information, the more probable its historical accuracy. Thus, Jesus' betrayal by one of his chosen followers and the denial by Peter have a high degree of historical probability, for they are highly embarrassing incidents.

Fourth, material found in separate sources should be judged likely to be historical. The likelihood here is not so great as in the previous criteria, but this test allows us to compensate somewhat for the biases of the individual sources. This criterion does not validate specific events or sayings, so much, as typical kinds of things. Is the same sort of material found in different sources? Obviously, material in Mark and Matthew, for example, cannot be counted as separate sources since one was probably the source of the other. But strata of material found in all our supposed sources (Mark, Q, M, L, and John) would seem to be firmly rooted in the earliest tradition. We may be fairly certain that Jesus did not keep the Sabbath well and that he associated with all the wrong sorts of people, because such behavior occurs in all the sources.

The fifth criterion represents a move of a

different kind by building on the results of the first four. Having established a reasonable core of material that is quite likely to be historical, other material which is coherent with it should be used to form a broad portrait of Jesus. While the other criteria emphasize analysis, this one attempts synthesis. Can we integrate the various data around the one man, Jesus? In this final stage the narrative aspect of history comes closest to the narrative aspect of literature. The results of this final stage are only *possible,* perhaps approaching *probable* if sensitively handled. While it is beyond our scope here to reconstruct such a portrait, I will briefly indicate the results of others.

History, Myth, and Literature

One of the earliest attempts to come to terms with the historical ambiguity of the gospels used a certain concept of myth. David Friedrich Strauss (1808–1874) argued that the gospels are mythic documents, which attempt to portray ideas as if they were historical events (see 1972 reprint, 52, 81–82). He understood myth as a story created to teach a truth, rather like a parable. The most influential commentator of the modern period, Rudolf Bultmann, picked up this concept and, in order to make the gospels accessible for our time sought to "demythologize" them, that is, to translate them back into ideas (1963:1–44). Obviously, Bultmann did not think it possible to speak meaningfully about the historical Jesus.

While there is much to be learned from this endeavor to find meaning behind the historical reports, to dissolve the historic material into timeless truths seems in some tension with the basic thrust of the gospel as a literary form. Even if we concede that ultimate meaning lies behind these stories, so that we may speak of them as myth, the gospel form seems to require not myth *as* history but myth *in* history, and this requires a more adequate definition of myth than that of Strauss. Such a definition might draw on Plato's concept of myth as a representation of a reality

that cannot be known directly, that is, it can only be known as the myth itself (*Timaeus* 29). It cannot be translated, because "the meaning of the myth is inseparably associated with its mythic form" (R. M. Frye, 1973:30). As noted earlier, this concept of myth is closely allied with the concept of mimesis, which is the basis of literature (p. 107). Literature uses the particular to present the universal; literature re-presents (mimesis) reality in such a way that the reader learns and infers the meaning of the events.

To the extent that the gospels are literature, imaginative presentations of reality, they do not seek to present the reader with the facts for a life of Jesus, but to so present Jesus that his real significance becomes clear. They are mythic in the sense that they reveal a reality beyond the events themselves, but a reality that abides in the events. This understanding of myth does not solve the problem of myth and history in the gospels, since it does not prove that a given element is historical. Yet it does resolve some of the tension in the older formulation, which regarded history and myth as mutually exclusive categories. They are not necessarily, and the concept of mimesis presents a fruitful alternative to this dichotomy by transcending, yet incorporating, myth and history.

Aristotle observed: "Poetry . . . is more philosophical and more significant than history" (*Poetics* 1451b; see his complete discussion in chapter IX). He meant that it was more valuable to see the significance of actions than to know who did what and when. But we have seen that modern history insists on meaning as well as facts, and to that extent it is poetry—art. As one modern literary critic has cogently argued, it is not a question of history *or* literature: "We can only get back to the Jesus of history through the Jesus of literature" (R. M. Frye, in Walker, 1978:302). This is true in two senses: the gospels are literally all we have. If we cannot get to Jesus through literature, we cannot get to him at all. More importantly, the gospels as literature seek to present *their* views of Jesus as a real person. While each presents a unique view of Jesus, the reader recognizes the same person in all four works. Frye wishes not to delve behind the gospels to reach Jesus, but to go through the gospels to Jesus.

The Jesus of Story, Canon, and History

If we were to begin with the kinds of evidence suggested by the scholars who have developed the criteria discussed above, we could begin to sketch a picture of Jesus. He was a man from Nazareth who became associated with the movement of John the Baptist, a movement looking for the coming of God's kingdom. He had a great power over people, undoubtedly drawing a large following, but one that included many of the social outcasts of his time: prostitutes, traitors, revolutionaries, rowdies, common folk, working-class people. Some of these people were transformed by their contact with him, believing he had the power to heal and to exorcise demons. This power was understood as the dawning of God's kingdom, which would be implemented not by the violent overthrow of evil but by turning the other cheek. Living such a life brought Jesus to a dismal end, crucified by the occupying power as a revolutionary. His activities of healing and exorcism, and his teaching, were focused on the coming kingdom; thus there is little wonder that his death was understood as being related to that kingdom.

Scholars who have gone beyond this minimal core to try to elaborate a coherent portrait of Jesus by using other material that has some probability of being historical speak of Jesus as a prophet of God's coming kingdom. His characteristic activities (healing and exorcism) are not merely humanitarian acts; they demonstrate the overthrow of Satan's kingdom. His teachings center on the nature of that kingdom, now present in the world. In trying to live out the implications of that kingdom, he did not fail to give his own life.

The Jesus story we find in the New Testament is far richer than this historical summary, and more diverse. Matthew, Mark, and Luke were not content merely to pass on the traditions they re-

ceived. They reshaped it, reordered it, even invented new material to adequately interpret Jesus as they knew him. John went even further, transforming the whole of the Jesus tradition into a certain way of viewing Jesus. Paul did not use much of the Jesus tradition in his letters, though he perhaps did in his proclamation. For Paul, however, it was clearly the death of Jesus, an act of human obedience, which reversed the human disobedience of Adam that grants righteousness to all those who take part "in Christ" and in his community. For Hebrews, Jesus became the great High Priest, and for Revelation he was the transcendent, heavenly Lord; James had little to say about him.

Yet all this rich variety has a certain unity, a unity enhanced by the centuries of canon making. Behind all the New Testament writings, there stands a real, recognizable Jesus—identifiably the same person. Writings in which the vision of Jesus wandered too far from this common representation were finally relegated to the sidelines in the long and arduous process of canon making. Extraordinary imagination is at play, but in each case this imagination is disciplined by historical recollection. If we were to imagine the situation had all the gospels and other writings about Jesus been accepted, we would understand this point. For we would then be confronted with such a fantastic array of possibilities that all hope of recognizing the historical person would vanish. If only one gospel had been preserved, however, we would feel we knew Jesus exactly, mistaking the literary representation for the man himself. Having four gospels, and other accounts as well, allows us to avoid this error and to obtain a richer picture of the subject of these works.

A modern man of letters offers us an insightful observation in this regard. This Oxford medievalist observed:

☙ ☙ ☙

There are characters whom we know to be historical but of whom we do not feel that we have any personal knowledge—knowledge by acquaintance;

such are Alexander, Atilla, or William of Orange. There are others who make no claim to historical reality but whom, none the less, we know as we know real people: Falstaff, Uncle Toby, Mr. Pickwick. But there are only three characters who, claiming the first sort of reality, also have the second. And surely everyone knows who they are: Plato's Socrates, the Jesus of the Gospels, and Boswell's Johnson. (Lewis, 1967:156)

For Lewis this was primarily a literary insight, but it is also a historical conclusion. Now no one would claim that Plato's Socrates is the historical Socrates pure and simple. Yet he is, recognizably, the same Socrates.

And so it is beneath, or rather within, all the creative diversity of the New Testament. There too we encounter recognizably the same person. But proof of that can never be found in a book like this. Here we can only provide some hints on how to read these ancient works. It would be a great mistake to substitute the reading of this for the reading of them. If you wish to hear their stories, you must read them. Read.

RESOURCES FOR FURTHER STUDY

The Canon: One of the best discussions is R. Grant, 1965, *The Formation of the New Testament.* See also Farmer and Farkasfalvy, 1983. The early dating of the Muratorian Canon has been challenged by A. C. Sundberg, Jr., 1973, "Canon Muratori: A Fourth–Century List." Sanders, 1984, *Canon and Community,* introduces the new concern for canon criticism (the concern to interpret the Bible within the context of the believing community).

Jesus: The literature attempting to reconstruct historical information about Jesus is so vast I can only present the introductory and more recent studies. Tatum, 1984, provides a fine summary of the literature and a complete bibliography. Jeremias, 1964, gives a cogent introduction to the issues involved. Harvey, 1966, treats the issues of historical knowledge about religion in a clear and provocative fashion.

Significant recent studies include:

Aulen, 1976, *Jesus in Contemporary Historical Research.*
Duling, 1979, *Jesus Christ through History.*
Farmer, 1982, *Jesus and the Gospel* also treats the canon.

Grant, M.,1977, *Jesus: An Historian's Review of the Gospels.*
Harvey, 1982, *Jesus and the Constraints of History.*
Marshall, 1977a, *I Believe in the Historical Jesus.*
Reumann, 1983, *Jesus in the Church's Gospel.*
Vermes, 1981, *Jesus the Jew.* (Also see his 1984).

A standard synthetic treatment of Jesus is Bornkamm, 1960; the analytic analysis of Perrin, 1967, has been a major influence on those concerned with Jesus' teaching.

Two rather different attempts have been made to combine philosophy and literary studies with historical questions: Breech, 1983, *The Silence of Jesus;* and Greunler, 1982, *New Approaches to Jesus and the Gospels.* Neither is easy reading.

Unity and Diversity: One of the best treatments of the unity behind the real diversity of the New Testament writings is Dunn, 1977.

The classic work of Bauer, *Orthodoxy and Heresy in Earliest Christianity,* is now available in English, 1971.

The methodology of Robinson and Koester, 1971, *Trajectories through Early Christianity,* has had enormous influence on later studies.

For Further Study of the New Testament

Should you wish to pursue some particular aspect of the New Testament further than the general resources listed at the ends of the chapters, one of the best works to begin with is the *Interpreter's Dictionary of the Bible,* 4 vols., Abingdon, 1962, with a supplemental volume in 1976. It will provide both a summary of current scholarly thinking on most topics and a short bibliography of the most important works on that topic.

Two related reference sets are *The Oxford Classical Dictionary,* Oxford University Press, 1970; and *Encyclopedia Judaica,* 16 vols. plus supplement, Jerusalem: Keter Press, 1972.

The basic journal index for all aspects of religion studies is *Religion Index: One* (formerly known as *Index to Religious Periodical Literature*). Its references are arranged alphabetically by topic. (See "Bible, New Testament.") New Testament topics are also treated in the annual bibliographic guide to the ancient world, *L'Année philologique,* especially in section I (Histoire Litteraire, and its subdivision Litterature judeo-chretienne) and section V (Histoire, and its subdivision D, Histoire religieuse et mythologie). It covers works in English, French, and German. More comprehensive, but not as widely available, it *Elenchus Bibliographicus Biblicus,* a topical index to over one thousand journals, published in Rome by the Biblical Institute Press. The *Arts and Humanities Citation Index* indexes the citations, footnotes, and references in scholarly articles, providing a very useful means for developing a bibliography once you have a few basic sources. Both it and *Religion Index: One* are available on-line. Check with your librarian.

Another very valuable reference work is *New Tes-* *tament Abstracts.* It provides short abstracts of articles from most of the important journals that deal with the New Testament. It is arranged by biblical writing rather than by topic, with periodic indexes. There are three issues a year.

The more important journals for the study of the New Testament include:

The *Journal of Biblical Literature,* the professional journal of the Society of Biblical Literature.
New Testament Studies, the professional journal of the *Societas Novi Testamentum Studiorium,* based in England.
The *Catholic Biblical Quarterly,* the professional journal of the Catholic Biblical Association.
Interpretation, published by Union Theological Seminary in Virginia, this journal deals with all aspects of biblical literature. Issues often focus on a specific problem or kind of literature.
Novum Testamentum, a New Testament journal published by E. J. Brill, Leiden.
Semeia, an experimental journal devoted to literary and structuralist studies of biblical literature. Issues are devoted to specific themes or methods.
Harvard Theological Review, which despite its name covers all aspects of the study of religion.
American Academy of Religion Journal, the professional journal in general religion studies.

In addition, journals focusing on the study of Judaism and on classical antiquity often cover topics important for the study of the New Testament. Some of the more important ones are listed below.

On Classical Antiquity:

American Philological Association, Transactions and Proceedings, a major journal for the study of classical Greece and Rome.

Aufstieg und Niedergang der Römischen Welt, published in Germany but contains many English articles. Specializes in major treatments of specific themes.

And others, such as *Antiquity, Classical Journal, Classical Quarterly, Classical World, Gnomon, Greece and Rome, Greek, Roman and Byzantine Studies, Hermes, Isis,* the *Journal of Roman Studies,* and *Yale Classical Studies.*

On Judaism:

The *Hebrew Union Annual,* published by the Hebrew Union College, deals with all aspects of the study of Judaism.

The *Jewish Quarterly Review,* the *Journal for the Study of Judaism, Judaism: A Quarterly,* and the *Journal of Jewish Studies* are all useful references.

Finally, reviews of important monographs may be located by using the *Book Review Index.*

Bibliographic guides are also available. Two of the best are F. W. Danker, *Multipurpose Tools for Bible Study,* Third edition (Concordia Publishing House, 1970) and R. T. France, ed., *A Bibliographic Guide to New Testament Research* (Sheffield: JSOT Press, 1979). Both are annotated. Also useful is the minimally annotated listing of D. M. Scholer, *A Basic Bibliographic Guide for New Testament Exegesis,* Second edition (Grand Rapids, MI: Eerdmans, 1973).

A few specialized bibliographies are also available; see the following bibliography for complete details:

On the bible as literature—Gottcent, 1979.
On Jesus and the Gospels—Aune, 1980.
On the Sermon on the Mount and the parable—Kissinger, 1975 and 1979.
On the study of Judaism—Neusner, 1972b.
On the Dead Sea scrolls—Fitzmyer, 1977.
On the pseudepigrapha—Charlesworth, 1981.

Bibliography

Abel, E. L.
1971a "The Psychology of Memory and Rumor
Transmission and Their Bearing on Theories of
Oral Transmission In Early Christianity," *JR*
51:270–81.
1971b "Who Wrote Matthew?" *NTS* 17:138–52.

Abrams, M. H.
1953 *The Mirror and the Lamp: Romantic Theory and the Critical Tradition*. New York: Oxford University Press.

Achtemeier, P. J.
1970 "On the Historical-Critical Method in New
Testament Studies," *Perspective* 11:289–304.
1972 "The Origin and Function of the Pre-Mar-
can Miracle Catenae." *JBL* 91:198–221.
1975 *Mark*. Philadelphia: Fortress Press.
1978 "Mark as Interpreter of the Jesus Tradition," *Interpretation* 32:339–52.
1985 *Romans*. Interpretation Commentary. Atlanta: John Knox Press.

Adams, R. M., ed.
1973 *To Tell A Story: Narrative Theory and
Practice*. Los Angeles: William Clark Andrews
Memorial Library, UCLA.

Aland, K.
1961 "The Problem of Anonymity and Pseudonymity in Christian Literature of the First Two
Centuries," *Journal of Theological Studies* NS
12:39–49.

Albright, William and C. S. Mann
1971 *Matthew*. New York: Doubleday.

Apuleius
The Golden Ass. (Also called *The Metamorphosis*)
W. Adlington, tr. Cambridge: Harvard Univer-
sity Press/Loeb. (See also Lindsay, 1962.)

Aristotle
Poetics. W. H. Fyfe, tr. Harvard University Press/
Loeb. (See also Golden, 1968.)
The Art of Rhetoric. J. H. Freese, tr. Cambridge:
Harvard University Press/Loeb, 1936.

Auerbach, Eric
1953 *Mimesis: The Representation of Reality in
Western Literature*. Princeton: Princeton University Press.

Augustine
*Harmony of the Gospels. The Works of Aurelius
Augustine*. Vol. 8. M. Dods, ed. Edinburgh: T
& T Clarke, 1873:198–480.

Aulen, Gustaf Emanuel H.
1976 *Jesus in Contemporary Historical Research*. Philadelphia: Fortress Press.

Aune, David
1972 *The Cultic Setting of Realized Eschatology
in Early Christianity*. Leiden, the Netherlands:
E. J. Brill.
1980 *Jesus and the Synoptic Gospels: A Bibliographic Guide*. Madison, Wisc.: Theological
Students Fellowship, 1977.
1983 *Prophecy in Early Christianity and the Ancient Mediterranean World*. Grand Rapids, Mich.:
Eerdmans.

Bacon, B. W.
1930 *Studies in Matthew*. New York: Henry Holt.
1933 *The Gospel of the Hellenists*. New York:
Henry Holt.

Bailey, John A.
1978 "Who Wrote II Thessalonians?" *NTS*
25:131–45.

Bailey, Kenneth
1980 *Through Peasant Eyes: More Lucan Parables, Their Culture and Style*. Grand Rapids,
Mich.: Eerdmans.

Balch, David L.
1981 *Let Wives Be Submissive: The Domestic
Code in 1 Peter*. Chico, Calif.: Scholars Press.

Balsdon, J. P. V. D.
1969 *Life and Leisure in Ancient Rome*. New
York: McGraw-Hill.

Banks, Robert
1975 *Jesus and the Law in the Synoptic Tradition*. New York: Cambridge University Press.
1980 *Paul's Idea of Community, the Early House*

Churches in Their Historical Setting. Grand Rapids, Mich.: Eerdmans.

Barbour, Ian G.
1974   *Myths, Models, and Paradigms.* New York: Harper & Row.

Barker, Glenn et al.
1969   *The New Testament Speaks.* New York: Harper & Row.

Baron, S.
1952   *A Social and Religious History of the Jews.* Vols. 1 and 2. New York: Columbia University Press.

Barr, David L.
1976   "The Drama of Matthew's Gospel: A Reconsideration of its Structure and Purpose," *Theology Digest* 24:349–59.
1984   "The Apocalypse as a Symbolic Transformation of the World: A Literary Analysis," *Interpretation* 38/1:39–50.

Barr, David L. and Judith L. Wentling
1984   "The Conventions of Classical Biography and the Genre of Luke-Acts," *Luke-Acts: New Perspectives from the SBL Seminar.* C. H. Talbert, ed. Los Angeles: Crossroads Press: 63–88.

Barr, James
1976   "Story and History in Biblical Theology," *JR* 56:1–17.

Barrett, C. K.
1957   *A Commentary on the Epistle to the Romans.* New York: Harper & Row.
1961a   *The New Testament Background: Selected Documents.* Harper Torchbooks.
1961b   *Luke the Historian in Recent Study.* London: Epworth.
1963   *The Pastoral Epistles.* New York: Oxford University Press.
1968   *Jesus and the Gospel Tradition.* Philadelphia: Fortress Press.
1971   "Paul's Opponents in II Corinthians," *NTS* 17:233–54.
1974   *The First Epistle to the Corinthians.* New York: Harper & Row.
1975a   *The Gospel of John and Judaism.* Philadelphia: Fortress Press.
1975b   *Jesus and the Gospel Tradition.* London: SPCK.
1975c   *The Second Epistle to the Corinthians.* New York: Harper & Row.
1978   *The Gospel according to St. John.* Philadelphia: Westminster.

Barth, Markus
1974   *Ephesians,* 2 vols. Anchor Bible. New York: Doubleday.
1979   "St. Paul—A Good Jew," *Horizons in Biblical Theology* 1:7–45.

Bauckman, Richard J.
1983   *Jude, 2 Peter.* Word Biblical Commentary. Waco, Tex.: Word Books.

Bauer, Walter
1971   *Orthodoxy and Heresy in Earliest Christianity.* R. A. Kraft et al., eds. and trs. Philadelphia: Fortress Press.

Beardslee, William
1970   *Literary Criticism of the New Testament.* Philadelphia: Fortress Press.

Beare, F. W.
1962a   *The Earliest Records of Jesus: A Companion to the Synopsis of the First Three Gospels.* Nashville: Abingdon.
1962b   *St. Paul and His Letters.* Nashville: Abingdon.
1970   *The First Epistle of Peter.* Oxford: Blackwell.
1982   *The Gospel According to Matthew.* New York: Harper & Row.

Beck, Norman A.
1983   "The Lukan Writer's Stories about the Call of Paul," *SBL Seminar Papers, 1983.* Chico, Calif.: Scholars Press: 213–18.

Beckwith, I. T.
1919   *The Apocalypse of John: Studies in Introduction.* New York: Macmillan.

Beker, J. Christian
1980   *Paul the Apostle: The Triumph of God in Life and Thought.* Philadelphia: Fortress Press.
1982   *Paul's Apocalyptic Gospel: The Coming Triumph of God.* Philadelphia: Fortress Press.

Belo, Fernando
1981   *Materialist Reading of the Gospel of Mark.* Maryknoll, N.Y.: Orbis Books.

Berger, Peter and Thomas Luckmann
1966   *The Social Construction of Reality: A Treatise in the Sociology of Knowledge.* New York: Anchor/Doubleday.

Best, E.
1965   *The Temptation and the Passion: The Markan Soteriology.* SNTS Monograph Series, 2. New York: Cambridge University Press.
1967   *The Letter of Paul to the Romans.* New York: Cambridge University Press.

1971   *I Peter*. London: Oliphants.

1972   *I and II Thessalonians*. New York: Harper & Row.

1977   "The Role of the Disciples in Mark," *NTS* 23:377–401.

1978   "Peter in the Gospel according to Mark," *CBQ* 40:547–58.

1981   *Following Jesus: Discipleship in the Gospel of Mark*. JSOT Supplement Series, 4., Sheffield, England: JSOT.

1983   *Mark: The Gospel as Story*. Edinburgh: T&T Clarke.

Bettenson, Henry, ed.

1963   *Documents of the Christian Church*. New York: Oxford University Press.

Betz, Hans Dieter

1968   "Jesus as Divine Man," *Jesus and the Historian,* F. T. Trotten, ed. Philadelphia: Westminster Press: 114–33.

1979   *Galatians: A Commentary on Paul's Letter to the Churches in Galatia*. Philadelphia: Fortress Press.

Bilezikian, Gilbert

1977   *The Liberated Gospel: A Comparison of the Gospel of Mark and Greek Tragedy*. Grand Rapids, Mich.: Baker.

Black, Matthew

1973   *Romans*. London: Oliphants.

Bogart, John

1977   *Orthodox and Heretical Perfectionism in the Johannine Community as Evident in the First Epistle of John*. Chico, Calif.: Scholars Press.

Bonsirven, Joseph

1964   *Palestinian Judaism in the Time of Jesus Christ*. W. Wolf, tr. New York: Holt, Rinehart & Winston.

Boomershine, Thomas E.

1974   *Mark, the Story Teller: A Rhetorical-Critical Investigation of Mark's Passion and Resurrection Narrative*. Union Theological Seminary, Ph.D. dissertation.

Booth, Wayne

1961   *The Rhetoric of Fiction*. Chicago: University of Chicago Press.

1974   *A Rhetoric of Irony*. Chicago: University of Chicago Press.

Borgen, P.

1963   "Observations on the Midrashic Character of John 6," *ZNW* 54:232–40.

1965   *Bread from Heaven: An Exegetical Study of the Concept of Manna in the Gospel of John and the Writings of Philo*. Leiden, the Netherlands: E. J. Brill.

Borgman, Paul

1980   "Story Shapes That Tell a World: King David and Cinema's Patton," *Christian Scholars Review* 9:291–316.

Bornkamm, Gunther

1960   *Jesus of Nazareth*. New York: Harper & Row.

1970   "Authority to 'Bind' and 'Loose' in the Church in Matthew's Gospel: The Problem of Sources in Matthew's Gospel," in Miller and Hadidian, 1970, I: 37–50.

1971   *Paul, Paulus*. New York: Harper & Row.

Bornkamm, Günther et al.

1963   *Tradition and Interpretation in Matthew*. Philadelphia: Westminster Press.

Bouquet, A. C.

1953   *Everyday Life in New Testament Times*. New York: Charles Scribner's.

Brandon, S. G. F.

1967   *Jesus and the Zealots: A Study of the Political Factor in Primitive Christianity*. New York: Charles Scribner's.

Breech, James

1983   *The Silence of Jesus: The Authentic Voice of the Historical Man*. Philadelphia: Fortress Press.

Bright, John

1953   *The Kingdom of God*. Nashville: Abingdon.

1959   *The History of Israel*. Philadelphia: Westminster Press.

Brinsmead, Bernard H.

1982   *Galatians: Dialogical Response to Opponents*. Chico, Calif.: Scholars Press.

Brown, Colin

1976   *History, Criticism, and Faith*. Downers Grove, Ill.: Inter-Varsity Press.

Brown, Peter

1971   "The Rise and Function of the Holy Man in Late Antiquity," *JRS* 61:80–101.

Brown, Raymond E.

1966   *The Gospel according to John*. 2 vols. New York: Doubleday.

1971   "Jesus and Elisha," *Perspective* 12:85–104.

1975   "The Meaning of the Magi, the Significance of the Star," *Worship* 49:574–82.

1977   *The Birth of the Messiah: A Commentary on the Infancy Narratives in Matthew and Luke*. New York: Doubleday.

1979 *The Community of the Beloved Disciple*. Ramsey, N.J.: Paulist Press.

1982 *The Epistles of John*. New York: Doubleday.

Brown, Raymond, Karl Donfried, and John Reumann
1973 *Peter in the New Testament*. Minneapolis: Augsburg.

Brown, Schuyler
1978 "Mission to Israel in Matthew's Central Section (Mt. 9:35–11:1)," *ZNW* 69:73–90.

1984 *The Origins of Christianity: A Historical Introduction to the New Testament*. New York: Oxford University Press.

Bruce, F. F.
1954 *Commentary on the Acts of the Apostles*. Grand Rapids, Mich.: Eerdmans.

1963 "When is Gospel Not a Gospel?" *Bulletin of the John Rylands Library* 45:319–39.

1963b *The Epistle of Paul to the Romans*. Grand Rapids, Mich.: Eerdmans.

1964 *The Epistle to the Hebrews*. Grand Rapids, Mich.: Eerdmans.

1972 *New Testament History*. Grand Rapids, Mich.: Eerdmans.

1974 *Jesus and Christian Origins Outside the New Testament*. Grand Rapids, Mich.: Eerdmans.

1977 *Paul: Apostles of the Heart Set Free*. Grand Rapids, Mich.: Eerdmans.

1980 *Peter, Stephen, James and John: Studies in Non-Pauline Christianity*. Grand Rapids, Mich.: Eerdmans.

1984a *Epistles to the Colossians, to Philemon, and to the Ephesians*. (New International Commentary) Grand Rapids, Mich.: Eerdmans.

1984b *The Gospel of John*. Grand Rapids, Mich.: Eerdmans.

Buechner, Frederick
1977 *Telling the Truth: The Gospel as Tragedy, Comedy, and Fairy Tale*. New York: Harper & Row.

Bultmann, Rudolf
1931 *The History of the Synoptic Tradition*. London: Blackwell. (Reprint, 1972.)

1953 *Kerygma and Myth: A Theological Debate*. New York: Harper & Row.

1951 *The Theology of the New Testament*. New York: Charles Scribner's.

1971 *Gospel of John*. Philadelphia: Westminster Press.

1973 *The Johannine Epistles*. Philadelphia: Fortress Press. (German original, 1967.)

Burkill, T. A.
1959 "Anti-Semitism in St. Mark's Gospel," *NT* 3:34–53.

1963 *Mysterious Revelation: An Examination of the Philosophy of St. Mark's Gospel*. Ithaca, N.Y.: Cornell University Press.

Butcher, S. H.
1951 *Aristotle's Theory of Poetry and Fine Art*. New York: Dover.

Butler, B. C.
1951 *The Originality of St. Matthew*. New York: Cambridge University Press.

Cabannis, Allen
1970 *Liturgy and Literature*. Tuscaloosa: University of Alabama Press.

Cadbury, Henry J.
1920 *The Style and Literary Method of Luke*. Cambridge: Harvard University Press.

1937 *The Peril of Modernizing Jesus*. New York: Macmillan.

1958 *The Making of Luke-Acts*. London: Allenson.

Caird, G. B.
1963 *The Gospel of St. Luke*. New York: Penguin Press.

1966 *A Commentary on the Revelation of St. John the Divine*. New York: Harper & Row.

Callan, T.
1985 "The Preface of Luke-Acts and Historiography," *NTS* 31/4:576–81.

Calloud, Jean
1976 *Structural Analysis of Narrative*. Semeia Supplements, 4. Philadelphia: Fortress Press.

Cameron, Ron
1982 *The Other Gospels: Non-Canonical Gospel Texts*. Philadelphia: Westminster Press.

Cannon, George E.
1983 *Use of Traditional Material in Colossians*. Macon, Ga.: Mercer University Press.

Carcopino, J.
1940 *Daily Life in Ancient Rome*. New Haven, Conn.: Yale University Press.

Carrington, Philip
1957 *The Early Christian Church*, vol. 2. *The Second Christian Century*. New York: Cambridge University Press.

Cartlidge, D. and D. Dungan.
1972 *A Sourcebook of Texts for the Comparative Study of the Gospels*. Chico, Calif.: Scholars Press.

Casson, L.
1974 *Travel in the Ancient World*. London: Allen & Unwin.

Charles, R. H., ed.
1913 *The Apocrypha and Pseudepigrapha of the Old Testament*. 2 vols. New York: Oxford University Press.
1920 *A Critical and Exegetical Commentary on the Revelation of St. John*. New York: Charles Scribner's.

Charlesworth, James H., ed.
1972 *John and Qumran*. London: Geoffrey Chapman.
1981 *The Pseudepigrapha and Modern Research*. Chico, Calif.: Scholars Press.
1983, 1985 *The Old Testament Pseudepigrapha*. 2 vols. New York: Doubleday.

Chatman, Seymour.
1978 *Story and Discourse: Narrative Structure in Fiction and Film*. Ithaca, N.Y.: Cornell University Press.

Cicero
The Education of the Orator. H. M. Hubbel, tr. Cambridge: Harvard University Press/Loeb, 1939.
Letters. 7 vols. E. O. Winstedt, W. G. Williams, M. Cary, et al., trs. Cambridge: Harvard University Press/Loeb, 1912–72.

Clark, K. W.
1947 "The Gentile Bias in Matthew," *JBL* 66:165–72.
1960 "Worship in the Jerusalem Temple After A.D. 70," *NTS* 6:269–80.

Clarke, M. L.
1953 *Rhetoric at Rome: A Historical Survey*. London: Cohen & West.

Clement
"The Epistle of Clement to the Corinthians," (I Clement) *The Apostolic Fathers*. J. B. Lightfoot, tr. Grand Rapids, Mich.: Baker, 1957. (See also Loeb, 1912.)

Coleman-Norton, Paul R., ed.
1966 *Roman State and Christian Church: A Collection of Legal Documents*. 2 vols. London: Allenson.

Collins, Adela Yarbro
1976 *The Combat Myth in the Book of Revelation*. Chico, Calif.: Scholars Press.
1979 *The Apocalypse*. Wilmington, Del.: Michael Glazier.
1984 *Crisis and Catharsis: The Power of the Apocalypse*. Philadelphia: Westminster Press.
1986 *Early Christian Apocalypticism: Genre and Social Setting*. Semeia 36 (ed.). Decatur, Ga.: Scholars Press.

Collins, John J., ed.
1979 *Apocalypse: The Morphology of a Genre*. Semeia 14. Chico, Calif.: Scholars Press.
1983 See Nickelsburg and Collins, 1983.
1984 *The Apocalyptic Imagination: An Introduction the Jewish Matrix of Christianity*. Los Angeles: Crossroads.

Colwell, Ernest Cadman
1970 *The Gospel of the Spirit*. New York: Harper & Row.

Conzelmann, Hans
1961 *The Theology of St. Luke*. G. Buswell, tr. New York: Harper & Row. (German original, 1953.)
1975 *First Corinthians*. Philadelphia: Fortress Press.
1979 *Galatians*. Philadelphia: Fortress Press.

Cook, Michael J.
1978 *Mark's Treatment of the Jewish Leaders*. Leiden, the Netherlands: E. J. Brill.

Cook, S. A., F. E. Adcock, and M. P. Charlesworth, eds.
1924 *The Cambridge Ancient History*. 12 vols., 1924–1939. New York: Cambridge University Press.

Cope, Oliver Lamar
1976 *Matthew: A Scribe Trained for the Kingdom of God*. CBQ Monograph 5. Washington, D.C.: Catholic Biblical Association.

Corley, Bruce C., ed.
1983 *Colloquy on New Testament Studies: A Time for Reappraisal and Fresh Approaches*. Macon, Ga.: Mercer University Press.

Court, John M.
1979 *Myth and History in the Book of Revelation*. Atlanta: John Knox Press.

Creed, J. M.
1930 *The Gospel According to St. Luke*. New York: Macmillan.

Crites, Stephen
1971 "The Narrative Quality of Experience,"
JAAR 39:291–311.
1975 "Angels We Have Heard," *Religion as
Story*. J. B. Wiggins, ed. New York: Harper
& Row.
Crossan, John Dominic
1973 *In Parables: The Challenge of the Historical Jesus*. New York: Harper & Row.
1979 *Finding Is the First Act: Trove Folktales
and Jesus' Treasure Parable*. Philadelphia:
Fortress Press.
Crowe, Jerome
1979 *Acts*. Wilmington, Del.: Michael Glazier.
Cullmann, Oscar
1953 *Early Christian Worship*. London: SCM.
1956 *The Early Church*. London: SCM.
1958 *Immortality of the Soul or Resurrection
of the Dead? The Witness of the New Testament*. London: Epworth.
1962 *Peter: Disciple-Apostle-Martyr*. Philadelphia: Westminster Press.
1963 *The Christology of the New Testament*.
Philadelphia: Westminster Press.
1976 *The Johannine Circle*. Philadelphia:
Westminster Press.
Culpepper, R. Alan
1975 *The Johannine School: An Evaluation of
the Johannine-School Hypothesis Based on an
Investigation of the Nature of Ancient Schools*.
Chico, Calif.: Scholars Press.
1983 *Anatomy of the Fourth Gospel: A Study
in Literary Design*. Philadelphia: Fortress Press.

Dahl, Nils A.
1976 *Jesus in the Memory of the Early Church*.
Minneapolis: Augsburg.
Danby, Herbert
1933 *The Mishnah*. New York: Oxford Uni-
versity Press.
Danker, Frederick W.
1976 *Luke*. Philadelphia: Fortress Press.
Daube, David
1949 "Rabbinic Methods of Interpretation and
Hellenistic Rhetoric." *Hebrew Union College
Annual* 22:239–64.
Davids, Peter H.
1982 *The Epistle of James: A Commentary

on the Greek Text*. Grand Rapids, Mich.:
Eerdmans.
Davies, W. D.
1964 *The Setting of the Sermon on the Mount*.
New York: Cambridge University Press.
1977 "Paul and the People of Israel." *NTS* 24:4–
39.
1980 *Paul and Rabbinic Judaism: Some Elements in Pauline Theology*. Fourth edition.
Philadelphia: Fortress Press.
1983 *Jewish and Pauline Studies*. Philadelphia: Fortress Press.
Davis, Charles Thomas
1973 "The Fulfillment of Creation: A Study of
Matthew's Genealogy," *JAAR* 41:520–35.
Deissmann, Gustav A.
1957 *Paul*. New York: Harper Torchbooks.
DeRidder, Richard R.
1971 *The Dispersion of the People of God: The
Covenantal Basis of Matthew 28:18–20 against
the Background of Jewish Proselytism* . . . .
Kampen, the Netherlands: J. H. Kok.
Derrett, J. Duncan M.
1971 "Law in the New Testament: The Palm
Sunday Colt," *Novum Testament* 13:241–58.
1973a "Figtrees in the Testament," *Heythrop
Journal* 14:249–65.
1973b "The Good Shepard: St. John's Use of
Jewish Halakah and Haggadah," *Studia Theologica*. 27:25–50.
1973c "The Manager at Bethlehem: Light on
St. Luke's Technique from the Contemporary
Jewish Religious Law," *Studia Evangelica* 6:86–
94.
1974 "Allegory and the Wicked Vinedres-
sers," *Journal of Theological Studies* 25:426–
32.
1975a "Cursing Jesus: The Jews as 'Religious
Persecutors,'" *NTS* XXI 1975:544–54.
1975b "Midrash in Matthew," *Heythrop Journal* 16:51–56.
1982 "Trees Walking, Prophecy, and Christology," *Studies in the New Testament*. Leiden,
the Netherlands: E. J. Brill.
1983 "Binding and Loosing (Matt. 16:19; 18:18;
John 10:23)," *JBL* 102:112–17.
Dewey, Joanna
1980 *Markan Public Debate: Literary Technique, Concentric Structure and Theology in
Mark 2*. Chico, Calif.: Scholars Press.

Dibelius, Martin
1935 *From Tradition to Gospel.* New York: Charles Scribner's.
1953 *Paul.* Philadelphia: Westminster Press.
Dibelius, Martin and H. Greeven
1976 *James.* M. A. Williams, tr. (Hermeneia Series) German original, 1920, rev. 1964. Philadelphia: Fortress Press.
Dibelius, Martin and Hans Conzelmann
1972 *The Pastoral Epistles.* P. Buttolph and A. Y. Collins, trs. (Hermeneia Series). Philadelphia: Fortress Press.
Dio Cassius Cocceianus
Roman History. E. Cary, tr. Cambridge: Harvard University Press/Loeb, 1961.
Diogenes Laertius
Lives of Eminent Philosophers, 2 vols. R. D. Hicks, tr. Cambridge: Harvard University Press/Loeb.
Dodd, C. H.
1946 *The Johannine Epistles.* New York: Harper & Row.
1951 *The Apostolic Preaching and its Development.* New York: Harper & Row.
1953 *The Interpretation of the Fourth Gospel.* New York: Cambridge University Press.
1963 *Historical Tradition in the Fourth Gospel.* New York: Cambridge University Press. (Reprint, 1976.)
Donahue, J. R.
1973 *Are You the Christ?* SBL Dissertation Series 10. Chico, Calif.: Scholars Press.
Donaldson, Terrence L.
1985 *Jesus on the Mountain: A Study of Matthean Theology.* Sheffield, England: JSOT.
Donfried, Karl P., ed.
1977 *The Romans Debate.* Minneapolis: Augsburg.
Doty, William G.
1972 "The Concept of Genre in Literary Analysis," *The Genre of the Gospels.* Denver, Colo.: Society of Biblical Literature.
1973 *Letters in Primitive Christianity.* Philadelphia: Fortress Press.
Doughty, D. J.
1979 "Women and Liberation in the Churches of Pauline Tradition," *Drew Gateway* 2:1–21.
Douglas, Mary
1969 "Social Preconditions of Enthusiasm and Heterodoxy." In *Form of Symbolic Action.* Seattle: University of Washington Press: 69–80.
Drower, E. L.
1962 *The Mandaeans of Iraq and Iran.* Leiden, the Netherlands: E. J. Brill.
Drury, John
1976 *Tradition and Design in Luke's Gospel.* Atlanta: John Knox Press.
Duling, Dennis C.
1979 *Jesus Christ Through History.* New York: Harcourt Brace Jovanovich.
Dungan, David
1971 *The Sayings of Jesus in the Churches of Paul.* Philadelphia: Fortress Press.
Dunn, James D. G.
1977 *Unity and Diversity in the New Testament.* Philadelphia: Westminster Press.
1980 *Christology in the Making: A New Testament Inquiry into the Origins of the Doctrine of the Incarnation.* Philadelphia: Westminster Press.
Dupont-Sommer, A.
1962 *The Essene Writings from Qumran.* Chicago: World.

Ebeling, Gerhard
1985 *The Truth of the Gospel: An Exposition of Galatians.* Philadelphia: Fortress Press.
Edwards, O. C., Jr.
1981 *Luke's Story of Jesus.* Philadelphia: Fortress Press.
Edwards, Richard A.
1985 *Matthew's Story of Jesus.* Philadelphia: Fortress Press.
Efird, James M.
1978 *Daniel and Revelation: A Study of Two Extraordinary Visions.* Valley Forge, Pa.: Judson Press.
Eliade, Mircea
1959 *Cosmos and History: The Myth of the Eternal Return.* New York: Harper & Row.
Elliot, J. H.
1981 *A Home for the Homeless: A Sociological Exegesis of First Peter, Its Situation and Strategy.* Philadelphia: Fortress Press.
Ellis, E. Earle
1961 *Paul and His Recent Interpreters.* Grand Rapids, Mich.: Eerdmans.
1967 *The Gospel of Luke.* Huntington, N.Y.: The Attic Press.

1972   *Eschatology in Luke*. Philadelphia: Fortress Press.

1984   *The World of St. John*. Grand Rapids, Mich.: Eerdmans.

Ellis, E. Earle and Max Wilcox

1969   *Noetestamentica et Semitica: Studies in Honour of Matthew Black*. Edinburgh: T&T Clarke.

Ellis, Peter F.

1974   *Matthew: His Mind and His Message*. Collegeville, Minn.: Liturgical Press.

1982   *Seven Pauline Letters*. Collegeville, Minn.: Liturgical Press.

Else, G. F.

1957   *Aristotle's Poetics: The Argument*. Cambridge: Harvard University Press.

1967   *Aristotle: Poetics*. Ann Arbor: University of Michigan Press.

Enslin, Morton Scott

1927   "Paul and Gamaliel," *JR* 7:360–75.

Epictetus

Discourses, 2 vols. W. A. Oldfather, tr. Cambridge: Harvard University Press/Loeb, 1925–28.

Epp, Eldon J.

1978   "Paul's Diverse Imageries of the Human Situation and His Unifying Theme of Freedom," *Unity and Diversity*. Robert A. Guelich, ed. Grand Rapids, Mich.: Eerdmans: 100–16.

Eusebius

The History of the Church from Christ to Constantine. G. A. Williamson, tr. Minneapolis: Augsburg, 1965. (See also Loeb, 1932.)

Evanson, E.

1792   *The Dissonance of the Four Generally Received Evangelists*. Scnochenberg.

Farmer, W. R.

1974   *The Last Twelve Verses of Mark*. Leiden, the Netherlands: E. J. Brill.

1976a   *The Synoptic Problem: A Critical Analysis*. Dillsboro: Western North Carolina Press.

1976b   "The Post-Sectarian Character of Matthew and Its Post-War Setting in Antioch of Syria," *Perspectives in Religion Studies* 3:235–47.

1982   *Jesus and the Gospel: Tradition, Scripture, and Canon*. Philadelphia: Fortress Press.

Farmer, W. R. and D. M. Farkasfalvy

1983   *The Formation of the New Testament Canon*. Ramsey, N.J.: Paulist Press.

Farrer, Austin

1949   *The Rebirth of Images: The Making of St. John's Apocalypse*. Gloucester, Mass.: Dacre.

1964   *The Revelation of St. John the Divine*. Oxford: Clarendon Press.

Fee, Gordon D.

1984   *First and Second Timothy, Titus*. (Good News Commentary) New York: Harper & Row.

Fenton, John C.

1963   *The Gospel of St. Matthew*. Pelican Series. New York: Penguin Books.

1970   *The Gospel According to John*. Oxford: Clarendon Press.

Ferguson, John

1970   *The Religions of the Roman Empire*. Ithaca, N.Y.: Cornell University Press.

1980   *Greek and Roman Religion: A Sourcebook*. Park Ridge, N.J.: Noyes Press.

Filson, Floyd V.

1956   "Broken Patterns in the Gospel of Matthew," *JBL* 75:227–31.

1960   *The Gospel According to St. Matthew*. New York: Harper & Row.

Finegan, Jack

1969   *Handbook of Biblical Chronology*. Princeton, N.J.: Princeton University Press.

Fischel, Henry

1969   "Story and History: Observations on Graeco-Roman Rhetoric and Pharisaism," *American Oriental Society, Midwest Branch, Semi-Centennial Volume*. Denis Sinor, ed., Asian Studies Research Institute. Bloomington: Indiana University Press.

Fitzmyer, Joseph A.

1970   "The Priority of Mark and the 'Q' Source in Luke," *Jesus and Man's Hope*, Vol. 1. D. Miller and Y. Hadidian, eds. Perspective, Pittsburgh Theological Seminary.

1977   *The Dead Sea Scrolls: Major Publications and Tools for Study*. Chico, Calif.: Scholars Press.

1981–86 *The Gospel according to Luke*. 3 vols. (Anchor Bible Series) New York: Doubleday.

Flusser, David

1958   "The Dead Sea Sect and Pre-Pauline

Christianity," *Scripta Hierosolymitana* 4:215–66.

1975 "Two Anti-Jewish Montages in Matthew," *Immanuel* 5:37–45.

Foakes-Jackson, F. J.
1931 *The Acts of the Apostles*. New York: Harper.

Foerester, Werner
1972 *Gnosis: A Selection of Gnostic Texts*. 2 vols. New York: Oxford University Press.

Forster, E. M.
1962 *Aspects of the Novel*. New York: Penguin Books.

Fortna, R. T.
1970 *The Gospel of Signs: A Reconstruction of the Narrative Source Underlying the Fourth Gospel*. New York: Cambridge University Press.

Fowler, Robert M.
1981 *Loaves and Fishes: The Function of the Feeding Stories in the Gospel of Mark*. Chico, Calif.: Scholars Press.

1985 "The Rhetoric of Indirection in the Gospel of Mark," *Proceedings of the Eastern Great Lakes Biblical Society* 5:47–57.

Francis, Fred O.
1973 *Conflicts at Colossae: A Problem in the Interpretation of Early Christianity*. Chico, Calif.: Scholars Press.

Francis, Fred O. and J. P. Sampley
1984 *Pauline Parallels*. Second edition. Philadelphia: Fortress Press. (Original, 1975.)

Franklin, Eric
1975 *Christ the Lord: A Study in the Purpose and Theology of Luke-Acts*. Philadelphia: Westminster Press.

Frederick, Gerhard
1965 "Evangellion" *TDNT* vol. II:707–37. Gerhard Kittel, ed., Grand Rapids, Mich.: Eerdmans.

Frei, Hans W.
1966 "Theological Reflections on the Gospel Accounts of Jesus' Death and Resurrection," *The Christian Scholar* 49:263–306.

1974 *The Eclipse of Biblical Narrative: A Study in Eighteenth and Nineteenth Century Hermeneutics*. New Haven: Yale University Press.

Frend, W. H. C.
1967 *Martyrdom and Persecution in the Early Church*. New York: Oxford University Press.

Freyne, Sean
1980 *The World of the New Testament*. Wilmington, Del.: Michael Glazier.

Frye, Northrop
1957 *Anatomy of Criticism: Four Essays*. New York: Atheneum.

Frye, Roland Mushat
1973 "On the Historical-Critical Method in New Testament Studies: A Reply to Professor Achtemeier," *Perspective* 14:28–33.

1971 "A Literary Perspective for the Criticism of the Gospels." In *Jesus and Man's Hope*, II:193–221. Pittsburgh Theological Seminary.

Fuller, Reginald H.
1962 *The New Testament in Current Study*. New York: Charles Scribner's.

1980 *The Formation of the Resurrection Narratives*. Philadelphia: Fortress Press.

Funk, Robert W.
1982 *Parables and Presence: Forms of the New Testament Tradition*. Philadelphia: Fortress Press.

Furnish, Victor Paul
1979 *The Moral Teaching of Paul*. Nashville: Abingdon.

1984 *Second Corinthians*. (Anchor Bible) New York: Doubleday.

Gaechter, Paul
n.d. *Die Literarische Kunst im Matthaus-Evangelium*. Stuttgart: Verlag.

Gager, John G.
1974 "Gospels and Jesus: Some Doubts About Method," *JR* 54:244–72.

1975 *Kingdom and Community: The Social World of Early Christianity*. Englewood Cliffs, N.J.: Prentice-Hall.

1983 *The Origins of Anti-Semitism: Attitudes toward Judaism in Pagan and Christian Antiquity*. New York: Oxford University Press.

Gamble, Harry
1975 "The Redaction of the Pauline Letters and the Formation of the Pauline Corpus," *JBL* 94:403–18.

Garland, David E.
1979 *The Intention of Matthew 23*. Leiden, the Netherlands: E. J. Brill.

Gärtner, Bertil
1954 "The Habakkuk Commentary (DSH) and

the Gospel of Matthew," *Studia Theologica* 8:1–24.

Gasque, W. Ward
  1975 *A History of the Criticism of the Acts of the Apostles*. Grand Rapids, Mich.: Eerdmans.

Gaston, L.
  1970 *No Stone On Another: Studies in the Significance of the Fall of Jerusalem in the Synoptic Gospels*. Leiden, the Netherlands: E. J. Brill.

Georgi, Dieter
  1985 *The Opponents of Paul in 2 Corinthians: A Study in Religious Propaganda in Late Antiquity*. Philadelphia: Fortress Press.

Gerhardsson, Birger
  1979 *The Origins of the Gospel Tradition*. Philadelphia: Fortress Press.

Getty, Mary Ann
  1980 *Philippians and Philemon*. Wilmington, Del.: Michael Glazier.

Glatzer, Nahum N.
  1959 *Hillel the Elder: The Emergence of Classical Judaism*. Washington, D.C.: Bnai Brith Hillel Foundation.
  1969 *The Judaic Tradition*. Boston: Beacon Press.

Golden, Leon
  1962 "Catharsis," *TAPA* xciii:51–60.
  1965 "Is Tragedy the Imitation of a Serious Action?" *Greek, Roman, and Byzantine Studies* VI:283–89.
  1968 *Aristotle's Poetics: A Translation and Commentary for Students of Literature*. Commentary by O. B. Hardison. Englewood Cliffs, N.J.: Prentice-Hall.
  1969 "Mimesis and Katharsis," *Classical Philology* LXVI 3:147–52.
  1976 "The Clarification Theory of Katharsis," *Hermes* 104, Band 4, 437–52.

Goldstein, H. D.
  1966 "Mimesis and Catharsis Reexamined," *Journal of Aesthetics and Art Criticism* XXIV 567–77.

Goodenough, Erwin R.
  1953 *Jewish Symbols in the Greco-Roman World*. 13 vols. Princeton: Princeton University Press.

Goodspeed, Edgar J.
  1959 *Matthew, Apostle and Evangelist*. Minneapolis: Winston Press.

Goodspeed, Edgar J. and Robert M. Grant
  1966 *A History of Early Christian Literature*. Chicago: University of Chicago Press.

Gottcent, J. H.
  1979 *The Bible as Literature: A Selective Bibliography*. Boston: G. K. Hall.

Goulder, M. D.
  1974 *Midrash and Lection in Matthew*. London: SPCK.
  1978 "Mark XVI:1–8 and Parallels," *NTS* 24:235–39.

Grant, Frederic C.
  1926 *The Economic Background of the Gospels*. New York: Russell & Russell.
  1953 *Hellenistic Religions: The Age of Syncretism*. (ed.) New York: Bobbs-Merrill.
  1957 *The Gospels: Their Origins and Their Growth*. New York: Harper & Row.
  1962 *Roman Hellenism and the New Testament*. London: Oliver, Boyd.

Grant, Michael
  1977 *Jesus: An Historian's Review of the Gospels*. New York: Charles Scribner's.

Grant, Robert M.
  1952 *Miracle and Natural Law in Greco-Roman and Early Christian Thought*. Amsterdam: North Holland.
  1961 *Gnosticism*. New York: Harper.
  1963 *Historical Introduction to the New Testament*. New York: Harper & Row.
  1965 *The Formation of the New Testament Canon*. New York: Harper & Row.
  1976 *Perspectives on Scripture and Tradition*. Notre Dame, Ind.: Fides.
  1977 *Early Christianity and Society*. New York: Harper & Row.

Grant, Robert M. and David Tracy
  1984 *A Short History of the Interpretation of the Bible*. Philadelphia: Fortress Press.

Green, H. Benedict
  1975 *The Gospel according to Matthew*. New York: Oxford University Press.

Gros Louis, Kenneth R. R.
  1974 "Revelation." In *Literary Interpretation of Biblical Narratives*. Nashville: Abingdon.

Grube, G. M. A.
  1965 *The Greek and Roman Critics*. Toronto: University of Toronto Press.

Gruenler, Royce Gordon
  1982 *New Approaches to Jesus and the Gos-*

pels: A Phenomenological and Exegetical Study of Synoptic Christology. Grand Rapids, Mich.: Baker.

Gundry, Robert H.
1967 *The Use of the Old Testament in St. Matthew's Gospel.* Supplements to Novum Testamentum 18. Leiden, the Netherlands: E. J. Brill.
1982 *Matthew: A Commentary on His Literary and Theological Art.* Grand Rapids, Mich.: Eerdmans.

Gunther, John J.
1973 *St. Paul's Opponents and Their Background.* Leiden, the Netherlands: E. J. Brill.

Guthrie, Donald
1975 *New Testament Introduction.* Downers Grove, Ill.: Inter-Varsity.
1981 *Galatians.* Grand Rapids, Mich.: Eerdmans.

Hadas, Moses and Morton Smith
1965 *Heroes and Gods.* New York: Harper & Row.

Haenchen, Ernst
1971 *The Acts of the Apostles: A Commentary.* Philadelphia: Westminster Press.
1984 *John: A Commentary.* 2 vols. Philadelphia: Fortress Press.

Hanson, A. T.
1982 *The Pastoral Epistles: Pastoral Bible Commentary.* Grand Rapids, Mich.: Eerdmans.

Hanson, Paul D.
1979 *The Dawn of Apocalyptic: The Historical and Sociological Roots of Jewish Apocalyptic Eschatology.* Philadelphia: Fortress Press.

Hanson, R. P. C.
1967 *The Acts.* New York: Oxford University Press.

Hare, Douglas R. A.
1967 *The Theme of the Jewish Persecution of Christians in the Gospel of St. Matthew.* Vol. 6 NTS monograph series. New York: Cambridge University Press.

Hare, Douglas and D. Harrington
1975 "Make Disciples of All the Gentiles (Mt. 28:19)," *CBQ* 37:359–69.

Harrington, Daniel J.
1979 *Interpreting the New Testament: A Practical Guide.* Wilmington, Del.: Michael Glazier.

Harrington, Wilfrid
1979 *Mark.* Wilmington, Del.: Michael Glazier.

Harrison, J.
1922 *Prolegomena to the Study of Greek Religion.* New York: Cambridge University Press.

Harvey, A. E.
1982 *Jesus and the Constraints of History.* Philadelphia: Westminster Press.

Harvey, Van A.
1966 *The Historian and the Believer: The Morality of Historical Knowledge and Christian Belief.* New York: Macmillan.

Hawkin, J. D.
1972 "Incomprehension of the Disciples in Markan Redaction." *JBL* 91:491–500.

Hawkins, John Caesar
1909 *Horae Synopticae: Contributions to the Study of the Synoptic Problem.* New York: Oxford University Press (1968 reprint).

Hays, Richard B.
1983 *The Faith of Jesus: An Investigation of the Narrative Substructure of Galatians 3:1–4:11.* Chico, Calif.: Scholars Press.

Held, Heinz Joachim
1964 "Matthew as Interpreter of the Miracle Stories," *Tradition and Interpretation in Matthew.* Philadelphia: Westminster Press.

Helgeland, John
1975 "Roman Army Religion," *Society of Biblical Literature Seminar Papers, 1975*:199–205. Chico, Calif.: Scholars Press.

Hemer, C. J.
1977 "Luke the Historian," *Bulletin of the John Rylands University Library* 60:28–51.

Hengel, Martin
1974a *Judaism and Hellenism.* 2 vols. Philadelphia: Fortress Press.
1974b *Property and Riches in the Early Church: Aspects of a Social History of Early Christians.* Philadelphia: Fortress Press.
1977 *Crucifixion: In the Ancient World and the Folly of the Message of the Cross.* Philadelphia: Fortress Press.
1979 *Acts and the History of Earliest Christianity.* Philadelphia: Fortress Press.
1980 *Jews, Greeks, and Barbarians: Aspects of the Hellenization of Judaism in the Pre-Christian Period.* John Bowden, tr. Philadelphia: Fortress Press.
1983 *Between Jesus and Paul: Studies in the History of Earliest Christianity.* J. Bowden, tr. Philadelphia: Fortress Press.

Hennecke, E. and W. Schneemelcher
    1963   *New Testament Apocrypha*. 2 vols. Philadelphia: Westminster Press.
Herford, R. Travers
    1903   *Christianity in Talmud and Midrash*. Hoboken, N.J.: Ktav, reprint.
    1952   *The Pharisees*. Boston: Beacon Press.
    1971   *Talmud and Apocrypha*. Hoboken, N.J.: Ktav.
Heschel, Abraham J.
    1962   *The Prophets*. New York: Harper & Row.
Higgins, A. J. B.
    1967   "The Priestly Messiah," *NTS* 13:211–39.
Hill, David
    1972   *The Gospel of Matthew*. The New Century Bible. London: Oliphants.
    1976   "On Suffering and Baptism in I Peter," *NT* 18/3:181–89.
Hill, J. H.
    1894   *The Earliest Life of Christ*. Edinburgh: T&T Clarke.
Hirsch, Eric D., Jr.
    1967   *Validity in Interpretation*. New Haven: Yale University Press.
Hock, Ronald R.
    1980   *The Social Context of Paul's Ministry: Tentmaking and Apostleship*. Philadelphia: Fortress Press.
Hoffman, R. Joseph
    1984   *Marcion: On the Restitution of Christianity*. Chico, Calif.: Scholars Press.
Hollenbach, Paul W.
    1983   "Recent Historical Jesus Studies and the Social Sciences," *Seminar Papers of the Society of Biblical Literature, 1983*. Chico, Calif.: Scholars Press.
Holmberg, Bengt
    1980   *Paul and Power: The Structure of Authority in the Primitive Church as Reflected in the Pauline Epistles*. Philadelphia: Fortress Press.
Hooke, S. H.
    1935   "The Myth and Ritual Pattern in Jewish and Christian Apocalyptic." In *The Labyrinth*. New York: Macmillan.
Hooker, M. D.
    1972   "On Using the Wrong Tool," *Theology* 75:570–81.
    1980   *A Preface to Paul*. New York: Oxford University Press.

Horace
    1966   *Art of Poetry*. H. R. Fairclough, tr. Cambridge: Harvard University Press/Loeb.
Horbury, William and Brian McNeil, eds.
    1981   *Suffering and Martyrdom in the New Testament*. New York: Cambridge University Press.
Horst, P. W. Vander
    1972   "Can a Book End with GAR? A Note on Mark XVI 8," *JTS* 23:121–24.
Hoskyns, Sir Edwin
    1947   *The Fourth Gospel*. London: Faber.
Houlden, J. L.
    1970   *Paul's Letters from Prison*. Philadelphia: Westminster Press.
    1973   *The Johannine Epistles*. New York: Harper & Row.
Howard, George
    1979   *Paul: Crisis in Galatia*. New York: Cambridge University Press.
Howard, Virgil
    1977   "Did Jesus Speak About His Own Death?" *CBQ* 39:515–27.
Howe, Margaret
    1980   "Interpretations of Paul in the Acts of Paul and Thecla," *Pauline Studies: . . . Presented to Professor F. F. Bruce*. Grand Rapids, Mich.: Eerdmans.
Hubbard, David A. and Gerald F. Hawthorne
    1983   *Philippians*. Waco, Tex.: Word Books.
Hultgren, Arlend J.
    1979   *Jesus and His Adversaries: The Form and Function of the Conflict Stories in the Synoptic Tradition*. Minneapolis: Augsburg.
Hunt, A. S. and C. C. Edgar, ed. and tr.
    1932   *Select Papyri: I, Nonliterary Papyri, Private Affairs*. Cambridge: Harvard University Press/Loeb.
Hurtado, Larry
    1983   *Mark*. (The Good News Commentary Series) New York: Harper & Row.

Ignatius
    "The Epistles of Ignatius," *The Apostolic Fathers*, vol. 1:165–277. K. Lake, tr. Cambridge: Harvard University Press/Loeb, 1912–13.
Irenaeus
    "Against Heresies." In Library of Christian Classics, vol. 1: *The Early Christian Fathers*.

C. C. Richardson, ed. and tr. Philadelphia: Westminster Press, 1953.

Isaac, B.
1984 "Judea After AD 70," *Journal for Jewish Studies* 35/1:44–50.

Isenberg, S. R.
1974 "Millenarianism in Greco-Roman Palestine," *Religion* 4:26–46.

James, M. R.
1924 *The Apocryphal New Testament*. Oxford: Clarendon Press.

Jeremias, Joachim
1955 *The Eucharistic Words of Jesus*. Oxford: Blackwell.
1963 *The Parables of Jesus*. S. H. Hooke, tr. New York: Charles Scribner's.
1964 *Problem of the Historical Jesus*. Philadelphia: Fortress Press.
1969 "Paulus als Hillelit." In *Neotestamentica et Semitica*. Edinburgh: T&T Clarke: 88–94.

Jervell, Jacob
1972 *Luke and the People of God*. Minneapolis: Augsburg.
1977 *God's Christ and His People*. New York: Columbia University Press.
1984 *Unknown Paul: Essays on Luke-Acts and Early Christian History*. Minneapolis: Augsburg.

Jewett, Robert
1979 *Chronology of Paul's Life*. Philadelphia: Fortress Press.
1981 *Letter to Pilgrims: A Commentary on the Epistles to the Hebrews*. New York: Pilgrim Press.

Johnson, Luke T.
1977 *The Literary Function of Possessions in Luke-Acts*. Chico, Calif.: Scholars Press.

Johnson, M.
1969 *The Purpose of the Biblical Genealogies*. New York: Cambridge University Press.

Jonas, Hans
1963 *The Gnostic Religion: The Message of the Alien God and the Beginnings of Christianity*. Boston: Beacon Press.

Jonge, M. de
1977 *Jesus: Stranger from Heaven and Son of God*. J. E. Steely, ed. and tr. Chico, Calif.: Scholars Press.

Josephus, Flavius
Antiquities. R. Marcus et al., trs. Cambridge: Harvard University Press/Loeb, 1930–65.
Autobiography. Cambridge: Harvard University Press/Loeb.
Jewish War. H. Thackeray, tr. Cambridge: Harvard University Press/Loeb, 1927–28.

Judge, E. A.
1968 "Paul's Boasting in Relation to Contemporary Professional Practice," *ABR* 16:37–50.
1982 *Rank and Status in the World of the Caesars and St. Paul*. University of Canterbury.

Juel, Donald
1977 *Messiah and Temple*. In SBL Dissertation Series 31. Chico, Calif.: Scholars Press.
1984 *Luke-Acts: The Promise of History*. Atlanta: John Knox Press.

Justin Martyr
Dialogue with Trypho. In *Saint Justin Martyr*. T. B. Falls, ed. and tr. Edmonds, Wash.: Christian Heritage, 1948.

Juvenal
Satire. Hubert Creekmore, tr. New York: Mentor, 1963.

Kahler, Martin
1896 *The So-Called Historical Jesus and the Historic Biblical Christ*. Philadelphia: Fortress Press. (Reprint, 1964.)

Kalin, E. R.
1975 "Early Traditions About Mark's Gospel: Canonical Status Emerges, the Story Grows." *Current Trends in Mission* 2:332–41.

Käsemann, Ernst
1964 *Essays on New Testament Themes*. London: Allenson.
1968 *The Testament of Jesus: A Study of the Gospel of John in the Light of the Chapter 17*. Philadelphia: Fortress Press.
1971 *Perspectives on Paul*. Philadelphia: Fortress Press.
1980 *Commentary on Romans*. G. W. Bromily, tr. Grand Rapids, Mich.: Eerdmans.
1984 *Wandering People of God: An Investigation of the Letter to the Hebrews*. Roy A. Harrisville, tr. Minneapolis: Augsburg.

Keck, L. E.
1966 "Introduction to Mark's Gospels," *NTS* 12:352–70.

1971   A Future for the Historical Jesus: The Place of Jesus in Preaching and Theology. New York: Abingdon.

1979   *Paul and His Letters*. Philadelphia: Fortress Press.

Keck, L. E. and V. P. Furnish

1984   *The Pauline Letters*. Nashville: Abingdon.

Keck, L. E. and J. L. Martyn, eds.

1966   *Studies in Luke-Acts*. Nashville: Abingdon. (Reprinted, 1980.)

Kee, Howard Clark

1973a   *Understanding the New Testament*. Fourth edition, Englewood Cliffs, N.J.: Prentice-Hall, 1983.

1973b   "Aretalogy and Gospel," *JBL* 92:402–22.

1973c   *The Origins of Christianity: Sources and Documents*. ed., Englewood Cliffs, N.J.: Prentice-Hall.

1977a   *Jesus in History: An Approach to the Study of the Gospels*. Second edition. New York: Harcourt Brace Jovanovich.

1977b   *Community of the New Age: Studies in Mark's Gospel*. Philadelphia: Westminster Press.

1980   *Christian Origins in Sociological Perspective: Methods and Resources*. Philadelphia: Westminster Press.

1984   *The New Testament in Context: Sources and Documents*. Englewood Cliffs, N.J.: Prentice-Hall. (Original, 1973c.)

Kelber, Werner H.

1974   *The Kingdom in Mark*. Philadelphia: Fortress Press.

1976   *Passion in Mark: Studies on Mark 14–16*. (ed.) Philadelphia: Fortress Press.

1979   *Mark's Story of Jesus*. Philadelphia: Fortress Press.

1983   *The Oral and the Written Gospel: The Hermeneutics of Speaking and Writing in the Synoptic Tradition, Mark, Paul, and Q*. Philadelphia: Fortress Press.

Kelly, J. N. D.

1969   *A Commentary on the Epistles of Peter and Jude*. New York: Harper & Row.

Kennedy, George A.

1972   *The Art of Rhetoric in the Roman World (300 BC–AD 300) A History of Rhetoric*, vol. 2. Princeton: Princeton University Press.

1984   *New Testament Interpretation through Rhetorical Criticism*. Chapel Hill: University of North Carolina Press.

Kermode, Frank

1967   *The Sense of an Ending: Studies in the Theory of Fiction*. New York: Oxford University Press.

1979   *The Genesis of Secrecy: On the Interpretation of Narrative*. Cambridge: Harvard University Press.

Kilpatrick, G. D.

1946   *The Origins of the Gospel According to St. Matthew*. Oxford: Clarendon Press.

Kim, Chan-Hie

1975   "The Papyrus Invitation," *JBL* 94: 391–402.

Kingsbury, Jack Dean

1969   *The Parables of Jesus in Matthew 13: A Study in Redaction-Criticism*. Atlanta: John Knox Press.

1975   *Matthew: Structure, Christology, Kingdom*. Philadelphia: Fortress Press.

1979   "The Figure of Peter in Matthew's Gospel as a Theological Problem," *JBL* 98:67–83.

1983   *The Christology of Mark's Gospel*. Philadelphia: Fortress Press.

1986   *Matthew as Story*. Philadelphia: Fortress Press.

Kissinger, Warren S.

1975   *The Sermon on the Mount: A History of Interpretation and Bibliography*. Metuchen, N.J.: Scarecrow Press.

1979   *The Parables of Jesus: A History of Interpretation and Bibliography*. Metuchen, N.J.: Scarecrow Press.

Klausner, Joseph

1955   *The Messianic Idea in Israel from Its Beginning to the Completion of the Mishnah*. New York: Macmillan.

1961   *From Jesus to Paul*. Boston: Beacon Press.

Klijn, A. F. J.

1980   *An Introduction to the New Testament*. Leiden, the Netherlands: E. J. Brill.

Knox, John

1935   *Philemon Among the Letters of Paul*. Chicago: University of Chicago Press.

1939   *Chapters in a Life of Paul*. Nashville: Abingdon-Cokesbury.

1942   *Marcion and the New Testament: An Es-*

say on the Early History of the Canon. Chicago: University of Chicago Press.

Koch, Klaus
1969 *The Growth of the Biblical Tradition: The Form-Critical Method*. New York: Charles Scribner's.

Koester, Helmut
1972 "Romance, Biography, and Gospel." In *The Genre of the Gospels*. Denver, Colo.: Society of Biblical Literature.
1982 *Introduction to the New Testament*. 2 vols. Philadelphia: Fortress Press.

Kohler, Kaufmann
1973 *Origins of the Synagogue and the Church*. New York: Arno Press.

Kraeling, C. H.
1951 *John the Baptist*. New York: Charles Scribner's.
1964 *Rand McNally Bible Atlas*. Skokie, Ill.: Rand McNally.

Krause, Martin
1977 *Gnosis and Gnosticism: International Conference on Patristic Studies*. Leiden, the Netherlands: E. J. Brill.

Krentz, Edgar
1975 *The Historical-Critical Method*. Guides to Biblical Scholarship Series. Philadelphia: Fortress Press.

Krieger, Murray
1964 *A Window to Criticism*. Princeton: Princeton University Press.

Krodel, Gerhard, ed.
1978 *Ephesians, Colossians, II Thessalonians, the Pastoral Epistles*. Philadelphia: Fortress Press.

Kümmel, Werner Georg
1966 *Introduction to the New Testament*. (14th rev. ed. of the work of Paul Feine & Johannes Behm.) Nashville: Abingdon.
1972 *The New Testament: The History of the Investigation of its Problems*. Nashville: Abingdon.

Kysar, Robert
1975 *The Fourth Evangelist and His Gospel: An Examination of Contemporary Scholarship*. Minneapolis: Augsburg.
1976 *John: The Maverick Gospel*. Atlanta: John Knox Press.
1984 *John's Story of Jesus*. Philadelphia: Fortress Press.

Laistner, Max Ludwig Wolfram
1977 *Greater Roman Historians*. Berkeley: University of California Press.

Lambrecht, Jan
1981 *Once More the Astonished: The Parables of Jesus*. Los Angeles: Crossroads.

Lane, Michael, ed.
1970 *Introduction to Structuralism*. New York: Harper (Basic Books).

Lane, William
1974 *The Gospel according to Mark*. Grand Rapids, Mich.: Eerdmans.

Lapide, Pinchas
1984 *Paul: Rabbi and Apostle*. L. W. Denef, tr. Minneapolis: Augsburg.

LaSor, W. S.
1956 "The Messiahs of Aaron and Israel," *VT* 6:425–29.

Lattimore, Richmond
1967 *The Odyssey of Homer: A Modern Translation*. New York: Harper Torchbooks.

Laws, S.
1981 *The Epistle of James*. New York: Harper & Row.

Leaney, A. R. C.
1958 *A Commentary on the Gospel According to St. Luke*. London: Black.
1984 *The Jewish and Christian World: 200 BC to AD 200*. Cambridge: Cambridge University Press.

Leon, H.
1960 *The Jews of Ancient Rome*. Philadelphia: Jewish Publication Society.

Levi-Strauss, Claude
1967 "The Effectiveness of Symbols," *Structural Anthropology*. New York: Anchor/Doubleday, 181–201.

Lewis, C. S.
1958 *Reflections on the Psalms*. Harcourt, Brace, and World.
1967 "Modern Theology and Biblical Criticism." In *Christian Reflections*. W. Hooper, ed. Grand Rapids, Mich.: Eerdmans.

Lewis, J. P.
1964 "What Do We Mean by Jabneh?" *Journal of the Bible and Religion* 32:125–32.

Lightfoot, J. B.
1891 *The Apostolic Fathers*. New York: Macmillan; Baker Book House. (Reprint, 1956.)

1950   *The Gospel Message of St. Mark.* New York: Oxford University Press.

1956   *St. John's Gospel: A Commentary.* New York: Oxford University Press.

Lightstone, Jack N.

1984   *Commerce of the Sacred: Mediation of the Sacred among Jews in the Greco-Roman Diaspora.* Brown Judaic Studies 59. Chico, Calif.: Scholars Press.

Lindars, Barnabas

1961   *New Testament Apologetic: The Doctrinal Significance of the Old Testament Quotations.* Philadelphia: SCM Press.

1981   "John and the Synoptics: A Test Case," *NTS* 27:287–94.

Lindbloom, Johannes

1972   *Prophecy in Ancient Israel.* Philadephia: Fortress Press.

Lindsay, Jack, tr.

1962   *Apuleius' The Golden Ass.* Bloomington: Indiana University Press.

Lindsell, Harold

1976   *The Battle for the Bible.* Grand Rapids, Mich.: Zondervan.

Lipman, Eugene J., ed. & tr.

1974   *The Mishnah: Oral Teachings of Judaism.* New York: Shocken Books.

Lischer, Richard

1984   "The Limits of Story," *Interpretation* 38 Univ/1:26–38.

Lofink, G.

1979   *The Bible: Now I Get It! A Form Criticism Handbook.* New York: Doubleday.

Lofland, John

1966   *Doomsday Cult: A Study of Conversion, Proselytization, and Maintenance of Faith.* Englewood Cliffs, N.J.: Prentice-Hall.

Lohse, Edward

1971   *Colossians and Philemon.* Philadelphia: Fortress Press.

1976   *The New Testament Environment.* Nashville: Abingdon.

Longstaff, Thomas W. R.

1980   "Crisis and Christology: The Theology of the Gospel of Mark," *Perkins Journal* 33: 28–40.

Lucian

Works, 8 vols. A. M. Harmon et al., trs. Cambridge: Harvard University Press/Loeb, 1915–21.

Luck, Georg

1985   *Arcana Mundi: Magic and the Occult in the Greek and Roman Worlds.* Baltimore: Johns Hopkins University Press.

Lucretius

On the Nature of the Universe. R. E. Latham, tr. New York: Penguin Books (1951).

Luedemann, Gerd

1984   *Paul, Apostle to the Gentiles: Studies in Chronology.* Stanley F. Jones, tr. (forward by John Knox) Philadelphia: Fortress Press.

Lund, Nils

1931   "The Influence of Chiasmus Upon the Structure of the Gospels," *ATR* 13:27–48.

MacDonald, Dennis R.

1982   *The Legend and the Apostle: The Battle for Paul in Story and Canon.* Philadelphia: Westminster Press.

MacDonald, J. J.

1969   "Was Romans xvi a Separate Letter?" *NTS* 16:369–72.

MacMullen, Ramsay

1974   *Roman Social Relations: 50 BC to AD 284.* New Haven: Yale University Press.

1981   *Paganism in the Roman Empire.* New Haven: Yale University Press.

Malbon, Elizabeth Struthers

1980a "Mythic Structure and Meaning in Mark: Elements of a Levi-Straussian Analysis," *Semeia* (1979) 16:97–132.

1980b " 'No Need To Have Anyone Write'?: A Structural Exegesis of I Thessalonians," *SBL Seminar Papers.* P. Achtemeier, ed. Chico, Calif.: Scholars Press.

1983   "Fallible Followers: Women and Men in the Gospel of Mark," *Semeia* 28:29–48.

1985   *Narrative Space and Mythic Meaning in Mark.* New York: Seabury Press.

Malherbe, Abraham J.

1977   "Ancient Epistolary Theorists," *Ohio Journal of Religion Studies* 5/2:3–73.

1983   *Social Aspects of Early Christianity.* Philadelphia: Fortress Press.

Malina, Bruce J.

1981   *The New Testament World: Insights from Cultural Anthropology.* Philadelphia: Fortress Press.

1986   *Christian Origins and Cultural Anthro-*

pology: Practical Models for Biblical Interpretation. Atlanta: John Knox Press.

Maly, Eugene H.
1979   *Romans.* Wilmington, Del.: Michael Glazier.

Manson, T. W.
1966   *The Servant Messiah.* New York: Cambridge University Press.

Maranda, Pierre and K. Maranda
1971   *Structural Analysis of Oral Tradition.* Philadelphia: University of Pennsylvania Press.

Marshall, I. Howard
1977a   *I Believe in the Historical Jesus.* Grand Rapids, Mich.: Eerdmans.
1977b   *New Testament Interpretation: Essays on Principles and Methods.* Grand Rapids, Mich.: Eerdmans.
1978a   *Acts and the History of Earliest Christianity.* Philadelphia: Fortress Press.
1978b   *The Gospel of Luke.* Grand Rapids, Mich.: Eerdmans.
1978c   *The Epistles of John.* Grand Rapids, Mich.: Eerdmans.
1982   *The Acts of the Apostles: An Introduction and Commentary.* Grand Rapids, Mich.: Eerdmans.
1983   *1 and 2 Thessalonians.* Grand Rapids, Mich.: Eerdmans.

Martin, Ralph
1973a   *Mark: Evangelist and Theologian.* Grand Rapids, Mich.: Zondervan.
1973b   *Colossians: The Church's Lord and the Christian Liberty: An Expository Commentary with Present Day Application.* Grand Rapids, Mich.: Zondervan.
1975   *The Four Gospels.* New Testament Foundations: A Guide for Christian Students. Grand Rapids, Mich.: Eerdmans.

Martyn, J. Louis
1979   *History and Theology in the Fourth Gospel.* Nashville: Abingdon.

Marxsen, Willi
1969   *Mark the Evangelist.* Nashville: Abingdon.

McArthur, H. K.
1971   "Burden of Proof in Historical Jesus Research," *Expository Times* 82:116–19.

McIntire, C. T.
1977   *God, History, and Historians: Modern Christian Views of History.* New York: Oxford University Press.

McKenzie, John L.
1968   *Second Isaiah.* New York: Doubleday.
1976   *Light on the Gospels.* Chicago: Thomas More Press.

McKnight, Edgar V.
1969   *What is Form Criticism?* Philadelphia: Fortress Press.

McNeile, Alan Hugh
1915   *The Gospel According to St. Matthew.* London: Macmillan.

Meeks, Wayne
1972   *The Writings of St. Paul.* New York: Norton.
1975   "Am I a Jew? Johannine Christianity and Judaism." In Neusner, 1975b, vol. 1:163–86.
1983   *The First Urban Christians: The Social World of the Apostle Paul.* New Haven: Yale University Press.

Meier, John P.
1976   *Law and History in Matthew's Gospel: A Redactional Study of Matthew 5:17–48.* Rome: Biblical Institute Press.
1977   "Nations or Gentiles in Matthew 28:19?" *CBQ* 39:94–102.
1979   *The Vision of Matthew: Christ, Church, and Morality in the First Gospel.* Ramsey, N.J.: Paulist Press.

Merkley, P.
1970   "New Quests for Old: One Historian's Observation on a Bad Bargain," *Canadian Journal of Theology* 16:203–18.

Metzger, Bruce M.
1971   *A Textual Commentary on the Greek New Testament.* New York: United Bible Society.
1972   "Literary forgeries and Canonical Pseudepigrapha," *JBL* 91:3–24.

Meye, R. P.
1969   "Mark 16:8: The Endings of Mark's Gospel," *Biblical Research* 14:33–43.

Miller, Donald G. and Y. Hadidian
1970   *Jesus and Man's Hope.* 2 vols. Pittsburgh Theological Seminary.

Minear, Paul
1966   "Luke's Use of the Birth Stories," in *studies in Luke-Acts.* Nashville: Abingdon.
1981   *New Testament Apocalyptic.* Nashville: abingdon.
1982   *Matthew: The Teacher's Gospel.* New York: Pilgrim Press.

1983   "The Original Function of John 21," *JBL* 102:85–98.

Mink, L. O.
1969   "History and Fiction as Modes of Comprehension," *New Literary History* 1:541–58.

Mitton, C. L.
1976   *Ephesians*. London: Oliphants.

Moessner, David P.
1983   "Paul and the Pattern of the Prophet Like Moses in Acts," *SBL Seminar Papers. 1983*. Chico, Calif.: Scholars Press: 203.

Mohrlang, Roger
1984   *Matthew and Paul: A Comparison of Ethical Perspectives*. New York: Cambridge University Press.

Momigliano, Arnaldo
1971   *The Development of Greek Biography: Four Lectures*. Cambridge: Harvard University Press.
1977   *Essays in Ancient and Modern Historiography*. Middletown, Conn.: Wesleyan University Press.

Montefiore, Claude G.
1927   *The Synoptic Gospels*. 2 vols. Second edition. Hoboken, N.J.: Ktav.

Montefiore, Claude G. and H. Loewe, eds.
1974   *A Rabbinic Anthology: Selected and Arranged with Comments and Introductions*. New York: Shocken Books.

Moore, G. F.
1927   *Judaism in the First Centuries of the Christian Era*. 3 vols. Cambridge: Harvard University Press.

Morgan, R.
1974   "New Testament in Religious Studies," *Religious Studies* 10:385–406.

Mounce, Robert H.
1977   *The Book of Revelation*. Grand Rapids, Mich.: Eerdmans.
1986   *Matthew*. New York: Harper & Row.

Mowinkel, S.
1956   *He That Cometh*. New York: Oxford University Press.

Mullins, Terence Y.
1980   "Topos as a NT Form," *JBL* 99:541–47.

Munck, Johannes
1959   *Paul and the Salvation of Mankind*. Atlanta: John Knox Press.
1967   *The Acts of the Apostles*. New York: Doubleday.

Munro, Winsome
1983   *Authority in Paul and Peter: The Identification of a Pastoral Stratum in the Pauline Corpus*. New York: Cambridge University Press.

Muratorian Canon
See Hennecke and Schneemelcher, 1963:43.

Murphy-O'Connor, Jerome
1975   "The Structure of Matthew XIV–XVII," *Revue Biblique* 82:360–84.
1984   *St. Paul's Corinth: Texts and Archaeology*. Wilmington, Del.: Michael Glazier.

Murray, Gilbert
1955   *Five Stages of Greek Religion*. New York: Doubleday.

Nag Hammadi Library
See Robinson, 1977.

Neill, Stephen
1964   *The Interpretation of the New Testament 1861–1961*. The Firth Lectures. New York: Oxford University Press.

Neubauer, Adolf and S. R. Driver
1969   *The Fifty-third Chapter of Isaiah According to Jewish Interpreters*. 2 vols. Hoboken, N.J.: Ktav.

Neusner, Jacob
1962   *A Life of Rabban Yohanan ben Zakkai, ca. 1–80 C. E*. Leiden, the Netherlands: E. J. Brill.
1972   *There We Sat Down: Talmudic Judaism in the Making*. Nashville: Abingdon.
1972b   *The Study of Judaism: Bibliographic Essays*. ed., Hoboken, N.J.: Ktav.
1975a   *First Century Judaism in Crisis*. Nashville: Abingdon.
1975b   *Christianity, Judaism and Other Greco-Roman Cults: Studies for Morton Smith at 60*. vol. 1. *New Testament;* vol. 3 *Judaism before 70*. (ed.) Leiden, the Netherlands: E. J. Brill.
1977   "History and Structure: The Case of Mishnah," *JAAR* XLV:161–92.
1978   "From Scripture to Mishnah. The Origins of Tractate Niddah," *Journal of Jewish Studies* 29:135–48.
1981   *Judaism: The Evidence of the Mishnah*. Chicago: University of Chicago Press.
1984   "Messianic Themes in Formative Judaism," *JAAR* 52:357.

Nicholson, Godfrey
1984   *Death as Departure: The Johannine De-*

scent-Ascent Schema. Chico, Calif.: Scholars Press.

Nickelsburg, George W. E.
1972 *Resurrection, Immortality, and Eternal Life in Intertestamental Judaism*. Cambridge: Harvard University Press.
1981 *Jewish Literature Between the Bible and the Mishnah: A Historical and Literary Introduction*. Philadelphia: Fortress Press.

Nickelsburg, George W. E. and John J. Collins, eds.
1980 *Ideal Figures in Ancient Judaism: Profiles and Paradigms*. Chico, Calif.: Scholars Press.

Nickle, K. F.
1966 *The Collection: A Study of Paul's Strategy*. London: SCM.

Nineham, D. E.
1964 *The Gospel of St. Mark*. New York: Penguin Books.
1965 *Historicity and Chronology in the New Testament*. London: SPCK.

Nock, A. D.
1937 "The Genius of Mithraism," *JRS* 27:108–13.
1964 *Early Gentile Christianity and Its Hellenistic Background*. New York: Harper & Row.

O'Brien, Peter Thomas
1977 *Introductory Thanksgivings in the Letters of Paul*. Leiden, the Netherlands: E. J. Brill.

Oliver, R. P.
1951 "The First Medicean Manuscript of Tacitus and the Titulature of Ancient Books," *TAPA* (1951) 82:232–61.

Onasander
Strategikos. Illinois Greek Club, tr. Cambridge: Harvard University Press/Loeb, 1923.

Osiek, Carolyn
1980 *Galatians*. Wilmington, Del.: Michael Glazier.

O'Toole, Robert F.
1984 *Unity of Luke's Theology: An Analysis of Luke-Acts*. Wilmington, Del.: Michael Glazier.

Pagels, Elaine H.
1973 *The Johannine Gospel in Gnostic Exegesis: Heracleon's Commentary on John*. Nashville: Abingdon.

1975 *The Gnostic Paul: Gnostic Exegesis of the Pauline Letters*. Philadelphia: Fortress Press.

Painter, John
1981 "The Farewell Discourses and the History of the Johannine Community," *NTS* 27:525–43.

Patte, Daniel
1976 *What Is Structuralist Exegesis?* Philadelphia: Fortress Press.
1983 *Paul's Faith and the Power of the Gospel*. Philadelphia: Fortress Press.

Patzia, Arthur G.
1984 *Colossians, Philemon, Ephesians*. (Good News Commentary) New York: Harper & Row.

Perkins, Pheme
1981 *Hearing the Parables of Jesus*. Ramsey, N.J.: Paulist Press.

Perrin, N.
1967 *Rediscovering the Teachings of Jesus*. New York: Harper & Row.
1969 *What is Redaction Criticism?* Philadelphia: Fortress Press.
1970 "Literary Gattung Gospel: Some Observations," *Expository Times* 82:4–7.
1971 "Christology of Mark: A Study in Methodology," *JR* 51:173–87.
1972 "Evangelist as Author: Reflections on Method in the Study and Interpretation of the Synoptic Gospels and Acts," *Biblical Research* 17:5–18.
1976 *Jesus and the Language of the Kingdom*. Philadelphia: Fortress Press.
1977 *The Resurrection According to Matthew, Mark, and Luke*. Philadelphia: Fortress Press.

Perrin, Norman and Dennis Duling
1982 *The New Testament: An Introduction*. New York: Harcourt Brace Jovanovich. (Revision of 1974 edition.)

Perry, Ben Edwin
1964 *Secundus the Silent Philosopher*. American Philological Association. Ithaca, N.Y.: Cornell University Press.

Petersen, Norman R.
1970 "So-called Gnostic Type Gospels and the Question of the Genre 'Gospel,'" Denver, Colo.: Society of Biblical Literature.
1972 "Composition and Genre in Mark's Narrative," *Genre of the Gospels*. Denver, Colo.: Society of Biblical Literature.
1974 "On the Notion of Genre in Via's

'Parable and Example Story': A Literary-Structuralist Approach," *Semeia* 1:134–81.

1978   *Literary Criticism for New Testament Critics*. Philadelphia: Fortress Press.

1980   *Perspectives on Mark's Gospel*. *Semeia* 16 (ed.). Chico, Calif.: Scholars Press.

1985   *Rediscovering Paul: Philemon and the Sociology of Paul's Narrative World*. Philadelphia: Fortress Press.

Philo
Collected Works. 10 Volumes. F. H. Colson, tr. Cambridge: Harvard University Press/Loeb, 1924–62.

Philostratus
Life of Apollonius of Tyana, 2 vols. F. C. Conybeare, tr. Harvard University Press/Loeb, 1912.

Piaget, Jean
1970   *Structuralism*. New York: Basic Books.

Pines, S.
1966   *The Jewish Christians of the Early Centuries According to a New Source*. Leiden, the Netherlands: E. J. Brill.

Plato
Collected Dialogues of Plato, E. Hamilton and H. Cairns, eds. Princeton: Princeton University Press, 1961.

Plescia, Joseph
1971   "On the Persecution of the Christians in the Roman Empire," *Latomus* XXX:120–32.

Pliny The Elder
Natural History. H. Rackham, W. Jones, and D. Eichholz, trs. Cambridge: Harvard University Press/Loeb, 1938–63.

Pliny The Younger
Letters. 2 vols. W. Melmoth, tr. Cambridge: Harvard University Press/Loeb, 1915.

Polycarp
Philippians. The Apostolic Fathers. K. Lake, tr. Cambridge: Harvard University Press/Loeb, 1912.

Polzin, Robert
1977   *Biblical Structuralism: Method and Subjectivity in the Study of Ancient Texts*. Semeia Supplements 5. Philadelphia: Fortress Press.

Pomeroy, Sarah
1975   *Goddesses, Whores, Wives, and Slaves: Women in Classical Antiquity*. New York: Shocken.

Praeder, Susan Marie
1981   "Luke-Acts and the Ancient Novel," *SBL Seminar Papers, 1981:* 269–92. Chico, Calif.: Scholars Press.

Price, Reynolds
1978   *A Palpable God: Thirty Stories Translated from the Bible with an Essay on the Origins of Life of Narrative*. New York: Atheneum.

Priest, John
1963   "The Messiah and the Meal in 1Qsa," *JBL* 82:95–100.

Pritchard, James B., ed.
1955   *Ancient Near Eastern Texts Relating to the Old Testament*. Princeton: Princeton University Press.

Pritchard, John Paul
1972   *A Literary Approach to the New Testament*. Norman: University of Oklahoma Press.

Przybylski, Benno
1980   *Righteousness in Matthew and His World of Thought*. New York: Cambridge University Press.

Quintilian
On the Training of Orators. 4 vols. H. E. Butler, tr. Cambridge: Harvard University Press/Loeb, 1920–22.

Rad, Gerhard von
1965   *The Message of the Prophets*. New York: Harper & Row.

Ramsay, William M.
1960   *The Cities of St. Paul, Their Influence on His Life and Thought: The Cities of Asia Minor*. Grand Rapids, Mich.: Baker.

Reedy, C. J.
1972   "Mark 8:31–11:10 and the Gospel Ending: A Redaction Study," *CBQ* 34:187–97.

Reicke, Bo
1968   *The New Testament Era: The World of the Bible from 500 B.C. to A.D. 100*. Philadelphia: Fortress Press.

Reumann, John
1977   "A History of Lectionaries: From the Synagogue at Nazareth to Post Vatican II," *Interpretation* 31:116–30.

1983   *Jesus in the Church's Gospel: Modern Scholarship and the Earliest Sources*. Philadelphia: Fortress Press.

Rhoads, David
1976   *Israel in Revolution 6–74 C.E.: A Polit-*

ical History Based on Josephus. Philadelphia: Fortress Press.

Rhoads, David and Donald Michie
1982   *Mark as Story: An Introduction to the Narrative of a Gospel*. Philadelphia: Fortress Press.

Rice, David G., and John Stambaugh
1979   *Sources for the Study of Greek Religion*. Chico, Calif.: Scholars Press.

Riches, John K.
1983   "The Sociology of Matthew: Some Basic Questions Concerning its Relationship to the Theology of the New Testament," *SBL Seminar Papers, 1983:*259–71. Chico, Calif.: Scholars Press.

Risenfeld, H.
1970   *The Gospel Tradition*. Philadelphia: Fortress Press.

Rist, John M.
1978   *On the Independence of Matthew and Mark*. New York: Cambridge University Press.

Robbins, Vernon K.
1973   "The Healing of Blind Bartimaeus in the Markan Theology," *JBL* 92:224–43.
1978   "By Land and By Sea: The We-Passages and Ancient Sea Voyages," *Perspective on Luke-Acts*. Charles Talbert, ed., Danville: Association of Baptist Professors of Religion (also, Edinburgh: T&T Clarke): 215–42.
1984   *Jesus the Teacher: A Socio-Rhetorical Interpretation of Mark*. Philadelphia: Fortress Press.

Roberts, T. A.
1966   "Gospel Historicity: Some Philosophical Observation," *Religious Studies* 1:185–202.

Robinson, James M.
1959   *A New Quest of the Historical Jesus*. London: Allenson.
1971   "Dismantling and Reassembling of the Categories of New Testament Scholarship," *Interpretation* 25:63–77.
1977   *The Nag Hammadi Library in English*. (ed.) New York: Harper & Row.
1982   *The Problem of History in Mark: And Other Marcan Studies*. Philadelphia: Fortress Press. (Partial reprint of 1957 edition.)

Robinson, James M. and Helmut Koester
1971   *Trajectories Through Early Christianity*. Philadelphia: Fortress Press.

Robinson, John A. T.
1962   *Twelve New Testament Studies*. London: SCM.
1976   *Redating the New Testament*. Philadelphia: Westminster Press.

Roetzel, Calvin J.
1982   *The Letters of Paul: Conversations in Context*. Atlanta: John Knox Press.

Rolland, P.
1972   "From Genesis to the End of the World: The Plan of Matthew's Gospel," *Biblical Theology Bulletin* 2:166

Rollins, Wayne G.
1963   *The Gospels: Portraits of Christ*. Philadelphia: Westminster Press.

Roloff, Jurgen
1981   "Luke's Presentation of Paul." *Evan. Theologie* 39:510–31.

Rosche, T. R.
1960   "The Words of Jesus and the Future of the Q Hypothesis," *JBL* 79:210–20.

Rose, H. J.
1951   *A Handbook of Greek Literature*. Fourth edition. New York: Dutton.

Rose, H. R.
1959   *Religion in Greece and Rome*. New York: Harper & Row.

Rostovtseff, Mikhail I.
1957   *The Social and Economic History of the Roman Empire*. 2 vols. Oxford: Clarendon Press.

Roth, Robert P.
1973   *Story and Reality*. Grand Rapids, Mich.: Eerdmans.

Rowland, Christopher
1982   *The Open Heaven: The Study of Apocalyptic in Judaism and Early Christianity*. Los Angeles: Crossroads.

Rowley, H. H.
1963   *The Relevance of Apocalyptic*. New York: Association Press.

Rudolph, Kurt
1983   *Gnosis: The Nature and History of Gnosticism*. New York: Harper & Row.

Russell, D. A.
1981   *Criticism in Antiquity*. Berkeley: University of California Press.

Russell, D. A. and M. Winterbottom
1972   *Ancient Literary Criticism*. Oxford: Clarendon Press.

Russell, D. S.
1964   *The Method and Message of Jewish Apocalyptic 200 BC–AD 100*. Philadelphia: Westminster Press.

Safrai, S. and M. Stern
1974   *The Jewish People in the First Century: Historical Geography, Political History, Social, Cultural and Religious Life and Institutions*. 2 vols. Philadelphia: Fortress Press.
Saldarini, S. J. and Anthony J. Saldarini
1974   "The End of the Rabbinic Chain of Tradition," *JBL* 93:97–106.
Sampley, Paul J.
1978   "The Letter to the Ephesians." In Krodel, 1978.
1980   *Pauline Partnership in Christ: Christian Community and Commitment in Light of Roman Law*. Philadelphia: Fortress Press.
Sanders, E. P.
1977   *Paul and Palestinian Judaism: A Comparison of Patterns of Religion*. Philadelphia: Fortress Press.
1983   *Paul, the Law, and the Jewish People*. Philadelphia: Fortress Press.
1984   *Jesus and Judaism*. Philadelphia: Fortress Press.
Sanders, E. P. et al.
1980–83   *Jewish and Christian Self-Definition: Aspects of Judaism in the Greco-Roman World*. 3 vols. Philadelphia: Fortress Press.
Sanders, James A.
1984   *Canon and Community: A Guide to Canonical Criticism*. Philadelphia: Fortress Press.
Sanders, James T.
1971   *The New Testament Christological Hymns*. Philadelphia: Fortress Press.
1975   *Ethics in the New Testament*. Philadelphia: Fortress Press.
Sandmel, Samuel
1961   "Parallelomania," *JBL* 81:1–13.
1969   *The First Century in Judaism and Christianity: Certainties and Uncertainties*. New York: Oxford University Press.
1970   "Prolegomena to a Commentary on Mark." In *New Testament Issues*. R. A. Batey, ed. New York: Harper & Row.
1978   *Anti-Semitism in the New Testament*. Philadelphia: Fortress Press.

1979a   *Philo of Alexandria: An Introduction*. New York: Oxford University Press.
1979b   *The Genius of Paul: A Study in History*. Philadelphia: Fortress Press.
Schaberg, Jane
1985   *The Illegitimacy of Jesus: A Feminist Theological Perspective*. New York: Seabury Press.
Schick, Edwin A.
1977   *Revelation: The Last Book of the Bible*. Philadelphia: Fortress Press.
Schmidt, Karl Ludwig
1919   *Der Rahmen der Geschichte Jesus* (The Framework of the Story of Jesus). Berlin: Trowitsch.
Schmithals, Walter
1972   *Paul and the Gnostics*. J. E. Steely, tr. Nashville: Abingdon.
Schnackenburg, Rudolf
1968   *The Gospel According to St. John*. St. Louis: Herder & Herder.
1980–82   *The Gospel according to St. John*. 3 vols. New York: Seabury.
Schneidermeyer, W.
1971   "Galatians as Literature," *Journal of Religious Thought* 28:132–38.
Schoeps, Hans-Joachim
1961   *Paul: The Theology of the Apostle in the Light of Jewish Religious History*. Philadelphia: Westminster Press.
Scholes, Robert and Robert Kellogg
1966   *The Nature of Narrative*. New York: Oxford University Press.
Schürer, Emil
1973   *A History of the Jewish People in the Age of Jesus Christ (175 BC–AD 135)*. Vols. 1 & 2. A new English version revised and edited by Geza Vermes, Fergus Miller, and Matthew Black. Edinburgh: T&T Clarke. (Vol. 2, 1979.)
Schüssler Fiorenza, Elizabeth
1973   "Apocalyptic and Gnosis in the Book of Revelation and Paul," *JBL* 92:565–81.
1977   "Composition and Structure of the Book of Revelation," *CBQ* 39:344–66.
1981   *Invitation to the Book of Revelation*. New York: Image Doubleday.
1983   *In Memory of Her: A Feminist Theological Reconstruction of Christian Origins*. Los Angeles: Crossroads.

1985 *The Book of Revelation: Justice and Judgment.* Philadelphia: Fortress Press.

Schweitzer, Albert

1906 *The Quest for the Historical Jesus: A Critical Study of its Progress from Reimarus to Wrede.* New York: Macmillan. (Reprinted, 1964.)

Schweizer, Eduard

1961 *Church Order in the New Testament.* London: Allenson.

1965 *The Church as the Body of Christ.* London: SPCK.

1969 "Eschatology in Mark's Gospel." In *Neotestamentica et Semitica.* E. E. Ellis and M. Wilcox, eds., Edinburgh: T&T Clarke: 114–18.

1970 *The Good News according to Mark.* Atlanta: John Knox Press.

1975 *The Good News according to Matthew.* Atlanta: John Knox Press.

Scobie, Alexander

1969 "Aspects of the Ancient Romance and its Heritage: Essays on Apuleius, Petronius and the Greek Romances," *Beitrage zur Klassischen Philologie,* Heft 30. Königstein, F.R.G.: Verlag Anton Hain.

Scroggs, Robin

1977 *Paul for a New Day.* Philadelphia: Fortress Press.

1983 *The New Testament and Homosexuality.* Philadelphia: Fortress Press.

Senior, Donald

1975 *Jesus: A Gospel Portrait.* Cincinnati: Pflaum-Standard.

Sevenster, J. N.

1975 *The Roots of Anti-Semitism in the Ancient World.* Leiden, the Netherlands: E. J. Brill.

Shepherd, Massey H., Jr.

1960 *The Paschal Liturgy and the Apocalypse.* Atlanta: John Knox Press.

Shubert, Paul

1939 *The Form and Function of the Pauline Thanksgiving.* Berlin: Alfred Topelmann

Shuler, Philip L.

1982 *A Genre for the Gospels: The Biographical Character of Matthew.* Philadelphia: Fortress Press.

Sidebottom, E. M., ed.

1967 *James, Jude, and 2 Peter* (The New Century Bible). Nashville: Thomas Nelson.

Simon, Marcel

1967 *Jewish Sects at the Time of Jesus.* Philadelphia: Fortress Press.

Smart, James D.

1975 *Doorway to a New Age: A Study of Paul's Letter to the Romans.* Philadelphia: Westminster Press.

Smith, Dennis E.

1981 "Meals and Morality." In *Paul: His World. SBL Seminar Papers, 1981:*319-40.

Smith, D. Moody

1965 *Composition and Order of the Fourth Gospel: Bultmann's Literary Theory.* New Haven: Yale University Press.

1974 "Johannine Christianity: Some Reflections on its Character and Delineation," *NTS* 21:222–48.

1976 *John: Proclamation Commentary.* Philadelphia: Fortress Press.

1984 *Johannine Christianity: Essays on its Setting, Sources and Theology.* Columbia: University of South Carolina Press.

Smith, Morton

1971 "Prolegomena to a Discussion of Aretalogies, Divine Men, the Gospels, and Jesus," *JBL* 90:174–99.

1973 *The Secret Gospel.* New York: Harper & Row.

Sophocles

"Oedipus The King." In *Sophocles I,* David Greene and Richmond Lattimore, eds. New York: Washington Square Press, 1954.

Soulen, Richard N.

1976 *Handbook of Biblical Criticism.* Atlanta: John Knox Press.

Spencer, R. F.

1969 *Form of Symbolic Action.* Seattle: University of Washington Press.

Spivey, Robert A. and D. M. Smith

1974 *Anatomy of the New Testament: A Guide to Its Structure and Meaning.* Second edition. New York: Macmillan. (3rd ed. 1982.)

Stacey, Walter David

1977 *Interpreting the Bible.* New York: Hawthorn Books.

Stambaugh, John E. and D. Rice

1980 *Sources for the Study of Greek Religion.* Chico, Calif: Scholars Press.

Stanton, Graham, ed.
1983   *The Interpretation of Matthew*. Philadelphia: Fortress Press.

Starr, J.
1932   "The Unjewish Character of the Marcan
Account of John the Baptist," *JBL* 51:227–37.

Stein, Robert H.
1981   *An Introduction to the Parables of Jesus*.
Philadelphia: Westminster Press.

Stendahl, Krister
1964   "Quis et Unde," *Judentum, Urchristen-
tum, Kirche: Festschrift für Joachim Jeremias*.
Second edition. Berlin: Alfred Topelmann.
1968   *The School of St. Matthew and its Use of
the Old Testament*. Philadelphia: Fortress Press.
1976   *Paul Among the Jews and Gentiles, and
Other Essays*. Philadelphia: Fortress Press.

Stewart, A. F.
1977   "To Entertain an Emperor: Sperlonga,
Laokoon, and Tiberius at the Dinner Table,"
JRS 67:76–90.

Stock, Augustine
1984   *Call to Discipline: A Literary Study of
Mark's Gospel*. Wilmington, Del.: Michael
Glazier.

Stone, Michael E.
1980   *Scriptures, Sects, and Visions: A Profile
of Judaism from Ezra to the Jewish Revolts*.
Philadelphia: Fortress Press.
1984   *Jewish Writings of the Second Temple
Period*. (ed.) Philadelphia: Fortress Press.

Stowers, Stanley K.
1982   *The Diatribe and Paul's Letter to the Romans*. Chico, Calif.: Scholars Press.
1984   "Social Status, Public Speaking and Private Teaching: The Circumstances of Paul's
Preaching Activity," *NT* 26/1:59–82.

Strauss, David F.
1972   *The Life of Jesus Critically Examined*
(reprint). Philadelphia: Fortress Press.

Streeter, Burnett H.
1924   *The Four Gospels: A Study in Origins*.
New York: Macmillan.

Suetonius Tranquillus
The Lives of the Caesars. 2 vols. J. C. Rolfe,
tr. 1914. Cambridge: Harvard University Press/
Loeb.

Suggs, M. Jack
1970   *Wisdom, Christology, and Law in Matthew's Gospel*. Cambridge: Harvard University
Press.

Sundberg, A. C., Jr.
1973   "Canon Muratori: A Fourth-Century List,"
HTR 66:1–41.

Swain, Lionel
1980   *Ephesians*. Wilmington, Del.: Michael
Glazier.

Sweet, J. P. M.
1979   *Revelation*. Philadelphia: Westminster
Press.

Tacitus
Annals. 4 vols. J. Jackson, tr. Cambridge: Harvard University Press/Loeb, 1937.

Talbert, Charles H.
1974   *Literary Patterns, Theological Themes,
and the Genre of Luke-Acts*. Chico, Calif.:
Scholars Press.
1975   "The Concept of Immortals in Mediterranean Antiquity," *JBL* 94:419–36.
1977   *What is a Gospel? The Genre of the Canonical Gospels*. Philadelphia: Fortress Press.
1978   *Perspectives on Luke-Acts* (ed.). Danville, Va.: Association of Baptist Professors of
Religion.
1982   *Reading Luke: A Literary and Theological Commentary on the Third Gospel*. Los Angeles: Crossroads.
1984a   *Luke-Acts: New Perspectives from the
SBL Seminar* (ed.). Los Angeles: Crossroads.
1984b   *Acts*. Atlanta: John Knox Press.

Talmon, Shemaryahu
1971   "Typen der Messiaserwartung um die
Zeitenwende" (Types of Messianic Expectation
at the Turn of the Era). In *Problems Biblischer
Theologie: Festschrift fur Gerhard von Rad*. Pp.
571–88. H. W. Wolff, ed. Munich: Kaiser
Verlag.

Tannehill, Robert C.
1975   *The Sword of His Mouth*. Philadelphia:
Fortress Press.
1977   "The Disciples In Mark: The Function of
a Narrative Role," *JR* 57:386–405.

Tarn, W. W.
1952   *Hellenistic Civilization*. Chicago: World.

Tatum, W. Barnes
1984   *In Quest of Jesus: A Guidebook*. Atlanta:
John Knox Press.

Taylor, Vincent
   1935   *The Formation of the Gospel Tradition.*
   New York: Macmillan.
   1966   *The Gospel According to St. Mark.* New
   York: Macmillan.
Teixidor, Javier
   1977   *Pagan God: Popular Religion in the
   Greco-Roman Near East.* Princeton: Princeton
   University Press.
Theissen, Gerd
   1978   *The Sociology of Early Palestinian
   Christianity.* Philadelphia: Fortress Press.
   1983   *The Social Setting of Pauline Christianity: Essays on Corinth.* Philadelphia: Fortress
   Press.
Thesleff, H.
   1965   *The Pythagorean Texts of the Hellenistic
   Period.* (Acta Academie Aboensis, Humaniora
   30/1) Abo, Finland: Abo Akademie.
Thomas, K. J.
   1977   "Torah Citations in the Synoptics," *NTS*
   24:85–96.
Thomas, Robert L. and Stanley N. Gundry, eds.
   1978   *A Harmony of the Gospels with Explanations and Essays.* Chicago: Moody Press.
Thompson, G. H. P.
   1972   *The Gospel According to Luke.* New York:
   Oxford University Press.
Thompson, William
   1970   *Matthew's Advice to a Divided Commu-
   nity.* Rome: Biblical Institute Press.
Thorpe, James, ed.
   1970   *The Aims and Methods of Scholarship in
   Modern Languages and Literature.* Second
   edition. New York: Modern Language
   Association.
Throckmorton, Burton H., Jr.
   1961   *Romans for the Layman.* Philadelphia:
   Westminster.
   1967   *Gospel Parallels: A Synopsis of the First
   Three Gospels,* RSV. Third edition. Nashville:
   Thomas Nelson.
Tiede, David L.
   1972   *The Charismatic Figure as Miracle
   Worker.* Denver, Colo.: Society of Biblical
   Literature.
   1980   *Prophecy and History in Luke-Acts.* Phil-
   adelphia: Fortress Press.

Tilborg, S. van
   1972   *Jewish Leaders in Matthew's Gospel.*
   Leiden, the Netherlands: E. J. Brill.
Tolbert, Mary Ann
   1978   *Perspectives on the Parables: An Approach to Multiple Interpretations.* Philadelphia: Fortress Press.
Trepp, Leo
   1982   *Judaism: Development and Life.* Third
   edition. Belmont, Calif.: Wadsworth.
Trocmé, Étienne
   1975   *The Formation of the Gospel according
   to Mark.* Philadelphia: Westminster Press.
Trotter, F. Thomas, ed.
   1968   *Jesus and the Historian.* Philadelphia:
   Westminster Press.
Tuckett, Christopher
   1983   *The Messianic Secret.* Philadelphia: Fortress Press.
Tzventan, Todorov
   1975   *The Fantastic: A Structural Approach to
   a Literary Genre.* Ithaca, N.Y.: Cornell University Press.

Urbach, E. E.
   1975   *The Sages: Their Concepts and Beliefs.*
   Jerusalem: Magnes Press.

Vallée, Gérard
   1981   *A Study in Anti-Gnostic Polemics: Irenaeus, Hippolytus, and Epiphanius.* Waterloo,
   Ont.: Wilfrid Laurier University Press.
Vermes, Geza
   1968   *The Dead Sea Scrolls in English.* New
   York: Penguin Books.
   1978   *The Dead Sea Scrolls in Perspective* (with
   Pamela Vermes). Philadelphia: Fortress Press.
   1981   *Jesus the Jew: An Historian's Reading of
   the Gospels.* Philadelphia: Fortress Press.
   1984   *Jesus and the World of Judaism.* Philadelphia: Fortress Press.
Verner, David C.
   1982   *The Household of God: The Social World
   of the Pastoral Epistles.* Chico, Calif.: Scholars Press.
Via, Dan Otto, Jr.
   1967   *The Parables: Their Literary and Exis-
   tential Dimension.* Philadelphia: Fortress Press.

1973 "Parable and Example Story: A Literary-Structuralist Approach," *Linguistica Biblica* 25: 21–30.

1975 *Kerygma and Comedy in the New Testament*. Philadelphia: Fortress Press.

Vielhauer, Phillip

1966 "On the Paulinism of Acts," *Studies in Luke's-Acts*. L. E. Keck and J. L. Martyn, eds. Nashville: Abingdon: 33–50.

Votaw, Clide W.

1970 *The Gospels and Contemporary Biographies in the Greco-Roman World*. Philadelphia: Fortress Press.

Waetjen, Herman C.

1976 *The Origin and Destiny of Humanness: An Interpretation of the Gospel according to Matthew*. San Rafael, Calif.: Omega Books.

Walker, W. O.

1969 "Quest for the Historical Jesus: A Discussion of Methodology," *ATR* 51:38–56.

Warner, Rex

1958 *The Greek Philosophers*. New York: Mentor.

Watson, G. R.

1969 *The Roman Soldier*. Ithaca, N.Y.: Cornell University Press.

Weeden, Theodore

1971 *Mark: Traditions in Conflict*. Philadelphia: Fortress Press.

Welch, John W., ed.

1981 *Chiasmus in Antiquity: Structures, Analyses, Exegesis*. Hildesheim, F.R.G.: Gerstenburg.

Wellek, Rene and Austin Warren

1956 *Theory of Literature*. Third edition. Harcourt, Brace and World.

Wells, George Albert

1976 *Did Jesus Exist?* Buffalo: Prometheus Books.

Westcott, Brooke Foss

1958 *The Gospel According to St. John*. London: James Clark.

Whiston, William, tr.

1960 *Josephus: Complete Works*. (Kregel reprint of 1867 edition.)

White, Hayden

1972 "The Structure of Historical Narrative," *Clio* 1/3:5–20.

1973 *Metahistory: The Historical Imagination of Nineteenth-Century Europe*. Baltimore: Johns Hopkins University Press.

White, John L.

1982 "The Greek Documentary Letter Tradition: Third Century B.C.E. to Third Century C.E.," *Semeia* 22:89–106.

1984 *Studies in Ancient Letter Writing: Semeia* 22 (ed.). Chico, Calif.: Scholars Press.

Whittaker, Molly

1984 *Jews and Christians: Graeco-Roman Views*. Cambridge: Cambridge University Press.

Wiefel, Wolfgang

1977 "The Jewish Community in Ancient Rome and the Origins of Roman Christianity." In Donfried, 1977.

Wilder, Amos N.

1971 *Early Christian Rhetoric: The Language of the Gospels*. Cambridge: Harvard University Press.

1976 *Theopoetic*. Philadelphia: Fortress Press.

1981 *Jesus' Parables and the War of the Myths*. Philadelphia: Fortress Press.

Wilken, Robert L.

1984 *The Christians as the Romans Saw Them*. New Haven: Yale University Press.

Williams, C. S. C.

1957 *A Commentary on the Acts of the Apostles*. New York: Harper & Row.

Williamson, E.

1970 *Philo and the Epistle to the Hebrews*. Leiden, the Netherlands: E. J. Brill.

Williamson, G. A., tr.

1965 *Eusebius' The History of the Church from Christ to Constantine*. Minneapolis: Augsburg.

Wilson, R. McL.

1973 "How Gnostic were the Corinthians?" *NTS* 19:68–69.

Wilson, R. S.

1933 *Marcion: A Study of a Second Century Heretic*. Cambridge: Clarke.

Wilson, Stephen G.

1973 *The Gentiles and the Gentile Mission in Luke-Acts*. New York: Cambridge University Press.

Woll, D. Bruce

1981 *Johannine Christianity in Conflict: Authority, Rank and Succession in the First Farewell Discourse*. Chico, Calif.: Scholars Press.

Wrede, William
1901   *The Messianic Secret*. J. C. G. Greig, tr., Cambridge: Clarke (1971).

Yadin, Y.
1958   "The Dead Sea Scrolls and the Epistle to the Hebrews," *Scripta Hierosolymitana* 4:36–55.
1966   *Masada: Herod's Fortress and the Zealots' Last Stand*. New York: Random House.

Yamauchi, Edwin M.
1963   *Pre-Christian Gnosticism: A Survey of the Proposed Evidence*. Grand Rapids, Mich.: Eerdmans.

Zeitlin, Solomon
1940   "The Crucifixion of Jesus Re-examined," *JQR* 31:327–69.

Ziesler, John
1983   *Pauline Christianity*. New York: Oxford University Press.

Index

Note: Boldface numbers indicate pages where subjects are defined or identified.

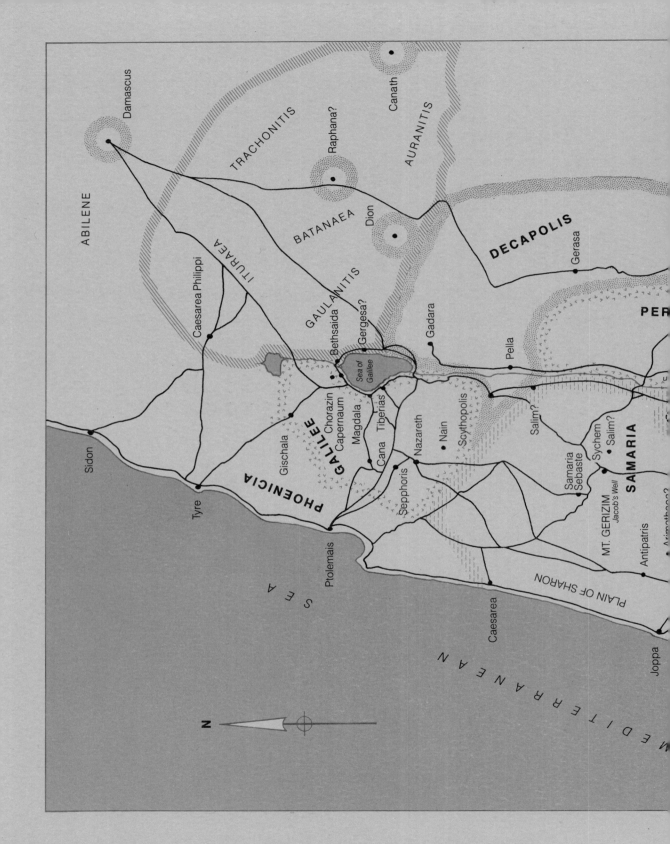